To Neil,

Wishing you a
Merry Christmas &
Happy New Year in 1996.

From Nick & Christopher.

ARSENAL

OFFICIAL HISTORY
ARSENAL

Phil Soar & Martin Tyler

HAMLYN

Photographic Acknowledgements

Action-Plus 213 top; Allsport/Russell Cheyne 230 top, /Shaun Botterill 226 top, 235; Arsenal Football Club 8, 10 bottom, 11, 14, 16, 19, 24 left, 25 top, 29 top and bottom, 32 (all three), 34 top, 42, 45 top and bottom, 46-47, 48 top and inset, 66 bottom left and right, 72 top left, 78, 79, 80, 82 top, 84 top, 85, 86 top and bottom, 88 bottom, 89 (all three), 93 top, 96 bottom, 99, 107 bottom, 108 top, 110, 112, 114, 125, 129 (all three), 136, 140 top and bottom, 145, 148-9, 152 top and centre, 153 bottom left, 156, 157, 160 top and bottom, 161 top right and bottom, 164 top and bottom, 165 top and centre, 167, 168-9, 169, 170, 172-3, 202-3, 226 bottom, 227, 230 bottom, 231, 247, 248; Colorsport 184 bottom, 184-5, 188 top and bottom, 193 bottom, 196 top and bottom, 197 centre and bottom, 198 bottom, 200, 201 top and bottom left, 203, 204, 212-3 bottom, 216, 218-9, 220-1, 223 bottom, 226 bottom, 227, 230 bottom, 231, 247, 248; *Daily Express*, London 2; Football Association 67 (all four); *The Guardian*, London 66 top, 142; Hulton Deutsch Collection 10 top, 16-17, 21 bottom, 31 top and bottom, 40 top and bottom, 43 bottom, 44, 49, 50, 51, 54-5, 56 top, 57 top and bottom, 58, 59, 61, 71 top, 83, 87 top and bottom, 88 top and centre, 90, 94 top and bottom, 97 centre; Mark Leech 232, 238 top, 242 top, 251 bottom, 251 top, /Andy Linighan 245; John Motson 72 bottom left and right; The Photo Source front endpapers, 13, 14-15, 62, 63, 64-5, 68 top, 69 top and bottom, 71 bottom, 73, 74 top, 75, 77, 92, 93 bottom, 94 centre, 95, 96 top, 103 top and bottom, 116, 117, 119, 123, back endpapers; Doug Poole 212, 215, 222, 223 top; Popperfoto 97 top and bottom, /Thompson 228; Press Associaton 106, 151, 152 bottom, 153 top, 155 top and bottom, 165 bottom, 176-7, 178-9, 179, 199 top and bottom; Royal Ordnance 24 right; *Sunday Times* 80-1, 107 top, 108 bottom; Syndication International 126-7, 144, 150, 153 bottom right, 161 top left, 166-7, 168, 191 top and bottom, 195, 201 bottom right, 224-5; Bob Thomas Sports Photography 208 top and bottom, 209 top and bottom, 214, 217, 229, /Bob Thomas 240, 244, 252 bottom, /Clive Brunskill 239 top and bottom, 246, /David Joyner 241, /Fresco 243, M. Thompson 249, 250, /S.G. Forster 237, 238 bottom.

Colour photography by Colorsport. Colour photographs from the Double season are the property of Arsenal Football Club.

It has not been possible to trace the original copyright owners of some of the photographs used in this history. Any questions relating to photographs used should be addressed to The Hamlyn Publishing Group Limited. We apologise should we have inadvertently infringed any copyright.

Records by John Burt and Daniel Feinstein with assistance from Jonathan Culverhouse and Kevin Connolly.

Title page: Hail the conquering heroes; the Double side brings the Championship trophy and the FA Cup home to Islington on 9 May 1971.

This edition published in Great Britain in 1994
by Hamlyn
an imprint of Reed Consumer Books Limited
Michelin House, 81 Fulham Road,
London SW3 6RB
and Auckland, Melbourne, Singapore and Toronto

Contents

Introduction
and Acknowledgements

It was the 92nd minute of the very last match of the 1988–89 season, probably the most significant and dramatic in English football history. For only the third time in the 101-year existence of the Football League the two leading teams were playing for the Championship on the final day of the season. Uniquely, there were no other games this day. It really was the last game of the season. Arsenal were winning 1–0 at Anfield, in any other circumstances an outstanding result. But here, at that moment, it meant that Liverpool were going to win the League and the Double by a single goal. Both clubs had the same number of points but Liverpool had a goal difference advantage of just one. It would be Liverpool's second Double in four seasons, an astonishing achievement in a season which will always be remembered primarily for the Hillsborough disaster.

It was all over bar the presentation of the trophy to Ronnie Whelan. A late injury to Kevin Richardson had taken the match into injury time. There were just seconds for the Kop to wait before they acclaimed their double-Double winning team as, perhaps, the greatest English club side ever.

And then Alan Smith, as he had been doing all night, cleverly picked up a pass from Dixon and moved it deftly on to Michael Thomas, some yards out from goal on the right side of the pitch. Thomas moved forward, went past Nicol by taking a rebound off the defender's body and sped into the penalty area. Grobbelaar, hero of so many similar situations, a keeper who had saved from the same Thomas just 10 yards out a few minutes before, came out and spread himself. Nicol and Houghton flung themselves at the Arsenal man. But Thomas deftly flicked the ball to his right, over Grobbelaar's body and into the corner of the goal. 2–0. Seconds left. Pandemonium. Arsenal were Champions by virtue solely of scoring more goals. On points and goal difference Arsenal and Liverpool had identical records. If goal average rather than difference had still been the arbiter, Liverpool would have been Champions and so winners of the Double. No Championship has ever had a closer finish. None has gone to the last 30 seconds. None has deprived a team of the Double in such an impossible-to-script manner.

History takes many years in the making and as long in the writing. It is probably too early to place Michael Thomas's goal securely in its rightful context. But it is already arguable that it will become the most famous goal ever scored in League football — comparable with Geoff Hurst's second in the 1966 World Cup final or Blackpool's fourth in the 1953 FA Cup final.

It was a game and a finale which no fantasist would have dreamed of writing. It was surely enough that these two teams had come together to decide the Championship in the very last game of the season, a season forever to be remembered for Hillsborough. For the season to end that way, with just seconds remaining, and at that venue, was to live and rewrite every boy's childhood fantasies.

It was inevitable that there should be reminders of another goal in another game against Liverpool. The comparisons were close: a yellow and blue shirted young star scoring in the dying minutes of the last match of the season; red shirted Liverpool were the opponents and the Double was at stake. But Charlie George lay down after his goal in 1971, while Michael Thomas turned a flying somersault of, in all probability, utter astonishment. And Arsenal were to win their Double of 1971, while Liverpool were to lose theirs of 1989. To have played each other twice for the Double; that alone is worth its place in the history books, particularly this book which was created to celebrate the first hundred years of Arsenal's history.

One hundred years is a long time. How long can perhaps the best be judged when we realise that 1886, the moment of Arsenal's birth, was also the year that the world's first motor car was built. And, even then, the fifteen young men who founded Royal Arsenal were probably well into their thirties before they actually saw a motor vehicle and certainly grandfathers before they would have seen an aeroplane.

Much can happen in a century. Too much to record fully here. To give our story meaning we must seek out landmarks, find moments when it is possible to explain much in a short space of time, perhaps even in a single game. That is why we begin our story not with 1886, or even the magical Double of 1977, but with the FA Cup

final of 1930. The story is more precise even than that. It homes in on the two captains that day, Tom Parker and Tom Wilson, walking onto the field together. In that one innocent gesture they told so much; in a way they revealed the underlying story of inter-war football. And that is the heart of Arsenal's story; a tale essentially of the 1920s and 1930s.

By some chronological freak, Arsenal's world changed at the turn of the 1930s. The glories that followed can probably be traced to a dramatic few minutes against a team of Second Division nobodies at Elland Road, the first of the games which are the real cornerstones in the Highbury story. Forty-one years later, on another ground in Yorkshire, those few minutes were to be eerily rerun. If we must pick landmarks, if that is how this history should be told, then these few minutes from these two matches shine like beacons from the dusk of history. It is these two games, rather than the 1971 FA Cup final or the last game of the 1989 League Championship, which will be the centre-points of our story.

Both were semi-finals. Both games had seen Arsenal, at half-time, 2–0 down and virtually out. Both finished 2–2. The first game eventually led to the 1930 final, the game which defined an era. It was Arsenal's first ever trophy and from it they went on to the glories of the next ten years. Without that conclusion, it is entirely possible the Arsenal of today would be no more significant than a middle of the road club.

The second game was dramatic for its dénouement, a last minute Peter Storey penalty which was perhaps the second most important goal in the club's long history. It was to lead to the 1971 FA Cup final and the Double, a feat Herbert Chapman's team of the 1930s could never achieve. We say this was the second most important goal for one simple reason. Peter Storey's penalty was not so much the moment the Double was won, but was certainly the moment it could have been lost; The Double is a central, vital and highly emotional part of the Arsenal story. But it is ultimately not as important as 1930. With or without the Double, Highbury would still be Highbury. The ground, the club and the worldwide reputation were built by Herbert Chapman, Tom Whittaker and the teams of the 1930s. The Double was the icing on an already substantial cake.

This book is about those men and those landmarks, and about more moments and matches and the players that created them. In particular it is about Herbert Chapman, the greatest manager the game has ever seen.

A first-class football club is a complex organism. It is of course about players, directors, grounds and games, but it is also about the far greater numbers who watch each week. A soccer team is often a deeply significant part of a man's three score years and ten. Having been born under the star of a football club, it is almost impossible to stray elsewhere in the mind, no matter where he may go physically. That one team will always slightly increase the pulse rate at 5pm on a Saturday evening. The heights of exultation that a Cup final or, in Arsenal's case, the Double, can bring to tens of thousands should not be doubted or devalued. For many it will be one of the two or three most emotional and moving moments they will ever experience in their lives.

All football clubs have their peculiarities; Arsenal's most interesting is one of location and historical accident. Football in England has long been about provincialism. Arsenal are not (at least since their move from Woolwich) a provincial club. Chapman's efforts, coupled with the lack of any alternative, allowed them to become the capital's club, at a time which corresponded with London imposing its economic as well as political dominance over the rest of a depressed and uncertain nation. It was this historical good fortune which was ultimately to determine the character of Arsenal. A team supported by rich and poor, but somehow, then and now, the rich relation. Herbert Chapman chose his time and his location well.

Since their foundation in 1886 Arsenal have played around 6,000 first-class games. We cannot talk about them all, but we can at least record them. At the back of the book you will find a complete match-by-match, week-by-week record (up to August 1994) of every first-class game the club has played. We have chosen 1919, the year the club's modern history began with that sensational start to their record-breaking unbroken spell in the First Division, as the year from which we cover not only all the games and their results, but also all the team line-ups and goalscorers. The statistical part of the book has been a massive undertaking for all concerned and we should like to thank John Burt, who provided the original material, and checked and corrected it; Daniel Feinstein, who prepared the players' records which give every first-class appearance since the club was founded; Kevin Connolly for his updates; Roger Walker for his work on the typography and layout; and Jonathan Culverhouse for his expertise.

Numerous people assisted us in our research and talked to us of their own experiences and recollections, including many Arsenal players, past and present, who kindly took time to help. There are simply too many to thank here. Instead we would like to mention just a handful — Bertie Mee, Don Howe, Don Roper, Billy Wright, Ken Friar, David Miles, and especially Bob Wilson who made his own archives available to the authors. At Hamlyn, we would like to mention our art director Chris Pow, editors Sarah Bennison and Peter Arnold, picture researcher Jean Wright, Diana Godwin-Austen, supporters Charles Fowkes and Terence Cross.

But above all others we would like to record our debt to Tony Bagley. It was he who originally commissioned the book, argued about its contents and enthused over its preparation. A great lover of the game, he sadly died before the book's completion.

Phil Soar and Martin Tyler

HERBERT
CHAPMAN

· CHAPTER 1 ·
Herbert Chapman

The beginning of everything can really be traced to 2.45 pm on Saturday 26 April 1930. The place was London's vast Empire Stadium. Two men stood together in the Wembley tunnel, tense with just fifteen minutes to go before the start of only the eighth FA Cup final to be played there.

Soon they were to emerge into the sunlight together, the first captains ever to lead out their teams side-by-side for a major football match. One of those men was Tom Wilson, captain and centre-half of Huddersfield Town, the dominant team of the age. In the brief decade since the First World War, Huddersfield had won a unique hat-trick of League Championships and reached four FA Cup finals. But, though no one could have believed it that day, the parade had already passed Huddersfield by. They would never again win a major honour.

The second man, Tom Parker, captained Arsenal, a north London club of no great distinction which, in nearly 50 years, had won absolutely nothing. And yet in the decade that remained between that April day in 1930 and the start of another world war, Arsenal, originally Royal Arsenal, later Woolwich Arsenal, briefly The Arsenal, would win five Championships, match Huddersfield's League hat-trick and reach two more FA Cup finals. By 1939 they would have become the richest, best supported and most successful club side in the world, a bright shining star that has yet to be dimmed in the football firmament.

For that fleeting moment in 1930 the pendulum stood still. Midway between the two world wars the centre of gravity of English football gently moved south. And, as if to mark such a uniquely symbolic game, the teams not only took the field together but crowded into the same dressing room at the end to congratulate the winners and even shared the same celebration dinner that night at the Cafe Royal.

There had to be more to it than that, of course; much more, certainly another reason for such a peculiarly portentous day. The reason was to be found in the slightly portly, commanding figure of the 52-year-old Arsenal manager, Herbert Chapman. It was he who had earlier led Huddersfield to their hat-trick in the mid-1920s, left that team before the end of it and moved to small, struggling, trophyless Arsenal. When he arrived at Highbury in May 1925 he

had said it would take five years to build a winning team. Here he was at Wembley, literally five years to the week later, presumably intending to make good his boast.

In retrospect, with the useful hindsight of half a century, it is easy to see what happened and provide explanations for why it happened. But it was not so clear then. Huddersfield were clearly the better team of the two; Arsenal were in the bottom half of the First Division and had survived several close shaves on their way to the final. If the Gunners had lost that day it is not unreasonable to argue that the whole history of Arsenal FC might have been very different. There may never have been the 1930s; we may never have had reason to speak of the marble halls of Highbury; Arsenal may have remained, at best, as they had since their 1927 FA Cup final defeat, a middle of the road First Division club. The 1930 FA Cup final might have been remembered primarily for the dramatic appearance of the *Graf Zeppelin*, another peculiarly poignant moment in this symbolic final midway between the two wars. The hopes and fears of years gone by, and of years to come, rested heavily on the shoulders of Tom Parker and Herbert Chapman that day.

It is the measure of this one game, of its remarkable portents, of the future that it promised for one of the two clubs and the past chapter that it closed for the other, that virtually the whole history of inter-war football can be told in its 90 minutes.

And, by the same token, the history of Arsenal FC, which remains in essence a tale of the 1930s, can be related in the day's dominant figure – Herbert Chapman. That is why we must start our story of Arsenal Football Club on this one day, with the life of that one man, and with one single, all-encompassing football match.

Saturday 26 April 1930 had begun fine and warm; temperatures were in the sixties, perfect for the 55th FA Cup final. The morning papers had said King George V would not be well enough to attend, but he surprised everyone by arriving to a rousing reception for his first outdoor appearance since an illness 18 months ago. The leading story in *The Times* that day had been the arrival home from India of the Prince of Wales, his plane actually touching down in front of the cameras in Windsor Great Park. But even

The bust of Herbert Chapman which stands in the legendary marble halls of Highbury, specifically inside the entrance to the East Stand. Modelled by the famous sculptor Jacob Epstein, it was commissioned and paid for by twelve of Chapman's friends including his physiotherapist and spiritual heir Tom Whittaker. The twelve would meet each year on 4 January, the anniversary of Chapman's death, to talk and lay a wreath on his grave in Hendon churchyard. The rituals of this 'HC Club', as it was called, were to continue until the death of its last members.

9

The Times took a more than passing interest in the day's football, pointing out to its readers that. . . 'The broadcast from Wembley Stadium this afternoon will begin at 2.30pm with community singing conducted by Mr T.P. Radcliff and accompanied by the band of the Welsh Guards. At 2.45pm Mr George F. Allison will open the commentary on the Cup final match between The Arsenal and Huddersfield Town, and this is expected to last until about 4.45pm. The position of the ball in the field of play and the score will be called at intervals by Mr Allison's assistant in the stand.'

George Allison was, as it happened, also an Arsenal director and the club's second biggest shareholder. It was only the fifth time that a game had been broadcast live and the effects of this exciting new medium, wireless, were far

Arsenal team was Charlie Preedy in goal, Tom Parker and Eddie Hapgood at full-back, Alf Baker, Bill Seddon and Bob John the half-backs, and Joe Hulme, David Jack, Jack Lambert, Alex James and Cliff Bastin the forwards. Nine of the eleven had been brought to Highbury by Chapman himself and, with the substitution of Moss for Preedy, Roberts for Seddon and Charlie Jones for Baker the team was probably close to the greatest one of an era that lives on in the memories of those fans still alive over fifty years later.

Huddersfield were, at the time at least, a rather more distinguished eleven. Former England captain Roy Goodall was at full-back, the magnificent centre-half Tom Wilson (a famous Huddersfield surname) remained as stopper, and the right-wing pair of Alex Jackson and Bob

Left: **The 1930 final** will be remembered for a remarkable number of reasons, not least the fact that the captains came out side by side for the very first time before a major game. Celebrating Herbert Chapman's association with the two finalists were captains Tom Parker of Arsenal (left) and Tom Wilson of Huddersfield. It was the Yorkshire club's fourth Cup final since the First World War, a period during which they had also won a hat-trick of Championships under Chapman's management.

Below: **King George V** is introduced to the Arsenal team by Tom Parker before the 1930 final. In the picture (left to right) are Bill Seddon, David Jack, Jack Lambert, Bob John, Alex James and, shaking hands with the King, Cliff Bastin. Bastin was one month past his 18th birthday, then the youngest player to appear in a Cup final. He sent his winners' medal to his schoolteacher in Exeter.

from being fully felt. For one thing, the Football League still organised a full programme on Cup final day. The crowds who stayed away to listen to the radio missed some good matches — Wolves drew 4–4 with Bradford Park Avenue, Fred Cheesmuir of Gillingham scored all six goals in his side's 6–0 defeat of Merthyr Town and Lincoln City beat New Brighton 5–3. Sheffield Wednesday stayed five points clear at the top of the First Division with a 1–0 defeat of Grimsby. Arsenal were little concerned about League results. With just two matches left of the season they were in twelfth place and the Wembley crowd of 92,488 was understandably only interested in what was about to happen there and then. Only one London club had won the FA Cup in the twentieth century (Spurs) and the capital had still never applauded a League Championship winner.

As a match, it was one of the better finals. The

Whatever the result, the 1930 final would always have been known as the Graf Zeppelin final. Towards the end of the first half the airship, pride of a German nation slowly rebuilding its self-confidence, suddenly appeared like a great cloud at 2,000 feet. It dipped in salute to the King and passed on. Most of the players apparently carried on oblivious. The picture, which shows W.H. (Billy) Smith (no relation to the bookshops) centring from the left, reveals only Huddersfield left back Spence and David Jack (far right) looking up.

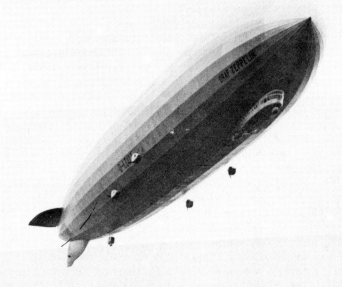

Kelly was the best in the country. 'Flying Scotsman' Jackson, scorer of a hat-trick in Scotland's famous 5–1 defeat of England at Wembley two years earlier, had also scored nine of Huddersfield's eleven goals on the way to the final. Eddie Hapgood was given the job of shadowing him wherever he went, Bob John taking the role of subduing Kelly. The defensive plan worked superbly, though it was in no sense a one-sided game.

Memories, however, are not made of defensive tactics but of goals, and never more so than in Cup finals. The first remains one of Wembley's most famous. In the team coach on the way from the club's hotel in Harrow, Alex James had spoken to winger Cliff Bastin: 'If we get a free-kick in their half early on, I'll slip it out to you on the wing. You give it me back and I'll have a crack at goal.' Most of the players thought James was joking – since joining the Gunners from Preston he had ceased to be anything other than a very occasional goalscorer. But in the 17th minute just such a free-kick occured; James was fouled 40 yards from goal, sprang to his feet and looked at referee Tom Crew, who nodded to the Scotsman to take the kick without any ado. Out went the ball to the left-wing, off hared Bastin, drawing Goodall out towards him. At just the right moment Bastin slipped the ball back inside for James, following through, to hit it into the corner of the net. The Huddersfield players protested briefly, but the referee had been quite correct in allowing the instant restart. It was, said *The Times:* 'The skill and bold tactics of James that turned the scale in favour of his side. . . to his remarkable control of the ball, he added the craft that both sees and makes openings.'

Some minutes later, in yet another incident redolent with symbolism, the *Graf Zeppelin*, Germany's giant airship and pride of a nation slowly rebuilding its self confidence, suddenly loomed over the stadium like a massive cloud. Flying at 2,000 feet, well below the legal limit, it dipped its nose in salute to the King and flew on. The players barely noticed; those that did were apparently annoyed at the break in their concentration.

Huddersfield attacked for the rest of the game, greatly helped by Arsenal's erratic goal-keeper, Charlie Preedy, who was deputising for the injured Dan Lewis. In the programme pen-notes he had explained how he liked coming out to meet the ball at the earliest opportunity. Unfortunately he appeared not to have explained this to his defence, used to playing in front of a more conservative keeper. Said *The Times* on Monday: '. . . at times Preedy took risks which hardly deserved to succeed as they did. Three times he let the ball slip from his hands as he was trying to clear.'

The Arsenal goal led something of a charmed life, often unguarded after a Preedy dash had failed to connect with the ball, and the Gunners' centre forward Jack Lambert spent much of the second half virtually alone on the centre line as his colleagues defended frantically. With just seven minutes left, a sudden long clearance from James found Lambert in the centre circle. Somehow he slipped between Goodall and Spence and the centre forward hared nearly half the length of the pitch towards the Huddersfield

Below: **Alex James'** (out of picture) **famous goal** in the 17th minute of the 1930 final. Fouled 40 yards out, he sprang to his feet, looked at referee Tom Crew and got a nod to restart instantly. He passed to Bastin (behind the near post) who slipped the ball back inside for James to score. The goal was a complete surprise, partially because James rarely scored, but more because of the speed of the free-kick. James had learned this habit in Scotland, where referees allowed it, and Chapman had become very irritated with him trying it south of the border. Because the officials usually called him back, Chapman had ordered James to desist. It was not the only controversial decision Tom Crew made that day. At half-time he sent a telegram to the manufacturer of the ball saying: 'I've chosen your ball.' It was later suggested that Cup final referees tended to expect some favour in return and the issue later lead as far as the resignation of the FA's treasurer.

Above: **David Jack heads wide** during the 1930 final. In 1923 Jack recorded the first goal ever scored at Wembley – for Bolton versus West Ham in the White Horse final. He also scored the only goal of the 1926 final and secured winners' medals in both games. He would presumably not have been nervous before the match, but most of the Arsenal team were. The appropriately named Highbury groundsman, Bert Rutt, had played gramophone records to the team in the dressing room for an hour before, hoping to take their minds off things. They were also to be encouraged through the game by the two mascots which became their supporters' trademarks during the 1930s – the bugler and the lucky white duck.

goalkeeper, Turner, who seemed suddenly dazed by this disastrous turn of events. Lambert shot from the edge of the area past the badly placed keeper, the ball hit the back of the net and Lambert turned, arms outstretched, expecting to greet his onrushing colleagues. But there was no one there; the rest of the side were still in their own half. So Lambert set off alone, applauding himself as he went, to provide one of football's more enduring memories at the end of one of football's most famous matches. It is probably no exaggeration to say that this game, which ended 2–0, along with the FA Cup final and semi-final in the Double year of 1971, is the most memorable in the history of Arsenal Football Club. It was not only the moment when the greatness began, it was also the moment when everything could so easily have slipped away.

The 1930 FA Cup final was the forerunner of two more in the decade that followed — 1932 and 1936 — and of five League Championships, 1931, 1933, 1934, 1935 and 1938. By the time Hitler's war began, Arsenal were without doubt the greatest, the most famous, the most widely supported football club in the world. In the half century since only Liverpool have managed a comparable dominance, and even then, it has to be said, without quite the same national promi-

nence or emotional commitment, for and against. One cannot begin to compare, for instance, Liverpool's two defeats by Brighton in the 1983 and 1984 FA Cups with the sensation caused by Walsall when they knocked the Gunners out of the same competition fifty years before. Since the 1930s the glories have inevitably been fewer, the trophies more widely spaced, but the reputation and image that Herbert Chapman built remain essentially as he left them. And so dominant is Chapman in Arsenal's history that, although it was nearly half a century before the club won a major prize, it is surprising to recall that it is also more than fifty years since Chapman died so tragically in 1934.

The history, status and wealth of the club is so bound up with this one man that it is surely necessary to go back and discover what we can about him, to find what it was that he brought to Highbury which was to generate such an amazing transformation and leave such a lasting legacy. The story of Arsenal must inevitably begin with the story of Herbert Chapman.

Herbert Chapman was born eight years before Arsenal, on 19 January 1878 in Kiveton Park, a small mining village on the borders of South (then West) Yorkshire and Nottinghamshire. His father was an illiterate miner who had five other sons and one daughter. Herbert was an

Charlie Preedy's handling, both safe (*left*, with Bill Seddon and Tom Parker looking on) and unsure (*below*, completely missing a corner) was to be one of the features of the game. Preedy was a late season replacement for the unlucky Dan Lewis, who had given away the dramatic only goal of the 1927 final, and the deputy had a reputation for erratic behaviour. Jack Crayston, who made his debut in a Third Division game against Preedy (then with Wigan), wrote afterwards: 'It was an odd start to my career; the goalkeeper played the deuce of a fine game against us – at right back!'

exceptionally bright child in an age when working class children had virtually no opportunities, so much so that he eventually reached Sheffield Technical College to complete a course in Mining Engineering. He was to use his academic qualifications, and hold down various jobs in industry, for nearly all of his life. Indeed, it was not until Huddersfield first became League Champions, when Chapman was already 46, that he finally turned his back on an engineering career.

He was a moderate footballer, a roly-poly inside forward or wing half, but nothing like as good as his brother Harry, who was a forward with the Sheffield Wednesday Championship winning sides of 1903 and 1904. Herbert remained an amateur through most of his playing career, which took him through a remarkable range of clubs and locations. In the ten years between 1897, when he was 19, and 1907, when he became player-manager of Northampton, he played for Stalybridge Rovers, Rochdale, Grimsby, Swindon, Sheppey United, Worksop, Northampton, Sheffield United, Notts County and Spurs.

In most of these towns he also took an engineering job, which was wise as his playing career could only be described as unmemorable. But ten clubs in as many years also had its advantages. He got to know people in the game throughout the country, he saw numerous styles of management (most of them poor) and he began to develop his own theories about how best to run a football club and win football matches. His longest spell in a single place was

Cliff Bastin was less humorous after the final: 'I am all in favour of a goalkeeper who advances at the right time (as Preedy had written in the programme notes for the final). On this particular occasion, however, Charlie was advancing all the time – whether it was the right or wrong time was purely incidental.' Arsenal survived Preedy's forays, though on several occasions he was to miss the ball completely when way outside the goal. Preedy was actually a taxi-driver. After the game it became a Highbury joke that: '...there's never one around when you need one.'

two years at White Hart Lane and, though he was usually in the reserves, the potential for a major club in North London (Arsenal were still south of the river) cannot have escaped his attention.

When he took over at Northampton in 1907 they had just finished bottom of the Southern League. In 1908–09 Northampton were Champions. Chapman finished playing the same year and in 1910 Northampton were fourth, in 1911 second and in 1912 third. By that time Chapman had returned to his native Yorkshire as manager of Second Division Leeds City. His first job was to canvass for votes at the League's AGM, where City were facing re-election. The club improved dramatically, just missing out on promotion in 1914 and then, in the rather different atmosphere of wartime football, being good enough to win the unofficial League Championship of 1918. Chapman had taken over the management of a munitions factory in 1916, a move which was probably and paradoxically to save his future career for, in 1919, Leeds were summoned before a League commission to answer allegations of making illegal payments between 1916

and 1918. This had always been, in theory, a major offence in the eyes of the League but was a much more sensitive issue in wartime. The club refused to release their books and were simply thrown out of the League. The club's officials, including their ex-manager, were suspended and Chapman remained in various industrial jobs for the next two years, suffering at least one spell of unemployment.

Chapman probably knew about the payments involved (he had been fined by the League once before, though on something of a technicality, in 1912) but as he was not at the club during the critical period the judgement seemed a little harsh. It was, understandably, to have a lasting effect on him and its echoes were to affect Arsenal in a truly dramatic way a decade later. That part of the story must, however, wait its turn.

When Leeds City were ejected from the League in 1919, Second Division neighbours Huddersfield Town sensibly decided to move up the road to Elland Road in their place ('From Leeds Road to Leeds City' went the headlines). Town were based in a rugby league stronghold,

had little support to speak of and were literally facing collapse. But in a classic instance of out of adversity coming strength, meetings of supporters rejected the decision to move towns (though the League had already approved), raised cash and reinvigorated the board. Co-incidentally there was a miraculous transformation on the field. Within a year Town were promoted to the First Division and were playing in the first post-war Cup final. Late in 1920 the Huddersfield secretary-manager, Ambrose Langley (an old playing colleague of Chapman's brother Harry) approached the then unemployed Chapman with an offer of a job as his assistant. Langley had been one of the main advocates of the move to Leeds and he was obviously aware that his own days must be numbered. Chapman had now been out of football for more than four years and the League cancelled his suspension without question, but it shows just how far his star had fallen that the appointment did not receive a single mention in even the local press.

Within a month Langley handed over the reins to Chapman (this must have been agreed in advance), within three years Huddersfield were League Champions and within five they had completed the first League hat-trick in history.

By that time, however, Chapman had again left Yorkshire and returned to North London. Though Arsenal advertised their manager's job in *The Athletic News* on 11 May 1925, Chapman had already been approached. Arsenal chairman Henry Norris offered him £2,000 a year to take the job, easily the highest salary in the game, and Chapman took little persuading. His days at Tottenham had shown him the potential of London, and when he had visited Highbury before the war he had been particularly struck by the adjacent underground station, only 12 minutes from Piccadilly. In a period of mounting unemployment he was also conscious of the better opportunities his two teenage sons would have in the capital.

So what sort of man was Herbert Chapman?

Above left: **Tom Parker renews** his acquaintance-ship with King George V at the end of the 1930 final. Second in line is future captain of club and country Eddie Hapgood.

Above right: **After the ball is over;** the terraces are covered in newspapers and rubbish, the fans are gone. All alone are the smiling victors, posing for a highly unusual final picture. Tom Parker holds the first major prize Arsenal have ever won; on his right are Alf Baker and the debonair David Jack. Herbert Chapman is on the far left, Alex James on the far right. They all went on to another highly unusual event – a joint banquet with the Huddersfield team.

The image that has come down to us over half a century is that of a strict authoritarian, the man who once refused to allow Joe Hulme to spend a weekend at home in Lancashire (though Arsenal were playing at Bolton) because Hulme's two goals on the Saturday were not enough, the man who insisted none of the staff at Highbury left at 6.00 pm before asking whether there was anything more he wanted them to do. But if he was an authoritarian, it was in a far more authoritarian age. Jobs were scarce, jobs at football clubs were good ones, particularly at Highbury. A player earned £8 per week, four times as much as the average working man. To be the most successful club in Britain, you had to have the best. There was no gainsaying that, and it applied across the board. Early on he called the fifty club stewards into his office and told them he was ending the various free perks they received. He wanted everything above board. Though his teams were tough, he was never an advocate of unfair play. There are two celebrated

incidents when Chapman immediately transferred players who had been guilty of very bad tackles – Islip from Huddersfield and Black from Arsenal.

He was a committed man. He wanted to build the greatest of all football teams. Bernard Joy said of him: 'There are two kinds of visionary; those that dream of a whole new world, and those who dream of just one thing. Chapman's vision was of the greatest football team in the world. His genius was in actually creating something close to that.'

His players, in their reminiscences, seem to regard him with affection rather than fear; some go even further. Cliff Bastin wrote in 1950: 'There was an aura of greatness about him. He possessed a cheery self-confidence. His power of inspiration and gift of foresight were his greatest attributes. I think his qualities were worthy of an even better reward. He should have been prime minister, and might have been but for the lack of opportunities entailed by his position in

the social scale.' An extreme view perhaps (and an inaccurate one as Ramsey Macdonald was PM at the time) but Chapman believed that his players were worthy of the very best, hence the tremendous facilities at Highbury and, in particular, the medical and physiotherapy side, years before its time, run by Tom Whittaker. He also insisted on his players having part of their earnings saved by the club. 'He was not a bully,' said Bastin, '. . . he gave few words of praise and fewer of blame.' The signing of Bastin himself also shows other essential elements in Chapman's success as a manager — his absolute commitment to the job and his willingness to back his judgement and take chances.

Chapman had first seen Bastin at Watford when the manager and George Allison had gone not to watch Bastin at all but to size up a member of the home side named Barnett. Bastin, playing for Exeter in a Third Division South game, was then only 16 but his amazing ball control and composure struck Chapman instantly and Barnett was completely forgotten. In the inter-war period youngsters developed much more slowly and it was very rare to see a teenager even in the Third Division. But Bastin was a natural (when he eventually arrived at Highbury the commissionaire wouldn't let him in, thinking he was a boy seeking autographs). Chapman set off immediately the following morning for Devon. Bastin, always a phlegmatic man, was unimpressed by Chapman's overtures, even though he had played just a handful of matches for his local club, Exeter City. He was more concerned with a tennis match he was due to play that afternoon. But Chapman persisted and persisted. 'I had visions of a lifetime spent sitting there listening to him,' said Bastin a quarter of a century later. Bastin, of course, eventually gave in, signed and became one of the all-time great names in British football, uniquely winning every honour in the game before his 21st birthday.

It was a good example of Chapman personally overseeing Arsenal as a close, family club. He had a very happy home life of his own. His wife was a teacher from the same Yorkshire village, and they had four children. His commitment to his family can be judged by the answer he gave immediately when asked what the proudest moment of such a successful life had been: 'When my son Ken qualified as a solicitor.' Oddly neither of his sons was to play soccer, but both were accomplished at rugby. Indeed, Ken, the eldest, was to become President of the Rugby Football Union. Perhaps the proximity to such tremendous success was a disincentive rather than an encouragement.

When Chapman joined Arsenal in 1925 he had been playing and managing in the senior game for nearly 30 years, apart from his four-year break. While it would be wrong to say that his conception of the ideal tactical approach was fully formed, it is certainly the case that, over this period, his successes had been based on certain constant themes.

Chapman was, above all else, a believer in great players. He brought Clem Stephenson to Huddersfield as soon as he became manager, and later won the signature of Alex Jackson. At Arsenal he immediately insisted on having Charlie Buchan, later David Jack and Alex James, among the greatest, if not the greatest, players of their generation. He believed that a great player could fit into any tactical system, and was to prove it, even with the complex Alex James. The fact that a player, like Stephenson or Buchan, might even be past his best was not in itself important.

It is arguable that Chapman was actually not a great tactician — when the offside law was changed from three defenders to two in 1925 Chapman was rather slow to spot the changes required to deal with the extra freedom it gave to attackers. The introduction of a centre-back and midfield link was suggested by Charlie Buchan, who could see the problem from the field, and it took Arsenal some time to settle down to the new system. Where Chapman was obviously magnificent was in fitting the man to the system required; to pursue the example, he then found and developed Herbie Roberts into the definitive stopper centre-back.

If there is another, simple key to understanding Chapman's view of the game it is perhaps in the phrase: 'A team can attack for too long.' He is first quoted as saying that when at Northampton in November 1907, after his side had attacked for most of a cup match but Norwich had stolen a 1–0 victory. Chapman soon instructed his wing halves not to press forward behind the attack quite so readily, and that the whole team should sometimes drop back to open out the game, bring the opposition forward and create the opportunity for a counter-attack.

Chapman was to say the same 25 years later: 'You can attack too long, though I do not suggest that the Arsenal go on the defensive even for tactical purposes. I think it may be said that some of their best scoring chances have come when they have been driven back and then have broken away to strike suddenly and swiftly.' That almost sums up a general view of Arsenal in the 1930s, the 'lucky' Arsenal of myth and legend. As with most myths, there is certainly something in it. The speed of Bastin and Hulme, the strength of Lambert and later Drake, the cunning of James, were all essential pieces of a clear plan. But in 1930–31 Arsenal scored 127 First Division goals — three per game. They can't all have come from breakaways.

Chapman has been misinterpreted in saying that a team goes on the pitch with one point and, if it doesn't concede a goal, keeps that point. He did indeed say almost exactly that, but not as an advocate. In fact he was criticizing the fact that so many teams, particularly in the early 1920s when goalscoring was at an all-time low, were basically defensive, off-side orientated tactical units. He once even advocated 11 up and 11 down as a means of forcing teams to look for

The victorious 1930 team, all of whom signed this picture. Standing, left to right: Alf Baker, Jack Lambert, Charlie Preedy, Bill Seddon, Eddie Hapgood, Bob John. Middle row: Herbert Chapman, David Jack, Tom Parker, Alex James, Tom Whittaker. Front: Joe Hulme and Cliff Bastin.

goals. There is no doubt, nonetheless, that Chapman was one of the first to put to really good effect the very obvious truth that the best side is the one which scores most goals, not the one which attacks longest or which the crowd thinks has shown most endeavour. This was a surprisingly difficult point for many fans to appreciate in the 1930s, and beyond.

Chapman was never reluctant to admit the necessity of strong defence above all else. As he wrote in 1933: 'I confess I am out to win, and so are my players. It is laid down by law that the team who scores the most goals wins. To accomplish this, you must be sure that the defence is sound. All this, I know, is elementary but it is also the rock bottom of football.' Arsenal's system was designed on a pivotal principle, wrote Chapman: 'First, as to the attack, we have ceased to use our wing forwards in the old style, in which they hugged the touchline. Not only is it the aim of Hulme and Bastin to come inside when the Arsenal attack, but also the aim of the wing halves. This gives us

seven men going up on goal. Now, as to defence, the team swing the other way, but the same principle applies so we have eight defenders when the goal is challenged. The defence pivots towards the position of attack, the opposite back coming in to support the centre. It is, of course, essential that the two insides should come back and it is on this account that you get what is called the W-formation. The two wing halves are therefore the key men, either in defence or attack, and no defence can be sound unless it has the support of two inside forwards.'

All of this is relatively familiar today, going under terms such as 'closing down space' or 'getting behind the ball'. In the 1930s it was genuinely still a mystery. Programmes were always printed with a 5-3-2 formation (five forwards and two full backs) and crowds continued to believe that this is how teams like Arsenal played right through to the 1950s — despite the clear weekly evidence to the contrary in front of their eyes.

Because Arsenal so completely dominated

English football in the decade after the 1930 Cup final, it is perhaps worth examining exactly what it was about the manager, the club and their tactics that brought such astonishing success.

First of all, it is nonsense to suggest that Chapman arrived at Highbury with a plan in mind and then went out to find the players to fit it. If anything, the reverse was the case. Between his arrival in 1925 and his first game in charge, three months later, the offside law was changed and a whole new era had begun. Chapman had achieved considerable success in refining and exploiting the old system and it would be unrealistic to have expected him, or any other manager, to understand all the implications of the law change overnight. His Leeds and Huddersfield teams had been tight, defensive units, and his roving centre half at Leeds Road, Tom Wilson, was a key, if now obsolescent figure. When Charlie Buchan forced the third–back tactic on the team (the phrase 'policeman' came in later) the other changes required were reasonably obvious — the full backs moving out to mark the wingers and one of the inside forwards dropping back to become the midfield link. Arsenal may have adapted to these changes better than most other clubs but there was nothing secret or particularly subtle about them and, by the end of Chapman's first season (1925–26), most of his opponents were using the same formation. The tactical reason for Chapman's successes definitely lay elsewhere.

While it is undeniably true that the use of Alex James as the link-man was the *key* to Arsenal's success, its *essence* was further forward. The added dimension in Arsenal's game was actually the use of the wingers Cliff Bastin and Joe Hulme, and the club's relative decline towards the end of the 1930s was due more to the fact that these two could not be replaced than for any other reason.

Chapman did not plan it that way. By the late 1920s it had simply become apparent to him that, in the astonishingly fast Hulme and the cool clever Bastin, he had two players of very unusual quality. The basic difference in Arsenal's game from that point on was they they generally played only three real front men. There was always a strong centre forward (Jack Lambert being the most celebrated), and behind him David Jack was a goalscorer of quality but not a true front-runner. The wingers did not play in the manner of their equivalents at other First Division clubs. Their role was not, in other words, to hug the touchline, beat the full back, get to the goal-line and cross for the centre forward to head home. They were both capable of doing this, but Chapman saw it as essentially wasteful. A normal winger spent too much time waiting. He must be used more extensively and far more effectively.

The result was that both Hulme and Bastin would cut in far more often than they would go outside, that Alex James's most famous pass would become the ball *inside* the full back, and that both wingers became goalscorers of impor-

tance (in the great era between 1929 and 1935 Bastin scored 116 League goals and Hulme 75; an average between them of almost exactly a goal a game — meaning Arsenal expected one or other of their wingers to score every week). As long as no other club played this way, it was always likely to work. The opposing full backs had 40 games a year dealing with conventional wingers going outside; twice a season they met Arsenal and had to deal with a totally different threat. But, and here is the rub, Chapman could only do it because he had Hulme and Bastin and, eventually, Alex James to feed them. His competitors couldn't match his success simply because they didn't have the players; nor could his successor George Allison continue it, because ultimately he couldn't replace them.

Chapman did not create all of this overnight. Parts of his post-1925 system — the stopper centre half, the midfield link — were quite straightforward and the manager's strength here was finding the perfect men for the job. The more subtle development involving the wingers was probably largely chance but, having seen the potential, Chapman worked at the conclusions and maximised them. He didn't just win an odd League Championship, he completely dominated the game. What happened, bluntly, was that he moved one player back through each department of the team. The stopper centre half actually meant a line of three at the back rather than two. The need to replace the centre half in midfield meant one of the inside forwards had to fall back to create three in midfield and four up front. This is where most teams left it — at 3-3-4. As they continued to use conventional wingers they had to have at least two goalscoring forwards — otherwise there was no one for the wingers to serve. Chapman went further by dropping another man some way back as well, creating a system far closer to 3-4-3 than 3-3-4.

The benefit (as was also to be seen in the 1970s when 4-4-2 became the norm) was that the extra man in midfield helped Arsenal gain much more possession of the ball. In purely technical terms, it was a defensive alteration. It moved a man backwards. But Arsenal could make it work and scored a lot of goals because they had the genius of James, Hulme and the phenomenal goalscorer Bastin. Any other club trying the same thing was almost certain to fail for precisely those reasons. Hence, in general, they didn't try.

Chapman knew it was a scheme perfectly geared for scoring goals on the break. It was arguably the ultimate fulfilment of his old belief that '. . . you can attack for too long.' It was, in many ways, an away team's approach (in the six great seasons between 1929–30 and 1934–35 Arsenal won 187 points at home and 147 points away) but, at the same time, it in no way blunted the greatness of the other parts of the team when they wanted to attack and faced opponents who were their inferior. Their goalscoring record was second to none in the 1930s. Nevertheless, one can see the seeds of the tactics of the 1960s (using wingers in such unconventional ways

reserve, third and junior teams all tried to play, within their capabilities, to the same pattern. The reasoning was obvious — if a reserve came into the first team he would be familiar with the behaviour of the players around him. This was obviously most important in defence, but was not insignificant in attack. The club's classic moves, the ball from James inside the full back, or the cutting in of the wingers and the playing of the ground ball sideways, would not have come naturally to any player had they not also played that way in the reserves.

To ensure the tactical messages came across, Chapman turned part of his desk into a plan of the field, with models to represent the players. When players came to see him, it was easy to discuss moves, ideas and developments in a practical way. Chapman introduced weekly team talks for the whole side; everyone was invited to contribute, and it was from these meetings that many of the best ideas emerged.

One needs to put all this in perspective if one is to understand its significance. This was an era when directors chose the team, whether or not they knew a thing about the game. There was no such animal as team manager — technically he was secretary-manager, deputed basically to run the club. Attempts to integrate tactics, combine the best team (as opposed to the eleven players the directors might have thought were best in eleven individual positions) and develop a pattern of consistency were largely outside the control of the average manager, or were easily frustrated if he tried. Chapman, having seen over his playing career how not to run a whole range of clubs, was probably the first real professional in a world of semi-amateurs. These were the days when success was a Cup semi-final here and there, finishing fifth or sixth in the League now

found remarkable echoes in Alf Ramsey's seminal Ipswich side of 1962) and one can surely understand how the cries of 'Lucky Arsenal' arose from the unsophisticated and unseeing terraces of the era. Chapman's instinct for both fitting the right man to predetermined parts of a plan, while being able to adapt and develop other parts of that plan to the particular skills of the men available was, of course, the mark of footballing genius.

Another important part of Chapman's philosophy was that the whole club should play to the same system — in other words the first,

and again, and bringing in large enough crowds to balance the books. If further proof is needed, and with the possible exceptions of Wolves' Frank Buckley and Charlton's Jimmy Seed, who now can name any other manager of the inter-war era?

What was really remarkable about Chapman was his influence on, or attempts to influence, the game outside the playing area as well. Many of his proposals were firmly opposed by the FA, to whom he must have seemed a constant irritation. He introduced numbering on the Arsenal shirts on 25 August 1928, when the Gunners visited Hillsborough. This was the first time a team had ever been numbered and the FA told him to desist. He had a minor revenge by having the reserves continue to wear the same shirts. He introduced a 45-minute clock and was told to stop that (it was simply turned into the 60-minute clock still standing on the southern terracing), he wanted to start floodlit matches (midweek games then kicked off at 3.00 pm with the obvious loss of revenue) but was not allowed to, and Arsenal proposed the 10-yard penalty semi-circle ten years before it was finally adopted. Other ideas he put forward have still to come to fruition — goal judges (which he felt very strongly about), two referees rather than one, and far more clubs promoted and relegated (although the number was increased from two to three in 1973–74). He was a keen advocate of a single England manager, rather than a selection committee. In 1932 he wrote: 'The idea may be startling, but I would like the England selectors to bring together 20 of the most promising young players a week under a selector, coach and trainer. The idea would be to practise definite schemes and . . . at the end have them hold a conference at which views might frankly be exchanged. I would keep these players together during the season, . . . if this proposal were carried out, I think the result would be astonishing. I may say that I have no hope of this international building policy being adopted.' Note that not even Chapman dared suggest that a single manager actually pick the players. It was, of course, 30 years before these ideas began to be put into practice, and we are still some way from the ultimate conclusion but, surprisingly, the FA did give Chapman a chance to carry out some of his ideas in 1933. He travelled with the England party to Italy and Switzerland and, despite the objections of some of the selectors, was allowed to act as team manager, giving pre-match talks and trying to decide tactics in advance. With several Arsenal players in the team, this was obviously reasonably practical and the tour was a success — England drawing 1–1 with future world champions Italy in Rome and beating a strong Switzerland side 4–0.

The idea was not repeated, though there is no reason to suppose it might not have been eventually because Stanley Rous, secretary of the FA from 1934 and later, of course, President of Arsenal, was very much in favour. Chapman's death might have ended a good idea prematurely; with no obvious candidate to take his place the possibility died with him. It is arguable that, had Chapman lived longer, the principle might have been accepted and the whole history of post-war English international football could therefore have been very different.

The exploits of Arsenal as a team are covered elsewhere in this history, but to end a celebration of Herbert Chapman, the man who made the team and the club we know today, we should perhaps mention the most symbolic and yet most visible of all the man's achievements. When he took Leeds City to Highbury for the first time (on 6 December 1913) he had been particularly struck by the fact that the club had an underground station virtually in the ground. It was minutes from Piccadilly on the quickest and most direct of all the tube lines. The station, on what was then the Great Northern, Piccadilly and Brompton Railway, was actually opened in December 1906, when Chapman was playing for Spurs. There was only one problem, the station was called Gillespie Road. This was obviously a major advertising opportunity missed; what if all of the millions of people who travelled by the Piccadilly Line or looked at maps of the underground could see the name Arsenal right in front of their eyes? There was not much Chapman could do about it when he arrived at Highbury, but by 1932 the club was celebrated enough, and well supported enough, that he could invite the London Electric Railway (as it was by then called) to discuss the matter. Changing the name was not as simple as it sounds. In those days the destination was printed on each ticket, not to mention on all of the maps, in all of the time tables, and in all of the carriages. The LER was also no doubt wary of numerous other clubs requesting similar things (Chelsea are close to Fulham Broadway, then called Walham Green, though Fulham FC are not, West Ham are actually nowhere near the station of that name). On the other hand, Arsenal drew so many supporters that, Chapman argued, actually promoting the name might bring more passengers for the LER. Initially the railway proposed a compromise of Highbury Hill, but Chapman persisted and, on 5 November 1932, Arsenal became a fixture on maps throughout London. It remains the single greatest tribute to the skill, persuasion and perseverance of the man and Arsenal celebrated the honour with a 7–1 win at Molineux on the same day.

By the time Arsenal's half century came around Chapman was gone, dying from pneumonia at the age of 55. His bust, by the famous sculptor Jacob Epstein, was later placed in the magnificent entrance hall of the new East Stand, from where, for the last half century, he has watched over the club he raised to greatness. There are few clubs who can say with any certainty that they have already had their greatest manager and most influential era. It may not even be true of Arsenal, but it seems unlikely that there will ever be another Herbert Chapman.

· CHAPTER 2 ·
Royal Arsenal

All in all, 1886 was a memorable year for football. Blackburn Rovers completed the last ever hat-trick of FA Cup wins, winning a replay against West Bromwich Albion 2–0 on Derby Racecourse in the first final to be played outside London. It was the initial year of professionalism and, though the Scots banned their clubs and players from any involvement with English professional teams, there did not seem to be any obvious ill-effects south of the border. But when James Forrest, a professional with Blackburn Rovers, played at half-back for England in Glasgow the Scots objected and the England selectors made Forrest wear a different shirt to distinguish him from the ten England amateurs. The Football Association was already 23 years old, the FA Cup fifteen, but the game was still very different from the one we know today. Apart from the centre line, there were no pitch markings; there was no need to provide a crossbar; there were no nets or penalties; a goalkeeper could handle the ball anywhere on the pitch, and the referee had no power to award a free-kick or even a goal unless the players appealed to him. There was not even any requirement that all members of a team wear the same coloured shirts.

In the wider world, 1886 was not particularly momentous. Prime Minister William Gladstone introduced his first Irish Home Rule Bill, saw it defeated in the Commons and was replaced by Lord Salisbury, after whom the new capital of Rhodesia was to be named. Great Britain extended her African empire even further by annexing Zanzibar, and the Severn railway tunnel, then the longest in the world, was opened. Frances Burnett wrote Little Lord Fauntleroy, Robert Louis Stevenson published

Dr Jekyll and Mr Hyde and, on the sporting front, the foundation of the Lawn Tennis Association remains the most significant fact that the history books record.

But, tucked away in a backwater on the borders of rural Kent and the southern sprawl of the largest city in the world, other events were taking place of which the newspapers and public at large were, understandably, totally ignorant.

It was a small group of Scotsmen which was really behind what happened at the Woolwich Arsenal towards the end of 1886, first among them one David Danskin from Kirkcaldy in Fife. What he actually did was to found a works football team. At that time Kent was firmly rugby and cricket country, both alien games to a lowland Scot like Danskin. The only local clubs which can claim a prior place in football history are Blackheath and Blackheath School, both attenders at the historic first meeting of the Football Association in 1863. Both quickly defected to play rugby and Blackheath are, oddly, the only founder members of the FA still in existence. The local cricketers were no more sympathetic to Danskin — earlier in 1886 one Joseph Smith had tried to persuade the cricket club at the Woolwich Arsenal to allow part of their pitch to be used for football, but they would not hear of it. None of this was perhaps too surprising. The Arsenal, one of the government's main munitions factories, was rather out of place in both Kent and the Home Counties, as were many of the men who came to work there.

The real spur came with the arrival in Woolwich of two Nottingham Forest players, Fred Beardsley and Morris Bates. Forest were already one of the leading sides in the country, having been the first northern club to reach the semi-finals of the FA Cup, which they did in 1879, 1880 and 1885. On that last occasion they had forced the great Queen's Park to two matches with Fred Beardsley as their goalkeeper. Nottingham also had (and still has) an ordnance factory next door to the old Forest ground at Trent Bridge, and no doubt this was where Beardsley and Bates had worked before they moved to similar jobs in Woolwich. Their arrival pushed Danskin and three friends, Elijah Watkins, John Humble, and Richard Pearce, into action. They asked around to see who might be interested and 15 men were prepared to pay

6d (2½p) each to start up a club. Danskin added another three shillings (15p) out of his own pocket (a tenth of the weekly wages of a working man at the Arsenal at that time) and the club bought a football with the money. Apparently they had 1s 3d (6p) change.

It is interesting to relate that Fred Beardsley had worked for a previous spell at Woolwich Arsenal, back in 1884, and had helped form another team then. Beardsley told his grandson, R. A. Beardsley-Colmer, many years later that this club had been called Woolwich Union and had played on 'Piggy' Walton's field in Plumstead. Beardsley was always a football fanatic — he changed jobs in 1887, going to work for Siemen's Engineering, but they quickly dis-

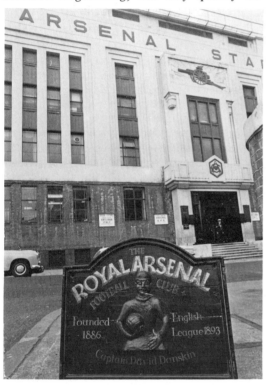

missed him because he took too much time off to play the game. Although it is possible that many of the same men who played for Woolwich Union also joined the new club, it would not be accurate to say that the one was the forerunner of the other, particularly as Danskin and John Humble were apparently not involved.

The likelihood is that there was more than one football team comprised of men from the Arsenal at that time. The better players probably turned out for several of them and the team that eventually became Royal Arsenal was no doubt a composite of some or all of these teams. The reason we today regard Danskins' Dial Square as the forerunner is that John Humble (and, to a lesser extent, Danskin himself) became the club's unofficial historian by virtue of eventually being associated with Arsenal longer than anyone else. Humble and Danskin naturally related their own experiences, the story of their earliest involvement with organised football in the Arsenal as they knew it. If another of the players, Beardsley for instance, had happened to

become honorary secretary, then he might have handed down a slightly different story for us to ponder today.

It is important to try and put ourselves in the position of those 15 founding fathers a century ago. As far as they were concerned, the team was a means of providing themselves with a little fun, exercise and, no doubt, a convivial social circle. They gave no thought to the future, of what their team might become. This was entirely sensible, for how could men who had yet to see a motor car and who would be grandfathers before they saw an aeroplane, possibly envisage an FA Cup final watched by thirty million people?

There were, to be sure, thousands of similar groups of young men dotted around the country whose identical efforts would never reach a history such as this. Naturally, only a tiny number of these sides were to rise, by good fortune and some genuine endeavour, to the national prominence of the next century.

The closest date we have for the initial subscriptions to Danskin's new club is October

Above left: **David Danskin effectively founded** the club by taking subscriptions in October 1886. This board was thought to have hung on the wall of the Royal Oak pub in Woolwich, where the club's name was changed to Royal Arsenal on 25 December 1886 and where its members regularly met. The sign found its way to Highbury in the 1950s.

Above: **Dial Square** today; for the first few weeks of the team's existence they had no name and were later referred to by Danskin as Dial Square simply because many of the 15 founders worked there. The workshop had been erected as long ago as 1717 and it was a worthy progenitor of such a famous club, for it had

Continued opposite ▷

Right: **A team line-up** at the Manor Ground in 1906. The framed figure is Fred Beardsley, then a director but earlier a key member of the 15 original founders. It was his arrival from mighty Nottingham Forest which prompted David Danskin to try to organise a team. Beardsley was the goal-keeper and one of his duties was to keep the goalposts in his garden, adjacent to Plumstead Common. It was also Beardsley who asked Forest for the loan of some old shirts. Instead they sent a full set of kit and Arsenal play in red to this day as a consequence of Beardsley's request. Beardsley had helped form an earlier club, Woolwich Union, at the Arsenal in 1884.

been designed by Vanbrugh, who also built Blenheim Palace for Marlborough and the facade of Kensington Palace for William and Mary. It acquired its name when the large sundial, still in place, was added in 1764.

Centre right: **John (or Jack) Humble,** for many years the club's secretary, chairman and director. At the age of 18 he walked to London from Durham, found a job at the Arsenal and became one of the 15 founders and Beardsley's understudy in goal. Largely responsible for recording the early details of the club, it was Humble who took it into the professional ranks of the League and who, after Chapman and Norris, must be regarded as the most important figure in its history.

1886, but it is unlikely that the founding of the Arsenal can accurately be attributed to any single day. Apart from the seven names mentioned earlier, others who paid at that point were named Price, Whitehead, Porteous, Gellatly, Ratcliffe and Brown (the other two must remain unrecorded by history). Danskin, Humble, Beardsley and Brown all lived to see Arsenal's first honour, the FA Cup victory in 1930. David Danskin himself was fortunate enough to witness all the successes of the decade that followed, writing to manager George Allison from his hospital bed after listening to the 1936 Cup final on radio, an arrangement surely not even vaguely imagined by his colleagues exactly half a century before when he put the whole thing in motion.

The first game of the new club was actually arranged against a team called Eastern Wanderers on 11 December 1886. There were one or two problems, such as the lack of a name, a pitch and any kit. For the time being the side, if it called itself anything at all, had simply used the name of one of the workshops within the Arsenal where many of the players were employed — Dial Square. The actual Dial Square had been erected as long ago as 1717, and acquired its name when a large sundial was built over its entrance in 1764. The facade of the building still exists, as does the sundial. The building is actually situated between Woolwich and Plumstead which in part explains why, despite their name, Woolwich Arsenal never played a single match in Woolwich itself.

Sadly, the historic first game did not take place anywhere near the Arsenal or Woolwich. The players crossed the Thames by the famous ferry to a piece of open ground someone had found on the Isle of Dogs. Elijah Watkins, whom Danskin had asked to be the first secretary, described it as follows: 'It eclipsed any

pitch I ever heard of or saw; I could not venture to say what shape it was, but it was bounded by back-yards for two thirds of the area and the other portion was . . . I was going to say a ditch, but an open sewer would be more appropriate. We had to pay handsomely to have . . . the mud cleaned out of our dressing-room afterwards!'

There was some dispute about the result, as there were no crossbars, hardly any pitch markings and the ball apparently spent a fair amount of its time in either the back gardens or the sewer. Nonetheless, Dial Square decided they had won 6–0 and met in the Royal Oak, next to Woolwich Arsenal station, on Christmas Day 1886 (a Saturday that year) full of enthusiasm. They immediately set about solving what they saw as their three major problems; a shortage of name, kit and somewhere to play. The name was easy — Dial Square was clearly far too unprepossessing and nothing less than Royal Arsenal would satisfy their ambitions. The name probably came from simply combining that of the pub they were sitting in with their place of work, though that was also referred to on occasions as the Royal Arsenal. It was to remain Royal until 1891, when Woolwich Arsenal was formally adopted though, strangely, the Football League insisted on calling the club Royal Arsenal until 1896.

The kit was almost as easy. Red was adopted because Beardsley and Bates already had shirts of that colour (first-class goalkeepers, like Beardsley, wore the same shirts as their colleagues until 1909), and in future players were supposed to provide their own shorts (several continued to wear knickerbockers) and real boots, as opposed to working boots with bars nailed across them. As the regal Royal Arsenal could not actually afford any of this kit, Fred Beardsley wrote to Nottingham Forest asking if

Right: The main entrance to the Woolwich Arsenal as it is today. Note the cannons on either side of the gateway. Most of the Arsenal is no longer in use and the club's grounds were one mile away in Plumstead anyway. Despite their name, Woolwich Arsenal never played a game in Woolwich itself.

Left: After their 6-0 success on the Isle of Dogs on 11 December 1886, the fifteen team members from Dial Square met in the Royal Oak (next, as the picture shows, to Woolwich Arsenal station) on Christmas Day 1886. It was there that they adopted the grand title of Royal Arsenal and, despite assumptions to the contrary, it is likely that the name came from a simple combination of the words in the picture – Royal from the pub and Arsenal from Woolwich. It is interesting that they were quick to drop Royal in 1891 when they turned professional.

they could help. Forest, who were the first team in the country to adopt uniform red when they began wearing caps of that colour in 1865, generously sent a complete set of red shirts and a ball and Arsenal have worn red and white, like Forest, for 100 years in consequence. The white sleeves, to add just a little extra distinction, were added by Chapman before a Highbury match against Liverpool on 4 March 1933.

Forest's ball was also useful, for the club didn't have one of those either, having lost the original somewhere along the line, but now all they lacked was somewhere to kick it. The only option was to use any convenient public land nearby and the obvious choice was Plumstead Common. This is not the flat, pleasant recreation area that the name conjures up, though it was also where Woolwich Union had played. Not only is it rather uneven and hilly, it was then also stony and rutted owing to it often being used by

the Royal Horse Artillery as a manoeuvring ground. While part of the old Common still exists, housing has been built on much of it in the intervening century and it is no longer possible to determine exactly where Royal Arsenal raised their goalposts. One thing we do know, however, is that the said goalposts were kept nearby in Fred Beardsley's back garden during the week. Many current League clubs started the same way. Spurs played on the Tottenham Marshes for five years before they were able to fence off an enclosure, being forced to do so by a combination of unruly spectators throwing mud at the players, their inability to take money and finding, on more than one occasion, that their carefully marked pitch had simply been stolen by another pair of teams.

The Reds (as they were then nicknamed) invited nearby Erith to Plumstead Common for a match on 8 January 1887, the first under the

Right: **Despite its name,** Plumstead Common is neither particularly flat nor particularly green. Very little of it remains undisturbed today and it was never a very good place to play football because of the ruts and damage caused by the Royal Horse Artillery, who used it for manoeuvres. It was, however, the closest public space to the Arsenal and that it why the team played on it during their first season, 1886-87. They played nine games after forming Royal Arsenal – winning six and drawing one. There is no record of exactly where their pitch was; indeed, it is possible that they played in different spots on the Common each week.

Left: **While playing on Plumstead Common,** the team would change in the local pubs. Of the three they were known to have used, only The Star, though altered, remains. The Common can be seen in the background, where the first ever game under the name Royal Arsenal was played (against Erith) on 8 January 1887.

without having kicked a ball, but that's another story). Within seven years of their foundation, Woolwich Arsenal were members of the Football League, a tribute to their entrepreneurial foresight rather, it must be said, than to their playing record.

The first few seasons, nonetheless, had their fair share of local success. As early as 1889 the club reached the semi-final of the London Senior Cup, where they were beaten 0–2 by Clapton. The following season they won the Kent Senior Cup, the Kent Junior Cup and, more significantly, the London Charity Cup. The latter was concluded with a 3–1 win over Old Westminsters (the old boys of Westminster School) at the Manor Field in front of 10,000 people. The team was Beardsley, McBean and Connolly (both full backs were from Kirkcaldy, Danskin's home town), Howatt, Bates (the captain) and Julian, Offer, Christmas, Robertson, Barbour and Fry. The Old Westminsters had their revenge in the London Senior Cup final, winning 1–0 in what was then the premier competition for clubs in the capital. These four competitions were no easy option, though it must be remembered that the London FA at this time was fiercely amateur and that Arsenal had the advantage of being a works team. Good players were found jobs at the Woolwich Arsenal by a sympathetic management and, on occasion, the club even bought out the contracts of footballing soldiers who they discovered stationed at the nearby barracks or enlisted with the Horse Artillery.

The next season, 1890–91, the Gunners won the London Senior Cup for the first time, beating Casuals 3–2 in the quarter-finals, Clapton 3–2 at the Oval in the semis (having been 2–0 down 25 minutes from the end) and St Bartholomew's Hospital 6–0 in the final, also at the Oval. This was the first really important

name Royal Arsenal, and their first formal 'fixture'. The first team ever to play under the name Arsenal was: Beardsley, Danskin and Porteous at full-back, Gregory, Price and Wells at half-back, and Smith, Moy, Whitehead, Crighton and Bee as forwards. Another eight fixtures had been completed by end of the season. The strength of Beardsley and Bates (who was known as the 'iron-headed man' because he regularly used his forehead, rare in an era of solid, heavy balls) was at the core of the team's early success, helped by the skills and occasional experience of several of the Scots, and they lost only two of their 10 matches that season.

Progress from here onwards was more than steady. Despite their humble origins, Arsenal actually had one of the fastest rises of all the early League clubs (Chelsea and Bradford City later went straight into the Football League

success for the club and, as the *Kentish Independent* reported: 'Excitement is a mild description for the scenes in Woolwich and Plumstead on the return of the football champions on Saturday night. A host of admirers met them at the Dockyard Station and drove them in open carriages, shouting and singing. There were celebrations everywhere all evening and, we fear, a good deal of drinking was mixed with the rejoicing and exultation.'

It was when they came up against the professionals, or even the leading amateur sides, that Royal Arsenal were made aware of their status. The club first entered the FA Cup, by far and away the most prestigious competition throughout the country, as early as 1889–90. Their first three ties were relatively easy, against Lyndhurst (an 11–0 victory in their first ever FA Cup match), Thorpe (who could not afford to come to London from Norwich for a replay after a 2–2 draw) and Crusaders. But Swifts beat them easily 5–1 in the next round and Derby County won 2–1 at the new Invicta ground in the first tie of the next season. Two Arsenal players, Peter Connolly and Bobby Buist, played so well in that game that John Goodall, the Derby captain and acting secretary-manager, offered them contracts. In the end they did not

THE WEEKLY HERALD.
FRIDAY, November 25, 1887.

origin in personal disappointment to the fact, that ... comprises a good third. The number of persons ... parity of the ratepayers ... Does the writer ... persons were desirous ... importance and were ... the objects of their ... say that his state-ment, I fail to see any ... is not as "A Correspondent" the care of the public ... of the word "primary" ... other duties—whether ... matters little—which the ... and, and to insist upon ... performance of these ... Green ratepayers in ... Parliament for Separa-... to the roads, and asks, footpaths, lighting, and ... that they are much ... years ago?" and he further ... say that because two ... repair that that circum-

course, and I therefore think "West Green" has been premature in lecturing the members upon their duty to the ratepayers in this matter.
I feel confident that our members will make themselves acquainted with the feeling of the Ward before pledging themselves, either to support or oppose the proposed scheme, and "West Green" would have done well to have waited until such feeling had been ascertained.—I am, Sir, yours faithfully,
ALF. A. ROBINSON.

FOOTBALL.

TOTTENHAM HOTSPUR v. ROYAL ARSENAL.—This match was played on the ground of the former at Park, Nov. 19th. The Spurs at once began to attack, but 10 minutes from the start, the Arsenal scored a lucky goal. From this point, the visitors were pressed throughout, and, had it not been for the splendid defence of F. Beardsley (Notts Forest), in goal, the score would have been much larger. Through darkness, the game was stopped 15 minutes before time, the Spurs winning by 2 goals to 1.
TOTTENHAM HOTSPUR (2nd XI) v. CHESHUNT.—This match was played on the ground of the former at Park, on Saturday, Nov. 19th, and after a pleasant game of 60 minutes, resulted in a draw, no goals being scored.

177, Salmon's L

BEST
We have as usual ob ... that o

BEST
2s 0d,
Compare our 2s Tea with t ... Tasted by E

The only known match report on the first ever meeting between Spurs and Arsenal, on 19 November 1887. The game was played on the Tottenham Marshes and Spurs won 2-1. As Arsenal arrived late the game lasted only 75 minutes but this was by no means unusual in those days, as can be seen from the second report. Since that day (and up to August 1985), the clubs have met 185 times, Arsenal winning 73, Spurs 78, with 34 draws. Note that Arsenal are already being described as 'lucky'.

***This page:* The Manor Ground was Arsenal's main home** south of the river until 1913. They moved there on 11 February 1888. The site was next door to what is known as Royal Arsenal East (*upper left*), which explains why the club played in Plumstead rather than Woolwich. Plumstead station is behind the far embankment and the previous pitch (Sportsman Ground) was the next field on the left. Apart from the name of the main road (Manor Way) there is nothing left to give any indication that crowds of 25,000 once watched First Division football on this very site. It is now occupied by Manor Way, a roundabout, and the Plumstead Bus Garage. The game *above* was against Liverpool on 2 September 1905 (Arsenal won 3-1) and the view from exactly the same position

Right: **An altogether more impressive line-up,** taken in the summer of 1890. The trophies are the Ken Senior Cup, the Kent Junior Cup, the London Charity Cup (probably the Shield in fact) and a cup won in a six-a-side competition at the Agricultural Hall, Islington. The picture seems to have been taken at their new ground, the Invicta, to which they moved that summer. Founder David Danskin is second left on the bottom row. These are the only two known pictures of the club's founder.

Below: **The first known team picture,** probably taken before the London Association Cup match against Phoenix on 3 November 1888. The line up is, seated: Morris, Barbour, Brown, Connolly, Danskin, Chatteris. Standing: Horsington, Wilson, Beadsley, Bates, McBean, Scott. At back: Parr

today is seen *left*. The strange shaped roof of the engineering works on the horizon is the only remaining identifiable landmark. The embankment from which the picture *left* was taken and which can be seen in the centre of the picture *upper left* is not part of the railway but is, in fact, the Southern Outfall Sewer, the main liquid waste disposal for the whole of South London. When it was

constructed above ground at the turn of the century, it provided a perfect spot from which to watch the Reds (as they were then called) free of charge. As a result the club built a new, steeply banked terrace at the west and south ends of the ground, largely to cut off the view from the sewer bank. This was completed in 1904 and the many local soldiers who came to games quickly dubbed it

Spion Kop, after the famous Boer War battle in which hundreds of British soldiers had been slaughtered in crowded trenches on the top of a South African hill. The name Kop was later adopted on other grounds (most notably Anfield) but the one in Woolwich was the first large earth terrace and the original.

go, but the event set the alarm bells ringing in the Arsenal committee and was to begin the train of events which took Royal Arsenal into the Football League and also led to the foundation of the Southern League.

By this stage the club had settled at a formal address, the Invicta Ground (Invicta is the motto of the county of Kent). After playing on the Common in 1886–87, for the 1887–88 season they had occupied the Sportsman Ground in Plumstead, an old pig farm situated on the edge of Plumstead Marshes, but this pitch had a predictable tendency to become waterlogged. On the morning of their first home game against prime local rivals Millwall (to be precise on 11 February 1888), the committee arrived at the Sportsman Ground to find it under water.

Looking up Manor Road towards Plumstead Station, they noticed that the field next door, which was used as pastureland, appeared dry. Jack Humble rushed round to the owner, a Mr Cavey, and asked permission to use it. He agreed, Woolwich Arsenal drew 3–3, and for the next two years (1888–90) they played on the Manor Field, which they rather grandly called the Manor Ground. After the Cup successes of 1889 and 1890, they decided to move just across Plumstead High Street, to a new ground which already had a stand, terraces and dressing rooms — the Invicta. At the Manor Field, they had to rope off the pitch and bring in wagons (borrowed from the nearby barracks) if they expected a big crowd, which would mean around 500 to 1000. The players usually changed at the Green Man in Plumstead High Street or at the Railway Tavern beside the station (neither exists today), and often had to help with collecting the money.

All this seemed behind them at the Invicta, particularly when, on Easter Monday 1891, they attracted 12,000 fans to see a game against Scottish Champions Hearts. But when the landlord put a massive increase on the rent (from £200 to £350 per annum) hoping to exploit the club's election to the Football League in 1893, they could not pay and had to move again. The Invicta's owner was one George Weaver, of the Weaver Mineral Water Company, and after Arsenal left two rows of houses were built on the site named Mineral and Hector Streets. The old Manor Ground was repurchased and club and supporters worked through the summer of 1893 to get it ready for the Second Division. The club stayed there, opposite Plumstead Station, for 20 years until a final move far further afield than anyone could have envisaged in these early days.

Back in 1891, committee member and occasional goalkeeper John Humble was very shaken by the ease with which his better players could be lured away by a Football League club if they were playing well. As Royal Arsenal were nominally amateur (though their players were undoubtedly paid 'expenses') there was nothing to stop any of them accepting an offer from a professional club. The next step was a bold one, for everyone knew the obsessive hatred the London FA had of that evil northern virus professionalism, and few had yet dared challenge it. This was to be a problem for another decade and a half, eventually ending in virtually a complete break when the London, Surrey and Middlesex FAs formed the Amateur Football Association as an entirely separate body from the official FA in 1907.

Jack (as he was usually known) Humble deserves something of a diversion for, apart from being the most important influence on the club's history after Herbert Chapman and his chairman Henry Norris, he seems to typify the men who worked at the Arsenal and who founded the football club. He was born in a village called East Hartburn in County Durham in 1862. His father and mother died within three months of each other in 1880 and Jack and his elder bother decided to leave the relatively depressed North East. Not being able to afford the train fare, they walked from Durham to London and had both found jobs as engine fitters at the Arsenal by the time of the 1881 census. Their's was a hard but common story of the times. The Arsenal drew large numbers of poor men from the Midlands, the North and Scotland, of whom Danskin, Beardsley and Humble were unusual probably only in their devotion to, and skill at, football. Humble was to remain connected with the club for four decades, for much of that time the last link with the real working men who had founded the club.

At the 1891 AGM, held in the Windsor Castle Music Hall, Humble proposed taking the chance of going professional to ensure they kept their best players and this was carried by a large majority. Jack Humble declared at this meeting

that: 'The club (has been) carried on by working men and it is my ambition to see it carried on by them.' This was in objection to an additional proposal that a limited liability company should be formed simultaneously. Though this was to be adopted two years later, in 1893, it seems to have been regarded as a retrograde step, against the sporting ethos of the club and (rightly as it proved) endangering the control of the working men who had founded it. Humble, nonetheless, remained a director until a scandal in 1927 forced him, though wholly innocent, to resign.

The London FA were apoplectic about professionals in any form, and immediately banned Arsenal, their previous Cup winners, from all competitions under their auspices and expelled them into the bargain. The only modern-day equivalent is the reaction of the Rugby Union to anyone who has ever played rugby league or written a book (and taken payment) about his experiences as a player. But for Woolwich Arsenal (the AGM had also changed the name — presumably because calling a professional club Royal might have invoked even more fury from above) the arguments were not as arcane as they are today; the problems were very practical and very real.

They were effectively banned from playing in all competitions except the FA Cup or in friendlies against professional clubs from the North or Midlands. The FA Cup was therefore financially critical, but their first round tie in January 1892 took them to Small Heath (later renamed Birmingham) and they went down ignominiously 5–1. The following year was even worse — a first round proper 6–0 defeat by Sunderland.

There seemed only one solution — to try to form a southern version of the Football League, providing real competitive fixtures, and thus to staunch the ebb of support that the club was experiencing. In February 1892, just after their Cup ejection by Sunderland, Woolwich Arsenal called a meeting of possible southern members and, initially at least, there was real enthusiasm. Twelve sides were elected: Chatham, Chiswick Park, Crouch End, Ilford, Luton, Marlow, Millwall, Old St Mark's, Reading, Swindon, West

Above: **Between their foundation in 1886** and the move to Highbury in 1913, Arsenal played in four different locations in Plumstead. There is now no trace whatsoever of three of these pitches (the Common, Sportsman Ground and Manor Ground) and the only remaining trace of the fourth is some terracing in the back gardens of one or two houses in Hector Street, Plumstead. This was once the Invicta Ground (named after the motto of Kent) and was Arsenal's home between 1890 and 1893. When the club was elevated to the Football League in 1893, the landlord, one George Weaver, tried to increase the rent from £200 per year to £350. The club refused and moved back to the Manor Field. Weaver gave up his dreams of sporting glory (or profit) and built houses on the site, completely obliterating it except for these few feet of eerily nostalgic concrete.

Right bottom: **In April 1948** the Gunners invited the only three living members of their first professional team of 1891 to a game versus Chelsea. The three are (*left to right*) Bill Julian, Gavin Crawford and John McBean. Julian had gone to work at the Arsenal in 1889 and became the first professional captain two years later. The picture (*centre*) shows him in the kit of the era, though the star suggests he had just appeared as a guest for Luton. Gavin Crawford was a Scot who became the first professional imported by the club in 1891. John

Continued opposite ▷

McBean and Julian said in 1948 that the club grew so quickly in the 1890s because of government rearmament policies (to counter the perceived Imperial threat of the French rather than the Germans) which obviously brought thousands of men to work in the Arsenal and to serve in local army units. This created a supply of players but, more important, also a base of support from displaced Scots, Northerners and Midlanders whose natural game was ill-served in London; Woolwich was hence something of a sporting oasis in the unsympathetic Home Counties, and a natural to host the first Southern member of the League.

Herts (forerunners of Watford) and Arsenal. If the inclusion of Old St Mark's and Crouch End suggests that the meeting was not particularly priescient, then this is further confirmed by the fact that Spurs came bottom of the poll, un-elected with just one vote (presumably their own). Nine years later Tottenham were to become the first Southern professional club to win a major honour, the FA Cup. The meeting was held on 24 February 1892 in Anderton's Hotel, Fleet Street. There was an obvious symbolic significance in the location, for it was in the very same hotel that the Football League itself had been formed four years before.

The London FA predictably exploded again, threatening to ban the other eleven clubs as well as Arsenal. Surprisingly, they all backed down, though the idea was successfully revived a year later by Millwall. Arsenal, with no one local to play against, were now getting desperate. There seemed only one gamble, and that a tremendous long shot at best. This was to apply for membership of the Football League, though the Woolwich club had never previously played in any league competition.

At the end of the 1892–93 season the Second Division was extended from 12 to 15 clubs. This created three vacancies, and two more sur-prisingly yawned when Bootle resigned and Accrington (a different club from the later, ill-fated, Stanley) refused to play in the Second Division after being relegated from the First. Newcastle United and Rotherham Town were given places without a vote, and Liverpool, Arsenal and Middlesbrough Ironopolis were elected at a later meeting. There were actually only seven recorded new candidates, the others being Doncaster Rovers and Loughborough Town. The simultaneous addition of Liverpool, Newcastle and Arsenal, who were to win an astonishing 26 of the next 80 Championships of the organisation they joined together, must surely be the most distinguished of all the League's annual elections. It was also clearly Arsenal's good fortune to have applied at a time when there were so many vacancies. In a typical year they would have stood no chance, and even in a year with two new vacancies (the most at any normal time) they could have had little hope of success. On such random chances do great stories depend.

As there were no League clubs south of Birmingham and Burton, it was a considerable step for the League to take. Most journeys would be overnight, costs would be high, Woolwich Arsenal had no record of massive crowd support and they were hardly attractive visitors. On the playing front, the FA Cup was usually the acid test for new applicants, and here Arsenal could only be said to have failed dismally. They had never progressed beyond the first round proper and, oddly, were never to achieve even that small distinction in the re-mainder of the nineteenth century. Nonetheless, someone on the League Management Committee had the foresight to recognise the benefits. Firstly, if the League was ever to become a national institution, it must have members in London, the capital and the country's dominant city. Secondly travel was becoming less onerous. Cities like Manchester and Liverpool were now only four and a half hours from London by the fastest trains (even if Plumstead was nearly another hour on the other side). And thirdly, and perhaps the telling point in the end, to admit Arsenal would be to reward the club's brave stand on professionalism and to encourage others to do the same.

All in all, the summer of 1893 was a critical moment for the future of football. The Scottish FA finally accepted professionalism at their AGM the same month as Arsenal's admittance to the League, and 16 southern clubs were also persuaded to form the Southern League, though only half were professional at the time. All three decisions were major stepping stones on the road to legitimacy for the League and the FA in creating a general acceptance of professionalism and, a mere seven years old, Arsenal were playing a major part.

It was Arsenal's first significant contribution to the history of football. For the club and its board, however, one rather more immediate consequence of the club's arrival in the League, and the raising of the rent at the Invicta, was the decision to try and buy a ground of their own. The only way to raise enough money was to form a limited liability company, and this, despite those earlier objections, happened in the summer of 1893. The new company had a nominal capital of 4,000 £1 shares. In all 860 people subscribed for 1,552 shares (the rest were left unissued) and most of the shareholders were manual workers at the Arsenal who lived locally. There were only three holdings of 20 shares or more, the highest being 50 by a coffee house proprietor. The first board contained a surgeon, a builder and six engineers from the Arsenal. At that moment, without a ground, large crowds, or obvious playing resources, the problems were actually just about to begin.

· CHAPTER 3 ·
Woolwich Arsenal

The twenty years between Woolwich Arsenal joining the Football League in 1893 and their departure for Highbury in 1913 could not exactly be described as a period of unqualified success. Indeed, apart from the six-year spell following Harry Bradshaw's arrival as manager in 1901, it could better be termed one of financial struggle and footballing mediocrity. The Gunners were never a bad Second Division side. They chuntered along in mid-table until Bradshaw's arrival resulted in a fourth, third and second in successive seasons, the last gaining them promotion to the top division for the first time in 1904. They stayed there nine years, but never finished better than sixth and even that performance was not as outstanding as it sounds for they won 14, lost 14 and drew 10. Indeed, in only one of the nine First Division seasons between 1904 and 1913 did they win more League games than they lost.

The FA Cup is perhaps a better guide to their real status, for Arsenal were to go beyond the second round (the equivalent of today's fourth) only twice between 1893 and the First World War. Admittedly, these years, 1906 and 1907, were the highlight of the whole era, for Arsenal reached the semi-final in both seasons, but that proved the last gasp of the team Bradshaw built. He had already left, being lured away to Fulham in 1904, of whom we shall hear much more later.

So, 1904 to 1907 apart, the era was really the story of a struggle against geography and the rise of the other professional London clubs. Geography was perhaps the more insoluble of the two. Despite seeming to be relatively close to the middle of London, Woolwich is actually something of a backwater. No one passes through, it is difficult to reach from the eastern side, and the river effectively cut Arsenal's geographical circle of support by half. It was also a good 20 to 30-minute tram ride further out than the nearest major club (at the time Millwall Athletic), and was always a particularly inconvenient place to get to by rail, despite the Manor Ground being literally across the road from Plumstead Station.

George Allison was a junior sports reporter with Hulton's before the First World War and was given Woolwich Arsenal as his regular team. He told more than a few amusing stories about trying to get there: 'From Fleet Street to Plumstead was heavy going. Other sports writers

were more than happy when I offered to undertake all the reporting of Arsenal's home games — meaning I wrote about them for most of the Saturday, Sunday and daily papers, often doing ten different reports (on the same) match. The payment I received softened the monotony of the long and tedious journey (Allison was, in consequence, often called George Arsenal by his colleagues). One could travel on the South Eastern and Chatham Railway from London Bridge, Cannon Street or Charing Cross. The trains stopped at every station. There were the same halts on the return journey, with the added difficulty that no one knew where the trains were going. I once travelled back with a soldier, who asked a porter on Plumstead Station where we were going. "London Bridge," he was told. At the next station he asked another railwayman. "Charing Cross," was the answer this time. He asked again at the next station and was given a third answer. Eventually he told one railway

Below: **Some of the early season tickets** from the Manor Ground covering seasons 1894-95, 1895-96 and 1896-97. The holder simply showed them on entry and the club was noted for encouraging their use – for many years Arsenal had more season ticket holders than any other club in the country.

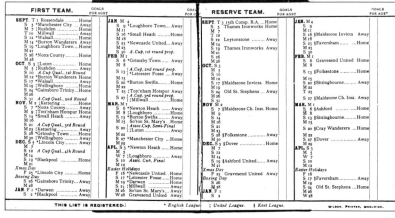

FIRST TEAM.	GOALS FOR AGST			RESERVE TEAM.	GOALS FOR AGST		
SEPT. T 1 Rossendale ....Home		**JAN.** M 4		**SEPT** T 3 15th Comp. R.A. ....Home		**JAN.** M 4	
S 7 *Manchester City ...Away		S 9 ‡Loughboro Town... Away		S 5 Thames Ironworks Home		S 9	
M 7 ‡Rushden ....Home		M 11		M 7		S 11	
T 10 Millwall ....Away		S 16 *Small Heath ....Home		T 10		S 16 ‡Maidstone Invicta Away	
S 12 *Walsall.................Home		M 18		M 12		M 18	
M 14 *Burton Wanderers ...Away		S 23 *Newcastle United... Away		M 14		S 23 ‡Faversham ....Home	
S 19 *Loughboro Town ...Home		M 25		S 19 Thames Ironworks Away		M 25	
M 21		S 30 A.Cup, 1st round prop.		M 21		S 30	
S 26 *Notts County ....Home		**FEB.** M 1		M 26		**FEB.** M 1	
M 28		S 6 *Grimsby Town ... Away		M 28		S 6 Gravesend United Home	
OCT. S 3 ‡Luton .... Home		M 8		**OCT.** S 3		M 8	
M 5 ‡Rushden ....Away		S 13 { A.Cup, 2nd round prop.		M 5		S 13 ‡Folkestone ....Home	
S 10 A.Cup Qual., 1st Round		*Leicester Fosse ... Away		S 10		M 15	
M 12 *Burton Wanderers Home		M 15		S 12		S 20 ‡Sittingbourne..... Away	
S 17 *Walsall...............Away		S 20 *Burton Swifts.......Home		S 17 ‡Maidstone Invicta Home		M 22	
M 19 ‡Wellingboro ....Away		M 22		M 19		T 25	
S 24 *Gainsboro Trinity ...Home		T 25 { A.Cup, 3rd round prop.		S 24 Old St. Stephens ... Away		S 27 ‡Maidstone Ch. Inst. Away	
M 26		‡Millwall ....Away		M 26			
S 31 A.Cup Qual., 2nd Round		**MAR.** M 1		M 31		**MAR.** M 1	
NOV. M 2 ‡Kettering ....Home		S 6 *Newton Heath ......Home		**NOV.** M 2 ‡Maidstone Ch. Inst. Home		S 6 ‡Ashford ....Home	
S 7 *Notts County ....Away		M 8 ‡Loughboro ....Home		S 7		M 8	
M 9 ‡Tott'nham Hotspur Home		S 13 *Burton Swifts.......Away		S 9		S 13 ‡Sittingbourne.........Home	
S 14 *Small Heath .... Away		M 15 So'ton St. Mary's...Home		S 14		M 15	
M 16		S 20 { A.Cup, Semi-Final		S 16		S 20 ‡Cray Wanderers ...Away	
S 21 A.Cup Qual., 3rd Round		‡Luton ....Away		S 21		M 22	
M 23 ‡Kettering ....Away		M 22		S 23		S 27 ‡Dover .... Away	
S 28 *Grimsby Town ....Home		S 27 *Manchester City ...Away		S 28 ‡Folkestone .... Away			
M 30 ‡Wellingboro ....Home		M 29		M 30			
DEC. S 5 ‡Lincoln City ....Away		**APL.** S 3 *Newton Heath ......Home		**DEC.** S 5 ‡Dover ....Home		**APL.** S 3	
M 7		M 5		M 7		M 5	
S 12 A.Cup Qual., 4th Round		W 7 ‡Loughboro ....Away		S 12		W 7	
M 14		S 10 Assoc. Cup, Final		M 14		S 10	
S 19 *Blackpool ....Home				S 19 ‡Ashford United...... Away		S 17	
M 21				M 21		M 19	
Xmas Day		*Easter Holidays*		*Xmas Day*		*Easter Holidays*	
F 25 ‡Lincoln City ....Home		F 16 *Newcastle United...Home		F 25 Gravesend United Away		F 16	
Boxing Day		S 17 *Leicester Fosse....Home		*Boxing Day*		S 17 ‡Faversham ....Away	
S 26 *Gainsboro Trinity... Away		M 19 *Darwen ....Away		S 26		M 19	
		M 28		M 28		S 24 Old St. Stephens ...Home	
JAN. F 1 *Darwen ....Away		S 24 *Millwall ....Away		**JAN.** F 1		M 26	
S 2 *Blackpool ....Away		M 26 So'ton St. Mary's ...Away		S 2		W 28	
		W 28 *Gravesend United ...Home					
THIS LIST IS REGISTERED.]				* *English League*	‡ *United League.*	§ *Kent League.*	
						WILSON, PRINTER, WOOLWICH.	

official "You're a bloody liar, you don't know where it's going".'

When Woolwich Arsenal joined the League in 1893, they were London's only professional club. Fifteen years later, there were five in the Football League alone (Chelsea, Spurs, Fulham and Clapton Orient were the others — Spurs having already won the Cup), plus a range of good Southern League sides like Millwall Athletic and Crystal Palace not to mention excellent local amateur clubs such as Clapton and Dulwich. Amateur football remained strong in South London for many years, not only drawing support but also many of the good players who emerged. Arsenal's unique position had been eroded remarkably quickly.

Additionally, there was the Boer War between 1899 and 1902, an enormous blow to a club whose dependence on the military, in its earlier days, cannot be over-estimated. This took both players and support out of the area, particularly as the Arsenal itself introduced a Saturday afternoon shift. The tradition throughout the country at that time was for men to knock-off at Saturday lunch-time (there was no such thing as a full two-day weekend), have a drink and go to the game. The war was to prove almost as much a disaster for Arsenal as it was for the British troops in South Africa.

By the turn of the century the Reds (as they were then nicknamed) had so far managed to hold their own in the Second Division. The long distances were something of a help to them, for they rarely lost at home (only 13 defeats in the first five seasons). On the other side of the coin, they did not pick up many points away, never winning more than three games on the road in a single season until 1897–98.

There were occasional highlights — the very first game of their League career was on Saturday 2 September 1893 against another newly elected club, Newcastle. It ended 2–2, Shaw and Elliott being the scorers. Arsenal's first League win did not come until 11 September, at home to Walsall Town Swifts, when John Heath scored a hat-trick in a 4–0 home victory. Almost exactly two years earlier (on 14 September 1891) Heath had written his own ineradicable place in the history books when he scored from the first penalty ever awarded in an English first-class match (he was then playing for Wolves against Accrington). Newcastle scored six against the Gunners at the end of the month, and Burton Swifts did the same in November, but Arsenal returned the compliment twice during the season — against opponents Middlesbrough Ironopolis (away from home) and Northwich Victoria, both long since gone from the Football League. All in all,

Below: **The first team squad** at the start of the 1895-96 season; top: Boyle, Powell, Storer, Caldwell, Hollis; centre: Davis, Jenkyns, Ward; bottom: Mills, Hare, Buchanan, O'Brian, Mortimer. It was an average season, the side finishing seventh in the Second Division. John Boyle's season was particularly interesting – he played six times at half back and four times in goal. The club tried six men between the posts during the season in an attempt to replace the departed Storer.

Right: **Harry Storer, the first choice keeper** in 1894 and 1895. When he was chosen to represent the Football League against the Scottish League on 13 April 1895, he became the first Arsenal player to win representative honours. Storer is wearing the red and light blue striped shirt that the club briefly tried in 1895. As the idea was not pursued, one can only assume that just the single set of kit was ever purchased. Goalkeepers wore the same shirts as the rest of their team until 1909.

ninth place out of fifteen in their first season, with 28 points from 28 games, was acceptable, though Liverpool took all the attention by winning the division undefeated — the last time this was to occur in English football history.

The next few seasons were similarly unspectacular, though consecutive home games on 6 and 12 April 1895 did see a 7–0 victory over Crewe and a 6–1 victory over Walsall Town Swifts.

The club soon gained its first representative honours. Goalkeeper Harry Storer was chosen between the posts for the Football League against the Scottish League in April 1895 and the gloriously named Caesar Llewellyn Jenkyns became the first current full international when he represented Wales against Scotland on 21 March 1896. Typically, both men were too good for the club and had been transferred within a year. Also too good were, surprisingly, Loughborough Town, who beat the Gunners 8–0 away in a Second Division game on 12 December 1896. The Loughborough defeat came during a peculiar spell which has never been surpassed before or since by the club. Between October 17 and Christmas Day 1896, their League results went as follows: a 3–5 defeat at Walsall, a 6–1 win over Gainsborough Trinity, a 4–7 defeat by Notts County, a 2–5 defeat by Small Heath, a 4–2 win over Grimsby, a 3–2 victory over Lincoln, the 0–8 defeat at Loughborough, a 4–2 win over Blackpool and a 6–2 Christmas Day romp past Lincoln. In nine

34

games they had scored 32 goals and conceded 34.

Imagine how enthusiastic fans would be today if they could count on seeing seven goals per game — and with very little idea of who would score the most. There was no obvious excuse for the Loughborough defeat (that team's only claim to fame nearly 100 years later) except that, perhaps, Arsenal's regular keeper Fairclough had been replaced by Leather. On the other hand Fairclough had conceded 23 goals on his last six appearances so this hardly counts as an excuse at all. Goalkeepers had long been Arsenal's achilles heel — as early as 1893–94 they had no recognised custodian and full back William Jeffrey played 12 games at left back and another 10 in goal!

The result at Loughborough remains Arsenal's record defeat, but the compliment was quickly returned on 12 March 1900 when Loughborough came to the Manor Ground and were themselves beaten 12–0. This is still Arsenal's record victory and is one of only 18 occasions when a side has scored a dozen goals in a Football League fixture. The peculiarity of having a record defeat and record victory against the same team, particularly only four years apart and against a club which left the League as long ago as 1900, is not surprisingly also unparalleled.

Sadly, these talking points only serve to brighten an essentially dour, unspectacular period. A disastrous FA Cup defeat by non-League Millwall (2–4 away) on 16 January 1896 proved one turning point for the committee. They decided to appoint a secretary-manager, one T.B. Mitchell from Blackburn, who was quickly succeeded by George Elcoat from Stockton. When Harry Bradshaw took over at the turn of the century the club were going nowhere very fast. He soon brought in the two most notable players of the period, an Australian left back, Jimmy Jackson, who became both club

captain and a leader determined to control everything on the pitch, and a new goalkeeper from Sheppey United, Jimmy Ashcroft. When Ashcroft played in all three internationals in 1905–06, he became the first Arsenal player to be capped for England. Results and support improved slowly. By February 1903, over 25,000 were prepared to turn out to see Cup holders Sheffield United win a first round FA Cup tie 3–1 in Plumstead. The receipts were a healthy £1,000, the first time the club had passed the four-figure mark.

The following season, 1903–04, led to promotion. This was almost entirely the result of an excellent home record, with an astonishing goal average of 67 to 5. Not a match was lost at home (all were won but the last two) and there were 8–0 wins over Burton United and Leicester Fosse. The away record was not so impressive, with just six wins, but the overall goal tally of 91–22 could still be regarded as the best in the club's history, it being very difficult to compare seasons with differing numbers of matches. Proud Preston won the division a point ahead of Arsenal, with Manchester United another point behind third. The team which gained promotion was Jimmy Ashcroft (who played in every game), Archie Cross (a local lad from Dartford), captain Jimmy Jackson, John Dick, Percy Sands (an amateur schoolteacher who taught in Woolwich), Roddy McEachrane (a neat Inverness-born schemer who played left half), Tommy Briercliffe (signed from Blackburn), Tim Coleman, Bill Gooing (the centre forward, who was another ever present), Tommy Shanks (the leading scorer with 25 League goals) and Bill Linward (signed from West Ham). Of the twenty players to appear in the promotion season, only two had been with the club before Bradshaw's arrival as manager. Shanks was not only Arsenal's leading scorer, he was also the League's. Only two other Arsenal players have

subsequently led the Football League's lists in a single season — Ted Drake in 1934–35 and Ronnie Rooke in 1947–48.

Woolwich Arsenal's success quickly brought problems in its wake. Bradshaw was lured away to Fulham for a large salary before the next season had even begun and his Woolwich successor, Phil Kelso, was also to go to Craven Cottage five years later. Fulham have a strange affinity for Arsenal when choosing their managers — no less than nine of the first 14 at Craven Cottage either played for or managed the Gunners.

Kelso was a Scotsman, previously manager of Hibernian, and he reinforced the side, as many have done before and since, with his fellow countrymen. Initially gates were good (averaging over 10,000) and the club made a particular point of encouraging season-ticket holders, one result being that for a time they had more than any other club in the country.

Those supporters were well rewarded in 1906 when the club managed to get past the second round for the first time in their 20-year history and reach the semi-finals of the FA Cup. Nor was it an easy run: West Ham were beaten away after a home draw, then Watford 3–0, Sunderland (already having been League Champions four times) 5–0, a sensational result at the time, and then Manchester United 3–2 away in the quarter final. Charlie Buchan, a Woolwich lad, later wrote that he sold one of his school books to pay for his admission to that Sunderland game, and was beaten for it afterwards. He could not have realised that he was watching the two clubs which would span most of his famous career.

The semi-final was at Stoke, against all-conquering Newcastle. Between 1905 and 1911 the Magpies were to reach five FA Cup finals and Arsenal did not really stand in their way. Newcastle won 2–0 with goals from the great Colin Veitch and Jimmy Howie, though they then lost the final 1–0 to Everton. Arsenal had fielded one of their best ever forward lines and, early on, centre forward Bert Freeman hit the bar before Newcastle had scored. Arsenal could not hold Freeman for more than a couple of years, and had to sell him to Everton. He was to lead the Football League's goalscorers three times between 1908 and 1913 and finally won an FA Cup winner's medal when he scored the only goal of the game for Burnley v Liverpool in 1914. The two wingers were also internationals — Bill Garbutt on the right (capped for England later when with Blackburn) and the unpredictable Scot Bobby Templeton on the left. Templeton had won caps when with Aston Villa and Newcastle and is sadly perhaps best remembered for his part in the 1902 Ibrox disaster during the game there between England and Scotland. He had set off on one of his mazy runs down the wing and was doing so well that thousands on his side of the field pressed forward to get a better look. The movement caused a wooden stand to sway and collapse, and 25 people died as they fell through to the ground.

Considering that they had never before gone beyond the second round, it was a great surprise to see Arsenal pop up in the semi-final again the following year. This time their progress was easier, past Grimsby, Bristol City (at the time lying second in the First Division), Bristol Rovers and Barnsley. They met mighty Wednesday at St Andrew's in the semi-final and Arsenal went one up after only ten minutes when Garbutt headed in a Satterthwaite cross.

Left: **The Wednesday (they did not add Sheffield until 1929)** attack from a corner during the 1907 FA Cup semi-final at St Andrew's. It was the second consecutive year that Arsenal had reached the semi-final stage – a great surprise to their supporters as they had never previously gone beyond the second round. The Wednesday forward heading goalwards is actually Harry Chapman, Herbert Chapman's brother, and the Arsenal keeper is Jimmy Ashcroft. In the previous season, 1905-06, Ashcroft had become the first Arsenal player to be capped for England when he appeared in all three home internationals. Standing next to the goal-line is the famous 16-stone Charlie Satterthwaite; Satterthwaite's power became legendary after a 25-yard shot against Sheffield United hit the bar so hard that it bounced back, knocked the keeper out cold and still rebounded into the net. Against Wednesday, Satterthwaite provided the cross for Garbutt to open the scoring but Wednesday came back to win 3-1 and Arsenal had to wait another 20 years before they won a semi-final.

Football at Highbury.

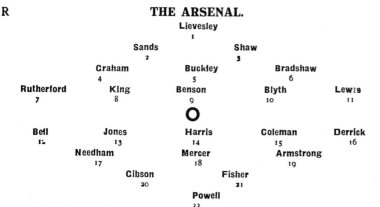

TEAMS FOR TO-DAY.

R   THE ARSENAL.   L

Lievesley
1

Sands   Shaw
2   3

Graham   Buckley   Bradshaw
4   5   6

Rutherford   King   Benson   Blyth   Lewis
7   8   9   10   11

O

Bell   Jones   Harris   Coleman   Derrick
12   13   14   15   16

Needham   Mercer   Armstrong
17   18   19

Gibson   Fisher
20   21

Powell
22

NOTTS FOREST.   R

Linesmen : J. North and W. H. Walton.

Referee : H. T. Yates.

Right: **Perhaps the most valuable of all Arsenal programmes** – that from the last game the club ever played in the Second Division. The match was against Forest on 24 April 1915 and, happily, the centenary year of 1986-87 marks 68 years in the top flight, equalling Sunderland's long standing record. The programme also announced manager George Morrell's resignation and the effective closure of the club and first-class football for the duration of the war. It turned out to be a remarkable game to match an historic moment. Arsenal won 7-0 with four goals for King and two for the out-of-position full-back Bob Benson. Within a year Benson was dead, collapsing during a wartime game at Reading and dying in trainer George Hardy's arms. The League table in the same programme showed Arsenal as sixth in the Second Division and this position was not altered in the official Football League records after the game had concluded the season. Arsenal were thus quoted, and printed, as finishing sixth in 1915 for the next 65 years until, in 1980, the Association of Football Statisticians pointed out that the 7-0 win had taken them over Birmingham on goal average and they actually finished fifth. In normal circumstances this might have seemed irrelevant but because of what happened in 1919 the repetition of the error for six decades was astonishing.

Then came tragedy; keeper Ashcroft was injured in a collison with centre forward David Wilson when coming outside his area to collect a loose ball (at this time keepers could handle anywhere in their own half) and Wilson scored from the free-kick which referee Jack Howcroft had controversially awarded Wednesday. The incident turned the game and Wednesday scored twice more (making it 3–1) to reach Crystal Palace for the final, which they won by beating Everton 2–1.

Nonetheless, it had seemed to be a very successful season for the Reds, perhaps a sign of things to come. They were seventh in the First Division, the reserves had won the London League and the South Eastern League, inside right John 'Tim' Coleman had played for England and full back Jimmy Sharp for Scotland. As it happened, it was actually the top of the roller-coaster, not part of a careful ascent. The club's support and finances were not strong enough to survive a decline in results, and, once things started to go wrong, they accelerated virtually out of control.

The problems were initially much more acute off the field than on it, where the side finished 15th, 6th and 18th between 1907–08 and 1909–10. Phil Kelso resigned, initially to run a hotel in Scotland, but almost immediately joined Fulham instead, replacing Harry Bradshaw (who had turned down a new contract and became secretary of the Southern League). The new Arsenal manager, George Morrell, found himself having to sell to survive. Within 12 months virtually all the important names had gone — Coleman, Freeman, Sharp, Ashcroft and

Garbutt. After leaving Woolwich for Blackburn, William Garbutt moved further and further afield. In 1914 he went to Genoa as coach, where his team won the Italian League the following year. By 1927 he was in Rome, and two years later went on to Naples. In 1935–36 he coached the Spanish champions Athletic Bilbao but the Spanish Civil War drove him back to Italy. During the Second World War he was hidden there by friends and in 1946 took up his old post again at Genoa.

Morrell's first full season in charge began on 2 September 1908. The first programme of the season was not shy about discussing the fact that the best players had all gone: 'Here we go again,' began the editor 'and the followers of Arsenal look forward to the advent of another season with a great number of the players on whom we rely practically unknown quantities. The "Reds" will look somewhat strange without such faces as Ashcroft, Sharp, Coleman, Freeman, Kyle and Garbutt but we believe capable men have been engaged to replace them and we look forward to a successful season.'

The hope was misplaced for it was to be nearly two decades before the 'Reds' had another genuinely successful year. Nonetheless, the editor did go on to comment: 'If we do not have a back of the same calibre as Sharp, we have one likely to prove a worthy successor in the person of (Joseph) Shaw.' Worthy indeed. Even the greatest of all the pre-war Gunners, Andy Ducat, eventually had to be transferred to Villa. Right-half Ducat appeared for England in all three internationals in 1909–10, when he was only 23, and after the war also played cricket for his country. Appearing at centre forward, Ducat scored a hat-trick in his first ever game for Arsenal, on Christmas Day 1905, versus the mighty Newcastle United, the best side of the era. It was particularly sad that his best playing days were lost to the First World War. For their part Woolwich Arsenal never recovered from those sudden sales in 1908, particularly missing keeper Ashcroft. The crowds melted away, as did the results, and by 1910 the club was effectively bankrupt and up for sale.

For the next decade the Arsenal story is really to be told off the field rather than on it. The main reason for this was one Henry Norris, the chairman of Fulham. As we have seen, the links between the two clubs were already close, if not necessarily friendly, and in 1910 Norris was able to use the Woolwich club's problems to effect a takeover of Arsenal as well.

Fulham had experienced a remarkably rapid rise since Norris became chairman. In 1902 and 1903 they won the Second Division of the Southern League, were then elected to the First and, under Bradshaw, won that Division in 1906 and 1907, upon which they applied to join the Football League and were immediately accepted. This was the first concrete evidence of Henry Norris' remarkable powers of political persuasion where the Football League was concerned. At the 1907 election Fulham easily received the

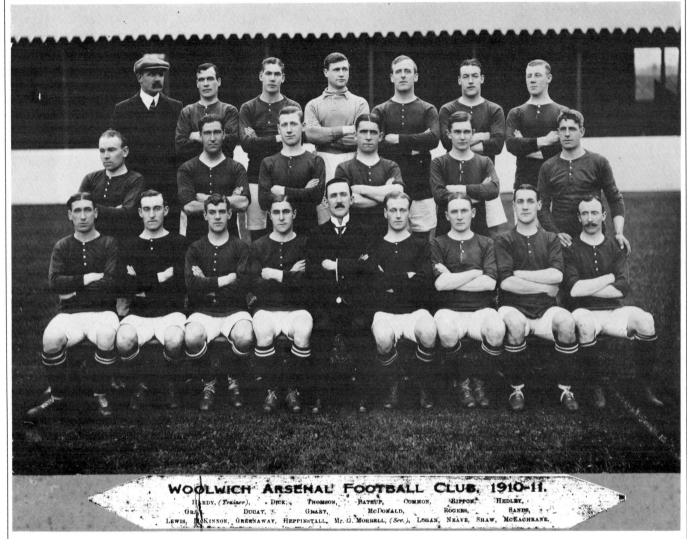

WOOLWICH ARSENAL FOOTBALL CLUB, 1910-11.

HARDY, (*Trainer*), DICK, THOMSON, BATEUP, COMMON, RIPPON, HEDLEY,
GRANT, DUCAT, GRANT, McDONALD, ROGERS, SANDS,
LEWIS, McKINNON, GREENAWAY, HEPPINSTALL, Mr. G. MORRELL, (*Sec.*), LOGAN, NEAVE, SHAW, McEACHRANE.

George Morrell's hard-pressed team of 1910-11. This was the season the club went bankrupt and were bought by Henry Norris, who tried to persuade the League to let Arsenal and Fulham play alternate weeks at Craven Cottage. Virtually all of the players who had taken the side to the 1906 and 1907 semi-finals had been sold by Morrell, but one or two famous faces remain. Alf Common had been the first £1,000 footballer when transferred from Sunderland to Middlesbrough in 1905, while Andy Ducat was perhaps the greatest of all the pre-war Reds. Scoring a hat-trick versus mighty Newcastle on his debut, Ducat was one of the rare sportsmen to be capped for England at soccer and cricket.

highest number of votes (28) and replaced Burton United.

Norris was a self-made man, his fortune based on property development in south-west London. He was Mayor of Fulham for seven years, was knighted in 1917 and represented Fulham East in Parliament from 1918 to 1922. A dictatorial man, he ran his football clubs like his businesses. A thin autocrat with a walrus moustache, he welcomed neither criticism nor advice; nonetheless, he was influential and persuasive, as will be seen later. Over the years he developed very close friendships with members of the League Management Committee, particularly president John McKenna, and while an MP he was able to represent the interests of football, and himself, with some success.

Leslie Knighton, Arsenal manager to Norris' chairman between 1919 and 1925, has left us perhaps the best descriptions of Norris. Knighton said in his autobiography: 'I soon found out that everyone was afraid of Sir Henry. And no wonder! I have never met his equal for logic, invective and ruthlessness against all who opposed him. When I disagreed with him at board meetings and had to stand up for what I knew was best for the club, he used to flay me with words until I was reduced to fuming, helpless silence. Then, as I sat not knowing what to say, and trying to bottle up what I was tempted to say, he would whip round and shout: "Well Knighton, we pay you a great deal of money to advise us and all you do is sit there as if you were dumb".' But afterwards, says Knighton: 'Sir Henry would ask my advice, smile, wheedle. . . . . and I was falling over myself to help him again. He did it with everyone. Those board meetings took years off my life.'

Like many influential Londoners with lower-class roots in the Edwardian era, Norris was sensitive to the fact that London appeared to be unable to compete with the provinces in what had become the national winter sport. For whatever personal reasons, he became determined to create a side capable of competing with

the best from the North and Birmingham. His attention first turned to his local club, Fulham, but by 1908 he had obviously become convinced that they would never have a strong enough base for the success he sought.

Though Fulham had not been unsuccessful on the field, they, like Arsenal, were quite poorly supported. By 1910 the Cottagers had an accumulated overdraft of over £3,000 while the Woolwich club were to all intents and purposes completely bankrupt.

Though this was the year Norris took over Arsenal, he remained a Fulham director until the war. His co-director at Woolwich, William Hall, was also Fulham chairman until the same date and the two men obviously controlled both clubs. It was partially because of this that the League later insisted no one could have a controlling interest in two League members.

One may debate why Norris turned to Woolwich Arsenal rather than more promising sides to further his dream. The reasons were probably three-fold. The first was that the obvious alternatives were in the hands of equally autocratic men — Charlie Roberts at Tottenham and Gus Mears at Chelsea — and he was unlikely to wrest control of either club from them. The second reason was the Woolwich club's financial weakness and lack of a strong support base, which he would have known about from the two managers he had poached. And while this was not a long-term advantage, it did render the club susceptible to takeover. The third reason was, in the short term, crucial; Woolwich Arsenal were in the First Division and seemed to have established a relatively safe base there. In 1908 London had only Chelsea and Arsenal in the top Division.

Norris had no doubt been putting out feelers for some time, but it was not until the summer of 1910, with the Gunners having escaped relegation by only a couple of points, that he was able to take control. His initial plan was very simple — he wanted to amalgamate Woolwich Arsenal with Fulham, move them to Craven Cottage and have a First Division team play there. When the League said no, he proposed an even more financially attractive solution — Arsenal and Fulham could play at Craven Cottage on alternative Saturdays. The other London clubs objected and that was turned down as well. The League also pointed out the obvious disadvantages of having one man controlling two clubs (there was technically nothing to prevent this at the time) and Norris was in the position, having failed to achieve either of his objectives, of being informally forced to choose one club or the other.

In the end he came down in favour of the Woolwich club, no doubt because they were still in the First Division. Sadly, this was not to be the case for much longer. After a couple more years of mid-table insignificance, 1912–13 was a disaster. Arsenal finished bottom with only 18 points, 26 goals scored and three wins. The points, goals and wins were all the lowest ever recorded in the First Division and remained

records, though equalled, until the end of the two point system, after which the Stoke side of 1984–85 managed an even more disastrous season. In 1912–13 Arsenal won only one League game at home all season, still a record for any Football League club.

By the end of the 1912–13 season, the club was reported as having only £19 in the bank. The size of the disaster had been clear from the first few matches and Henry Norris and William Hall had been looking for some rapid solution to their plight throughout the year.

Their conclusion was as dramatic as it was simple. If the club was to have any chance of becoming the power in the land that Norris desired, then it would simply have to move.

There were four necessary guidelines for a new location. It should be within greater London so as not to lose all of the support the club had relied upon over the years; it should be in a heavily populated area, preferably not bounded by the river or any other restriction to access (while Arsenal had the river to the north, Fulham also suffered from it being immediately to the south-west); thirdly, it should not be too close to another major club; and, most important of all, it should be very easy to reach by public transport. In 1913 the last point was a prerequisite for any side which hoped to attract really big crowds. Among the open spaces that Hall and Norris negotiated for were ones in Battersea and Harringay, but they found nothing that met all of their requirements. Nor were they to, in the end, accepting that they would probably have to be in the north or west and therefore inevitably close to either Spurs or Chelsea.

Exactly when and how Highbury came into the reckoning is not known. The land in question was actually the site of St John's College of Divinity, but relatively little of it was built upon. Most was taken up by the two football pitches, two cricket pitches and various tennis courts used by the students. The keys to the site, as far as Hall and Norris were concerned, were its availability and the underground station. Negotiations were not exactly easy and went on for several months, Norris bringing all his considerable influence to bear on the very important Ecclesistical Commissioners. In the end, Arsenal paid a massive £20,000 for a mere 21-year lease and agreed not to stage matches on Good Friday and Christmas Day (this restriction was eventually lifted in 1925 when the club paid another £64,000 to buy the whole site outright). The college itself remained at the southern end of the ground until it burned down at the end of the Second World War, after which the large blocks of flats behind the clock were built.

The actual deed of transfer was signed by the Archbishop of Canterbury, but if Norris thought that this implied heavenly blessing for his plans then he was quickly to discover others disagreed. The objections to Arsenal moving to Highbury came from three main sources. The most pre-

dictable was from the other clubs, particularly Tottenham and Clapton Orient, then playing at Homerton. Both were within four miles of Highbury but Arsenal would be closer to the centre and, with that vital underground station, much easier to reach. Spurs had only joined the League five years before and had just spent enormous sums (around £50,000) on improving their ground. The old main stand at White Hart Lane (pulled down in 1981) had been finished only three years before.

Local residents joined in the outcry — it was one thing having a college of divinity on the doorstep, quite another to see it suddenly turn into a football ground. It is impossible to imagine such a transfer being approved today, but at that time there was very little in the way of planning permission required. If there had been, Norris would never have stood a chance, for Islington Council joined with the other objectors on the grounds that football clubs exploited their players for dividend purposes and because the value of the whole area would drop.

Tottenham, Orient, the local residents and even Chelsea appealed to the League Management Committee and a special meeting was

called in March 1913. It went on until two in the morning, by all accounts a not too friendly and highly argumentative debate. To cut a long story short, Arsenal won the day. This was arguably less because the Management Committee agreed with their plans (there is some evidence to suggest that one or two members didn't) than because they concluded they were: '. . . of the opinion that under the rules and practice of the League (we) have no right to interfere.'

Many clubs had moved in the past — very recently Notts County had crossed the Trent to Meadow Lane — but no one had ever objected before and the transfers had usually been local and to everyone's benefit. Nonetheless, the fact remained that clubs had never *asked* to move and the League had never claimed the right to prevent them. It was the club that was in membership, not the ground. Arsenal's case was, by any standards, different. It is only 10 miles as the crow flies from Woolwich to Highbury, but in terms of travelling times within greater London that is very different from Blackburn Rovers or Sunderland moving a mile up the road. In no previous case had there been a clear incursion into a competitor's catchment

Above: **The Manor Ground at Plumstead,** club home from 1893 to 1913. Because the ground was so hard to get to, few pictures of it were taken or survive. These two were taken during a game versus Bolton on 14 September 1912 and are interesting because they show the two stands. Arsenal lost the game 1-2, a familiar enough result as they won only one game at home all season (still a League record), won only three in all, finished bottom of the First Division and amassed only 18 points, also a First Division record until Stoke went one worse in 1984-85. This was the period when George Allison, then the programme editor among other roles, claimed he stood outside the ground with the sparse crowd jollying them to come in, and then rushed inside to shake their hands when they did. If that's true, it was all in vain. At season's end, in April

area, nor was there to be again. The only partly comparable example since is South Shields' move to Gateshead in 1930, and by then the League had already acted following the Arsenal furore to prevent clubs moving without permission.

The last first-class game at the Manor Ground was on Saturday 26 April 1913. The opponents were Middlesbrough and Woolwich Arsenal said goodbye to their name, their home and the south-east of London with a 1–1 draw, a rather better result than most that season for they had won only two games in all first-class competitions at the Manor Ground in the previous 12 months.

Woolwich was dropped from the name and, though the club apparently never officially called itself The Arsenal, that was to be the name under which it was publicly known until Herbert Chapman insisted on the single word some dozen years later. Oddly, the official *Football League Fiftieth Anniversary History* said: 'Thus the new Arsenal club was reborn and, on 3rd April of the following year (1914) it was given permission to drop the Woolwich from the name and was henceforth known as "The Arsenal".' This history then went on to point out that Sheffied Wednesday called themselves The Wednesday for many years, thus implying that the club had actually asked to be called *The Arsenal*.

Now the spending really began. In four months the new pitch was levelled (the north end had to be raised eleven feet, the south end lowered five feet), a new grandstand was partly built and turnstiles and terracing installed. It cost Norris another £80,000. Including bank guarantees and loans, by the time the first match was played at Highbury on 6 September 1913 he had found an astonishing £125,000 to put into the club. In 1986 terms that is well in excess of £2 million. Cash was so short that the builder of the stand agreed to take a percentage of the weekly gate in order to pay for its construction.

All Norris had to show for this investment at that time, of course, was a Second Division football team. The first game was against Leicester Fosse and the Reds did well enough, winning 2–1. Scottish international inside left Andy Devine scored the first goal, but it is centre forward George Jobey whose contribution that day has gone down in the history books. He sprained an ankle during the game and was helped off by trainer George Hardy. As there were no dressing rooms or running water (the single stand was not even half built), Hardy decided to take Jobey to the player's lodgings nearby. To do so, and not wanting the player to walk, he borrowed a cart from the local milkman David Lewis, who lived in Gillespie Road (and being Welsh, was known as Lewis the Milk), and Jobey was observed being trundled off home in conditions which were to change rather dramatically in the next 20 years.

All in all, the team did quite well in that Second Division season — finishing third and failing to go up only on goal average behind

1913, Woolwich Arsenal shut up shop, abandoned Plumstead, and headed north of the river to the hopes, dreams and destiny of distant Highbury.

Bradford Park Avenue. The critical game was the last home match of the season, on 18 April against Clapton Orient, who were sixth in the division. In a bitter hangover from the controversy over Arsenal's move a year before, Orient fought like tigers to draw 2–2. The following week, though Arsenal won 2–0 at Glossop (the Hill-Wood family club), Bradford beat Blackpool 4–1 and were up.

But a far greater shock was about to face Norris. He desperately needed First Division football and seemed to have a team that might achieve it but, within a year of that first game at Highbury, Europe was at war. The result was disaster. Players, particularly the many with Woolwich Arsenal connections, went back to munitions work, others joined the forces, the crowds declined and the League, though it was contested in 1914–15, was something of an irrelevance.

The most notable players of the era were right back Joe Shaw, who was to stay with the club during and beyond the inter-war period as assistant manager and be a critical part of the glories that followed, and his full back partner Bob Benson. Benson was one of the many players who went back into munitions work and therefore lost his match fitness. Having gone to watch the club play at Reading in February 1916, Benson volunteered to take Joe Shaw's place as Shaw himself could not get away from his own job. Benson was clearly unfit, had to leave the field and, having gone to the dressing room, died a few minutes later in the arms of George Hardy. In a sad, but fitting, tribute he was buried in an Arsenal shirt.

Benson's was a personal tragedy and there were many more in that 'war to end wars'. For the club, having taken such a gamble only a year before, the war was a source of total despair. At the end of the 1914–15 season manager George Morrell was unceremoniously sacked to save money and, financially, things just got worse. By 1918 the club was £60,000 overdrawn and Norris was, not surprisingly, again desperate. His five years with Arsenal had so far been nothing but a catalogue of disasters.

On Saturday 24 April 1915 Arsenal had played their last game of the season against Nottingham Forest at Highbury. That very day's programme gave the details of George Morrell's departure and the club's plight. It was to be, nonetheless, their best display of the year, a convincing 7–0 win with Harry King scoring four goals, Jock Rutherford one, and the tragic Bob Benson, less than a year before his death, playing up front and getting two. Beyond that, it was not apparently a match of any great consequence — though one result was that Arsenal just squeezed into fifth place in the division. What no one knew at the time (and who can blame them) was that it was to be Arsenal's last game in the Second Division. Over 70 years later, Arsenal have still to make their next appearance in anything but the highest company.

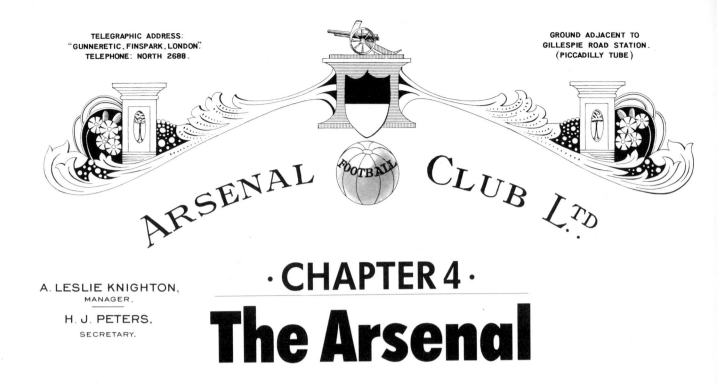

TELEGRAPHIC ADDRESS:
"GUNNERETIC, FINSPARK, LONDON".
TELEPHONE: NORTH 2688.

GROUND ADJACENT TO
GILLESPIE ROAD STATION.
(PICCADILLY TUBE)

A. LESLIE KNIGHTON,
MANAGER.

H. J. PETERS,
SECRETARY.

· CHAPTER 4 ·
The Arsenal

When the long, terrible conflict known then as the 'War to End All Wars' reached its exhausted conclusion in the November of 1918, first-class football had effectively ceased to exist. Three quarters of a million young British men had been killed, and of those no small number had been professional footballers.

Amid all this, The Arsenal's problems were clearly small ones, but to Sir Henry Norris they were real enough. When the war began the club had been fielding a side which should have quickly fought its way back into the First Division and hence helped with the £60,000 standing debt and Norris' immense £125,000 investment. But those players who survived the war were all five years older and there was absolutely no telling how any club would perform in the season that was to begin in September 1919.

It was at this point that Henry Norris set out on the single most outrageous enterprise ever to be conceived in the history of English football. His remarkable political successes in obtaining Fulham entry to the League and Woolwich Arsenal entry to North London were minnows compared with the audacious whale he was about to float. Nearly 70 years later there is still no convincing explanation of how Norris achieved his object and it is almost inconceivable that any other individual, before or since, could have carried it off at all. Norris's aim, very simply, was to talk The Arsenal back into the First Division.

In 1914–15 the team had finished fifth in the Second Division (for 60 years that League table was invariably copied showing Arsenal finishing sixth but, in actual fact, they finished just above Birmingham on goal average by virtue of that 7–0 win over Forest in their final game). Above Arsenal were Derby, Preston, Barnsley and Wolves. In 1919 it was decided to extend the First Division from 20 to 22 clubs. Extensions of the divisions had happened on several occasions since the League was founded in 1888 and the almost invariable procedure when extending the First Division was to re-elect automatically the bottom clubs from the previous season and promote the top clubs from the Second Division. Given the unfortunate intervention of the war, there seemed every reason to suppose that this is exactly what would happen, and little cause even to discuss it. And this was, indeed, what almost everyone assumed (and were told) would happen.

By chance, two other London clubs, Chelsea and Spurs, had finished nineteenth and twentieth in the First Division in 1915. Showing remarkable stealth and political judgement, Norris used the eight months between the end of the war and the Annual General Meeting in mid-1919 to canvass the other major clubs and various influential friends in the game. He had received his knighthood in 1917 and became a Tory MP in 1918, and one must assume that many were flattered by the attentions of this successful luminary in a game which then had few figures of note outside its own confines.

Norris seemed to have little to work on. But there was just one small chink of hope. At the end of the 1914–15 season it had become obvious that the League would have to be abandoned for the duration of the war. There had been allegations of some match fixing by one or two players (who had bet on the results) and, in one instance, this was proven after lengthy court cases. That particular game was Manchester United versus Liverpool, and United had won it 2–0 to finish 18th, just one point ahead of Chelsea. Though United would have dropped below Chelsea if Liverpool had beaten them, they would still have finished ahead of last

Above: **The official club letter-heading** used from 1921. Apart from the club badge and the pointed reference to the tube station, then called Gillespie Road, the document is interesting for what it does not say rather than what it does. In other words, though the press, public and even the Football League in its official records all insisted on calling the club The Arsenal, clearly Highbury itself was content with plain Arsenal. Herbert Chapman insisted on universal usage of the single word in 1927, intelligently realising that Arsenal would always come first in any alphabetical list of clubs. What he did not foresee was Aldershot joining the Third Division South in 1932. After the Second World War, interestingly, the official name reverted to The Arsenal and new share certificates were issued in that name (information courtesy of Malcolm Davis).

Above: **The date is 31 August 1913;** the view is from the corner of the North Bank across to the main stand and Avenell Road (which has clearly remained unchanged to this day). Six days later, on 6 September, the club played its first game at Highbury, beating Leicester Fosse 2-1. From the evidence of this picture, it is difficult to see how they managed it.

Right: **Some six months later,** on 14 February 1914, Huddersfield were the visitors in the first of many famous Highbury encounters between the two sides. Though this shot went wide, Huddersfield won 0-1. It was a costly defeat for Arsenal, as even a draw would have seen them promoted at the end of the season. They came third on goal average behind Notts County and Bradford PA. As can be seen, the main stand (actually the only stand until 1932) was now half built, though it had no walls. Massive tarpaulins theoretically kept out the rain. Norris had already spent £125,000 on leasing and levelling the land and was so hard pressed that the builder agreed to take a percentage of the gate receipts each week as his payment. This is one reason why the stand took so long to complete.

placed Spurs, but the whole business did serve to create an understandable uneasiness that the 1914–15 season was not quite all it should have been. It should be said that there was not the slightest suggestion that Spurs or Chelsea were ever involved in any wrongdoing at the time, and none has ever been suggested since.

What Norris said to the other chairmen has never been revealed, but his desperation for First Division status plus the size of the investment at risk clearly persuaded enough of them that he had a worthwhile case. Leslie Knighton described his chairman's technique at the time thus: 'His influence was enormous. (He would) speak to an important person there, suggesting

a favour, remind a certain financier who was interested that he had once done him a good turn and been promised something in return.'

When the AGM was convened, Norris' strategy became clear. It must have been agreed with League President 'Honest' John McKenna, a close friend of Norris and the owner of Liverpool, in advance. Firstly, Chelsea were detached from Spurs and their position taken separately. There was no vote, and the fact that Chelsea would have finished third from bottom in 1915 had Liverpool beaten United in the fixed match undoubtedly influenced the meeting. McKenna proposed they they be re-elected on the nod and this was accepted. Then Derby and

Preston, first and second in the Second Division in 1914–15, were elected to the First Division without debate. Then came the bombshell. McKenna, who might have been more reticent given that he was the force behind Liverpool FC, made a brief speech recommending that Arsenal be given the remaining First Division place because of their service to the League and their longevity, particularly pointing out that Arsenal had been in the League 15 years longer than Spurs.

The arguments were, of course, complete nonsense. The League is not run on the basis of the most experienced clubs being given the higher places, and, in any event, Wolves, who finished fourth, had been members of the League four years longer than Arsenal. Spurs chairman Charlie Roberts found it (not surprisingly) very difficult to counter the illogicalities of this Alice in Wonderland meeting in which he had suddenly, unexpectedly and inexplicably become entrapped. The vote was taken; Arsenal got 18 (the League minutes still insisted on referring to them as Woolwich Arsenal), Spurs got 8, Barnsley (who finished third) 5, Wolves 4, Forest (who finished 19th and had no claim to a place whatsoever) got 3, Birmingham 2 and Hull 1. Hence Arsenal were elected and Norris had his First Division club again. It is interesting to note that Arsenal got well under half the vote, suggesting that if Spurs had received advance warning they might have persuaded the five other clubs, who stood no real chance, to withdraw.

To this day it is impossible to explain what went on at that AGM. The most plausible explanation is actually the most irrational; the individual representatives assumed that, if McKenna was prepared to support so unlikely a cause, then he must have some very good, if well-hidden, reason for doing so. If there was such a reason, it has remained very well-hidden indeed, though it would clearly have been assumed to be something to do with the results at the end of the 1914–15 season. For the sake of completeness, it should be mentioned that for many years there were rumours of the involvement of significant sums of money. Nothing has ever been discovered in writing, of course, and there has never been any other documentary proof, so it must remain a mystery.

Paradoxically, it was a conclusion that probably favoured Spurs more than Arsenal. Only six years after failing to prevent the upstart's arrival on their patch, the Tottenham board went back to White Hart Lane pondering the injustice of it all. Their response was on the field. In 1919–20 they scored 102 goals and broke all the records for points (70) and wins (32). Straight back in the First Division, they finished sixth, and won the FA Cup at Stamford Bridge. Until Chapman was bedded in at Highbury, Spurs were clearly North London's leading club. There was, not surprisingly, a heavy residue of bitterness between the clubs, unparalleled before or since in the English game.

In September 1922 a particularly vicious match led to two sendings off (very rare at the time — twenty sendings off in a whole League season was high), censures, suspensions and an FA Commission of Inquiry.

As late as 1928, Arsenal were accused of throwing games at the end of the season to ensure Spurs went down. The games concerned in that 1927–28 season were both at home — a 0–2 defeat by Portsmouth (who finished 20th) on 28 March and, more relevantly, a 0–1 defeat by Manchester United (who finished 18th) on 28 April, the last week of the season. Both those clubs finished one point above Spurs, who had finished their programme early, and if Arsenal had managed even a draw with either Portsmouth or United then Spurs would have stayed up. On the other hand, the table in 1927–28 was astonishingly tight. Seven points covered Derby, who finished fourth, and Middlesbrough, who finished bottom. Arsenal, in 19th place, were only three points ahead of Spurs themselves and would therefore, one must assume, have endangered their own position by such unlikely behaviour. The Gunners rarely got the better of Spurs in the inter-war period anyway; between Chapman's arrival in 1925 and October 1934 Spurs did not once lose at Highbury.

The Arsenal did not exactly enjoy a successful spell for the few seasons after 1919, but at least they stayed where they were. It is a happy coincidence that the centenary is also the point that Arsenal equal the record for the longest unbroken spell of First Division membership. Sunderland stayed there from 1890 to 1958, a run of 68 years. Arsenal's 68th year comes in the second half of the season 1986–87.

Norris had appointed Leslie Knighton as manager in June 1919. Knighton, who had

The moment Henry Norris feared he would never see – Arsenal back in the First Division. Arsenal captain Joe Shaw (left) and his Newcastle equivalent Bill McCracken shake hands before the first post-War First Division fixture at Highbury on 30 August 1919. Arsenal's last League fixture had been four and a half years before in the middle ranges of the Second Division. The club's magical transformation from Second Division also-ran to membership of the elite without touching go is perhaps the most unlikely story in the history of English League football. Shaw, of course, went on to become team manager after Chapman's death, while McCracken retained a close affinity with Highbury. He was manager of the Hull side which, though at the wrong end of the Second Division, reached the semi-final of the FA Cup in 1930 and lead Arsenal 2-0 with only 30 minutes left. At the age of 90 he was invited to a reception at Highbury. Naturally the club offered to arrange hotels and transportation but McCracken politely refused, explaining that he had a breakfast appointment back home the following morning.

This page: **Before and after;** the top picture shows the ground as it was at the time of Leslie Knighton's departure and Herbert Chapman's arrival in 1925. The lower picture was taken just after the Second World War and shows the new East and West Stands. The first North Bank Stand was built in the 1930s but was destroyed in an air raid. The club rebuilt it to an identical design as soon as it could obtain permission (materials were scarce) after the war. Although the terracing looks similar in the two pictures, it was all built up quite considerably before the new stands were erected. One contractor who was dumping rubbish into a hole on the North Bank got too close to the edge and his horse and cart toppled in. It proved impossible to save the injured animal, which had to be destroyed where it lay and was left to be buried in the middle of the terracing. There is one other titbit of interest in the upper picture. Though there appears to be a full house for the game, and though there were no parking restrictions of any sort, there is not a single car to be seen anywhere.

previously had quite successful spells with Huddersfield and Manchester City, was, however, rarely allowed to manage. Among Norris' other edicts, Knighton was not allowed to sign players smaller than 5ft 8in, was not allowed to spend more than £1,000 on anyone (Norris was either not prepared to spend any more money or, more likely, was running short of it), was expected to sign and create a team of purely local players and, to compound all these problems, had to save money by abandoning the scouting system. The task tended to verge on the impossible and the playing record reflects this.

The best position between 1919 and Chapman's arrival six years later was ninth in 1921, the only time the club won more games than they lost. In the Cup Arsenal got beyond the second round just once, in 1922, when they lost to Preston in the quarter-finals after a replay. Knighton's last FA Cup game as manager (and probably one of the reasons behind his dismissal soon afterwards) actually provides one of the funniest stories in football history.

The Arsenal were drawn against West Ham in the first round in January 1925 and Knighton told how he was surprised to be approached by a Harley Street doctor who was also an Arsenal fan: 'I trust you agree that we have a poor chance of survival against West Ham, Mr Knighton,' said the doctor. 'What the boys require is something in the nature of a courage pill. They do no harm, but tone up the nerves to produce the maximum effort.' Knighton investigated the doctor, who was genuine, and his remedy, which did not appear poisonous or illegal, and decided to go ahead. The team were, naturally enough, reluctant. Knighton tried to reassure them by promising to take one of the pills himself. At 2pm on the Saturday of the match they all took their pills. At 2.50pm the referee came into the dressing room and told them he'd called the game off because of fog. 'Getting the boys back to Highbury that afternoon was like trying to drive a flock of lively lions,' said Knighton. 'The pills not only left us raring to go but also developed the most red-hot, soul destroying thirst I've ever known. We drank water until I thought the Thames would dry up.'

On the following Monday Arsenal went to Upton Park again and went through the same routine. Down went the pills. . . and down came the fog. The game was called off again. The after effects were the same.

On the Thursday the game finally began, the Arsenal team and their manager having taken their pills for a third time. By half-time the Gunners were running around like maniacs. 'They were giants suddenly supercharged. They tore away with the ball and put in shots like leather thunderbolts. They monopolized the play — and yet they couldn't score. . . For West Ham there was no defence against the pluck-pills. The ball crashed and bounced against the West Ham goal. The Arsenal players ran like Olympic sprinters, jumped like rockets to reach the high ones and crashed in shots from all

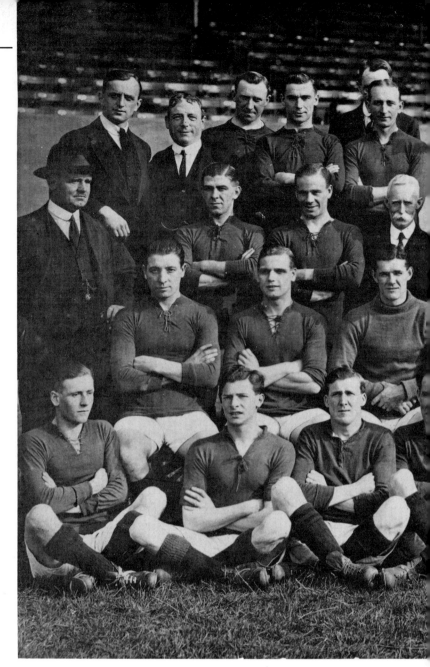

Key to photograph above: 1 Ratcliffe **2** Ewan **3** Buckley **4** Counley **5** Jim Peters **6** Bill Smith **7** Lewis **8** Peart **9** Kempton **10** Dunn **11** Wood **12** North **13** Plumb **14** Walden **15** George Hardy (trainer) **16** White **17** Blyth **18** William Hall **19** Sir Henry Norris **20** Jack Humble **21** C Crisp **22** G Peachey **23** Jewett **24** Butler **25** Paterson **26** Leslie Knighton **27** Graham **28** Baker **29** Williamson **30** Bradshaw **31** Rutherford **32** Joe Shaw **33** Hutchins **34** Pagnam **35** McKinnon **36** Hopkins **37** Voysey **38** Rosebotham **39** Rose **40** Groves **41** Greenaway **42** Burgess **43** Toner **44** Tom Whittaker **45** Coupland

The club line-up in 1920.
The picture is unusually interesting because, with the exception of Chapman, all of the major managerial and administrative names of the first half of the twentieth century happen to have come together at the same moment – Henry Norris, William Hall, Jack Humble, Joe Shaw, Leslie Knighton, Tom Whittaker and John Peters.

angles and distances. It is no disparagement to West Ham to say that they had the most incredible luck that half. Sometimes in Cup games, you must have noticed, fortune is completely one-sided.' The game ended as a goalless draw. But Knighton's troubles were only just beginning. 'I forgot my frightful thirst,' he recounts, 'croaking out congratulations and sympathy to the team. But you should have heard them! Running about had made their thirst and bitter throats a thousand times worse. That night those pills created a riot.'

An hour before the replay began at Highbury Knighton took out his box of pills. The team refused point-blank to go through it all again. They drew 2–2. The fifth attempt was at Stamford Bridge. There were no pills and no goals for Arsenal. With the last kick of the game, George Kay scored from a Jimmy Ruffell corner and West Ham won 1–0. The doctor never told Knighton what was in the pills, nor ever offered them again. He remained convinced that Arsenal would have won the Cup had they persevered. Assuming the doctor was right, Knighton would surely have stayed manager, Chapman would

presumably never have come to Highbury, and who knows where Arsenal would be today?

Knighton's team had its strengths, despite the poor playing record. Joe Shaw was still at full back, Scots utility player Billy Blyth was used anywhere and everywhere and Tom Whittaker was a very reliable, highly intelligent, wing half or full back until a knee injury in Woolongong, Australia, while on tour with the FA party, ended his playing career and directed him towards becoming the most famous trainer/physiotherapist soccer has known. Knighton also made one or two clever and surreptitious signings. Alf Baker, later an England international at right half, signed for Arsenal after Knighton had met him at the pithead in Ilkeston (near Nottingham) to forestall other clubs waiting at Baker's home. Baker was to play in all eleven positions for the club during his career.

Another international who was whisked away for nothing from under the noses of others was Bob John. He came from Caerphilly, where Knighton painted a glowing picture of the glories of the capital (which John was, indeed, later to enjoy with the club) compared with

Cardiff, to whom John was pledged. He was in the Welsh national side within six months. Also from South Wales (though he was born in Bristol) came Jimmy Brain, who was to lead the attack for several seasons. Both Knighton and Peter McWilliam, manager of Spurs, reputedly had to disguise themselves when they visted South Wales because of the anger expressed when the two London clubs had stolen away Jimmy Seed, Cecil Poynton and Bob John, and Spurs were at a crucial disadvantage because all their negotiations for Brain had to be carried out in secret. It was a good time for South Wales football, of course. In 1923–24 Cardiff lost the championship to Huddersfield only on goal average, and would have won it had goal difference been operating then, or if a penalty given ten minutes from the end of their last League game had not been saved by Birmingham keeper Dan Tremelling. In 1925 and 1927 Cardiff were also to reach the FA Cup final, on the latter occasion defeating the Gunners. By that time, Chapman had effectively dispensed with almost all of Knighton's team, the only regular survivors being Baker, John and Brain.

Because of Norris' transfer edicts (he tried in both 1922 and 1924 to get the League to impose a limit on fees of £1,650 — rarely for a League AGM, they chose to ignore Norris' wishes), Knighton also had to indulge in some rather unusual transfers. Dr Jimmy Paterson was an amateur winger with Queen's Park in Glasgow, when his sister happened to marry the Arsenal club doctor, J. L. Scott. Paterson joined Scott's practice (based in Clapton) and also started to play for the club. Added to his then unique appearance (as a Scot) for the Football League against the Scottish League in 1921, he was presumably also the only man to have been a player for the club of which he was simultaneously one of the medical team.

A more celebrated transfer was that of the

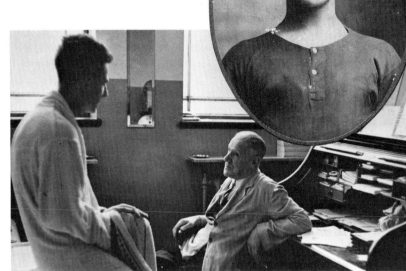

Right: **Joe Shaw** at the time he entered the first team as a full back in 1908.

Below: **Forty-five years on,** in 1953, Shaw remained part of the Arsenal set-up. For most of that period he had been assistant manager and had been team manager in reality after Chapman's death in 1934.

famous 'Midget' Moffat of Workington. Again, this is a story worth telling largely in Leslie Knighton's words.

Knighton had been told about Midget Moffat, the five foot tall Workington winger, by an old Huddersfield colleague, who had also warned him that other sides were beginning to take an interest. But chairman Norris had recently imposed one of his absolute edicts — no small men, all new signings had to be at least 5 feet 8 inches tall and weigh in at a minimum of 11 stone. Nonetheless, Knighton trusted his source enough to go to Workington by an overnight train and watch the player.

The manager was as mesmerised as the opposing full back: '. . . a tiny footballer

Left below: **The infamous Arsenal team bus** which was to begin Sir Henry Norris's slide into obscurity. The chairman is second from left, trainer George Hardy is on his right and manager Leslie Knighton on his left. The complex and lengthy series of FA hearings and High Court cases between 1927 and 1929 actually began with an accusation that Norris had sold the bus (for £125) and the receipts had somehow found their way into his wife's bank account. Norris did not deny this as such, but said it was repayment for the money he paid Charlie Buchan to come to Highbury in 1925 as well as being something of a consideration for the £17,000 the club actually owed him personally at the time (the club probably owed him rather more but whatever the sum it was enormous for the time). Further accusations and allegations followed and in 1929 Norris was eventually drummed out of the game he loved and had so influenced. The accusations were technically correct but essentially unfair. He had certainly done nothing that was not common practice elsewhere in the game. Norris' problem was the number of enemies he had made in various places, particularly with his amazing conjuring trick in 1919, and

Continued opposite ▷

spinning rings around two perfectly competent full backs, a midget with a kick like a horse,' Knighton said later. He immediately offered the player a job but Moffat strangely failed to turn up at Highbury the following day. Knighton arrived at the ground the subsequent morning to find the groundsman waiting for him. 'I've got a little tiny chap waiting for you. Says he's come to play for Arsenal. He's asleep in the dressing room.' And, said Knighton: 'There was Moffat, fast asleep on some kit in a corner, his shock of hair sticking out like a squirrel's tail.' Moffat had arrived at Euston and gone straight to Woolwich, thinking the club still played there (they had moved 12 years earlier). When he arrived it was dark. A road-sweeper explained things, and offered Moffat a lift on his cart all the way to Highbury.

Knighton took Moffat straight off on a continental tour to Scandinavia, where the winger was apparently a great success. Norris, who had been on a summer holiday in Nice, returned at the start of the new season to find a midget in his midst. 'Norris smiled and said nothing,' wrote Knighton, 'but, as always, he got his way. Moffat had to go, to Luton and thence on to Everton.'

Sadly, Midget Moffat rather sums up Knighton's career at Highbury — clever, thoughtful, but bound hand and foot by Norris' peculiar restraints. Whether Knighton would have been a more successful manager in different circumstances is difficult to assess; it certainly seems possible, for he went on to achieve a fair deal with Chelsea and Birmingham.

For his part, it appears that Norris could not work out what was going wrong. As far as we can tell, it doesn't seem to have occurred to him that his restriction on transfers could be affecting the team's potential. He saw the game with an outsider's eye — each of the players seemed good enough, why wouldn't they knit together properly, why did they keep losing by the odd goal? There were other pressures on Norris. As we have seen, Spurs had recovered well from the shenanigans of 1919 and were established as the leading, and best supported, club in the area

(between 1921 and 1925 Spurs finished sixth, second, twelfth, fifteenth and twelfth).

And Norris wasn't getting any younger. If he was ever to do it, to realise the dreams of the past two decades, it would have to be soon. He was no longer an MP, no longer Mayor of Fulham. Highbury had become his career and, in his own eyes perhaps, the remaining symbol to crown a successful life. If Arsenal were ever to achieve anything, there was now only one place to go and one man to go to. All the seeds of Norris' own personal tragedy had now been sown. They were to be reaped in the next five years.

Knighton was dismissed towards the end of the 1924–25 season. In his autobiography, the manager gives his own explanation of the event. Early on in his Highbury days, he had decided to get married. As his future wife lived in Manchester, and a house was available there, Knighton decided to move back north. Norris, according to Knighton, persuaded him to stay by offering his own apartment for Knighton's use (which Knighton accepted) and a benefit game in 1925–26, specifically the Arsenal versus Spurs match that season. This game could be expected to bring in perhaps £3000 to £4000 for Knighton, as a benefit then meant that the player or manager simply kept the takings of a regular season fixture. As it happened, the Arsenal-Spurs match proved to be the first of the 1925–26 season. Knighton believed that Norris fired him simply to avoid paying over the gate receipts of this game. Knighton actually wrote: 'I believe Norris sacked me to get round offering me the big benefit he promised. . . when I tackled him about it, he made it clear I had nothing but a verbal promise, but he offered me £500 "without prejudice".' It is worth mentioning that Norris remembered Knighton in his will nine years later, by which time Knighton appears to have forgiven him.

It is certainly an interesting story, but matters are rarely so simple and it does not ring entirely true. A more likely explanation surely lies in the fact that The Arsenal had been knocked out of the Cup by West Ham in the first round, and had finished 20th in the League. As it happens, they have never finished so low in the 60 years since.

Norris probably approached Chapman in April 1925. The chairman managed one final dig at everything he had railed against with a superfluous advertisement in the *Athletic News* on 11 May 1925. It read: 'Arsenal Football Club is open to receive applications for the position of TEAM MANAGER. He must be experienced and possess the highest qualifications for the post, both as to ability and personal character. Gentlemen whose sole ability to build up a good side depends on the payment of heavy and exhorbitant (sic) transfer fees need not apply.'

It was a final restatement of at least one of his beliefs before they were allowed to rest in peace. From this point on, Arsenal and Sir Henry Norris were in the hands of the first football professional.

· CHAPTER 5 ·
Legendary Arsenal

Herbert Chapman's first few months at Highbury were not exactly uneventful. In the close season the old offside law was changed. Previously to remain onside required three defenders between the frontmost attacker and the goal, and now this was reduced to two. This was in response to the deadening effect of the offside game, refined during the early 1920s by teams such as Newcastle and Notts County. The immediate effect was a flood of goals and a change in tactics which allowed far more goal-scoring in the English game until around the late 1960s. To take one good example of the effect of the change, Huddersfield's first two championships (1923–24 and 1924–25) under Chapman had been achieved with 60 and 69 goals scored. Chapman's two Championships with Arsenal saw the Gunners score 127 in 1930–31 and 118 in 1932–33.

Chapman does not appear to have developed any immediate tactical variations in the light of the new law. His first season started relatively poorly — the very first game was a 1–0 home defeat by Tottenham though this was followed by 1–0 away wins at Manchester United and Leicester. However, on 3 October 1925 came a truly critical match, a resounding 7–0 defeat at Newcastle. This defeat so upset Charlie Buchan, new to Arsenal from nearby Sunderland, that he demanded a tactical change by dropping the centre half (previously the free-ranging link between defence and attack) back between the full backs. The centre half could thus cut out forwards coming through the middle who hoped to exploit having to be behind only one defender rather than two. Apparently Newcastle, with Charlie Spencer at centre half, played this very system during their 7–0 win and Buchan, who had suggested the idea at every Arsenal team meeting since the opening day of the season, clearly thought himself vindicated.

A handshake begins one of the most symbolic games ever played at Highbury. The date was 29 August 1925, the captains Charles Buchan of Arsenal and Arthur Grimsdell of Spurs. It was Chapman's first game as Arsenal manager, Buchan's first as an Arsenal player and the first day of the revolutionary new offside law. A combination of the three, among other things, was to change Arsenal within a decade from First Division also-rans to the greatest side in the world. These things take time though – Spurs won this game 0-1.

Charlie Buchan is beaten to the ball by his old colleague and Sunderland keeper McInroy at Highbury on 20 November 1926. Arsenal lost the game 2-3 with Buchan and Ramsey getting the home side's goals. Buchan, born in Plumstead, had played four games for Arsenal reserves back in the Woolwich days but left over a dispute about 11 shillings (55p) expenses and made his name with the great Sunderland team of the pre-war era. He moved to Highbury in 1925, the transfer fee being perhaps the most celebrated of all time. Sunderland manager Bob Kyle had asked for £4,000, insisting that Buchan may be 33 but he would still score 20 goals in a season. Henry Norris asked Kyle to put his money where his mouth was and accept £2,000 down and £100 for every goal Buchan did score. Kyle accepted and did well on the deal, for Buchan scored 21 and Sunderland made a £100 bonus.

Charlie Buchan was a player Chapman would always listen to, a good example of Chapman's determination to bring the very best players, irrespective of age or price, to his clubs. He had used Clem Stephenson at Huddersfield in the same way in 1920 (Stephenson later took over from him as manager there) and Chapman also took the great Alex Jackson to Leeds Road. At Highbury he paid a record fee for David Jack and eventually captured Alex James, the outstanding schemer of the inter-war period.

Charlie Buchan was Chapman's first purchase at Highbury, and one that was to reverberate round the club for many years. Buchan had actually been born in Plumstead, had watched Arsenal as a boy, studied at Woolwich Polytechnic, and had played four games for Arsenal Reserves. He walked out on the club in 1909 when the notoriously mean George Morrell turned down an expense claim for 11 shillings (55p). He joined Northfleet, then Leyton, and was transferred to Sunderland (after turning down Norris and Fulham) for a massive £1,200 when aged only 18. He played in their Championship side of 1913 and in the Cup final that year, became captain of England and, after his retirement, became a very well known journalist and broadcaster, famous to the post-war baby boom generation for *Charlie Buchan's Football Monthly*. He was nearly 34 when he came to Highbury, and had, a couple of months before, already been the subject of an approach by Leslie Knighton, who had clearly decided to go out with a bang by (unbeknown to Norris) offering £7,000 for Buchan's signature. Buchan's main concern was his sports shop in Sunderland,

from which he took a great deal of income. The maximum wage at the time was only £8 per week and the need for sweeteners and compensations was not uncommon in persuading very good players to move.

Chapman was presumably a much more persuasive negotiator than Knighton, for Sunderland were eventually prepared to consider and accept a much lower fee. The signing has, of course, gone down as one of the most celebrated in football history and is worth recounting. Buchan was serving in his shop in May 1925 when in walked Chapman. 'I've come to sign you for Arsenal,' he told Buchan immediately, and the player assumed he was joking. On being told that Chapman had spoken to the club, Buchan telephoned Sunderland manager Bob Kyle, finding it difficult to believe that the club would release him so easily. It was another ten weeks before he put pen to paper and in the meantime the deal had been thrashed out. It was actually Norris, and not Chapman, who had insisted on handling the financial negotiations. Sunderland had asked for £4,000, but Norris was not prepared to pay that for a 33-year-old player. Norris had originally interviewed Buchan in 1910 when he was chairman of Fulham and Buchan was 18 — Norris offered 30 shillings a week and Buchan insisted on £2 so their paths diverged for 15 years. Kyle argued that Buchan might now be 33 but that he would still score 20 goals in his first season with Arsenal. Norris asked Kyle to put his money where his mouth was — £2,000 down and £100 for every goal scored. Kyle agreed and Buchan scored 19 League goals and two in the Cup. So Kyle got

his £4,000 and £100 interest on top. For Arsenal the deal was a publicity godsend, a ready-made headline every time Buchan scored. The crowd responded as well: 'There goes another £100,' they would chant whenever he got near goal.

Norris must already have given Chapman *carte blanche* on transfer fees, for within a few weeks the manager had also bought the Scottish international keeper Bill Harper from Hibs for £5,000. The Buchan transfer dragged on for those ten weeks because of the player's insistence on somehow being compensated for the likely loss of revenue from his shop.

Chapman, no doubt remembering only too clearly what had happened when Leeds City were suspended in 1919 and how difficult it had been for him to find work afterwards, would not get involved in any illegal payments but, according to Norris, pleaded for the chairman to meet Buchan's demands. The chairman later claimed that Chapman left the room when this delicate point was reached. The scene is interesting to imagine; the chairman, desperate for success and prepared to bend the rules; the manager, sensing and needing success just as much, but frightened to risk his livelihood and reputation again. The payments involved came to light as part of a much wider League commission two years later, which found Norris and William Hall guilty of various financial irregularities (it would be harsh to call them anything worse). Though the hearing was supposedly secret, the *Daily Mail* published the details and Norris sued the FA for libel in suggesting he had acted dishonestly. Norris had a reputation for being quick to take legal action, which he usually won, but in February 1929, the case having gone as high as the Lord Chief Justice, the FA were vindicated and were able to exclude Norris from any further involvement in football. No doubt the cluckings of chickens coming home to roost were heard loud and clear at FA headquarters; the ghosts and resentments of 1913 and 1919 had stalked London football as sharply as any other disagreement in the history of the game and there were many who were anything but displeased at the outcome.

The significant findings of the commission were that between 1921 and 1924 Norris' chauffeur had been paid by the club, and that in 1926 the club had paid for his motor car. During the case, Norris and Chapman clashed, the chairman saying that the manager and club had known about various payments and Chapman (perhaps again with his mind on 1919) denying it. Norris called Chapman a liar and particularly mentioned that £125 for the team bus was the sum he had given to Buchan, under the counter, to come to Highbury. It should be said that Buchan, in his autobiography, disputed this — though only in general terms: 'Let me say here that I made nothing out of my transfer. . . In fact, I lost rather a lot of money through changing quarters like that.' One is, nonetheless, struck by Buchan's careful choice of words, which seem chosen to cloud rather than clarify.

When asked why he had done it, Norris replied very simply and obviously: 'Because (otherwise) we would not have got the players.' It all sounds desperately petty now, but at the time there were many scores to be settled and, in the fashion of a true Greek tragedy, the opportunity was not regretted by some. It was a genuine tragedy for Norris; since 1910, in addition to the money he had found for the club via various business ventures and from his own companies, he had sunk over £15,000 directly from his own pocket and no one could seriously claim that he was alone or unique in his supposed misdemeanours. Most of the leading clubs were doing the same thing one way or another.

During the case Norris declared that: 'I only made one mistake in my career, and that was sacking Knighton.' Leslie Knighton took this as a signal compliment, but in its context one is tempted to believe that it was a none-too-subtle jab at Chapman. Nonetheless as a final epitaph to the man who, almost as much as Herbert Chapman, built the modern Arsenal, we should return to the manager he fired, Leslie Knighton: 'Despite everything,' said Knighton in his autobiography, 'I still say he was the best Chairman I ever had (Knighton managed eight clubs). He did miles more for football and for footballers than the public will ever know. If he had not been (such) a rebel against petty authority he would have risen to the greatest position in the game. A financial genius, football was his hobby and delight, even though only a bagatelle compared with some of his business deals. The game was immensely the poorer for his passing out of it, and it was a tragedy indeed that such a man should have gone under a cloud.' In a sense the greater regret was that the dreams were about to come true — the year after his exclusion saw the first major trophy at Highbury. Norris lived to see the FA Cup and League won before dying, an outcast from the game, just six months after Chapman on 30 July 1934. His estate, £71,733, was still the equivalent of a seven-figure sum today.

The new Chairman was Sir Samuel Hill-Wood, whose family had run Glossop North End before the war as a sort of works team, and with some success. Glossop, in Derbyshire, remains by far the smallest town ever to have hosted a First Division club. Hill-Wood had his own place in the sporting record books already. Playing for Derbyshire versus the MCC at Lord's in May 1900, he had scored 10 runs off a single ball, the highest ever recorded before or since from a single hit. He was content to leave the running of the club to a Herbert Chapman who was no doubt greatly shaken by the court case but mightily relieved at its outcome. It is certainly possible to put down Chapman's relative lack of success between 1927 and 1930, in part at least, to the tensions and pressures created within the club by this long-running and highly emotional affair.

But back to October 1925 and to the team

meeting after that appalling 7–0 thrashing by Newcastle; it was here Buchan persuaded Chapman that centre half Jack Butler had to drop back. The meeting was in the Royal Station Hotel in Newcastle and Buchan had started the debate by refusing to catch the train back to London. 'Oh no,' said Chapman. 'You're playing at West Ham on Monday. I know what you want so let's discuss it.' Buchan outlined his ideas to the team. He didn't actually want a centre half 'policing' the centre forward, rather a man given a geographical 'beat' on the edge of the area. The rest of the defence would wheel around him to provide support. Buchan then pitched hard to be given the now necessary roving inside forward job needed to replace the centre half's attacking role (he described it as being like the fly half in rugby) but Chapman refused, wanting Buchan to continue as a goalscorer up front. There was no other obvious candidate for the job, so Chapman apparently put it to Buchan: 'It's your plan Charlie, do you have any suggestions?' Buchan suggested occasional inside forward Scotsman Andy Neil, who, though not fast ('slow as the post', said Buchan) could kill the ball instantly and distribute it quickly and accurately with either foot. After some argument (obviously everyone's role was affected, and someone had to drop out for Neil) the plan was accepted and Neil took on the role for the following day's match at West Ham. The plan worked perfectly, Arsenal won 4–0 and, for a year at least, they barely looked back. Jimmy Ramsey and then Billy Blyth later took over the link man's job from Neil.

It would not be true to say that the new system was in any sense invented by Buchan and Chapman. As we have seen, Newcastle were already experimenting, as were Queen's Park and several other sides, including Spurs. What Chapman did do, of course, was to refine it and find the players to fit the positions as perfectly as was ever likely to be possible.

He quickly moved his full backs out to mark the wingers (that job had regularly been done by the half backs), dropped a second inside forward back halfway between the midfield line and the forwards, and decided that three very fast moving and adaptable forwards were probably the best attacking answer to the new defensive formations and the revised offside law. This was not developed overnight, but over a period of years, ending with the 3-4-3 or WM formation of the great Arsenal teams. The key was never the scheme itself, but the players who fitted into it.

Chapman had retained relatively few of the men he inherited from Knighton. Alf Baker continued at right half, Bob John for a time at left back and then at wing half. Bernard Joy said of John that: '. . . next to Joe Mercer, he is the finest wing half Arsenal have had and I have played alongside giants like Jack Crayston, Wilf Copping and Archie Macaulay. There was nobody like him for plucking the ball out of the air with his foot, whatever its height or pace, and bringing it to the ground. He did his job quietly,

efficiently and unobtrusively, and there lay his strength.' Charlie Buchan was equally unstinting in his praise of John, whom he regarded as the core of the Arsenal side: 'He deserves a place in any list of famous players. . . yet one rarely hears him mentioned nowadays (this was in 1955). You could depend on Bob in every game but this dapper player was not showy. He just got on with the job.' Bob John eventually played 421 First Division matches (a club record until surpassed by George Armstrong) over 16 seasons, won three Cup medals, three Championship medals and 16 caps. If there was a cornerstone of the great teams, it was surely Bob John.

Chapman moved Jimmy Brain, who had recently been playing as an inside forward, to centre forward and Brain immediately established a new club scoring record with 33 goals in 1925–26. By February 1926 another of the critical influences had arrived — right winger Joe Hulme. Reputed to be the fastest winger in British football, Hulme had previously played for York and Blackburn and eventually won nine England caps, a lot for a winger at the time (it was always one of the obvious, more detached, positions that the selectors liked to change time and again). Hulme was not only the joker of the team, he was also a very good cricketer. The most famous story concerning him was when he was batting for Middlesex against the very fast West Indian bowler Learie Constantine. Hulme had completely missed three consecutive bumpers and, on the fourth, the umpire called: 'No ball.' 'So that's what's happening — I knew something was wrong,' shouted Hulme. He had happier cricketing days — in 1934 he set up a record sixth wicket stand for Middlesex of 212 with Gubby Allen.

All in all, 1925–26 proved to be a successful first season for Chapman. The results were not spectacular, but kept going the right way and Arsenal finished with 52 points, which took them to second place in the League. They never really challenged Huddersfield though, who took their third consecutive Championship and the first ever hat-trick, later to be matched by the Gunners and Liverpool. It would no doubt have surprised their fans and directors to be told, at the moment of their greatest triumph, that Huddersfield would never again win a major prize. Arsenal's 52 points was the most they had ever achieved in the First Division (eight more than in 1920–21) and the greatest number ever achieved by a London club. Second place was also the highest ever reached by a club from the capital, equalling Spurs' performance of 1922.

But if anyone at Highbury thought that here was the brave new world, then they were wrong. Chapman said it would take five years to win a trophy and he was right, though quite why he was right remains elusive despite the speculations about the gathering legal storm clouds over Norris and his manager. The next four years in the League were almost a definition of mediocre — 11th, 10th, 9th and 14th. Perhaps it was because the team was always in a state of flux as

Chapman added to it, or tried to incorporate the skills of a Jack or a James. Certainly it was to continue to be a period of team building.

The next significant purchase was Tom Parker, Southampton's right back. Relatively slow but very good positionally, Chapman particularly wanted him as a steadying, intelligent captain. He played 155 consecutive League games and was easy to pick out (there were no numbers in the League until 1939) because of his bald head. Chapman always had a perchant for miners, not surprisingly given his own mining background, and there were over a dozen on the staff during his regime. One of the most popular was the ungainly but highly effective Jack Lambert, acquired as an inside forward for £2,000 from Doncaster Rovers. Chapman was always trying to find the perfect centre forward and constantly seemed to be buying, or trying to buy, Lambert's replacement. But he always returned to the big fellow and the quest for the ideal was not actually satisfied until after the manager's death, with the arrival of Ted Drake. Lambert stayed with the club after his playing career had finished, going down to Margate to manage Arsenal's nursery club in that town (they played in the Southern League from 1933, winning their sections in 1936 and 1937). Tragically the big centre forward was to be killed in a road accident at the start of the Second World War.

For the other side of the field from Hulme, Chapman originally bought Welsh international Charlie Jones from Nottingham Forest. Jones was a very intelligent, worrying type of player, but an odd choice in the long term for outside left as he lacked speed. Chapman later moved him to right half, where he became a permanent fixture in the great team of the early 1930s. Jack Butler, on the other hand, failed to adapt to his new stopper centre half role, all too often venturing upfield and being caught out of position. In December 1926 Chapman somehow found a tall 21-year-old redhead playing for Oswestry on the Welsh borders and bought him for just £200. Roberts became such a feature of Arsenal's success that he has remained identified forever as the basic mould for the stopper, policeman, centre half. Rarely moving upfield, he performed his central defensive role consistently and effectively season after season.

Roberts was never a particularly skilful player, but he became an essential part of the tactical formation. As Cliff Bastin said: 'As an all-round player he may have had his failings, but he fitted in perfectly with the Arsenal scheme of things. Seldom was it that he wasted a ball. . . Alex James picked up ball after ball from him in midfield.' Roberts rarely scored a goal, though he won the 1932 FA Cup quarter-final at Huddersfield with a totally unexpected header from a corner right at the start of the match. He is also remembered for scoring two identical own goals in the same game for Derby at Highbury. His case is an interesting one for, by everyone's admission, not only was he not a skilful player, he was a relatively poor kicker of the ball.

Whittaker said that: 'Roberts' genius came from his intelligence and, even more important, that he did what he was told.' His orders were to stay in the centre of the defence, to intercept all the balls down the middle and either head them clear or pass them short to a team-mate. 'Because he carried out his orders,' said Whittaker, 'his inability to kick a ball hard or far was camouflaged.'

While 1926–27 was not a notable year in the League, it did end on a high note. After forty years, Arsenal made their first appearance in an FA Cup final. It was, incidentally, Chapman who at this time insisted on changing the common name from The Arsenal to plain Arsenal, arguing that it would mean the club always came first in any alphabetical list — a point which remained valid only until 1932, when Aldershot joined the Third Division South.

In forty years the club had only gone beyond the second round/fourth round stage (i.e. last 32) on four occasions, frankly à dreadful record for a first-class club, so the Wembley appearance was certainly something to celebrate. The run to the final was a tough one. Sheffield United were beaten 3–2 at Bramall Lane, then Port Vale 1–0 in a replay. Liverpool were beaten 2–0 at Highbury in the fifth round (the old first round or last 64 had become the third round in 1925–26) with both goals coming from headers at free-kicks. Wolves also came to Highbury for the quarter-final. Arsenal won the game 2–1, the winning goal being a remarkable one. A Joe Hulme centre was headed straight into the net from around 25 yards by centre half Jack Butler, who was yet to be replaced by Roberts. Arsenal were in the semis for the first time in 20 years and were lucky enough not to have to leave London as they were drawn against Southampton, then in the middle of the Second Division, and the game was played at Stamford Bridge. The Gunners were even luckier to win on a blustery, wet day. Southampton pressed for much of the match but could only score once, late in the match, through their centre forward Rawlings, who had played for England while Southampton were still a Third Division side. By that time Hulme and Buchan had made the game safe.

The final is remembered for three things. One is the very first Cup final radio commentary, the second is Cardiff City taking the Cup out of England for the only time. The third is the tragic goal, the only one of the match, that, in truth, lost it for Arsenal rather than won it for Cardiff. Keeper Dan Lewis, a Welshman himself, had only come into the side for the third round tie at Sheffield. He replaced Bill Harper, who immediately set off for the States in search of fame and fortune (and returned to the club slightly disillusioned four years later). Lewis was also to find fame in the final, but not the kind he would have sought.

It had not been a very good game, played on a greasy pitch with much commitment but little skill. Arsenal had been the better side, winning all of the game's eight corners.

At Stamford Bridge on 26 March 1927, forty years after their foundation, Arsenal finally won a semi-final. Their opponents were Southampton and the goals in a 2-1 success were scored by Joe Hulme and Charlie Buchan. Hulme's goal (*above* – he is out of picture) was the first and is being celebrated by Arsenal players (left to right) Billy Blyth, Jimmy Brain and Syd Hoar.

With just 16 minutes left, Cardiff skipper Fred Keenor took a throw and found his Scots centre forward Hugh Ferguson around 25 yards out. Ferguson advanced and tried a half-hearted, weak ground shot which should have given Lewis no trouble. The keeper did indeed stop the ball but, turning away slightly to avoid the oncoming Ferguson, it slid out of his grasp and under his left arm. Even now the situation was not lost but, in an attempt to gather the ball up again, Lewis turned and simply knocked it with his elbow so that it trickled gently over the line. The film of the incident is appalling to behold — the whole thing happens in slow motion, as if the projector was running at half speed.

Even then the game was not over, for Arsenal were soon to be offered the best chance of the match. Sid Hoar put in a long, high centre. Cardiff keeper Tom Farquharson misjudged the flight, it bounced once and passed over his head. Brain and Buchan both rushed in to nod the ball into the empty net. But as Buchan then describes it: '. . . at the last moment Jimmy left it to me; I unfortunately left it to him.' The ball bounced harmlessly away past a post and, with it, Arsenal's remaining hopes.

After the presentations, Lewis threw his losers' medal to the turf, from where it was retrieved by fellow Welshman Bob John. 'Never mind, you'll have another chance,' said John,

Above: **A delightful picture of the Arsenal** first team taken behind Highbury's southern terracing two days before the 1927 FA Cup final. Left to right: Billy Blyth, Bob John, Horace Cope, Andy Kennedy, Tom Parker, Dan Lewis, Bill Seddon, Jack Butler, Alf Baker, Joe Hulme, Jimmy Brain, Syd Hoar and Charlie Buchan. Horace Cope had been injured two weeks before the final at Huddersfield and was replaced at full back by Kennedy. Though only 5ft 9in, Cope weighed over 13 stone and when he arrived at Highbury from Notts County special shorts had to be made for him as the club had none that would fit. Alf Baker remains unique among all the men who have played for the club in 100 years, for he is the only one ever to have appeared in all eleven positions in first-class games.

Left: **An Arsenal corner** during the 1927 FA Cup final against Cardiff City. The attackers are Buchan, Blyth and, challenging keeper Farquharson, Jimmy Brain. Arsenal won all eight corners awarded in the game, evidence of their dominance in every department except goals.

but he was wrong and Lewis was to be injured just before the 1930 final. The Arsenal team in 1927 was Lewis, Parker, Andy Kennedy, Baker, Butler, John, Hulme, Buchan, Brain, Billy Blyth and Sid Hoar. Grease on Lewis' new jersey was partly blamed for the disaster, and when Arsenal reached the 1930 final Tom Whittaker told Charlie Preedy to wear an old, unwashed jersey rather than a new one. The ritual was observed in all the subsequent finals through the Chapman, Allison and Whittaker eras.

Chapman was not discouraged. He had lost important matches before. The team building continued. The left full back position was something of a weakness, the current incumbents being Horace Cope and Andy Kennedy. To fill the slot, Chapman showed another of his strengths, that of finding rare talents in unlikely places. He had shown this with Roberts and was to show it again with Bastin. Eddie (actually Edris Albert) Hapgood was particularly special because he had played only 12 games for non-League Kettering and in no way looked the part. A 19-year-old milkman who had not been signed at the crucial moment by his home town club, Bristol Rovers, he weighed only 9 stone 6 pounds. Although he was, and remained, a physical

Above and right: **The moment that was to haunt** keeper Dan Lewis for the rest of his life. He had stopped a weak, speculative shot from Cardiff forward Hugh Ferguson in the 1927 final but, somehow, the ball slipped from his grasp and gently rolled towards the line. Turning to gather it, he caught the ball with his elbow and knocked it over the line. The time the virtually slow motion incident took can be judged from the positions of Tom Parker in the two pictures. The Cardiff forward is not Ferguson, but winger Len Davies. It was the only goal of the game and the only occasion the Cup has ever left England. Lewis was himself a Welshman and lost his chance of retrieving his reputation when he played right through to the semi-final stage in 1930 but was injured before the final. Grease on his jersey was blamed for the error, but the belief that Arsenal always wash new jerseys before a final is not accurate. What Tom Whittaker insisted afterwards was that the keeper should wear an *unwashed* (and hence ungreasy) shirt.

fitness fanatic, he was relatively weak and was often literally knocked out when heading the wet, heavy, leather ball of the period. Arsenal invested heavily in their £750 signing, Tom Whittaker forcing the ex-vegetarian to eat steaks and build up both his strength and weight. A few years later, after an accident in which Hapgood had been burned quite badly, Tom Whittaker built a special leather harness for his body so that he could play without the burns rubbing the whole time, proof of Hapgood's remarkable physical courage and unswerving commitment to the game and to the club.

It was sad that Hapgood eventually became

rather estranged from the game. His relations with Allison were never as good as with Chapman, and between him and Whittaker strains gradually developed as they appeared rivals for future senior roles at the club. This was a great pity, as Hapgood had written in 1944 (before Whittaker took over from Allison as manager) that: 'Tom Whittaker has, perhaps of all the people who helped me at Highbury, been my closest friend.' Hapgood was later manager at Blackburn, Watford and Bath but, after losing the Bath job in 1956, he asked Arsenal for a retrospective benefit and was very upset when the club was unable to agree. In his commitment and obsession

with physical fitness there was a boyish naivety which was best illustrated on his very first trip to Highbury after Chapman had signed him from Kettering. On the train journey he lost his whole signing on fee (£10) to a gang playing the three-card trick. In some ways, it was a lesson he never entirely benefitted from.

Whatever else he now had, by 1927 Chapman clearly felt he lacked the great names and, with the exception of perhaps Buchan and Hulme, the great players. His two great transfer coups were still to come — David Jack and Alex James. The David Jack story has been told so often that it has become part of soccer folklore, but no doubt it bears repetition.

By 1928 David Jack was one of the great names of English football. A cultured, stylish (he used to turn up at the ground in spats) inside forward, he was one of those rare animals, an automatic choice for England. He had scored the first ever goal at Wembley, in the 1923 Cup final, and won winners' medals with Bolton in that year and again in 1926. Bolton were one of the handful of top teams at the time, but in the close-season of 1928 informed other clubs that they would consider offers for any player, excepting only David Jack. Chapman and George Allison went to Bolton to see their board, initially meeting a blank refusal. Eventually, however, the question was asked: 'How much would we have to offer for you to change your minds?' Bolton, probably to get Chapman and Allison to go away, said £13,000 — almost double the existing record.

Allison and Chapman returned to the Midland Hotel in Manchester for dinner, eventually invited the Bolton chairman and secretary to join them and haggled until the small hours. In the

end an offer of £11,500 plus the accrued benefit to be paid to Jack was accepted (players then received a benefit after five years, but if they left a club after, say, three years, they could be given a sum to represent three fifths of what they might have expected to receive). Oddly, the fee is usually quoted as £10,670 or £10,890, but all the parties agree in their memoirs that it was £11,500. David Jack was roused from his bed and belatedly asked his opinion. After talking to his father (then the Plymouth manager) he was amenable and agreed to come to London the following day to sign.

That day was coincidentally the first time Bob Wall had ever been involved in a transfer. He had just been taken on as secretary/assistant to Herbert Chapman. Wall takes up the story as he and Chapman headed off for the Euston Hotel to meet the Bolton party off the Manchester train: 'We arrived at the hotel half-an-hour early. Chapman immediately went into the lounge bar. He called the waiter, placed two pound notes in his hand and said: "George, this is Mr Wall, my assistant. He will drink whisky and dry ginger. I will drink gin and tonic. We shall be joined by guests. They will drink whatever they like. See that our guests are given double of everything but Mr Wall's whisky and dry ginger will contain no whisky and my gin and tonic will contain no gin".' According to Bob Wall, their guests were in a cheerful mood by the time the deal was finalised and were not inclined to question anything further.

Charlie Buchan had by now retired, his last game being the famous 3–3 draw at Everton on 5 May 1928 when Dixie Dean got a hat-trick and broke the League scoring record with 60 goals in a single season. Without Buchan, Chapman

Above: **The classic Arsenal golfing party** of the great years – Tom Parker, David Jack, Herbert Chapman and Alex James. The picture was taken at Hatch End on 14 November 1929. It was not a good period for the club – they were to win only three of their next 16 League games but had still, by season's end, won a first major trophy and laid the foundations for the decade that was to follow.

lacked a commander on the field. There was actually no obvious candidate whom Chapman could pay the earth for. David Jack was Buchan's counterpart in goalscoring ability, but not as a leader, the intelligence on the pitch. As Bernard Joy rightly pointed out, the way the Arsenal system had developed, the key man had become the foraging inside forward, the centre of the W, the man who picks up clearances from the defenders and sends the forwards away. Clem Stephenson had done a similar job for Chapman at Huddersfield, but there were very few players in the game with either the technical or strategic skills, never mind both.

One player who did have the vision was Alex James, the creator behind the Scots Wembley Wizards of 1928, infamous 5–1 humiliators of England. He had gone from Raith to Preston, where he was less a schemer than an attacking inside forward. In four years there (admittedly in the Second Division) he had scored 60 goals and he was known to have often commented along the lines of: 'I'm never going to chase an opponent in possession.' In June 1929 Preston, surprisingly, put him up for sale. Maybe they decided that being known as 'Alex James and the other ten' was not good for the club in the long run. Chapman beat most of the big clubs — including Villa, Liverpool and Manchester City — for his signature.

George Allison said of James: 'No one like him ever kicked a ball. He had a most uncanny and wonderful control, but because this was allied to a split second thinking apparatus, he simply left the opposition looking on his departing figure with amazement.' The small size of the transfer fee (£8,750) was such a surprise that the Football League held an inquiry before

Arsenal were allowed to register James. With so many clubs interested it had naturally been assumed that the fee would break the David Jack record, and the Lancashire clubs, possibly with the recent Norris case in mind, were muttering about inducements. The inquiry showed Arsenal were completely clean — all they had done was to help find James a job in Selfridge's, the London store. But even the inquiry had more to it than met the eye. Chapman knew he would face rumours about the impending transfer (he had already secretly obtained James' signature) and it was actually the manager himself who quietly asked the League to set up the inquiry. He then publicly insisted he would not sign James (something of a deceit) until *after* such an investigation.

It could not be said that James was the perfect club man. It took a season for him to settle in to his new role, after which he virtually gave up scoring goals. Chapman always treated him slightly differently from the other players (he was allowed to stay in bed until noon on matchdays, for instance). Alex was the key, that was the message; and it is certainly true that the side did not win anything before James arrived but started winning everything soon afterwards.

Chapman's patience was, nonetheless, sorely tested. In the summer of 1931 James refused to re-sign, presumably looking for some sort of extra inducements. In August the club sent him on holiday, then Chapman called him back saying the club had decided to despatch him on a cruise instead. He hurried back to London Docks, only to find that Chapman had booked him a berth on a banana and general cargo boat. John Peters, the assistant secretary, somehow persuaded James to go on board and he was finally released in Bordeaux. He always claimed to have quite enjoyed it. James eventually signed the week before the season began. When the team, who were training, heard the news they raided the Arsenal band room and serenaded James into the ground by murdering 'See the Conquering Hero Comes.' More serious was James' failure to turn up at the celebration banquet after the Championship success of 1933. He had refused to go to Belfast to play Cliftonville in the last week of the season and was dropped. As club captain he should have received the trophy from League President John McKenna (the same man who had done so much to help put Arsenal where they were 14 years before). James' place was left empty and Charlie Jones accepted the award as vice-captain.

James is probably one of the ten or so greatest players in British football history — ranking alongside the likes of Matthews, Greaves, Charlton, Bloomer, Morton, Best, Blanchflower and Goodall. It is always necessary to ask whether such players would be as great in another age. The philosopher Hegel, in a rather profound answer to the question, said: 'The great man of his age is the one who can put into words or actions the will of his age, tell his age what its will is, and accomplish it. What he does

is the heart and essence of his age.' Hegel was speaking of the great statesman, but on the narrower canvas of a football field Alex James *was* the heart and essence of his age. Arsenal were the team of the era, and James was the heart of the team, the definition of football success. Without him the style, the system and the successes would probably never have been achieved. Whether James would have done as much in another era is an interesting point. Some of the greats would arguably not have achieved as much at a different time — Matthews in the 1970s, for instance — but James was probably a player for any age and every era.

All of this is probably rather peripheral to the essential truth about Alex James — that at the critical time he was the hub of the whole team. He foraged so far back that he was no longer an inside forward, and Bastin therefore had no one inside him for most of the time. For many teams this would have caused problems, but for Arsenal it was an encouragement to develop different moves. The classic was the James/Hulme/Bastin triangle. James, often facing his own goal, would hit a long pass up the right wing. Hulme would race past the defence, and hit his centre way over to the left for Bastin either to shoot or dribble in on goal. Up the middle would steam Lambert, looking for any crumbs that might fall from the table. In 1932–33 Bastin and Hulme scored 53 goals between them, perfect evidence that Arsenal did play the game very differently from their contemporaries, who tended to continue to rely on the wingers *making* goals for the centre forward, rather than scoring themselves. By playing the wingers this way, Chapman was able to have one more man in midfield, and thus control the supply of the ball, primarily through James. But it was only possible because both wingers were exceptional footballers — Hulme because of his speed and Bastin because of his tactical brain and coolness. Bastin's calm was legendary. Tom Whittaker said of him in 1950: 'Coupled with his sincerity and his loyalty to all his bosses, he had a trait few of us are blessed with — that is, he had an ice-cold temperament.'

Boy Bastin was the very last of the major signings, coming a couple of weeks after James. Bastin is very amusing on his first meeting with the Scotsman. James was already a star, while Bastin was hoping just to play for the reserves. James came up and introduced himself to Bastin in an accent which, Bastin says: 'I have never heard rivalled, before or since. I must confess,' Bastin goes on, 'that my chief reaction, apart from feeling rather more at home than I had a few moments earlier, was of trying to understand just what Alex was saying. Alex and I may have developed a well-nigh perfect understanding on the field, but off it I always found him a trifle incomprehensible.' Bastin knew him well of course, and had enormous admiration for the man, particularly for his self-confidence. 'Nobody had greater faith in the qualities of Alex James than Alex James himself — not even

Herbert Chapman, and that is saying something. Alex needed all his self-confidence during his first few months at Highbury, for he was very slow to settle down.'

As part of the settling down process, James further established his own trademark — the baggy shorts. They were apparently not his idea at all. Cartoonist Tom Webster drew him playing for Preston in the *Daily Mail* one Monday with rather long shorts, possibly to emphasize James' small stature. James liked the idea, and insisted on going out to buy a pair to fit the cartoon. They also kept his knees warm, he would tell admirers.

By 1930 James was indeed beginning to fit, but there must have been frustration in the boardroom as well as on the terraces. In five years under Chapman, Arsenal had spent a fortune but the world remembered them only for an excruciating goal in the 1927 Cup final and a chairman permanently banned from the game.

It is interesting to speculate what would have happened if Chapman had died exactly four years earlier, in January 1930. Certainly his own reputation would have been dramatically lessened, his days at Huddersfield perhaps questioned as a peculiar fluke or the work of Clem Stephenson (just as Jimmy Seed was, at that very moment, receiving the credit for Sheffield Wednesday's Championships of 1929 and 1930).

But would the team have gone on to greatness in the 1930s? Who can say, but in the last month of the 1920s no one would have predicted anything very much for the club, Chapman or not. The season had begun so badly that relegation looked the only sort of news Arsenal were likely to make. The forward line (now temporarily including David Halliday from Sunderland for £6,000) had cost £34,000, by a mile the most expensive in football history, and yet it couldn't score goals. But perhaps there was something magic in that new decade, in the rather less than celebrated (away from Highbury at least) 1930s. For it was the turn of the year, the passing of the 'gay twenties', that was the turning point for Arsenal. In the League they achieved no more than respectability (finishing 14th), but in the Cup they truly achieved glory.

The second week of the new decade saw the third round of the FA Cup. Arsenal drew Chelsea at Highbury, never an easy game. Chapman made a courageous decision, possibly the most difficult in his career, and dropped James. If the team wasn't scoring with the class of forward they had, then it had to be the provider who was at fault. Halliday was also dropped, in came John, Thompson and Lambert. Arsenal won 2–0 in a rainstorm. Two weeks later Chapman simply ordered James to bed. The Scotsman had always suffered from a form of rheumatism in the ankles, which made it difficult for him to play golf, and Chapman felt James needed a complete rest. In the fourth round Birmingham (who reached the final the following year) came to Highbury and went

The date: Saturday 25 January 1930.

The place: Highbury. The game: a fourth round Cup tie against Birmingham. Charlie Preedy punches away a Birmingham cross in one of only two FA Cup ties he ever played for Arsenal. The other was the final that year. The match ended 2-2 with Jack and Bastin scoring the goals. That Saturday night, Herbert Chapman made the decision that was, according to Bernard Joy, the turning point in the modern history of Arsenal Football Club. The manager went round to see Alex James, who had been dropped and sent home to bed (the Gunners had won only five of their previous 20 games). He told James that Arsenal could not succeed without him and that the whole season, and by implication both their futures, rested on the replay at Birmingham the following Wednesday. James responded, came back and the replay was won 1-0 with an Alf Baker penalty. Arsenal never looked back. The first month of the new decade had indeed been the turning point.

away with a 2-2 draw. Leslie Knighton was now their manager and Chapman knew the replay would be a tough one. If Arsenal lost it, then the whole season would have gone and Chapman's judgment on his big signings could only come into serious question.

Bernard Joy, who was with the team in the 1930s and whose opinion has always been highly respected, argued in 1952 that Chapman's decision after the first Birmingham game that Saturday night, 25 January 1930, was the turning point in the modern history of the club. Thirty-three years after Joy, one has not only to agree but to go further; it was, with the semi-final a few weeks later, probably the most critical moment in the whole hundred years.

Chapman had to win the replay at St Andrew's the following Wednesday. On the Sunday morning he went round to Alex James' home, got him out of bed and took him off to Highbury for training. Chapman gambled that James would react to the crisis, to the obvious placing of responsibility on his shoulders. It worked, not spectacularly, but it worked. Alf Baker scored from the penalty spot, the only goal of a hard game. The fifth and six rounds were no easier — a 2-0 win away at Ayresome Park and a convincing 3-0 win at West Ham, banishing memories of the pep-pill farce of five years before. The semi-final looked easy — Hull City at Elland Road. Hull were at the bottom of the Second Division and were relegated to the Third a month later. It was also their first semi-final. Quite what they were doing there was anyone's guess, but most knowing observers put it down to the wily management of Bill McCracken, the full back who had perfected the offside game ten years before. All the interest was in the other semi-final between the two Yorkshire giants, Huddersfield and League Champions Wednesday (between them they had won five of the seven most recent championships). This was indeed to

be a famous match; with Huddersfield leading 2-1 a Wednesday shot entered the net just as the whistle blew for full time. The referee disallowed the goal but many of the crowd went home not knowing whether there would be a replay or not.

Back at the supposedly less interesting semi-final at Elland Road, shocks were in store. After 15 minutes keeper Dan Lewis cleared a ball from the edge of his area. It was a poor kick, travelling only 30 yards or so, and it went straight to the Hull inside left Howieson. He lobbed it straight back on the volley and it flew over Lewis' head into the net from a full 45 yards out. After 30 minutes Eddie Hapgood sliced a Duncan shot into his own net and Arsenal were 2-0 down at half-time. In the second half, the goals just wouldn't come. And it was not until twenty minutes from the end that whichever gods control football ended their little joke. Those last few minutes are among the most important in the club's history, and they bear a remarkable similarity to the last minutes of the 1971 semi-final against Stoke at Hillsborough, when the Gunners also came back from a 2-0 deficit with two Peter Storey goals and went on to perform the Double. In both 1930 and 1971, the semi-final result was vital to the history of the club, just as vital as the finals themselves.

Firstly Alf Baker got Joe Hulme away on the wing, he crossed and David Jack finally defeated McCracken's offside trap and converted the centre. Twelve minutes later Cliff Bastin picked up a ball from Alex James, took on the defenders in a solo run and hit the ball into the top right-hand corner. Arsenal were unlucky not to get a third, but the teams met again for a midweek replay at Villa Park. Hull seemed bitter about being robbed so late in the first game and the tackling was fierce. So much so that, in the second half, the Hull centre half Arthur Childs became the first (and for another 50 years the only) man to be sent off in a semi-final. He was despatched for

taking a kick at Jack Lambert. That was the end for Hull. Soon afterwards Joey Williams (taking the place of the injured Hulme) hared off down the right wing, pulled the ball back from the goal-line and David Jack connected with a right-foot volley to score the game's only goal. Arsenal were at Wembley for the second time in four years, Huddersfield were there for the fourth time in a decade.

The defeat of Hull seemed to lift a great weight from the Arsenal attack. Two weeks before the Cup final the Gunners ran up their biggest First Division win to date, 8–1 over Sheffied United (they were to equal this margin against the very same team three years later). And five days before the final they set yet another record when, having been 3–1 down at half-time, they eventually drew 6–6 at Leicester. It remains the highest scoring draw in any English first-class game, having only been equalled by Charlton v Middlesbrough in 1960. Oddly Lambert's deputy, David Halliday, had an excellent game at Leicester, scoring four times to justify his remarkable record at Sunderland, where he had recorded 155 goals in 167 matches. But the centre forward spot was firmly Jack Lambert's by now, a decision that was to be fully justified five days later at Wembley.

The final against Huddersfield (for all the details of the game see the first chapter of this book) was formally the start of the great decade, but it was the following year that has always been known as the great season. 1930–31 saw the establishment of the record points total for a Championship side (66 — later to be surpassed by Leeds United under the now defunct two-point system), and the remarkable total of 127 goals scored would have then been, and remained for all time, a First Division record had Aston Villa not, incredibly, scored 128 the same year. In London, Birmingham and elsewhere it was a wonderful season for spectators.

The season was a massive success for the Gunners from start to finish. The first two games were away, at Blackpool and Bolton. They were both won 4–1. Arsenal were not defeated until their tenth game, at the Baseball Ground against one of the consistently best sides of the 1930s, Derby County. Despite Arsenal's tremendous performance through the whole season, strangely they were never clear of challengers and were not sure of the trophy until two weeks before the end of the contest, when Liverpool went down 3–1. Villa were, of course, the biggest threat, countering a 5–2 defeat by the Gunners at Highbury with a 5–1 win at Villa Park and the friendly rivalry between the clubs was marked by Villa's attendance at the season's end celebration banquet. Villa were also the first opponents in the Cup, and went 2–0 up at Highbury before Lambert and Jack forced a draw. Arsenal played well to win the replay 3–1 but surprisingly went out 2–1 at Stamford Bridge. It certainly was a surprise — Arsenal had beaten Chelsea there 5–1 in the League in November. Though a disappointment, it did not upset the team. Four days later they beat Grimsby 9–1 at Highbury, still their biggest ever First Division win (they also beat Sheffield United 9–2 in 1932–33) and, a week later, won 7–2 at Leicester, to make it

13 goals in consecutive appearances at Filbert Street.

The Gunners lost only four games in all, and their home and away records were identical — 14 wins, 5 draws and 2 defeats. The team for the final game of the season is probably the one that is best remembered as the great team of the whole era — Ted Harper in goal, Tom Parker and Eddie Hapgood at full back, Herbie Roberts at centre half, Charlie Jones and Bob John at half back, Joe Hulme and Cliff Bastin on the wings, Alex James, as the provider, David Jack and Jack Lambert up front.

Harper had just returned from his four year sojourn in the United States, and was re-signed. He replaced Dutchman Gerry Keyser, a wholesale fruiterer who was an amateur with both Arsenal and Charlton. Cliff Bastin described Keyser as mildly crazy: '. . . Gerry was utterly reckless, whether between the posts or crouched behind the wheel of one of the huge American cars which were his heart's delight.'

Jack Lambert was now reasonably established as Chapman's first choice, and the manager let David Halliday go to Manchester City in November. The first of the two meetings between Arsenal and Villa at Villa Park in the 1930–31 season was the celebrated occasion when the Midlanders' magnificent England international centre forward Pongo Waring cheerfully taunted Chapman with his obsession for buying centre forwards: 'I bet you'd like to get me Herbert, wouldn't you?' said Waring. And Chapman would have, for Waring was the best in the country until Drake came along, but

he was also one of the few players Chapman could never manage to get his hands on. Underrated Jack Lambert actually set up an Arsenal record in 1930–31 with his 38 League goals, though this was soon to be beaten by Drake.

Those eleven names for the last game of 1930–31 would certainly have to be supplemented by one or two others to complete the real first-class roll of honour for the era. The three obvious omissions are George Male, Wilf Copping and Frank Moss. Male became Hapgood's full-back partner late in 1932 before Tom Parker went to Norwich as manager. Male actually played in the 1932 Cup final in his normal position, left half, but with Parker ready to retire Chapman needed a replacement and selected Male, who already had a reputation for all-round skill, strength and steadiness. Male told how Chapman called him into his office and astonished him by explaining how Male was about to become a right back. Chapman was so convincing about Male's skills that, said Male: 'I wasn't only convinced I was a right back, I knew I was the best right back in the country!' And so it proved, Male eventually taking over the England captaincy from Hapgood. He played his first game at right back on 15 October 1932 and within months he had been chosen for an international trial. Bernard Joy argued that the success of the Male/Hapgood combination was a matter of contrasts: 'Hapgood was enthusiastic, volatile and poised, the born captain. Male was determined, rugged and fast in recovery; as a person quiet, retiring and modest, the ideal first mate.' Not only did they both captain England,

Arguably the most important goal in the history of Arsenal Football Club. The only goal of the game, it was scored by David Jack in the second half of the semi-final replay against Hull at Villa Park on Wednesday 26 March 1930. Joey Williams, deputizing for Joe Hulme, ran the ball down the right wing right to the touchline and crossed for Jack (centre) to volley right-footed into the left-hand corner of the net past keeper Gibson. Williams had overrun the goalline and is out of the picture to the left. On the right, arms aloft, is centre forward Jack Lambert. A few minutes earlier, Hull centre half Arthur Childs had aimed a kick at Lambert and been sent off for his pains. Childs thus acquired the sorry distinction of being the only player ever sent off during an FA Cup semi-final or final in the first 100 years of that competition. The goal took Arsenal to the 1930 final, their first major success, and onto the decade that became theirs. The story of Arsenal remains essentially a story of the 1930s and the tie against Hull was, in retrospect, the moment of truth at the beginning of that decade. Had they fallen at this hurdle, 2-0 down at Elland Road, then it is entirely credible to argue that the whole history of the club would have been very different. The importance of David Jack's volley, of Joey Williams' brief appearance on centre stage, can never to minimised.

16 **SPORTS GUARDIAN**

FA CUP COMMENTARY: David Lacey

Arsenal: Nation mourns

JUST before teatime on Saturday the news spread rapidly through the press boxes, press rooms and those dingy corners of football grounds where men with note-books await the pleasure of men with words to fill them.

Even the strong-minded struggled to hide their emotions. There was a trembling of lower lips and a hasty simulation of coughs. Some gave up altogether and turned away, shoulders heaving. But sooner or later the fact had to be faced : Arsenal were out of the FA Cup.

Unluckily too by all accounts, their predictable goalless draw at Goodison Park

because of who they are and what they are, and following their easy dismissal of Altrincham their position will only be affected if they are given a difficult away tie in today's fourth round draw.

Visits to Southampton and West Bromwich Albion would fall into this category and Manchester City's form is such that even they might be able to sake off their perennial of Liverpool suf them a h Saturday United in thi have

ing football of such high quality that it appears they have just invented the sport and are introducing it to natives who are allowed only the occasional glimpse of a strange, white, round object that appears to be controlled by invisible wires.

Often, however, this period of supremacy is nothi

Shaw to Withe, who promptly collided with the 6ft 4in defender and laid him out. On being revived Butcher had to change his ripped shirt and in doing so bared to the audience two ugly weals on the back which suggested that he had either offended the seventh Cardigan or been

several years the cover was identical with no mention of the participants) and Newcastle again in 1952 (*bottom right*) were all controversial defeats.

The 1936 success against Sheffield United (*right*) was a happier moment. The Gunners also appeared in two lesser known Wartime Cup finals at Wembley. In 1941 they played Preston in front of 60,000 people and drew 1-1 (Denis Compton

scored the goal) though the replay was lost 1-2 at Blackburn. In 1943 75,000 turned out to see Arsenal crush Charlton 7-1 in the Southern Cup final. Reg Lewis scored four, Ted Drake two and Compton got the other. They lost the play-off to Northern champions Blackpool 4-2.

Top left: **After another FA Cup defeat,** in the third round against Everton on

3 January 1981, *The Guardian*'s David Lacey beautifully encapsulated half a century of 'Lucky Arsenal'. In just one headline and two paragraphs, Lacey summed up the provincial attitudes which were born in the 1930s and have never entirely died. Arsenal had reached the previous three FA Cup finals, the first club this century to achieve such a hat-trick.

A selection of some of the programmes from Cup finals which featured Arsenal. By 1986, the Gunners had appeared in 15 major finals (eleven FA Cup, two League Cup, two European) but had won just six of them. It is interesting to compare this record with that of Spurs, who have won far fewer Championships but succeeded in twelve out of fourteen Cup finals. The games against Cardiff in 1927 (*bottom left*), Newcastle in 1932 (*right*, the inside page as for

FINAL TIE

OF THE
FOOTBALL
ASSOCIATION
CHALLENGE CUP
COMPETITION

AT THE

Empire Stadium Wembley

SATURDAY, APRIL 25th, 1936

ARSENAL
v.
SHEFFIELD UNITED

Kick-off 3 p.m.

OFFICIAL PROGRAMME SIXPENCE

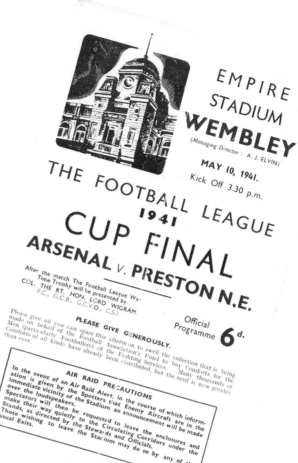

EMPIRE
STADIUM
WEMBLEY
(Managing Director : A. J. ELVIN)

MAY 10, 1941.
Kick Off 3.30 p.m.

THE FOOTBALL LEAGUE
1941
CUP FINAL
ARSENAL v. PRESTON N.E.

After the match The Football League War
Time Trophy will be presented by
COL. THE RT. HON. LORD WIGRAM.
P.C., G.C.B., G.C.V.O., C.S.I.

Official
Programme 6d.

PLEASE GIVE GENEROUSLY.

Please give all you can spare this afternoon to swell the collection that is being made on behalf of the Football Association's Fund to buy Comforts for the Men (particularly Footballers) of the Fighting Services. Many thousands of Comforts of all kinds have already been distributed, but the need is now greater than ever.

AIR RAID PRECAUTIONS

In the event of an Air Raid Alert, in the course of which information is given by the Spotters that Enemy Aircraft are in the immediate vicinity of the Stadium, an announcement will be made over the loudspeakers. Spectators will then be requested to leave the enclosures and make their way quietly to the Circulating Corridors under the Stands, as directed by the Stewards and Officials. Those wishing to leave the Stadium may do so by any of the usual Exits.

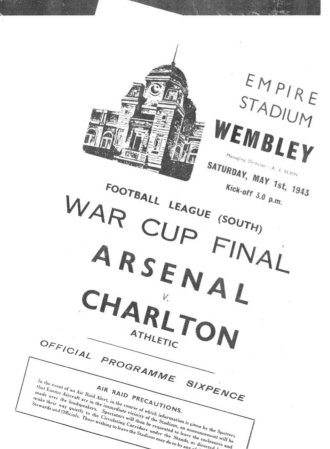

EMPIRE
STADIUM
WEMBLEY
Managing Director : A. J. Elvin

SATURDAY, MAY 1st, 1943
Kick-off 3.0 p.m.

FOOTBALL LEAGUE (SOUTH)
WAR CUP FINAL
ARSENAL
v.
CHARLTON
ATHLETIC

OFFICIAL PROGRAMME SIXPENCE

AIR RAID PRECAUTIONS.

In the event of an Air Raid Alert, in the course of which information is given by the Spotters that Enemy Aircraft are in the immediate vicinity of the Stadium, an announcement will be made over the loudspeakers. Spectators will then be requested to leave the enclosures and make their way quietly to the Circulating Corridors under the Stands, as directed by the Stewards and Officials. Those wishing to leave the Stadium may do so by any of the usual Exits.

THE FOOTBALL ASSOCIATION CHALLENGE CUP COMPETITION
FINAL TIE
ARSENAL v NEWCASTLE UNITED
SATURDAY, MAY 3rd, 1952 KICK OFF 3pm

EMPIRE STADIUM
WEMBLEY
OFFICIAL PROGRAMME · ONE SHILLING

they also played together for their country 14 times. They are, in all probability, the finest club full back pair that their country has ever fielded.

Wilf Copping was already an international when he came from Leeds in 1934, he and Jack Crayston (from Bradford) effectively replacing Charlie Jones and Bob John. Copping is probably best remembered for his remarkable display in the 'Battle of Highbury' against Italy on 14 November 1934 when Arsenal provided seven of the England team and the World Cup holders were beaten, in a bitter game, 3–2.

Frank Moss was actually only the reserve keeper at Second Division Oldham when Chapman signed him. Apparently Chapman pretended to be pursuing the first team keeper Jack Hacking and, when Oldham wouldn't release him, switched his interest to the reserve as an apparent afterthought (this story has been told about several of Chapman's signings). He was another agile keeper, totally fearless and a natural for the England jersey. His career was sadly cut short because of a recurrent shoulder injury. His last effective game for the club was at Everton on 16 March 1935, when he was injured, dislocating his troubled shoulder early on and playing the rest of the match on the wing. He was always a very good forward (for a time he hoped to continue in the game as an outfield player) and scored an excellent goal, cutting in past his defender and shooting into the corner for a peculiarly unfitting end to a goalkeeper's career. He did try to come back for a few games the next season, but the shoulder and collarbone were continually causing problems and he was forced to give up the game completely.

The team that brought the League Championship to the South of England for the very first time in 1931 was hardly anonymous, but it was unusual in that its back up was far more sophisticated than at any other club of the period. The cornerstone was Tom Whittaker, who eventually became manager after George Allison in 1947. It is almost impossible to do full justice to Whittaker either as coach, physiotherapist or inspiration. The stories about him are legion, almost invariably extremely complimentary. Bernard Joy said that: 'Chapman's success would have been impossible without Whittaker,' but George Allison reaches the essential Whittaker more succinctly. Allison was once asked: 'Is it true, what Tom Whittaker says?' 'Of course it is,' was Allison's reply. 'What did Tom say?'

Cliff Bastin was as effusive: 'I can never thank him enough for the care and expert treatment he lavished on me whilst I was at Highbury. Perhaps 'expert' is a badly chosen word, for Tom was something more than an expert. There was about him a touch of genius.' Bastin explained how men who would have remained on the injured list for three or four weeks at another club would be fit at Highbury within three or four days. Bastin, on one occasion, scalded his foot in a boiling hot bath and

couldn't stand on it. The foot was agony, but Whittaker built a special soft cast inside Bastin's boot so that the winger felt no pain. His only sensation when he ran, as he explained, was the water inside the blister running up and down his foot. Whittaker also used to snap Bastin's cartilage back into place on the field, doing this on at least a dozen occasions, and when Bastin eventually had to have an operation, Whittaker attended and assisted. The cartilage itself, having been removed, was apparently so unusually deformed that it has become a permanent exhibit at the Royal College of Surgeons.

Tom Whittaker was born in Aldershot in 1898. His father was a sergeant-major and Tom also had a military career, studying as a marine engineer and joining the Royal Artillery as, very appropriately, an ordnance engineer. It was while he was playing for the Army (he later transferred to the Navy to exploit his marine engineering) that Arsenal spotted him and brought him to Highbury, where he played as a wing half and later full back until his injury in Australia in 1925. His arrival at Highbury, on 11 November 1919, has a touch of the times about it — Leslie Knighton, newly installed as

manager, met him off the tube!

The surgeon who told Whittaker he would never play again in 1925, Sir Robert Jones, was so impressed by the player that he arranged a year's course in anatomy, massage and electrical treatment of injuries, particularly associated with muscles. Whittaker returned to Highbury after that injury unsure about his future. Arsenal had apparently been intending to let him go in 1925, but he was retained so that he could go on the FA tour (players without clubs were not allowed to represent the FA). Because he had been injured in a representative game, the FA was paying his wages. For six months Whittaker was unable to train and helped in the treatment room. Officially, he was just a player under treatment. One day in February 1926, Chapman called Whittaker up to the top of the stand. For a few moments there was silence, says Whittaker, then Chapman turned and, with his arm stretched out towards the pitch and emphasising every word, said: 'I am going to make this the greatest club ground in the world, and I am going to make you the greatest trainer in the game. What do you say to that?'

Whittaker later built the most modern treatment room in football, and possibly in the country, at Highbury. It was full of sunlamps, heating and electrical apparatus and attracted all sorts of sportsmen who had no association with Highbury. Whittaker was, for instance, also the official trainer for Britain's highly successful Davis Cup tennis team in the 1930s, as well as the regular England soccer team trainer.

He worked seven days a week and would treat anything short of a broken limb. His ability to get players back quickly, and hence help Chapman keep as settled a team as possible, was a crucial element in the club's consistent pattern of success between 1930 and 1936. The other great contribution Whittaker made to Chapman's personal success was relieving the manager of day to day control of the players. This was vitally important for it allowed Chapman time to watch new players, negotiate transfers and consider other essential matters for the club like trying to get the name of the tube station changed.

Whittaker actually became first-team trainer in February 1927. George Hardy, who had held the job since before the First World War, shouted a tactical switch to the players from the bench during a Cup match against Port Vale on 2 February 1927. Chapman said he wouldn't tolerate the trainer influencing tactics and relegated Hardy to the reserves, giving the 29-year-old Whittaker the job. Straight after that Port Vale game Chapman marched into the dressing room and, in front of everyone, told Whittaker to take over the first team immediately. Whittaker, who lodged with Hardy, was shocked, but he and Hardy remained friends, even after the latter left Highbury and went to White Hart Lane. Chapman's action was only an excuse. Hardy was of the old school, Whittaker was obviously the man Chapman wanted and,

more to the point, needed. The shout from the dugout, if it really happened, was merely the trigger.

Whittaker remained as trainer, apart from a spell during the Second World War, for twenty years. He finally took over as manager from Allison in 1947. Almost his first act that year was to call back Joe Shaw from Stamford Bridge as assistant manager. Shaw, the longest serving man on the staff, was the crucial third member of the management team in the 1930s. The fourth was John Peters, the second assistant manager who actually performed much of the secretary's role through to his death in 1952.

Before the 1931–32 season began the talk was of the chances of the Double, not performed since Aston Villa in 1896–97 and not to be performed again for another three decades. After a month the talk was what happened to the League Champions? Arsenal lost their opener at home to West Bromwich and didn't take both points until their fifth match. They never made up the gap that had already opened up and, although it was a good season, eventually finishing second was something of an anticlimax. Everton were champions, two points ahead. Bernard Joy says the team was over confident, pushing forward too eagerly, leaving too many holes for the counter-attack. It was a lesson that was learned for subsequent seasons.

The Cup should have provided compensation, but failed to do so after the most controversial goal in British domestic football (only the third England goal in the 1966 World Cup final possibly ranks above it.)

The run to the 1932 final was straightforward but hard work, and there were to be no replays. Lancashire Combination side Darwen (they had been in the League as recently as 1899) provided an 11–1 walkover in the third round, then Plymouth, with Ted Harper in goal, were removed 4–2. After a 2–0 away win against gradually improving Portsmouth (they reached the final in 1929 and 1934) the quarter-final brought Arsenal back to old adversaries Huddersfield at Leeds Road. After only two minutes Hulme won a corner; the winger held the ball until Herbie Roberts came up on a rare (but obviously pre-planned) foray, placed it right on Roberts' forehead and Arsenal had scored the only goal of the game.

The semi-final at St Andrew's also saw just one goal, this time at the end of the game rather than the beginning. The opponents were Manchester City, who were to reach the next two finals as compensation. The 1932 semi-final was already in time added on, with City frantically attacking, believing that they had to win there and then and would not do so well in a replay. But they left their defence relatively under-manned and as a final clearance came out from the Arsenal penalty area Bastin picked it up and hopefully knocked it towards the right-hand corner. The defender let the ball go, thinking it would go over the line, but Lambert suddenly appeared, hooked it back and there

This page: The opening of the two new stands (the West on 10 December 1932 and the East on 24 October 1936) was football's equivalent of the unveiling of the Taj Mahal. There was nothing like them anywhere in the country and it says much for the club and its architects that they remain as comfortable and efficient today, having served the club for more than half its life. One oddity of the club programme through the 1930s was that the cover remained identical, with only the reference to the season being changed. There was a supplement for the West Stand opening (*bottom left*) which highlighted another of Chapman's great public relations coups – persuading the Prince of Wales to perform the ceremony. Royalty was, apart from the Cup final, rarely associated with football at the time. The game was against Chelsea and the Prince met the players before the match. Hughie Gallacher, the opposing captain, is seen (*centre picture*) in a less than respectful pose with his arm round the future King Edward VIII. Herbert Chapman, to Gallacher's left, seems unsure of the protocol relating to Gallacher's behaviour. Many of the players signed this picture – Alex James top left, Hughie Gallacher centre (programmes by courtesy of John Motson).

ARSENAL·FOOTBALL·CLUB·LTD

DIRECTORS:
THE RT. HON. THE EARL OF LONSDALE, K.G., G.C.V.O., D.L. (*Chairman*)
J. J. EDWARDS, Esq. (*Vice-Chairman*)
THE RT. HON. THE EARL OF WESTMORLAND
THE RT. HON. THE EARL OF GRANARD, P.C., K.P., G.C.V.O.
COL. SIR MATHEW HILL, C.B.E., V.D., D.S.O.
MAJOR SIR SAMUEL HILL-WOOD, Bart., D.L., J.P.
J. D. PEMBERTON, Esq., J.P.
MAJOR-GENERAL J. D. McLACHLAN, C.B., C.M.G., D.S.O.
H. S. E. VANDERPANT, Esq.

Colours: RED SHIRTS WITH WHITE COLLARS AND SLEEVES WHITE KNICKERS

Secretary-Manager: GEORGE F. ALLISON

Telegraphic Address: "GUNNERETIC" FINSPARK, LONDON

ARSENAL STADIUM, HIGHBURY, N.5.

Vol. XXV. No. 12.   Saturday, October 24th, 1936   Two-pence

The Inauguration of The East Stand.

This afternoon the new East Stand, which we have seen gradually developing before our eyes for the last two months, is inaugurated and takes its part as a portion of the Arsenal Stadium. Its predecessor, demolished last Spring, witnessed many a sternly-contested game and looked down through the years on many a brave player toiling and battling in the service of his club. Now it has gone, yielding place to a successor which in its turn will view the fortunes of the club as it passes down the years.

The East Stand is a noble thing, a building of wonder and unparalleled in Football. Together with its slightly older companion on the West side, it will for many a day bear testimony to the craft of those who wrought it and to the skill and vision of the architects who dreamed it and then brought it to reality. Claude Ferrier, who brought the West Stand into being, is unhappily no longer with us, but to him also, as well as to William Binnie, the Stand inaugurated to-day stands as a monument of great work nobly achieved.

But we would err if we regarded the new Stand merely as an isolated structure, however wonderful. It is the completion of a labour of ground-improvement which has been spread over ten years. Although we recall it, we can only with difficulty visualise once more the Arsenal ground of 1926. A world of difference lies between that and the Arsenal Stadium of 1936. Step by step a new thing has been raised up for our use and this afternoon we have reached the culminating point. Yet there is a wider significance in the East Stand. It crowns not only the last ten years. In the autumn of 1886 a tiny football gathering first met in Dial Square at Woolwich Arsenal. The fifty years which separate us from them contain a varied history of mingled triumphs and falls of the club which started on that far-off day. Half a century of honourable struggle stands behind the edifice which starts upon its history to-day.

Above: **An unusually shy Alex James** poses for the camera before a reserve team game at Highbury on 13 April 1932. His fitness was being tested before the Cup final, then ten days away. A week later one final tackle by Tom Whittaker, in a practice game to please a photographer who had arrived late, caused James' knee to break down again and he left the field in tears, unable to play at Wembley. In the background the foundations of the new West Stand are well advanced.

was Bastin to touch it home with the last kick of the match. It was an interesting illustration of Chapman's belief that a team can attack for too long.

The final was to be against Newcastle. The preparations were dominated by whether or not Alex James would be fit. He had damaged knee ligaments against West Ham a couple of weeks earlier, being rushed back to Highbury by Tom Whittaker before the game at Upton Park was even over.

Three days before the Cup final Chapman announced his team — James and Hulme were not fit enough so in came George Male and Pat Beasley. The news was a surprise, and L. V. Manning, sports editor of the *Daily Sketch*, got James and Hulme to jog around the Highbury pitch and published a picture captioned: 'The two fittest men in football.' Chapman was furious, and ordered the pair down to Brighton, where the team were staying. Tom Whittaker gave them both a tough try-out the following morning on the Brighton ground, in front of 40 or so photographers. Both came through and were reinstated in the team for Saturday's final. Then, as everyone was making their way back to the dressing room, another photographer, whose car had broken down, came rushing into the ground to plead with Whittaker for a final shot. Whittaker agreed, tackled James once more and, suddenly, James fell to the ground clutching his

knee. He was carried to the dressing-room where, says Whittaker: '. . . almost crying with pain and disappointment, he would not let the doctor touch him and shouted at me to get everyone out of the room. Even Chapman had to go.' George Male, signed from the London amateur side Clapton earlier that season, had been in, out, and back in a Cup final side within the space of an hour. Male played left half, and it was on that side that the critical moment was to occur.

It was almost half-time (with Arsenal 1–0 up after Bob John had headed the ball home when United had made a hash of a clearance) when Newcastle centre half Davison over-hit a long pass up the right wing for inside forward Jimmy Richardson to chase. The ball appeared to cross the goal-line and the Arsenal defenders relaxed, but Richardson carried on and hooked the ball into the centre. Eddie Hapgood could probably have intercepted it, but didn't bother. Centre forward Jack Allen did bother, flicking it neatly into the net. Referee Bill Harper gave a goal, the Arsenal players were incredulous but did not argue. L. V. Manning said in the *Sunday Graphic* the next day: 'One cannot praise too highly the restraint of the Arsenal players when the first Newcastle goal was scored. Every man must have known what was so clear to the onlookers — that the ball had crossed the line — but there was not the slightest attempt at a demonstration

or protest.' Tom Parker got their minds back on the game but the timing was perfect for Newcastle, who came out for the second half a different team and Allen scored again for United to win 2–1. Arsenal had thus finished runners-up in both major competitions, only the second time this had ever happened, the first being Huddersfield's misfortune in 1928.

Though it has always been claimed that the ball was over the line, in fairness it must be said that no convincing photograph exists (unlike the 1966 goal, where the evidence clearly shows that England's third goal should not have been allowed) and the angle of the most reproduced photograph is not necessarily a good one. The *whole* of the ball must be over the line, which means that it is perfectly possible for a bouncing ball to seem to be beyond the line in even a slightly angled picture, but not actually 100 per cent beyond in reality. Newcastle were the first team to win the final at Wembley after being behind in the match, and the first to come from behind in any final since they did the same thing themselves in 1910.

The disappointment of 1932 was only short-lived. For many years afterwards regret was expressed that, despite their dominance of the decade, the Arsenal of the 1930s never performed the Double. 1931–32 was to be the nearest they came for, like Liverpool in the 1970s and 1980s, they did not seem to be able to concentrate on the FA Cup when they were leading the League. And for the next three seasons Arsenal were to do exactly that, equalling Huddersfield's hat-trick with an impeccable period of dominance covering 1932–33, 1933–34 and 1934–35.

Above: **The first of the Cup final records**, half a century before they became tedious. The Arsenal team were photographed in the Columbia recording studios a month before the 1932 final. Captain Tom Parker is closest to the microphone. Arsenal recorded one side, Newcastle the other: there is no trace of its commercial success, as there were no record charts for another 20 years.

Left: **The shield which hangs** outside the boardroom at Highbury commemorating the hat-trick of Championships between 1932 and 1935. Huddersfield and Liverpool have almost identical trophies. The bust is of Denis Hill-Wood.

Most clubs which have such a successful spell do so with a very settled side. Indeed, it is almost a truism of the game that a great side lasts for no more than three good seasons. The Arsenal of the first half of the 1930s were almost exactly the opposite. By 1935 no more than three of the regulars of 1932 were still in the team — Hapgood, Roberts and Bastin. Most of the missing had simply succumbed to age, though Frank Moss was an exception. Much more significantly, Herbert Chapman was dead and had been replaced by George Allison. Yet the period was one of remarkably consistent results, with only 24 League games lost and a points average of 58. By Championship standards, none of the three seasons was particularly outstanding, certainly not to be compared with the record breaking 1930–31, and their number of defeats (9, 8 and 7 in the three seasons) was no better than average for a Championship side. On the other hand, the pattern of consistency during a period of team rebuilding was most certainly outstanding; against that, while there were other good sides around such as Sheffield Wednesday, Manchester City, Sunderland and Derby none of them managed to put together a settled team for long enough in the early 1930s. If this sounds like grudging praise, it is only so in the context of the heady two years which followed the 1930 Cup win.

Many of the individual replacements proved to be the match of their predecessors. George Male was already a Highbury stalwart when he replaced Parker in 1932, Eddie Coleman and an ageing Jimmy Dunne appeared in Lambert's shirt, though neither truly became a fixture, and the great David Jack played only 14 games

in 1933–34 and then went to Southend as manager. He was replaced by Ray Bowden, who arrived from Plymouth in March 1933. Bastin was still a youngster, though he suffered from periods of injury and his deafness was beginning to be a worry, but Joe Hulme proved very difficult to duplicate.

The Arsenal wingers had performed very different jobs compared with men in the number 7 and 11 shirts at other clubs and it was not easy to slot new men into Arsenal's unique system. They had not only to be very fast in the conventional sense, but also significant goal-scorers as well. Only Alex James was allowed the liberty of not appearing on the scoresheet. As has been said before, it was the role of Hulme and Bastin, more than any other aspect of their style, which marked the Arsenal of the early 1930s apart from their competitors. That meant the club's wingers could, and would, often also double up as inside forwards. Pat Beasley, who arrived from Stourbridge, would play in either Bastin or Hulme's place if they were injured, or act as Bastin's inside forward. He would have played in the 1932 Cup final if Hulme had not recovered from that injury but, ironically, he and Hulme then played on opposite wings for Huddersfield in the 1938 Cup final. Ralph Birkett, who later won an England cap while with Middlesbrough, was bought from Torquay specifically to take over from Hulme, but was never an adequate replacement, and by 1935 Alf Kirchen from Norwich was on the right wing.

The midfield men were more easily replaced, Jack Crayston from Bradford and Wilf Copping from Leeds coming in for Charlie Jones and Bob John with remarkably little disruption in the

summer of 1934. When Alex James was unavailable the remarkable Peter Dougall would take his place. By all accounts he was an even cleverer player, but could never consistently harness his fabulous ball skills to the team effort, but then it was perhaps unfair to expect anyone to replace the hub of the wheel. In goal Alex Wilson replaced Moss in a quiet, competent way. He had come from Morton in May 1933. When Moss was injured at Goodison in March 1935, however, Wilson was also hurt and George Allison had no other first-class keeper. That day also happened to be the transfer deadline, so he asked Everton if Arsenal could sign their reserve keeper George Bradshaw there and then. Bradshaw was a little bemused by this sudden turn of events, but eventually agreed and came to Highbury for a number of years.

The first year of the hat-trick, 1932–33, did not start particularly well. Charlie Jones was injured and, in their first home match, Arsenal lost to West Brom for the second consecutive year. But this season was to be different, with 32 of the next 36 points finding their way back to Highbury. Yet again, though, Villa managed to score five goals in Birmingham and the 5–3 defeat was Arsenal's only setback in that 18-game run. The final match in the sequence was the Christmas Eve 9–2 thrashing of Sheffield United at Highbury. Jack Lambert scored five, his best ever for the club, in what was virtually his valedictory performance. That particular game is often recalled as the height of Arsenal's powers in the whole inter-war period, though, oddly, two days later they went down 1–2 at home to Leeds. Villa and Wednesday continued to press until April when, though Arsenal were ahead, both their challengers had games in hand. By chance both came to Highbury in April, where Arsenal finished things off in fine style. Villa went down 5–0 and ended four points behind, Wednesday lost 4–2 and were eventually three points further back. The month saw five wins in a row and the last, 3–1 versus Chelsea at Stamford Bridge, confirmed the Gunners' second title in three years. The forwards had been magnificent all season, and the total of 118 goals was the club's second highest ever and included one 9, two 8s and one 7. Cliff Bastin's 33 goals still remain a Football League record for a winger.

The next season, 1933–34, was a strangely subdued one compared with those before and after. It was marred, of course, by Herbert Chapman's death, but, though it saw one more point won (59 rather than 58) the goalscoring record was completely different. Only 75 were scored compared with 118 the season before and 115 the season after. One major reason was Alex James' injury against Birmingham in the first match of the season. He was out for half of the campaign, as was Joe Hulme. However, Arsenal quickly went to the head of the table, putting together a spell of 27 points out of a possible 32. Derby and Huddersfield both took the lead briefly, but they had to play the Gunners in

consecutive matches in Easter week. Arsenal beat Derby 4–2 at the Baseball Ground and followed up with a 3–1 defeat of Huddersfield at Highbury. In the end only Huddersfield kept up the challenge, eventually finishing three points in arrears. Spurs finished third.

It was actually one of those strangely quiet seasons when not a lot seems to happen and no team can really impose its authority. Both Villa and Wednesday had lost their sparkle, finishing mid-table, and Arsenal, despite the loss of Chapman, were able to hold their ground by virtue of their established patterns of play and their consistency. Even so, they had to survive a number of poor results — home defeats by Everton and Spurs within the space of four days, a 4–1 crushing at Leicester and a 3–0 defeat at Sunderland — and were perhaps lucky that their crisis season coincided with a corporate lethargy among their competitors.

The third year of the hat-trick saw a genuine new star in the making. He was Ted Drake, George Allison's first signing (from Southampton) in March 1934. Drake was to score a record 42 goals with the Gunners in this, his first season. That total included four matches in which he scored four goals and three in which he notched mere hat-tricks. The newcomer almost carried the team. There were numerous major injuries — Dunne, Copping and Bastin all had cartilage operations and even the two trainers, Tom Whittaker and Billy Milne, both had to be hospitalized during the season. Most of the reserves had fair spells in the first team, but still went on to win the Football Combination for the seventh time in nine seasons. Had Chapman lived, he would have seen it as the perfect validation of his insistence that the reserves play to the same patterns and tactics as their seniors.

The 1934–35 season had started well with an 8–1 crushing of Liverpool (how Highbury would applaud such a result today) and the first four home games produced 21 Arsenal goals. Away matters did not give rise for similar congratulations, with only a single victory prior to the New Year. But none of their regular challengers could put together anything like a convincing set of results and Arsenal headed the table until March when Sunderland, inspired by the young Raich Carter, went a point ahead. Arsenal had games in hand, however, and though Sunderland held them to a goalless draw at Highbury, Arsenal made Sunderland's task almost impossible with a 2–0 win at Everton on 16 March 1935. This was the game in which Frank Moss scored Arsenal's second, magnificent goal as a highly inappropriate finale to his mainstream goalkeeping career. Sunderland ended the season four points behind with Sheffield Wednesday, perhaps Arsenal's most dogged challengers in the Chapman era, another five adrift.

Chapman was always surprised, and perhaps a little distressed, that Huddersfield could not get to a Cup final during their hat-trick years. The Yorkshiremen were there in 1920 and 1922, and

The planning department:
Bob John, Herbert
Chapman and Alex James
discuss the forthcoming
FA Cup final against
Newcastle early in
April 1932.

again in 1928 and 1930, but in the middle years, 1924 to 1926, when they should by rights have made it, they were nowhere to be seen. Arsenal had a peculiarly similar record. They reached the final in 1930, 1932 and 1936, but missed out in 1933, 1934 and 1935. Oddly, they never even reached a semi-final in those seasons. In 1934 Villa played well to win 2–1 at Highbury in the quarter-final. It is odd that the paths of Villa and Arsenal seemed to be constantly crossing, and that Villa appear to leap from the pages of history as the Gunners most prestigious and difficult rivals. Odd, because Villa did not win a single prize between 1920 and 1957. It was Wednesday, the other major challengers, who knocked Arsenal out in 1935, also 2–1 but this time at Hillsborough.

We have skirted around what happened on 14 January 1933. It is not usual in the history of a great club, when there is so much to tell, to dwell for very long on a game that was lost, particularly in the third round of the Cup, but this one is an exception. Fifty years later, when Walsall came to Highbury, still as a Third Division side, and surprisingly won again (this time in the Milk Cup) no one tried to make any

serious comparison between the two matches. There was no way they could. Walsall's 2–0 defeat of Arsenal in 1933 remains, very simply, the greatest act of giant-killing in English club history. This is vaguely peculiar. There have been giant killers whose performances have seemed far more praiseworthy since, there have been non-League clubs knocking out First Division sides, but whenever a giant-killer arises, the comparison is automatically made, above all other games, with Walsall 2 Arsenal 0.

We need to stand back a little to judge the real significance of this result. Arsenal, it should be remembered, had just gone through a run obtaining 32 points from 18 matches. Three weeks before meeting Walsall, they had crushed Sheffield United 9–2. They were well clear at the head of the First Division and were, in a sense, at their very peak, for they had no obvious rivals. It is difficult to find comparisons, because there are none, but perhaps Liverpool in 1983 come closest. In the three previous seasons Arsenal had won the Cup, then the League, then been runners-up in both. The Double in 1932–33 seemed a very strong possibility.

The game must also be put in a social and economic context. This was the height of the depression. Three million were out of work, a far higher percentage of the work force then than 50 years later, and benefits were far less generous where they existed at all. As in the 1980s, there was very real resentment in the provinces against London, Westminster, 'them' as opposed to 'us'. Walsall may not have corresponded with Lancashire or Tyneside today, but it was a moderate sized provincial town with problems enough of its own. Arsenal, in its way, was a very visible representative of London, a symbol of the richness of life there compared with the provinces. The fact that this was unfair, that most of the players were from the north and many had been miners, was not the point. What mattered were the symbols, what people wanted to believe was true.

It is also realistic (and it should not be ignored) to point out that Arsenal were not a popular club outside London, compared with, say, the Spurs side of the early 1960s. This was a difficult attitude to analyse, for it was a feeling abroad without any rational base, rather than a justifiable dislike. In part it was due to the 'Bank of England' reputation, Chapman's and later Allison's apparent desire to buy success at almost any price, though many clubs had gone the same route and failed dismally. In part it was also the tactical style; the holding back, occupying midfield space, the numerous goals which came from quick breaks from James to Bastin and Hulme, rather than the constant attacking pressure which was the traditional approach of the day. Spectators, having come to expect fast dribbling wingers crossing from the goal-line for thundering centre forwards in the Dixie Dean or Pongo Waring mould, found Arsenal's style odd and, therefore, somehow 'lucky'.

Fans had yet to realise the simplest of all football truths, that the winning team is, by definition, the one which scores most goals. Eighty-five minutes of unrewarded but naive pressure may somehow seem more valuable than a single breakaway goal, but that isn't what the laws of the game say. Actually, such perceptions as they related to Arsenal were not only extremely unfair but, very simply, wrong — Arsenal scored 127 League goals in 1931, 118 in 1933 and 115 in 1935, overall considerably more than any of their competitors, and, to repeat the obvious, they couldn't all have come from lucky breakaways. What is true is that, like all teams, Arsenal tended to play differently away from Highbury than at home. Equally, other sides would attack them more on their own grounds, forcing Arsenal towards the use of their 'smash and grab' style. It is very difficult for the generation of fans born after the Second World War to imagine how little exposure pre-war crowds had to the big clubs. North London fans could watch Arsenal every other week but a Liverpudlian or a Mancunian was only able to see this dominating force once or twice a year —

thus his views about the sort of team they were, and the way they played, could only be based on very limited evidence. He had no opportunity of seeing Arsenal 20 or 25 times a year on television (as he certainly would in the early 1980s) and thus building a more balanced view. Arsenal at Villa, Hillsborough or Roker would always face a hard game, would always be forced to defend, and would probably rely on Hulme and Bastin for a winning goal. It was the fact that they succeeded so often which bred the resentment.

In any event, the key to the Walsall result, the way it was greeted and the reason it has remained the giant-killing feat *par excellence*, lies as much in the times as in the football. Walsall were the small, underprivileged, provincial David overthrowing the rich, lucky London-based Goliath and the Midland side's success was feted far and wide, often by people who probably had not the slightest idea where Walsall was.

Chapman has been accused of underestimating Walsall, but there is little evidence to support this contention. Walsall had been watched, and, though their last four matches comprised three draws and a 5–0 defeat, Chapman was under no illusions as to the kind of game he was facing. His real problem had been influenza, earlier claiming Bob John, Jack Lambert and Tim Coleman. Eddie Hapgood and Joe Hulme had also been injured and Chapman therefore had to decide whether to play recently unavailable men or some of his well-prepared reserves. He chose the reserves — it would be a hard match but here would be a good opportunity for the second-teamers to push their claims for a first team place. In many respects, they were less likely than the internationals to be upset by rough Third Division tackling. So in came Scot

Left and right: **The cover and first page** of the programme for the greatest giant-killing feat in English club history. Arsenal came to Walsall on top of the First Division, having reached two of the three previous finals. The guns and reproduction of James confronting the teddy bear are a delight for a Third Division programme of half a century ago. The programme editor could not possibly have realised how right he was when he wrote: 'When the history of our club comes to be written, there is little doubt that January 14, 1933 will be a . . . Red Letter Day.' Even now, whenever the name Walsall is mentioned, the instant thought is of that one afternoon long ago. What the editor could not have realised, however, was just how largely this day would feature in the history of Arsenal as well.

OFFICIAL PROGRAMME ·   PRICE 2ᴰ

'BIG GUNS' IN WALSALL!

'THE FIELD·MARSHENAL' OF THE ARSENAL:- 'IS THIS THE WAY TO WEMBLEY'

THE TEDDY BEAR (SHALL WE SAY A TRIFLE INTIMIDATINGLY) 'YES! FOR ONE OF US'

THIRD·ROUND·FOOTBALL·ASSOCIATION·CUP

WALSALL v ARSENAL

FELLOWS·PARK · JANUARY·14·1933

Tommy Black at left back, Norman Sidey at left half, Billy Warnes at outside right and Charlie Walsh at centre forward. The last two had both been recruited from local amateur clubs. Too much has been made of the side's inexperience — it still contained Moss, Male, Roberts, Jack, James and Bastin. Tom Whittaker later dismissed the suggestion that the first-teamers were unavailable, though, afterwards, Chapman seems to have encouraged this belief. Everyone travelled to Walsall says Whittaker, in the team's own railway coach the day before. During the journey Chapman announced the team to, in Whittaker's own words: '. . . murmurs of amazement.'

The newspapers, always loving a David versus Goliath, gave the game the usual build-up and their angles were predictable enough. Said one:

'Arsenal, the Rich, the Confident, the League leaders, the £30,000 aristocrats, against the little Third Division team that cost £69 all-in. Arsenal train on ozone, brine-baths, champagne, gold and electrical massage in an atmosphere of prima donna preciousness. They own £87 worth of football boots. Walsall men eat fish and chips and drink beer, and the entire running expenses of the club this season have been £75.'

The players didn't quite see it like that. One or two of the reserves were particularly edgy. Just before leaving the dressing-room Chapman came over to Charlie Walsh: 'I'm expecting a lot of you today, son, we're relying on you to show us your best.' Walsh, who had been nagging Chapman for a first team chance for months, replied: 'OK Mr Chapman, I'm ready to play the game of my life.' Chapman answered: 'Good lad, you'll do,' and then, just as he was turning away, paused: 'Oh, and by the way, you'd better put your stockings on or the crowd will laugh at you.' Walsh was so nervous he had put on his boots before his socks. Walsh's apprehensions were more justified than his team-mates would have guessed. Walsall employed classic cup-tie tactics. Their enthusiasm was overwhelming, their tackling, especially on James, could only be described as grim. Arsenal failed to settle throughout the match, but should still have won it. Walsh, now complete with socks, made a complete hash of the easiest chance of the first-half when he missed a simple Bastin centre and the ball came off his shoulder. In the second the centre forward's intervention was even more disastrous when he took the ball off David Jack's toe just as Jack seemed certain to score.

As Arsenal failed to score, Walsall became more confident, the inches of mud which covered the pitch being much more to their liking. After 60 minutes Gilbert Alsop, the home side's centre forward, headed home a Lee corner-kick to put Walsall a goal up. Fifty years later Alsop, still marking out pitches at 73, remembered: 'We had a corner and their full back (Black) was marking me. He didn't get up. The ball was just a big plum pudding that day and I headed it off my forehead straight into the corner of the net. I'd been watching Dixie Dean play for England.' Alsop also remembered the foul which, five minutes later, sealed the game for Walsall. He could still point to a scar on his knee which, he claimed, was caused by Tommy Black's violent tackle after 65 minutes. It was in the penalty area and, as a result, Billy Sheppard scored from the spot.

The Arsenal players had been getting more and more irritated by the Walsall tactics. 'They could not have complained if five of their men had been sent off in the first quarter of an hour,' said Bastin afterwards, 'We had ten free-kicks in the first ten minutes.' Black had become particularly irate, the more so after failing to prevent Alsop's goal, and Arsenal paid the penalty.

The Gunners could do nothing to retrieve the two-goal deficit in the last 25 minutes and the packed 11,000 crowd chaired the Walsall players

off at the end. For the Arsenal team, retribution was swift. Chapman was apoplectic. He refused to let Black return to Highbury and had transferred him to Plymouth within a week. Whether this was because of Chapman's anger at Black's tackle on Alsop, or because of his all-round performance in the match, was never absolutely clear, though Chapman certainly said the former. Walsh, whose display was almost as wretched as Black's, was sold to Brentford by the end of January, having, despite his ambitions, played just that one first-team match for Arsenal. Warnes went to Norwich at the end of the season. Only Sidey remained in the reserves, a competent back-up for Roberts.

For Walsall the game was something of an inspiration. Though they were knocked out by eventual finalists Manchester City in the next round, they managed to finish the season third in the Third Division North. For Arsenal it was a hiccup, though one that was to echo down the years as, in all probability, the most famous Cup tie the club have ever contested. Exactly fifty years later the fact that it was Walsall, rather than any other Third Division club, who knocked the Gunners out of the Milk Cup at Highbury must have made some small contribution to Terry Neill's departure from the manager's office.

Walsall was the last FA Cup defeat Herbert Chapman ever suffered. By the time Villa defeated the Gunners in the quarter-final of 1934 Chapman was dead. It was so sudden, so unexpected, that it was almost prosaic. There is somehow very little than can be said about it. On Saturday 30 December 1933 Arsenal had drawn 0–0 at Birmingham. They were a comfortable four points clear at the top of the League. It was

to be a typical, perhaps slightly busy, week for Chapman. On the Monday, New Year's Day, he went to see Bury play Notts County, who had someone in whom he was interested. He then crossed the Pennines to watch Sheffield Wednesday play Birmingham on the Tuesday. Wednesday were the visitors at Highbury the following Saturday and were Chapman's greatest fear for the title. By the Wednesday he had clearly developed a heavy cold but ignored the advice of Dr Guy Pepper, the club doctor, and went down to Guildford to see the third team. 'I don't get a chance to see the lads very often,' he commented. On returning home to Hendon he was much worse and went to bed. By Friday, 36 hours later, he seemed rather better but the pneumonia, as it presumably was, suddenly worsened and he died at 3 am on the Saturday morning.

The news came as a complete shock. The players arrived at Highbury a few hours later to discover suddenly that the Boss, who was perfectly healthy when they had last seen him in Birmingham, was dead. Bastin told of the terrible blow the players felt: 'As I approached the ground, the newspaper-sellers were shouting out the news of Chapman's death. It seemed just too bad to be true. In the dressing-room, nobody had anything to say, yet each of us knew what (the others) were thinking. Herbert Chapman had been loved by us all.' George Male was walking past a tube station when he saw the newspaper board: 'Herbert Chapman Dead.' . . . 'That was the first I knew about it. I couldn't believe it.' Arsenal and Wednesday stood to attention before the game. 'I suppose Arsenal gave quite a good display that day, considering that to the players the game was

The most famous of all Arsenal pictures: Alex James leaves a trail of Manchester City defenders behind him during a game at Highbury on 13 October, 1934. The left-hand member of the trio is Matt Busby. The view is towards the North Bank, then graced by the famous clock. The FA had recently told the club to change it from a 45-minute timer to a proper clock. It was eventually moved to the southern end when the North Bank stand was built. Arsenal won this particular game against City 3-0 and ended the season as Champions for the third consecutive time (picture by courtesy of *The Sunday Times*).

just an unimportant incident,' said Bastin. 'Even the crowd was practically silent throughout the ninety minutes of a game which seemed to go on for ninety years.' Arsenal and Wednesday drew 1–1, but the team collapsed afterwards and lost three consecutive games, including two home matches against Spurs and Everton.

Herbert Chapman was buried at Hendon, the church he had attended regularly, four days later. The pall-bearers were among the greatest names in the game's history — David Jack, Eddie Hapgood, Joe Hulme, Jack Lambert, Cliff Bastin and Alex James. The crowds were huge and the Reverend A Hunt Cooke, a close friend of Chapman's at St Mary's, recalled that the scenes were a little shocking: 'There were

people climbing all over the graves with cameras. Mr Chapman would not have approved.'

Bob Wall, then Chapman's secretary, said that, for several years afterwards, he regularly heard Chapman's measured footsteps in the Highbury corridors late in the evening, along the upper landing, through the boardroom and cocktail bar, into the Press Room and on into the stand. He, and other members of the staff, often looked down the corridors to see if anyone was there — but no one ever was. If there are such things as ghosts, then Chapman's at Highbury would be perfect. In every sense, he has continued to live on in the club and the ground that he raised, just as he promised Tom Whittaker, to the very heights of football.

· CHAPTER 6 ·
Allison's Arsenal

Chapman's death was so unexpected that there was no obvious successor. The players probably favoured Joe Shaw, who was deservedly popular and fully versed in Arsenal's ways. Shaw, apparently, was not particularly keen on the glare of publicity that was now an essential part of the job as manager at Highbury and stayed behind the scenes. Whether George Allison, the director in charge, actually formally offered him the job is unclear. The choice of a successor was an almost impossible one for the board — to follow Chapman was the hardest task in football. As it turned out, the problems were not as intractable as the board probably imagined. The club was run on a day to day basis by Joe Shaw, Tom Whittaker and John Peters, all of them highly competent, and the fact that between Chapman's death and the outbreak of war Arsenal won three Championships and the FA Cup (more trophies, interestingly, than when he was alive) is largely due to them. It was also true, of course, that the players were much more responsible now than they had been earlier, or, indeed, were probably to be later, and the club had established a style and approach to the game that could survive even the passing of a Herbert Chapman.

The solution that the board came up with, while unlikely, proved in the end to be rather clever. George Allison, who had been involved with the club since its Woolwich days and became a director in the early 1920s, moved from the board room to the manager's office. For some months after Chapman's death, Allison had been acting as Managing Director/Secretary. He did not actually become manager until the end of the 1933–34 season. It was a clever move because it avoided any great disruption, it allowed Shaw and Whittaker to continue to manage the team, the training and the tactics, it saved the club from facing any new broom that an outsider would probably want to bring, even to so successful a club as the Gunners, and it allowed the team to continue playing exactly as before. And the proof of the pudding has to be in the eating — the results showed that it worked.

Technically Joe Shaw had become team manager, John Peters secretary and Tom Whittaker trainer. The 'official' job of secretary-manager was not actually advertised, but there

Left upper: **George Allison ponders the future** at Highbury soon after the death of Herbert Chapman in 1934. Allison did not succeed Chapman immediately, taking the title of Managing Director until the end of the year. Joe Shaw was team manager for most of 1934, until Allison resigned as a director and officially became secretary-manager. At the time directors could not be paid employees of the club.

Left lower: **Allison (left) puts on** his broadcasting gear before a radio commentary. His assistant is Derek McCulloch, later better known as Uncle Mac on BBC's Children's Hour. McCulloch's job was to call out the position of the ball on the field and the listener matched this to a numbered grid published in the *Radio Times*. Allison first came to public prominence as the commentator on FA Cup finals, and handled both the 1927 and 1930 finals despite being an Arsenal director. The first game on which there had ever been a live commentary was from Highbury on 22 January 1927, though the commentator on this occasion was H. B. T. Wakelam. The match was a 1-1 draw between Arsenal and Sheffield United and it fell to Charlie Buchan to score the first goal ever broadcast live. Highbury was always chosen for experimental radio and television broadcasts, not because of the club's importance but because it was so close to the BBC studios at Alexandra Palace.

were hundreds of applications anyway, to which Allison had to reply. One from Wales claimed the ability to run 14 miles in an hour, a mile in 3½ minutes and '. . . to have developed a private system of team control on the field by verbal orders that will break any defence or attack that does not use my methods. . .' Allison was asked to reply promptly to this application, stating what he would offer for '. . . serving as (a) manager, (b) trainer, (c) recruiter and (d) player, as I am considering taking up heavily paid posts overseas for opulent salaries. . .' As Allison said, presumably tongue in cheek, being the only one who saw the applications gave him ample opportunity to put examples like that to one

assistant was Derek McCulloch, who went on to become the BBC's premier 1940s and 1950s children's broadcaster under the name Uncle Mac.

Bernard Joy, who played for Allison, described him as: '. . . tactful, friendly and good-hearted. But he fell short in his handling of footballers and lacked the professional's deep knowledge of the game. (Allison) wisely left dressing-room discipline in Tom Whittaker's hands and it was Whittaker and Joe Shaw who took the brunt of the strained relations which occasionally developed between management and players. The two of them were loyalty itself to Allison — they had to be or the club would have fallen

Right: **The months after Chapman's death** saw a great outflowing of emotion in North London. Gates were closed for game after game despite the fact that the club suffered an inevitable reaction to events and a slump in form. The picture was taken from the North Bank a full hour before the kick-off against Spurs on 31 January 1934. Spurs won 1-3, Bastin getting the only home goal. The Gunners didn't win a First Division game that tragic January.

side, lest they endanger his prospects.

Allison was actually three years older than the Arsenal, having been born in Darlington in 1883. He had built a reasonable reputation for himself as a journalist, and had for a time been the manager's assistant at Middlesbrough, but his name came to national attention when he was chosen to be Britain's first ever radio sports commentator. The very first major event to be broadcast live was to be the 1927 Cup final, played on 23 April between Arsenal and Cardiff City. In actual fact there was a trial broadcast earlier of an Arsenal game versus Sheffield United on 22 January 1927 but this had a very small audience (Highbury was always used for pre-war radio and television trials because of its proximity to the studios at Alexandra Palace, not because of Arsenal's reputation). Oddly, no one seemed to think it unreasonable that the commentator for the Cup final should also be a director of one of the teams playing. Allison's

apart.' Cliff Bastin, who also played for the next five years under Allison, clearly agreed with Joy, but there is a slight edge to comments in his autobiography. Having pointed out that Joe Shaw was unhappy with the glare of publicity, Bastin comments: 'The man who did take over the position was one to whom the limelight was far from unwelcome. . . he was not, however, a successor shaped in the Chapman mould. Indeed, relations between him and Mr Chapman had not always been of the happiest. . . He (Allison) had the name of Arsenal splashed across the front pages of the press, but he lacked Herbert Chapman's gift of getting the best out of his players.'

These were commonly held views when Allison took over, and were to be heard often enough through the rest of the decade. But others were prepared to look at the results and accept what was plain to see; few men, if any, could have taken over from Herbert Chapman,

and there were still plenty of trophies on the board room sideboard. Frank Carruthers, one of the leading journalists of the period, wrote in 1937: 'The continuance of Arsenal's power is a wonderful tribute to Mr George Allison, who has borne his office through a period of extreme difficulty which would have taxed the ingenuity of a Herbert Chapman to surmount.' And to sum up his views about George Allison's success he said, simply: 'Well, we have all been wrong.' The public image of Allison was never to change. The publicity blurb for his autobiography declared: 'Famous director and manager of Arsenal FC, broadcaster and journalist, for 40 years a pioneer in the success of one of the greatest teams ever to take the field; the friend of Kings and statesmen, the confidant of players, the brain behind a hundred transfers, George Allison has now written his story.'

For the season and a half after Chapman's death things went as well as they could have done for anyone. No other man has come into a manager's seat and won the Championship in his first two seasons. But while Arsenal clearly remained the team to beat through the rest of the 1930s (as, say, Manchester United were in the 1960s) they were no longer unquestionably the best. In the last four seasons prior to the outbreak of war in 1939 their record was a creditable sixth, third, first and fifth, though the Championship of 1938 was won with a mere 52 points, the lowest ever in a full 42-match season. The Cup was again highly creditable, but arguably not outstanding compared with the impossibly high standards set by Chapman between 1930 and 1934. There were, nonetheless, three quarter-finals and the 1936 final victory over Sheffield United.

When Allison's third season in charge began in August 1935 success had become a habit. It was seven seasons since Arsenal had not won or threatened to win one or both trophies. In 1930 there was the FA Cup, in 1931 the League, in 1932 the runners-up slot in both, in 1933, 1934 and 1935 the Championship. Could they do it again? After seven matches and only two wins it didn't look likely.

All great teams come to the end of their eras. Some settle slowly, as Arsenal did, some rapidly, as Manchester City did after their Championship of 1937. For Arsenal, as we have seen, nearly all of the major players had already gone. Alex James and Herbie Roberts were approaching the end of their careers, Frank Moss' shoulder injury recurred in a Cup tie against Blackburn and his career was finally over, reserve centre forward Ronnie Westcott, of whom great things were expected, injured a knee in only his second League match and never played again.

Allison later wrote that, just before the manager's death, Chapman had told him: 'The team's played out Mr Allison, we must rebuild.' At the time the club was top of the First Division and half way through the hat-trick. In many ways the quote rings untrue. Perhaps it was just Chapman's way of loosening up a

director for yet more major expenditures, or perhaps it was a throw-away line after a single poor game. Nonetheless, the team was rebuilt, and not so much because of Allison's desire to buy new players as the ageing of the first-team squad. Allison's first signing was Ted Drake, the reluctant gas inspector from Southampton, in March 1934. And the highlight of the 1935–36 season was to be one game involving the same Ted Drake.

The date was 14 December 1935 and the match was one of the standard classics of the decade — Aston Villa versus Arsenal at Villa Park. About 70,000 were packed inside the ground to see another instalment in a rivalry which provided a series of highly memorable encounters since 1930. They were not to be disappointed though, for once, neither Arsenal nor Villa were heading the League. The Gunners were already eight points behind Sunderland while Villa, having conceded 52 goals in 18 games were bottom. Founder members of the

Arsenal versus the World Champions Italy on 14 November 1934. No less than seven Gunners were chosen to play on their own ground against the recently crowned Jules Rimet Trophy winners. Seven men from one club in the same England team is a modern day record (though equalled by Liverpool forty years later) and it fully reflected the balance of football power in the mid-1930s.
Left: The line-up, left to right, of the seven: George Allison (club manager), Wilf Copping, Ray Bowden, George Male, Frank Moss, Ted Drake, Eddie Hapgood, Cliff Bastin and Tom Whittaker (trainer for both club and country). As can be seen from the programme, Drake was not originally selected but came in when George Hunt of Spurs (and later Arsenal) was injured. England won a brutal match 3-2 with Eric Brook (2) and Drake getting all three goals in the first 15 minutes.
Right: So many players were injured that the Arsenal dressing room was said to resemble a battlefield for much of the following week. Among the casualties being treated by Tom Whittaker were (left to right) Copping, Moss, Bastin and Drake.

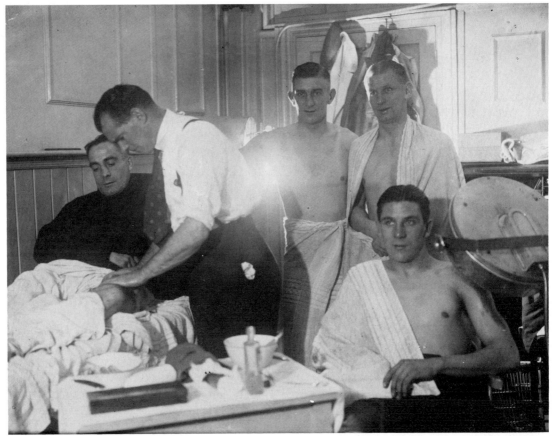

League in 1888, Villa had never been relegated and, in an attempt to stave off that ignominy, had recently spent so heavily that Chapman's and Allison's earlier behaviour looked like that of paupers by comparison. Between November 1935 and January 1936 Villa were actually to spend £35,000 on five players, more than the cost of Arsenal's famous 'Bank of England' forward-line. Villa were fielding six internationals, Arsenal were without James and Hulme. Centre forward Ted Drake had been in the reserves and was carrying a knee injury, which was heavily strapped for the first time.

For the first quarter hour Villa were the better team, but at half-time they went in 3–0 down and Drake had a hat-trick. All the goals were classic Arsenal — a long-ball from Pat Beasley for Drake to run on to, a long pass from Bastin which Drake picked up and ran with to the edge of the area before scoring, and a rebound from a Pat Beasley shot from the wing. At the end of an hour Drake had a double hat-trick and Arsenal were 6–0 up. This time the goals came from a mistake by Villa centre half Tommy Griffiths, who assumed a ball was going over the goal line only to see it rebound off the post for Drake, another pass from Bastin to Drake and an instant return from a bad goalkeeping clearance.

Drake was controlling the ball perfectly, beating defenders at will and shooting so accurately that the Villa keeper, Merton, had no chance. It was the exhibition of a complete centre forward. By this stage the entire Villa half back line was marking Drake, but it made little difference for his seventh shot actually hit the bar and bounced down to be cleared. It was one of only two goal attempts of the whole afternoon which missed its mark (the other was saved). Villa did score once, but Drake had the last word in the final minute with yet another goal from a Bastin cross-field pass; seven goals away from home with just nine shots.

One reason it was the season's highlight for Drake was that he was injured for much of it. As the 1936 Cup final approached, in which Arsenal were to play Sheffield United, Allison needed to test Drake's fitness after a cartilage operation. The game before the final was against Villa at Highbury. Ted Drake scored the winning goal and it was the final nail in Villa's relegation coffin.

Drake's seven goals in Birmingham were a League record, equalling Jimmy Ross Junior's alleged total for Preston against Stoke set way back in 1888 (and since found to be incorrect). By one of those peculiar statistical coincidences, however, Drake's was to remain the record for just 12 days, when Bunny Bell of Tranmere scored nine against Oldham in the Third Division North, though Drake's record remains for the First Division. Drake's goals made little difference to the title race — Sunderland beat the Gunners 5–4 in an exciting game at Roker and went on to win the Championship easily. Arsenal finished sixth, their worst position since 1930, with Derby, Huddersfield, Stoke and Brentford also in front of them.

The Cup was to be a different story. Bristol Rovers were defeated 5–1 at Eastville, then Liverpool 2–0 at Anfield. 'Recorder' in the Arsenal programme was particularly effusive about that display: 'It will go down in Arsenal

history as one of the most glorious performances. The form of our team . . . was superb and would probably have accounted for any team in the land.' The next game was again away (the seventh consecutive away draw) at Newcastle, whom Arsenal had never beaten in the Cup and who had, of course, beaten them in the 1932 final. Moss, Roberts and Drake were all out injured, and the Gunners did well to draw 3–3. The replay at Highbury was easier, a 3–0 win including two Bastin penalties. The sixth round finally saw a home draw and a 4–1 defeat of Barnsley. The semi-final was at Huddersfield against highly unfashionable Grimsby (but then a First Division club) and there were some concerns that this might be another struggle like the one against the other Humberside team, Hull, in the semi-final six years before. It was certainly a hard game, Bastin's goal being the only one of the match and taking Arsenal to Wembley for the fourth time in ten years. Bastin had a habit of scoring the critical goal in semi-finals and in this case, he shot past Grimsby's centre half Hodgson whom Alex James had spotted (while on a scouting mission for Allison) was rather weak on his right side. Bowden and

A Smart Alec!

By TOM WEBSTI

THE ARSENAL PERFORMER – SAT IN HIS CORNER EATING HIS APRIL PIE HE PUT IN HIS THUMB – AND PULLED OUT A PLUM AND SAID " WHAT A GOOD BOY AM I."

[Daily Mail Copyright.

Left: A cartoon commemorating the famous game against Sheffield Wednesday on 2 February 1935, in which Alex James scored a hat-trick in 20 minutes. That morning James' nine-year-old son had come home to tell his father that he had scored seven goals in a school game and wanting to know why his father never scored anymore. James produced his only Arsenal hat-trick that afternoon, also provoked by finding out that Wednesday manager Billy Walker had told his defenders not to bother with James near to goal as:'. . . he never scores these days . . .' Cliff Bastin wrote to Harry Homer, the programme editor, a week later saying: 'Alex surprised us all by scoring a hat-trick, much to the amusement of the crowd.' James soon slipped back into his old ways and by December that year Trevor Wignall was writing of him in the *Daily Express*: 'Alex James was, as usual, magical and marvellous, but if he had to depend for a living on finding the net he would starve to

THE YOUNGER GENERATION—By Cumberworth

THERE IS KEEN RIVALRY BETWEEN ALEX. JAMES AND HIS SON AGED NINE YEARS. RECENTLY THE LATTER ARRIVED HOME AND SHOOK THE PATERNAL PRESTIGE BY— ANNOUNCING THAT HE HAD SCORED 7 GOALS. To RECOVER

BAGGED THREE GOALS TODAY! / SEZ YOU! / HIS POSITION IN THE HOUSEHOLD PA JAMES MADE HIS DESPERATE EFFORT OF LAST SATURDAY.

TOMORROW, ALL FATHERS WILL HOPE THAT ALEX DOES NOT SLIP BACK TO HIS OLD NON. SCORING GAME.

IF HE DOES WE SUGGEST THAT HE WAITS ON THE DOORSTEP TILL HIS OFFSPRING HAS BEEN PACKED OFF TO BED.

Bastin practised playing on this weakness at Highbury the day before the semi-final, with Bowden working on how to draw Hodgson to the right, going past on the outside and slipping the ball back inside for Bastin coming into the gap. Bowden tried the move exactly as practised in the 40th minute; it worked just as planned and Arsenal won the game 1–0.

With no chance of winning the League, Allsion had been resting his injured players (such as Roberts and Drake) between Cup ties. This did not please the League, who fined Arsenal £250 in a show of displeasure which became almost an annual ritual directed at some club or other between the wars. When the final came round Drake, Roberts, James and Hapgood were all unwell. Drake was barely recovered from a cartilage operation and had only played his comeback game one week before. Allison decided he had to risk the centre forward and reshuffled his attack — putting Ray Bowden at inside forward and moving Bastin back to the left wing (he had been playing inside). The

upshot was that Pat Beasley, who had been in Bastin's spot for much of the season, was dropped before the final, just as he had been hours before the 1932 game. The FA again refused to mint an extra medal for him. The team that therefore took the field was Wilson, Male, Hapgood, Crayston, Roberts, Copping, Hulme, Bowden, Drake, James, Bastin.

Their opponents were Second Division Sheffield United, who had beaten Burnley, Preston, Leeds, Spurs and finally Fulham to get to Wembley. For most of the game United were on top, almost going ahead in the first minute when Alex Wilson dropped the ball in the 6-yard box, and later unluckily hitting the bar with a Jock Dodds header after half an hour. There were no goals until the 74th minute, when Bastin picked up a clearance and passed the ball through the middle to Ted Drake. Drake side-stepped past United captain Tom Johnson and hit the ball hard, left-footed, past keeper Smith. United attacked for the rest of the match and suffered further wretched luck when Dodds hit the

death. The corner flags were, as usual, more in danger of being struck than the goal-posts . . .'

Above left: **Another James cartoon,** this time by Tom Webster, who was responsible not only for prompting James' long shorts but also the design of Arsenal's shirts. This cartoon was published on 22 April 1935, two days after a 1-0 Highbury win had guaranteed Arsenal their third consecutive League title. Pat Beasley had scored the goal and it was highly appropriate that the opponents had been Huddersfield, the only other team to perform such a hat-trick and also, of course, under Chapman's management.

Top right: **James, dressed in unlikely garb,** watches the Barnsley keeper Ellis during an FA Cup quarter-final tie at Highbury on Leap Year's Day, 1936. Arsenal won 4-1 with goals from Bastin, Bowden and Beasley (2).

Bottom right: **More Yorkshire connections** at Kings Cross three weeks later on 21 March 1936, as the fans gather to catch the special trains to Huddersfield for the semi-final against Grimsby. They were rewarded by a single goal from Ray Bowden and a trip to Wembley.

Left: **The 1936 FA Cup final** against Sheffield United was not to prove the most glittering moment in the club's history, but the demand for tickets never faltered. The Monday after those fans had set off for Huddersfield (previous page) the Highbury staff faced this postbag of requests for Cup final tickets. Some things never change. The post obviously worked well in those days – particularly the Sunday collections. 1936 did have a particular significance for the club, of course; it was the 50th anniversary of their foundation and, hence, the mid-point in this history.

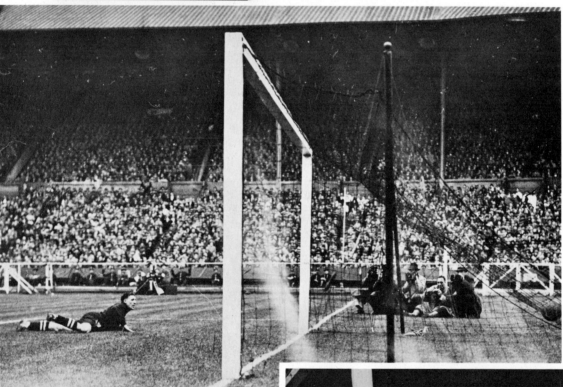

Above: **The only goal of the 1936 FA Cup final:** Drake picked up a pass from Bastin, side-stepped the Sheffield captain Tom Johnson and hit the ball hard, left-footed past keeper Smith. Drake, strapped and barely recovered from a cartilage operation, had struggled for much of the game and could not get up after the goal. He took no further part in the game. The moment, *right*, is often described as the goal but was actually a very similar incident earlier in the match when Drake's shot went just wide of Smith's post.

Right: **Celebrations at the end of the 1936 final.** From left to right the players are Hapgood (who had been told that James would replace him as captain only that morning), James, Hulme and manager Allison. It was only Arsenal's second Cup success.

Below: **The evening was spent** at the Café Royal, where the club always had their celebration dinners. A cheerful crowd includes George Male (complete with obligatory cigarette – how times change), Alex James and, at the far right, Mrs James.

Below right: **The victorious team.** Back row: George Male, Jack Crayston, Alex Wilson, Herbie Roberts, Ted Drake, Eddie Hapgood;

centre: George Allison, Joe Hulme, Ray Bowden, Alex James, Cliff Bastin, Tom Whittaker; bottom: Pat Beasley and Wilf Copping. Beasley had been dropped days before the Cup final for the second time (1932 was the first). The club asked permission to mint a special medal for him, but the FA refused. Beasley was eventually to play in a final in 1938, when he was on the opposite wing to Joe Hulme in the losing Huddersfield team against Preston. If it was a first for Beasley, for Hulme it was a last. It was Hulme's fifth Wembley FA Cup final, a record equalled but not surpassed, and he never played in another first-class game.

woodwork a second time. Drake, who had been uncomfortable for the whole game, said afterwards that when he got the ball from Bastin he knew it was now or never. After he had scored James and Bastin were the first to reach him, but he was on his hands and knees in the grass, unable to get up because of the pain in his injured knee. Drake stayed on the field for the rest of the game, but took no further part. It was the only goal of the game and Alex James took the trophy. Hapgood had not realised he wouldn't be captain until he read the morning papers, a communication slip by Allison which appears to have rankled with Hapgood afterwards.

The captain and the manager never had a particularly close relationship, Hapgood being another who has described Allison as lucky to take over when he did and not possessing the football knowledge of Chapman (but then who could have compared, one is forced to ask?) Later Hapgood was particularly hurt that Allison was prepared to let him go to Luton at the start of the 1943–44 season, when the player wanted a final year with the Gunners. But the full back tells a good story about Allison in his autobiography, admitting that the manager was also very amused by it. Shortly after taking over, Allison was running a team talk preparing for the following day's match: 'The danger man for Wednesday is Charlie Napier,' he told Jack Crayston, 'and you have the job of marking him and not letting him have the ball.' Crayston tried to interrupt but Allison stopped him: 'Wait a moment, let me finish and then give me your views.' When Allison had finished he asked what Crayston wanted to say. 'Napier does play well for Wednesday, Mr Allison,' the half back commented, 'but we're playing Blackpool tomorrow.'

Having been largely outplayed by a Second Division side in the 1936 final, Arsenal were forced to face the realities of their new position. They were no longer *the* outstanding side. Others, having watched what Chapman had achieved, had begun to copy many of his methods. Arsenal's tactical game was no longer a surprise, particularly when Bastin, Hulme and James became older, slower and less effective. Individual players retired, others were injured. The strain of a decade with every game played like a Cup tie was taking its toll.

And yet there was still no single club ready to take over the mantle — Sunderland were always in at the kill, Preston often looked good, Huddersfield kept popping up, Wolves and Derby threatened to win everything and eventually won nothing. So, at the end of the day, Arsenal still maintained a better overall record than any other club — it is just that we are tempted to judge them by the standards not of the Chapman era as a whole, but solely against the 1930–34 period. None of the other sides really approached Arsenal for more than a single season; it was Arsenal's decade from beginning to end.

The realities of Arsenal's slightly diminished status were clear in the first few games of 1936–37. The Gunners won only two of their initial nine matches and, by the end of October, were 17th. In a now familiar story, though, the side fought back until, by mid-March, they were on top and seemed to be on the way to a seventh trophy in eight years. But, in true fairy story tradition, Manchester City came with an astonishing run of 36 points out of 40 from the New Year onwards. The crucial game was at Maine Road on 10 April 1937, when the Gunners went down 2–0 and left City clear to take the title. The following season City scored the highest number of goals in the First Division (80) and somehow managed to get themselves relegated, the only time the Champions have gone straight back down. For Arsenal, the season's most significant event was probably Alex James' retirement. His last League game was against Bolton on 1 May 1937 and was hardly the send off he or the club might have wished. Bernard Joy, now in the team in place of the injured Herbie Roberts, called the Mayday goalless draw 'dismal'. James' final match was actually played at Feijenoord on a summer tour a month later.

It is impossible to underestimate James' contribution to the successful Arsenal side of the 1930s. He was simply the key man. Before he arrived, as has often been repeated, they had won nothing, despite the big signings. In the six years after his arrival they won four Championships and reached three FA Cup finals. 'You might have suspected,' said Don Davies in an obituary in the *Manchester Guardian*, 'when you saw him shuffle onto the field for the first time that there was one who might lay claim to genius. Some held that James' slovenly appearance was natural, others said it was a pose. But it was in sharp contrast to one of the tidiest minds

Alex Wilson and Herbie Roberts combine to stop Everton's Dixie Dean during a League match on 29 August 1936. Hapgood, Bowden and James scored in a 3-2 victory. Roberts became the definitive 'policeman' stopper centre half, serving Arsenal in that position for a decade, though he was acknowledged to be a player with weaknesses. Whittaker said of him: 'Herbie's genius came from his intelligence and, even more important, that he did as he was told. His orders were to stay in the centre, intercept balls down the middle and head them clear or pass them short. His inability to kick a ball hard or far was thus camouflaged.' The picture also shows the revised strip with red shirts, white sleeves and red and white socks (previously the socks had been blue because the club couldn't find a red that matched and wouldn't run). Cartoonist Tom Webster, who inspired Alex James' shorts, was also responsible for the new shirts. Webster had turned up for a game of golf with the Chelsea chairman wearing a blue sleeveless sweater over a white shirt. The chairman, whose team wore blue shirts and white shorts at the time, liked this original combination and wanted to introduce it at Stamford

ridge. Dave Calderhead, hen the Chelsea manager, disagreed and efused to allow it. When Vebster told the story to Chapman, he picked up he idea instantly and sent ut his team in the listinctive style which has asted to this day – Arsenal happily ignoring he almost annual osmetics that too many lubs indulge in owadays. The new shirts vere first worn on 4 March 933 at Highbury against iverpool and could not be aid to have had exactly a alismanic effect. Liverpool von 0-1 and Arsenal, hough they won the Championship, did not enjoy a single success hat March. That the change came so soon after Walsall may not be entirely coincidental.

in football. James hated waste, particularly wasted effort. To him it was the surest mark of inadequate technique. "Let the ball do the work" was his motto.' After he had begun to heed Chapman's advice to: '. . . . . cut out the circus tricks until we're winning 3–0,' James was at the centre of everything. That was why he was always treated slightly differently from the rest. Chapman would not have put up with his antics, his disappearances in the night and his lying in bed until noon from any other player. When he finished playing he took up a job with one of the pools companies. As a result, he was banned from playing or managing for a while, including a petty objection to his turning out for Northampton in wartime games. He later became a Sunday paper reporter and eventually returned to Highbury as a coach. He was to live only until 1953, aged 51, one of several of the great names of the 1930s to die tragically young.

James proved almost impossible to replace, though Allison tried. He bought Bobby Davidson from St Johnstone, but he was not to be the playmaker Arsenal needed. Nor, in the end, was Cliff Bastin, who featured for most of the 1936–37 season where he had started out, at inside forward. Allison searched further afield, buying Leslie Jones from Coventry (already a Welsh international) and George Drury from Sheffield United to fill the gap, but they didn't work either. In the end, he made the move which was, to a large extent, to become the albatross around the neck of his reputation — the purchase of Bryn Jones from Wolves.

Bob John retired on the same day as Alex James, Herbie Roberts never came back from his injury and a bloodclot complication and Joe Hulme was out for virtually a year and a half after injuring his back when he ran into a concrete wall at one end of the Huddersfield pitch. Oddly, it was back there to Leeds Road that Hulme eventually went in January 1938, and within three months he was playing outside right in the famous FA Cup final against Preston, won by the latter with a last minute George Mutch penalty. Hulme was the first man to play in five Wembley FA Cup finals, a record later to be equalled by Pat Rice. The 1938 Cup final was actually Joe Hulme's last ever first-class match, a wonderful way to end any career. Denis Compton almost did the same in 1950 (and got a winner's medal into the bargain) but he eventually played one more League match, against Portsmouth, after the Wembley finale.

Herbie Roberts had a less happy sequel to his Arsenal career, which ended after that bad injury on 30 October 1937 versus Middlesbrough. He became part of the backroom staff, moving down to train the nursery club at Margate. After only a brief time there, shortly after the outbreak of the war, he was to die of erysipelas, a rare bacterial infection of the skin which penicillin can cure relatively easy today. He was a great loss to Arsenal and to football and was the second (after Jack Lambert) of the great team to die soon after moving to Margate.

The nursery club idea had been another of Chapman's brainwaves. It was much better to have your youngsters competing in a real League than against other juniors, he reasoned. His first move was to try to take over Clapton (later Leyton) Orient, then a Third Division South club, who were threatened with expulsion by the FA in 1931 unless they paid off their debts. Chapman effectively took over the club late that year and all of the players were registered with Arsenal. It was a nice, if short-lived, irony as, 20 years before, Orient had been one of the main objectors to the move to Highbury. Needless to say, the League objected strongly and ordered Chapman to desist (they had clearly had enough of Arsenal bosses running two clubs twenty years earlier). The upshot was that Jimmy Seed, Orient manager since April 1931, found himself just a few weeks from the start of the 1932–33 season with no team, no directors and no registered players.

It was not Chapman, but Allison, who later turned to the Southern League, which was not concerned about the two clubs idea, and Arsenal acquired Margate instead. Seed was to have his own revenge on Arsenal — between 1934 and 1936 he took Charlton from the Third Division to the First and in 1936–37 he squeezed into second place between Manchester City and the Gunners.

So, having finished third in 1936–37 and been knocked out of the Cup in the quarterfinals at the Hawthorns, it did appear that Arsenal were in decline. All the more surprising, then, was their Championship in 1937–38, the fifth in eight years. Their record was almost identical to that of 1936–37, with exactly the same number of points, 52. They lost as many as 11 games (their highest number of defeats in any season in the 1930s to date, with the sole exception of 1935–36 when they lost 12) and scored only 77 goals, their lowest total since 1929–30 apart from the 75 in 1933–34, that peculiarly quiet season containing Chapman's death.

The side was not in any sense a settled one and the season was tough and inconsistent. At the end the Gunners were to just squeeze past Wolves and Brentford, who were performing the surprise Charlton role one season later. George Hunt had been bought from Spurs (one of the rare transfers between these two clubs at that time) to partner Drake up front and did so well that it was a surprise when Allison transferred him to Bolton at the end of the season. Joy had replaced Roberts and Bastin and Male were now the only survivors from the great days, making another Championship both more surprising and impressive. By February, Arsenal and Wolves were favourites for both major competitions and found themselves drawn together in the Cup one week after meeting in the League. Wolves won the League game 3–1 to go ahead of Arsenal in the table, though both were then several points behind Brentford. In the Cup the roles were reversed, Arsenal winning a very

tough game 2–1 with goals from Drake and Kirchen in what Bernard Joy called the most exciting tie he ever played in. It must have exhausted them, for they went out 1–0 to eventual winners Preston in the next round at Highbury.

Brentford, despite having been seven points ahead of Arsenal at one stage, were like many other clubs who have risen through the divisions quickly. The elements of unfamiliarity and surprise carry them so far for so long, but the lack of strength in depth tends to tell in the end. Brentford walked the tightrope for a long time, but when they fell they fell heavily. In eight games Brentford took only two points and were out of contention.

At Highbury new names were making their mark — Mel Griffiths at outside right, Eddie Carr, a successful centre forward when Drake was injured, as he so often was. A long run of success put Arsenal three points clear of Wolves, at Easter, but then came disaster. Over the holiday period the Gunners could only draw 0–0 at Birmingham and then lost both games against Brentford. The matches against their London rivals, who were back in form now that their chance had virtually gone, were particularly inept, notable for Ted Drake's injury at Griffin Park, where he was knocked out and then came back on the field despite having blood pouring down his face from a head wound. That was the Drake of Arsenal inter-war legend. He ended this particular game being carried off the field half-conscious hung over Tom Whittaker's shoulder.

The Easter debacle put Wolves back on top

and the contest went to the last match. Preston had made a late run from behind and were being tipped for the Double. Arsenal were perhaps fortunate to go to Deepdale a week before the Cup final (in which Preston defeated Huddersfield) and, with the Preston players no doubt tense and afraid of injury, as teams always are at that point, the Gunners won 3–1 when, on form, the game should have seen the end of their title hopes. On the very last day Wolves were away to Sunderland. If Wolves won, they were champions no matter what the opposition did, but if they drew, and Arsenal beat Bolton at Highbury, then Arsenal would be champions again. It was one of those odd moments when all the hopes and all the fears of perhaps years of effort come together in a single match.

The Bolton game was easy for a committed Arsenal, who won 5–0. But, though Sunderland had nothing to play for, they threw themselves into their game with Wolves with a vengeance. So determined were they that one of their defenders was sent off and they still won 1–0. Wolves, who had come so close, were thus to win absolutely nothing in the 1930s. The game at Roker had kicked off 15 minutes before that at Highbury, and when the result came through on the scoreboards and the crowd started cheering Bernard Joy called to Eddie Hapgood: 'They've lost Eddie.' Hapgood, typically, was so embroiled in the game, though Arsenal were already 4–0 up, that he simply didn't understand what Joy was talking about.

The final season before the Second World War proved to be notable for little but the purchase of Bryn Jones. This was really the

Bottom left: **Demolition work begins** on the old Main (East) Stand at Highbury on 21 April 1936. It had stood since 1913 and its replacement was complete the following October.

Top right: **Television comes to Highbury;** the first match shown live anywhere in the world was played at Highbury on Thursday 16 September 1937. Excerpts were shown on the BBC from a practice game between the first team and the reserves.

Bottom right: **George Allison demonstrates** on the famous tactical table during a midweek session in September 1938. The picture was taken in the boardroom, which retains the identical features to this day, down to the hat-rack. By this time Allison was not only manager but also the club's second largest shareholder (with 566 shares – J. J. Edwards had 752). Out of 470 shareholders, over 400 held just one share. The cost of the two new stands had put enormous financial pressure on the club and by August 1939 they were in debt to the tune of £22,960 and had only £3 18s 6d in the bank (£3.92). As in 1914-15, they found themselves going into a world war in a precarious financial state.

point at which Allison was accused of taking over Chapman's 'money bags' reputation with a vengeance. Interestingly such criticisms were a source of unusual irritation to Allison, who usually took disagreements and press comment in his stride. He was very quick to point out that, between 1925 and 1934, Chapman spent £101,000 in fees and received £40,000 for those he sold — a balance of around £7,000 per annum. Between Allison taking over and the war, Arsenal spent £81,000 and received £51,000, a net expenditure of £30,000. This was certainly more than manageable when,

during the six seasons 1933–39, the total profit amounted to £136,000, a massive sum for any football club or moderate sized company of the period. In 1934–35 the club became the first ever to have gate receipts of over £100,000, and made a profit of £35,000. Of the other clubs only Portsmouth, with £14,961, even got into double figures. The financial reserves were then £60,000 and even programme sales brought in nearly £2,500.

Financially more debatable, as it happened, was the building of the stands. The West Stand cost £45,000 and was opened by the Prince of Wales (later the Duke of Windsor) on 10 December 1932. It had actually been first used on 12 November for a game against Chelsea (Arsenal won 1–0) and was, by a large margin, the grandest and most expensive structure on any League ground at the time. It incorporated three flats, an electric lift, and had 4,100 seats and the lower level, which was originally all standing, could theoretically hold another 20,000. Work had actually begun on redeveloping the ground in 1931, when the club started building up the banking on all four sides. Local inhabitants were encouraged to bring in their rubbish to help the process and, as Simon Inglis mentions in his invaluable *The Football Grounds of England and Wales,* one coal merchant backed up too close to a hole in the North Bank and saw his horse and cart disappear into the cavity. The animal was so badly injured that it had to be destroyed and it is buried where it fell, in the middle of the North Bank terracing.

The North Bank roof was originally built in 1935 (the clock then being moved to the South Bank) but was destroyed by bombs in the war. The new East, or Main, Stand was not planned to be built until 1941, but the original stand was deteriorating so fast, and the finances appeared to be so favourable, that the decision was made to rebuild in 1935 (it was first used for the game v Grimsby on 24 October 1936).

As the club had already borrowed quite heavily to erect the other stands, by early 1937 Arsenal had debts of £200,000 and needed average crowds of 40,000 simply to pay the running expenses and finance the debt. The Main Stand, though planned to be identical to the West Stand, finally cost far more (£130,000 to be precise) and when the war came in 1939 the club found themselves in a similar position to that of Henry Norris in 1914. The war years clearly left the problem unsolved but, with the enormous boom in attendances between 1945 and 1952, and some intelligent management, the problem happily, and perhaps a little fortuitously, solved itself. One reason why the East Stand cost more than the West was that it had an expensive public frontage — the West is built entirely behind a row of houses and is effectively invisible from that side.

When George Allison finally decided he had to buy Bryn Jones in August 1938, the record fee was still the £11,500 he and Chapman had paid out for David Jack ten years before. Eventually

This page: Left, right and out. The magnificent Ted Drake was probably the greatest of all Arsenal centre forwards. His 42 goals in 1934-35 have never been surpassed, nor have his seven goals for the club at Villa Park on 14 December 1935, the most ever scored by a single player in any First Division game. The top picture shows Brentford keeper Crozier deflecting a shot from Drake at Griffin Park on 8 September 1938. Brentford defeated the Champions 1-0. The middle picture was taken a year earlier, against Sunderland at Highbury on 18 September 1937 and shows Drake's goal in a 4-1 win (Hulme, Davidson and Milne got the others). The lower picture is a classic, also taken at Brentford but on 18 April 1938, when the home side won 3-0. Arsenal lost twice to Brentford in the space of three days but still just squeezed in to win the League by a point, their total of 52 being the lowest which has ever headed the Championship in a 42-match season. Drake was injured three times in the match, was twice carried off, finished with two broken bones in his wrist, nine stitches in his head and was eventually (pictured) carried off unconscious over Tom Whittaker's shoulder. It was an extreme performance even by the tough and brave standards of Ted Drake. A young Denis Compton looks concerned on the left, Cliff Bastin on the right. Players were (as can be seen) still unidentified but shirt numbering was introduced for all games the following year.

Wolves forced Allison up to £14,000, and Jones was left to carry the very distracting tag of 'most expensive player'. Many players before and since have found this difficult, not least Bryn's own nephew Cliff Jones when he came to Spurs for £35,000 two decades later. Bryn started well enough though, scoring in his first game, against Portsmouth, and getting two more in the next three matches. But he never really settled that season, not enjoying the limelight as much as an Alex James and feeling the crowd and club's expectations weighing very heavily on his light shoulders.

It was the sort of pressure he could never escape from at Highbury — when he and Allison agreed that a run in the relative calm of the reserves might improve his form, 33,000 turned up to see his second team debut. As they had nearly all come to see Jones, this was even worse than being in the first team and the experiment was never repeated. Allison was understandably unrepentant about his purchase, pointing out that: '. . . he was not a prolific goalscorer (though he had scored 52 goals in 163 games for Wolves) just like Alex James, because his chief asset was the holding together of the line and the making of openings for the more vigorous of his team-mates.'

Allison said that Jones often asked to be saved from the ever-present, ever-insistent limelight, and believed that, given time to settle down, he would have made the grade: 'My faith never failed and I have never for a moment considered him a bad buy. Please don't think I'm going to say that I've never had bad buys. I have, but Bryn was not one of them.' Allison's point seems a fair one. It took Alex James a season to settle down and there was no reason to expect Jones, just as important a buy, to adapt any faster. He played exceptionally well on the team's close-season tour of 1939 but never really had another chance except in the very different atmosphere of wartime football. Like many great players, notably Stan Cullis of Wolves, his best years were inevitably lost to the war.

Interestingly, other members of the club did not share Allison's optimism. Cliff Bastin, in his autobiography, said: 'I thought at the time this was a bad transfer, and subsequent events did nothing to alter my views. . . I had played against Bryn in club and international matches and had ample opportunity to size him up. To my mind, he was essentially an attacking player, who was successful at Wolverhampton largely because the rest of the team was playing well.'

Bastin argued that James had a first-class footballing brain and that Jones, while being a first-class footballer, did not. James, whom

Below: **Leslie Jones** (second left) scores for Arsenal against Grimsby on 19 March 1938. Jones was a regular Welsh international but should not be confused with his compatriot and namesake Bryn Jones, whose arrival in August of the same year was to be the most controversial of all the major transfers in the inter-war period. Arsenal beat Grimsby easily 5-1, with the other goals coming in pairs from Griffiths and Bastin.

Bastin of course called one of the most self-confident people he had ever met, was able to weather the bad patch of the transition, while Jones, quiet, modest and self-effacing, was not. Bastin was the wing partner of them both, of course, so his judgement is possibly the most reliable available. Sadly, his conclusion is rather dismissive: 'It was his (Jones) natural instinct to play as far upfield as I. Arsenal's attempt to curb that instinct failed. . . (He) would have been much happier if he had never left Wolverhampton.'

Apart from Jones, the goalkeepers were also in the news in the last season before the war. George Marks, hailing from the non-footballing town of Salisbury, became the first-team keeper and was England's first choice for much of the war, losing his place only after a bad head injury sustained against Wales towards the end of hostilities. Much more serious was the tragedy that befell the reserve keeper David Ford. Aged only 18, he had played well in a Combination game for the second team against Portsmouth at Highbury. On the way home, he collapsed in the tube station, was rushed to hospital and found to have a duodenal ulcer, the pain of which he had foolishly kept quiet. He never recovered and died the following Saturday. More were to die in the hostilities that followed — of the 42 players on the staff in 1938–39, nine were dead by the end of the war. Nearly all the players joined the forces (Whittaker had served in the First World War and Bastin's deafness disqualified him so the two of them manned the Air Raid post on top of the main stand). The ground was bombed several times — Eddie Hapgood recalled one occasion when the incendiaries missed the stands but somehow managed to set fire to both sets of goalposts. Soon afterwards a barrage balloon arrived and was moored on the practice pitch. This did not prevent a 1,000-pound bomb hitting the same pitch, nor various other aerial objects destroying both the North Stand and some of the terracing. If this seems like bad luck, Birmingham were much worse off — St Andrew's was hit no less than 18 times! Arsenal and Spurs shared an undamaged White Hart Lane for most of the war and Arsenal won

the London League in 1941–42, the League South in 1942–43 and the League South Cup in 1942–43.

Arsenal were to conclude their inter-war glories with a flourish in 1939. Though they had never been in the hunt for the League title (Everton won it easily) the Gunners did win five of their last six games to finish, as in 1914–15, fifth. By this time Hitler had already invaded Czechoslovakia and the normality of football already seemed a little unreal. Although three games were played at the start of the aborted 1939–40 season, it was fitting that the last official pre-Second World War match should have been as peculiar, in its own way, as the last game in 1914–15. That was at Highbury on 6 May 1939, against bogey team Brentford, and was used to film the playing sequences for a thriller called *The Arsenal Stadium Mystery* by one Leonard Gribble. Brentford wore white shirts and black shorts instead of their usual change strip (to provide contrast for the black and white cameras) and played the part of the mythical Trojans. Several Arsenal players, as well as George Allison, enlivened the plot. Whether the script called for a 2–0 home win is not clear, but that's the way the game ended. It was Arsenal's last official first-class match for over six years.

Above: **The last League game before the Second World War** was as peculiar, in its own way, as its equivalent before the break for the First World War. It was against Brentford on 6 May 1939 and Arsenal won 2-0 with goals from Alf Kirchen and Ted Drake, but it was more notable for the fact that it was used to make the film 'The Arsenal Stadium Mystery'. Brentford, in unusual change strip, played the fictional part of 'The Trojans' and several Arsenal personalities took part in the film, including Cliff Bastin, Tom Whittaker and, seen being made up, George Allison.

Below: **One of Ted Drake's two goals** in the 1943 League South Wartime Cup final on 1 May 1943. Arsenal won 7-1, the highest victory recorded in a first-class Wembley final. Blackpool then beat Arsenal 4-2 in a North-South play-off at Stamford Bridge. The war was to prove a tragic time for a heavily bombed Highbury. No less than nine of the 42 professionals on the books in 1939 failed to survive it, the highest loss of any club. The nine were Henry Cook, Bobby Daniel, William Dean, Hugh Glass, Leslie Lack, William Parr, Sidney Pugh, Herbie Roberts and Cyril Tooze.

Above: **Charlton on the attack** against Arsenal at White Hart Lane during a Regional Wartime League South match on 2 November 1940. The game was drawn 2-2 with Arsenal ending the season fourth in the League (Crystal Palace won the League that season). Arsenal shared White Hart Lane with Spurs throughout the War. Highbury was used as an air-raid lookout post (largely because of the marshalling yards nearby) and was also bombed on several occasions. Among the damage was the total destruction of the original North Stand.

Dennis Compton, like most of the Arsenal players, joined the forces, becoming (appropriately) a gunner in the army.

Arsenal captain George Male shakes hands with his Charlton counterpart, Don Welsh, before the Football League South Cup final on 1 May 1943. Arsenal won the game 7-1, completing a hat-trick having previously won the Football League (South) and the League Cup (South).

· CHAPTER 7 ·
Whittaker's Arsenal

Forty-two of Arsenal's 44 professionals in September 1939 had gone into the services. The administrators at Highbury followed, and the ground itself played a part in the war effort — Arsenal Stadium was transformed into a stronghold for ARP (Air Raid Precautions). The club was temporarily based at White Hart Lane, though for a time George Allison converted the referees' room at Highbury into a small flat. Amid the confusion of wartime competitions and the difficulties of finding who was able to play when and where, Arsenal's success nonetheless continued.

In 1939–40 the South 'A' League was won, and in the following season the club reached another Wembley final in the Football League War Cup. With young Laurie Scott partnering Hapgood at full back and Bernard Joy at centre half, the attack was led by Les Compton, who at Wembley against Preston North End missed a penalty. Brother Denis' goal earned a replay, but with Drake now replacing the elder Compton Arsenal lost the replay at Blackburn 2–1.

The football honours, such as they were in such austere circumstances, continued: Champions of the London League in 1941–42 and the Football League South the following season, when there was also a successful return to Wembley, this time in the Football League South Cup final. Reg Lewis, who was to make his mark at the Empire Stadium in more illustrious peace-time circumstances, contributed four goals in a 7–1 thrashing of Charlton Athletic. The gifted forward whose casual approach and happy knack of scoring was to make him such a popular figure at Highbury in the early post-war years finished the 1942–43 season with a remarkable tally of 53 goals, which were partly responsible for the high total attendance of 670,000 at Arsenal's 39 games.

Two seasons later Lewis was not available and Arsenal's scoring honours were shared by Drake and Stan Mortensen from Blackpool, one of many guest players. Stanley Matthews was another in one wartime league game — he scored. For Ted Drake, though, a slipped disc proved to be one injury that even that gallant forward could not overcome, and his dramatic career ended.

The effort of continuing football in the war years proved extremely costly. Pre-war debts of some £150,000 were a millstone when the 1945–46 season began with regional Leagues retained and the return of the FA Cup the major concession to normality. White Hart Lane was still the home venue for the most remarkable match of that confused season. Late in 1945 Moscow Dynamo arrived on an unprecedented tour. With regular European football still more than a decade away, the visit was greeted with a sense of mystery mingled with anticipation. The Russians themselves were singularly suspicious of their hosts. The drama of the plot was heightened by the prevailing weather for much of their stay, a London pea-souper fog.

George Allison's own account of the events surrounding the match tell of the scurrying around to find a team worthy of the illustrious pre-war standards that Moscow Dynamo would expect and the opposition's misunderstanding of these efforts.

The manager's dealings finally produced six 'guests': goalkeeper Bill Griffiths from Cardiff, left back Joe Bacuzzi from Fulham, left half Reg Halton from Bury and three illustrious forwards — Matthews, Mortensen and Ronnie Rooke, whom Allison would sign from Fulham the following season. George Drury, now 31, and Horace Cumner, both survivors from the Arsenal pre-war scene, were the other two forwards, while Joy was at centre half, 33-year-old Cliff Bastin at right half and Scott at right back.

The crowd of 54,620 had only sporadic views of the proceedings as the fog occasionally lifted. So did the referee, a Russian, and his two linesmen who used the Soviet system of controlling the match with both linesmen on the same side of the field and the senior official operating from the other side.

Moscow Dynamo scored in their first attack, through Bobrov, but Rooke equalised and then the ebullient Mortensen struck twice. At halftime it was 3–2 but sinister whisperings reached the ears of George Allison that the referee would abandon the match if Dynamo fell further behind. On the other hand, if they were to recapture the lead the match would be played to a finish, however thick the fog.

The Russians did score twice in the second half, and the match did run its allotted span; the suggestion of subterfuge could not disguise the flair and discipline glimpsed through the fog.

George Male retired as a player in 1948. His very last first-class game was a perfect ending to a great career; it was on 1 May 1948 at home to Grimsby and Arsenal won 8-0, confirming their status as League Champions. Though Male played two more games on tour that summer, the Grimsby match was the last formal appearance of any of the players from the Chapman era. Like many of his colleagues, Male then went onto the coaching staff and became a tough task-master.

Conventional League fare resumed in August 1946, and for the first match at Highbury, a Football Combination fixture against Clapton Orient, the programme notes had a poignant ring:

'Our last programme was published on the second of September 1939 and not one of us will want to be reminded of what happened on the third. We beat Sunderland that day and Ted Drake scored a hat-trick. And it happened almost seven years ago. Where have we all been since then and what have we not seen. . . .'

First Division football returned to Arsenal Stadium on 4 September against Blackburn Rovers and Marksman summed up the mood of joy, without forgetting 'You who talked Arsenal with me over a campfire in Assam and the chap with the Italy Star on the train in India who informed me of Herbert Roberts passing on, the fellow in the Skymaster on the long hop from Ceylon to the Cocos Islands who told me about our Cup Final win and all those who played with or against Tom Whittaker's Arsenal Arps in the very early days of ARP. And the older ones who

stuck to the job in London through bomb and fire and rocket yet still made the long trek up to White Hart Lane to give the boys a cheer. We're home again now!'

On the field the resumption was inauspicious. It began with a defeat at Wolves where six goals and one of Bernard Joy's eyeteeth were lost. Reg Lewis, after scoring, ended up in goal, but at least his eleven goals in the first ten matches papered over some of the cracks. But others ran deep with little young talent immediately available; the move to White Hart Lane had temporarily ended the production line at Highbury. Icelander Albert Gudmundsson, an amateur, was one of 31 players used in the League. The charismatic Doctor Kevin O'Flanagan, an international at football and rugby, on one occasion on successive weekends, was another. Walley Barnes made his debut early in November, but it was two signings in the subsequent weeks which lifted Arsenal from the bottom of the First Division.

Joe Mercer, who had been in the England team as an attacking wing half at the outbreak of war, was in dispute with Everton. At 32 he had virtually decided to retire from football to concentrate on a grocery business in Wallasey. Surprise interest from Arsenal reawakened his ambition. He signed on one condition, that he could live and train in Liverpool. Allison and Tom Whittaker were not worried about his ageing, bandy legs. They had purchased a football brain, and by converting Mercer to a defensive half back they got full return for an investment of £7,000. Mercer also gave value to his team-mates off the field; it was not unknown for him to arrive in London on a match day with some extra provisions acquired through his grocery connections; in times of severe rationing such generosity made the genial Merseysider even more popular.

Two weeks after Mercer Arsenal added another bargain. At 35 Ronnie Rooke looked an even more unlikely buy, but the short-term need for goals was critical. Rooke struck 21 in 24 League games and the details of his transfer — a fee of £1,000 plus two players moving from Highbury to Fulham — emphasised again the shrewdness of the Arsenal management. Rooke did not finish top scorer. That honour fell to Lewis with a splendid 29 in 28 First Division matches. From the foot of the table the two lifted Arsenal to the respectability of mid-table; in thirteenth place they still finished top of the London pecking order, although in the third match of a five-hour FA Cup third round saga Chelsea finally triumphed on 'neutral' soil at White Hart Lane with two goals from Tommy Lawton.

For two tremendous servants, however, the road had come to an end. Cliff Bastin had been restricted to just six League matches, and he needed a major operation on his middle ear in April 1947. The dreadful winter led to an extension of the season into June. It was too much for an already wearied George Allison who, after

an intimate association with the club of four decades, announced his resignation: 'Now I feel the need for a less strenuous life and I leave the future of Arsenal in other hands.'

Those hands had already cared for so many Arsenal players and other sportsmen of great renown. Tom Whittaker, the master-trainer, had modestly stayed in the background, vastly influential on the football side of the club while Allison had shown his considerable talents in the business and publicity departments. Now, for all his personal reluctance to step into the limelight, the time was right for him to accept the demanding post of secretary-manager.

Bob Wall always recalled Whittaker at work in shirt-sleeves with a pot of tea never far away. A gentle, kindly man, he had spent the war in the RAF. As a qualified engineer he had repaired aircraft, sending them out to battle again with the painstaking detail which had aided the recovery of so many Arsenal footballers. Having fought in the First World War, he was awarded the MBE for secret work in connection with the D-Day landings in the Second.

Joe Shaw returned from Chelsea, where he had been assistant manager, to become Tom Whittaker's right-hand man. The 1947–48 season began with a temporary captain. Les Compton still had cricket responsibilities for Middlesex, so Joe Mercer led out Arsenal for the opening League game at home to Sunderland. The pitch had been reseeded, the running track around it re-surfaced. There was optimism in the air and it was to be well-founded.

The playing strength was augmented by two more signings. Archie Macaulay from Brentford had starred for Scotland at Wembley the previous April and also represented Great Britain against the Rest of Europe. The cultured, red-haired wing half had much of the spirit of the Scottish terriers depicted on the lucky charm he carried with him all the time.

After much persuading — Whittaker made eleven trips to see him before the deal was done — forward Don Roper arrived from Southampton and a football family. His grandfather played for Chesterfield, his father for Huddersfield Town and Royal Marines, with whom he won an Amateur Cup medal. Rejection by Hampshire County Cricket Club after trials during the summer of 1947 had sharpened Roper's appetite to make a career in football.

What was to become a historic season began on 23 August with a 3.30 kick-off at Highbury against Sunderland. Three goals, from Ian McPherson, Jimmy Logie and Rooke, all in the opening 15 minutes of the second half, produced a 3–1 victory. Four days later Charlton were swept aside 4–2 at The Valley, with McPherson running riot against the FA Cup holders, scoring one and laying on the other three for Roper, Lewis and Logie. The Scottish winger had returned to football with impressive war-time credentials as an RAF pilot, his bravery winning him the DFC and bar. Though naturally an

outside right, his early contributions to Whittaker's bright start to the season were on the opposite flank.

A third successive victory came at Bramall Lane, Rooke levelling the score before Roper's 35-yarder was fumbled by the home goalkeeper Smith with only three minutes remaining. Reg Lewis then took centre stage with four goals — Rooke claimed the other two — in a 6–0 demolition of Charlton in the return match at Highbury; the visitors were handicapped by an eighth-minute injury to defender Peter Croker who went off with knee ligaments damaged trying to curb McPherson.

The buoyant mood at Highbury was maintained by news from Hastings that Denis Compton had struck the 17th century of his golden summer representing the South of England against the touring South Africans — and by the prospect of Manchester United's forthcoming visit to challenge the 100 per cent record that had lifted Arsenal to the top of the First Division. Ten thousand fans were still outside when the gates were closed and they missed another victory, by 2–1 with goals from the forceful pairing of Rooke and Lewis. The sense of expectation at the club was highlighted even more by the decision of Bryn Jones to turn down a move to Newport County. 'I'll stay until they chase me away, first team or not,' was the retort of the skilful Welsh international for whom the advent of war had forever rendered theoretical the question of whether his record transfer fee was justified.

For the first time Arsenal extended a sequence of wins at the start of a season to six — Bolton Wanderers, the next victims, were defeated 2–0 at Highbury. McPherson and a Rooke penalty contributed the goals in a match which Arsenal finished with only seven fit men. Lewis, recently watched by England selectors, pulled a thigh muscle after ten minutes. Before half-time Alf Fields strained tendons leaping over his own goalkeeper, George Swindin. Rooke and McPherson were also limping at the end of the match. Tom Whittaker sensed the need for the return of Les Compton, who had been given permission to continue his cricket with Middlesex.

The tall wicket-keeper was back in the Arsenal dressing room at Deepdale for match number seven and, as club captain, was given a ball by Whittaker to lead out the team. Modestly Compton passed it to Mercer saying: 'If you don't mind Tom, I think Joe should have this. He's not done too badly with the job so far.' Thus Mercer retained the captaincy which was to bring more than a touch of romance to the twilight days of his career. Without Lewis at the sharp end of the attack the first point was dropped at Preston in a goalless draw, but the following week Stoke City were on the receiving end of a three-goal first-half performance, with Bryn Jones enjoying a rare first-team appearance.

Lewis was back but Mercer missing because of food poisoning for a tough trip to Burnley,

which brought a hard-fought success, with Barnes making one desperate clearance off the line. The winning goal from Lewis came against the balance of play. With two reserves, Paddy Sloan and the loyal George Male, as wing halves, Arsenal could only draw the next match at home to Portsmouth, but victory had been there for the taking when Rooke's 39th-minute penalty was brilliantly saved by Butler.

Goals remained hard to come by throughout October, a time when the flair of Denis Compton might have added an extra spice to Whittaker's recipe for success. But Britain's most glamorous sports star was confined to a hospital bed for the removal of some floating body from a troublesome knee. Aston Villa's visit to Highbury drew a 61,000 capacity crowd and a 1–0 win, but the goal was disputed with Rooke getting away with a push on centre half Moss before racing clear to score. A thumping penalty from Rooke brought a share of the points at Molineux — Roper fouled by Shorthouse — after Jesse Pye had given Wolves the lead right on half-time. It was a penalty against Arsenal, conceded by Leslie Compton and converted by Eddie Wainwright, that cost a point in the next match against Everton at Highbury. The brilliance of visiting goalkeeper Ted Sagar had restricted Arsenal to a solitary score from Lewis in the 65th minute.

With football such an attraction after the sacrifices of war, Arsenal, as First Division leaders, had already become the major draw. Stamford Bridge played host to a crowd of 67,277 for Chelsea's clash with the Gunners on 1 November. Astonishingly some 27,000 also watched the reserve game between the two clubs at Highbury on the same afternoon; the appearance of Tommy Lawton in the Chelsea second string heightened the appeal of the fixture.

In the senior match Arsenal came away with a goalless draw, the unbeaten record still intact. It remained so seven days later when Blackpool, with Mortensen and Matthews, were beaten 2–1 at Highbury through another Rooke penalty and a goal for Don Roper. That week — in November 1947 — the Football Association had written to all clubs with warnings about hooliganism! Before the Blackpool match Tom Whittaker addressed the Highbury crowd with a request to 'Keep up your reputation for sportsmanship. Don't barrack the referee.'

Arsenal's colours were lowered 4–3 by the Racing Club in Paris, when the traditional meeting reached unprecedented heights of excitement — but the League record still had two more matches to run. A splendidly struck 25-yard drive from Rooke brought back both points from Blackburn Rovers, then Rooke was also a scorer along with the diminutive Logie in a 2–0 Highbury triumph over Huddersfield Town.

With more than a third of the season gone Arsenal stood proudly six points clear of Burnley at the top of the tree, with a record of: Played 17, Won 12, Drawn 5, Lost 0, goals for 31, against 8. Yet the tag of 'lucky' was still being pinned on the team. Public opinion held the view that progress had come from efficient organisation and defensive discipline rather than football of a higher level than the opposition.

Thus the inevitable first defeat, on 29 November at Derby County, did not come as shattering news. The Baseball Ground was packed to the rafters to see the pursuit of a record (22 games unbeaten from the start of a season) held by Preston and Sheffield United collapse to a goal in the 32nd minute. Steel and Morris both had shots blocked but finally the loose ball was despatched past Swindin by winger Reg Harrison.

A goal in the same minute a week later, by Black of Manchester City at Highbury, threatened another defeat, but five minutes from time Les McDowall, who was later to manage the Maine Road club, was penalised for hand-ball. Rooke sent his penalty unerringly past Frank Swift, and there was no disputing that, on this occasion, Arsenal were fortunate.

In such circumstances a visit to bottom club, Grimsby Town, could only be viewed as a welcome opportunity to return to the groove of earlier in the season. The Blundell Park club had conceded three goals per match on average over the first half of the seaon; Arsenal managed four through the reliable Rooke 2, Logie and Roper.

The Saturday before Christmas has now been accepted an an attendance low spot with the demands of shopping for the festivities ahead. It was not so in 1947 when more than 58,000 flocked to Roker Park to watch Arsenal in the flesh. The vast majority of them almost had an early holiday treat when Davis sent Sunderland into the lead with only ten minutes remaining, but five minutes later the limping Barnes, a passenger at centre forward, helped create an equaliser. Bryn Jones was to play only seven times in the Championship season but his Roker Park equaliser, his solitary goal of the campaign, held great significance; a second defeat with the congested holiday fixture list ahead might have badly disturbed the Arsenal momentum.

Instead the two Christmas matches produced typically contrary results. The Football League in pre-computer days, with scant regard for the family life of footballers, paired Arsenal home and away with Liverpool! Only Mercer with his Merseyside base could have relished the Christmas morning start at Anfield, but the team responded to the challenge with two goals from Rooke and another from Roper which ended Liverpool's unbeaten home record. Two days later though, revenge was claimed. Albert Stubbins and Billy Liddell struck to stop Arsenal's invincible run at Highbury; Lewis replied too late to salvage a draw from a match for which touts did a roaring trade, with reports of tickets valued at 7s. 6d. (37p) changing hands at more than four times that price!

On New Year's Day, Arsenal, 1–0 winners at Bolton, stood five points clear at the top. Thirty-seven-year-old George Male was pressed into

service at Burnden Park and gave a sound performance. Bolton claimed that they had equalised a 32nd minute goal from Lewis in a late scramble when the ball appeared to have crossed the line before Swindin pulled it clear. The crowd was allowed in only half an hour before an early start on a pitch flooded by melted snow and the referee dispensed with the half-time interval.

Arsenal's quest for football honour continued with a 3–2 victory over Sheffield United in the last game of the holiday programme. United were down to ten men when Rooke grabbed an important second goal; the player off the field was Alex Forbes, the flame-haired wing half shortly to return to Highbury as part of Whittaker's team strengthening. Forbes had been concussed and remembered nothing of his return to the pitch, during which time United scored twice in the last five minutes to give the scoreline a rather flattering look.

With the FA Cup providing a new challenge and a break to the slog for the Championship, Tom Whittaker was not the sort of man to underestimate a kindly draw, a home tie with Second Division Bradford Park Avenue. Consequently, he took his players to Brighton (shades of pre-war delights) for a few days' preparation in the bracing sea air. It did not have the desired effect. In Billy Elliott, the Yorkshire club possessed a locally born left winger who would later play for England after a transfer to Burnley; the 22-year-old Elliott knocked in a first-half goal. Bradford also included a centre half whose involvement in post-war football would span almost 40 years, many at a very high level of influence. Ron Greenwood became the cornerstone of Bradford's rearguard action in that third round tie at Highbury, and Arsenal's FA Cup ambitions perished.

There was little time for despondency. The next two First Division opponents also had their eyes on the League title, Manchester United and Preston. United still played their home matches at Maine Road, because of war damage at Old Trafford, and the interest in the visit of the leaders was massive. More than 80,000 crammed into the ground for a game that finished level after Lewis had drawn first blood and Jack Rowley equalised. The attendance remains the highest ever recorded for a Football League fixture, to be precise, 83,260.

Lewis was now operating at inside right and he retained the position for the tussle with Preston, striking two more valuable goals. Rooke was also on target, while Don Roper enjoyed an inspired afternoon. With those three important points in the bag since the Cup disappointment, Arsenal continued to set a blistering pace at the top of the League. In February Stoke City took the unusual step of making their home match all-ticket against the leaders, but the 41,000 ticket-holders did not witness a goal, largely due to a succession of saves from Swindin.

For the Valentine's Day fixture against Burnley, the Arsenal team appropriately contained a touch of romance. Denis Compton, who had turned out in only one post-war League match, was called into the senior side in place of the injured McPherson. For such a charismatic performer it was a perfect opportunity against a side which came to Highbury needing a win to close the gap at the top. Compton's return captured the imagination of the paying public; 20,000 arrived too late to get into the packed ground and with shades of Wembley 1923 a policeman mounted on a white horse strove to maintain order in the streets around Highbury.

It took Compton only fourteen minutes to play his part. His lob was punched by goalkeeper Strong straight to Roper who drove the ball into the Burnley net. Rooke added two more, with Compton also involved in the move that led to Arsenal's third goal. With 13 matches still to play, the Gunners now held an eight-point advantage over their closest challengers.

Meanwhile, Tom Whittaker had not grown complacent about the depth of talent at the club. Because of the immediate post-war circumstances Arsenal were fielding one of the oldest sides ever to win the Championship, with Rooke, now 36, Les Compton 35 and Mercer 33 holding three of the key roles. Quietly, Whittaker was adding to his staff. Cliff Holton, an amateur from Oxford City, was signed in November 1947. Peter Goring, eternally to be dubbed as the butcher's boy, gave up his part-time football with Cheltenham Town to join the Arsenal staff the following January, and the next month a senior player arrived in the shape of Alex Forbes, whose swashbuckling performances for Sheffield United had often caught the eye of the Highbury crowd.

Forbes' debut was delayed until after the third defeat of the League campaign, at Aston Villa on 28 February, which should really not have happened at all. An own goal by Moss and another from Rooke gave Arsenal a 2–1 lead when Denis Compton was tripped in the Villa penalty area. Rooke put his penalty wide, and Villa revelled in the second chance they had been given. Les Compton had been injured in training and played with one leg strapped from ankle to knee. In Trevor Ford, the fiery Welsh international, the home side had the perfect forward to capitalise on a weak link. Ford roasted his marker, and scored twice as Villa raced home 4–2.

Alex Forbes was chosen at inside left for his debut, with Wolves the opposition on a foggy Highbury afternoon. Many of the crowd were still settling down when Hancocks caught Arsenal cold with a goal after 80 seconds, but Forbes immediately began to justify his £12,000 transfer fee. His equaliser in the eighth minute delighted his new supporters and his dance back to the centre won him a place in their hearts. It was a tremendous start for a player who had once turned his back on football in favour of ice hockey. Whittaker had sent Macaulay to persuade him come to Highbury when Forbes was in hospital recovering from appendicitis.

Wolves led again but with Denis Compton in irrepressible form in the second half Arsenal bounced back to win 5–2. A week later at Goodison Park the cricketing footballer did even better, scoring his first two post-war League goals in a 2–0 triumph over Everton.

After only three defeats in 32 games, it came as a surprise that two more followed in the next three matches. The first came at Highbury where Chelsea chalked up a 2–0 victory. John Harris did a magnificent job containing Rooke and Chelsea carried enough venom in their attack to strike through Bobby Campbell and Roy Bentley. The other loss was sustained at Blackpool, where two goals from Stan Mortensen took him to the top of the First Division scorers list, with one more than the 27 of Rooke, who had to observe at close quarters his tally being overtaken.

A week earlier fate had not been kind to Bob Anderson, whose misfortune it was to make his League debut in the Middlesbrough goal against Arsenal at Highbury. Smarting from the home defeat by Chelsea, Arsenal confronted the untried keeper in a mean mood. Among the seven goals that flashed past Anderson were two more from Denis Compton, and a hat-trick from Rooke, which was completed when he headed a tentative clearance from the goalkeeper straight back past him. So one-sided was the match that newspaper reports at the time make reference to several thousand supporters leaving at half-time. Poor Bob Anderson, for whom Good Friday in 1948 hardly lived up to that billing; he never played again in the First Division, although he did reappear in League football in the 1950s with Crystal Palace, Bristol Rovers and Bristol City. Goodfellow, the regular keeper that season, had returned on the Easter Monday when Arsenal made the long journey to Ayresome Park. Rooke had to settle this time for just one goal and Middlesbrough recovered some dignity in a 1–1 draw.

With fewer and fewer fixtures available for the chasing pack to close on their prey, Arsenal moved a step nearer to safety by completing the double over Blackburn Rovers at Highbury, Logie's sixth goal of the season and Rooke's 29th providing a margin of sufficient comfort; on 10 April Arsenal took the field at Huddersfield nine points clear with just five matches left. A win at Leeds Road would see Whittaker's men breasting the tape. The conclusion, however, was not so decisive.

A goal from Don Roper brought only one point, and the players had to bath and change so quickly to catch the London train that they could not discover the day's other results. It was Denis Compton who broke the glad tidings. At Doncaster he ran for a paper which reported defeats for Manchester United, Burnley and Derby County. Arsenal were Champions, and had led from start to finish. George Male, the last of the great pre-war side, played at Huddersfield, and as ever turned in a highly polished performance.

Inevitably anti-climax followed, with Derby winning at Highbury the following Saturday, and two successive goalless draws at Portsmouth and Manchester City. There was, however, a celebration on 1 May, though only 35,000, the smallest home gate of the season, were there to see it. Yorkshire-born Lionel Smith was given his League baptism at centre half, but it was the attack which made the headlines. Arsenal ripped into Grimsby to the tune of 8–0, and four goals for Rooke confirmed him, with 33, as the Football League's leading scorer — and this at the age of 36! Grimsby were scuppered into the Second Division and are still waiting to return.

George Swindin had conceded only 32 goals in the full League programme and added a second Championship medal to that gained in 1938. Rooke was the only other ever-present, though Macaulay, Mercer and Roper missed just two matches and Logie and Laurie Scott three. Les Compton collected a League winners' medal to go with his memento of cricket championship success the previous September (a rare double). So too did brother Denis, though he had to wait until October to receive his because of doubts as to whether his 14 appearances were sufficient qualification (hereafter 14 was regarded as the acceptable minimum).

Undoubtedly the tremendous consistency of the big-hearted Rooke proved to be a marvellous attribute throughout the season, but much of Arsenal's success came from the reliability of their defensive method. Joe Mercer labelled it as the 'retreating' defence. The prevailing style of the day was to try to win the ball in midfield with an attempted tackle on the opponent in possession. If that tackle was lost then there was little sophisticated covering. Mercer, with Macaulay as a shrewd ally, preferred Arsenal to leave the ball with the opposition and back off, packing the centre of the defence. Arsenal's captain had noted the success of such manoeuvres in basketball during the war, when he'd played service games with Americans. The crowd did not always like the tactic, newspaper comment denounced it as negative, but the rest of the First Division, with the exception of Derby County, who beat Arsenal twice, could not fathom out a solution. The seven-point margin at the end of the season was ample testimony to Arsenal's worth as champions. It was no more than an extension of everything Chapman had taught the club.

The players presented Tom Whittaker with a silver cigarette box inscribed 'To Tom/In Appreciation/From The Boys'. The manager, however, was already aware that the side had not been built to last. Before the end of May 1948 he had acquired the potential of Doug Lishman, a regular scorer for Walsall in the Third Division South. Nevertheless, the 1948–49 season began with the air still full of anti-climax. It took a run of wins in the autumn to lift the club from the bottom half of the table to fifth place, where Arsenal stayed. Derby County again proved to be a bogey team, taking three of the four League

points and knocking Whittaker's side out of the FA Cup at the Baseball Ground in the fourth round.

One match did stand out, an extravagant 4–3 victory in the Charity Shield against the Cup holders Manchester United at Highbury. Incredibly Arsenal led 3–0 after just five minutes — Jones, Lewis and Rooke — but United's resolve stood the test. Lewis scored again for Arsenal, a splendid solo goal, but the destiny of the Charity Shield was not finally settled until the last blast of the referee's whistle.

Rooke's magnificent contribution to the history of Arsenal Football Club ended in June 1949. Sixty-eight goals in 88 First Division games were ample evidence of his contribution. At 37 he refused to contemplate retirement, and moved as player-manager to Cystal Palace, his pre-war club, where he paid his way in goals for two more seasons. A man of iron who never flinched from the physical contact of those who tried to stop him, he left Highbury with the satisfaction of having more than answered the call of George Allison: 'Ronnie, we're in trouble. We've got to get goals, by hook or by Rooke.'

The other half of the duo who turned the tide at Highbury in 1946 remained at the club. Joe Mercer passed his 35th birthday during pre-season training prior to the 1949–50 season, and if one target drove him to continue playing it was a search for the honour which had eluded him, an FA Cup winners' medal. Mercer had been a young reserve at Everton when they had won the most romantic of the game's trophies in 1933. The following day a kindly Albert Geldard, who had played in that final, was cleaning his boots beside Mercer at Goodison Park and offered the youthful Mercer a piece of Wembley turf. 'No thanks, I'll get some myself one day,' was the confident reply. It seemed that those words would haunt him.

Four defeats in the opening five matches may well have concentrated the players' minds on the FA Cup; the only win during that dismal start had come at Chelsea where Peter Goring scored on his debut and Swindin captained the side in the absence of Mercer and Les Compton. Brother Denis had ended speculation that he had played his last for Arsenal by signing for the new season on the eve of the third Test against New Zealand, thus becoming one of 54 professionals on the staff.

League performances improved sufficiently to achieve a respectable sixth place at the end of the season but it was the Cup which cheered all at Highbury. A run began which contained all the superstitions and omens which somehow surround the competition. For example, it began on an anniversary. Sheffield Wednesday came to north London on 7 January 1950, sixteen years virtually to the day when they had been the opposition for an Arsenal devastated by the loss of Herbert Chapman. In 1950, that was an anniversary remembered as if it were yesterday.

Now, in the FA Cup third round, they were in-form opponents, unbeaten for three months.

Their team-work almost came to their rescue in spite of losing right back Vince Kenny, injured in the tie. Reg Lewis finally made the breakthrough with 13 seconds left on the referee's watch. Oddly the crowd was ten thousand less than capacity because publicity suggesting a huge attendance had deterred many from what they believed would be a wasted journey.

The signs remained good in the draw for the fourth round, another home game against Swansea Town, who were labouring in the lower half of the Second Division. On a frosty pitch the underdogs performed gallantly while Arsenal again looked anything but potential winners of the competition. The decisive goal in a fortunate 2–1 win came ironically from a Welshman. Keane handled and Walley Barnes, whose career had been rescued from persistent knee trouble by little more than his own strength of will, slotted the penalty past the left hand of goalkeeper Jack Parry.

George Swindin, the dry Yorkshireman who had been signed from Bradford City in 1936, had added the role of prophet to his more usual occupation of goalkeeper. Before each round so far he had foretold that Arsenal would be given a home tie. Again his words rang true when Burnley came out of the hat to visit Highbury in round five. In a small way the visitors had contributed to the Cup aspirations of the team they now faced, because on the opening day of the season it had been Burnley who had beaten Arsenal in the capital and thus set the Highbury League campaign off on a flat note.

The lure of the Cup, not for the first or last time, produced an indulgence in preparation. There was no seaside training in the traditional manner; instead the Arsenal squad were treated to sessions under sunray equipment to tone them up. Goals from Lewis and Denis Compton did the trick, though Mercer remembers getting away with hand-ball in his own goalmouth.

Swindin forecast another home draw with the added prediction that Leeds United would be the opposition. Incredibly it came true, and it looked as though, in football parlance, Arsenal's 'name was on the FA Cup'. Leeds also languished in the Second Division, but their reaction to a first Cup tie at Highbury produced a creditable display. Lewis, who was to finish behind Goring in the League charts, added to his catalogue of significant Cup goals by darting between two defenders to score. Arsenal were into the semi-finals and they had not been forced to leave Highbury to get there.

A semi-final pairing with Chelsea meant that they still did not have to leave North London, and the saga of the tie remains as memorable as the final itself. At White Hart Lane Chelsea brought back the former England international Len Goulden; at 37 he had been out of favour for six months. When Chelsea sprinted into a 2–0 lead after 25 minutes, both goals from Bentley, Goulden must have been dreaming of a fairytale visit to Wembley. Arsenal had other ideas, although it needed an outright stroke of good

fortune to help put those ideas into effect.

Outside right Freddie Cox knew White Hart Lane well; he had been signed from Spurs in September 1949 in an attempt to halt the slide at the start of the season. The best years of his footballing life had been sacrificed in wartime when he had flown Dakotas in Transport Command. His interest in aerial subjects extended to birds; Freddie was a keen ornithologist. In the semi-final he took a corner, the aerodynamics of which must have surprised even him.

In the dying seconds of the first half Cox struck this corner with the outside of his foot. The ball veered in towards the Chelsea goal and was over the line before Harry Medhurst, the goalkeeper, made a vain attempt to keep it out. Cox, who died in 1973 after a career in League management, never claimed any deliberate intent, but Arsenal gratefully accepted the touch of luck, and came out for the second half in determined vein.

Yet with a quarter of an hour remaining they were still trailing. Another corner, this time from the left wing, came to the rescue. Again the goal had a story behind it. As Denis Compton prepared to take the flag kick he waved forward brother Leslie. Joe Mercer countered by telling the centre half to stay back, but blood being thicker than water and the need for an equaliser pressing, Compton the elder ignored his captain's instructions. The fraternal pair emphatically won the argument when Denis' corner found the forehead of Les and the ball sped into the Chelsea net. On balance of play Arsenal had been fortunate to earn a replay, but this had been Chelsea's chance and it had gone.

Arsenal's form was much improved in the replay, which also took place at Tottenham, the following Wednesday. George Swindin's ability to predict the future passed, it seemed, to Eileen, the wife of Freddie Cox. On the Tuesday night she dreamed that her husband would score

the goal that took Arsenal to Wembley. And so he did, but not until the 14th minute of extra time, with his weaker left foot.

The journey to the Empire Stadium, therefore, became the longest Arsenal had had to make in the entire Cup run. By an odd coincidence Liverpool had reached the final without leaving Lancashire, beating Blackburn at Anfield, after a replay, winning home ties against Exeter, Stockport and Blackpool, then a semi-final success, of extra satisfaction, over Everton at Maine Road, Manchester. Bob Paisley, later to become the most successful of all Liverpool managers, had scored the vital goal against Everton, but he was left out of the team for the final. His only memento was to be in the Wembley match programme, in which he was listed as left half.

That job in the Arsenal team went of course to Mercer, with most of the country's neutrals hoping that one of the game's most-loved characters would at last complete his collection of medals. Yet unwittingly Arsenal's captain found himself in the midst of a potentially embarrassing situation. He had continued to train in the north-west — with Liverpool! Understandably he was asked not to join the Liverpool first team at Anfield for fear that he would find out too much about their Wembley battleplan. He was not banned from the ground, but his access was restricted to afternoon sessions, often with Jimmy Melia, who was then on the Liverpool groundstaff.

Liverpool were managed by George Kay, West Ham's captain in the first Wembley final in 1923. Kay had nurtured a team the majority of whom had come through the ranks, notably the Scottish international forward Billy Liddell. Liddell, reckoned the Arsenal players, was the most likely barrier to their winning the Cup. Moreover, Liverpool held an important psychological advantage. They had won both League meetings with Arsenal, 2–1 at Highbury in

The goals that brought the Cup back to Highbury in 1950, both scored by inside left Reg Lewis. Both the first (top right) and second (bottom right) were sharp breaks which left Liverpool keeper Cyril Sidlow with little chance. It had been a good Cup year for Arsenal; they were drawn at home throughout, played both semis against Chelsea at White Hart Lane and thus never left London. Twenty-one years later, when they again met Liverpool in the final, they were drawn away in every round and compounded this by again reaching the final the following year without a single home draw (photographs by courtesy of *The Sunday Times*).

George Swindin saves at the near post from Liverpool right-winger Jimmy Payne's diving header during the 1950 FA Cup final. It was the closest Liverpool came, Arsenal winning the match 2-0 for their third success in the competition. The defenders are Joe Mercer and Leslie Compton, wearing the unfamiliar orange or old gold (the dye was somewhere between the two) change strip that, unusually, Arsenal adopted for the final.

September, 2–0 at Anfield on New Year's Eve.

On the eve of the final itself Mercer was hailed Footballer of the Year by the Football Writers' Association. Tom Whittaker had already decided upon his team. Lishman, McPherson, Macaulay and Roper had their merits considered but were passed over; Goring kept his place, the Wembley setting being a perfect ending to his first season at senior level, and his mother, father and seven of his eleven brothers and sisters travelled up from the West Country to see the match.

Rain fell heavily on 29 April 1950. Wembley was bursting at the seams, though the ticket allocation for each club ran to only 11,500 (4,500 seats, 7,000 standing) of the 100,000 capacity stadium. Arsenal assembled in the North dressing-room where a telephone link enabled the betting members of the team, of whom there were several, to settle their nerves with calls to their bookmakers about that afternoon's racing.

Both teams had to change from their usual red shirts; Liverpool opted for white with black shorts, Arsenal took the field in shirts of old gold with white shorts. Two pre-match decisions

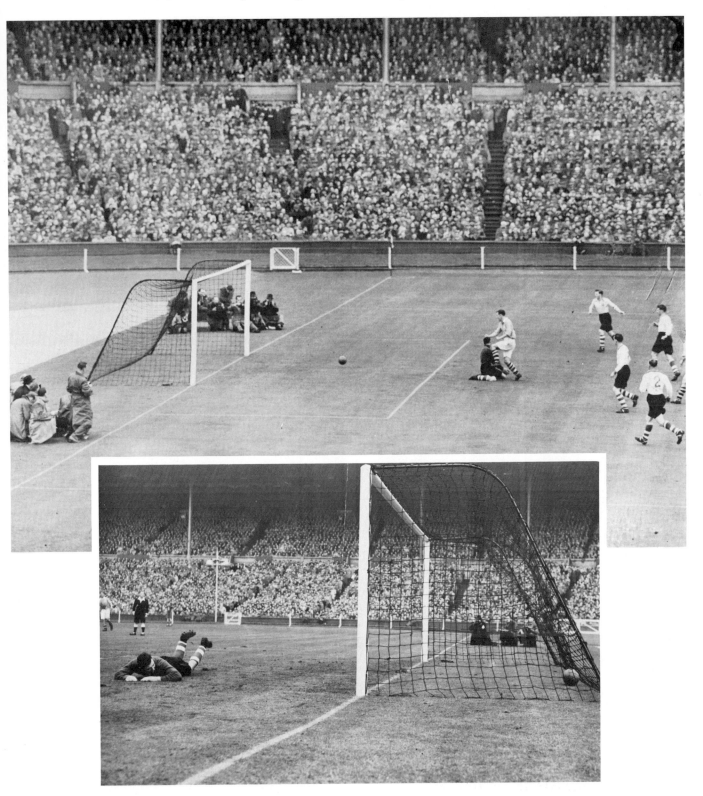

The victorious 1950 Cup winning team; from left to right: Reg Lewis (scorer of the two goals), Freddie Cox, Peter Goring, Walley Barnes, Denis Compton, George Swindin, Joe Mercer (with the Cup), Laurie Scott, Alex Forbes, Leslie Compton and Jimmy Logie.

A mood of grey austerity presides over the Highbury of 1950 as Leslie Compton, Joe Mercer and the Cup depart for a triumphal tour of North London (photograph by courtesy of *The Sunday Times*).

helped turn the tide of the battle towards the north London club. Forbes had been given the task of subduing the threat of Liddell, and after some early alarms the forceful wing half, who had been recalled by Scotland two weeks before the final, coped splendidly.

An even more significant decision had been to keep faith with the 30-year-old Reg Lewis. It had not been taken lightly. Lewis undoubtedly scored goals, but at times he could look lazy and lethargic. His skill had not been in question from the moment he had begun his League career with a debut goal against Everton on New Year's Day 1938. Yet Whittaker often dropped him, and Mercer's voice among others was heard in defence of Lewis before his place was finally confirmed.

At Wembley he became the match-winner, collecting both goals, coincidentally for a father of twins, at identical times in each half. The first, after 17 minutes, came when Goring moved away, distracting the attention of Liverpool defenders. Jimmy Logie had the ball at his feet; the tiny inside right, who weighed little more than nine stone but was a giant in this match, immediately slotted a pass through a square defence for Lewis to chase.

It was a knife into the heart of Liverpool. Lewis comprehensively beat their Welsh international goalkeeper Cyril Sidlow. Seventeen minutes into the second half it was Lewis again, this time with assistance from Cox, and from then on there was little doubt that Joe Mercer would at last lay his hands on the FA Cup.

The medal to go with it almost escaped Arsenal's captain. His Majesty King George VI presented the trophy, and the personal memento came from the Queen. Joe was just about to go down the Royal Box steps with a *loser's* medal when the error was spotted.

One Arsenal player did retire a few days later but it was not Joe Mercer. Approaching his 32nd birthday Denis Compton realised that the combination of international cricket, top-flight football and a knee that was protesting more and more about wear and tear was no longer viable. He had already decided to abdicate from football before the Cup final, a fact used to Arsenal's advantage by Tom Whittaker at half-time at Wembley.

Compton's first-half contribution had been less than memorable. 'Now,' said the Arsenal manager, weighing each word carefully, 'you've got 45 minutes left of your soccer career. I want you to go out there and give it every ounce you possibly can.' Denis Compton rarely lacked confidence, but this time he needed fortification. A glass of whisky was produced, and Arsenal's outside left played a full part in a strong second half performance. Nor was it quite his football finale. The following week Portsmouth came to Highbury needing points to win the Championship. Compton gave a brilliant performance; Goring scored twice in a 2–0 victory, though Pompey eventually took the title.

While Denis Compton, after knee surgery,

turned his thoughts towards representing England's cricketers in Australia in 1950–51 (a tour which incidentally also robbed Arsenal of the services of an aspiring inside forward, Brian Close, who had been signed from Leeds United) football's international selectors sought the services of Les Compton. On 15 November 1950 at the astonishing age of 38 Arsenal's veteran centre half represented his country for the first time, England's oldest international debutant. England beat Wales 4–2 at Sunderland with Lionel Smith also winning his first cap and Ray Daniel, Compton's club deputy, called up for Wales. Compton retained his place a week later when Yugoslavia forced a 2–2 draw at Highbury, but the next international was five months later so a short but remarkable international career was over.

Arsenal led the First Division at the half-way mark of the 1950–51 season, but two injuries on Christmas Day against Stoke City turned a Championship sprint into a stumble. Lishman broke a leg, thus robbing the team of its leading scorer; four of his 16 goals had come in one match against Sunderland in November. Swindin was also hurt, allowing Ted Platt an extended run in goal. Although Whittaker turned again to Lewis — who typically responded with a sequence of four games in each of which he scored twice — and for the first time to the raw Holton, the team unit did not function as smoothly in the second half of the season. Arsenal finished fifth in the League, which was won for the first time by Spurs, and lost their grip on the FA Cup to a Stan Pearson goal for Manchester United in the fifth round.

Arsenal's Double of 1970–71 is of course well documented in this history and elsewhere. Less easily recalled are the events of the 1951–52 season when the Gunners stood three games away from what would have been the first Double of modern times. Had those three games been won instead of lost the season would have been legendary. Instead it was a marvellously bold attempt which foundered in the final analysis on injuries.

Swindin had shrugged aside his injury from the previous year and played a full season in goal, Barnes was absent for just one League game though the fallibility of his knee became a major factor in the last chapter of the story. Mercer, Forbes, Logie and Roper added further threads of continuity. By now Daniel had superseded Compton at centre half, and the goalscoring department lay at the feet and heads of Lishman and Holton. The cricket connection had not entirely disappeared with the Comptons; Arthur Milton, the Gloucestershire batsman, operated on the right wing on a semi-regular basis. Indeed after just 13 League appearances he played for England against Austria, and though his football career did not develop to the heights promised he opened the innings for his country, joining the distinguished list of double internationals.

Progress in the First Division was steady,

always in the challenging bunch of clubs, occasionally on top. Lishman enjoyed a golden spell of hat-tricks in three consecutive home games; Fulham, West Bromwich Albion and Bolton were his victims. The League matches were punctuated by occasional prestige friendlies, with floodlights installed at the ground, treating the Highbury faithful to the new experience of watching evening matches. The ground also enclosed the biggest post-war attendance at the club; the visit of Spurs luring 72,164 to see whether the Champions could be toppled.

The FA Cup run began at Carrow Road, where Norwich City could not rise up above their Third Division South status. Barnsley in round four provided no more testing opposition; Lewis, now a weapon to be used only occasionally, added to his personal store of Cup-tie memories with a first-half hat-trick. Lishman claimed the other in another confident triumph.

On paper the fifth round draw brought a more testing problem. Leyton Orient in the lower reaches of the Third Division South were on the giant-killing trail. The homely East London club had beaten two high-flying Second Division outfits, Birmingham City and Everton, both slain on their own territory. Now the 'O's' were at home and the prospect of a meeting with Arsenal attracted massive interest.

Whittaker's side, however, did not capitulate, although Lewis was injured scoring the first goal and limped through more than half the match; averaging a goal a game in the League at the time plus his four in the FA Cup, he might have forced his way into another Cup final team until this misfortune. Arsenal, however, coped easily with the handicap at Brisbane Road, and Lishman hit two more to kill off the giant-killers.

Arsenal had to travel again in the sixth round, again not very far and the draw against Second Division Luton Town meant that the top clubs were again avoided. After only nine minutes Luton became the first side to put the ball past Swindin in the 1952 FA Cup. Moore headed in a corner taken by Mitchell. Without Jimmy Logie to orchestrate their midfield play, Arsenal were still trailing at the interval, during which Whittaker reshuffled his forward line.

Freddie Cox was switched to the left wing and lived up to his billing as a Cup tie specialist. Arthur Milton came back to his sparkling best. Cox equalised from a very acute angle and with Luton handicapped by injuries to Davies and Owen the match tilted away from them. Three goals inside five minutes completed the scoring with Cox cutting in again to find the back of the net from an oblique position and then crossing for Milton to collect Arsenal's third. A penalty

The crowd rather than the players is the focus of this unusual shot taken on 16 September 1950. Peter Goring (number 9) is seen completing his hat-trick in a 6-2 thrashing of traditional rivals Huddersfield. Jimmy Logie and Doug Lishman got the others.

from Mitchell was Luton's last reply in a rivetting match.

What Mrs Cox dreamed before the semi-final has not been recorded but the match certainly produced a case of *deja vu* for her husband. Again Chelsea provided the opposition. Again White Hart Lane was the venue. And again the first match, postponed this time by snow from its original date, finished in a draw. In truth it rarely held the imagination of the crowd; no corners in the first hour during which Arsenal scored in the 35th minute. Almost inevitably Cox was the marksman, served with a touch of subtlety by Logie. Chelsea equalised 27 minutes from the final whistle through Billy Gray.

Forty-eight hours later the teams reassembled at Tottenham, and, as two years earlier, Arsenal won through, this time 3–0. The Cox-Logie combination eased the tensions by conjuring an early goal, and Cox broke the back of the Chelsea resistance with his second 20 minutes from time. Roper, operating at outside left, took his only corner in either game and the diminutive Cox found space to head home. Lishman made sure of Arsenal's return to Wembley with another header.

The final itself offered a showdown between the competition's two most recent super-powers, the holders Newcastle United against the winners from the previous year. It was a match which had statisticians trotting out comparisons with 20 years earlier. Then Arsenal had been beaten in the 'over the line' match in which Newcastle had become the first side to concede the opening goal in a Wembley final and come from behind to win.

In 1932 Arsenal had also sought the Double, only to fall between the two stools of cliché. They also had to meet Newcastle at home in the League between the semi-final and final just as they had to do in the fixture-congested April of 1952 (drawing 1–1 with Milton, who did not play at Wembley, Arsenal's goalscorer). By then injuries were beginning to damage hopes of bringing the League title to Highbury.

On Good Friday, 11 April, Ray Daniel broke his arm in a goalless draw at Blackpool. The next day Lionel Smith wrenched a knee at Bolton; Arsenal lost 2–1. Leslie Compton stepped out of the shadows to help out in the crisis.

Three home games brought a fine return of five points, but at the cost of wearying key players. Mercer felt the strain so keenly that Whittaker persuaded his captain to stand down from the crucial visit to West Bromwich Albion, the clubs eighth game in 17 days. Understandably the flesh was weak, even if the spirit was strong. Albion won 3–1 with Arsenal giving Scottish forward Jimmy W. Robertson his only First Division outing.

That defeat effectively ended the League challenge; only a seven-goal victory at Old Trafford on the Saturday before the Cup Final would take the title from Manchester United. Reg Lewis turned out for his last senior appearance; Lionel Smith proved his recovery from injury; but United celebrated their title with a runaway 6–1 victory. Nor did Arsenal escape unscathed physically. Arthur Shaw, who might have pipped Daniel for the centre half spot in the Wembley line-up, suffered a fractured wrist, a similar injury to his rival. Nevertheless, had the Gunners won those two last games, against West Bromwich and United, they would have been champions.

Newcastle United's passage over the run-in to the final had been as smooth as Arsenal's had been choppy. Moreover, the holders were able to relax at the seaside while Tom Whittaker and his medical team were checking the casualty list at Highbury. Daniel had not played for more than three weeks, but with a plaster supervised by the manager so that it would pass the scrutiny of the referee the Welsh international was chosen for the fray. So too was Logie, who had been hospitalised earlier in the week leading up to the final.

Lishman, the ex-commando, who had just missed selection two years earlier, tried quickly to make up for lost time with a hooked shot that passed just wide of Newcastle's goal. Arsenal settled quickly and were looking good when fate took a hand, as so often happened in FA Cup finals during the 1950s. Barnes twisted a knee so painfully that though he returned with the joint bandaged, he could not continue. Arsenal faced the prospect of surviving for the last 55 minutes with ten men.

Roper, strong and robust, was immediately switched from outside left to right back; his heroic display typified Arsenal's tenacity. Smith had to clear a Milburn effort off the line when for once the supreme Swindin was beaten, but the depleted team did not just settle for survival. Cox forayed infield and Forbes added to his usual labour with many attempts to support the undermanned attack. Eleven minutes from the end Lishman rose to meet a corner from Cox but the ball skimmed the bar.

Five minutes later the gallant stand ended. Of the ten Arsenal players remaining Holton and Roper both went down, in urgent need of the trainer's attention. Daniel's arm was aching; Logie's damaged thigh could no longer be concealed. Mercer yelled at referee Arthur Ellis to stop the game to allow treatment for Holton and Roper. The ball was still in play and Mitchell was allowed to cross into the middle where George Robledo climbed above Smith to send in a header which dropped in off the post. Roper, still on the ground, could only sit and watch it happen. There was still time for Forbes to hit the bar, but Newcastle became the first club in the twentieth century to win the FA Cup in consecutive seasons.

Mercer made sure his team left the pitch together to tremendous appreciation from the crowd. Later that night he addressed the guests at the traditional banquet, speaking with great emotion: 'I thought football's greatest honour was to captain England. I was wrong. It was to captain Arsenal today.'

The only goal of the 1952 FA Cup final; Chilean George Robledo beats Lionel Smith to a Mitchell centre and squeezes the ball off the post past George Swindin to give Newcastle a 1-0 victory and allow them to become the first club to retain the FA Cup in the twentieth century. Number 9 is the great Jackie Milburn. Smith made 181 first-class appearances for the club at both centre half and left back and, though he never became an automatic club choice at full back, won six England caps in that position.

Perhaps some of the resolution forged over those 90 minutes at Wembley brought the players even closer. Certainly those who represented the club in the following 1952–53 First Division campaign proved to be too good for their rivals. The title came to Highbury for the seventh time, setting a new record, but it was to be mighty close.

Barnes was missing for the entire season, though Joe Wade and John Chenhall made light of his absence. Others made meaningful contributions, like Don Oakes who marked his League debut on the opening day of the season at Aston Villa by scoring the winning goal. A tall inside forward from Rhyl, Oakes had waited almost seven years for his chance. He kept his place of course for the following match but suffered injury helping in another winning cause at home to Manchester United. Such are the vagaries of football that he did not reappear at first-team level until the last nine matches of the 1954–55 season, when he operated at wing half. With a regular place beckoning at long last, he contracted a serious illness on tour in the summer of 1955. After protracted treatment, he had to accept medical advice to retire.

With two victories in those first two matches, Arsenal failed to build on such an optimistic start, winning only once in the next six outings. Sunderland and Charlton both plundered two points at Highbury. Only the return of Milton with almost 2,000 runs banked for Gloucestershire in a prolific season of batsmanship inspired a victory in this dismal spell; the cricketer-winger struck the bigger ball cleanly with one of the goals in a 3–1 home success against Portsmouth. The return match, however, encapsulated the uncertainties at that time. Holton struck twice before half-time only for Arsenal to allow Pompey to fight back for a draw.

A victory at White Hart Lane, always an occasion to savour, promised an upswing, with Milton on the scoresheet for the third time in four games. Don Roper, in particular, enjoyed the three matches in October: two goals at home to Blackpool, another against Sheffield Wednesday and two more in a 3–0 success over Newcastle United, which had more than a hint of extra satisfaction. But Roper reserved his virtuoso performance for another of the popular floodlit friendlies, with this time Hibernian coming to Highbury like lambs to the slaughter. To the delight of a 55,000 crowd Roper scored five times, one straight from a corner, in a 7–1 triumph, Lishman being responsible for the other two goals. It was a feast to set before the Duke of Edinburgh, the guest of honour at a match played for the National Playing Fields Association and the Central Council of Physical Recreation, two organisations of which the Duke was president.

In November the spotlight turned on Jimmy Logie. His impish genius was recognised at last by Scotland's selectors. The Alex James of his generation, Logie wore the blue jersey against Austria at Hampden Park. In the same month as his 33rd birthday the honour came far too late. It was his only cap, but at least it conferred much deserved international status on a man whose talents put him alongside many players from

Arsenal, or anywhere else, who won more caps.

Ten days after Logie's international, Arsenal put on a display of their own from the very top drawer, demolishing Liverpool 5–1 at Anfield. Ben Marden, one of many professionals at the club who might have earned a regular berth away from Highbury, struck twice in his first senior match of the season and Holton weighed in with a hat-trick. Holton also marked a return to Stoke, where he had made his League debut two years earlier, with a last-minute equaliser in a 1–1 draw. Arsenal maintained the routine of winning at home and drawing away, often the recipe for League success, until the turn of the year.

The last match of 1952 deserves special mention, not just because it brought the bonus of an away victory. On Christmas morning the Arsenal players were again a long way from their families, at Burnden Park, Bolton. The first half was above average but not exceptional. Willie Moir sent the home side into the lead but by the interval Milton had equalised and Holton, whose power of shot was formidable, had edged the visitors ahead.

In the second half those who might have had their minds on their Christmas dinners were first able to gorge themselves on a glut of goals. Within the opening five minutes of the half Logie and Roper had increased the Arsenal advantage to 4–1. Then it was Moir making it 4–2 before a Daniel penalty restored the lead to three goals. The action of the final eight minutes was even more frantic. Bolton's defensive generosities extended to the conceding of another goal to Holton, before Nat Lofthouse ended the year in which he had been tagged The Lion of Vienna for his England heroics with two late replies for Bolton. Believe it or not there was still time for Bolton to earn a penalty, which could have made it 6–5, but Kelsey, facing a spot kick for the first time in League football, saved Langton's attempt. Sadly the action of a marvellous match was never captured; all the local photographers preferred Christmas at home!

Goodness knows what the return match two days later might have produced, but the London fog descended and Arsenal had to wait until April for a 4–1 win. Incidentally, Kelsey had no such success when he met a second penalty in the next match. Trevor Ford sent the ball past him in an important 3–1 win for Sunderland, who started 1953 at the top of the First Division. Yet it was the Gunners' only defeat in eight League and Cup matches starting at the turn of the year. Lishman in particular responded to the consistency of the team play by scoring in all eight games.

His goal in the FA Cup third round against Doncaster Rovers had looked blatantly offside, but the eventual four-goal margin whetted the appetite for another attempt to reach Wembley for what would have been the third time in four seasons. With a similarly easy passage at home to Bury, memories of the shortest route to Wembley in 1950 were awakened, only to be stopped by the toughest draw of the fifth round — Burnley, away! The sharpshooting combination of Holton and Lishman solved the problem; a goal each at Turf Moor was enough for a victory that made many at Highbury believe that this was Arsenal's year.

A home draw, even though it was against Blackpool, finalists in 1948 and 1951, did little to dispel that belief. Yet Tom Whittaker looked for a little extra luck when a colour clash in both first and change strips meant a new design of shirt. Whittaker plumped for the black and white stripes of Newcastle United, hoping that some of their FA Cup fortune would rub off on his team, but maybe the fact that Arsenal wore white shorts and not the black of the Magpies worked against the scheme. The Gunners lost by the odd goal in three, all of which arrived in a frantic last ten minutes.

Ernie Taylor made the breakthrough for Blackpool only for another small but wily schemer, Logie, to equalise two minutes later. Blackpool's winner brought sadness not only to Highbury but also to the scorer. Allan Brown, the powerful Scottish international inside forward, broke a leg colliding with Kelsey as he sent the ball past Arsenal's goalkeeper. Brown had missed the 1951 final against Newcastle through injury and, sure enough, his misfortune at Highbury made him a spectator again for the magnificent Matthews final two months later. In 1959, Allan Brown did finally reach Wembley, but in the colours of Luton Town he collected a loser's medal.

A week before the Cup tie at Highbury, Blackpool had also interrupted Arsenal's progress in the League. Lishman's scoring sequence finally came to an end, but one Arsenal goal in their 3–2 defeat at Bloomfield Road was a collector's item; more than six years after his move from Everton Joe Mercer finally opened his First Division account for the Gunners.

Convincing wins over two traditionally difficult opponents, Spurs and Derby County, had kept the club in the Championship race, and the reaction to the Cup exit could hardly have been more positive. Cliff Holton brushed aside Sheffield Wednesday at Hillsborough with four goals, two with the right foot, one with the left and one with his head. The recalled Freddie Cox made some of the bullets for Holton to fire.

Mercer, suitably encouraged, struck another vital goal that brought a 1–1 draw with close rivals Preston North End in a rearranged match that was staged on a Thursday afternoon, but it came in a spell of six games without a win that threatened disaster. Five successive wins then righted the ship. Liverpool were hit for five goals for the second time that season, then Chelsea beaten 2–0 with Marden, who had been dropped after his two goals at Anfield, marking his return after almost five months by hitting the target again. A cheeky backheel from Logie brought a crucial breakthrough during a 4–2 battle against Manchester City.

Centre half Bill Dodgin was summoned into

the first team four months after signing from Fulham; Daniel was away with Wales, and missed the excitement of the rearranged Bolton game — the win that took them to the top of the table. It was now 15 April and four games remained.

A Lishman hat-trick settled the first of those, at home to Stoke City. Two away matches produced no goals, but the first brought one point from a draw at Cardiff. The fixture list with rare good sense included on the last Saturday of the League programme a meeting between the two current pretenders to the title: Preston versus Arsenal at Deepdale. The points situation meant the Gunners' title ambitions could survive a defeat but not a heavy beating. Preston won 2–0 with goals from their two most revered forwards, Tom Finney and Charlie Wayman. Both clubs now had one match left but not on the same day.

Preston were first into action on the Wednesday before the Cup final. Away to bottom club Derby County, they won 1–0 and left for an end of season tour not knowing their fate. Arsenal's finale was staged before a packed Highbury two days later on Cup final eve; only a win would be enough. Burnley, the opposition, were in the top six of the table. It took only three minutes for the drama to take its first twist.

Roy Stephenson, Burnley's outside right, who was to win a Championship medal nine years later with Ipswich Town, drove in a crisp, low, centre. Confident of his own touch on the ball but not yet in tune with the pace of the match, Mercer tried to cut out the danger. He succeeded only in diverting the ball into his own net. At that moment the title looked bound for Deepdale.

It was no time for patience. Arsenal threw caution to the winds in a display of forceful attacking football which brought goals for Forbes, in one of his most passionate performances for the club, Lishman and Logie. Burnley then cut the deficit in the second half, and the all-out policy gave way to the tactics of entrenchment, and what they had Arsenal held. When the sums were done Tom Whittaker's team had won the League on goal average — by less than one-tenth of a goal.

Mercer, Logie and Roper of the regulars in 1948 had survived as helmsmen on the voyage five years later. Swindin, now second string to Kelsey, also made enough appearances to qualify for a medal, his third, fifteen years after his first. Among the goalscorers five players had got into double figures, with Holton's striking rate of 19 goals in 21 matches the most impressive statistic.

Don Roper had been at the forefront of both post-war Championship triumphs: 'The defensive side of our game was probably better in 1948. We went out then for every match not expecting to concede a goal. Both times we were very well organised by Tom Whittaker. As a winger I was expected to come deep and help the full back defend, and of course I did fill in as a defender when there were injuries. Like in the

1952 Cup final. When it happened in League games it always seemed to be against the likes of Finney or Matthews! Joe Mercer obviously played an enormous part in both those successes. We never saw him in the week at all because he trained at Liverpool. He did not do pre-season work with us either. But he was our godfather. A great man.'

Joe Mercer's third championship success — the two Arsenal titles added to one achieved with Everton in 1939 — seemed the perfect time for him to retire to the shop counter of the grocery business on Merseyside. Joe certainly thought so himself, but such was his influence in the Highbury dressing-room that he was persuaded to sign for one more year. He had played 19 further League matches in a topsy-turvy season when on 10 April 1954 he broke a leg.

Ironically the injury occurred in an innocuous collision with a team-mate, Joe Wade. Ironically, too, the opposition was Liverpool, the club he had seen more of while training than Arsenal. He took his leave on a stretcher from the stage he had graced, with a wave of goodbye that brought tears to the eyes of many who loved him among the Highbury crowd. Everyone in the ground knew that the curtain had finally come down on an illustrious playing career. To come, of course, were management successes with Manchester City, and, for a short spell, with England.

Football quickly rings out the old and rings in the new. Derek Tapscott, a bright young Welsh forward acquired from Barry Town, was given his debut in the same match. The sadness at Mercer's fate was mingled with excitement at Tapscott's two goals in a 3–0 victory. From a family of 17, where speed around the house might have been necessary to be noticed, Tapscott, perhaps not surprisingly, had a style of perpetual motion. He followed up his promising first appearance with two more goals in his next League outing against Portsmouth.

Indeed it was very much a time for change.

Jimmy Logie scores the all important third goal against Burnley on 1 May 1953. It was the goal that won the Championship, for with it Arsenal overcame Burnley 3-2 on the day and pipped Preston on goal average for the title. The other goals were scored by Forbes and Lishman. On 25 April, a week before, Arsenal had lost 2-0 at Preston to give the Lancastrians hope of the title. A win in the final game of the season was thus vital for the Gunners, and they got it with nothing to spare to take the Championship by a goal average of 1.516 against Preston's 1.417. Had Preston won 5-0 rather than 2-0 a week earlier they, and not Arsenal, would have taken the title.

The 1953–54 campaign was clouded at the outset by the death in the summer of Alex James. The obituary writer who recalled the brains behind so much of Arsenal's football in the 1930s summed him up perfectly as the 'pawky little Scot with the Chaplin manner of comic genius'. James had lived his life to the full but his loss from cancer at the age of 51 seemed dreadfully premature. The following October Arsenal met Preston, James' former club, in a match in honour of his memory and that of North End's Derek Lewis, a forward of great potential whose sudden demise from illness had shocked the football world.

Arsenal's attempt to defend their title began dreadfully. Six of the first eight matches were lost, the other two drawn. The club's predicament reached a crisis point at Sunderland in what turned out to be Swindin's last League match. Lishman had given Arsenal the boost of a goal before the veteran goalkeeper was hurt in a collision with Trevor Ford, with Sunderland by then leading 2–1. Swindin was, in all, beaten seven times, and the match must have been relished by Daniel, who had been sold to Roker Park in the close season, complaining that he did not like the style Arsenal expected of their centre half.

Dodgin had accepted the tactics more readily, and Barnes, who had not played since his Wembley injury, battled back to sufficient fitness to earn a recall though his problems were to persist. To strengthen his hand in attack Tom Whittaker sought a short-term solution. Tommy Lawton, the nation's pin-up centre forward throughout the 1940s, was struggling as player-manager of Brentford. At 34 his best years were clearly behind him, but Ronnie Rooke had more than risen to the challenge of a late call to Highbury. Could Lawton do the same?

The deal was done in secret and Lawton was unveiled to the Highbury public on 19 September 1953, against Manchester City. He could not, however, in his two and a half seasons with the club, sustain a regular place; it was almost seven months before his first League goal against Aston Villa. Yet Lawton loved the glamour attached to being an Arsenal player and recalled that his biggest mistake in football had been in not signing for the club when George Allison wanted him from Burnley in 1936 (he chose Everton instead).

The early traumas of that season were cast aside by a run of much more consistent form which lifted the League position from bottom to seventh; but the blend was missing and twelfth place at the end was a fair reflection of the ups and downs. The low moments included a shock home defeat in the fourth round of the FA Cup by Norwich City. Alex Forbes was sent off early in the match along with Bobby Brennan of Norwich, who had already missed a penalty. Tom Johnston scored two fine goals for City, who created a classic Cup upset by winning 2–1.

The transitions continued into the next campaign, where the League position rose only marginally to ninth and the Cup exit again came in round four — to Wolves at Molineux. February 1955 saw the departure of two distinguished servants. Logie left for non-League action with Gravesend and Northfleet; Milton linked up with Bristol City, an easier base from which to continue with his cricketing career.

Lishman and the loyal Roper continued to supply the goals, with help from the energetic Tapscott. Kelsey was firmly established among the top flight of goalkeepers, and one of Whittaker's tactical ploys paid dividends; Goring who had been unlucky with injury and illness was switched from a forward role to right half. The unluckiest player of all was surely the Irish half back Bill Dickson, who suffered in quick succession a badly dislocated shoulder, a damaged knee and appendicitis; and could not develop what had started to be a promising career.

One match in 1954 does remain in the memory, though not for the result. The prestige of Arsenal Football Club around the world made it the number one choice for the Soviet Union when the Iron Curtain was lowered to invite guest opponents for Moscow Dynamo. The fixture was finally scheduled for Tuesday 5 October, and the simple tale is that Arsenal were hammered 5–0. The circumstances, ignored by some of the popular press which panned the performance at the time, were certainly extenuating.

The players took off in two BEA Viscounts from Northolt airport before nine o'clock on the Sunday morning, but they did not arrive in their Moscow hotel until lunch time the following day. There were stops at Frankfurt, Prague, Warsaw and Minsk, and the deeper the journey into Soviet territory the poorer and less frequent the refreshments. Sunday night was spent at Minsk in dormitory accommodation, and it was an exhausted squad of players who took the field in the Dynamo Stadium. The Russians were held at bay until almost half-time but Arsenal fell apart in the second half. A month later there was a reciprocal visit to England from Spartak Moscow, but there was no revenge on the pitch. Arsenal were beaten by the odd goal in three.

Lawton gave the 1955–56 season an optimistic start with a hat-trick against Cardiff City in the opening home game, but by January he was on the move again. There were frequent other changes as Whittaker, not enjoying the best of health, wrestled with the problems of finding a team to live up to the standards which had won seven Championships. Wingers Mike Tiddy and Gordon Nutt (a former Arsenal schoolboy) were purchased from Cardiff City with Brian Walsh moving in the opposite direction. Another double signing acquired the services of defender Stan Charlton and the versatile Vic Groves from Leyton Orient. Later in the season Lishman's eight years of excellent achievement, marked by 125 goals in 226 League matches, was ended by a transfer to Nottingham Forest. A link with the past was also broken when Barnes gave up the

Ted Ditchburn saves at the feet of Derek Tapscott on 10 September 1955 at White Hart Lane. Arsenal lost 3-1, Don Roper scoring the goal. Tapscott was a prolific scorer for the club in a relatively unsuccessful era. he recorded 68 first-class goals in 132 appearances.

struggle with his knee, asking for his contract to be cancelled so he could join the BBC as part of their broadcasting team on football.

Roper ascended to the captaincy, which then passed to Holton for a time, with the striker who had been converted from full back in his early Highbury days now performing at left half. The chopping and changing brought inconsistent results, until a finale with a genuine flourish hoisted the club rapidly up the table to fifth place. FA Cup ambitions were kindled by a run into the last eight before eventual defeat at Birmingham. Ignominy was avoided in the third round, but only just. Bedford Town of the Southern League came away from Highbury with an astonishing 2–2 draw. In the replay the non-Leaguers were five minutes away from a sensation which might have eclipsed even the defeat by Walsall in 1933; Groves then equalised and in extra time Tapscott hurled himself forward to head in the goal which saved Arsenal's face. It was the first game ever transmitted by Independent Television.

One game which epitomised the youthful policies pursued by the club management saw Blackpool, then League leaders, swept aside 4–1. The forward line that day, full of exuberance, was Clapton, Tapscott, Groves, Bloomfield and Tiddy. Con Sullivan was having a successful spell in goal deputising for Kelsey, but he was denied another clean sheet in extraordinary circumstances. Left back Dennis Evans believed he had heard the final whistle as the goalkeeper threw the ball to him; he drove it back into his own net. Sullivan had heard it too and was picking up his cap from the side of the goal. But the blast had come from the crowd, from a railway guard in uniform encouraging the referee to end the match. Having played two previous matches without conceding a goal, Sullivan was far from amused at this particular fan's trick.

Evans' version of the episode says much about the Arsenal of the time: 'I was playing against Stan Matthews, which was always such a test, so I was so relieved to hear what we all thought was the final whistle. Derek Tapscott was already up the tunnel! I was regarded as a hard player, but my style against Matthews was more restrained. When I was to mark him for the first time, Tom Whittaker called me upstairs to his office. The message was not what I expected. He told me *not* to set out to kick Stan off the pitch! "Even your own fans will hate you if you do that," he said. So I had to take care to defend in other ways.'

Arsenal continued to be the glamorous club, which attracted the famous to the guest seats in the directors' box; Malenkov, the president of the Soviet Union, attended a match against Manchester United. Yet slowly the club was moving away from the era of pre-war invincibility and the links with the immediate post-war triumphs were gradually diminishing. The number of young players in the team was one indication, and in 1956 the strongest link with past glories was abruptly severed.

Tom Whittaker died on Wednesday 24 October 1956 in University College Hospital, where he had undergone an operation the previous Easter. Like his great mentor Herbert Chapman he passed away in harness, as he would have wished; and like Chapman he had sacrificed his health in the cause of a club which meant more to him than his own life.

Both had died tragically young (neither reached 60); both in differing ways had been the very heartbeat of Highbury. Tom Whittaker perhaps had a premonition that he would not outlive his job, once admitting: 'Someone has to drive himself too hard for Arsenal. Herbert Chapman worked himself to death for the club,

and if it is to be my fate I am happy to accept it.'

Joe Mercer had been lured back into football as manager of Sheffield United; his moving tribute to the guardian angel who had extended his career at Highbury to such glorious heights appeared in the *Daily Express*:

'Meeting Tom Whittaker was the best thing that ever happened to me; he was the greatest man I ever met.

As the news of his death goes around the world thousands, perhaps millions, of people will say the same thing. And how so very deeply they will mean it. Arsenal was his kingdom but in every soccer-playing country in the world he was acknowledged as a prince of the game. There never has been a greater man in football. It is a game full of hard knocks. But Tom never hit anybody. He never shirked making a hard decision, like sacking or dropping a player, or any of the other things that can hurt deeply. But the way Tom did it, it never did.

Tom made bad sportsmen into good sportsmen. He made good footballers into great footballers.

Tom was responsible for none of the bad things in football. Cynics may smile and say "I wonder". But I know.

I know that he never did a bad thing. All problems had only one solution; the one done with kindness . . .

After Newcastle beat us in the 1952 final, Tom came into the dressing-room, looking as happy as we had ever seen him. He said: "I am really proud of you chaps. You played great football. I am as proud of Arsenal today as ever I have been." Damn it, he made us feel we had won the Cup.

The last time I saw Tom was a couple of months ago. He looked very ill, but he had already started a new phase in Arsenal history. He realised the days of big buying were over. His plans only included youngsters. And every youngster who ever went to Highbury quickly learned one thing. The only thing that mattered was the club.

Tom Whittaker never thought of the chairman, a player or anyone individually when he made a decision. If it was good for the club then it was right . . .'

Others wrote of his 'simple charm', his 'tolerance' and his 'sense of fairness'. Denis Compton recalled that he had never seen him lose his temper, 'although there were often occasions when he would have been justified in doing so. He took infinite trouble with everyone whom he considered to be his responsibility. In my early days at Highbury I often saw him there till eight, nine or ten o'clock at night, personally working to get players fit for the following Saturday. He'd do the work himself and wouldn't delegate it to anyone else. He had a kind of genius for it, I think . . .'

The late Bob Wall remembered a genial side to his nature, and his huge physical strength. On one playful occasion he lifted the Compton brothers, '. . . one under each arm as if they were babies, over a wall and dropped them into the team bath. He was a big man in many ways.'

Tom Whittaker's reputation had spread way

Anxious faces at Highbury in 1951 for manager Tom Whittaker (right) and his assistant Jack Crayston. Whittaker had been awarded the MBE for his wartime service as a Squadron Leader in the RAF, notable also because he had thus seen service through both wars in all three of the armed forces. He formally became manager in 1947 when Allison stepped down. He remained as manager until his death in 1956, departing, like Chapman, in harness. His managership had been no less successful than that of his mentor. Both were in full charge for nine years, both won two Championships, both reached two FA Cup finals, both won the first and lost the second two years later. The coincidences are, to say the least, interesting. Crayston succeeded Whittaker as manager, though he lasted only two years before George Swindin took over.

beyond the confines of English football. When Arsenal took on the role of ambassadors on expeditions around the globe, the secretary-manager was the perfect head of the delegation. In 1949, for example, the summer tour took the club to Brazil where in Sao Paulo many supporters of the local team were of Italian extraction; Italy and the rest of the football world had just been stunned by the Superga aircrash which wiped out the brilliant Torino team. Whittaker's sensitivity recognised the need for a tribute and before the match, at his suggestion, the two teams and the crowd stood, heads bowed, to the music of *Ave Maria*.

Yet his kindness never became weakness. Centre half Bill Dodgin returned from the 7–1 humiliation at Sunderland in that dreadful opening to the 1953–54 season feeling that he had let down the side — Arsenal, remember, had collected only two points from eight matches. Dodgin wanted to be left out, and went to see Whittaker: 'I left his office quicker than I entered it. He told me very firmly that if there was any dropping to be done, he would do it.'

In February 1956, Arsenal had tried to lighten the load on Tom Whittaker. Alec Stock, who had played for Yeovil Town in their famous Cup victory over First Division Sunderland, had moved into management at Leyton Orient and impressed many sound judges in the game. Stock came to Highbury as assistant manager. He lasted less than two months because Leyton Orient tugged at his heart strings and called him back and there was no sign of Whittaker taking any less of the responsibilities.

Tom Whittaker was not a man who sought personal publicity for his efforts; he did not have the flair for that of a George Allison or indeed Chapman himself. His upbringing from a military family had bred a character of scrupulous honesty. Arsenal and football dominated his life; only his war career as a Squadron Leader in the RAF had interrupted his service to the football club. Tributes poured in from all over the world. Desperately saddened Arsenal were beaten by four goals at Everton on the Saturday after his death.

No one felt the loss more keenly than Don Roper who, like many players, was not aware that Whittaker's health was in such decline: 'I don't know about all the others but I only found out that he had died by reading it in the papers. It was a terrible shock. I had been his second signing in 1947, and for me he alone created that great atmosphere at Highbury. With him gone I didn't feel I wanted to be there any more.'

In fact Roper had played his last League game for the club eight weeks before Tom Whittaker died, at home to Preston. After his death the prospect of spending much of the time in the reserves carried no appeal, and on 7 January 1957 Don Roper returned whence he came, to Southampton; he was seven months short of ten years of tremendous commitment, three League games short of 300 for Arsenal in the First Division. He had represented England 'B' and

the Football League and in 1950 came close to selection for England's World Cup squad in Brazil: 'Obviously I would have loved to have played in a full international, but in a way I'm glad I didn't get called up for just one cap. In 1947 I was given one County match for Hampshire and then told they did not want me. That was so disappointing that I rather wish that I had not played at all. But my time at Arsenal was marvellous. George Swindin was my room-mate on away trips. We got on very well. Laurie Scott and Reg Lewis were other good friends. So too was Leslie Compton. He was everyone's friend. Great days. Arsenal football club was life itself.'

So Don Roper moved out of his club house in Southgate, like many players very appreciative of the standards set by Arsenal in all aspects of running a football club. Bill Dodgin had been immediately struck on signing at Highbury by the quality of the training kit. Roper remembered rushing to a sports-shop on a tour to Switzerland to buy the latest streamlined football boots manufactured in Germany. Club officials wanted only the best for their performers.

The obvious stress of the dual role of secretary-manager persuaded the Arsenal board to split the two jobs. Bob Wall was promoted to secretary. Jack Crayston, a member of two League Championship teams and the 1936 FA Cup winning side, took over as manager. Crayston had been an assistant to Tom Whittaker, his man 'downstairs at Highbury' helping particularly with the scouting and at times, because he had received some training as an accountant, with book-keeping.

Crayston had also won eight England caps before the war. Famed for his long-throws he was a strapping wing half, over six feet tall, weighing 13 stones and needing specially constructed boots for his size 12 feet. His nickname was 'Gentleman Jack', though he often disclaimed the validity of such a tag: 'It was coined by the newspapers but I used to mutter some horrible things to myself even if they weren't directed at my team-mates'.

Like so many others his playing days had been curtailed by the war which broke out a month before his 29th birthday. Born in the north of Lancashire and signed from Bradford he had become part of the Highbury family, and in choosing him to succeed Tom Whittaker the Highbury board were aiming for the continuity they had found in Allison and Whittaker.

An even longer servant, Joe Shaw, finally retired. He had been signed as a player in 1907 from Accrington Stanley, hanging up his boots in 1923. Following a short spell with Chelsea he had resumed his Arsenal connection under the title of Head Coach and Chief Representative, in effect Whittaker's number two.

On 13 March 1957, George Allison passed away; he had lived with indifferent health over the ten years since he had resigned from his football career at Highbury. 'George Arsenal', as he had been widely known, had risen from his humble start in the club ranks as the writer of

Cliff Holton rises above Jimmy Scoular and the Newcastle defence to score in a First Division game on 30 November 1957. It was a poor season for the Gunners and this game was no better than many, Newcastle winning 3-2. Danny Clapton (whose brother Dennis, though playing only four games for the club, served to confuse statisticians for years) scored the other. Holton was also to find statistical fame when, playing for Watford three years later, he scored hat-tricks in consecutive matches on consecutive days.

the match programme to Secretary-Manager. His knowledge of the game might never have been deep, but he was clever enough to realise his limitations, not frightened to consult the opinions of others. Yet as a front person for the prestigious Arsenal organisation he had been perfect. His rapport with the media would have been a strength in any era.

The following day another death was recorded, that of J. W. Julian, club captain back in 1890 and the first to lead a professional side at Woolwich. He had been an enthusiastic and regular spectator at matches at Highbury right up to the time of his demise.

Jack Crayston's appointment was confirmed in December 1956. How can one tell whether he felt the shudders of history at that time? He was part of the lineage being put to rest with the deaths of Julian, Whittaker and Allison. He had much to live up to — Chapman won two Championships and the FA Cup, Allison three Championships and the Cup, Whittaker (like his mentor) the League twice and the Cup once. Could Crayston maintain the succession? In the circumstances the final League position, fifth, was more than satisfactory, as was reaching the sixth round of the FA Cup, although losing at home to West Bromwich Albion after forcing a replay at the Hawthorns was disappointing. Tapscott had his best scoring season with 25 League goals, and David Herd emerged from the shadows of reserve team football to justify faith shown him by Whittaker.

Herd's instincts for the game were in his blood. His father Alec had been a pre-war Scottish international, and David had the most unusual experience of lining up for his Football League debut alongside his dad, for Stockport County in 1951; he was then 17 and Alec 39. Herd junior progressed so well at Highbury that

he, too, represented Scotland, the last of his five appearances coming just before his departure from Highbury to Manchester United in the summer of 1961.

David Herd had been finishing his National Service in the RAF when Tom Whittaker brought him south; his shooting was spectacular and he averaged better than a goal every other game in Arsenal's colours.

The gradual decline in the number on the Highbury professional staff continued for the 1957–58 season. Jack Crayston could call on 42 players compared to the 55 retained two seasons earlier. He named full back Evans as his new captain, and among those to whom he gave a first taste of First Division football was a South African winger, Dan Le Roux, and a goalkeeper who was also a fine cricketer, Jim Standen.

Crayston was also able to produce more from Groves, who had suffered severely from injuries in his first season and a half with the club. His absence had angered a section of Arsenal fans who expected more from the club's investment of £23,000; he received abusive letters accusing him of malingering. The downward spiral had reached rock bottom in December 1956 when he asked for a transfer. The board of directors agreed to sell but only when he had proved his fitness. Subsequently a move into a club house following his marriage produced a more settled outlook. Crayston also helped by selecting him in a deeper role at wing half, and Vic Groves recaptured his appetite for the game which had made him such an infectious player to watch.

That Arsenal were trying to move with the times was emphasised by the appointment, in December 1957, of Ron Greenwood as coach. Greenwood, still remembered at Highbury for his performance for Bradford Park Avenue in 1948, had retired from playing the previous year

and had been cutting his managerial teeth with Eastbourne United. David Herd remembered the reaction of the playing staff: 'It was a very exciting time for us. Ron Greenwood had so many coaching ideas which at the time were very new. It was very stimulating for us.' One Greenwood experiment involved equipping players with receivers in training so that they could take instructions from the coach.

Yet Arsenal slumped to their lowest points total since 1930, slipping to twelfth place. It was 30 years since Arsenal had conceded so many goals. The Cup was no better, with a sensational 3–1 defeat at Third Division Northampton in the third round.

On the coach journey to the match Evans, at Crayston's request, had passed the captaincy to Dave Bowen, who had been bought from Northampton in 1950. The Welsh international wing half kept the captaincy until he returned to Northampton 18 months later. No one has achieved more than Dave Bowen, as player, manager and administrator, to keep League football alive in the town. It was he who took them from the Fourth Division to the First in the 1960s.

One match typified the two faces of Arsenal's nature that season, the 5–4 defeat by Manchester United at Highbury. Coming on the Saturday before the Munich air tragedy, the United performance is rightly remembered as the perfect epitaph for the Busby Babes. Five of their team on 1 February 1958 perished five days later: left back and captain Roger Byrne, the entire half back line of Eddie Colman, Mark Jones and Duncan Edwards and centre forward Tommy Taylor.

From the Arsenal viewpoint the first half summed up the defensive frailties which were to be such a barrier all season to real progress. For all the brilliance of Matt Busby's superb young side they might have expected stiffer resistance. After ten minutes Edwards, a colossus who could never be replaced, thrashed a shot past Kelsey from the edge of the penalty area. On the half hour a swift counter-attack initiated by fast direct running from left winger Albert Scanlon saw Bobby Charlton arrive in the centre for another exhibition of explosive finishing. Before half-time Scanlon and right winger Kenny Morgans carved out the opening from which Taylor sent Manchester United into a 3–0 lead.

It stayed that way until 15 minutes into the second half. Then Arsenal's unpredictability took another turn. From lacking harmony they were suddenly in tune. Inside three astonishing minutes the score was transformed from 3–0 to 3–3! Herd struck a goal which might have caught the admiring eye of Busby who was to later whisk him off to Old Trafford. The springheeled Groves headed down a cross from Nutt for Bloomfield to beat goalkeeper Harry Gregg. With the ground in uproar, Arsenal regained possession from the kick-off; Nutt's next foray produced another centre from the Arsenal left and Bloomfield launched himself into a diving header which had the dourest fan yelling in delirium.

It was a measure of the greatness of United that they took three such forceful blows flush on the chin, but still recovered to land the knock-out punch of a champion. Dennis Viollet, an inside forward with a sharp eye for goal, responded to interplay between Charlton and Scanlon to restore their lead. Taylor slotted in his second and United's fifth from an improbable angle. Arsenal deserved to make the margin of defeat closer, and Tapscott was able to do so when his never-say-die attitude carried him clear to strike the ninth and final goal of a match that would have been unforgettable even without the subsequent sorrow.

Dennis Evans prevented another United goal with a soaring header to clear off the line and his recollection of the match had a poignant touch: 'Duncan Edwards, who was built like a giant, flattened Danny Clapton on to the track around the ground. Danny was too slight really to look after himself, so I went across and told Duncan to cut it out. A few minutes later Duncan got the ball and came charging at us. I was the nearest defender. As he knocked it just too far ahead of him it flashed through my mind that I really could get revenge for Danny. It was the perfect situation for defenders like myself to whack an opponent when you look as though you are going for the ball.

'But Duncan was already a legend in the game and instinct took over. I simply slid the ball away from him and out of play. Had I gone through with the tackle I know I could have hurt him. Perhaps then he wouldn't have been fit to go to Belgrade, and he wouldn't have been on that plane at Munich.'

Jack Crayston was not blind to the shortcomings of his team. He regularly asked the board for money to strengthen his hand, but it was not forthcoming. Cliff Jones was just one of a number of players he pursued, but Swansea realised the value of their winger who was to play 59 times for Wales, and were determined not to sell him cheaply. When he finally became available it was Spurs who struck the deal, and Jones became part of the 1960–61 Double side whose rampaging success made Arsenal's lack of progress at that time more difficult to bear.

The match programme outlined the Arsenal philosophy at the time: '. . . a policy not to bid for a player's transfer. We always ask the fee required, and having been told make up our mind whether the player is worth that fee.' Yet with increasing pressure for success in a market which was naturally declining after the post-war boom, the ethics of football business were changing.

Crayston believed that the club did have the money to invest in the transfer market. At a board meeting at the end of the season clearly the frustrations became too much. 'Gentleman Jack' Crayston resigned, severing a tie with the club that had lasted almost 25 years. He moved back to Yorkshire for a spell as secretary-

manager to Doncaster Rovers, before using his accountancy skills in a business career and finally retiring to live in the West Midlands. In 1985 he looked back on the changes in football with a twinkle in his eye: 'In my time players had short hair, wore long shorts and played in hob-nailed boots. Now they have long hair, short shorts and play in slippers.'

Towards the end of Crayston's short reign Arsenal managed to preserve one of the club's pre-war records. Wolves were assured of the Championship and threatening to break Arsenal's total of 66 points achieved in 1930–31. By winning at Molineux, where reserve striker Tony Biggs made an encouraging first appearance, Arsenal prevented that possibility.

There was no disguising who topped Arsenal's list to fill the post of manager. Joe Mercer fitted the bill perfectly but when Joe left Bramall Lane it was for Aston Villa and by then the manager's office at Highbury was occupied by one of his old team-mates.

George Swindin had established his credentials for the post by bringing Peterborough United of the Midland League into the national limelight with FA Cup giant-killing feats. A strong-minded Yorkshireman who did not suffer fools gladly, the former Arsenal goalkeeper hardly lacked the courage to pick up the reins at the club at a difficult time.

He was to keep the job for four seasons, and the first, 1958–59, turned out to be the most successful by far. Arsenal finished third while at the same time the playing staff underwent a drastic overhaul. Money was made available and scarcely had the season got underway when £27,000 was spent on a wise-cracking, fast-talking highly competitive wing half from Preston North End.

Tommy Docherty had spent the summer in Scotland's squad at the World Cup finals in Sweden, but he had done so without Preston's permission. Unthinkable as it is today, the club had insisted that he travelled on their own tour to South Africa. Docherty's forthright manner was not just part of his public persona during his later flamboyant managerial career. His response was a transfer request, as well as his refusal to miss out on the World Cup opportunity. Consequently he sat out Preston's opening game of the 1958–59 season against Arsenal at Deepdale, his customary number four shirt passing instead to Gordon Milne.

Swindin seized the opportunity of attracting an unsettled top-class player to Highbury. Docherty himself grasped the chance so eagerly that he forgot to ask what his wages would be! He marked his first appearance in Arsenal's colours with his only League goal for the club in a 3–0 victory at home to Burnley. His chattering on the field at first was greeted with disapproval by his new set of supporters, but then they took to such an extrovert display. Once, off the field, Tommy Docherty did speak out of turn to a referee after an away match; he was reported to the FA and suspended for a fortnight.

Swindin's next major move involved a dash by car to entice another Scottish international, Jackie Henderson, to become part of his rebuilding plans. Henderson had made his name with Portsmouth, but his move to Wolves seven months earlier had not been successful. Like Docherty, he took an instant liking to the Highbury stage, soon scoring twice in a 4–3 victory over West Bromwich Albion. The two new Scots, together with Herd, who had staked claims for his first international call-up by scoring four goals in a 6–1 triumph at Everton, represented their country against Wales at Cardiff. In the opposing ranks were Kelsey and Bowen. On the same day the club could still field a team good enough to hold Champions Wolves to a 1–1 draw, with Biggs scoring on another rare senior opportunity.

With a 21-year-old Irish full back Billy McCullough arriving from Portadown, the incomings had to be balanced by outgoings. Tiddy moved from the first team fringe to Brighton, and two more senior players also said their farewells. Tapscott was not in Swindin's plans and he returned to Wales, taking to Cardiff City a pedigree of 62 goals in 119 First Division matches for Arsenal. Cliff Holton's time was also up, sold to Watford almost eleven years after he had come to Highbury from amateur football with Oxford City. During that time his versatility had offered a whole range of attributes to many different Arsenal teams. Nor was Holton finished; with Watford in two spells, Northampton, Crystal Palace, Charlton and Orient, he increased his total of League goals by more than 200, many of them with the venomous power which had characterised his shooting at Highbury.

Both Herd and Holton attributed their marksmanship to countless hours spent in the shooting 'box' which was constructed on the training area which was then in the open behind the Clock End. It was cleverly designed so that the ball rebounded at varying angles to be struck again. Herd swore by it, but it did not survive the rebuilding of the facilities there. He does remember its design, however, should any future Arsenal manager wish to pep up a shot-shy attack!

Another aspect of training no longer in use is the practice of measuring the feet of every new signing, which enabled a footwear firm based in Bolton to provide made-to-measure running shoes with spikes for use on the shale track around Highbury. Sprinting and shooting were virtues which were much encouraged at Arsenal in the 1950s.

In November Danny Clapton reflected the upswing in the club's fortunes, by becoming the first player at the club for five years to be chosen by England. The skilful winger from London's East End played against Wales, but it was to be his only selection. Joe Haverty's appearances for the Republic of Ireland raised the number of current internationals on Swindin's staff to seven.

Len Julians was another 1958 addition. Though he scored on his debut on Boxing Day, a 6–3 defeat at Luton, he did not enjoy the best of fortune at Highbury, and left 18 months later for Nottingham Forest. He was on target in a 2–2 draw in the fifth round of the FA Cup against Sheffield United, but in the replay at Bramall Lane Kelsey broke an arm, Evans had to deputise in goal, and Arsenal were out of the competition.

In Kelsey's absence, Standen was again given the chance to show his potential, and when he too was stricken with injury third choice Peter Goy performed with credit in a 1–0 win over Leeds United in which Goring was recalled for his last senior game, nostalgically back in his old position in attack. His partner in that match was Roy Goulden, son of the former West Ham and Chelsea international Len Goulden; Goulden senior was now also on the club's payroll as manager of the 'A' team in the Metropolitan League.

It was Goulden's only appearance. Goy only took part in one further League match for Arsenal, though he later continued his career with Southend, Watford and Huddersfield. Again he was on the winning side at home to Birmingham City in a match re-arranged for the Monday after the Cup final because of the tragic death from polio of Jeff Hall, Birmingham's England international right back. In common with all professionals, the Arsenal players were immediately inoculated against the disease.

By then Swindin had made another expensive purchase which did not pay real dividends. Mel Charles of Swansea looked a carbon-copy of his brother John, a genuinely great player who performed towering feats particularly in the colours of Leeds United, Juventus and Wales. The younger Charles was blessed with similar versatility, but not durability. In London he was dogged by bad luck, needing two knee operations in the space of a year. It was only in this third season that he was fit enough for a regular place; he did not complete that campaign, Arsenal cutting their losses by selling him to Cardiff City.

By the end of Swindin's first season, 17 players had left the club, including the loyal Bowen who had returned to Northampton Town as player-manager. Vic Groves succeeded Bowen in the post of club captain with Docherty his vice-captain. On the list of new recruits, Ian McKechnie was unusually billed as a forward goalkeeper, though it was only in the latter role that he played in the First Division. For George Swindin, however, the right blend remained elusive.

It might have all been very different if Docherty had not broken an ankle against his old club Preston in October 1959 when Arsenal were cruising in fourth place. From the end of that month to 6 February 1960 Swindin's side went without a home win, and relegation was a worry by the time Docherty had regained his fitness. The highly competitive Evans also frac-tured an ankle during the season on two occasions, and Charles succumbed to his cartilage weaknesses.

It might have been different again if Huddersfield Town had responded to Arsenal's overtures for Denis Law. An offer was made to the value of £50,000, but Manchester City topped it, and Law's subsequent glittering career only served to emphasise the missed opportunity.

It might still have been different if a few miles north of Highbury, Tottenham Hotspur had not been building a team to make history. Any shortcomings at Highbury were brought into sharper focus by Bill Nicholson's magnificent Spurs' side which set unprecedented standards for the modern game by finally nailing the growing belief that the Double could not be done. Two wins over Arsenal were just part of an all-conquering march to the First Division title in 1960–61, though Tottenham did not have the added satisfaction of topping the record of 66 points; they did, however, equal the Arsenal total of 30 years earlier.

It would take Arsenal ten years to put the record straight with their fiercest rivals. Unknowingly one change in the Highbury personnel for that particular season, which was as disjointed at Arsenal as it was cohesive at Spurs, began the recovery. Billy Milne, the long-serving physiotherapist who had carried on the task of healing the injured after Tom Whittaker's promotion had retired the previous season. His replacement himself had known injury, which had cut short his playing days as a winger with Derby County. Six years in the Royal Army Medical Corps had been followed by very impressive work, together with Dr Alan Bass, at a rehabilitation centre in Camden Town. Those were the credentials which brought Bertie Mee to Highbury in 1960.

There was a new training ground in 1960 for the players and their new physiotherapist; the centres for preparation were switched from Highbury and Hendon to the University College Grounds at London Colney. Peter Goring, though, was among the absentees when the squad reported for pre-season work; he had been released, though as the programme recorded: 'no club had a more faithful employee.' For those retained the future was somewhat uncertain. Newspapers were full of gossip about Arsenal and proposed transfers, and there was no smoke without fire.

George Eastham had sent shock waves through the traditional management of professional football in England by demanding to leave Newcastle United, for whom he had performed skilfully at inside forward from 1956 to 1960. He asked simply for the right of working men in other trades or professions, to change his place of employment after giving due notice that he wanted to leave. Football, though, had never reflected the democracy of the rest of the nation; the game was governed by the 'retain and transfer' system, which left the employers literally holding all the cards. If any club wanted to

keep a member of its playing staff, it could do so by preventing that footballer from joining any other Football League club. Transfers only took place when both the selling and the buying club were in agreement. There could be no auction on players' salaries either; the League still operated a maximum wage, then £20 per week, which meant that the pay structure was theoretically the same in the Fourth Division as in the First.

It was not the abolition of the maximum wage that Eastham set out to challenge, though at the same time through the skilful negotiation of the Professional Footballers Association headed by its chairman, Jimmy Hill, that battle was simultaneously being fought and won. Eastham simply wanted to find another club and was prepared to go to court to fight for his right to move. The game's establishment branded him a rebel and a villain; as Eastham said at the time: 'According to which side of the fence you are on I've become a martyr, a big-head, a rebel or — as Charlie Mitten, the manager of Newcastle United, insisted — "The guy with the biggest head, the shortest arms and the deepest pockets in the business".'

George Eastham moved to London, where a sympathetic friend employed him for six months as a salesman; his benefactor was Ernie Clay who later became a director and then chairman of Fulham. The League initially treated the affair as an internal matter for Newcastle, who, in the week leading up to the opening of the 1960–61 season made a conciliatory gesture. Eastham could continue to live and train in London, and keep his job outside football, if he re-signed.

Despite pressures from friends and foes to accept, Eastham believed that the dispute had gone too far for reconciliation. George Swindin tried to solve the dilemma with a conventional transfer approach; Newcastle wanted two international forwards and £25,000. Arsenal were prepared to include Herd in a package, and this had unfortunate repercussions. Herd was to score 30 goals that season, but at the end of it, his faith in the club shaken, he left for Manchester United.

In November 1960 the deal was finally done with no other player involved. For one of the country's most astute creators of chances, Arsenal paid Newcastle United £47,500; Eastham's share was a £20 signing-on fee! But that was far from being the end of the story. The PFA encouraged Eastham to continue his fight against the system, to free footballers from 'slavery'. In June 1963 Eastham versus Newcastle United was heard in the High Court before the aptly-named Judge Wilberforce. The evidence presented on behalf of the League Management Committee spoke of 'the situation being hopeless without the retain and transfer system. Regulated football would be finished.' Gerald Gardiner QC, representing George Eastham, likened that system to life in the Middle Ages.

On Thursday, 4 July, Independence Day in the United States, Mr Justice Wilberforce ruled in favour of independence for footballers — that the FA and Football League were responsible for an unreasonable restraint of trade. Instead of the old practice of signing-on for each season, players were now to be bound to clubs by contract, the length of which would be negotiable.

Finally getting to play football after the long legal wrangle which led to the abolition of the 'retain and transfer' system, George Eastham scores for Arsenal versus Manchester United on 21 October 1961. The other goals in a 5-1 win came from Gerry Ward, John Barnwell and Alan Skirton (right). When Newcastle would not transfer Eastham to Arsenal a year earlier, the player refused to turn out for the Magpies again and, with Jimmy Hill of the PFA advising him, effectively sued the football authorities for restraint of trade. He was to win the case and Arsenal were to get their man.

With the maximum wage by then abolished, professional football became governed by market forces; the best supported clubs could, and did, acquire the better players and were able to reward them appropriately.

Ironically Eastham's single-mindedness had already been felt in the Highbury boardroom. He had first worn the famous red and white shirt in a reserve match at Highbury, putting thousands on the gate; then on 10 December he marked his return to the First Division with two goals in a 5–1 victory over Bolton Wanderers. Yet at the end of the season, with the retain and transfer system not yet challenged in court, he refused the first offer made by Arsenal to their players after the abolition of the maximum wage.

Eastham rejected a basic wage of £30 a week, with incentives: a bonus for each first team appearance of £10; £4 for a win (unchanged from the previous year); £1 per each thousand on gates between 35,000 and 45,000; and £2 per thousand for attendances above 45,000. Mel Charles also held out against these terms, which were accepted by every other member of Swindin's first team squad. Eastham, who was to win all his 19 England caps during his six years at Highbury, was the first to relent. Charles, who began the new season with a flurry of goals, then followed suit.

A future Welsh international, Arfon Griffiths, was signed from Wrexham in February 1961, but he stayed just 19 months. Another newcomer to the first team who was to stay longer made his first appearance at Sheffield Wednesday a fortnight after Eastham's debut; Terry Neill wore the number four shirt and scored in a 1–1 draw.

The spring of 1961 saw two departures among Arsenal's senior personnel. Ron Greenwood's perceptive coaching talents had already attracted a legion of admirers, and when the offer to manage West Ham United came along his employers did not stand in his way. Two months earlier Tommy Docherty, who had lost a little of his enthusiasm for playing, was recruited as first team coach by the Chelsea manager Ted Drake.

Also in 1961 Sir Bracewell Smith stood down from the Chairmanship of the club through the strain of too much travelling, and was appointed Life President. Denis Hill-Wood was elected in his place, continuing the family tradition which encompassed his father Samuel and later his son Peter. But on the field the 1960–61 and 1961–62 seasons did not produce potency to match potential. Alan Skirton drew good reviews, comparing his wing play to that of Alf Kirchen, and he succeeded Herd as top scorer. Johnny MacLeod from Hibernian and Eddie Clamp, a stern-tackling wing half from Wolves, came to Highbury as established players. But the blend was not right, and the debut of an industrious winger from the north-east called George Armstrong almost passed unnoticed.

With criticism mounting, George Swindin accepted the responsibility for the shortfall, and in March 1962 he resigned. Terry Neill tells how

Swindin discovered what everyone else knew when he saw a speculative newspaper hoarding at Euston. It precipitated a summer of change and by the start of the 1962–63 season Arsenal not only had a new manager, they also had a new coach, a new team captain and, in a fanfare of publicity, a new centre forward.

The choice of manager certainly captured the public's imagination. Billy Wright typified the best values in British football. Hard but fair, he first played for England in the initial peace-time international in 1946. His subsequent feats took him into the game's Hall of Fame, with a record 105 caps at wing half and later centre half, and the captaincy of his country on 90 occasions. He played in 70 consecutive internationals, a record never likely to be beaten. More than that, he acted as a perfect ambassador not only in international football but for Wolverhampton Wanderers, for whom he performed with great distinction until an emotional retirement in 1959.

Billy Wright took football from the back pages to all other parts of the daily papers. His genial nature, added to the stature he had achieved in football, made him one of the nation's leading personalities. His marriage to Joy Beverley, one of the singing trio of sisters who were topping bills in the world of show business, was supposed to be secret. Yet thousands were there in Poole to salute the happy couple.

Three times Billy Wright had skippered Wolves to the League Championship, the last in his final year; he had been part of the FA Cup winning team in 1949. In 1952 he had been elected Footballer of the Year. He was recognised in the honours lists with a CBE.

When the call to Highbury came his response was immediate and positive. Before dedicating himself to the cause of Wolverhampton Wanderers, the young Billy Wright had been intoxicated by reports of Arsenal's triumphs in the 1930s. They became 'his team'; he admired the club immensely. Though Arsenal had broken from the tradition of making their appointments from within, they could scarcely have chosen someone with a greater awareness of the club's traditions.

His coach also had first-hand experience of the standards expected at Highbury; Les Shannon, who had been working for Everton, had been in the Burnley side which tried so hard in that frantic last match of the 1952–53 season to deprive Arsenal of the Championship. Nine years had elapsed without further success, so the incoming management were well aware of what was expected from them.

To that end Wright invested £70,000 in Joe Baker, a Liverpudlian who had made his name in Scotland and was signed from Torino. Baker, then 22, had already captured the headlines by winning his first England cap while playing for Hibernian, the first man to win an England cap while playing outside the country.

Baker took his place as centre forward in

Billy Wright, then England and the world's most capped player, took over the manager's chair from George Swindin (who had held it for four years) in 1962. He, in his turn, was to last another four, by which time directors and fans were becoming restless as the club had not finished higher than seventh since the turn of the 1960s. Wright was the only one of the eight managers after Herbert Chapman not to have previously had strong links with Highbury. This may have worked against him, as would putting the paper into the typewriter the wrong way round.

had marred his first League game by putting five goals past him.

One of several players of his era who enjoyed a cigarette, Kelsey is remembered by many ex-team-mates for one exceptional show of agility. It came when he was caught off guard and thrown into a swimming pool. Jack clambered out soaked from head to toe, but the cigarette was bone dry!

Ian McKechnie was charged with the responsibility of following in such famous footsteps in that opening match at Orient. He had been signed originally as an outside left but Swindin spotted his potential in goal during training sessions.

Billy Wright began his Arsenal career with a 2–1 win, Baker supplying the winning goal, to the delight of many tipsters who were busily forecasting that this would be Arsenal's best season since the 1953 Championship. But there was to be no overnight success. Though Baker and Strong scored 52 goals between them, Arsenal finished only seventh.

The following season Arsenal's powerful pair of attackers were even more impressive; they finished level on 26 goals in the First Division, plus five more each in Cup competitions. Geoff Strong relished the rivalry: 'Joe and I hit it off from the start, and we enjoyed the race between us to see who could be top scorer. Our partnership blended well, and it was, I think, the start of playing two central strikers at the club. Before that it was one centre forward and two inside forwards. In my day the forward line was brilliant. The goals flowed. But unfortunately we kept letting them in at the other end.' In 1963–64, Arsenal dropped one place, to eighth; only the Champions Liverpool netted more goals in home matches than the 56 struck at Highbury. Yet in First Division games 89 goals were conceded, more than Bolton Wanderers, who were relegated.

Billy Wright was already aware of the problems within the club but, by his own later admission, too inexperienced in management to be able to solve them quickly enough: 'I began to realise that I had some senior players who did not want to play for Arsenal. They wanted to do well for themselves, but they weren't Arsenal through and through. I wanted the types who lived for the club, and by continuing the good work started by George Swindin with the youth policy I could see the potential in the youngsters who were coming through.' Three of the players later to win the double in the club's very finest hour were given their debuts during Wright's second season: Peter Simpson, John Radford and Bob Wilson.

Simpson's baptism arrived at home to Chelsea, the match in which he was given the job of marking the free-scoring Bobby Tambling; Tambling's reply was to score all four goals in Chelsea's 4–2 victory, but Simpson did enough to ensure that his first team career was not immediately nipped in the bud.

Wilson, too, began inauspiciously, though he

Wright's first League match at Orient; he was flanked by two inside forwards from the north-east who had both come to Highbury in the 1950s, Geoff Strong and John Barnwell. The side was captained by Terry Neill, with two more Ulstermen at full back in Magill and McCullough. Laurie Brown, the former amateur international star operated at right half, with young Scot John Snedden to the left of Neill. The two wing positions went to Armstrong and Skirton.

Unfortunately for the new manager his arrival coincided with the end of Jack Kelsey's marvellous career, though that was not confirmed until the following November. Kelsey had played a then record 327 League games over eleven years. His 41 international appearances for Wales also constituted a record for a British goalkeeper, and it was while representing his country that he sustained the back injury which caused his downfall.

Wales had been asked to provide opposition for Brazil in their preparation for the World Cup finals. The match took place in Sao Paulo and Kelsey collided heavily with Vava, Brazil's famous striker. Four years earlier in the World Cup in Sweden one of his finest hours had come against Brazil when only a deflected shot from the 17-year-old Pele had found its way past him in a gripping quarter-final. He'd come a long way from the night when he had sneaked away from Highbury distraught that Charlton Athletic

made a winning debut: 4–2 at home to Forest. The goalkeeping problem was developing into a crisis. Jack McClelland, who had taken over from McKechnie, had broken a collar-bone at Leicester, and Baker, who took over the jersey, was beaten five times in a 7–2 defeat. McKechnie's lack of experience became exposed when he was recalled. Both Wilson and his manager realised that he was not ready either, but until the acquisition of Jim Furnell from Liverpool half-way through the season there was no viable alternative.

Bob Wilson, though, had one attribute appreciated by students of goalkeeping history. He was born in Chesterfield, the breeding ground of many fine keepers of whom Gordon Banks remains the most notable. Wilson, though, came from a family so Scottish that when he was chosen to play for England Schoolboys, in the same side as Nobby Stiles, his father refused to watch the match. Wilson senior also played a significant role in the unusual path his son had taken to Highbury, advising him to turn down an offer to join the groundstaff of Manchester United so that he could continue his studies at Loughborough College.

A year's probationary teaching at Paddington in West London had brought Bob Wilson south. He had been attached to Wolves as an amateur, and his arrangement at Highbury was initially on the same unpaid basis. Later Wolves received £7,000 when he was offered a professional engagement.

The club continued to provide the very best to prepare the playing staff for action. The training area behind the Clock End was covered during the summer of 1963 to provide splendid all-weather facilities. But the team were inconsistent. This spread to Arsenal's first European campaign, in the Inter-Cities Fairs Cup (later to become the Fairs Cup, then the UEFA Cup). It took Johnny Macleod only nine minutes to record the club's first goal in Europe — against Staevnet, a team of Danish part-timers. Arsenal were five up at half-time in Copenhagen and the deadly duo of Baker and Strong both came home with hat-tricks in a 7–1 triumph. Astonishingly Staevnet, with no hope of redressing the balance, won the return at Highbury 3–2. In the next round RFC Liege offered a sterner test, defending successfully at Highbury to obtain a 1–1 draw; a goal from the adventurous McCullough was all Arsenal could manage in a 3–1 defeat in the second leg.

In April 1964 Billy Wright's search for greater commitment took him back to his Black Country origins. Don Howe had been born in Wolverhampton, but his name had been made at nearby West Bromwich Albion, his only club. Howe's technique and determination at full back had won him 23 England caps, many of them alongside Wright, who saw him as a man who could help put the fire back into the dressing-room: 'As a player Don was a bit static by then, but I knew he would be very good for the Arsenal. A lovely man, a passionate man! I

bought him not just for the present but for the future, and for some £35,000 I think you'll agree the club got excellent value.'

Howe joined forces with Wright in April 1964, but after the transfer deadline, so his first appearance had to wait until the start of the 1964–65 season. The fixture list made it an awesome beginning, away to Liverpool who were setting out to defend their League title. It was a splendid match, a perfect choice for BBC Television to start their new experiment with Saturday evening highlights called *Match of the Day*. Liverpool led 2–0, were pulled back to 2–2, but struck a winner in the dying seconds. Peter Thompson, their elusive winger, gave Howe a baptism of fire, which was greeted with great amusement in the Highbury dressing-room 20 years later when the match was screened again to commemorate the anniversary. By then Don Howe was manager of a generation of footballers who had never seen him play, and some of whom were not even born that day at Anfield.

That same game had another repercussion; it confirmed Bill Shankly's admiration of the qualities of Geoff Strong, who had again been an Arsenal scorer. With typical determination Shankly set out to get this man, and by November Strong was sold to Liverpool: 'I jumped at the chance of the move because at the time I just could not see any future at Highbury

Willy Irvine backheels the ball past keeper Tony Burns to open the scoring for Burnley on 17 October 1964. It was Burns' debut, but it was to end happily as Peter Simpson, Jon Sammels and Joe Baker scored to help end the match 3-2 in favour of the home side. The picture is also interesting because of the figure on the right, one Don Howe, who was to become manager almost exactly 20 years later. He played 74 first-class games for the club, scoring just once.

in terms of success. Everything at the club was marvellous in so many ways, but it was too good really. It lacked the spark that was necessary to win trophies. Funnily enough, I had just a few weeks at the club with Frank McLintock and I could see that maybe he was bringing the drive that was needed.'

Six months later Strong collected an FA Cup winners medal, as Liverpool beat Leeds United at Wembley, but not as a striker; Shankly converted him into a wing half and his career developed from there. Frank McLintock had always been a wing half, and his stock had risen from his contribution to the two FA Cup runs which had taken unfashionable Leicester City to Wembley. There, however, he had been a loser both times. In 1963 he had also played three times for Scotland, twice alongside Ian Ure, who had recently joined Arsenal.

With Highbury supporters raising their voices in demands for an improvement on the field, McLintock's arrival for £80,000 was the latest attempt to appease them. Moreover, the new-comer's signature had been won against stern competition from other First Division clubs, including Spurs. Nottingham Forest spoiled McLintock's debut party by winning 3–0 at Highbury, with John Barnwell, an Arsenal player only seven months earlier, directing the Forest traffic towards the home goal.

Time would show that McLintock, then a foraging and at times ill-disciplined player, had the backbone to overcome such a dismal start. But there was no disguising that in his first season Arsenal were a soft touch. Baker continued to be among the country's leading scorers, but Strong, who had not been the favourite of every Arsenal fan, was badly missed. The League position plummeted to 13th and the FA Cup exit brought bitterness and recrimination, a shameful 2–1 defeat at Third Division Peterborough United. Accusations about lack of commitment were spread thickly by those reporters who covered the downfall.

It was left to the club's youngsters to provide one ray of sunlight through the gloom. The Youth team reached the final of the FA Youth Cup, beating Everton 1–0 at Highbury in the first leg only to lose 3–1 in the return in front of 30,000 spectators at Goodison Park. Radford provided the spearhead, and from the rest David Jenkins and Gordon Neilson were to become members of the first team squad. A year later the next generation of young Arsenal players, including Pat Rice and Sammy Nelson, won the trophy, beating Sunderland 5–3 on aggregate. None of the other ten who played reached the first team, but the later success of these few players mark one contribution Wright made in his four years at the helm.

Season 1965–66 was the last in first-class football for the genial, kindly Billy Wright, whose playing days had been almost devoid of failure, but whose management days were as short on success. Maybe the writing was on the wall the previous summer with the decision to change the club colours to all-red shirts, with the only white being on the collar and the cuffs; white shorts with red seams and red stockings completed the design which was seen as a return to the style of Nottingham Forest. The change was soon reversed and, to Arsenal's credit, they have been the only major club to ignore the money-chasing detail changes of recent years.

As most of football awaited the 1966 World Cup with an increasing sense of anticipation, Arsenal's and Wright's fortunes reached unprecedented depths. A home fixture against Leeds United was misguidedly rearranged for Thursday 5 May 1966, the same evening Liverpool contested the European Cup Winners Cup final against Borussia Dortmund at Hampden Park, shown live on television. That attraction, combined with Arsenal's dismal form, resulted in the Gunners attracting what is still the lowest First Division crowd since the First World War — 4,544 against the second placed club in the League! And they lost 3–0. Only a win over Leicester two days later elevated the club to 14th, their lowest place since 1930.

At the end of the season Billy Wright took a holiday; apart from his responsibilities at Highbury he had also been contracted by BBC Television to take part in their coverage of the World Cup finals. While he was away the board decided that recent results 'justified a change in management'. Denis Hill-Wood broke the news to him on his return. Outwardly it was accepted with the gentlemanly nature with which Wright, the player, had wooed the hearts of the football world. Inwardly it hurt bitterly: 'It was heartbreaking for me. Maybe I was too nice, but that is the way I am. But I wanted so much to make Arsenal great again, and I did feel that with the young players we were moving along the right lines.'

There is no doubt that the softness in Wright's approach was taken advantage of by senior players. In turn he found it easier to bring the best out of the youngsters. A caring man who would think nothing of inviting his players to the West End to see the Beverley Sisters and other show business friends, his Highbury heartbreak happily did not alter the very essence of one of football's amiable heroes. Straight after the World Cup of 1966 he accepted an offer from ATV (later Central TV) to use his knowledge of the game in television. Twenty years later he remained a much loved figure in that industry, and had just completed another World Cup, his sixth in television to go along with his three as England's captain.

In 1966 his sacking at Arsenal merely deflected the back pages of the newspapers away from speculation as to whether England could win the World Cup. Which major figure in football, wondered Fleet Street, would be summoned to Highbury to accept the challenge of trophy-hunting for Arsenal?

127

· CHAPTER 8 ·
Arsenal's Double

Many decisions were involved in the construction of the Double-winning side, which took Arsenal Football Club to the highest of all domestic achievements. Yet surely the most inspired was taken by the board of directors in the summer of 1966. While the media indulged in fruitless speculation about which of the game's big names would be appointed to succeed Billy Wright, the Highbury decision-makers were recognising a quality of leadership within the fold.

Bertie Mee was offered the manager's job at a private meeting with Denis Hill-Wood. The choice of the physiotherapist caught Fleet Street off their guard (though Whittaker was a precedent of course). It had the majority of the playing staff believing that it could only be a stop-gap appointment, and even surprised the recipient of the offer: 'It was a surprise, but a very pleasant one. I had not planned to become a football club manager. I was very happy in the career of my special interest, and I was enjoying a great deal of job satisfaction from it. But I was used to positions of responsibility. I had run organisations of various types. So my response was that if that's what the board would like, then I would give it a go.'

With two successful careers already behind him — in the military and medical spheres — Bertie Mee was the right man at the right time for a club which needed an urgent injection of authority. Yet though Bertie Mee was by no means a household name, he was very well known inside the game. He had been running the treatment of injuries courses for the Football Association for almost 20 years. At establishments such as Lilleshall he had lectured to all football's leading managers and coaches, and he had their respect. Such experiences had given the new Arsenal manager a sound working knowledge of the highways and byways of the Football League.

Bertie Mee also brought to the job an immediate insight into what was wrong inside the dressing room. After all, it had been his area of operation for six years. The players also knew that he stood for no nonsense in the discipline of recovering fitness. Most significant of all, he was not overawed at what he had been chosen to do, but with a characteristic and sensible touch of caution he did make sure that an exit was

available should it be required: 'I asked the chairman if I could initially take the job for twelve months, and that if it didn't work out, I could revert to my previous position. He was most agreeable. So I began by approaching the task in terms of management, from purely a management point of view. It was my belief that there was nothing radically wrong, but the club had to be more professional from all angles. We needed a general tightening-up. The players were a good crowd, but I felt that they could be more dedicated to the job, and certainly could care more about Arsenal. The danger was that mediocrity was being perpetuated.'

With Les Shannon also leaving the club following the change of management, Mee required a new coach, and successfully sought the services of an old friend, Dave Sexton, then with Fulham. Frank McLintock, in his 1969 autobiography *That's The Way The Ball Bounces* summed up the players' response to Sexton: 'I haven't come across many people in the game who have his ability to get through to players without shouting the odds and screaming at them. I don't know what it is that Dave has, maybe it's a gift of leadership. That is perhaps simplifying his effect, all I know is that he could have persuaded us to do anything. He thinks deeply about football and pointed out things I wouldn't have dreamed of — and before he came I thought I knew most of it.

'In his sixteen months at Highbury he had us eating out of his hands, and we were happy with the manager too. In a way, Dave's impact made us respect Bert even more. After all, it was he who brought Dave in. He must have known about him and recognised his talent. I felt we could trust both of them, which is saying something in this game.'

The first change made by Bertie Mee was to dispense with the skilful but at times erratic Eastham, who was sold to Stoke City. Eastham had once admitted that he knew within the first five minutes whether he was going to have a good game or not. The new manager did not deny Eastham's talent but wanted those who would roll up their sleeves and battle in all weathers.

A further pruning came with his decision to cut one team from the club's commitments. Arsenal withdrew from the Metropolitan League,

Not everything was wine and roses . . . the great years of 1968-72 were to see no less than five major cup finals, one in each season. The memories are firmly of 1971, but three of the five were lost by tight margins. The 1968 Football League Cup final was decided by a single goal (above) from Leeds United full back Terry Cooper (hidden in picture) after a corner. A year later Arsenal were back at Wembley for the final of the same competition and this time hot favourites to defeat Third Division Swindon Town, with nine of the previous year's twelve

appearing again. The result was a shock 3-1 win by the underdogs, Don Rogers, with two, and Roger Smart scoring their goals. The only Arsenal response was from Bobby Gould, who left the field in tears (above) comforted by John Radford. Gould, a popular player with colleagues and crowd alike, made 83 first-team appearances in a four-year career with the club and scored 23 goals. Sadly, he was never to obtain that winner's medal.

Bottom left: **In 1972 Arsenal came back** to Wembley looking to retain the FA Cup, a feat performed this century only by Newcastle and Spurs. They again failed by one goal, again to a Leeds United then at the height of their powers. The goal was a header from Allan Clarke which gave Geoff Barnett no chance. Barnett was deputizing for Bob Wilson, who had been injured in one of those interminable semi-finals against Stoke.

though this did not take effect until the 1967–68 season. With the abolition of the maximum wage, the increased cost of employing players meant that those who shuttled between the Reserves and the 'A' team with little hope of becoming first team material could no longer be accommodated.

The reign of Bertie Mee began in style with a 3–1 win at Sunderland. Alan Skirton scored twice but within a month he was also on the move, to Blackpool. Four of the Double-winning team played at Roker Park — Storey, at left back, McLintock, Radford and Armstrong, who was the other scorer. Don Howe was the new club captain, but, following a broken leg, he was to play just one First Division match under Mee, at Manchester City on 10 September 1966.

The home campaign began with a match which attracted a 40,000 crowd drawn to Highbury partly by the win at Sunderland but also by the presence of the World Cup triumvirate of Moore, Peters and Hurst, who lined up for West Ham. Arsenal won 2–1, Radford contributing both goals, and a win over Aston Villa gave the new regime an auspicious start. It was not until match five that the team was beaten, and it was Spurs who enjoyed inflicting that first defeat 3–1 at White Hart Lane.

In that season Arsenal entered the League Cup for the first time. In common with some other First Division teams, the club had looked at the fledgling competition designed by League Secretary Alan Hardaker as an unnecessary extra. In 1966–67 the competition achieved the respectability that was being sought for it by the scheduling of a Wembley final; previously the outcome had been decided on a home and away basis. Victory also now included an automatic entry into the Fairs Cup, another considerable attraction.

Yet Arsenal's debut in the League Cup scarcely suggested that the club had warmed to the experience. It took three games to beat Gillingham, with a 1–1 draw at Highbury being matched in the replay before a 5–0 triumph on the Third Division club's ground. The games were barely regarded as first team fixtures with the inclusion of several fringe players. Arsenal went out in the next round, losing 3–1 at home to West Ham.

Tommy Baldwin had the distinction of scoring the club's first three goals in the League Cup, and four in all in the Gillingham saga, but they were parting shots. As Bertie Mee continued his rebuilding, the young striker from the northeast left for Chelsea, swapped for a taller, more elegant forward, George Graham. The move worked well for both parties. Two days after Graham's arrival, Mee spent £50,000, then a record fee for a full back, on Bob McNab from Huddersfield Town. Two more pieces were fitted into the jigsaw.

Not every deal was to reap such returns. Colin Addison was an expensive buy from Nottingham Forest, but left 15 months later for Sheffield United without establishing a regular place. The transitional nature of the season did produce an eneven pattern of performance; at the half-way mark Arsenal had dropped to sixteenth place. But a run in the FA Cup to the fifth round perked morale, and the season was finished with an unbeaten run of 12 matches, which improved the final League placing to seventh. Moreover, there was one trophy to the club's name. In BBC Television's popular football show *Quiz Ball* two players were paired with a celebrity and Ian Ure and Terry Neill romped away with the title for Arsenal. Ure, in particular, was an intellectual revelation.

The playing staff had already realised that the promoted physiotherapist was no push-over in the manager's office. Mee had set high standards and established a reputation for being strict but fair in the pursuit of them. It was significant that Peter Simpson performed regularly in the first team during the 1966–67 season. The new manager had delivered a few well-chosen words to the player whose gifts were not initially matched by his ambition: 'I'd known Peter Simpson since he was 14 or 15. In my previous work at the club I'd already had to kick his backside from time to time. So one of the first things I did was to ask him whether he was going to be a regular in the team or poodle around the place unsure of whether he really wanted a career in the game. I also told him I was not going to give him much longer to decide.'

An easy-going character from East Anglia, Simpson tightened his approach and was very unlucky not to add an England cap to his subsequent honours with Arsenal; only the perennial Bobby Moore and his regular deputy Norman Hunter prevented full international recognition.

Bertie Mee was not a man for fads or fancies. He discouraged the usual dressing room superstitions in his players, and Ure's concern for a particular 'lucky' shirt in a match against Coventry City became a factor in Arsenal's eventual decision to sell the Scottish international defender to Manchester United.

For the opening game of the 1967–68 season, Mee, now over his self-imposed trial period, wrote in the programme: 'No manager could wish for a more dedicated team. The record of the defence speaks for itself, but we would all agree that we were not scoring enough goals to make ourselves a serious threat from a Championship point of view. Our forward position must be strengthened if the right type of player becomes available.' Certainly the goals from midfield — ten from Jon Sammels, nine from McLintock and seven from the winger Armstrong — had been essential to helping Mee end his first season in the top half of the table.

The major purchase of a striker did not happen until February 1968 when the big-hearted approach of Coventry goalscorer Bobby Gould attracted a record Arsenal bid of £90,000. By then Dave Sexton had already left to become manager at Chelsea, wanting, as Mee put it, 'to paddle his own canoe'.

McLintock, now the club captain, felt the departure keenly. So too did many other senior players, and picking up the pieces was not an easy task for his successor. Don Howe, who had been in charge of the reserve team, was promoted to chief coach, and within a matter of weeks had wiped away much of the distress at Sexton's departure. The team's form in the League showed no vast improvement, but the signs of progress did appear elsewhere, ironically in the competition which Arsenal had only recently learned to value.

Arsenal were paired in the Football League Cup quarter-final with Burnley. Coincidentally the tie, at Turf Moor, was scheduled for three days prior to Arsenal's First Division visit there. A replay in the League Cup thus meant that the two clubs were involved in three incident-packed meetings in the space of six days. The intensity of competition did not leave a pleasant taste.

When Burnley raced into a two-goal lead through Andy Lochhead and Brian O'Neill after only nine minutes, Arsenal's interest in the League Cup appeared to be over. Earlier in the decade it might have been so, but now Arsenal were developing resilience. Those two Scottish friends, Graham and McLintock, rattled in goals (two for Graham) in a frantic ten minutes which astonishingly saw Arsenal leave the field at half-time 3–2 in front. Twelve minutes into the second half McNab was sent off and Burnley's Willie Irvine managed a late equaliser which meant that battle was to be resumed at Highbury.

All might have been well but for the unfortunate timing of the First Division match. Feuds that had been simmering came to the boil again, and Arsenal finished the League game with nine men. McLintock was the first to be despatched by Sheffield referee Jim Carr for an apparent punch which left Frank Casper, the Burnley forward, flat on the ground. Arsenal's captain disputed the official's interpretation of the incident, and later won an appeal at a personal hearing in front of the FA Disciplinary Committee; Bertie Mee's testimony in his defence helped carry the day.

Peter Storey was the other player to be sent off, protesting too vigorously about the validity of the only goal of the match scored by Gordon Harris following a free-kick. Storey's tackle, which looked legitimate to millions of television viewers who saw the game on *Match of the Day*, had been penalised, though that did not excuse his subsequent outburst.

Both McLintock and Storey lined up in the League Cup replay the following Tuesday, but McNab was missing. His place went to a young, extremely enthusiastic London Irishman whose ebullient nature had won him an apprenticeship in the days of Billy Wright, over more naturally gifted schoolboys lacking such an infectious attitude. Against Burnley in 1967 Pat Rice showed no fear of the 'big time', and Arsenal scraped through 2–1 with Radford and Neill on target.

Huddersfield Town in the middle of the Second Division provided, on paper, easy opponents in the semi-final. But a timely goal from McNab was the only difference between the two sides at Highbury after a five-goal affair which kept the 40,000 crowd on edge to the last. The second leg at Leeds Road was by no means a formality, but Arsenal added to their aggregate lead with a 3–1 success, and after 16 years were back at Wembley.

Leeds United had also won both legs of their semi-final, and the Wembley occasion was billed as a battle between two teams desperate for success. Already Leeds, under Don Revie, had earned the tag of 'being the bridesmaid, never the bride'. Twice recent runners-up in the First Division they had been Wembley losers to Liverpool in the FA Cup Final in 1965. With football entering a cynical age, the antics of Revie's players had led to constant accusations of gamesmanship. With Arsenal coming to grips with the realities of that era in a new, methodical approach, a classic final was never really a possibility.

In many ways the match was the forerunner of titanic battles to come between the two clubs — much marauding in midfield but few clear-cut chances, and the outcome determined by a disputed goal. At a corner, Leeds' two tallest players, Jack Charlton and Paul Madeley, engaged in what Mee referred to as 'basketball' manoeuvres in front of goalkeeper Jim Furnell. When Gray's corner, perfectly struck as a left-footed in-swinger, curved in towards goal Furnell found his route to the ball was blocked. Graham helped out with a clearing header right on the line. The ball dropped perfectly for Terry Cooper, towards the edge of the area, and his superb volley flew into the Arsenal net. McLintock and Ure led the protesters but Les Hamer, the referee, pointed to the centre spot.

Bertie Mee was not downcast, but the disappointments for the season were not over. A week later came another Cup tie against Birmingham City in the fifth round of the FA Cup; Arsenal went out after a replay, the loss of a late goal at home leading to Mee's decision to give Wilson another run between the posts. The League programme did finish on an upswing with five consecutive victories, and a rise to ninth place.

The 1968–69 campaign began with the first victory at White Hart Lane for eleven seasons; an own goal by Phil Beal and a Radford effort injected a sense of anticipation for the months ahead. But there was still dissatisfaction in the stands. The chairman addressed it in the programme:

'There appears to be a misconception abroad that Arsenal managers, since Tom Whittaker, have been stifled and restricted by the Board of Directors and refused money with which to go into the transfer market. I can deny this absolutely. In the past twelve months alone, we have made approaches for four top class players and offered, in each case, a fee that would have

been a British record. In each case the club concerned said that they did not want the money and would not part with the player.'

Much of the criticism levelled at the club concerned its 'obsession' with the glories of the past; others sniped at Bob Wall for holding too much authority. Brian James, the best writer of the period, summed-up much of the prevalent feeling in this tongue-in-cheek comment in the *Daily Mail*: 'It would help of course if Arsenal were to win the European Cup. But they'd have to do it here at Highbury. Against, say, a combined Real-Benfica XI and then it would need Bob Wilson to break from his goal to score a hat-trick for victory in the last eight minutes. Only a match like THAT could possibly stand comparison with the great performances of the past.'

Arsenal did conjure up their best start to a season for 20 years, eleven games unbeaten until defeat at Elland Road emphasised again the growing rivalry with Leeds United. The new tightness of the Highbury community was emphasised by the fact that only 15 players started First Division games, one of whom, Jenkins, was swapped for another, Jimmy Robertson. The new recruit from Spurs arrived with a reputation as a strong character in the dressing room, not always easy to handle, but Mee did not flinch from that type of challenge.

McNab's selection for England in four internationals reflected the improvement at Highbury, and Radford wore the number seven shirt for his country against Rumania at Wembley, though he would play only once more for Sir Alf Ramsey.

The solidity that was binding Arsenal together did not always please the neutrals but Mee had already established his first priority; his team was never likely to capitulate. Wilson was making great strides as a goalkeeper, his strength of character growing in the face of regular teasing from his team-mates about his background as a schoolteacher. He was an ever-present in the 1968–69 League campaign. So too was the cold-eyed Storey and the resident chatterbox, McNab. Court, who was to be sold to Luton on the eve of the Double, missed only two matches in midfield. Simpson was emerging as a more complete central defender than either Ure or Neill. The options in midfield were increased by experimenting in that area with Graham, who was blessed with a sure touch and sharp football brain, but whose lack of explosive pace was making life up front increasingly difficult for him.

The interest in the FA Cup ended once more in the fifth round, but hardly in disgrace, a 1–0 defeat away to West Bromwich Albion, fellow First Division rivals. Against a background of such consistency it is unfortunate that the season will ultimately only be recalled for another Wembley defeat in the League Cup final. Unlike the Leeds experience the players could not walk off this time with heads held high. This time it was a shaming experience.

The two-leg semi-final with Spurs had produced more evidence of the competitive nature of Mee's team. In front of a full house of 55,000 at Highbury, Spurs were only seconds away from the sanctuary of a goalless draw when Radford popped up with what turned out to be a crucial goal. Tottenham pinned their hopes of turning the tables at White Hart Lane on the mercurial Jimmy Greaves, who scored in a tough, and at times brutal, encounter, but so did Radford and Arsenal won 2–1 on aggregate.

The final was still three months away, and Mee and his players had to wait a fortnight to learn whom their opponents would be. When the news came, any thoughts that the hard part had been done by eliminating Tottenham could have been forgiven. Third Division Swindon Town had battled their way to Wembley.

No one was keener to win at Wembley than Frank McLintock. His career had been punctuated by Wembley finals, two for Leicester City and one for Arsenal. Yet he was a three-time loser. The playing surface at Wembley had lost its reputation. Once impeccable, it had been badly damaged the previous autumn by the staging of the International Horse of the Year Show. Repairs were underway but heavy rainfall again destroyed the conditions underfoot. Three days before the League Cup final England entertained France at the Empire Stadium and gallons of water had to be pumped from the pitch for the match to take place. More rain tested the groundstaff beyond their capabilities. When the teams visited the ground the day before the match they realised the final would be staged on a mud-heap.

As expected Arsenal carried the fight to Swindon from the outset, a series of attacks that in such treacherous conditions took more energy to mount than to defend against. With eight of the side still touched by the after-effects of a flu virus which had caused the postponement of a League match the week before, such energy spent was not easily recouped. For some it was not recouped at all. At this point in their League programme Arsenal had let in just 18 goals in 30 matches, all of them chiselled out of the granite of their organisation. Thirty-four minutes into the League Cup final they allowed Swindon to take the lead with a mix-up between Ure and Wilson which presented Smart with the most open of open goals.

Swindon kept the lead until only four minutes from time. Then goalkeeper Downsbrough, a superman on the day, ventured out of his area in an attempt to kick the ball to safety, away from the on-rushing Gould. Instead, the ball rebounded off the Arsenal forward, who reacted quickly and headed it into the unguarded net. With extra time beckoning, relieved Arsenal fans believed that their team now had a psychological advantage that they would not squander.

Down at pitch level Don Howe was not so sure. He wanted extra time to be abandoned by referee Bill Handley to spare the players the slog in the cloying mud. It was no philanthropic gesture. He recognised the weariness in his own

players, aggravated by their recent illnesses. McLintock, usually a natural athlete, had cramp in both legs. McNab was also in distress. Others felt they were running in treacle. Graham had already replaced the weary Simpson.

For a team of Swindon's humble status it would have been forgivable if they had not seized their opportunity. It was a measure of their quality that they grasped it firmly. After 15 minutes of extra time, Don Rogers poked the ball home from a corner, though McNab on the line almost prevented the ball crossing it. Rogers had been peripheral for much of the match, and is pictured in a strip unsullied by dirt surrounded by defenders covered in mud when he put Swindon into the lead. In the second period he etched his trademark onto a Wembley final, running half the length of the pitch for a memorable solo goal. It was like sticking a knife into a dying body.

Stan Harland went up the Wembley steps to collect the League Cup from Princess Margaret. McLintock — now a four-time loser — was stunned. He had not contemplated defeat this time. A good-luck telegram from Don Revie wishing that he could 'be first up the steps this time' had an ironic touch. The Leeds United manager had forgotten that the League Cup final's formalities have the losers collecting their mementoes first.

Mee and Howe began the arduous task of reviving morale which had once been so high. Only the strong would swim and not sink after such a distressing experience. Among them was Bob Wilson, whose fierce pride was aroused by the humiliation. Sixteen years later he put the desolation of defeat into perspective: 'I truly believe that the rise of the Double side stemmed from that afternoon at Wembley. We came home to headlines about the "Shame of Arsenal", and a lot of us were determined that it would never happen again. We craved success with even more intensity because of it.'

The club started the 1969–70 campaign with another small alteration in colours; red socks with a white band on the turnover replaced the blue and white hoops which had been introduced in the Chapman era because blue was a fast dye and did not run whereas red did.

Ure's colourful and at times turbulent stay at Highbury came to an end after six years. In August 1969 he was sold to Manchester United for £80,000. John Roberts, a product of Swansea Town, was signed from Northampton in November as a potential successor. In the quest for goals Mee turned to an 18-year-old brought up in Islington on the club's doorstep. Charlie George had already shown exceptional talent as a schoolboy and youth player. No one was surprised when he made his League debut on the opening days of the season in a 1–0 home defeat by Everton, and struck his first League goal in the third match at West Bromwich Albion.

Ray Kennedy, nine months younger than George, tasted first team action in September in Northern Ireland; Kennedy was introduced as a substitute for Radford against Glentoran in the first round second leg of the Fairs Cup. George showed another side of his nature by being sent off for dissent.

Geoff Barnett, recently signed from Everton, saved a penalty in a European debut against Sporting Lisbon and kept a clean sheet in a goalless draw that set up the home leg, when Radford and Graham (2) quickly put the tie beyond the reach of the Portuguese club.

Meanwhile, in the First Division the absence of a regular goalscorer was still keenly felt. George, in some disgrace after his dismissal against Glentoran, had properly been removed temporarily from the spotlight to continue his education in the reserves. Even the defence had not settled to its normal grudging efficiency. Neill and Roberts were vying for the berth in the centre and when neither were fit, McLintock found himself switched there. The impact was not immediate but the seeds had been sown, and the four-time loser at wing half would soon make a permanent switch which would lead to finally collecting silverware while wearing the number five shirt.

A particularly dismal autumnal run of 10 matches without a win was ended in style with a 5–1 triumph at Crystal Palace, a performance which was highlighted by three more goals for Radford, and one from Graham with a delightful one-two exchange which won him ITV's regional *Big Match* trophy for the London area's 'Golden Goal'.

Excluded from all the permutations to find the right blend up front was Bobby Gould. He was axed from the first team squad and made open to transfer, but had to spend most of the season on the sidelines before Wolves stepped in to sign him. He survived the disappointment and continued to score goals wherever he wandered throughout the Football League. The enduring Arsenal image of the 1960s is probably Gould leaving the field in tears at the end of the 1969 League Cup final, in which he scored Arsenal's only goal.

If one match pinpointed McLintock's switch to the middle it was a 1–0 victory at Anfield at the end of November. Later he recalled that the move was not what he wanted: 'Gordon Clark, our chief scout, had seen the potential of me playing centre half, but I was dead against it. It seemed a reflection that I was not doing the job properly in midfield. But now I look back I think I was a better wing half for Leicester than for Arsenal. I came for a record fee at a time when we weren't a very good team, and I got caught up in the chase for honours. I lost some of the discipline in my play, and I used to chase all over the place trying to make us successful.

'Going back to centre half meant that I had to be more controlled. I did tend to stray forward at the start, and I remember getting caught out of position by Leeds United in one match, and that cost us the game. But Bob McNab was particularly helpful, and he used to yell at me about my positional play. Thanks to him and the

other defenders I learned the job quite quickly and we became very well organised at the back.'

Terry Neill was back in the middle of defence when Rouen were held goalless in France just before Christmas in the third round of the Fairs Cup. Arsenal had to be at their most patient in the return leg to make the breakthrough, which arrived late in the match from Sammels. It was the second of four matches in a very eventful week. The previous Saturday Peter Marinello, billed as the first six-figure signing of the decade, had marked his first appearance by scoring at Manchester United, a goal that turned out to be the high point of his much-publicised stay at Highbury.

Marinello was not yet eligible for FA Cup action, and therefore could not be considered for the fixture two days after the Rouen second leg. Arsenal were beaten at Blackpool in a rearranged third round replay after leading 2–0 at half-time. The congestion of the action was completed by another defeat, 3–0 at home to Chelsea the following Saturday, but the match deserves recording because it marked the first full appearance of Ray Kennedy.

The investment of £100,000 on Marinello from Hibernian stands comparison with the acquisition of Charlie Nicholas 13 years later. The management recognised a need to improve the image of the team, to add a sprinkling of flair to spice up the recipe from solid fare to a more extravagant dish to set before the fans. As a teenager Marinello's wing play with Hibernian had brought him the tag of the 'Second George Best'. His long hair added to the image, but sadly the image was eventually no more than an illusion.

He had made his League debut in Scotland as a 17-year-old and was only 19 when Arsenal brought him south. At the time Bertie Mee stressed that the immediate expectations must not be too great: 'We have purchased Peter with an eye to the future. First of all, though, we must re-educate him. He has picked up some bad habits in Scottish football. But once we have straightened these out he will prove an invaluable member of the Arsenal staff. We must first of all make him aware that he is a member of a team and so harness his individual skill to our pattern of play.'

The media, however, were not prepared to wait. The goal at Old Trafford only served to sharpen the interest, coming as it did on George Best terrain. One of Mee's strongest suits was protecting his players from outside influences, but on this occasion even he was caught out. A relative of Marinello's worked in the features department of the *Daily Express*, and when the manager agreed to what seemed like a simple request for a one-off interview, the publicity machine went into full swing. The new signing was given his own column; there were regular photograph sessions. Modelling offers flowed in, and he was chosen for a national advertising campaign to market the drinking of milk. Peter Marinello was understandably too immature to cope.

Marinello's third game for the club came in Rumania in the quarter-final against Dinamo Bacau. Arsenal were given a tremendous welcome at the airport by girls in national costumes dispensing bouquets of flowers. The team was clapped on to the pitch and off it after a 2–0 victory. Sammels opened the scoring following up on a George drive that rebounded out from the underside of the bar. Radford headed the second from McNab's left wing cross.

The potential of Marinello allowed Arsenal to release Robertson to Ipswich just before the transfer deadline, and the European campaign gathered further momentum with a rip-roaring seven-goal slaughter of Bacau at Highbury, a perfect way to mark the club's 50th competitive game of the season. McLintock was now firmly bedded in at centre half allowing another youngster who had come through the ranks to wear the number four shirt. Eddie Kelly, still only 19, had masses of Glaswegian grit and benefited greatly from McLintock's assistance and encouragement.

The semi-final was not so clear cut. Ajax from Amsterdam were about to be triple European Cup winners. The team which travelled to Highbury in April 1970 included Johan Cruyff, Rudi Krol, Wim Suurbier, Piet Keizer and Gerrit Muhren.

Arsenal were well prepared for the task. Charlie George was often to be inspired by the big occasion, and in the first half he deceived goalkeeper Bals from long range. In the second half Sammels again produced an important goal from midfield. George, the teenager, accepted the responsibility of scoring the third from the penalty spot when Graham was tripped. On a cold night in Amsterdam a week later Arsenal contrived a warming result, restricting Ajax to a solitary score from Muhren.

The imminence of the Mexico World Cup meant that the season had been compressed to finish in April. Ramsey had already announced his squad, choosing Simpson and McNab in the original party of forty but not in the 28 who would travel to Mexico. McNab subsequently joined the travelling band when Paul Reaney of Leeds United broke his leg, only to be let down again when the squad was reduced to 22. His return home before the finals were underway did, however, produce a silver lining. His talkative nature marked him down as a perfect television pundit. In the year of the 'panel' he became a popular part of the ITV team alongside Malcolm Allison, Derek Dougan and Pat Crerand. On the rival channel Bob Wilson was carving out a broadcasting future as another World Cup analyst.

The appeal of both to the media was heightened by their presence in the Arsenal side which ended the run of 17 years without a major trophy. The first leg of the Fairs Cup final took place just a week after the semi-final victory; it meant another short trip into Europe to Belgium, this time to face Anderlecht in the Parc Astrid in Brussels. There was much mutual respect.

Interestingly Anderlecht insisted that they would change their own mauve shirts in both matches, so that they could face the north London club in the red shirts and white sleeves which remain a recognisable and respected emblem all over the world. For their part Arsenal knew that in Jan Mulder, a Dutchman, they were meeting a forward as gifted as any in the world.

Mulder did not disappoint. He was the hub of an uninhibited performance by Anderlecht which on other days would have been good enough to build up an unassailable advantage. The Belgian club could support Mulder with Belgium's own golden boy, Paul van Himst, who would later manage the club to European success. Devrindt undermined Arsenal with an opening goal. Mulder was too elusive and he twice produced finishing touches past Wilson. At 3–0 a third defeat in a major final in three seasons was looming.

With time ticking away Arsenal's fighting spirit gave them a toehold on the tie. Kennedy had come on for the tiring George, one raw recruit for another; but he found a header which beat goalkeeper Trappeniers, and the slide down a slippery slope to disaster had at least been slowed. Nevertheless the mood was sombre back in the Arsenal dressing-room as Wilson vividly recalled: 'Even with the late goal we were all downcast. It looked as though we could be foiled yet again in our efforts to bring the club a trophy. Initially Frank McLintock felt it the most keenly, and he was cursing about being in another losing final. But Frank was always impulsive. If he saw you in a suit he liked he had to get one like it straight away. If you'd been to a great restaurant he'd have to go there the next night. But just as suddenly the mood would change. In Brussels his initial despair turned straight into optimism. He came out of the bath yelling that we were going to win. He lifted everybody, and by the time we left the ground, nobody had their heads down. You could say that the second leg was won at that point.'

McLintock, by his own admission, finds specific matches hard to remember but his attitude that night remained in his memory: 'Anderlecht were good. Mulder and van Himst were special players. But defensively that had looked vulnerable when we had been able to attack. Their centre half looked poor in the air. I believed we could do it, and I wanted to make sure the rest of the lads did.'

McLintock's captaincy was based on such strength of purpose. Others would have been broken by the succession of disappointments. Though he had thought seriously about seeking fresh pastures after the League Cup final defeat by Leeds, he had eventually withdrawn his transfer request. His hunger for honours was about to be satisfied.

The second leg of the Fairs Cup final took place at Highbury on Tuesday 28 April 1970. In the match programme Bertie Mee paid tribute to McLintock's new role at centre half, which earlier in the month had earned him a recall by Scotland after three years out of the international limelight. The manager also wrote of the crop that was being harvested from the youth policy which had been tended by Billy Wright and himself after George Swindin had sown the seeds. George, Kennedy and Kelly were singled out for special mention.

Eddie Kelly repaid the compliment. A stunning early shot brought Anderlecht within reach. Arsenal tore into their opponents with such frantic commitment that McLintock was asked afterwards by one of the Belgians if Mee's players had taken drugs. But the stimulus was not artificial; it was the desire for achievement. In the dressing room the talk about Arsenal's past glories had become more than wearisome.

Anderlecht deserved their place in the final. In the quarter-final they had eliminated Newcastle United, the holders. In a last four that would not have disgraced the European Cup itself, the Belgian club overcame Inter Milan while Arsenal were tussling with Ajax. But at Highbury they could not match the home team's desire for victory.

The weakness in the air spotted by McLintock was exploited in the second half, and the muscular Radford found space to head Arsenal's second. Thanks to Kennedy's 'away' goal, Arsenal now led, but were in no position to relax as Mulder hit a post. The complexities of the two-legged scoring system kept the 51,000 crowd anxious to the very last. Sammels, who was to lose his regular place during the Double year, ensured a deserved place on the roll of honour by adding a third. Had Anderlecht managed just one in reply they would have been level on aggregate. Even Bertie Mee's considerable ability to detach himself from the emotion of match action was tested to the limit.

When the final whistle eventually sounded, the floodgates opened. Delirious supporters surged on to the pitch. George for one had his shirt pulled from his back by souvenir hunters. Sir Stanley Rous, then FIFA's President, presented the Fairs Cup, which stayed in England for the third successive year following the victories of Leeds United and Newcastle United. For Arsenal it was the end of 17 barren years. McLintock had his hands on a trophy at last and there they stayed as he was carried shoulder-high around the pitch. Oddly, despite its significance, it was not a much-heralded victory at the time and it is not particularly well remembered now. There were two good reasons. One was that the season had been shortened because of the World Cup and England's defence of that trophy was claiming everyone's attention. The other reason was not clear for a year — the glow from the Double was eventually to dull everything around it.

Don Howe's words that Highbury night held great significance: 'This can be the big breakthrough. We can go on and on and on from here. The tension is off the players now. They have proved they can play football. I think this is just

The 1970 Fairs Cup final against Anderlecht was a happier occasion. Arsenal lost the first leg 3-1 in Brussels and were left with a lot to do in the return. No team had ever come back from a two-goal deficit to win a two-legged European final, nor from a three-goal deficit at any point in a final. Nor has any team done either since, a tribute to the Gunners' outstanding achievement in a match which is often overlooked because of the drama which followed a season later. The goals in the second leg at Highbury were scored by Kelly, Radford and Sammels and John Radford is seen celebrating his with the help of Charlie George.

the beginning.' Bertie Mee was never given to wild prophesy but even he admitted: 'The experience we gained tonight will be invaluable for winning our next objective — the Football League.'

McLintock was overwhelmed, his personal jinx broken. Older supporters weaned on the 1930s and Championships won under Whittaker were in tears. The effect on the club was immeasurable. Shame at Wembley 13 months earlier had set a test for all concerned. That examination had now been passed with flying colours. A date with destiny was just round the corner.

The 1970–71 season followed the dramatic World Cup finals in Mexico. England had lost their grip on the trophy despite leading West Germany 2–0 in the quarter-final. Brazil had captivated the watching world with a succession of thrilling performances, but they bore little relevance to the prevalent style in the English First Division.

In the latter part of the 1960s, winning matches had become more and more a priority. Managers, a relatively new concept given the long history of the professional game, were being given less and less time to construct their teams. Alf Ramsey's England, the model to copy since the 1966 World Cup triumph, concentrated on strengthening the midfield. With three or four men deployed in that department, there were fewer berths for strikers; but with defensive strategies becoming more sophisticated one goal was often enough to win.

Cynical attitudes, increasingly pervading society in other forms, were also becoming part of football. Leeds United's rise to the forefront of the national game had been based on huge helpings of skill, but the taste had been soured by what was delicately called gamesmanship. Winning was the drug, and if that was what the supporters wanted, the cost at times seemed unimportant.

Arsenal, in particular, had suffered from the change of emphasis. The past was embroidered with trophies in the days when the British were renowned for their sportsmanship in defeat. When losing became less acceptable, the trophies had stopped, until that emotional night in 1970 when the Fairs Cup was paraded around Highbury.

Few in that vast crowd, if any, could have predicted the further consequences of ending that famine. The hunger in the dressing room was only partly assuaged. Up to that time the Double of League and FA Cup had been achieved only three times. 'Proud' Preston North End, 'The Invincibles', first did the trick in 1888–89, winning the twelve-team Football League without losing a match, and the FA Cup without conceding a goal. Aston Villa emulated Preston with a Double in 1896–97, by which time the First Division had blossomed into a 16-team competition.

It had long appeared that dreams of such success were applicable only to those formative years of the game, particularly when club after club (including Arsenal) fell between the two stools in the 20th century. The mould of failure had finally been broken by an exceptional team. Tottenham Hotspur, under the wise guidance of Bill Nicholson, had the League Championship buttoned up by the middle of April 1961, having started the 1960–61 season with a record-breaking eleven straight wins. Another First Division landmark was reached with 31 wins, 16 of them away, another record. Arsenal's points total (66) of 30 years earlier was also equalled.

With the League title in the bag so early, there was less pressure in the FA Cup final for Tottenham. With Leicester City, their opponents, handicapped by an injury to defender Len Chalmers, the first Double of modern times was attained. In 1960–61 Bill Nicholson's side stood head and shoulders above their rivals. Their all-conquering progress was watched by crowds totalling a staggering 2½ million over a remarkable season.

In the ten years since 1961, football had lost some of its swagger and increased its tactical appreciation, particularly defensively; another Double looked most unlikely, particularly with the fixture list now swollen by other competitions — the League Cup for all and European involvement for the best.

If you were looking for a team on which to stake a few pounds to accomplish such a feat, Arsenal would not have been among the favourites. Twelfth in 1969–70, averaging just one point per game with 51 goals scored and 49 conceded, was hardly the foundation to suggest such glories. A much better bet would have been Leeds United, runners-up in both competitions in the previous season, or perhaps Chelsea, FA Cup winners and third in the League, or even Everton, the 1970 League Champions.

With a touch of irony, the Double year began at the home of the defending champions. On paper it could hardly have been a tougher start, but Bertie Mee's policies of stabilising Arsenal into a side that did not readily concede defeat had already paid dividends. From the outset of his management every goal let in had been put under an analytical microscope. Those days of capitulation away from home which had marred the early 1960s were long gone.

With the benefit of hindsight the events at Goodison Park on Saturday 15 August 1970 said much about the qualities which were to provide the basis for such an historic campaign, the extraordinary resilience which was to shine through so many battles in the months ahead.

The manager's team selection had already been affected by pre-season injuries. Peter Simpson required a cartilage operation. Jon Sammels had a leg in plaster. John Roberts, the strong-man from Wales known as Garth, came into the defence alongside McLintock. The strength of Everton's midfield trio of Howard Kendall, Colin Harvey and Alan Ball was recognised in the role given to Peter Storey, who was deputed to shadow Ball throughout; Storey's job at right back was passed to Pat Rice, who had played just 13 League games in the previous three seasons.

Everton began the match with the confidence of Champions. Wilson's stint in the television studios had done nothing to impair his agility, and as Arsenal were reduced to conceding a succession of free-kicks, the goalkeeper produced a catalogue of saves. His standards rarely dropped over the next nine months. Yet approaching the half-hour mark in the first half, Everton acquired the lead their pressure deserved. Tommy Wright, just back from England duty in Mexico, overlapped on their right; his cross evaded Wilson and Joe Royle dived forward to head home.

Everton continued to dominate. McNab once cleared off the line from Alan Whittle amid a series of skirmishes around the Arsenal goal. Nineteen minutes from time, however, with Everton's forces again well forward, the visitors regained possession, and broke quickly and clinically. Radford set up the chance. George took it, but in doing so cracked two bones in his ankle as he collided with goalkeeper West. The Arsenal scorer left the field on a stretcher.

The pattern resumed with Everton furiously seeking the lead again, and six minutes from time they recaptured it. Again Wright, the right back, swung over a telling cross. Wilson could only deflect the ball on to the inside of his right hand post. What happened after that became a matter for debate.

The nearest Everton player was Ball, who via head and hand sent the ball to Johnny Morrissey,

who restored the champions' advantage from close range. Wilson was understandably upset, and at the final whistle asked Ball for his version. The England midfield star admitted that he had used an arm but only accidentally. It might have caused an even greater furore, but for the fact that Arsenal equalised a second time.

Roberts provided a pass that caught Everton square, and Graham, with the subtle touch which often characterised his work, floated his shot over West. There was still time for Graham to hit the bar, and that final flourish prompted McLintock to tell reporters after the match that: 'This is the best Arsenal side in my six years with the club.'

Two days later that side took the field again at West Ham, but with Marinello and Kennedy included because of the injuries. Upton Park boasted new floodlights, and beneath them Jimmy Greaves sparkled for the home side and Arsenal resisted with all the determination of the previous Saturday. Two points from two away matches was certainly a satisfactory return from such a difficult start to the season.

While the match reports found plenty of space in the national press, the characters of bygone days at Highbury still remained good copy. Alf Kirchen was discovered taking part in the English Bowls Association Championships at Mortlake. A winner of three England caps in 1937, his skill at bowls was rewarded with an England trial 33 years later.

Kirchen would have been proud of the performance Arsenal produced to open their season at Highbury. Manchester United were thrust aside on a baking afternoon in front of a crowd of 54,000. Storey again operated in midfield with more than an eye on George Best, while for Ian Ure it was an unhappy return to his old club.

Arsenal struck after 14 minutes: Ure was penalised and McNab clipped an accurate free-kick on to the head of Kelly, who guided the ball for a surprisingly unattended Radford to score. Four minutes later Radford again supplied the finish, shooting beyond Alex Stepney and past a defender on the line.

Arsenal bombarded United in the air, and the understanding between Radford and Kennedy was taking shape; it would become an integral factor in the months ahead. Armstrong's willing running in the team cause held more sway than Best's occasional sinewy sortie, though one such Mancunian burst produced a save at Best's feet that was to become Wilson's trademark, the clip from the televised match being instantly recognised in BBC's A Question of Sport over 15 years later.

For Wilson's opposite number, the afternoon held far less pleasant memories. Stepney had been hurt in a collision with the score at 2–0, and when Radford completed his hat-trick from Kennedy's astute flick, the goalkeeper handed the jersey to David Sadler and left the pitch clutching a damaged shoulder. The deputy was beaten just once, when Graham headed in off the post from a cross by Armstrong.

Don Howe paid tribute to McLintock's leadership after the match: 'They talk about Dave Mackay and Bobby Moore as great captains, but for my money McLintock is more inspiring than either of them. I am beginning to feel obsolete in the dressing room. Frank is doing as much talking as I am — and working wonders with his words. He lifts players up and makes them feel inches taller and he continues to inspire them out there on the pitch. His influence runs right through the team. His guidance and encouragement is, for instance, responsible for the tremendous form of John Roberts in the back line. I cannot speak too highly of the job Frank is doing.'

After such a pulsating performance against Manchester United, Arsenal were expected to demolish their next opponents at Highbury the following Tuesday, but newly promoted Huddersfield Town refused to be sacrificial lambs. Howe was warned for over-enthusiastic coaching from the line; Radford, Saturday's hero, had to give way to substitute Sammy Nelson because of a calf strain. Wilson was called into action to save smartly from Colin Dobson and Jimmy Nicholson.

Yet those irritations were forgotten when Kennedy, accepting a greater share of responsibility with Radford's departure, headed in the winning goal with just 15 minutes remaining. It was not a pretty triumph, but it was the first of many that season where the opposition, however eager, were worn down; more significantly it took Arsenal to the top of the table on alphabetical order, equal in every other respect with Liverpool.

The first defeat of the season came in game five against Chelsea, who had been a bogey team in seasons past. It was a high-octane affair, football at a furious pace fuelled by outbursts of hot temper. The match was watched by the victorious Brazilian World Cup coach Mario Zagalo who commented cryptically at the end that it was no wonder the English game produced no Peles.

Chelsea went ahead close to half-time when John Hollins burst from midfield, outpaced Roberts and lobbed his shot over Wilson. The ball hit the bar and stayed out but the effervescent Hollins, later to grace Highbury with the same enthusiasm, turned and chased after it to hit the target with a second effort with Arsenal unable to regroup. It was another moment that TV was to repeat often.

Kelly equalised with a header six minutes into the second period, but another Chelsea goal won the points. Peter Osgood swept a pass across the pitch into the stride of full back Paddy Mulligan who cut inside McNab before striking his first League goal. Wilson had been kicked on the knee in the first half but even with full mobility he would not have saved it. With intensive treatment he was passed fit for the next match, in midweek. Arsenal needed him because the visitors to Highbury came with a one hundred per cent record and had taken over at the top of the table.

In many ways the clashes between Leeds United and Arsenal typified the period. For three or four years, they were always the matches of the season. No shoot-out in a western movie held more drama, though neither team could claim to be the good guys taking on the bad guys. The importance of these meetings rarely brought the best behaviour out of either side. The defeated could often pay a high price; avoidance of defeat often became paramount.

Bertie Mee and Don Revie, the two managers, were different animals. Mee's view of life was realistic, uncluttered by superstition (as Ure discovered over his 'lucky' shirt). Revie, with his fetishes like 'lucky' clothing and 'lucky' dressing rooms at Wembley seemed burdened by such ritual. Yet he was closer to his players than the Arsenal manager, favouring a family atmosphere at Elland Road, and there was no disputing the talent at his disposal.

Leeds United never won the trophies that their talent seemed to deserve, and they rarely held the goodwill of the footballing public. They had played much the better football against Chelsea in the previous year's FA Cup final, yet lost after leading on three separate occasions. Since winning promotion in 1964, they had three times been runners-up in the First Division, and twice finished in fourth place; their only Championship in a long succession of title races had come in 1969.

On 1 September 1970 Arsenal had the honour of ending Leeds' perfect record so far that season. Geoffrey Green in *The Times* encapsulated the tone of the night in the pithy introduction to his match report: 'There were no goals and no broken legs at Highbury last night, and there might well have been one or two of both. Most of the plaudits of heroism went to the home side. Referee Iowerth Jones from Treharris, Glamorgan, quite properly sent off Kelly for kicking Billy Bremner; that senseless episode after 28 minutes seemed to have condemned Arsenal to defeat. The ten men, however, resisted manfully with the raw Rice, in particular, responding to the challenge. Leeds were not allowed to make use of their advantage. Bertie Mee was never given to exaggeration so his after-match comment deserves recording: "This was the best performance I have ever seen by an Arsenal team against a side of the calibre of Leeds. I am tremendously proud of all of them, and if we can live through an occasion like this we can live through anything".'

With the next match a resumption of north London rivalries with Tottenham, the Leeds experience appeared perfect preparation. For once, though, guns and tin helmets were not required against the old enemy. The derby game was the most placid for many, many years. Tottenham folded at Highbury with reserve goalkeeper Ken Hancock beaten by two moments of opportunism from the non-stop Armstrong, which was bad news for Armstrong's deputy Marinello, who also struck twice that afternoon in the reserve match at Spurs. The only blot on the Arsenal horizon was an injury collected by McLintock.

Arsenal's captain took part in the following game, a League Cup tie at Ipswich, broke down again, but refused to succumb to the damage. His defensive marshalling in front of more notable goalkeeping from Wilson earned a replay. Lack of variety in midfield, however, was troubling the management. Arsenal bid a club record of £125,000 for the Scottish international Bobby Hope, which was turned down by Hope's club West Bromwich Albion. How different the season might have been if it had been accepted.

If the win against Spurs had surprisingly turned out to be the easiest of the season so far, the visit to Burnley, at the bottom of the table, became the most fortunate. It did not look that way when Kennedy headed Arsenal into a fourth-minute lead, but Burnley, who had begun the match without a goal in their previous 623 minutes of action, did not lie down. Wilson kept them at bay with a string of athletic leaps and dives to adorn his 100th League game. He was only beaten when Roberts headed an inswinging corner from Dave Thomas into his own net. It was rough justice on Burnley when Roberts, to his own relief, set up an Arsenal winner for Radford late in the game.

There was no doubt at Highbury, from the Chairman downwards, that the club's main aim was to win the League Championship, the trophy that is the hall-mark of a great club side. To that end, the start of the season had been encouraging, but the busy programme of early season matches also included the defence of the Fairs Cup. It began in Rome against Lazio, a team with a track record of riotous indiscipline. The atmosphere in the Olympic Stadium could be very hostile indeed. Bertie Mee was concerned about intimidation, but even he did not foresee such a distasteful episode as that which followed the match.

Lazio were far from being a good side; that season they were to be relegated from the Italian First Division. Yet in Giorgio Chinaglia, who was born in South Wales of Italian ancestry and who had played briefly for Swansea Town, they possessed a formidable forward. Chinaglia belied his bulk with a good touch and a genuine eye for goal, which in his later career would shatter scoring records in the North American Soccer League. Chinaglia plus the unwelcoming Rome crowd were Lazio's main weapons.

Arsenal refused to be intimidated, and two goals from Radford silenced the firework-throwing spectators. In the 49th minute Kelly invited the muscular striker to fight for a cross, and Radford headed past goalkeeper Sulfaro. Five minutes later Kelly was the provider again; this time Radford steered the ball in at the near post. Only Chinaglia kept the tie alive, and in the last six minutes he equalled Radford's feat. First he belied his ponderousness by firing low past Wilson. Then he was the beneficiary of refereeing generosity. McLintock dived full length to head another Chinaglia drive off the line. Gerhard

The season that was eventually to become the most celebrated in even Arsenal's famous history, 1970-71, began quietly. The first four games saw two draws and two wins. The fifth game was at Stamford Bridge, where Arsenal suffered their first defeat at the hands of Cup holders Chelsea, 2-1. 54,000 people saw Mulligan and Hollins score for Chelsea and Eddie Kelly respond for the Gunners. They also saw Frank McLintock and Peter Osgood in argumentative mood. This was the game about which Mario Zagalo, manager of the victorious Brazilian World Cup team, later commented that if it was typical of the Football League then it was no wonder that the English game produced no Peles.

Schulenberg from West Germany ruled that Arsenal's captain had handled. Chinaglia sent home his penalty for the equaliser.

Much the better side, Arsenal had accepted their fate with disappointment but not with concern. The players were sure that the job would be finished properly in the second leg. It is important to stress that, for their part, there were no feuds simmering when the two teams attended an after-match reception in a nearby restaurant. The evening was drawing to a close when Kennedy was suddenly set upon by a Lazio player. That unprovoked attack erupted into a full-scale brawl, starting inside but becoming a street battle as the Arsenal party made for the coach which was parked outside. McNab was hurled to the ground, Armstrong flung against the side of the bus.

Through the battlefield strode Bertie Mee ushering his players on to the coach, concerned that Italian policemen were armed and that what was a despicable scene might turn into total tragedy. No one would have wished the incident to happen, but it did reaffirm the togetherness of the squad. Players who protected each other on the field rushed to the aid of their team-mates off it. This was no affair of high spirits which required a cover-up. Arsenal were innocent victims of the frustrations which Lazio felt, having failed to take advantage of the home leg.

Lazio made noises about refusing to play the second leg a week later unless Arsenal 'retracted the insults they hurled at the Italians'. The European governing body, UEFA, sided with Arsenal and fined the Italians. With eminent good sense they appointed Rudi Glockner of East Germany, the 1970 World Cup final referee, to officiate at Highbury. Herr Glockner cautioned five Italians, including the cynical English-born defender Guiseppe Wilson, and Arsenal, in total control, won 2–0.

The outcome was never seriously in doubt from the moment Radford contributed his third goal of the tie, a close-range header from a Storey cross after ten minutes. From then on only over-anxiety to punish Lazio with an emphatic win could explain so much pressure without further score. There was one more goal when Armstrong, 17 minutes from time, torpedoed forward to divert a pass from Rice past the beleaguered Sulfaro.

Sandwiched between the two legs of the Fairs Cup tie, Arsenal had found their shooting-boots against West Bromwich Albion, who came to Highbury with 19-year-old Asa Hartford deputising for Hope, who was injured. To Albion's credit they became the first of only two teams to score twice at Highbury in the First Division that season — through Reed and Brown — but they conceded six goals along the way. Graham and Kennedy each struck twice; Armstrong and an own goal from Cantello completed the tally.

The reaction to the Lazio experience came not after the first leg, but after the victory had been completed. Arsenal slipped below their standards of application and organisation and were hammered 5–0 at Stoke, of whom we shall hear more later. Wilson, the television analyst, had to endure the embarrassment of being beaten five times in front of the BBC cameras. For once the BBC did not invite the Arsenal goalkeeper to 'talk through' the goals on that night's *Match of the Day*, but he was big enough to discuss them in front of the cameras for the following Saturday's lunchtime preview programme.

Bertie Mee was far from pleased. He felt it was a betrayal of inside information which should have stayed within the club. He and Don Howe had hammered the team in training as a result of the Stoke defeat, but criticism was confined to the privacy of Highbury. The manager believed in protecting the players from outside comment, but only as long as they themselves did not breach the security.

The matter was quickly resolved, and in the long term harmed neither Bob Wilson's goalkeeping nor his prospects of a career in the media. The defeat at Stoke increased the side's determination, and only three days later Ipswich felt the backlash. Three goals in 35 minutes wiped away some of the taste of the Saturday defeat and ensured a place in the third round of the League Cup. Arsenal's aerial strength brought goals from Roberts and Radford; Kennedy hit the third, and iced the cake with another in injury time.

Kennedy went one better the following Saturday as the season moved into October. Nottingham Forest, like Ipswich, left Highbury with a four-goal mauling. The only chord of disappointment was struck by an attendance which dropped to 32,000. Still only two months past his 19th birthday, Kennedy was taking to a regular First Division life with astonishing ease. His strength, allied to a comfort on the ball unusual in such a sturdy forward, dovetailed perfectly with Radford. Both offered themselves willingly as targets for clearances. Both could hold the ball until help arrived. Most important of all, both were finding the back of the net.

A miskick by Sammy Chapman gave Kennedy his first goal after ten minutes. Then, he was credited with beating Radford to the final touch amidst a bewildered defence in the first attack of the second half, before reaching his hat-trick with a typical show of strength. Armstrong completed the scoring. Kennedy accepted the acclaim modestly: 'You usually only dream about these things happening. I used to think that only John Radford was capable of getting a hat-trick.' Arsenal's eight home games so far in League and Cup had brought seven wins and a draw with 23 goals scored and only those two against, by West Bromwich Albion.

The third round of the League Cup, however, brought an away tie at Second Division Luton Town, and the gates were locked at Kenilworth Road with 5,000 outside. The home side included one Arsenal player of the future in Malcolm Macdonald, who forced Wilson into an acrobatic save after 18 minutes, and one ex-Gunner in David Court, who gave away the 26th minute

free-kick from which his former club won the match via a Graham header.

Graham earned Arsenal's gratitude again when the League programme resumed at Newcastle, where the home team were seeking a first win at St James's Park since the opening day of the season. They were on their way towards it too when 'Pop' Robson steered the Magpies in front early in the second half. Graham punished a mistake by Ollie Burton to bring home a share of the spoils.

The return match with Everton was the 100th League meeting between the two clubs, and the Champions had just spent £150,000 on Henry Newton from Forest in an attempt to inject some freshness into what had already become a doomed bid to retain their title. Newton had been at Highbury a fortnight earlier in Forest's colours; for him it was a case of *deja vu*; Everton were also despatched by four goals.

To accommodate their new acquisition in midfield Howard Kendall was switched into the back four, but Arsenal's power in the air was too much for him. Kennedy had already been left unmarked from Graham's flick to head Arsenal into an early lead; when the teenager towered above Kendall to find the net with another header Arsenal were two up after 20 minutes. In the second half Radford's long throw set another test for Everton's rearranged defence and the ball was cleared only as far as Kelly, who powered it back past Rankin. The visitors' uncertainty was emphasised by Kenyon's unnecessary handball. Storey unfussily scored from the penalty. The fact that three of Arsenal's goals had come from aerial moves prompted the most famous football *bon mot* of the 1970s. David Lacey of *The Guardian*, noting that Henry *and* Keith Newton were playing in the Everton defence, commented: 'With two Newtons in the side, one might have expected Everton to deal better with round objects dropping from the sky.'

Kennedy's eleven goals in 16 matches were recognised by his selection for England's under-23 squad. The whole team was entertained to dinner at the Houses of Parliament by Lord Fletcher, a life-long supporter, to commemorate the winning of the Fairs Cup.

The next step along the road towards retaining it took place against Sturm Graz. Arsenal had originally been drawn at home in the first leg but the considerable risk of snow in Austria by the scheduled date for the second leg brought about a request to swap. The Austrians were also guaranteed a good gate by playing at home first; a heavy defeat at Highbury would have wiped out much of the interest.

In the end it became a very interesting tie indeed. Sturm Graz got their gate, just under 20,000, and responded to their support by winning their home leg 1–0 with a second half effort from Zamut. Kennedy redressed the balance at Highbury, but the unheralded Austrians rose to the occasion, despite having to substitute their goalkeeper in the first half.

> running strongly and at oblique angles, began to lose Kendall and before the half-hour he had scored twice. After 14 minutes Graham, rising by the near post flicked on Armstrong's corner and Kennedy nodded the ball squarely past Rankin. Six minutes later, as Rice's free kick came over from the right, Graham ran forward, Everton followed him and Kennedy was left with time and space to head the second. The third goal came in the sixty-sixth minute when Radford's throw was nodded down by Graham for Kelly to score with an excellent half-volley, though the course of the shot was diverted by Keith Newton's knee. With two Newtons in the side Everton might be expected to deal better with round objects falling from the sky.

David Lacey's cryptic comment after the 4-0 defeat of Everton at Highbury on 17 October. The goals were scored by Kelly, Storey and Kennedy and all basically came from high balls pumped into the penalty area. Everton had just purchased Henry Newton and thus had two Newtons in the back four. It was the start of a run of 12 games during which just two points were dropped – the foundation stones of the Double. The game's other significance was that well-beaten Everton were the reigning Champions.

Arsenal for their part were guilty of wasteful finishing, and the match seemed bound for extra time when the 90 minutes were up.

However, the Dutch referee Boosten added on five minutes for injuries and stoppages, and in the fifth minute of that time Graham's volley was handled on the line. Storey's nerve stood the test again from the penalty spot, and Arsenal were through 2–1 on aggregate. Overall it had hardly been a performance to savour.

There was no such recovery though in the League Cup. Arsenal were dismissed from the competition in the fourth round, with added insult because it was from their first defeat at Highbury for ten months. A goalless draw at Crystal Palace, in a thrilling match, seemed to be according to script. Arsenal's progress looked assured with Palace reported to Highbury with two of their regulars, Steve Kember and Mel Blyth, injured. Skipper John Sewell lasted only 20 minutes, and three other players were swathed in strapping.

Yet Palace grabbed the lead, hung on to it by their fingernails, and were then presented with the cushion of a second goal. Gerry Queen opened the scoring when Wilson could only push out a shot from Jim Scott. Arsenal roared forward in search of an equaliser, only to be stopped in their tracks by a moment of stupidity which went some way towards losing Roberts his place in the team. Queen challenged Wilson with his elbows as both went for a high ball, but the goalkeeper gathered it safely. Roberts, however, chose to chase after the Palace striker and hurl him to the ground. Referee Norman Burtenshaw had no option other than to award Palace a penalty. Tambling accepted the gift, and Arsenal were out.

Meanwhile, the League performances were

uncluttered by such acts. At Highfield Road it was Coventry City who had the problems. Radford set up Kennedy's twelfth goal of the season, then wrote his own name on the score sheet, though in falling he broke a bone in his wrist; tough and uncomplaining he refused to miss any matches because of the problem. Later Graham ran clear to seal a 3–1 victory.

Derby County, like Coventry in the bottom half of the table (though they were to win the next Championship), were also beaten by two clear goals, at Highbury. Kelly scored after 37 minutes, courtesy of a badly hit back pass from Derby's highly rated centre half Roy McFarland. The other goal came from Radford, a textbook header to take him into double figures for the season. Frank McGhee in the *Daily Mirror* was impressed by the comment of a spectator alongside the Press Box: 'A great goal. Far too good for this game.' Arsenal could console themselves with the figures that marked them as the First Division's leading scorers at that point in the season.

Radford again wrapped up the points in the next League match. Blackpool had won only twice and were to win only twice more in a wretched season which inevitably ended in relegation. Arsenal's victory had a calculated look to it. Other teams might have indulged themselves. Bertie Mee and Don Howe had preached the lessons of Stoke. First of all Blackpool were dispirited and then killed off, Radford manufacturing a scoring header late in the game from a high Armstrong cross. The Bloomfield Road fans did not even have a corner to cheer from their side until injury time.

By a quirk of the fixture list Crystal Palace were scheduled to return to Highbury the Saturday after their extraordinary League Cup win. Arsenal's tilt at revenge brought little satisfaction. The plan was to vary the build-up, and not rely on the now familiar aerial ball into the penalty area. Mee said: 'I asked the boys to spread it around more and keep it low as well.'

Radford's success in front of goal continued and he drew first blood with the match only 15 minutes old. Palace's response was reminiscent of much of Arsenal's season; the South London side struck back immediately. Queen's pass into the penalty area should have been cut out by Roberts, whose week of personal disaster was completed when he lost his footing. Alan Birchenall seized on the error to leave Wilson helpless.

With two of Palace's three goals at Highbury attributable to mistakes by the blond Welsh defender, Bertie Mee left him out for the visit to Ipswich. Peter Simpson stepped into the slot alongside Frank McLintock as though he had never been away. Roberts returned only once that season, though he had played enough League games at that point to qualify for his Championship medal. 'Garth' Roberts is now barely remembered as a member of the Double-winning side, yet he contributed greatly in those early months of the season. Often his fellow

defenders had to scream and shout at him to galvanise him into action; he did seem more susceptible than others to the onset of injury. But for three months he had done more than simply plug a gap.

George Graham had also been below par, so the team at Ipswich also included Jon Sammels, for his first match of the season, as it was for Simpson. Graham was demoted to substitute. The team did not really respond to the mini-shake-up, and Ipswich threw everything but the kitchen sink at the goal guarded by Bob Wilson. Arsenal somehow kept them at bay, and mustered only three shots in the match. Yet the third, in injury time, turned a grateful draw into a victory that was almost embarrassing. Armstrong let fly with referee Wallace from Swindon ready to blow the final whistle. Nineteen-year-old Laurie Sivell went to catch the ball, which was not fiercely struck, but dropped it back over his head — and over the line. The linesman immediately signalled a goal. Their manager, Bobby Robson, was exasperated: 'Arsenal should be ashamed to walk away with the points,' he complained. 'I can't believe it. We pulverised them. A moral victory? If I get three more moral victories like that I'll get a moral sacking.'

On Sunday 22 November, Bertie Mee took the players to Jersey for a golfing break. It was much needed. Some staleness had set in, understandably because in three months Arsenal had played 27 competitive matches. Only four had been lost and the defence had kept 16 clean sheets.

The change of routine did not have an immediate impact when Arsenal returned to work with a home fixture against Liverpool. For more than an hour the team, unchanged from that which had won at Ipswich, was unable to move up from second gear. It took a substitution to inject more acceleration. Graham took over from Kelly in the 65th minute with the purpose of a man with a point to prove. He had been dropped because his scoring rate from midfield had fallen.

Six minutes after his entry, Sammels, who had been promoted to the starting line-up ahead of Graham, snaffled the ball from Liverpool's Ian Ross. It was midfield harrassing which was very much Arsenal's style. Graham gained possession, avoided an attempted tackle by Tommy Smith and sensed the opportunity for a one-two as he strode towards the Liverpool penalty area.

Sammels acted as the 'wall' and returned Graham's short, sharp pass into the path of the substitute. The ball arrived invitingly for a volley, and Graham could not have struck it better, on his left instep. It flew past Clemence at searing pace for an outstanding goal.

Sixty seconds earlier Wilson had produced a crucial save from Steve Heighway, Liverpool's most potent attacking force in the match. As was becoming a very useful habit, Arsenal were difficult to catch once they nosed in front. Graham had not finished either. He played a part in the move which finished with Radford,

Anxious moments for (left to right) Don Howe, trainer and physio George Wright and Bertie Mee during the 2-0 defeat of Liverpool on 28 November 1970.

looking suspiciously offside, scoring Arsenal's second. The match also saw the number of spectators watching Arsenal that season pass the million mark.

Graham was understandably in from the start for the home leg of the Fairs Cup third round tie. The opposition, Beveren Waas, came from a small town in Belgium, and their team of part-timers was no match for an authoritative Arsenal. They could even shrug aside an early penalty miss by Storey, when Sammels was tripped, to cruise home by four goals to make the second leg a formality.

In the League the pursuit of Leeds United continued with a significant win at Manchester City, champions two years earlier. Though the season was just reaching its half-way point, City's defeat was enough for Malcolm Allison, one half of the managerial partnership with Joe Mercer, to concede that the title was a two-horse race: 'There are just two teams left in it. Leeds because they are the most powerful team in Europe and Arsenal because their number has come up and goalkeeper Bob Wilson is second only to Gordon Banks.'

Wilson's display at Maine Road was described as 'staggering'. City laid siege on the Arsenal goal, but could not pass a goalkeeper who was at his most commanding. For 75 minutes Wilson

kept his team-mates afloat before they started to swim against the tide. His opposite number Joe Corrigan was not so fortunate; he mishandled a Sammels corner and Armstrong punished the mistake with a cutely lobbed goal. In the last minute Armstrong measured a cross for Radford to leave Corrigan stranded again.

Arsenal's realistic policy had paid dividends once more. Don Howe had noted the sticky surface in his team talk: 'On a pitch like that you couldn't be too flash. It was dangerous to gamble and foolish to be adventurous. The only way to tackle the game was to base your planning on safety-first tactics. Just make it simple and cut out the mistakes.'

The fixture at Highbury the following Saturday, 12 December, was dominated by pre-match publicity. Bobby Gould was coming back to face Arsenal only six months after his £50,000 summer transfer to Wolves. For Gould it had been a good move. He had tucked away 15 goals for his new club. Now he intended to add to that tally past his 'best friend in football', Bob Wilson, and did not mind telling the press and television what was going to happen.

It made excellent copy and certainly spiced the atmosphere. In the event Gould had little chance to shine, though he outraged the home supporters with a typically brash challenge on

the goalkeeper with friendships forgotten in the heat of the battle; it was, incidentally, accepted in good part. The closeness between the two was to last and in December 1985 it was Gould, by then manager of Bristol Rovers, who persuaded the 44-year-old Wilson to help the Third Division club out of a goalkeeping crisis by signing for emergencies. It was 12 years since his last Football League game.

Arsenal won 2–1, Graham fashioning another breathtaking goal for himself, and Radford making light of a tight angle. With Leeds held at home by Ipswich that afternoon Arsenal were now just two points behind with exactly half the League programme completed.

Arsenal's credentials as Championship challengers were there for all to see in a thoroughly convincing 3–1 success at Manchester United. The discontent among a small section of the home crowd on the Stretford End led to the throwing

of a missile. Wilson was struck by a coin and required a stitch in a scalp wound, but he did his best to put the episode into perspective: 'The Stretford End crowd are a fabulous crowd, second only to the Kop at Liverpool and I wouldn't say a word against them. The fact that a very tiny minority step out of line and throw things doesn't alter my opinion. The incident happened in the second half when I was bending down to take a goal-kick. I rubbed my head and the ref came over. But I didn't want a fuss.' Referee Maurice Fussey from Retford took his cue from Wilson's reaction, and did not report the matter to the Football Association. Happier days.

There were problems of a different nature for the goalkeeper in the Boxing Day fixture at home to Southampton. Winter arrived in North London. Snow fell in sub-zero temperatures, and a holiday crowd of 34,000 got in despite a

Peter Storey, scourge of a generation of First Division attackers and whose contribution to the Double is impossible to overestimate. He was, apart from the Irish full backs, the only member of the squad to become an established international. Despite the well-documented personal problems that later beset him, Storey was known at Highbury as the quiet member of the team. Bertie Mee regularly gave him lifts from Cockfosters to the London Colney training ground and once said that he never heard Storey speak more than half-a-dozen words on a journey.

145

number of turnstile operators being unable to get to the ground. Wilson was among the frozen spectators for much of the match, and could only admire the performance of Eric Martin in Southampton's goal. Martin flung himself into the path of a fusillade of shots and became the saviour of the Saints in a goalless draw. Still, it was three months now since the last League defeat at Stoke.

The draw for the FA Cup third round brought Arsenal a tie that was steeped in romance: away to Yeovil Town. The part-timers from the Southern League were the competition's most consistent slayers of giants. They owed their place in round three to a characteristic upset of the form-book by winning at Bournemouth, who were to finish the season in a Fourth Division promotion spot. Moreover, once upon a time in the fairy stories of the game they had claimed a First Division scalp: Sunderland had perished on Yeovil's notorious sloping pitch in 1948.

Bertie Mee's players, however, were realists not romantics. Their competitive edge was sharpened by pre-match boasts from Norman Burnfield, the Yeovil chairman, that his team would win 4–1! The three-goal margin was correct. Arsenal were always too talented for their humble opponents, and they were also far too business-like to allow even the sniff of an upset. Radford's headwork brought him two more goals and Kennedy bundled in the other after a defensive mix-up.

A week later Arsenal had genuine reason to be grateful to Spurs, who surprisingly toppled Leeds United 2–1 at Elland Road. By beating West Ham at Highbury, the Gunners reduced the gap at the top to a solitary point and they had a game in hand. West Ham were outmanoeuvred by Arsenal's strengths in the air. Both goals in a 2–0 win came from headers; Graham and Kennedy were the marksmen. The Hammers had arguably helped Arsenal's cause. Bobby Moore, Jimmy Greaves and Brian Dear were missing for disciplinary reasons. They had been reported to manager Ron Greenwood after being spotted in a Blackpool night club on the eve of the 4–0 defeat in a third round FA Cup tie at Bloomfield Road.

McNab, absent against West Ham, was back for the visit to his former club, but for Arsenal it was not a happy return to Huddersfield Town. Frank McLintock felt most of the pain. Physically he was distressed when an elbow in the face early in the match meant finishing the weekend in the London Hospital, a broken nose in plaster after an operation to straighten it. Mentally the anguish came from the handball awarded against him 16 minutes from time, from which Frank Worthington scored to win the match 2–1.

McLintock gave his version of the incident thus: 'For a start the ball struck my arm. I did not deliberately propel it. Secondly I am positive that I was *outside* the penalty area at the time.' Television and photographic evidence certainly supported the second part of his claim.

Arsenal's goal came from what looked like a well-oiled free-kick routine. In fact Graham had miscued a shot at goal and Kennedy's glancing header came from pure opportunism.

The tempo of this extraordinary season allowed no time for rest or mulling over disappointments. McLintock was fit for the fourth round of the FA Cup, at Portsmouth, who were below mid-table in the Second Division. The Fratton Park pitch did not slope like that at Yeovil, but heavy rain gave it the texture of a bog.

In front of a crowd of 40,000 Radford hit a post, and then was denied by a finger-tip save. The referee believed that those fingers belonged to the Portsmouth goalkeeper John Milkins. It took massive protests by the Arsenal players to persuade him to consult a linesman. In fact, as most people in the ground had realised, it had been left back George Ley, diving full-length behind Milkins, who had pushed the ball aside. The decision was changed from corner to penalty and Storey's kick was immaculate.

The one goal seemed to be enough until Mike Trebilcock, who had scored twice for Everton in the 1966 Cup final, equalised with the game's final kick.

The excitement of that moment was rekindled throughout a marvellously enthralling replay nine days later. Portsmouth's self-belief was rekindled by a sixth-minute lead at Highbury, where they became only the fourth visiting club to score that season. For Arsenal, Charlie George was chosen to start a senior match for the first time since that August injury at Goodison Park. He immediately reminded the Highbury fans what they had been missing. The teenager with the flowing locks set off from the half-way line and matched a splendid run with a scoring shot that Milkins scarcely saw.

The goal sparked off constant Arsenal pressure. A second goal seemed inevitable; Simpson provided it with a sweet volley following a corner from Armstrong. However, Portsmouth made it 2–2, and the two teams slugged it out with the physical side of the match beginning to be a dominant force. Eoin Hand, Portsmouth's Irish defender, fouled Radford five minutes from time inside the area. Storey did not shirk from another penalty duel with Milkins and, as at Fratton Park, he won it. Sadly the match ended on an unsavoury note. Referee Jim Finney sent off midfield player Brian Bromley, though the Portsmouth manager, Ron Tindall, claimed that Bromley was only acting as a peacemaker following a scuffle between Rice and Ley.

Only two days before the replay, on Saturday 30 January, the Arsenal title hopes were being written off by a number of pundits. That afternoon Leeds were winning 2–0 at Manchester City while the Gunners were losing by the same score at Liverpool. Those two results spread the margin between the first and second in the table to five points. Leeds had become a byword for consistency and Arsenal, for all their vast improvement, did not have the pedigree to

suggest they could make up the wide deficit.

Liverpool played superbly to beat Arsenal, and Bob Wilson was so busy he left Anfield to glowing plaudits from the voluble Liverpool manager Bill Shankly: 'One save was brilliant. He must have sprinted half a dozen yards before he flung his arms up to deflect Toshack's header. A marvellous piece of quick thinking and agility. There are lots of good goalkeepers around. What makes Wilson outstanding is his courage. He'll dive at players feet and make quick decisions. He had his share of luck but bravery encourages luck.'

Joe Mercer was the next opposing manager to praise Wilson with this postscript to Manchester City's 1–0 defeat at Highbury: 'If we had swapped goalkeepers we would have won 2–1.' Wilson added to his growing list of critical interventions with two acrobatic stops from Colin Bell. Conversely Corrigan cost his side a point when he fumbled Simpson's 30-yard drive five minutes from time and Radford seized on the rebound. The match will not live long in the memory, but Bertie Mee saw the significance in the winning goal: 'We learned long ago from high-morale teams like Leeds and Liverpool that you really can make your own luck. Peter Simpson, for example, must have been tired when he cut out that ball. But he still had enough belief to run on and try his luck with a shot. And following up on other people's shots is something we demand of John Radford. It is easy to get players to do it at the start but to make what looks like a useless run in the last few minutes takes character. If Radford had stopped running no one would have noticed or blamed him. But by going flat out at the end he was on the spot to score.' The goal brought Arsenal four wins out of four against the Manchester clubs for the first time in fifty years.

At the same time the 'high-morale' battle between Leeds United and Liverpool at Elland Road was going in Liverpool's favour — and Arsenal's. The gap was back to three points. Charlie George caught the eye of Brian Glanville, *The Sunday Times* correspondent at the match: 'He must surely resemble the late Charlie Buchan; his height, his powerful physique, the delicacy of touch so astonishing in one so large. To see him receive a ball amidst a ruck of defenders and escape them with the skill of a Houdini is delightful.'

They were prophetic words. George was to settle the fifth round FA Cup tie against Manchester City ten days later. The match was put back from the Saturday to the following Wednesday because the Maine Road pitch was flooded, and it remained very heavy. Two goals from the precocious George, now operating as a raider from midfield in place of Graham, confirmed Arsenal's superiority in a thoroughly merited victory.

The exact date is not important but it was around this time, in February 1971, that Bertie Mee addressed his players. To a nation which believed that the twentieth century Double could only be achieved by a team with the swagger of the Spurs 1961 side, Arsenal were simply not contenders. There was some speculation about whether they could win the League. The pursuit of Leeds United was becoming one of the season's most fascinating features. But there were no public suggestions that Arsenal could emulate Tottenham and clear all the hurdles.

Inside Highbury it was a different matter. Mee saw the possibilities and had for some time: 'I told the players we could expect two matches a week for the rest of the season: "As this is the case now is the time for you to be really ambitious and to aim for the success which may never be possible for you as players again in your lifetimes." The point was forcibly expressed that all three trophies should be aimed for. Extra discipline and a dedication beyond that which even the most reliable modern professional soccer player is expected to give. They owed it to themselves and their colleagues to accept the challenge of the next three months.' They also owed it to the fans and to the tradition that was Highbury.

Arsenal's ambitions shone through an irresistible first half when Ipswich Town visited Highbury in the First Division on Saturday 20 February 1971. George added to his fast growing band of admirers with a near post header from Armstrong's accurate corner. Radford applied the finishing touches to some clever play by Kennedy. Another Armstrong flag-kick picked out McLintock whose move into the back four had not diminished his eye for an opening. Only a twisted knee for George marred the picture, with the injury forcing him to withdraw from England's under-23 squad to face Scotland.

With three goals under their belts, Arsenal suffered a quite uncharacteristic lapse in concentration. Ipswich hit back twice in the second half, missed an open goal and had another 'goal' nullified by the referee. Both genuine goals were credited to the returning Jimmy Robertson, whose curling free-kick also beat Wilson only for the referee fortunately to spot some pushing off the ball. But Robertson's corner which flew in off McNab did count. So too did his shot five minutes from time which created unnecessary anxiety in the home ranks before the two points were finally safe.

A week later at Derby Arsenal recaptured the mood of the second half against Ipswich and not the first. A 2–0 defeat had Fleet Street once more writing the obituary to any North London Championship challenge. 'Arsenal are right out of it now' was the headline in one national paper. 'Arsenal's dreams turn sour,' reported another. Leeds United now held a seven-point lead, though the Gunners still had two games in hand. In recent years, points in the bag had proved more valuable than games in hand.

The architect behind Derby's victory was no stranger to attempts to halt Arsenal. At 36 Dave Mackay had lost a little mobility but none of his competitive edge. It was as if he personally

resented that Arsenal were striving to emulate the Spurs Double side in which his buccaneering style played such a vital part, and it became a personal crusade to stop his old rivals.

It was fortunate that a rearranged fixture at Wolves was scheduled for just three days later. It afforded Arsenal the opportunity of ridding themselves of the taste of defeat. As one of the games in hand over Leeds it simply had to be won. On paper it was a harder task than that at the Baseball Ground. Wolves would finish the season in fourth place. Moreover the eager Bobby Gould was again straining at the leash to attack his old club.

Clearly Arsenal needed a good start, and they

got it, going a goal up inside the first minute. The boost to morale was immense, and it was the prelude to a dominant display. McLintock and Simpson presided at the back. Storey, Sammels, George and Armstrong ruled in midfield, where they had been overrun at Derby. Wolves were overcome 3–0.

Bertie Mee realised the importance of such a performance: 'This result showed the character of the side. They came back so well after the Derby setback to give one of their best performances of the season. It was absolutely wonderful. The title doesn't belong to Leeds yet. There are twelve games to go, and if we keep playing like this we must be in with a fine chance.' Frank

Charlie George scores the all important first goal of the fifth-round FA Cup tie against Manchester City at Maine Road on 17 February 1971. A free-kick had been given after Joe Corrigan handled the ball outside his area in the eighteenth minute. George simply shot past the City wall of George Heslop, Mike Doyle, Colin Bell, Tommy Booth and Tony Book. George scored another in the second half and one response from Colin Bell wasn't enough, the Gunners winning 2-1. It had been two weeks earlier, on 6 February, that Bertie

Mee made his celebrated speech in the Highbury dressing room after Arsenal had defeated the same City side 1-0 in the League. He told the team that he thought they had a chance of winning all three trophies (they were still in the Fairs Cup) but it would mean two hard matches a week from there onwards. And the appeal did not lack emotion, as Mee later wrote: 'I told them: "Now is the time for you to be really ambitious and to aim for the success which may never be possible for you as players again in your lifetimes".'

McLintock added: 'I am sick of people writing us off. A lot can happen before the season is over. Leeds need only lose a couple to start wobbling.'

The victory narrowed the gap to five points, Leeds now having played one game more. Both clubs still had the distraction of European competition, with Don Revie's side also in the Fairs Cup and bidding for Arsenal's crown. But Leeds were out of the FA Cup, the victims of the season's most sensational result. In the fifth round, with a team crammed full of internationals, they fell at Fourth Division Colchester United by three goals to two.

Arsenal's quarter-final opponents in the FA Cup were Leicester City, who were on their way to bringing the Second Division Championship to Filbert Street. Frank O'Farrell's side had been relegated two years earlier, but in the same season had reached the FA Cup final, losing narrowly to Manchester City. Five of the Wembley side remained to face Arsenal. Goalkeeper Peter Shilton, already an England international, had shown such marvellous potential that Gordon Banks, England's number one, had been allowed to move to Stoke. Left back David Nish would go on to win full international honours. Graham Cross, one of the breed of footballer-cricketers, was a reliable central defender. Forwards Rodney Fern and Lennie Glover could be match-winners on their day. Moreover the draw gave Leicester City home advantage.

They strove manfully to settle the tie at Filbert Street in arctic conditions in front of a crowd of 42,000. Wilson had a much busier afternoon than Shilton, and produced the save of the match in the 70th minute. Glover's pass found Fern in space and he took deliberate aim. Too deliberate because Wilson anticipated the direction of the shot and plunged to turn it aside. Two minutes from time Glover flung himself at a Willie Carlin cross but missed the ball completely when any sort of contact would have put Arsenal out of the competition.

Instead it was a replay, followed by talk of the impending fixture congestion which had cost Leeds United so much the previous season. The tie at Leicester was Arsenal's 46th competitive match of the season. Now they faced three critical matches inside a week — at home to Cologne in the Fairs Cup, at Crystal Palace in the First Division and then the replay against Leicester. Bob McNab however, summed up the feeling in the Highbury camp: 'We don't mind. It's better being in everything than cooling your heels for the rest of the season with nothing at all to play for.' The three games inside that week were all won.

The margin of victory over Cologne, however, was not enough to avoid eventual elimination from the Fairs Cup. The West Germans came without their key defender Wolfgang Weber, who had played against England in the 1966 World Cup final. But they did include another veteran of that tournament, Wolfgang Overath, in midfield, while striker Hannes Lohr had helped his country knock England out of the 1970 finals in Mexico. Bernd Cullman, Heinz Flohe and Josef Kapellmann were to become internationals in future World Cups.

Arsenal threatened to overrun Cologne at Highbury but the potential was not fulfilled. Yet they had started well. McLintock was again on target, capitalizing on a loose ball after goalkeeper Manglitz had lost a shot from Kennedy. The turning point, however, was an inswinging corner from full back Thielen which caught Bob Wilson unsighted by the number of players at the near post. The ball curved in by the far post off the woodwork. The half-time score was an injustice.

Graham replaced Sammels for the second half and played his part in incessant Arsenal pressure. It led to only one more goal, however. Radford screened the ball superbly from a gang of defenders and set up Storey whose low shot threaded its way through a congested penalty area.

After the match the words of the Cologne coach Ernst Ocwirk carried a hint of prophesy: 'Arsenal were as good as I expected, but they did not make the best of their chances. Their defenders McLintock and Storey had to show them how to score. We will win 1–0 in Cologne.'

And so, a fortnight later, they did, ending Arsenal's grip on the trophy through the away goals rule. But the manner of defeat was wholly unsatisfactory. Constantin Petres, a Rumanian referee, contributed a series of decisions which both mystified and infuriated the visitors. It began in the fourth minute when Kapellmann flung himself to the ground at the merest hint of contact from McNab. Werner Biskup despatched the penalty past Wilson for the goal that fulfilled the forecast of coach Ocwirk. Rice, George and Kennedy were booked for innocuous tackles or dissent.

Bertie Mee acted while the match was in progress: 'I appealed to the UEFA representative to talk to the referee at half-time. I wanted him to know that calling for the ball did not constitute an offence.' After the game the Arsenal manager turned his considerable anger on the opposition: 'The childish histrionics of the West Germans are bringing the game into disrepute. We saw this in the World Cup in 1966 and again in Mexico. I mean what I say.'

Arsenal did not go down without a tremendous fight in the second half. Graham twice came closest to a goal which would have meant survival. So upset was George at the final whistle that only quick thinking by Kelly, one of the substitutes, prevented further incident. He dragged his team-mate away as George was setting off after the referee.

If Europe had provided Arsenal with one bridge too far, the battle on the other two fronts was being fought with more success. The League campaign had seen two more victories, both without the loss of a goal. A 2–0 win at Crystal Palace was particularly welcome, following three previous unavailing efforts to beat the Selhurst Park club.

Graham was recalled to the starting line-up for the first time for six weeks in place of Sammels, who was relegated to substitute. Yet circumstances conspired to produce a goal from each of them. Graham gave Arsenal the lead, then on the hour George limped off, suffering from a kick on the ankle. Not for the first or last time this season the substitution brought reward. Sammels rapped in his only League goal of the campaign.

Blackpool were the next visitors to Highbury, on their way to the Second Division but with enough bravado to make Arsenal work very hard for the points. Wilson, described by visiting manager Bob Stokoe as 'the most improved player in football in any position' played a blinder to keep his goal intact. One save, from Craven's close range header defied belief. His opposite number, Neil Ramsbottom, also enjoyed a splendid match, but he made one mistake and Arsenal seized upon it.

Graham's cross was tailored for the goalkeeper's collection but the ball, as if charged

A timely interception for ex-schoolmaster Bob Wilson at Filbert Street during the quarter-final tie against Leicester on 6 March 1971. The game ended scoreless and Arsenal won the replay 1-0. It was Arsenal's fourth consecutive away draw in the competition. Wilson and Armstrong played in all 56 games during the Double season.

with electricity, squirmed from his grasp. Peter Storey was following in and he headed it over the desolate Ramsbottom. It was the first goal he had ever scored with his head.

For Storey it was welcome publicity at a time when his style of play was being criticised on television by Jimmy Hill and others. His relentless pursuit of the ball in his midfield role was to win him England caps in that position; inevitably, though, it led to the risk of late tackles. At times his appetite for victory also brought unnecessary dialogue with opponents and referees. If occasionally he did overstep the line between competitiveness and crudity, there was no doubt that he was a tremendous character to have on one's side. The trophies would not have been won without him.

By now Arsenal were into the semi-finals of the FA Cup for the first time for 19 years, though Leicester City in the quarter-final replay had once more proved to be a tough nut to crack. The match attracted Highbury's biggest crowd of the season, more than 57,000, and they witnessed a match that became the tale of two headers.

The first by Fern after 13 minutes was disallowed by referee Jim Finney on the evidence of his linesman. The Leicester forward was adjudged to have pushed Rice as he moved in to connect with Farrington's centre; it was a very close call. Then, with Mr Finney counting the seconds towards half-time, George rose perfectly to meet Armstrong's corner.

Such a blow right on the interval did not diminish Leicester's efforts. An absorbing contest continued to the very last kick and only then, were Arsenal sure of their place in the last four. McLintock locked out his old club in the end, and Leicester, gallant in defeat, certainly had a boost to their self belief which served them well in their run-in to the Second Division title.

The semi-final arrived in Arsenal's crowded schedule four days after the dejection of Cologne. The wounds to be licked were mental rather than physical; only the redoubtable Radford carried visible scars of that battle and he would be fit enough.

The draw had paired together Everton and Liverpool for a special derby, while Arsenal were drawn against Stoke City, on League form the weakest of the four survivors.

The matching of the underdogs and the Arsenal machine produced a rivetting contest at Hillsborough. Forty-one years earlier an FA Cup semi-final triumph in Yorkshire in dramatic circumstances provided the impetus to a decade of success; without that recovery against Hull City the glories of the 1930s might never have happened. Now, in the frantic pace of a semi-final in the 1970s the club wrote the most relevant page in the entire story of the Double season.

Quite simply Arsenal looked as though they had stumbled irretrievably at the penultimate hurdle. Stoke might have been nervously caught up in a desire to reach a first major final, or as the less fancied outfit they might have been the more relaxed team. Certainly Arsenal were at times tentative to the point of distraction in the first half, and their players left the field after 45 minutes trailing by 2–0.

Semi-finals by nature are cautious, inhibited affairs; the price of defeat is so high that few risks are taken; winning is all-important, the means scarcely matter. Arsenal began the match in that vein, with a greater share of possession in the first 20 minutes but no end product to show for it.

The cautious approach, though, had to be thrown out of the window after a most unusual goal which lifted this semi-final out of the rut. Wilson properly conceded a corner by pushing behind a teasing cross from Greenhoff. Arsenal did not deal conclusively with the corner kick, and as Storey booted the ball away, it struck Denis Smith and flew into the Arsenal net.

In the very next attack the flame-haired Conroy played a very effective one-two with Mahoney only to put his shot inches wide. Banks twice put his stamp on the game with sharp saves, foiling Kennedy on both occasions, before Stoke, fortified by their goalkeeper, were

'Charlie is their darling' screamed the predictably unoriginal headlines, but it was certainly true that this was George's golden era. This glorious header, executed while hanging four feet off the ground, was the only goal of the quarter-final replay against Leicester on 15 March 1971. George scored in the fourth, fifth and sixth rounds, then saved his finale for the perfect moment. The goalkeeeper, all those years ago, is Peter Shilton.

boosted further in the 29th minute. It was a gift from George. With time to spare the 20-year-old, stricken perhaps with butterflies in this most draining of matches, sent a dreadfully underhit back pass in the direction of Wilson. Ritchie pounced with the predatory instincts of a marksman playing for his moment of glory and reached the ball just before the Arsenal goalkeeper, took it past him and planted it in the yawning goal. It would have been a disaster for any Sunday morning team, let alone one which was pursuing the elusive dream of a League and Cup Double. Stoke should have gone 3–0 ahead when Greenhoff broke clear a few minutes later. Running through from the centre circle he bore down on Wilson carrying many decades of hope from the Potteries and all the fears of North London. But, at a poignantly vital moment for both himself and his club, he seemed to lose his nerve and shot high, wide and anything but handsome. Just like Elland Road in 1930, the tide had turned.

Early in the second half Mahoney charged clear yet again through the constantly square defence. Wilson this time was able to reach the ball. It was a good piece of goalkeeping from a splendid technician, but it carried greater import as Arsenal swept upfield. What might have been 3–0 suddenly became 2–1. Armstrong fed Kennedy, whose chip into the middle caused confusion in the Stoke ranks. Storey unleashed an instinctive drive from 20 yards and even Banks could do nothing.

Yet it was Stoke who reacted more positively to the goal. Arsenal were not allowed to dictate the play in their quest for an equaliser, largely because Greenhoff, in a supreme individual performance which contrasted with his finishing earlier, kept two and even three defenders constantly occupied. Twice on another day he might have brought Stoke the insurance of a

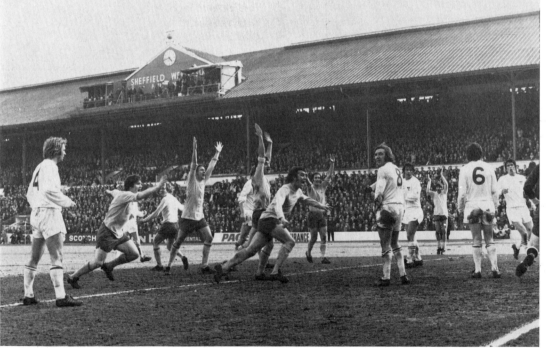

The moment of truth in the Double year. Just as the last minutes of the 1930 semi-final against Hull at Elland Road clearly altered the history of the club, so the last sixty seconds of the semi-final against Stoke at Hillsborough on 27 March 1971 were ultimately the key to the Double. It cannot be pointed out often enough how remarkably similar the last minutes of these two games were – obviously in their significance, but even down to their Yorkshire location, their final score, the venue of the replay, the eventual reckoning. In the history of all great clubs, there are such moments. The seconds were ticking away at Hillsborough with Stoke hanging on to their 2-1 lead. Arsenal won a corner on the right. George Armstrong took it. Up went McLintock (top) at the single most

important moment of his career with the club. He beat Denis Smith (5) to the ball, directed it towards the left-hand corner and saw Stoke's John Mahoney palm it off the line. Referee Pat Patridge (centre left) saw the same thing, as did the Arsenal players and the Stoke defence. The Staffordshire men (bottom left), the collapse of whose world can be seen in their expressions and postures, are, left to right, Jimmy Greenhoff, Mickey Bernard, Eric Skeels, Alan Bloor and John Ritchie, scorer of the first goal. But the most interesting thing about this picture is the clock on top of the Hillsborough stand. 4.44 pm it reads, four minutes beyond the normal final whistle. Of all the moments, of all the moves, of all the minutes, of all the matches that went to make

up the 1970-71 season, this was the one which won the Double.

For one man, however, the shouting was anything but over. That was Peter Storey, who said afterwards that: 'It was all very well them (his teammates) jumping about and going mad, but I had to stick the ball in the net. And against Gordon Banks (then the England keeper).' He did so easily (top), dummying Banks to move right while the ball sped to his left. The celebrations followed, particularly from Radford, Kennedy and Armstrong (centre left). Alan Bloor (6) and John Ritchie (9) seem less enamoured, their dreams shattered. They surely knew their chance had gone. So did the Arsenal supporters, and there was no doubt who was the hero of the hour (centre right).

Peter Storey had scored both the goals, one of them among the two or three most important in the club's history. Bertie Mee said after the game that: 'I shall never forget the two matches against Stoke –

the 5-0 thrashing and this success after being 2-0 down. After the 5-0 beating at Stoke we promised ourselves never again to enter a match with the casual feeling that it was half won before the kick-off.'

third goal. Arsenal's momentum was also interrupted by an injury to George, which brought Sammels on for the last 15 minutes. The resultant injury time proved to be an enormous blessing in disguise.

It was in the two minutes that Pat Partridge, the referee, added on, that the salvation came to keep alive Arsenal's appointment with history. Banks was pressed into conceding a corner, angrily protesting after the match that he had been fouled and that the decision should have been a Stoke free-kick. Armstrong took the corner from the Arsenal right, and this time Banks was nowhere. McLintock, a rescuing figure yet again, steered his header towards the left-hand post, where only the hands of John Mahoney prevented a goal. Referee Partridge

was perfectly placed to award the penalty.

The Arsenal players began to leap in jubilation. The thousands of supporters who had made the journey north to Sheffield roared. One Gunner was less than thrilled, however. Peter Storey had made the penalty job his own with a succession of nervelessly executed kicks. Even in the heat of the toughest battle he now realised the enormity of his task: 'The rest of the lads were all hugging each other as though we'd scored. But I was the one who had to stick it in. And past Gordon Banks too!'

At the other end of the ground Wilson dropped to his knees in prayer. The bedlam gave way to hush. It was one of those moments when the world stops. Had Storey missed, his name, like Bonetti's or perhaps Rix's, would have been engraved forever on the hearts of thousands. But Peter Storey was the man for Arsenal's hour of need. He repaid the faith of colleagues whose celebrations had looked so premature to the penalty taker. As Storey ran up, England's goalkeeper switched his weight on to his right foot and started to move in that direction. Storey sent his shot low, placed with the inside of his

right foot, to Banks' left. Stoke City 2 Arsenal 2, the rescue was complete.

If, from the whole season, we are to choose just one moment in which the Double was won but might have been lost, then it was Jimmy Greenhoff's miss in the first half. In a remarkable display of touch football, Greenhoff had been a giant that day ('You could have fired a cannonball at him, and he'd just have nodded it down to John Ritchie's feet,' said one report) but, at the vital moment, he had failed and Arsenal were saved. At 3–0 they must have been out. John Mahoney could have given Stoke the game as well, but he was neither a forward nor the star of the day, and Wilson was more than equal to the Welshman's abilities.

There can be no doubt that the semi-final was the moment of truth. A League match can be lost (even 1–0 at Elland Road, as we shall see) and the Double still won. But every Cup tie has to end positively. All Cup-winning teams have one match where luck plays its part, when they come through a game they could or even should have lost. This was Arsenal's.

Psychologically, after Hillsborough Arsenal were now in the ascendant. Deep down, for all their boasts that they would finish the job at Villa Park, the Stoke squad knew that they had missed their chance. Bertie Mee's players realised that their escape came almost from the pages of schoolboy fiction. There was another omen too. Liverpool had come from behind to beat Everton in the other semi-final, and would be waiting at Wembley just as they had been 21 years earlier, the last time Arsenal had won the FA Cup.

Both managers announced unchanged teams, George having recovered from his bruised ankle and spirits, but the match had a very different flavour. Arsenal assumed control from the start and maintained it.

Arsenal's skill at set pieces had kept their tally of goals ticking along for most of the season. In Armstrong the team possessed a master crafts-man at corners. Radford, Kennedy, Graham, McLintock and George all relished attacking his accurate crosses. So, in the 13th minute of the FA Cup semi-final replay, Armstrong's service was again a work of precision and Graham's header was so powerful that it completely beat Banks from fully 15 yards.

After the interval Arsenal quickly reaffirmed their grip with a second goal, which held special significance for the provider and the scorer. In terms of scoring the partnership of Radford and Kennedy were undergoing their most fruitless spell of the season. Neither had scored in the previous seven matches. But two minutes into the second half Radford darted down the left and as his cross slithered across the goalmouth Kennedy was in exactly the right place to turn the ball into goal. The two danced a jig of relief and triumph. It was the end of the scoring.

McLintock emerged from the dressing room, his own positive nature sharpened by the experi-ence: 'We are going for the Double! There is real character in this Arsenal side, and now we are

going to show we can win League and Cup. This will be my fifth time at Wembley and after being on the losing side in four finals the law of averages says I must have a great chance of a winners' medal this year. The way we are playing we can certainly do it.' Bertie Mee sat for the photographers in the dressing room posed between the two goalscorers, a bottle of champagne in hand. It was a night to enjoy, but the manager soon had to restore the concentra-tion. There were ten League games to be fitted in before the Cup final. What happened in those would determine whether Arsenal were going to Wembley simply for the Cup or for the Double.

While the dramas were unfolding at Hills-borough, Leeds United had been losing at Chelsea. Now they had 54 points from 35 games; Arsenal were on 48 points from three fewer matches. If they won them all, they would be level on points. Any projected forecasts about the outcome of the race had to take into account that Arsenal still had to visit Elland Road.

Arsenal did not have an easy fixture with which to pick up the reins in the First Division race. Chelsea were fresh from their comprehen-sive victory over Leeds. Arsenal had not won any of the previous eight matches between the two clubs. Highbury was packed with 62,000 fans for the meeting.

Arsenal allowed George even more attacking scope in a formation that often resembled 4-2-4 and the unpredictable youngster opened up the Chelsea defence two minutes after the break. He did so without touching the ball, but his extravagant dummy let Armstrong's cross run to Kennedy, who scored emphatically. 'No back lift,' enthused McNab about the goal. 'Most of us have to wind up for a shot. Ray hits them with hardly any foot movement. Jimmy Greaves used to do that.'

Kennedy had more time to set his sights for his second goal 15 minutes from time. George picked him out in a position that Chelsea claimed was offside, but there were no com-plaints from Dave Sexton about the first defeat he had suffered at the hands of Arsenal since he had left Highbury to become Chelsea's manager.

The match had a nasty conclusion. The tussle between McLintock and Peter Osgood ended with McLintock on the ground crying out that his left elbow had been broken in the fall. With the Cup final five weeks away had his Wembley jinx struck again? The damage was quickly diagnosed as a trapped nerve.

At Elland Road there was no faltering from Leeds United. Allan Clarke contributed all the goals in a 4–0 demolition of Burnley. Yet there were signs of edginess from the front-runners. Don Revie ordered his players not to mention the name of Arsenal. Jack Charlton confided: 'The situation is very tense. The Championship is on a knife edge. It is very difficult not to keep looking over your shoulder for a peep at the Gunners.' The old Leeds' superstitions were rearing their heads.

Three days later it was Arsenal who showed

The two goals which won the semi-final replay against Stoke on 31 March 1971. The first (top) came from George Graham (out of the picture) and the second (bottom picture) from Ray Kennedy (far right). Stoke could not respond, their moment of hope had dissolved four days before. Kennedy's arrival in the team had been as successful as it was swift. He had played only four League games in 1969-70 and came on as substitute twice in the Fairs Cup. In part he owed his early introduction in 1970-71 to a spate of injuries, but he took his chance perfectly.

the strain. The midweek match at home to Coventry City was one of the three the Gunners had in hand. It should not have been difficult, but twice Simpson had to clear from his goal-line with Wilson beaten. It was from one such clearance that Arsenal turned survival into success. Graham and Armstrong were the architects of the goal. Kennedy scored it, ignoring the close attention of two defenders to take the pace off the ball with his first sure touch and slam it past Bill Glazier with his second. It had taken 52 minutes to make the breakthrough, and Arsenal's resolution in defence of the lead was tested to the final whistle. The points were gathered and, if it had not been a match to savour, a healthy diet is not based entirely on rich food.

Kennedy's goal touch, four goals now in three games and 25 for the season, had closed the deficit on Leeds to four points with the leaders having played two games more. The goal aver-

ages were also very close, Leeds with 64 goals for and 27 against; Arsenal with 60 for and 25 against (only six of those in 18 matches at Highbury). The return to form in front of goal of Kennedy had also eased the pressure on Radford, who had now gone ten matches without finding the net.

Moreover, Radford was back in the groove in the away game at Southampton, where the narrow confines around the pitch tend to give The Dell a menacing look to unprepared visiting players. His goal arrived in the 34th minute when the home skipper, Terry Paine, lost possession to McNab. The ball was transferred to Armstrong, and Radford reached the cross before defender Denis Hollywood to force it home. But the lead lasted barely two minutes. Paine darted in to redeem his error with a close range header. The news that awaited the Arsenal players in the dressing room at half-time was that Leeds were also level at Newcastle.

Southampton had not been beaten at The Dell in the First Division since October. That did not daunt Arsenal and especially not McLintock. Ten minutes into the second half Radford's presence at a throw-in was his signal to race forward. Graham flicked on the striker's set-piece long throw and somehow McLintock stretched in front of Jimmy Gabriel to flick the ball into the net with the outside of his right foot. Southampton's ambitions were to win a qualifying place for Europe and the youthful Mick Channon led a late rally which kept Wilson on his toes. The Saints might well have had a penalty when Simpson seemed to grab Davies as he set himself for a header.

Arsenal's second half performance was more profitable than that of Leeds, who could only take one point from St James's Park. Facing seven games in three weeks the mathematics were in the Gunners' favour for virtually the first time. They had now won six League games in a row. Three points behind with two games in hand, the title was theirs if they could keep on winning.

There was no slackening of the Arsenal tempo in the face of the next challenge. Nottingham Forest had been an easy touch at Highbury in October. Much better performances approaching the return at the City Ground had relieved the danger of relegation with five wins in six matches.

Their confidence was evident in the opening minutes. Striker Neil Martin chased a through

Frank McLintock throws himself in front of Southampton's Jimmy Gabriel to score a vital goal at The Dell on 10 April 1971. Arsenal won the match 2-1, part of a sequence of nine consecutive League wins with only one goal (that by Terry Paine for Southampton) conceded. John Radford scored the other goal, his last of the season and the only one he recorded in the last seventeen matches of the Double year. Don Howe, then coach and number two to Bertie Mee, was unstinting in his praise of McLintock around this time: 'They talk of Dave Mackay and Bobby Moore as great captains, but Frank is more inspiring than either. I'm beginning to feel obsolete in the dressing-room. Frank is doing as much talking as I am, and working wonders with his words.' McLintock celebrates his goal (opposite).

ball to such purpose that Wilson had to hurl himself at the oncoming feet of the Forest forward. Both players needed lengthy attention. Neither had claimed the ball cleanly. It had rolled on towards the goal until Rice, chasing back, swept it to safety.

Armstrong's efficiency at corners once more produced a breakthrough in the 17th minute. McLintock's header was scrambled, it seemed, from the line. Kennedy, from a matter of inches, made sure of the goal which was initially credited to him, but later confirmed as McLintock's.

There was no doubt, however, that the second goal, two minutes before half time, belonged to the sturdy young front runner. Radford wound himself up for another long throw, Graham arrived at precisely the right moment to flick the ball on to Kennedy, and he applied the coup de grace for his 26th goal of the season. The effort was slightly tarnished by some late careless talk in the direction of a linesman which prompted a booking. It was quite a night for the young brigade in the Arsenal army, as Charlie George popped in a third goal five minutes from time.

Twenty-four hours earlier Leeds had been held goalless at Huddersfield, so another point

had been stripped from the grasp of the leaders. Leeds continuing involvement in the Fairs Cup had taken a hand. The match with Huddersfield took place on Easter Monday, 12 April. On the following Wednesday the first leg of the European semi-final was staged to make it a formidable week. The only consolation was that the draw had paired the two English survivors, so very little travelling was involved. Leeds went to Liverpool and came home with a magnificent 1–0 victory.

Leeds had four League games to play, Arsenal six. The gap had narrowed to two points. It brought the next set of matches for the clubs on 17 April into even sharper focus. By twenty to five that afternoon the lead had changed. Arsenal, seemingly always the more likely losers in the title race, suddenly found themselves topping the table.

The circumstances were very much in keeping with the story of the season for each contender. Leeds lost at home to West Bromwich Albion in a blaze of controversy. Arsenal beat Newcastle at Highbury with a display which did not easily bring poetic description to mind, but nonetheless brought the desired two points.

To deal with the events in North London first, the two precious points were gathered courtesy of a superb goal from George 19 minutes from the end of a mediocre match. Newcastle had drawn goalless at Highbury in each of the three previous seasons, and were intent on adding to that sequence. The first half contained more flare than flair, particularly when George reacted so angrily to a foul by Keith Dyson that the Arsenal man was booked. The other side of his nature appeared just when a goal was beginning to look beyond the home side. A packed penalty area ahead was not a daunting proposition when the ball dropped to George. He made sufficient inroads to disrupt the massed defence before turning sharply to drive a scorching left-footed shot past Iam McFaul. For the rest of the action George Armstrong provided the perfect postscript: 'I don't suppose anybody will remember the game, but they'll all remember the result.'

Conversely, at Elland Road everybody will remember one particular incident. The turning point of the match concerned a decision by referee Ray Tinkler. He allowed Albion's Tony Brown to burst forward with the ball from just inside the Leeds half on the West Bromwich right. In a more central position his team-mate Colin Suggett was clearly in an offside position, but not, ruled the referee, interfering with play. Brown ran on with the Leeds defence expecting the whistle, drew goalkeeper Gary Sprake out to meet him, and passed across the goal for Jeff Astle (also in an offside-looking position) to score at will. The crowd invaded the pitch. Chaos ensued.

The Leeds protests carried such venom that the Football Association subsequently fined the club £750 and ordered them to play their opening four home games the following season

away from Elland Road. Albion, who had not won away for 16 months, and were to finish the season sixth from bottom, eventually triumphed 2–1. For the Leeds morale it was a devastating blow, made worse by repeated television showings of the crucial episode which increased their sense of grievance. It is an interesting point for debate as to whether Arsenal would have more readily shrugged aside their disappointment. Leeds were to win their last three League matches and the Fairs Cup, but will always feel that the title was taken from them on a piece of refereeing interpretation.

This dramatic match, in a sense the perfect symbol of that whole period when Leeds dominated English football, was to continue to have repercussions 12 months on. The 1971–72 season ended with Leeds missing that Championship by just one point from Derby County. Of the four League matches the West Brom riot had caused them to play away from home, Leeds won two and drew two. It is perfectly reasonable to assume that they would have picked up that one point had those games been played at Elland Road (where they dropped only two points from their remaining 17 games). Hence it is still argued in Yorkshire today that Ray Tinkler's decision cost Leeds not one League title, but two.

If it was a piece of good fortune then Arsenal readily accepted it. Three days later another one-goal victory at Highbury condemned Burnley to the Second Division. With Storey and McNab on international duty for England against Greece in the European Championship, Kelly returned to midfield, and Roberts was given his only League outing over the second half of the season in defence. The absence of Storey in one other respect was covered by George because it was he, in the 26th minute, who accepted the responsibility of taking and scoring the match-winning penalty. The victory was less in doubt than some of Arsenal's one-goal successes during the season, and Wilson's only moment of real anxiety resulted from a careless back pass by Kelly. Paul Fletcher became the latest victim of the bravado of Arsenal's goalkeeper as he sped off his line to take the ball from the toes of the Burnley number nine. From 2 March to 20 April Arsenal had won all their nine League matches; the 18 points were captured with only 16 goals but in those 13½ hours of First Division hurly-burly the defence was penetrated only once, at Southampton.

It was at The Dell where Leeds returned to winning ways on Saturday 24 April, the day that the Gunners' run of victories was halted, ironically by West Bromwich Albion, at the Hawthorns. In some ways it was an unusual match, not least because Asa Hartford scored for both sides. His goal at the right end was the first of the four. For once Wilson's charge off his line could not rescue a square defence.

Albion held their lead for only four minutes. Yet again an Armstrong corner unsettled those defending against it, particularly goalkeeper Jim Cumbes. From his mishandling the ball dropped for George, who was denied a goal himself by a block on the line. McLintock, however, was first to the rebound to notch his third goal in five games, this one celebrating the announcement that he had been chosen as the Footballer of the Year.

Arsenal lost Rice at half-time, the legacy of a twisted ankle. Storey moved to right back but was still prepared to charge forward in the 55th minute in pursuit of a chipped pass from George. Hartford eagerly ran back, aware of the danger, only to increase it with a back pass. Cumbes was caught coming off his line and the ball rolled into goal with a simplicity which would have driven wild any Leeds United fans present. Five minutes from the end, however, Tony Brown, the scourge of the Elland Road supporters a week earlier, earned their gratitude with a thumping equaliser. Arsenal now had 61 points from 39 matches, Leeds were on 60 from 40 games.

Before leaving the Hawthorns, McLintock reflected philosophically on the impending clash of the Titans the following Monday: 'It's obviously going to be tough at Leeds, but the odds are still in our favour. I'm sure Leeds would be happy to swap positions with us. Our run of nine League wins had to end sometime. And Brown did it with a great goal. He hit the ball perfectly.'

Forty-eight thousand fans squeezed into Elland Road on Monday 26 April, packed like commuters on a rush-hour underground train.

Leeds had just reached the Fairs Cup final and a match with Juventus; against Arsenal they needed nothing less than victory for their Championship dreams to survive. A draw would be very much to Arsenal's liking, and for most of the game it looked the most likely outcome. The Gunners' sense of discipline and tactical organisation, a cornerstone of the season, served them well. Leeds, with Mick Bates deputising for Peter Lorimer, were kept at arm's length throughout a first half in which both teams were kept under excellent control by Norman Burtenshaw from Great Yarmouth, a late replacement for the elected referee Jim Finney, who had been hurt in a car crash.

Wilson's main task in the opening 45 minutes was to gather in a succession of crosses, but the pattern altered in the second half. The home side redoubled their efforts; Arsenal partly by design, partly because of Leeds' extra determination, opted to see out the siege rather than attack. And for all the creativity of Bremner and Johnny Giles, the best pair of midfield operators in the land at the time, Leeds were continually frustrated by a massed defence. It remained a stern, unrelenting battle, and though the prize was so great the conduct of the players was more orderly than in other meetings of the period between these two rivals.

It all changed in the dying moments. The ubiquitous Paul Madeley triggered off another Leeds foray. Bremner, who had never ceased in his quest for an opening, played his part, and

suddenly the ball broke for Jack Charlton all alone in front of Wilson's goal. England's World Cup centre half of 1966 directed the ball past the Arsenal goalkeeper as other defenders stood frozen, arms raised in a uniform appeal for offside. Even then the gods, for once, favoured Leeds because the ball struck a post and re-bounded out, only for a long Charlton leg to reach it before McNab. Instantly Norman Burten-shaw confirmed the goal.

Arsenal's protests were long in time and short in temper. George booted the ball into the stand and was rightly booked. Wilson and McLintock led the pursuit of the referee, and it was fully five minutes before he could restart the game. The linesman whose flag had stayed down was also turned upon by aggrieved visiting players. There was still time for Graham to send a back header inches over Gary Sprake's crossbar, before more furious words were directed at the referee when he blew the final whistle.

Many off the pitch queried the goal at the time though Bertie Mee confined himself to comment-ing that 'never was a defeat less deserved. Arsenal were fantastic, tremendous.' However, subsequent television re-runs convinced a number of the most bitter Arsenal players at the time that referee and linesman had been absolutely right. McNab, it seemed, had been too slow moving out. Mr Burtenshaw was able to look forward to his next Arsenal match with confidence; he had been appointed the FA Cup final referee.

Whatever the merits of the decision it meant that Leeds were back on top of the First Division, but William Hill, the bookmakers, still made Arsenal favourites for the Champion-ship at 4–5; Leeds were quoted as even-money.

May Day brought victories for both candidates in the race to be named Champions. Leeds struck twice in the first half at Elland Road, through Bremner and Lorimer, to make sure that their League season ended with a win over Nottingham Forest. Arsenal had to wait longer before gaining their reward against Stoke City.

It was the type of game which had become the norm at Highbury towards the end of the season. Stoke, like other visitors, were not brim-ming with ambition for victory. The cautious approach of five midfield players in support of the solitary attacker Greenhoff hardly indicated a team seeking revenge for an FA Cup semi-final defeat.

Arsenal began as though their boots were weighted down with tension. No opportunity was created until three minutes before half-time. George's forward pass caught the Stoke defence in a line, and Radford bore down on the Stoke goal and its guardian, Gordon Banks. He dallied so long that Smith was able to rush back and prevent the shot. It looked a significant miss and Radford later explained: 'Initially I stopped because I thought I was offside. Then I realised I wasn't and tried to lob the ball over Banks. But he started back-pedalling so I had to hold the ball. One of their blokes came in and I've the gash to prove it.'

Early in the second half Arsenal suffered again; Storey limped off with a groin strain and Kelly entered the congested midfield area. It was the start of a memorable week for the 20-year-old Scot. He had been on the field 12 minutes when he spotted the potential of a long ball into the goalmouth from Armstrong. Graham flicked it on to Radford who skilfully manipulated it into Kelly's path. The substitute blasted in the decisive goal.

Now at long last Arsenal knew exactly what they had to do to win the League for the first time for 18 years. Leeds had finished their First Division programme: Played 42, Won 27, Drawn 10, Lost 5, Goals For 72, Against 30, Points 64. Arsenal's record read: Played 41, Won 28, Drawn 7, Lost 6, For 70, Against 29, Points 63.

With a wonderful sense of occasion the last fixture was against the closest of foes, Tottenham Hotspur, at White Hart Lane. The game had been originally scheduled for the day of the FA Cup semi-finals and was now rearranged for the Monday night of Cup final week.

If Leeds had the chance to select a fixture to deprive Arsenal of the title it would surely be this one. Local rivalry alone would be enough to ensure maximum effort from the opposition, but there was even more at stake for Spurs. They needed three points from the meeting with Arsenal and a trip to Stoke to be sure of qualifying for the next European campaign. Bonuses of £400 per man (still a reasonable sum at the time) could depend on beating Arsenal.

The mathematical permutations were even more remarkable. A win would give the title to Arsenal, a defeat would send the trophy to Elland Road. But a goalless draw would mean success for Arsenal while (because of the peculiar-ities of the goal average system then in force) any scoring draw (even 1–1) would conclude matters in Leeds' favour. The mathematics meant it was more important for Arsenal not to concede a goal than to score one.

Arsenal's players had only reached this situa-tion through a deep yearning for success. The prospect of crossing another minefield did not alarm them. Frank McLintock rarely lost his sense of optimism: 'I'm sure we can make it. We always give good performances at White Hart Lane.' George Armstrong was equally confident: 'We're playing better away from home because we are not under the same tension, and it's in our favour that Spurs are not a defensive side.'

Alan Mullery, Tottenham's captain, reinforced the belief that it would be a mighty clash: 'Arsenal have got as much chance of being handed the title by Spurs as I have of being given the Crown Jewels. They are the *last* people we want winning the Championship. Everybody is on about the great season Arsenal are having. Well, we're not doing too badly. We have won the League Cup and reached the sixth round of the FA Cup. Now we mean to round off our season by beating Arsenal — and that will put us third in the table. That can't be bad.'

Manager Bill Nicholson recognised that the

League title could be the prelude to the Double
to which he had guided Spurs ten years earlier:
'We are tremendously proud of our Double
achievement. I suppose some other club has got
to do it again sometime but we will be doing our
best to see that it isn't Arsenal. My instructions
to the Tottenham players will be to go out to try
to win.'

Don Revie was glad to hear such words. The
Leeds manager declared: 'We have done all we
can and now we are helpless. My players have
been magnificent all season. I would hate to see
them pipped on the post again. We have got 64
points and there have never been runners-up
with a collection as big as that. We are not going
to sit around waiting for the result of the match

at Tottenham. The lads are playing in Chris
Chilton's testimonial match at Hull and I'll be
there watching them. It is now up to Tottenham.'
Revie was right — whichever side lost, they
would have amassed the biggest runners-up
points total ever.

The Arsenal players rested on the Sunday as
usual, but for Storey there was not enough time
for recovery. When the players reported for light
training on the morning of the match it was clear
that Kelly would be in the team from the start.
Sammels was chosen as substitute.

The players lunched at their own homes
before reconvening at the South Herts Golf
Club, the regular pre-match meeting place, at
4.30 pm. Already the football fans of North

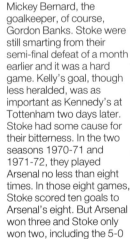

While both prizes were won in London, neither was secured at Highbury. On 3 May 1971 Arsenal went to White Hart Lane needing a win or a goalless draw to pip Leeds for the title. A scoring draw would have given the title to Leeds. Their fate rested on their near neighbours and rivals, the only other team to win the Double this century, the team they had displaced from the First Division half a century before. The crowd was enormous. Steve Perryman only just made the kick-off, taking an hour to travel 600 yards. The police estimated a crowd of around 150,000 tried to see the match; even the Spurs directors called it the biggest turn-out in the club's history. Those lucky enough to get inside saw just one goal (top left), a Ray Kennedy (out of the picture) header minutes from time. The desperate defenders are Knowles, Jennings and Kinnear. Statistically the goal made little difference – Arsenal still needed to *prevent* Spurs scoring. The Championship would have been theirs whether they had scored or not, just as long as Spurs didn't. At the final whistle the fans were to celebrate Arsenal's eighth Championship on the pitch (centre) while (top right) Armstrong, Kennedy and Radford preferred the champagne in the dressing room.

London were on the march towards White Hart Lane. The gates were locked more than an hour before the kick off with 51,192 lucky spectators inside. Twice that number were left on the outside.

The volume of traffic even surprised the police. The Arsenal team coach crawled along. Bertie Mee recalled: 'We gave ourselves an hour for a drive which normally takes 20 minutes. But even then it was a very difficult journey. I have never seen scenes like it. But there was never the pressure that we were going to be late, and seeing those thronging crowds increased the sense of occasion for us. There was no way we were going to be beaten.'

The referee, Kevin Howley, had to abandon his car a mile away to fight his way on foot through the crowds. It was the last League match in a distinguished career, a momentous occasion on which to bow out. Making his whistle heard in the din which echoed around the ground from start to finish became a problem for him. The vociferous McLintock

bellowed instructions to his team-mates which passed largely unheard.

McLintock had his hands full coping with the powerful Martin Chivers. The wise Alan Gilzean continually sought to steal a yard on Simpson. Jimmy Neighbour probed ceaselessly down Tottenham's left and stretched Rice to the full, and all the while Martin Peters hovered menacingly in the Spurs midfield, always likely to time a late run into a scoring position. For all the attacking intent clear cut chances were few. Peters flicked the top of the Arsenal bar with a swerving shot, and almost scored with a header. Joe Kinnear forced a courageous and painful dive from Wilson at his feet. Gilzean all but connected as the ball flashed across the Arsenal goalmouth.

At the other end George brought an athletic save from Pat Jennings in the opening minute. McLintock saw his goalbound shot bounce clear off the body of Collins. Graham's header curved on to the top of the Tottenham goal. Radford and Kennedy hustled and bustled at Peter Collins and Phil Beal. Armstrong was everywhere.

For all the energy imparted into the match by both teams, whose conduct had been first class, a goalless draw beckoned. But three minutes from time, Kinnear tried to dribble clear of trouble inside his own penalty area. George recaptured the ball from the Spurs right back, and twisted instantly to conjure a cross from an angle which would have defeated most players. Even then it seemed as though Arsenal had been denied. Jennings made the save of the night as Radford met the ball provided so cleverly by George.

Tottenham stopped to a man, perhaps in admiration of their goalkeeper, but also because they expected the ball to run behind for a corner. Armstrong had barely stood still all season, and was not going to break the habit now. Rescuing it from near the goalline his chip back across goal was met by Kennedy's soaring header. The ball sped high to Jennings' left, above the leap of Cyril Knowles behind him. It clipped the underside of the bar and was over the line.

The goal was greeted by an explosion of sound and instant exhilaration from every Arsenal player. But almost as quickly misgivings followed, particularly from the scorer. In one respect, the goal was irrelevant. A Tottenham goal would still give the Championship to Leeds, just as before, and there was still time for it. 'That was the longest three minutes I have ever known,' recalled Kennedy. 'I remember thinking to myself as Tottenham came back at us that perhaps it might have been better had my header not gone into the net.'

Spurs hurled themselves forward as the seconds ticked away. One last corner could still have deprived the Gunners, but Wilson's last act in an almost faultless series of performances throughout the 42-game First Division programme was to grasp the ball as though the lives of he and his team-mates depended upon it. As he fell to the ground he was surrounded by other players, half of them hoping for a fumble, the other half protecting their goalkeeper. For a few seconds it seemed that the match would end in acrimony but Kevin Howley stepped in firmly.

Moments later he blew a whistle in League football for the last time. The title belonged to Arsenal for a record eighth time. It had been won by a clear point at the last gasp of a marathon that had never been less than compelling. Leeds deserved sympathy for coming so close, but none could deny the magnificence of Arsenal's victory. Like a dog with a bone they had refused to let go right to the end.

Bedlam reigned on the pitch. George, close to the touchline, leapt into the arms of Don Howe. As thousands of fans raced to congratulate their heroes Bob Wilson found himself marooned. Unable to contain his joy he hugged the only participant he could reach — referee Howley! McLintock found a Leeds United scarf wrapped around his neck as he was chaired off shoulder high.

The celebrations became so protracted that

Don Howe found his own joy giving way to anxiety: 'My thoughts turned straight to the Cup final and I was worried that the crowd might injure our players. They were ripping at their shirts. Some wanted their boots, which of course they had to wear on Saturday. I was frightened that they would tread on somebody's foot and keep him out of the final.'

Twenty minutes after the end of the match some of the players still had not made it back to the sanctuary of the dressing room. Arsenal officials turned to the police for a rescue party but with the footballers unable to get off the pitch the constables were unable to make their way on to it. Eventually all were rounded up minus only a few shirts.

Bertie Mee lost his club tie as he returned to the directors' box to acknowledge the crowd's appreciation. Tottenham for their part were most magnanimous in defeat, which the Arsenal manager remembers with great affection: 'We were given champagne in the dressing room by Bill Nicholson. The club could not have done more to help us celebrate our great night. There had been a lot of petty rivalries between the two clubs in past years but in my time we did a lot of work to improve relationships. They must have been very disappointed that they had lost but they didn't let that spoil our evening.'

The party spirit continued long into the night. The team moved on to the White Hart in Southgate. There were no curfews posted or restrictions made. Tuesday, which had already begun by the time everyone reached home, would be a day for recharging batteries. Wednesday was the time really to begin the concentration on the FA Cup final.

Much of that day was given over to the needs of the media, but not for long. Bertie Mee's medical background gave him strong views about Wembley finals: 'Over the years so much had been said about the problems of playing there, particularly the victims of cramp. Now cramp is really an emotional problem. It does of course have physical symptoms, but they can often be a result of pressure. I wanted to protect the team from emotional stress, so there was no involvement with the press or television after Thursday.'

Don Howe concentrated on the physical preparation. Amidst the lush acres of the London Colney training ground, the players did their training on a pitch marked to the exact specifications of Wembley. The grass had been allowed to grow to cultivate as near as possible the feel of the Empire Stadium turf. Two recent League Cup final defeats had raised doubts about the team's ability to win at Wembley. No stone was left unturned in an attempt to create the right atmosphere this time.

For George Wright, the physiotherapist, it was becoming a race against the clock. Peter Storey's presence in midfield was vital to the construction of the side; his injury was responding to intensive treatment, but only slowly. On Friday night he joined up with the other players

at the Grosvenor Hotel in Park Lane. The hall porter reminded them that it had been a lucky venue for West Bromwich Albion three years earlier when they had brought the Cup back for their post-match banquet.

Bertie Mee had one major decision to make, and Storey was chosen to start the game. It was a risk but one that was calculated; the converted full back had become a fearsome opponent in midfield. Liverpool would not relish the bite in his tackles even if he was less than one hundred per cent fit.

There were psychological battles to be won. No one knew that better than Bill Shankly, Liverpool's manager, to whom the old cliche applied: 'a legend in his own life-time'. Shankly had surprisingly appeared by the side of the pitch the day before the final when Arsenal were taking a preparatory stroll to acclimatise to the Wembley environment. There was rain about, and Bob Wilson was greeted by one of the masters of gamesmanship and kidology with the comment: 'Bob, it'll be a nightmare for goalkeepers out here tomorrow.' Directed at a character with less perception that Wilson, it might have induced a sleepless night in a key opponent.

In fact 8 May 1971 was a stifling day. The Arsenal ritual did not include the customary lie-in of most Cup final teams. By ten o'clock the players were on the road to familiar surroundings. At the South Herts Golf Club they took their pre-match lunch with a sprinkling of words of encouragement from Dai Rees, the resident professional.

The opportunity to gain a spot of revenge on Shankly came 15 minutes before the kick-off. Arsenal had recent memories of the formalities of Wembley finals. Officials are keen to have the teams standing in the tunnel ready to walk out at the appropriate minute. Often the wait is so protracted that the nervous begin to suffer. So at 2.45 pm Bertie Mee politely but firmly told the FA representative that he was just finishing his team talk and his players would be out in a moment. A few minutes later the call came again. This time he replied: 'A couple of the players are just tying their boots, we won't be a minute.'

It was only at the third time of asking that Arsenal appeared. Liverpool had come out at the first request and been kept waiting. Shankly scowled, realising that for once he had been outfoxed. There was no delay for Arsenal; immediately they were led out into the sunlight and the wall of sound that was waiting beyond the end of the tunnel.

It had been six weeks since Liverpool had qualified for Wembley. While Arsenal's attentions had been very much elsewhere, at Anfield there had been no escape from the publicity machine. It had been one long round of interviews and discussions about the match in the weeks leading up to the great day itself. Arsenal's worries were whether the rigours of the League campaign would now begin to take their toll, and those unhappy memories of League Cup

defeats. They were playing their fourth major final in five years under Mee.

Liverpool's early promise brought no reward, only the bruises of battle as Storey came in high and late on Heighway. Toshack was then mis-used by Rice and McLintock. It took a telling pass from George to switch the balance of the opening minutes. Kennedy's running was never speedy, and recovering defenders forced him away from the goal and the danger evaporated.

Indeed it was not to be Kennedy's day, and six minutes into the second half he failed with another opportunity much closer to goal. In contrast Radford recaptured the form which had been elusive towards the end of the League season. No one contributed more to Arsenal's eventual victory than the muscular Yorkshireman in the number nine shirt. Though he did not score himself he was the provider of both opportunities which were taken; throughout the match he used the Gunners' possession to excellent effect.

Armstrong was another who could not quite capture his normal excellence, though once, arriving at the far post, he almost beat Clemence for a goal which would surely have spared the players extra time. Graham, however, strutted through the match with an arrogance that set him above others and he was awarded the Man of the Match prize. Twelve minutes from time he climbed characteristically to direct Radford's long throw beyond Clemence but it came off the bar. Smith hooked the rebound for a corner which Armstrong planted once more on Graham's head. This time left back Alec Lindsay cleared off the line.

Both sides used their substitutes. Storey, as expected, gave way to Kelly midway through the second half. Four minutes later Peter Thompson, with Chris Lawler, Tommy Smith and Ian Callaghan, a survivor from the 1965 Cup-winning team, was brought on in an attempt to inject more thrust into Liverpool's performance; the ineffective Alun Evans was replaced. Nevertheless, neither team could break the mould of the match in normal time. It had been a highly technical 90 minutes, with both sides cautious in their attempts to seek an advantage. The uncommitted neutrals, however, were seeking a more cavalier approach in the extra 30 minutes.

They had to wait only two minutes. Steve Heighway (he and Brian Hall were two university graduates in Liverpool's side) had rarely freed himself from the shackles imposed on the Arsenal right, but suddenly he slipped past Rice and Armstrong and from a tight angle cut in from the left. Wilson automatically took up position covering his near post. With his usually accurate sense of anticipation already predicting that Heighway should cut the ball back for Toshack arriving in the middle the goalkeeper slightly overcompensated for the cross. Heighway was nothing if not unorthodox and his shot fizzed into the gap that Wilson had left to his right. Only the beaten goalkeeper heard the nick as the ball glanced the post on its way in; it was

And so to Wembley;
Bertie Mee leads out his men for their tryst with destiny. More than one team had come to Wembley needing just one more victory to achieve the Double, and so far only Spurs had achieved it. In that sense the odds were firmly against Arsenal, as Manchester United found in 1957, as Liverpool were to discover in 1977 and as Everton were to regret in 1985.

Early on, the game was a tense one; referee Norman Birkenshaw and tattooed John Radford are pictured suggesting to Charlie George that he keeps his thoughts to himself. Radford was both a popular and an under-rated player, says Terry Neill: 'Very intelligent, very astute. When the tackle from behind was common-place, he was the first footballer I knew to put shin pads down the back of his legs.' One of Radford's particular skills,

the long throw into the goal mouth, became a trade-mark. So much so that using it as a decoy secured the only Arsenal goal of the first 1972 semi-final, again versus Stoke. Radford shaped to take a long throw, the whole Stoke defence retreated, Radford threw it short to an unmarked colleague instead and was himself still unmarked long enough to receive the return and set up the goal.

Goalmouth incidents in the first ninety minutes of the 1971 FA Cup final were not exactly numerous. One of Liverpool's closest shaves came when George Armstrong beat Tommy Smith to a close range header and Ray Clemence pushed the ball upwards (despite the keeper's apparent position in this picture) and caught it as it came down. Liverpool, though they finished only fifth, had an excellent defence that season. They scored only 42 goals but conceded just 24, then a First Division record.

There was no score in the 1971 FA Cup final until the first minute of extra time. Then Steve Heighway, a recent, rather unpredictable newcomer to the Liverpool first team from non-League football, broke down the left wing (left), slipped George Armstrong and shot for the near post before Pat Rice could cover. Bob Wilson had left just too much room (bottom picture) and the ball ended in the back of the net. Liverpool 1 Arsenal 0. Only four teams since the Second World War had won the Cup after conceding the first goal, and only three others have done so since 1971.

no fluke, Heighway had scored from a similar angle in a Merseyside derby earlier that season.

Wilson had little time for self-recrimination. Within moments he had saved Arsenal from certain defeat, plunging to keep out a close range shot from Hall. On the bench Don Howe was sending George Wright to the touchline with a vital message: 'My first reaction was here we go again, losing at Wembley, but anyway we'd had a tremendous season. But my next thought was that we'd got to change something to pull that goal back. I told George to get to the touchline and tell George Graham to go forward. Charlie George was nearly out on his feet because of the heat and was struggling to make any runs forward, so he was told to drop back into midfield.'

There were four minutes left in the first period of extra time when the move paid

dividends. Radford hooked the ball over his shoulder into a crowded Liverpool penalty area, where the congestion was perhaps too great for Clemence to risk an intervention. Larry Lloyd, Emlyn Hughes, Smith and Lawler were all between the Liverpool goalkeeper and the ball which fell for Kelly simply to touch it forward. It certainly could never be called a serious shot.

Yet on it rolled between a tangle of legs as Graham swept in to view. He swung a leg at the ball and Clemence, now very much the last line of defence, could do nothing to prevent its progress into the net. Graham wheeled away in celebration of the goal that everyone in the ground believed to be his. But football had entered a television age. The BBC and ITV were competing on the sporting front and the Cup final was the showpiece for each channel to show off its technical and editorial skills. New

Arsenal came back quickly. A seemingly hopeful ball into the crowded centre was pushed forward by Eddie Kelly (left in picture opposite). George Graham slipped between Tommy Smith and Emlyn Hughes and seemed to flick it past Ray Clemence. As he wheeled away in triumph (picture above) the goal was obviously credited to Graham. Liverpool 1 Arsenal 1. Later television replays encouraged an interesting, arguably unique, debate. Had George Graham actually touched the ball? In the end the goal was credited to Eddie Kelly, who remains the only substitute to have scored in an FA Cup final. Graham was naturally distressed that anyone should think he would try to steal a colleague's goal, and remains convinced he touched the ball. Further viewing of the film tends to support his case, or at least leave the matter unresolved. What probably happened is that he did get a slight touch to the ball, but the direction and speed were not varied at all. This was to prove vital. Ray Clemence's (centre right, top picture) advance had been made with an allowance for Graham changing the direction. Had Graham done so, Clemence might well have saved. In the end, what happened was effectively a dummy, the last thing Clemence expected.

camera angles were one area of that competition, and the day after the final the London Weekend Television look-back at the match included a 'revelation', from a camera behind the goal, that Graham had not touched the ball. The last certain touch came from Kelly, declared presenters Brian Moore and Jimmy Hill.

Thus the club credited the scoring of the equalising goal to Eddie Kelly. The research for the centenary history found still conflicting evidence. Fifteen years after the event George Graham still believes he made contact with the ball, and is understandably embarrassed at being recalled from time to time as the man who claimed a vital goal which apparently was not his. BBC Television's Barry Davies was stationed that afternoon among the photographers close to Ray Clemence's net. Watching with the eyes of a trained observer, he still believes that the goal should be Graham's. Ray Clemence, who ought to have been in the best position to judge, could throw no light on the subject. A recent study of the television pictures supports the Kelly theory but camera angles can be deceptive. It is certainly true that the ball did not change direction whether Graham touched it or not, so Graham's swing might at least have worked like a good dummy on Clemence.

The debate matters now only in the search for accuracy. At the time it did not matter in the slightest whose goal it was. Arsenal, yet again in this astonishing season, had refused to accept second place. But back on the bench the search for victory was not quite so immediate for Don Howe: 'Once we had equalised I settled for the draw. It hadn't really been our day overall, and I felt it would be better to steady ourselves and start out afresh for the replay. I decided to get

The **coup de grace,** that final dramatic moment towards which the whole of Arsenal's season had seemed to be building. And who else to supply it but the ex-North Bank supporter himself, Charlie George. With just nine minutes of extra time remaining, George picked up the ball around 25 yards out. He moved a few paces and,

despite the exhaustion which had dulled his game for the last half hour, hit a crisp right foot shot (top left). The ball took a tiny upward deflection off the top of Larry Lloyd's outstretched right boot and moved too quickly for a flying Ray Clemence (top right) to reach. Clemence just had time to turn in mid-air and see it hit the back of the net.

The game won, George (number 11 in bottom picture) turned and fell to the floor in the gesture for which he will always be remembered. McLintock and Radford ran to greet him. The Liverpool defenders are Peter Thompson and Tommy Smith. Note that the scoreboard gives the first goal to George Graham, who was to be voted Man of the Match.

George Graham back into midfield just to make sure he got behind the ball. Charlie still looked exhausted so I wanted him back up front. Out of the way really. He found his way forward because we were trying to protect our position for the draw.'

No one had explained the finer points of the theory to George himself. With the replay nine minutes away he interpassed with the magnificent Radford before letting fly from 20 yards with a right-footed shot which belied his weary appearance. The force in the drive would surely have beaten Clemence even if it had not taken a slight upward deflection off the lunging Lloyd. George marked the moment with a novel salute; his arms were outraised as in more conventional celebration, but he was lying flat on his back at the time! It remains the outstanding image of this unusual character.

How appropriate that Arsenal's Double was sealed by one of North London's own. Charlie George, born in Islington, a product of Holloway School, used to stand on Highbury's North Bank. With his flowing hair and his obvious mocking of convention he acted out the dreams of so many young Arsenal followers. At 20 years old he had earned himself and his team-mates an extra £12,000 a man with that winning goal. The money mattered, but the glory was priceless.

Frank McLintock became a Wembley victor at long last, at the fifth time of asking. Bill Shankly, generous in defeat, was quick to shake his hand. George did handsprings of jubilation. Kennedy embraced Lloyd in consolation. Wilson assured Clemence, a loser on his first Wembley visit, that he would be back and how right he was.

Bob Wilson later admitted that on a baking afternoon he had gone cold all over at the instant George had struck his momentous goal; such was the feeling of salvation after his earlier slip.

His recollections at the final whistle are also sharp: 'Frank was in so much of a hurry to go up and grab the Cup that I pulled him back. He'd waited so long. I shouted at him that it might never happen again and that he should savour every moment. Not to rush it.' Wilson was right, of course — it never did happen again for McLintock.

Wilson followed McLintock up to the Royal Box where the second leg of the Double was presented to Arsenal's captain by the Duke of Kent. On the way back to ground level the goalkeeper, by complete coincidence, spotted his older brother Hugh, who had been a great mentor in younger days. For the Wilsons it was a special moment on a special day at the end of a very special season.

For some it was too much to take. McLintock relished the ending of his Wembley hoodoo but years later he confessed that he had no emotion left: 'It may seem strange but I've never been able to feel that supreme thrill of winning the Double. Our Fairs Cup win the year before meant so much. And winning the League was terrific. Maybe I was just too drained at the end of it all.'

A quarter of a million people still had the energy to line the route from Highbury to Islington Town Hall the following day. Both trophies were displayed by the team from an open-top bus, along with the FA Youth Cup, the product of more success for the club's prospective stars. Arsenal Football Club was awarded the freedom of the Borough of Islington.

Bertie Mee had guided the club to a year of unprecedented achievement. It had taken 51 matches to win the Double, a longer road than that of any of the three previous holders of that accolade. 'I wanted the boys to win the Cup for Frank McLintock. The League Championship was for my chairman Denis Hill-Wood. For myself? I wouldn't mind the European Cup next season. I know we have done the Double, but at the moment it is too much to take in.'

For the next two weeks Mee felt like a zombie as the unwinding process began. The players came back to earth rather more quickly. On their holiday in Torremolinos it rained every day. It was as if the gods were saying enough is enough!

What was the chemistry that produced the Double-winning side triumph? George Graham admits that it was not a great team in the terms of Puskas' Hungary, di Stefano's Real Madrid or even Blanchflower's Tottenham. The Arsenal style was never going to make the public drool,

Period piece; Charlie George and girlfriend Susan Farge celebrate the Double at the Cafe Royal on Cup final night in unmistakeably 1971 style.

but the level of technical ability was high, and the team tactics carefully thought out and effective. Certainly the urge for victory was the extra ingredient which turned the above-average into the extraordinary. Bertie Mee paid special tribute to the morale of his players: 'They appreciated each other's weaknesses and would compensate for them. And they were able to play to each other's strengths. The chemistry both on the field and off it was just right.'

Though Don Howe held the reins at training, Mee could sense when the team was a little below par; his appearance at the side of the practice area would automatically induce extra effort. He was never at a loss for a quick-witted reply, an essential tool to maintain his authority amid the repartee of a professional dressing room.

Much of the competitive nature of the side stemmed from discussions during training. Good and bad was debated behind closed doors with an honesty that at times bordered on ferocious. It was a hard school and only the tough survived. The sensitive, like Wilson, and the naturally silent, like George, all had to play a part. Bonds were forged. They stood the test on the pitch, and on other occasions like the street fight in Rome. The togetherness created a solid base that saw the team to the Championship with those last four hard-fought 1–0 victories of the League season.

At Highbury, apart from the League Cup exit, Arsenal were invincible. Only three points were dropped from 21 First Division matches; draws against Leeds, Crystal Palace and Southampton. Only six goals were scored by visiting teams, 17 of the 21 visitors failed to score. Bob Wilson had much to do with this — he was the only player to take part in every minute of all 64 competitive games in the 1970–71 campaign. McLintock and Armstrong shared the distinction of being on the field for the complete duration of the 51 matches which made up the Double.

Originally the desperately keen amateur who did not look quite good enough for the job in his early days at Highbury, Bob Wilson blossomed into a superb professional. The search for knowledge which had taken him along the academic road to teaching was applied to the science of goalkeeping. To his skill he added a bravery which inspired those in front of him.

Pat Rice was another to whom a career in football had not come easily. The persistence he had needed to earn his apprenticeship stood him in good stead when the call came to League action. He had been capped for Northern Ireland at 19, but remained a reserve at his club until a vacancy was created at right back with the switch of Storey into midfield. Rice became a regular in 1970 and stayed throughout the decade, becoming a sterling captain along the way. After a spell at Watford he returned to Arsenal to join the coaching staff.

At left back Bob McNab sometimes disappointed with his passing but had few peers defensively. His outwardgoing personality was reflected in his smart attire and ceaseless chatter. He was always third man out onto the pitch. Both Wilson and McLintock paid tribute to his organising ability and to the help they received from 'Nabbers', with the goalkeeper particularly recalling the very last act of the Double season: 'Liverpool had a corner and Bob McNab whacked me on the backside, and yelled at me to go and get the ball — which was always our policy because we had a relatively short back four. On this occasion it was a wicked ball in at the near post, but he'd encouraged me yet again to be positive. I had to force my way past three players to reach it, but I caught the ball, dribbled it for a moment and kicked it upfield. Then the final whistle went.'

The two centre backs were differing characters but they complemented each other perfectly. No one had more confidence than Frank McLintock, a superb leader, whose natural impulsiveness was now kept in check in this team, whereas he had at times been indisciplined in his play in the past. His misgivings about his conversion to centre back were soon dispelled; in his defensive role he extended his First Division career past his 37th birthday, the last four seasons with a successful Queen's Park Rangers.

Peter Simpson rewarded the hours spent by Bertie Mee bullying him into realising his own talent. Known in the dressing room as 'Stan', his capacity for self-criticism was probably the one factor which prevented him forcing his way into the international reckoning; his skill certainly merited an opportunity at full level. A lover of champagne and a chain-smoker he continued to serve Arsenal until injuries took their toll in 1978.

In midfield Peter Storey epitomised the competitive nature of the side. His aggression on the field was in contrast to his quiet personality. He was followed loyally by his family wherever the team played. Storey was singled out for the awkward tasks of man-marking a difficult opponent. He stayed with Arsenal until March 1977 before a short, fruitless spell with Fulham and a fall into deeper problems.

George Armstrong left Highbury the same year, after 500 League games. He, earlier than any in the dressing room, had sensed that the Double year was going to happen. He held firm beliefs that Arsenal's name was written on the two trophies, and no one did more to turn dream into reality. His own mechanics, which produced his non-stop running, could hardly have been bettered by any of the huge cars that he loved to own. 'Geordie' Armstrong was a loyal lieutenant in the Arsenal cause. The descriptions of the goals in this chapter emphasise the major part he played. He was a master of chipping the ball accurately, and Radford and Kennedy in particular benefitted from his great gifts. In an era when wingers were a luxury, his all-round abilities and industry were a manager's dream.

Both George Graham and Charlie George lacked Armstrong's consistency but both adored the big occasion. Graham's tall upright style gave the impression of casualness and earned

The 1970-71 Arsenal squad, only the fourth ever to have won the Double. Back row, left to right: Pat Rice, Sammy Nelson, Peter Marinello. Centre: Bob McNab, Peter Simpson, Charlie George, Geoff Barnett, Bob Wilson, John Roberts, Ray Kennedy, Peter Storey.
Seated: George Wright (trainer and physiotherapist), George Armstrong, Eddie Kelly, John Radford, Bertie Mee (manager), Frank McLintock, George Graham, Jon Sammels, Don Howe. Of the players, only Geoff Barnett did not make any first-team appearances during the Double season.

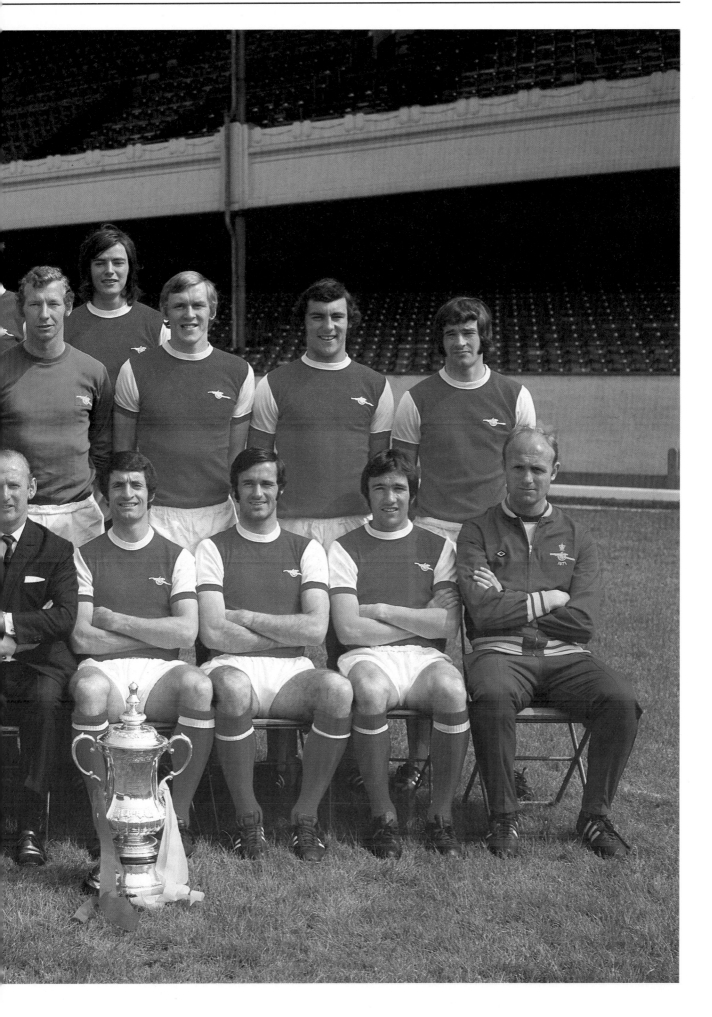

him his nickname 'Stroller'. As a former striker he never lost his eye for goal from midfield; his height added to Arsenal's aerial strengths. Whenever he was left out of the side he invariably marked his re-appearance with a vital contribution. He was also a particular favourite among Arsenal's female admirers!

Charlie George, above all others in the squad, had the capacity to alter the destiny of a match with moments of talent. As with many of the most gifted, that moment could never be predicted, and at times he could infuriate as well as inspire. His poker-face rarely betrayed the nerves he felt to the extent of being sick before matches. His hot temper more often came to the surface and at times it marred the majesty of his skill. But for the wear and tear of injuries his international career — one cap when he had moved on to Derby County — would surely have been more meaningful. The Double season was his most profitable; the rebel had had his cause.

The two strikers shouldered an enormous burden and they were both built to take it. The Arsenal style basically evolved around their work-load. Both Radford and Kennedy had the control to convert chances created for them; both had the instincts to hunt opportunities for themselves. Yet each was also prepared to run selflessly to make himself available for defenders to find, and to harrass the life out of opposing defenders. Maybe it was not a coincidence that both came from the north where the virtues of hard graft are more regularly preached. Radford from Pontefract was the senior partner, always catching out his team-mates with his dry sense of humour. Kennedy was contemplating becoming a chef, but relished his second chance to make a living from the game after he had been rejected by Stanley Matthews at Port Vale. Arsenal spotted his inherent ability, and his composure in finishing gave him the remarkable record of being top scorer in a Double-winning side at the age of 19!

It was five more years before he was called up by England, and then as a left-sided midfield player. The conversion had taken place at Liverpool where he had gone in 1974 as Bill Shankly's last signing. In a glittering career on Merseyside he added to his array of medals, but never claimed another Double of League and FA Cup, though in 1977 Liverpool lost in the final in a year they won both the Championship and the European Cup.

Three other players qualified for Championship medals in 1970–71. Eddie Kelly, five months older than Kennedy, was a regular until December, and his ability to add variety in midfield resurfaced in dramatic fashion at the denouement of both competitions. He also won a Cup-winners' medal.

John Roberts needed to be roused for battle but when he was, he made light of Simpson's absence early in the campaign. Jon Sammels built on his previous 200 League games for the club with a spell in favour through the mid-

winter months, but rarely held the full confidence of a group of fans whose barracking understandably eroded the quality of his performances in home matches.

Only Marinello and Sammy Nelson, the reserve left back, of the rest of the squad appeared in the first team. The lack of a crop of injuries obviously helped sustain the continuity. Arsenal were lucky in this respect, but there were many instances of regulars biting on the bullet and playing on through pain.

If public praise was grudging, Arsenal certainly won the wholehearted respect of the football world. Yet international managers were not besieging Bertie Mee for his players. No one stepped straight from the Double success to stardom for their country. Rice, at that time, would have played for Northern Ireland even from the reserves at Highbury. Nelson was regularly stepping from the Football Combination into the green jersey. It was the same for Roberts with Wales. McLintock ended the Double season with his final three appearances for Scotland.

Scotland beckoned for Graham and Wilson the following October, with the goalkeeper the beneficiary of a change of rules for qualification, which now embraced the nationality of parents. Radford had gained his first England cap in January 1969; his second and last, a brief substitute appearance, came the season after the Double. McNab's four caps were all won before the 1970 World Cup finals. Only Storey caught the eye of Sir Alf Ramsey because of Arsenal's success. In April 1971 he was chosen for his debut against Greece and went on to represent his country 19 times. The very lack of international stars is one of the interesting aspects of the whole success story. Preston and Villa were too distant to compare, but the Spurs Double team of ten years before contained many of the great names of their era —Blanchflower, Smith, Jones, Medwin, Mackay, White, Brown, even Norman and with Greaves to come a year later.

The Double was won through the strength of the whole being greater than the sum total of the individual parts. Arsenal were more functional than flashy, more efficient than exhilarating.

Don Howe, the chief coach, altered the style from the man-to-man marking preferred by Dave Sexton, his predecessor: 'I believed that being zonal at the back suited us better. It was an intelligent way to play, and in Bob McNab we had a tremendous defensive technician. We told our back four not to retreat into the box, and we played offsides by pushing up. Bob Wilson was a goalkeeper who was excellent at reading through balls and who loved to come and catch crosses. With Frank McLintock and Peter Simpson not the big type of centre halves, it suited them to let Bob take charge.

'Our midfield was solid with George Armstrong a good wide man who was willing and capable when it came to tucking in if the pressure was on us. George Graham turned into an old-fashioned

attacking left half who had the ability to score goals by timing his runs to the far post.

'We also got the ball to our front players very early. Teams are still trying to do it today. John Radford and Ray Kennedy were so strong that they could hold the ball brilliantly for supporting players. They were very mobile too, and in the match at White Hart Lane, when we won the Championship, Mike England, the Spurs centre half, marked Radford man for man and Raddy pulled him all over the pitch which in the end let Kennedy in for the winning goal.

'But what many people did not realise at the time was that we also played football from the back. Frank McLintock and Peter Simpson were both very comfortable on the ball. Bill Shankly realised it and Liverpool tried to copy us but at the time they didn't have the players to make it work.

'Above all we were blessed with a backbone of men with character who demanded excellence from the others.'

Those virtues had the support of a manager who preached discipline and who practised what he preached. The chief coach had a zealous approach and a tremendous tactical awareness. Behind Mee and Howe came an industrious staff who added to the backbone of the club — George Wright, Steve Burtenshaw, Gordon Clark, Brian Whitehouse, Alf Fields, Ernie Collett, Bert Owen and Tony Donnelly. Bob Wall and Ken Friar ran a tight ship on the administrative side. The medical back-up was first class. The Board of Directors supported the club by attending every game and by letting Mee manage.

Every piece fitted in the jigsaw. Arsenal Football Club had made history in the club's best-ever season. On top of the reputation built by Chapman and Whittaker as the greatest club in the land, Arsenal had now won the greatest prize in the land. Who could now dispute their place at the game's pinnacle? Moreover, there was every indication that the organisation this time had been built to last.

In any walk of life achieving success is only half the battle. Living with the difficulties it can create is another matter altogether. A month after the Double was won, North London was alive with rumours of the first split in a camp which had seemed rock-solid.

No member of the Highbury staff was fuelled with more ambition than Don Howe. Arsenal had lost Dave Sexton to become a manager in his own right four years earlier. It was understandable that other clubs looking to fill similar positions should be attracted by Howe's credentials. None of them knew him better than his old club West Bromwich Albion.

On 15 June Frank McLintock's words brought back memories of his feeling of loss when Sexton left for Chelsea: 'Don Howe mustn't leave Arsenal. I shall be very disappointed if he goes. I know the rest of the players feel the same.' But on 8 July Bertie Mee had to respond to the news that Albion had attracted Howe to the Haw-

thorns: 'There is little need for me to repeat how highly I value Don as a coach — and how sorry I am to see him leaving.'

The popular view at the time was that Don Howe had left because he wanted to step into Mee's shoes. Ten years later he strongly refuted those rumours: 'I did want to manage in my own right. That was only natural. But I wasn't in a hurry. Being manager of Arsenal was still my ambition but I would have been prepared to wait four, five, ten years if necessary. All it would have taken to keep me at Highbury would have been a promise that when Bertie decided to finish I would have been given a go as manager for a year or two. But nobody said that.'

He was speaking then as a Highbury employee, the right-hand man to Terry Neill. Later, when Neill was dismissed, Don Howe finally fulfilled his ambition. After an initial spell as caretaker-manager he was appointed almost 13 years after his departure for West Bromwich Albion. Back in 1971, what would have been a simple sense of loss became more acrimonious when Albion also head-hunted George Wright and the youth coach Brian Whitehouse. Denis Hill-Wood was angry enough to go into print. 'Loyalty is a dirty word, these days,' said the Chairman. 'There is nothing I can do about what West Bromwich have done in raiding our staff except just to ignore them.' There was to be an echo of irony for Hill-Wood's son, Peter, in these words when he effectively dismissed Howe 15 years later.

The directors promoted Steve Burtenshaw into Howe's place (not for the last time, as it happened), and appointed Fred Street from Stoke City as physiotherapist. Ian Crawford, a former Scottish under-23 winger, replaced Whitehouse in charge of the club's youngsters.

There was a departure too from the playing staff. Leicester City, now managed by Jimmy Bloomfield, invested £100,000 in the services of Jon Sammels. Neither player nor club really wanted the deal to go through but both recognised that it would be better for Sammels to be rid of the section of the Highbury crowd which continually barracked him.

For all the changes behind the scenes, 1971–72 began with a swagger in the Arsenal step. McLintock, Kennedy and Radford were all on target at home to Chelsea in front of a crowd of almost 50,000. Three days later Kennedy again found the back of the net for the only goal of the game at Huddersfield. Four points out of four, achieved without the assistance of George. Injured in the opening game of the Double season, he did not even make the first match this time because of cartilage trouble.

The buoyant mood, however, was wrecked by three successive defeats. The away game against Manchester United was staged at Anfield as part of an FA punishment. Arsenal led at half-time through McLintock but then conceded two uncharacteristically sloppy goals and lost 3–1. Newly promoted Sheffield United then became the first team to win a League match at Highbury for 19 months.

That in itself was no shame; United went on to take 18 points from their opening ten games and blazed a trail at the top of the table. But there were no excuses for another Highbury loss when Stoke took advantage of an insipid home performance to take the points with a goal from John Ritchie.

Such lapses, virtually non-existent in the Double season, re-emerged often enough to scupper the hopes of retaining the Championship. Perhaps the appetite had been slightly, almost subconsciously, dulled by the glories of the recent past. Certainly the departure of Howe did not help, though his new club felt the backlash of those two home defeats when Arsenal won at the Hawthorns the following week.

The response to a humiliating 5-1 hammering at Wolves (Arsenal led at half-time) was a 14-match unbeaten run which spectacularly closed the gap on the leaders Manchester City to four points. In February with Arsenal still in the FA Cup, there was wide speculation of another Double. Wilson's continued splendour in goal brought him two caps for his beloved Scotland. The selection of Graham, also for the first time, gave him a room-mate and an interpreter when he joined his international colleagues in Glasgow! Indeed on 13 October 1971 the club fielded six representatives in the European Championship, the two new Scots plus Radford on England duty, Rice and Nelson with Northern Ireland and Roberts representing Wales.

Others, however, suffered a loss of League form. Simpson, George and Storey were at different times omitted. Radford lost his place through injury and did not immediately win it back. He and George both served periods of suspension. Among the injured, Marinello needed a knee operation, and McNab was stricken with a pelvic complaint.

The fall in standards prompted Bertie Mee to delve into the transfer market. He aimed for the very top, and paid a Football League record fee of £220,000 in the week before Christmas for Everton's Alan Ball. After making his name in England's World Cup-winning side of 1966, Ball's combative brand of midfield skill had fired Everton to an FA Cup final in 1968 and the First Division Championship in 1970. He wore an Arsenal shirt for the first time at Nottingham Forest on 27 December 1971.

Ball arrived too late to be eligible for the European Cup quarter-finals which Arsenal had reached with some comfort in their initial venture in the Champions' competition. Peter Simpson had marked the baptism with a sweetly struck goal inside 90 seconds of the opening game in Norway against Stroemsgodset. Marinello, who had paved the way for Simpson, added a second in the 20th minute. Kelly was the other marksman in a 3-1 victory. Though a formality, the second leg had its moments, notably with a solo goal from Armstrong. Kennedy wrote his name on the scoresheet. Radford, who had completed a century

of senior goals for the club in the previous match, collected two towards his second hundred.

Grasshoppers of Zurich presented, on paper at least, a stiffer challenge. Arsenal met them, though, with all the determination of the previous season. In Switzerland Kennedy offered a quick reminder of his European success rate by netting in the second minute. Graham also scored to virtually finish the tie before the Highbury crowd set eyes on it. Kennedy, George and Radford exploited the relaxed atmosphere of the second leg for a 5-0 aggregate win.

The quarter-final draw did not spare the English champions. Ajax were the European Cup holders, with a superb collection of young players like Cruyff, Krol, Haan, Suurbier, Keizer and Rep. In Amsterdam, Gerrit Muhren scored twice for the Dutch club, one a penalty, but Ray Kennedy's aptitude for undoing European defences brought a valuable away goal. A 1-0 win at home would now be good enough. In for the suspended Radford, Marinello almost provided that goal in the Gunners' opening attack at Highbury. Instead it was Ajax who managed the one-goal win, thanks to an own goal from Graham.

Alan Ball's influence was most sharply felt in an FA Cup run which with a suitable touch of irony started at Swindon. Eight of the Swindon side which had inflicted so much agony on their First Division opponents at Wembley almost three years earlier took part in the match, as did a revered opponent, Dave Mackay, who in his last season as a player at 37 was also managing the Wiltshire club.

Ball was not ravaged by memories of the gloomy day at Wembley, and while the pundits waited for Arsenal to be toppled, the recent signing started to repay some of his transfer fee. He set up the game's first goal for Armstrong before opening his own account.

There was more of a scare in the fourth round, at Reading of the Fourth Division. Arsenal rather muddled through 2-1, the home club's Stuart Morgan heading an Armstrong corner into his own net, and Pat Rice bursting forward to strike Arsenal's winner, which was deflected.

The fifth round brought three skirmishes with Derby County. At the Baseball Ground Charlie George netted twice, as in the fifth round a year earlier, but Derby matched his two efforts with an Alan Hinton penalty and a goal from Alan Durban. Neither side could break through in the replay which went to extra time in front of a packed Highbury crowd of 63,077. Because of Arsenal's European commitments the third match was two weeks later, only five days before the quarter-final. On neutral soil at Leicester, Kennedy produced the crucial goal which eliminated a team which was on its way to the League Championship.

Away again in the sixth round, for the 18th time in the last 21 draws, Arsenal only had to travel a few miles. Orient were struggling to avoid relegation to the Third Division, but they

Arsenal were back again facing Stoke in the 1972 FA Cup semi-final at Villa Park on 15 April 1972. The game ended 1-1, George Armstrong scoring for Arsenal and Peter Simpson putting through his own goal for Stoke. The match's major talking point was, however, the injury to Bob Wilson 17 minutes from time. John Radford took over in goal and dealt

had thrilled the capital in the last round in a tie which epitomised the lure of the FA Cup. Two goals down to high-flying Chelsea at Brisbane Road, Orient had fought back splendidly to level the scores, then in a last-minute pandemonium to force in a winning goal.

East London was out in force to see whether Arsenal would go the way of Chelsea. With the League title now looking less likely, the Gunners had their hearts set on retaining the Cup. Orient thus met sterner opposition and shortly after half-time Ball, resplendent in the white boots which were briefly in fashion, ended Orient's dreams and kept Arsenal's alive.

By a strange coincidence Arsenal's semi-final opponents were once again Stoke City. Again the venue was Villa Park where the thrilling saga

had ended a year earlier. Arsenal's side showed only one change from the previous semi-final. Ball's inclusion meant Kennedy dropping down to substitute. The young forward had been feeling the strain of two demanding seasons in the matches leading up to the FA Cup tie. George wore the number nine shirt, and Radford, recently freed from suspension, partnered him. Storey had briefly been the player to stand down to accommodate Ball, but since March had reclaimed his place in midfield.

Stoke, who had won their first trophy in over 100 years of trying, the League Cup, included three players who had not been involved in the 1971 semi-final, all veterans: Alex Elder, Peter Dobing and George Eastham, whose return from South Africa into the First Division had

competently with everything a strangely subdued Stoke could throw at him. Here John Ritchie carefully keeps his distance after a Radford save. Radford was aware enough of Highbury tradition, before pulling on a spare jersey, to ask whether or not it had been washed. Again the clock is interesting – the game is already ten minutes over time.

given the season a certain romantic flavour.

Unlike at Hillsborough a year earlier it was Arsenal who received the boost of scoring first. Armstrong received a clearance just outside the penalty area, took the pace off the ball, and drove it past Banks.

That might have been the end of the matter but for an injury to Wilson, which left the goalkeeper hobbling in agony. He tore a cartilage but the decision was made to keep him on the pitch. It made reasonable sense. Wilson's courage was unquestioned. Better him on one leg than any outfield player with full movement.

That judgement, however, was faulty. Defenders suddenly tried to take too much care of the wounded Wilson. In the end Simpson aimed to cut out a cross he would normally have left for the goalkeeper, who moved out to try to gather it but not at sufficient speed. The end product was that Simpson nudged the ball into his own goal. With more than 15 minutes remaining it was time for a re-think. Wilson was pulled off and Kennedy brought into the action. The call for an emergency keeper was answered by Radford, a stern enough character to cope with the task of helping his team stay in the Cup in such an

The last act of the long-running Arsenal–Stoke saga was played out at Goodison Park on Wednesday 19 April 1972. Arsenal won 2-1 to end their fourth semi-final in two years against the Potters undefeated, though not without controversy. The first goal came from John Radford after a Charlie George break from a questionably offside position. The second goal was (opposite) a Charlie George penalty (Storey wasn't playing). As critical, and controversial, was a dramatic goalline save by Bob McNab (pictured above) from a Denis Smith header. Stoke claimed the whole ball was over the line before McNab made contact. In goal is Geoff Barnett, after Wilson's injury in the first semi-final.

unfamiliar role. He was sufficiently aware of Arsenal's tradition to begin by joking about the famous jersey which was blamed for the slip by Dan Lewis in the 1927 final. Radford coped admirably with the shots that Stoke managed as another opportunity to beat Arsenal ebbed away from them; the stand-in gave every impression of hugely enjoying the whole experience. Stoke once again seemed unable to believe their good luck.

The replay was set for Goodison Park, which was the perfect setting for Geoff Barnett's return to first team action after more than two years patience in reserve. Arsenal's other ex-Evertonian Alan Ball was invited to lead out the team on his return to the pitch he had graced so often. Ball had been a semi-final loser in Everton's colours a year earlier. Then Liverpool had come from behind. Now it was Arsenal's turn.

The first two goals were penalties: Greenhoff for Stoke, George for Arsenal, with Storey not required this time. It was fitting that Arsenal's winner fell to Radford; he had earned it with his goalkeeping stint at Villa Park. The goal was controversial, however, George breaking away from a seemingly offside position.

Leeds had already confirmed their place at Wembley with a one-sided 3–0 triumph over Birmingham City at Hillsborough. Arsenal's quest in the final had a double edge, not just to retain the FA Cup but to end Leeds' strong challenge for the Double, which if it was successful would take some of the glitter from the glories of 1970–71.

The Football League insisted that both clubs should fulfil an outstanding League fixture on the Monday before the Cup final. It was not an unreasonable request although neither manager looked kindly upon it. Arsenal would still be left with two First Division games after the final, Leeds with one.

At Coventry on Monday, 1 May, Arsenal fielded the side which booked their Wembley places by winning 1–0, McLintock being the scorer with his first goal since August. Barnett would keep goal at Wembley, with the unfortunate Wilson needing surgery. His involvement was restricted to organising the player's pool for the perks of the occasion, for which he was the unanimous choice of his team-mates. Kennedy could not force his way back into the attack and was named as substitute.

The bookmakers made Don Revie's team 4–7 to lift the Cup. Arsenal were the underdogs at 6–4. The news that Eddie Gray, who had given a virtuoso Wembley performance in the 1970 Cup final, was fit to play did nothing to shorten the odds against the Gunners.

There was added pageantry for this particular final, which commemorated the centenary year of the competition, not to be confused with the hundredth Cup final, which did not take place until 1981. The Queen and Prince Philip marked the occasion with their presence. Half an hour before the kick-off a parade representing the winning clubs over the 100 years increased the anticipation of spectators.

This year both clubs were able to wear their traditional colours, which might have been a bad omen. Both Arsenal's post-war triumphs in the FA Cup had been won in a change strip (indeed, the only Cups Arsenal have ever won wearing red shirts with white sleeves are the Fairs Cup in 1970 and the FA Cup of 1936). Neither team was new to Wembley, but sadly this did little to raise the tone of the contest.

Referee David Smith from Stonehouse had barely started the game when he was reaching for his notebook. McNab, who had made a splendid return to the senior side for the semi-final after a long absence, cut down Lorimer. From this undistinguished beginning the contest

rarely improved. The kindest interpretation of the drab 90 minutes would be to point to the respect that each team clearly felt for the other. Had it been a boxing match the referee would have called for more action.

The only abiding memory is of a winning goal of high quality which mercifully spared the frustrated crowd an extra 30 minutes. It did not come from Arsenal, whose attack rarely got out of second gear, even when Kennedy replaced Radford. Eight minutes into the second half the two Leeds central strikers pieced together a move which deserved to win the match. The foraging Mick Jones tricked McNab on the Leeds right. Allan Clarke met the driven cross with a diving header, stooping to conquer. Barnett and Wilson together would have had difficulty in keeping it out.

For Clarke it was a third time lucky affair. He had been voted Man of the Match as a loser for Leicester in 1969; the following year he had been beaten playing for Leeds against Chelsea. Now he had the decisive goal and another Man of the Match trophy. Jones deserved better than to collect his winners' medal in pain after dislocating an elbow in the dying minutes.

It was a costly injury. With the first leg of the Double in their pockets, Leeds now needed only a point from their trip to Wolves two days after Wembley. But they badly needed Jones to respond to a very competitive performance from a team with nothing to play for. Leeds were beaten 2–1, lamenting that they should have had two penalties. It was a very surprising result, and meant that for the second consecutive season Leeds missed the Championship by a point.

So Arsenal had lost the Cup and the League but happily not to the same club. The Gunners also had their say in the destiny of the Championship because, had Liverpool won at Highbury the night Leeds were losing at Molineux, Bill Shankly's men would have been Champions. The game, however, finished goalless, and to their astonishment Derby County, on a plane bound for an end of season holiday, heard that the League Championship was theirs for the first time. Derby finished with 58 points, one more than Leeds, Liverpool and Manchester City. Arsenal had to be content with fifth place with 52 points, the season closing on a dismal note with a 2–0 home defeat by Tottenham.

In many ways it had been a satisfactory season, though the placing in the League was not high enough to qualify for a spot in the UEFA Cup. But the standards had been set a year earlier and deep down the players who had discovered capacities for success beyond their wildest dreams knew that they had missed a great opportunity. It would not have taken too much more striving to have really challenged for a second successive League and Cup combination, a double Double. Now what a story that might have been!

· CHAPTER 9 ·
Modern Arsenal

It is often said that great teams last three seasons at the most. Truism it may be, but it was absolutely right as far as the Double side was concerned. Though, in retrospect, the great years seemed to encompass five finals in five years, that was more of a journalist's convenience than a reflection of footballing reality. The League Cup seasons of 1968 and 1969 could not be described as glorious and Arsenal's displays at Wembley were as likely to indicate slow decline in the years ahead as they were to foretell a glorious flowering. Even the Fairs Cup was not then what it seems with the benefit of hindsight.

Leeds had won the trophy in 1968, Newcastle in 1969 and the Gunners' triumph of 1970 (already overshadowed by World Cup preparations) was to be followed by three more years of English triumph via Leeds, Spurs and Liverpool. This was seen by the public at large as a vindication of one of the more irritating of English football cliches '. . . the Football League is the toughest/strongest/most competitive in the world. . . .' If this was the case, it was perhaps odd that only three English sides even reached the final in the next decade.

Arsenal's success was, nonetheless, seen at the time as an almost automatic continuation of English dominance — the surprise would have been if a League side had *not* won the trophy at the time. The mood seemed to be: World Cup in 1966, Celtic and United winning the European Cup in 1967 and 1968, Manchester City the Cup Winners Cup in 1970 and a whole string of Fairs Cup successes prove that the British game is back where it belongs — on top of the world. This devalued Arsenal's triumph, which was considerable, and 1969–70 should rightly be seen as the first of three excellent years. The third of these, 1971–72, was, as we have seen, not to end in triumph; it is a peculiar response which calls a runners-up place in one of the two major competitions a disappointment, but after the Double it could be little else. The Spurs Cup-winning side of 1962 suffered, if anything, an even greater deflation.

So, after a season which would have satisfied the ordinary mortals of the First Division, Arsenal and the fans of 1972 were in mourning. The Double success had set such an extraordinary standard for the side that was fifth in the table and a losing visit to Wembley amounted emotionally to failure.

There was unrest in the camp during the summer of 1972 too, which led to both George and Kelly being put on the transfer list. Both felt they were not being rewarded adequately in comparison with more senior players, who were then benefitting from the club's loyalty payments. By this time George, the cheeky Cockney of the media and darling of the North Bank, had become the problem child of Highbury, flitting from reserves to substitute's bench to first team and back again. An immense talent was going to waste, and there did not seem anybody capable of coping with a complex and unpredictable character who always had a young head on young shoulders and was rarely as confident as he appeared.

With hindsight, the months that followed were the turning point in Bertie Mee's managership. He was not to know, but it would be all downhill from that fifth Cup final in five years. He had a major decision to take: whether to keep faith with the men who had won the Double for him or build another side. He had already put the finger on his main fear by pondering that it might be possible for one man to motivate himself again . . . but all eleven?

Two months into the 1972–73 season he gave a distinct indication of the way his thoughts were turning when he bought Jeff Blockley, a stopper centre half in the traditional mould, from Coventry for £200,000. Mee was later to call the move his greatest mistake. Blockley, who was to make his only England appearance at the start of two generally unhappy years at Highbury, was obviously a replacement for McLintock. The news hit a nervous dressing room like a bombshell. Not only did McLintock feel his days at the top were far from over, but his team-mates still regarded the inspirational Scot as the best skipper in the League and capable of doing a first-rate job in defence.

Mee, although publicly defending his team's no-frills approach to the game, was privately stung by the persistent volleys of criticism that, for all their success, Arsenal were failing in their duty to entertain. Boring old Arsenal was the persistent cry throughout the land, particularly north of Watford. Mee's answer was an attempt to turn Arsenal into the total footballers of Holland, who had developed a revolutionary system in which players were encouraged to be flexible about positions and to use their skills

in an ever-changing pattern. Arsenal had discovered how effective it could be at first hand earlier in the year, when the European Cup holders, Ajax of Amsterdam, knocked them out on the way to retaining the title.

But Arsenal's flirtation with a style alien to their successful long ball game, and one equally unsuited to the consistently tough demands of English First Division football, was brief, and a 5–0 beating at Derby, hard on the heels of a 3–0 League Cup defeat at home by Norwich, prompted a tactical rethink. Arsenal, sacrificing general popularity in the cause of efficiency and results, went back to what they did best and the team, with Radford and Kennedy back in harness, went 15 games without defeat as they pursued Liverpool for the title through early 1973, and headed for Wembley again.

A chance to avenge the defeat by their old sparring partners from Leeds looked a distinct possibility when the Gunners were paired in the FA Cup semi-finals with Second Division Sunderland. A victory would also make Arsenal the first team this century to reach three consecutive Cup finals. But this was one of those years when the romance of the Cup defied logic all the way to Wembley and not only did Bob Stokoe's men dispose of Arsenal 2–1 at Hillsborough, they later shocked favourites Leeds in a memorable final thanks to Ian Porterfield's goal and goalkeeper Jim Montgomery's heroics. After overcoming the two hardest opponents in English football they surely deserved the Cup. The Hillsborough semi-final was an astonishing game, fraught with emotion and despair. Charlie George's goal was somehow never going to be enough to match what Sunderland had to offer and the Wearsiders won with goals from Halom and Hughes. Blockley played when not fully fit and his uncertainty set the mood for the success of the Second Division side.

Coming second was developing into a worrying habit and although Arsenal finished runners-up in the League to Liverpool, only three points behind, they could not even claim to be the most successful team in London, for the old enemy at Tottenham had beaten Norwich to win the League Cup. The result was that Mee became even more convinced he must rebuild and he allowed more key men to depart. McLintock, at 34, responded to a lucrative offer from QPR and proved his point by having four more good years and leading Rangers to within a whisker of the Championship in 1975–76 when Liverpool pipped them by a point. George Graham, striker turned elegant Scotland mid-fielder, became Tommy Docherty's first buy as Manchester United manager. That Graham, who was doing a valuable job in helping his younger teammates, felt in need of a fresh challenge, hinted at a less than perfect mood in the dressing room.

There was another departure with the new 1973–74 season only weeks old. Coach Burtenshaw resigned after two home defeats and a 5–0 thrashing at Sheffield United. The players had not been responding to him for some time. He

had never been able to lay the ghost of Don Howe, and it was an open secret that Mee wanted to replace him with the extrovert 36-year-old Bobby Campbell, who had helped Gordon Jago bring QPR up from the Second Division. Burtenshaw had not seen the last of Highbury's halls; on 28 March 1986 he was appointed caretaker-manager after the sudden departure of Don Howe.

But not even the most demanding fans expected the new partnership to conjure up a Championship side in one season and they suffered with the team as the wheel turned full circle in less than two years. The Fairs Cup winners of 1970, Double winners of 1971 and Wembley finalists of 1972 were dumped out of the League Cup in a second round tie at Highbury by little Tranmere Rovers, removed from the FA Cup in a fourth round replay at Villa Park and limped along to tenth place in a First Division campaign dominated by Leeds, who laid the foundations of their Championship with an unstoppable 29-match unbeaten run.

Defeat by Tranmere did have one blessing in disguise, for it allowed a young Dubliner called Liam Brady to break through into the first team where he was to benefit from the experience and influence of Ball. But fate had a cruel hand to play against these two in the last inconsequential match of the season against QPR. Bob Wilson's farewell appearance after eleven years and Brady's first League goal in a 1–1 draw were overshadowed by Ball breaking his leg in a tackle on Terry Venables. Instead of captaining Don Revie's England team on their summer tour, Ball spent the whole of the close season battling his way back to fitness.

During the summer there was another major rethink on tactics because the Radford-Kennedy partnership had faltered again in the second half of the season and the problem was an overweight and below par Kennedy. Even though he was still only 22, the physical punishment taken at the sharp end had dulled the big Geordie's appetite for the game, if not for the poor food which was taking the edge off his physical fitness. He would have done well to follow the example of the canny old campaigner Radford, who not only took to wearing shin pads down the front of his socks but also in the back. But an undoubted talent was still there to be tapped and the legendary manager of Liverpool, Bill Shankly, made a farewell present of Kennedy to Anfield, paying £200,000 for him just before the great man shocked football by announcing his retirement. It was left to another Geordie, new Liverpool boss Bob Paisley, to guide Kennedy into a career in midfield where he acquired another chestful of medals, won 17 caps for England and became one of the most feared competitors in European football.

Arsenal spent half the fee on Manchester United's abrasive Brian Kidd, another teenage prodigy who had scored in United's historic European Cup win on his 19th birthday six years earlier. But although he repaid Arsenal with 19

Ross, Armstrong, Brady and Ball form an apprehensive wall while Malcolm Macdonald breaks during the 3-1 defeat of Everton on 18 September 1976. Macdonald was then at his peak. He scored 25 goals that season in the League and his record five goals for England against Cyprus came on 16 April 1975. He had to retire prematurely in August 1979, at the age of 29, because of osteo-arthritis in the knee. Terry Neill commented that he was never bitter about this and remained surprisingly cheerful as he went on to a relatively successful career as manager of Fulham.

goals in his first season he never struck up a comparable understanding with Radford and it was quite plain that Liverpool had made the better investment. Kidd was to move back to Manchester to play for City after two years in London.

Ball worked hard to recover from his broken leg but hopes that he could knit old and new personnel together were dashed when the new club skipper suffered a fracture in the first match of a pre-season tour to Holland. This time, it was his left ankle and in the seven weeks he was absent, the new campaign, although launched by Kidd's winning goal against Leicester, headed for disaster. Blockley and George were on the transfer list — the defender was to move to Leicester in the spring — and what fragile confidence there was collapsed as the team sank towards the bottom of the table, accompanied by Tottenham, in ten games with-

out a win. With spirits at their lowest ebb, Mee, encouraged by former Rangers coach Campbell, managed to pull a masterstroke with a modest £20,000 outlay on a balding 31-year-old centre half who, in normal circumstances, would have never been regarded as Arsenal material. Terry Mancini had done a sterling job in the QPR success story. A member of the famous East End boxing family, he was Italian of name, Cockney of voice and of Irish parentage but, vitally for the Arsenal dressing room, he was a character and natural comedian who transformed the atmosphere and established himself as a folk hero on the terraces. Mancini was rarely found wanting on the pitch either, despite his detractors, and he was good enough to win five caps for the Republic of Ireland, one of them alongside Brady on his debut that same winter.

Mancini's purchase proved inspired, but Mee's next buy was fated never to fulfil his potential.

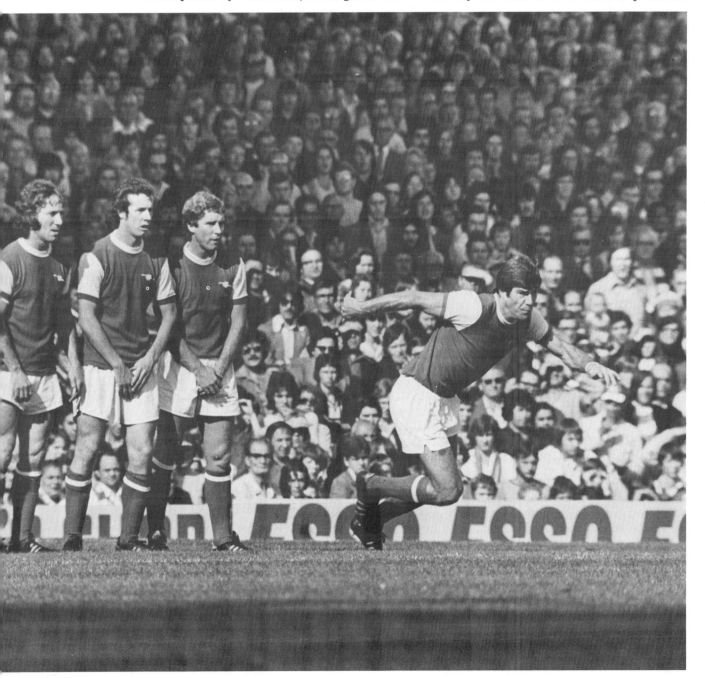

Alan Ball and Tom Ritchie of Bristol City tussle for the ball in the first game of the 1976-77 season on 21 August. City won 1-0. It was Ball's last season with the club, and a generally unsatisfactory one at that, for the Gunners finished only eighth with 43 points.

The Arsenal wall breaks during a visit to Stamford Bridge. By the 1974-75 campaign this team was breaking up. It was an unsatisfactory season for the club – they finished 16th which, with 17th place the following season, remain their poorest placings and spell since Herbert Chapman became manager in 1925. Indeed, Arsenal have finished in the bottom half of the First Division on only ten occasions in the past 60 years. It was a fall from grace which Bertie Mee had not envisioned when he wrote just three years before, in August 1971, straight after the Double: 'Our aim must be to maintain the situation where we are in the top two or three each season, winning something or other to keep the pot boiling. I would like my ambition to be to have a decade of Arsenal achievement on these lines. There is always the possibility that Arsenal as a team can flourish into something much more powerful in stature than they proved even in 1971. Then it might be our privilege to open out new concepts in this game of soccer.' Brave words, but sadly not to be fulfilled during the remainder of Bertie Mee's memorable reign.

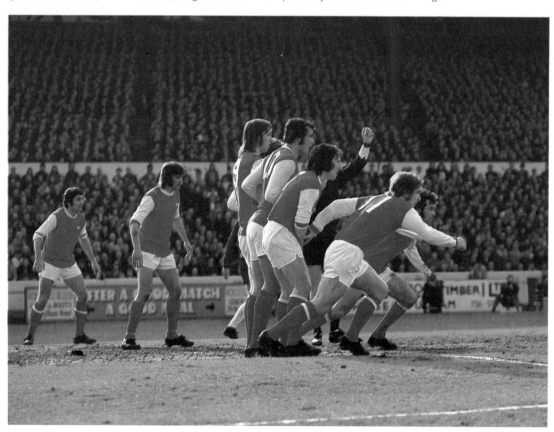

Alex Cropley, a neat Scottish midfield player came from Hibs for £150,000. He played only seven games before breaking his leg and was never the same player again. Cropley was much admired for his grit and determination. Although slight of build, he tackled like a bulldozer. One result was that he spent much of his career injured on the sidelines. He was to play only 34 first team games before moving to Aston Villa after 20 frustrating months at a less than appreciative Highbury.

The team's form was still erratic, but a promising FA Cup run lifted morale as the club moved into 1975. But not before York, struggling in the Second Division at the time, came to Highbury in the third round and fully deserved a 1–1 draw. It needed a hat-trick from Kidd and extra time to ease the Gunners through a difficult replay. Life became hard again in the fourth round and George Armstrong's first goals in 21 months arrived judiciously to put out Coventry in a replay at Highbury. Fingernails were down to the quick before Radford edged the Gunners into the quarter-finals in a second replay with Leicester.

But the celebrations were somewhat muted by the controversial match at Derby two days earlier which had plunged the club into turmoil.

To the background of Chelsea's brand new stand, Liam Brady and Charlie George stumble over a chance in September 1974. It was Brady's first full season in the first team (though he had started ten games the previous year) and George's last. Charlie left for Derby having achieved much but never really, in the eyes of the fans, having fulfilled his potential. In seven years he played just 169 first-class games, scoring 49 goals.

Both Ball and the equally experienced McNab had been sent off for dissent in a 2–1 defeat. It was only the second time since the war that two players from the same side had been sent off in the First Division, and the first had been McLintock and Storey in 1967. Ball and McNab felt they had fallen victim of over-zealous referee John Yates and wanted the club to back appeals which would allow them to play in the Cup quarter-final against West Ham. They were disappointed, owing to Arsenal's strong sense of responsibility.

At this time there was much consternation within football that clubs were taking advantage of the appeal procedure to make key players available for big games. After long deliberation Arsenal decided not to back their senior players and it was a decision which represented the beginning of the end of an uneasy relationship between Arsenal and the volatile and outspoken Ball. 'Arsenal and I can never be the same,' he was quoted as saying. Both he and McNab pressed on with appeals and played in the vital Cup game but a young lad called Alan Taylor, destined to score twice in quarter-final, semi-final and final, enabled the eventual 1975 winners to become the first London club ever to beat Arsenal at home in the FA Cup.

There was still a sting in the tail. Ball and McNab lost their appeals and were banned for three games.

When the dust had settled, the club still had to face the possibility of the unthinkable — relegation. Yet even though the teams were depressed and unhappy, feeling that Mee was becoming more and more remote and that Campbell had no more to offer as coach, they pulled themselves up from their bootstraps to beat the drop. In fact, they finished in a respectable 16th position but did not win too many friends in the process. Sheffield United manager Ken Furphy said after a 1–0 defeat at Highbury: 'I never thought I would see the day when Arsenal players fought among themselves, pulled shirts, wasted time and so freely indulged in foul tactics.' Desperate measures for desperate times. Elsewhere an old friend had lost the fight. West Brom, who never had the personnel to exploit Don Howe's tactical genius, had gone down the previous season and, when they failed to get back, Howe's contract was not renewed.

His erstwhile senior partner at Arsenal had only a season left in charge himself, and since the break-up of their famous partnership four years earlier both, it seemed, had lost a large measure of effectiveness. The Mee era was drawing to a close, but not before the manager, board, players and fans seemed close to an internal war, and the club was at its lowest ebb since the dog days of Billy Wright's reign exactly ten years before.

Two more major personalities from the Double side departed in the summer. Bob McNab had enhanced the long tradition of fine Arsenal full backs with his pace, astute tackling and reading of the game. This happy character

also acted as an able lieutenant to McLintock during the Double year. He was rewarded with a free transfer to Wolves. George finally got his wish to leave and such was his disillusionment that he even seemed destined to sign for Terry Neill, then manager at Tottenham. Spurs had planned a press conference to announce their coup but overnight George was tempted by a counter-offer from Dave Mackay to join Champions Derby for £90,000. That he never fulfilled the world class potential he clearly possessed was exasperating to all who worked and played with him at Highbury. Don Howe told him after seeing his virtuoso performances as a teenager that he could become the Di Stefano of English football. But he was never to achieve a level of consistency to command a regular place in the First Division, never mind be compared with the maestro of Madrid. When Ball arrived, the darling of the North Bank felt his nose pushed out of joint and the glimpses of greatness which had inspired Howe to such a lofty comparison became rarer and rarer. Then, there were his injury problems, particularly with his knees which were to trouble him in his subsequent spells with Derby and Southampton. George had just 169 games in six seasons for the Gunners, his flaws finally burying his genius.

Ball had been strongly linked with Manchester City in the summer and it was obvious he was losing heart for the Arsenal cause. His discontent led to a transfer request and he was dropped for the opening games of the 1975–76 season, with Eddie Kelly taking over the captaincy. The usual early season confidence proved fragile and once the team was beaten at home by Stoke in the third game of the season, all the tension and bickering returned. Ball was brought back and although Arsenal were desperately in need of his ability and experience, this had an adverse effect on Kelly. The players instinctively looked to Ball for leadership, a situation Kelly could not accept. He had welcomed the captaincy as the stimulus needed to revive his faltering career but within a year his love affair with Arsenal was over and he moved to join McLintock at QPR and was later to play under his managership at Leicester.

By November, the team had been knocked out of the League Cup at home by Everton and were four places off the bottom of the League. It was proving a real baptism of fire for two young Dubliners — Frank Stapleton, who was proving a brave and capable partner for Radford, and David O'Leary, a fine footballing defender who had the stamp of real class about him. When Wolves gave the Gunners a proper beating in the third round of the FA Cup, all that lay ahead was another relegation battle and the fans had long run out of patience with the team and manager. But for all the criticism nobody threw in the towel . . . until March. With the pressure really on, Peter Storey walked out for ten days and was suspended by the club. Storey, with the reputation of being one of the hardest men in

English football but good enough to be a key member of the Double side and an England player 19 times, could not take his or the club's decline any longer. He was not cut out to be a reserve player, and he had run into well-publicised troubles off the field.

Then came the real bombshell. Bertie Mee, soon after making a morale-boosting speech to the troops, described afterwards by Liam Brady as being of Churchillian proportions, announced in tears to a stunned press conference that he would retire at the end of the season. It was the first time, apart from a rare flash of temper, that Fleet Street had seen a show of emotion from this polite and reserved man. It had been clear to the club and players for some time that he had lost his appetite for the fray and the pressure of ten years in one of the hardest jobs in football had finally got to him. Mee had been greatly influenced by his friend Bill Nicholson, the other Double-winning manager of the modern game and one of the truly great figures of English football.

The Tottenham boss had retired two years earlier when all the enjoyment had gone for him, and Mee promised himself he would do the same if he ever woke up in the morning with that same feeling. Retirement allowed him the honourable way out. There were suggestions he might stay on to advise his successor, even become a director, but he decided it was best to leave the way clear for a new man and not make the same error as Manchester United did with Matt Busby. He severed his ties with Highbury, took a much-needed break from the game, and eventually was to lend his vast experience successfully to Graham Taylor as general manager at Watford and help complete their rise from Third to First Division. He was eventually to retire in 1986.

It would have been a tragedy if Arsenal, ever present in the First Division since 1919, had lost their place at the end of the Mee era. They had a narrow squeak with the key game coming at Highbury with the 17th-placed Gunners facing Wolves in 19th. Mancini's one and only first-team goal won the day, Arsenal stayed up, despite losing their last three games, and Wolves went down.

Survival, even if it was in 17th place and their lowest position since Chapman's arrival in 1925, did allow Mee to retire to the Highbury hall of fame alongside Allison and Whittaker. He had led them to the coveted Double, and the five cup finals, including the Fairs Cup win which remains Arsenal's only European trophy. But these were only the fruits of his work; he had restored pride, passion and power to the jaded giant of English football. More importantly for the future, he had laid the foundations, even in those last few difficult seasons, for the side who would be chasing the big prizes before the decade was out, and, at their best, would be favourably compared with the Double team.

In the three months it took Arsenal to find a successor to Mee, the speculation became intense and most of the top names in English football at the time found their way into the hat — Brian Clough, Jack Charlton, Wales manager Mike Smith and Bolton's Ian Greaves. The dressing room, or rather some key figures within it, had their own contender and a lobby led by Ball, Armstrong and Mancini pushed for Campbell to be promoted. But ironically the search, which took the club across the breadth of Europe, was to end almost at their back door.

Although English coaches have worked around the world with success and, in fact, established the game in many countries, the domestic game has always had an insular streak, which the Hungarian lesson in 1953 never really cured. So when it was discovered that Arsenal were attempting to prise away the celebrated Yugoslav Miljan Miljanic from Real Madrid the game waited eagerly to see if the mould would be broken. Miljanic had made his name with Red Star Belgrade and guided the Yugoslavs to the 1974 World Cup finals in West Germany. His teams were noted for their technical attacking brilliance.

Arsenal were confident they represented a tempting challenge, but it was not to be and there were strong suspicions that Miljanic used the Arsenal bid to improve his contract in Madrid. When Terry Venables, fast gaining the reputation as England's best young manager, turned Arsenal down because of his loyalty to Crystal Palace, chairman Denis Hill-Wood turned to an Highbury old boy who had always had his respect and was already a First Division manager.

Terry Neill had given Arsenal eleven years good service from 1959, when he joined them from Bangor in Northern Ireland as an enthusiastic 17-year-old wing half. Billy Wright was to switch him successfully to centre half and in 241 League games, until he lost his place to McLintock, Neill, who also had a spell as PFA chairman, proved a strong, intelligent and uncompromising opponent who could be physical or skilful as the situation demanded.

He was good enough to play for Northern Ireland at 18 and kept his place for 12 years, winning 59 caps and, in the latter years, acting as player-manager. One of his most memorable moments was to score the winning goal against England in his 50th international. He was obvious management material and cut his teeth in four years as player-manager at Hull until 1974 when, at 32, he succeeded Nicholson as Tottenham's youngest manager, a distinction he also holds for Arsenal. In his brief two-year reign at Spurs he never enjoyed a close or happy relationship with a rather distant board, headed by Sidney Wale. There were no major disagreements but a series of incidents led Neill to believe they did not have the drive or ambition to make Tottenham a great club again. So, when the offer came to take over at Highbury, Neill jumped at the chance, despite the obvious difficulties — particularly that of coming back in charge of old playing colleagues. A one-club man in his major League playing days, Neill had been seduced by Arsenal's history and reputa-

Liam Brady beats Bolton's Brian Smith while Frank Worthington and Willie Young look on.

Tottenham captain Steve Perryman is no match for a determined combination of Stewart Robson and Brian Talbot.

tion. When he left Highbury in 1970 for Hull, he had, not surprisingly, nursed a secret ambition to come back and manage the club.

Highbury needed a shake-up and with the full backing of Hill-Wood, affectionately known to him as the Old Man, Neill was the man to do it. His reign was to be studded with spectacular and often successful raids in the transfer market and much publicised disagreements with some of his difficult players. But the club was never out of the headlines and the majority were favourable to Arsenal FC.

Not surprisingly, he brought his number two, Wilf Dixon, from Spurs and Bobby Campbell, his position untenable, left within a couple of weeks. Ball, who led the dressing room faction in favour of the coach, lasted six months, in which he never saw eye to eye with Neill and to whom he was his usual outspoken self. In December, after being linked with Stoke, Norwich and his first club Blackpool, he joined Southampton for £60,000 and became Lawrie McMenemy's right-hand man as they rebuilt the 1976 Cup-winning side into a lasting First Division outfit.

Brian Kidd had joined Manchester City days before Neill's arrival and Neill's first task was to replace him with a big name personality. Much to his surprise, Malcolm Macdonald, near-legendary Supermac of Tyneside and the Geordies' biggest idol since Jackie Milburn, offered him the perfect opportunity to launch his reign with a spectacular transfer deal. Macdonald, originally a full back who had been turned into a swash-buckling centre forward at Fulham and Luton, had crossed swords with Newcastle manager Gordon Lee, who was to go down in the eyes of their fans (and never recover) as the villain who sold Supermac.

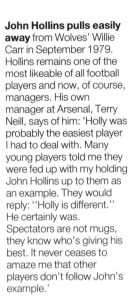

John Hollins pulls easily away from Wolves' Willie Carr in September 1979. Hollins remains one of the most likeable of all football players and now, of course, managers. His own manager at Arsenal, Terry Neill, says of him: 'Holly was probably the easiest player I had to deal with. Many young players told me they were fed up with my holding John Hollins up to them as an example. They would reply: "Holly is different." He certainly was. Spectators are not mugs, they know who's giving his best. It never ceases to amaze me that other players don't follow John's example.'

Neill's biggest problem was not to persuade Newcastle to part with the England international but to keep him out of the clutches of Arsenal's biggest rivals Tottenham. Keith Burkinshaw, their new manager in succession to Neill, had admired the centre forward's qualities when he was coach at Newcastle. For that reason, Arsenal hired a private plane to whisk Macdonald south to put his signature to a £333,333 transfer.

Macdonald was the larger-than-life character desperately needed at Highbury, where average gates of 40,000 in the Double year had dropped to 27,000. He arrived with a boast that he would score 30 goals in his first season and was almost as good as his word — grabbing 29 and missing a penalty which would have given him his target.

He was also to have a positive effect on the career of Stapleton, who first played alongside him in the second game of the 1976–77 season in place of Radford. This shy but determined young man from Dublin had shown great heading ability and was proving brave as a lion. He worked hard to dispel doubts about his pace and control in partnership with Supermac and later Alan Sunderland, and during the next two seasons he was to mature into the best all-round centre forward in Britain.

Neill's reign took off like a roller coaster. It was a time of highs and lows, comings and goings but when Chelsea were beaten 2–1 in the fourth round of the Football League Cup in front of a 52,000 crowd at Highbury in October there was a real belief that the club had finally turned the corner for the better. By the end of the season only two members of the Double side were playing in the first team, full back Pat Rice and the longest serving player, George Armstrong. The little winger, a man who had

given 100 per cent to the Arsenal cause for so many years was at loggerheads with the new manager and there was a running battle between them for the whole season because Armstrong was anxious to make a good move to see him through to the end of his career. He eventually got his wish the next summer, after playing the last of his 500 games for the Gunners against Manchester United at Old Trafford in the concluding game of the campaign. But by this time his love affair with the club was long over and it was sad that he seemed to leave for Leicester with a hint of bitterness.

Radford, at 29, was also close to the end of a distinguished career at the top and Arsenal were unable to hold Stapleton back any longer. Radford moved to West Ham for £80,000 in December and this down-to-earth Yorkshireman with the dry sense of humour, had clearly proved to be one of the best investments Arsenal had ever made. All he had cost Billy Wright as a 15-year-old in 1964 was a £10 signing-on fee and the train fare to London from Radford's home in the mining village of Hemsworth. He went on to play 383 League games and score 111 goals. Twenty-one of them came in the Double year as he and young Ray Kennedy became one of the most effective scoring double acts (literally) of post-war football. For all his success at club level, 'Raddy' was greatly under-rated and worth more than the two caps he won for England. In many quarters, he is still regarded as a better all-round player than his highly individualistic successor, Macdonald.

Storey was given another chance by Neill to try and save his career and shake off his problems outside the game, which already involved brushes with the law. But although he

worked hard to gain fitness he was unable to hold down a first-team place and moved to Fulham for £10,000. After only a handful of games at Craven Cottage he was to announce his retirement at 32 after 501 appearances for Arsenal and 17 for the Second Division club. It was a quiet and sad departure for one of the most controversial but successful figures of the 1970s.

Kelly was still only 25 but had never quite fulfilled the promise he had shown as a teenager when he burst into the Double side as an all-action midfield man with a taste for spectacular shooting. He had also suffered badly over the captaincy dilemma involving Ball and was happy to move and join McLintock at QPR. Of Mee's later signings, Neill showed his astuteness in the transfer market by recouping £135,000 from Aston Villa for Cropley, while Mancini, who knew his days were numbered, moved to Aldershot after his brief but successful mission for Arsenal in 52 League games.

Neill's first choice to fill the gap left by Mancini in the heart of the defence was Pat Howard, a team-mate of Macdonald's at Newcastle. But he had no hesitation in discarding him after discovering he could buy Willie Young, the big Scottish centre half whom he had acquired for Tottenham from Aberdeen. Young was very much his own man and had had his brushes with authority but he was an honest player with a wholehearted, no-frills approach. He also had an appetite for scoring goals and one of the abiding memories of Big Willie is his occasional sallies upfield showing off his dribbling skills. The Highbury fans quickly took him to their hearts.

After Ball's departure, Neill was in need of an experienced and skilful midfield player to augment the growing influence of the young Brady. The new manager decided to take a major gamble in the spring on Alan Hudson and paid £200,000 to Stoke for the privilege. Hudson had made something of a name for himself as a playboy at Chelsea (seemingly the foil for Osgood) but he possessed more natural skills than any of the current English-born midfield players. Yet already, at 25, he was being classed with George, Osgood and Bowles as one of the great wasted talents of his day.

Just as at Chelsea and Stoke, the Gunners were to be treated with only glimpses of his ability to control a game with vision, accurate passing and support play. The captaincy was given to Pat Rice, a quick and agile full back, who had survived all the upheavals at the club and was a reminder to players such as George and Hudson how enthusiasm and determination can bring a less gifted player out on top. Like George, he had lived within earshot of the North Bank roar and had been a fan since the age of ten when his family moved from Belfast to London.

His determination was such that Rice was to win international honours for Northern Ireland before he became a first team regular just prior to the Double year, and the Wembley epic against Liverpool was to be the first of a record five FA Cup final appearances. The most memorable was the 1979 meeting with Manchester United, which ended in the dramatic 3–2 win for Arsenal. It gave Rice his second winner's medal and the privilege of lifting the Cup to the ecstatic Arsenal following that day. Rice was a skipper who led by example and the team soon got right behind him. After finishing his playing career at Watford, he joined the Highbury coaching staff.

The Arsenal style had to be modified to revolve around the direct running of Macdonald and, with the help of some stunning goals from him, including hat-tricks against Birmingham and his old club Newcastle, Arsenal made steady progress in 1976–77 and reached fourth in the table and the fifth round of the FA Cup. But it was a risk to rely on one player so much and the inevitable happened in February — Macdonald hit a lean patch and the whole team struggled to the extent of an unprecedented 11 First Division games without a win including eight successive defeats. The Cup run ended with a lacklustre performance at Middlesbrough where the home team, recently re-established at the top after an absence of 20 years, put four goals past Jimmy Rimmer with Macdonald scoring the only reply. Neill's stinging public criticism of his players caused a real rift in the camp and although the Gunners finished a creditable eighth as Liverpool retained their title in Kevin Keegan's farewell season, it was clear that if Neill's valuable groundwork was not to be wasted, he would need a first-class lieutenant to take the bulk of the coaching and act as a buffer.

Arsenal were soon to acquire the services of one of the best again but not before they shared the summer's sensational headlines with Don Revie, the England manager who quit for Middle Eastern promise. Arsenal made their front-page news on an ill-fated tour of the Far East. When Neill jetted out for the trip, which would take in games in Singapore and a tournament in Australia, he believed he had persuaded the much-respected Dave Sexton to return to Highbury after ten years. The QPR manager wanted to leave Loftus Road and Sexton, always happier working with players than tackling managerial tasks, obtained his release and was set for Highbury as first team coach.

But Neill's hopes were dashed by Manchester United, who had just sacked Tommy Docherty after the dramatic treble-busting Cup final of 1977 (United beat Liverpool, who still won the League and European Cup). A cable to Singapore from his old friend Sexton informed Neill that he had been unable to resist the offer to take over at Old Trafford. Little could they know that as rival managers they would be leading out their teams at Wembley for an FA Cup final in two years time.

The tour, which climaxed with games against Red Star Belgrade and Glasgow Celtic in Australia, had not been welcomed by some of the players after a difficult season. The behaviour of Macdonald and Hudson deteriorated so much

Malcolm Macdonald is left behind by the pace and determination of Brian Talbot during the 1978 FA Cup final against Ipswich. The Suffolk side won with a single goal by Roger Osborne.

Below right: A year later Talbot was back at Wembley, just as determined but this time in Arsenal colours (again, oddly, yellow shirts for the third time in an FA Cup final in the 1970s). Here he (numbered 4) and Alan Sunderland collide in the scoring of Arsenal's first goal in the 1979 FA Cup final against Manchester United. Though the two appeared to strike the ball almost simultaneously, the goal was later credited to Talbot. Talbot was only the second man to appear in consecutive FA Cup winning teams for different sides. The first was Lord Arthur Kinnaird for Wanderers and Old Etonians in 1878 and 1879, exactly one hundred years before. Malcolm Macdonald's appearance in the 1978 final had prompted one of the funniest, but probably

fine job for Jimmy Armfield at Leeds, set the wheels in motion. Howe needed to be convinced there was no animosity remaining from his controversial departure to West Bromwich in the wake of the Double win. Arsenal had been incensed by Albion's raid on their back-room staff, which also took Brian Whitehouse and George Wright to the Hawthorns, but time had healed the wounds and within weeks Howe was back on familiar territory at the London Colney training ground with the new generation of Arsenal players.

Without doubt, Howe's return was one of the best decisions the club has ever made, for the old Highbury team-mates were to forge a partnership which, if not quite surpassing that of Mee and Howe, came very close for a time. Within a week in that month of August, Neill, with a little help from chairman Denis Hill-Wood, pulled off another major coup by bringing Northern Ireland goalkeeper Pat Jennings across north London

unfairest, *bon mots* of the era when a Mr. Lebor wrote to *The Guardian* saying: 'In answer to the question (in your football quiz) "What is always brought to the cup final but never used?" (the ribbons in the colours of the losing team) the answer should surely be "Malcolm Macdonald".' Macdonald had certainly had unfortunate experiences of finals in the previous few years – in 1974 he played in the Newcastle side which lost the FA Cup 3-0 to Liverpool, in 1976 Newcastle lost the League Cup final 2-1 to Manchester City, and in 1978 he had a frankly poor game for Arsenal. On the other hand, he had scored in every round except the final in 1978, getting seven goals in all, as Arsenal romped through without a replay and aggregating 17 goals to 4 in their five games. Hence the essential unfairness of the joke.

that Neill finally wielded the big stick and decided to send them home in shame for drinking and setting a bad example to their younger team-mates. They were both fined, suspended and transfer-listed on the manager's return and, although Macdonald was to make his peace, it was the beginning of the end for Hudson, who made only 20 more first team appearances, the last in an FA Cup final, before Neill sold him to Seattle Sounders in the North American League for £95,000.

After dealing with the bad boys of the tour, Neill's next priority was to find an alternative to Sexton and a call to Don Howe, then doing a

for a bargain £40,000. Jimmy Rimmer, that inveterate worrier, had given Arsenal three years' solid service and was probably the team's most consistent player when they battled successfully to avoid relegation in Mee's final season, but someone had to make way for one of the best goalkeepers in the world, and Rimmer moved to Aston Villa for whom he kept the number one jersey for five years and helped them win the 1981 League title and the 1982 European Cup.

Jennings, however, the man with the panhandle hands, and a masterful exponent of the goalkeeper's art, gave the Arsenal defence an air of impregnability and was a great reassuring presence

to his team-mates. The quiet Ulsterman had been first spotted by Watford, but after he had made just 57 appearances for the then Third Division side, Tottenham had moved in for him. During 13 years at White Hart Lane he had won an FA Cup winners' medal, appeared in two League Cup winning sides and helped Tottenham to their UEFA Cup win over Wolves in 1971–72. Spurs had had his understudy Barry Daines waiting in the wings for some time, and deciding that Jennings' career was drawing to a close at 32, they had let him depart. By his own admission, it was the worst mistake Keith Burkinshaw ever made. Jennings was to play over 300 games for the Gunners, bringing his career total to four figures and extending his international life to over 100 caps. At 40 he played in his second successive World Cup finals campaign in Mexico in 1986. Tottenham still wince whenever his name is mentioned, for Daines was never to establish himself at top level.

Howe came like a breath of fresh air to training and soon put a new spring in everybody's step. He demanded loyalty, discipline, hard work and consistently high standards. His contribution was to bring the best out of all the different personalities at his disposal. The style changed too, with Howe immediately recognising that success relied too heavily on Macdonald. He was asked to contribute more to overall team play but didn't always find it easy to comply, much to the coach's frustration on the bench.

The 1977–78 campaign opened with a 1–0 defeat in a freak hailstorm at Ipswich. What irony that this marvellous season, in which Arsenal were to figure in the Championship race, reach the League Cup semi-final and make it to Wembley in the FA Cup after an absence of six years would end with the same result against the same club in far more shattering circumstances. When two goals from Macdonald in a 3–2 victory put Manchester United out of the League Cup in a second round tie at Highbury the team were feeling sharp, highly organised and confident but Neill had one more piece of his jigsaw to rearrange. Trevor Ross had come through the apprentice ranks and played 57 games in midfield for the first team. He did a hard tackling, productive job on the right but Neill decided that the more powerful David Price, an England Youth international who had also come through the Highbury system, was the man for that position. Ross went to Everton for £170,000 and Neill added another £70,000 to buy Alan Sunderland from Wolves. One of the sharpest forwards in the First Division, Sunderland would add pace and fine technique to the forward line and was destined to score one of Wembley's most famous winners.

It was the League Cup that first gave Arsenal the Wembley feeling. They had put five goals past Hull and beaten Southampton 2–0 at Highbury before an outstanding performance by Pat Jennings earned a goalless draw at Maine Road. The replay drew 57,748 fans to Highbury and

was a night when Hudson produced the whole array of his skills to guide Arsenal through against a Manchester City side boasting such talents as Barnes, Channon, Hartford and old boy Brian Kidd.

Macdonald eventually won a penalty, put away by Brady to maintain his goal-a-round record. By this time, Arsenal were ploughing forward on three fronts — League Cup semi-finalists, Championship contenders and in the fifth round of the FA Cup after brushing aside Sheffield United and Wolves. The FA Cup paired them at home with Walsall, 45 years after the Third Division side had been responsible for the blackest day in Arsenal's history.

The two-legged League Cup semi-final proved the biggest test so far for Neill's exciting young side. Liverpool, English Champions for a tenth time and recently crowned European Champions for the first, were formidable opponents, although this was the furthest they had ever come in the competition. Ray Kennedy, playing with extra fervour against his old club, gave the Merseysiders a 2-1 advantage with the winning goal at Anfield. But although Arsenal were quietly confident of overturning the deficit, Liverpool's vast experience of European competition came into play and with Ray Clemence in majestic form and Stapleton scorning three good chances, they patiently kept a clean sheet to reach the final. But Wembley was not to prove a happy place for Liverpool, where they first discovered the hold Brian Clough's Nottingham Forest seemed to have on them. At the end of the season, Clough, of course, was to match Herbert Chapman's previously unique feat of taking different clubs to the Championship. In Chapman's case it was Huddersfield and Arsenal, in Clough's Derby and Forest.

But rather than undermine confidence, Arsenal's defeat by Liverpool had strengthened the belief in themselves because there was so little to choose between the sides. They had no trouble avenging the old Walsall score by 4–1 and it was the FA Cup giant-killers of that season, Wrexham, who gave more trouble, running them very close at the Racecourse Ground, before Arsenal reached 1978's second semi-final. It was then the gods smiled on them. Orient, using very effective counter-attacking tactics, surprisingly overcame Middlesbrough in a replay to reach their first semi-final. But by the big day they had shot their bolt and two goals from Macdonald and another by Rix in a one-sided game sent Arsenal to Wembley. Their opponents were to be Bobby Robson's Ipswich, who reached their first FA Cup final from Highbury, after a dramatic 3–1 victory over favourites West Bromwich.

Arsenal were now clearly expected to win the Cup and as the final approached news of Ipswich's walking wounded saw Arsenal installed as clear favourites. But the Gunners had worrying injury problems too. Sunderland was recovering from a broken bone in his foot, Rice, Nelson and Young were carrying knocks, Macdonald had

Liam Brady easily outpaces Wolves' Peter Daniel in 1979. In an Arsenal career which lasted from 1973 to 1980, Brady made 307 first-class appearances and scored a creditable 59 goals for a midfielder. His departure for Italy was, with Frank Stapleton's defection to Old Trafford, one of the two insurmountable blows Terry Neill had to counter at the beginning of the 1980s. He was never to find effective replacements, probably because, in reality, none was available.

Wembley again; the Arsenal end in the first of the three consecutive FA Cup finals, this one against Ipswich in 1978. The reference to the Irish is understandable. As well as Neill himself, no less than six of the team were from the island – Jennings, Rice, Nelson, O'Leary, Brady and Stapleton. Arsenal and Ipswich almost decided to arrange a joint banquet, so friendly are the two clubs with each other. It would have been a pleasing echo of the only similar event in modern times, the joint banquet of 1930, but it did not come to pass and Ipswich won the game 1-0.

been told he needed an operation on his right knee, which had begun to lock during games, and, during the Wembley build-up, Brady was carried off with a badly injured ankle at Liverpool.

They all played. Sunderland was not match fit, Macdonald lacked mobility and Brady needed to be substituted with the result that Ipswich and their delightful fans from Suffolk made the day their own with a winning goal from unsung local boy Roger Osborne. Neill ended the day with a defiant promise that Arsenal would be back next year, but for one man there would be no more chances to be a Wembley winner at club level after three heartbreaking defeats. Macdonald went into hospital three days after the final for the first of a series of knee operations that were to end his career at the age of 29 after only a handful of games the following season. It was also the last first team appearance for Hudson, who had begun brightly but faded.

Arsenal were surprisingly to fulfil Neill's post-Wembley prophesy (all losing managers say the same thing) but their qualification for the UEFA Cup was uppermost in their minds as they approached the 1978–79 season. Deep down they knew that the best prospect of putting some new silverware in the Highbury trophy cupboard was in cup competitions, for although they had finished fifth in the First Division, the squad lacked the strength in depth to be genuine Championship material. But, after relishing the prospect of the European games, Arsenal were not to meet the glamour clubs of Spain, Italy, West Germany and Holland but efficient teams drilled behind the Iron Curtain.

First came Lokomotiv Leipzig, who cracked in the last half hour at Highbury and were destroyed by Arsenal's swift counter-attacking in East Germany as they attempted to claw back three goals. It didn't get any easier in the second round against those old European campaigners, Hajduk Split, but Brady's first goal in Europe gave his side great hopes of progress despite a 2–1 defeat in Yugoslavia. Hajduk — literally translated as bandits — came to Highbury determined to defend their lead at any cost. That resulted in Brady and his 'close' marker being sent off and a second Yugoslav losing his head and being shown the red card when Willie Young, to everyone's delight and surprise, delicately chipped the goalkeeper for the winner on the night. Brady's first leg effort took the Gunners through on the away goals rule.

Back in the League, Arsenal were producing their best football since the heights of the Double year and had shot into the top four by Christmas. But the European experience was soon to end on a sour note against the sharp counter-punchers of Red Star Belgrade, who were to make it all the way to the final. Yugoslavia proved a cold, unfriendly place and the Gunners lost a drab game 1–0.

Red Star dug in at Highbury for the return before a 41,566 crowd and just when it seemed Alan Sunderland's goal had given Arsenal real hope of a place in the last eight Savic, Red Star's

international striker, broke away to equalise. With hindsight the loss of Brady through suspension to be replaced by the inexperienced Mark Heeley could well have been the deciding factor, but Red Star were to do exactly the same to West Bromwich in the quarter finals with breakaways at the Hawthorns. Red Star, guided from midfield by a future Arsenal import Vladimir Petrovic, met their match in the final against Borussia Moenchengladbach.

The Championship, and another crack at the FA Cup, soon took away the disappointment. This was a winter when Highbury's undersoil heating really earned its keep. As arctic conditions gripped the country, the Gunners played on and kept their rhythm while their rivals ground to a halt.

Arsenal were destined to reach Wembley and win what has become known as the Five Minute Final because of the dramatic climax to a game in which Arsenal thought they had two hands on the Cup by half-time. But Sunderland's last-minute winner to make it 3–2 was justice for not only a superb performance on the day but for the way Arsenal had negotiated eleven games on the road to Wembley. No opponents came any tougher than Sheffield Wednesday, then reviving themselves down in the Third Division under one of England's World Cup heroes, Jack Charlton. They matched Arsenal for effort in five unforgettable matches in a tie which gripped the public's imagination. Hillsborough's 1–1 draw was followed by a real fright at home until Brady saved the day. The teams then drew 2–2 after extra time at Leicester, and it was back to Filbert Street again to play out a thrilling 3–3 draw on one of the few pitches not ice-bound. The epic was finally decided on a fourth replay by first-half goals from Steve Gatting and Stapleton, with Wednesday having no more to give. A total of 143,996 fans had been enthralled by 540 minutes of classic cup action.

Two days after the first replay Neill completed the negotiations for the £400,000 transfer from Ipswich of Brian Talbot, whose industry and goals from the engine room of midfield had been one of the major reasons why Arsenal had finished losers at Wembley the year before. Talbot celebrated his Cup debut in red and white with the second goal in a comfortable 2–0 defeat of Notts County and was heading for the distinction of becoming only the second player to win Cup winners' medals in successive finals with different clubs.

The fifth round pairing with Clough's talented Forest side on their own ground tested the team to the full. They would have been happy with a replay but soaked up almost non-stop pressure, nullified the threat of winger John Robertson, then at his tantalising best, and broke out to win the game with a goal from Stapleton. After such a performance Arsenal's name seemed on the Cup already. It was Forest's first home defeat in 52 matches, the high point of Arsenal's late 1970s burst.

The omens became even brighter when Cup

Early season training for Alan Sunderland and Terry Neill in September 1979. Sunderland appears not to be taking matters too seriously, something which occasionally worried Neill. The manager said later of the player: 'He was the most sarcastic of all the players. Sundy's wit was frequently bitter. He was intelligent and sharp but his comments could hurt. In the end he was not a particularly popular player around the club.' Sunderland, after scoring 92 goals in 281 first-class appearances, left for Ipswich in 1984.

experts Southampton were brought back to Highbury and beaten 2–0 in a replay. The semi-final looked a difficult one. Wolves, relegation candidates for most of the season, had seemingly been revived by new manager John Barnwell and as so often happens, a lowly First Division side makes hay in the Cup. Wolves even had the advantage of playing in their own back yard at Villa Park but once Stapleton made the breakthrough there was only going to be one winner. How appropriate that Sunderland should put the final nail in his old side's coffin with a cheeky shot through Paul Bradshaw's legs. It was the most important goal in his career so far and the one that gave him most pleasure — at least for a couple of weeks.

Although in the final there was much to fear from Manchester United, conquerors of Liverpool in the semis, Arsenal, unlike the anxious men of the previous year, were eagerly anticipating the match in a relaxed and confident manner. On a hot stifling day, with Talbot running his heart out in midfield, and Brady and Stapleton looking world-class players, the Cup looked won with a joint effort from Sunderland and Talbot — they arrived at the same time for a shot though the goal was later given to Talbot — and Stapleton's fine header.

But with five minutes left the game was transformed by scrappy goals from McQueen and McIlroy. When Brady took the ball deep into United's half from the second kick-off, his only thought was to keep possession and hope for extra time, so fired up were United. But Graham Rix

had summoned up the energy for a marvellous run, took Brady's pass and slung over a perfect cross to the far post for Sunderland to slide the ball in for the winner. There was no time for United to come back again. Arsenal had done it. The excitement had all come in those frantic last five minutes.

The club just had enough time to savour their triumph before Brady, the kingpin of the team, confirmed the club's worst fears by announcing that he would be leaving Highbury after one more season when his contract ran out. He had seen Kevin Keegan leave Liverpool to make a success at Hamburg and hankered after such a challenge. He also believed that a move to the Continent could only improve him as a footballer. Arsenal's response was an offer to make him the best paid and most secure player in England. At 24, Brady had already matured into one of the world's finest midfield players, who could control a game or win it with that educated left foot of his. But his mind had been made up even before the Cup final, and after helping Arsenal to win a trophy again, he felt he could announce his intentions with a clear conscience. There was still much to savour from Brady in his final season, when he produced some exceptional performances on the way to the third successive FA Cup final and the European Cup Winners Cup final at the first attempt. But this was also a season that was to end in despair in the ill-fated Heysel Stadium, the Brussels venue where no English club has ever won a European final and which was to find its ineradicable place in football history five years later.

Pat Jennings clears from Manchester United's Joe Jordan in the 1979 FA Cup final. This was the game which was to become known as 'the five-minute final'. Arsenal were leading 2-0 in the 85th minute. United then scored twice, and Arsenal also got the winner, all in the next five minutes. Jennings, having been transferred by Keith Burkinshaw from Spurs when his career seemed near to an end, went on to play no less than 308 first-class games for his new club. He reached his 1,000th first class game versus WBA on 26 February 1983 and, by the time he set off for the Mexico World Cup in mid-1986, had made a home countries record 115 international appearances as well.

Jennings saves from Gordon McQueen in the 1979 final.

196

Another view of Brian Talbot's goal which gave Arsenal the lead in the 1979 FA Cup final against Manchester United. Arsenal were at the mid point of the first twentieth century hat-trick of FA Cup final appearances. The only teams to have done this before, all in the nineteenth century, were Wanderers, Old Etonians, Blackburn Rovers and West Bromwich Albion. Oddly Arsenal just missed by two months becoming the first team to achieve a hat-trick of first-class Wembley appearances. Nottingham Forest appeared in three League Cup finals in the same years (1978, 1979, 1980) and the League Cup final of 1980 was played two months before the FA Cup final.

Frank Stapleton scores Arsenal's second goal, a classic centre forward's header, against Manchester United in the 1979 final. Stapleton was to claim his own place in the record books when he scored *for* Manchester United against Brighton in the 1983 FA Cup final. He thus became the first man to score in an FA Cup final for two different teams (excluding own goals). His appearance in the 1985 final for Manchester United was his fifth, which equalled the record for Wembley FA Cup final appearances. This record is currently held by three Arsenal players (Pat Rice, Joe Hulme, Frank Stapleton) and Johnny Giles.

The third Arsenal goal of 1979 came in the dying seconds of the match with Alan Sunderland meeting a Rix centre at the far post and beating an astonished Gary Bailey. The sentiments of the United team, who had come back from 2-0 to 2-2 in the previous five minutes, are easy to read on Bailey's face.

At the start of the 1979–80 season, Arsenal returned to Wembley for the traditional Charity Shield pipe opener only to be given a lesson from Liverpool, who won 3–1. It was a typical performance from the Champions, highlighting the high standard of teamwork which has been the hallmark of Liverpool's continuing success. This Arsenal side were capable of playing as well as Liverpool on their day and were to prove even better in the FA Cup later in the season, but Neill's team never reached the same level of consistency which wins titles over the marathon League season.

Europe threw up an unappetising opener against the Turkish team, Fenerbahce. Howe, who had coached in Turkey, wrote them off as credible opposition but the reality was different. Arsenal had to work hard for a 2–0 first leg lead and needed nerves of steel to play out a goalless draw in the forbidding atmosphere of the Turks' own stadium in Istanbul. Juventus, Nantes and Valencia were all in the draw for the second round but Arsenal avoided them and were paired with the East Germans of Magdeburg. Willie Young's knack of scoring important goals, when they were least expected, proved priceless in establishing a slender 2–1 lead but the team did themselves proud away from home to earn a 2–2 draw and a place in the quarter-finals.

By this time Arsenal were being regarded as the best cup side in the League, although in the actual League Cup their old foes Swindon damaged the reputation in the fifth round when they won an exciting replay 4–3 with the help of own goals from Walford and Hollins and a winner from the prolific marksman of that season, Andy Rowland.

The Championship challenge was undermined by the distractions of three simultaneous cup runs but also by the inability to turn superiority into points at home, where the Gunners won only eight games and drew ten in finishing fourth. Liverpool won 15 and were unbeaten at Anfield while runners-up Manchester United won 17 at Old Trafford. The Gunners liked to counter attack, a major reason why they won ten away from home. Finally, there was the price of success in domestic competition and in Europe — fixture congestion towards the end of the season, a burden other top clubs, particularly Leeds, had already found too sapping.

Arsenal again avoided the really big boys in the Cup Winners Cup and celebrated at Highbury with a 5–0 eclipse of Gothenburg. The goalless draw in Sweden was a pure formality. But the semi-final draw paired them with the favourites and giants of Italian football, Juventus. In a controversial first leg at Highbury, Juventus took the lead through a twice-taken penalty, David O'Leary was put out of the game by World Cup striker Roberto Bettega and Marco Tardelli, another Italian international, was sent off for a foul on Brady. Justice was done when Bettega provided Arsenal with their equaliser by putting through his own goal.

Brian Talbot shields the ball from Liverpool's Alan Kennedy during the 1979-80 Charity Shield. Arsenal lost 3-1, Alan Sunderland getting their only goal. These two are the most successful of all teams in the early season curtain raiser; by 1986 Liverpool had won it on seven occasions outright with three shared and Arsenal on seven occasions outright. Oddly, the Gunners chose not to contest the event in 1971, after they had won both trophies, or they might be ahead in outright victories.

Frank Stapleton and Brian Talbot (bottom left) celebrate the FA Cup final victory with champagne in the dressing room. It was an unusual gesture for Stapleton, known as a hard-working, non-drinking, non-smoking professional. His departure two years later, to the team Arsenal beat that day, was a blow from which the attack could not hope to recover for many years.

The FA Cup tie against Liverpool in 1980 was eventually to become the longest semi-final in FA Cup history. There were four games in all, stretching from a goalless 12 April at Hillsborough through two 1-1 draws at Villa Park and finally reaching a conclusion at Coventry on 1 May 1980, just nine days before the FA Cup final. In the third game, on 28 April 1980, Alan Sunderland scored this goal (top picture) in just 13 seconds, the fastest semi-final goal ever. The tie was finally settled in the 12th minute of the fourth game by (bottom picture) a Brian Talbot header which left defenders Neal, Clemence and McDermott helpless. The tie lasted 420 minutes in all and would have been decided on penalties had there not been a result at Coventry. Arsenal now faced two League games in the nine days leading up to the final (they won one and drew the other) as well as two more after it, plus the Cup Winners Cup final.

Arsenal hardly had time to draw breath before they were pitched into an FA Cup semi-final with Liverpool after making steady if undemanding progress through the competition at the expense of Cardiff, Brighton, Bolton and Watford. Neither of the Reds could overcome excellent defensive work at Hillsborough in the first game. So it was off to Villa Park, but it finished level at 1–1 after extra time, so West Ham, who overcame Everton in their own replay at Elland Road, had a little longer to wait to know their Wembley opponents.

Hostilities were suspended for Arsenal's trip to Italy for the second leg against Juventus, now odds-on favourites to reach the final, especially with an away goal at their disposal. But Arsenal produced one of the outstanding results in 25 years of European competition by winning 1–0 in Turin on a ground where no British club had ever triumphed (nor, for that matter, had any other European opposition for ten years). Paul Vaessen, a professional for less than a year, was in the right place at the right time to score a famous winner two minutes from time. With Juventus having an away goal, the Gunners were two minutes from elimination. Vaessen must have felt the whole world was at his feet that night, but within two years his career was over, cruelly cut short by a serious knee injury.

The FA Cup semi-final struggle with Liverpool was renewed for a second time at Villa Park and Sunderland broke the deadlock after just 13 seconds (the fastest ever semi-final goal) but Kenny Dalglish equalised to make a third replay necessary. Off they went to Coventry's Highfield Road for another try with wild rumours being bandied about concerning American style shoot-outs, penalty kicks and probably tossing up to

see who went through. Neither side were happy about any of the suggestions and would have been quite content to play into the summer to settle it. But the problem was solved by Brian Talbot's lone goal at Coventry and they didn't even need extra time. To outlast Liverpool over four games had been some feat, and, taking into account the Juventus distraction, very creditable. The four games had been watched by 169,163 fans, paying £620,037. Interestingly, this is the highest aggregate attendance to watch a British cup tie, excluding finals, ever recorded.

Liverpool took defeat in their stride to retain their League title two days later by beating Aston Villa 4–1, but Arsenal's nine free days to prepare for Wembley were not to give them the edge against their old London rivals West Ham, who were still trying to escape from the Second Division at the time. The final was one to forget for Arsenal, who never came to terms with West Ham's astute tactic of using Stuart Pearson in a withdrawn centre forward role. Pearson had been a Neill discovery while he was at Hull, had won 15 caps for England while playing for Manchester United and was giving the Hammers a fine season at the end of his career. It was another veteran who finished off the Gunners with an unusual winning goal as Trevor Brooking stooped low to deflect a misdirected shot past Pat Jennings with his head. Brooking was to confirm later it was only the third goal he had scored with his head in a long and distinguished career for West Ham.

Never a classic, with Arsenal well below par, the match did make one piece of history when West Ham's Paul Allen became the youngest player to appear in an FA Cup final at 17 years and 256 days, taking the record away from Howard Kendall who had held it since 1964 playing for Preston in their defeat by . . . West Ham. Arsenal could have done with some young legs themselves. Talbot, the only ever present that season, gave so much in midfield that he collapsed with exhaustion on the coach leaving Wembley. The front runners, Stapleton and Sunderland, looked particularly weary and it was obvious the titanic struggles against Liverpool had taken their toll at the end of another long, hard season. If we are to be frank, it was really a final to forget. Young's professional foul on Allen, which denied the young player an excellent chance of a goal three minutes from the end, remains in the memory. This was doubly unfortunate as Arsenal were creating a record as the first side to appear in three consecutive FA Cup finals in the twentieth century.

The omens were not good for the Cup Winners Cup final four days later in the Heysel Stadium, Brussels, against Valencia, managed by Di Stefano and boasting the talents of Argentina's World Cup winning striker Mario Kempes and the West German international Rainer Bonhof. Defences dominated a tense game through 90 minutes and half an hour of extra time, Kempes being blotted out by the superb O'Leary. Neither side was able to score,

so one of the biggest nights in Arsenal's history was to be decided by the excruciating experience of a penalty shoot-out. The tension got to the biggest names on the field, Kempes and Brady, who both failed with the first attempts. The score reached 5–4 in Valencia's favour when their goalkeeper Pereira, who had moved for all Arsenal's attempts, did it again as Graham Rix approached.

This time he guessed correctly where the shot was going and the final was lost. Rix, who although only 22 had been through most experiences in football, was in tears and not even the thunderous ovation of the 15,000 Arsenal fans in Brussels that night could lift the desolation felt by a team which had been required to play 15 matches in 45 days before the big night.

But the footballing fates had not finished with Arsenal yet. They came home with a UEFA Cup place the next season still in the offing if they could win their two outstanding League games. Forty-eight hours after the Valencia match they went to Wolves and somehow won 2–1 but on

The ever dependable David O'Leary gives Jimmy Greenhoff and Lou Macari little chance in the 1979 FA Cup final. Out of the six cup finals Arsenal contested in the decade 1971-1980, they wore their own red shirts just once (versus Leeds in 1972). They appeared in yellow shirts and blue shorts in the other five. Arsenal have, peculiarly, played in their change strip in half of all their cup final appearances.

The month of May 1980 was to see Arsenal play seven first-class games, lose two finals and set up two records unlikely ever to be beaten. The first was that they finished the season having played no less than 70 first-class games, the most ever completed by an English side in a single year. The second was even odder; Arsenal failed to win the Cup Winners Cup having reached the final and not lost a single game in the tournament. Having passed Fenerbahce, Magdeburg, Gothenburg and Juventus (via Paul Vaessen's away winner seconds from time), they were to manage only a draw with Valencia in the Heysel Stadium, in Brussels, on 14 May 1980. Penalties were used to decide the match, for the first time in European club finals, and Valencia triumphed 5-4. From the Arsenal point of view, the culprits who missed were the two most surprising of their penalty takers – Liam Brady (seen walking away afterwards, bottom left) and Graham Rix. Valencia keeper Pereira moved early to Rix's shot (shown on the right), the final one in the tournament, and the Arsenal number 11 left the field wondering what might have been (bottom right) while Pereira was mobbed by his colleagues. It was Arsenal's fourth final in three years and sadly they won only one of them. The Heysel was to be the scene of a far greater tragedy for an English club almost five years to the day later.

Monday 19 May they were required to make the long trip north to Middlesbrough and finally cracked in their 70th match of the season. The UEFA Cup place disappeared in a 5–0 defeat to leave Arsenal so near yet so far in another competition — the League, in which they finished a creditable fourth to Liverpool. Can any team have worked and played so hard to achieve nothing at all? Those 70 first-class games remain the most ever played by a British club in a single season. It was the classic English football failure, and no less bitter for all its predictability.

The denouement in the Heysel was, in retrospect, clearly a watershed, though how can we tell whether it should have been? The irony was that it had been Brady and Rix who had missed the critical penalties, and they were then, and are now, rightly regarded as the most influential of all Arsenal players in the past ten years. Who can say what would have happened if either of them had scored — could Highbury now be different?

It was to be five years, virtually to the day, when the same Heysel Stadium staged its next one-legged European final, Liverpool versus Juventus in the 1985 European Cup. That shattering game was not just to conclude one club's brief period of success, as Arsenal's 1980

defeat had done; it effectively brought to an end the post-war history of British football. The double disaster of 1985 — Bradford and Brussels — plus the long-simmering dispute about televised football, finally flung the continued existence of the professional game as it had been known in the twentieth century into the melting pot.

For Arsenal the years between 1980 and 1985 had not been turbulent or traumatic so much as, according to many of their fans, tiresome and tedious. Average attendances fell from 36,371 in the 1978–79 season to 28,116 in 1983–84 and off a precipice through 1985. Charlie Nicholas came and Terry Neill went, but, standing in the marble hall looking at the bust of Herbert Chapman, one could be excused for thinking that this was not a period which history would compare favourably with what had gone before.

It is never easy to define turning points, to decide when the pendulum begins to swing back the other way, but for Terry Neill, Don Howe and the team that had memorably reached four Cup finals in three years, the moments that mattered were the days that Liam Brady and Frank Stapleton departed. Neither was effectively replaced, Stapleton's place proving an almost intractable problem with a whole stream of pretenders — Hawley, Chapman, Hankin to name but three — and less than perfect stopgaps. In the end, even an England centre forward in the shape of Paul Mariner could be seen only as a short term solution.

Frank Stapleton went in 1981. His contract was at an end, and he had a right to move wherever he wished. He is a somewhat unusual footballer, as Terry Neill says: '. . . a non-smoker, a non-drinker and a practising Catholic, a thoughtful, studious man.' Neill also relates how frustrating the negotiations were: 'Frank sat quietly and virtually all he said was "Make your best offer".' Arsenal did, though it wasn't to match Manchester United's. Even so, Martin Edwards, chairman at Old Trafford, commented afterwards that he was not sure how United could afford what they had offered. Neill, like most people in the game, has no objections to a player trying to obtain the best he can. It is a short career at best, and one that ill-fits a man in his late thirties to do anything else (what happens to all the players who *don't* become managers?). The ex-manager refers sympathetically to Paul Vaessen, who, at the age of 18, scored the critical goal in Turin in the semi-final of the 1980 Cup Winners Cup against Juventus. 'That proved to be the greatest moment of his career,' says Neill, 'for sadly he was forced to retire not long afterwards with a knee injury . . . one of the grimmest truths about football is that every player can be one tackle away from the end of his career.'

Liam Brady, the other critical departure, became a free agent in 1980 and went to Juventus for the maximum £600,000 that was allowed by UEFA and the EEC for international transfers. Arsenal's final offer to Brady would

have made him the highest paid player in England, but it was the challenge as much as the money that was motivating the Irishman. He was to settle extremely happily in Italy among the rest of the world's top players. The ability of the Italians to pay sums way beyond those on offer elsewhere in the world is a result of two financial advantages — the effective sponsorship of the clubs by major individual firms (such as Fiat with Juventus), and, perhaps more pertinently, that attendances are much higher than elsewhere (in the mid-1980s average Italian First Division attendances were more than double those in England and treble those in Scotland).

So United and Juventus got their men while Terry Neill and Don Howe got a mere £1½ million (very little by European superstar standards) and an almighty headache. Says Neill: 'It was a tragedy of monumental proportions for the club. No one can begin to understand the agony I went through during this period. It (then) meant years of travel as I searched for adequate replacements, and frequent criticism for having sold two such gifted players.' The criticism was, as we have seen, essentially unfair, though Neill never did find the right men. Against that, it is difficult to see, short of signing Bryan Robson and Ian Rush, where players of a similar standard could have been found. Stapleton was the best forward of his generation. Many memories of his skills will remain, but one which shows his value to the club perfectly is the late header which won the 1978–79 FA Cup quarter-final against Nottingham Forest at the City Ground. It was a classic effort, ten minutes from time, and it was the only goal of the game. The significance was in Stapleton's rare ability to win games which, by rights, Arsenal should have lost. Forest had not lost at home for 52 matches, were on their way to the European Cup, were clearly the team of the moment. Stapleton's goal took Arsenal past their most difficult hurdle. After that, anything was easy.

Another departure far sadder than that of Brady and Stapleton was to follow in 1982 when Chairman Denis Hill-Wood, much beloved throughout the game, died aged 76. He had taken over from his father 22 years before, had seen the glories of the Double, and handed the role on, in his turn, to his own son Peter.

For most First Division clubs — say a Leicester or a Newcastle — the first four seasons of the 1980s would not have been unsatisfactory. Arsenal finished 3rd, 5th, 10th and 6th in successive seasons, but at no point were they ever contenders for the title. Indeed, they were no closer than 16 points in arrears of the Champions under the new three points for a win system introduced in 1981.

The cups were also lacking their highlights, to say the least. Though 1982–83 was a poor year in the League, it was the best of the decade to date in the knock-outs. The Gunners reached the semi-finals of both cup competitions, only to come up against Manchester United in both. The Milk Cup (as the Football League Cup was

Stewart Robson, a West Ham supporter in his youth, takes on a West Ham defender in 1985.

renamed for a time) was never a contest. United won 4–2 at Highbury and 2–1 at Old Trafford. The FA Cup semi-final at Villa Park was tighter with United squeezing through 2–1. Tony Woodcock scored the Gunners' only goal and United went on to a final against Brighton.

The first half of the 1980s, however, will not be remembered for cup victories but for cup defeats. For a time there seemed a steady stream of embarrassing reverses; to Second Division Middlesbrough in the FA Cup in 1984, to Fourth Division York a year later (0–1 after Steve Williams gave away a penalty), to Second Division Oxford in the Milk Cup and, above all others, 1–2 at home to Walsall in the Milk Cup on 29 November 1983.

The second Walsall disaster has already become part of football folklore. It will never become as famous or as oft-quoted as the great giant killing act of 1933, exactly half a century before, but they will surely be automatically bracketed in any bicentenial history produced in the year 2086. The fame of that second disastrous night will rest more on the long arm of coincidence than on what actually happened on the pitch — one goal defeats by Third Division clubs over their First Division superiors in the League Cup had been anything but unexpected for at least ten years. The match owes its significance to its symbolism, to the fact that Terry Neill was already under intolerable pressure, that it was Walsall rather than another Third Division side who were the opponents and because Walsall will always mean 1933, a convenient and exact five decades in the past.

Whatever North London folklore passes down in the years to come (and it is always a temptation to ascribe great moment to single games) it was not the Walsall game on 29 November 1983 which was the point of no return for Terry Neill's managership. That had come nearly three months before, in a single week in early September. On 6 September Manchester United came to Highbury and won

3–2. Four days later it was Liverpool's turn, and they headed back up the M1 with a 2–0 victory under their belts.

The Gunners had already beaten Luton and Wolves in the League; after Liverpool they easily defeated Notts County and Norwich. But what counted was that they had clearly failed, before their own supporters, to beat the two clubs against whom all real comparisons had to be made. On this sort of form they could finish fifth or sixth quite easily, but they had no chance of the Championship. And that was what mattered; not that they necessarily *won* the title, but that at least they were seen to be in with a *chance*.

Through October 1983 results were inconsistent; on the impressive side Forest were beaten 4–1, Villa thrashed 6–2 away, Everton beaten at Highbury and Spurs knocked out of the Milk Cup 2–1 on 9 November. These were all good results. On the negative side, Sunderland and Coventry carried off the rare prize of a Highbury success; Ipswich, Leicester and West Brom added to the gloom. Strangely there were no drawn League games until after Christmas. Perhaps three points for a win did make a difference.

The pressures really came to a head after the 3–0 defeat at Leicester on 26 November. The mood of the times had, perhaps accidentally, been revealed by Terry Neill that same week when he had put up a notice informing staff that there would be no free turkeys that Christmas, due to ' . . . severe economic restrictions'. Anthony Holden surmised in the *Sunday Express* that: ' . . . the bird blight was (being) blamed on Charlie Nicholas, who had cost Neill £650,000 last summer and had yet to score at Highbury.' The team played dreadfully at Filbert Street, going down 3–0 in a game they should have won easily. Neill and Howe were furious. After the match Neill told Holden: 'What use is a £250 win bonus when they're on £1,500 a week and (seem to be) gambling half of it away on the bus?' (If

The Arsenal line-up in August 1980. Back row: Jennings, Hollins, Powling, Gatting, Sunderland, Young, O'Leary, Walford, Price, Nelson, Brady and Barron. Front row: Fred Street, Don Howe, Rix, Devine, Allen, Rice, Stapleton, Talbot, Terry Neill, Wilf Dixon. The picture contains all of the players who appeared in the four cup finals of the 1978-80 era except Malcom Macdonald and Alan Hudson, who both appeared in the 1978 final against Ipswich. The most interesting thing about the line-up is, of course, the appearance of Clive Allen for his only team photograph. He had been bought by Neill in June

The happy scene on 27 December 1986, when Arsenal Football Club was 100 years and two days old. Some of the ex-players who were guests of the club acknowledging the applause of the fans who had turned up to watch the match with Southampton. The birthday cake in the shape of the pitch contained 100 candles.

I heard the fans and I don't blame them. We were awful, but (three weeks ago) when we beat Spurs they sang a different song. And last night, apart from Rix, I fielded the same team. So why did they go out there and play like pantomime horses?'

The team lost twice more, to West Brom and West Ham, making it five defeats in six matches, before the axe fell. Peter Hill-Wood insisted that the decision was not because the team had lost a few matches. The reasons were broader. As David Lacey said in *The Guardian*: 'Arsenal were a potentially good team going nowhere and naturally the manager became the focal point for their anger.' Nonetheless, a dismissal at Highbury is always a shock. The club have (to date) had only eleven managers in 60 years and, of these, two died in office (Chapman and Whittaker) and only one (Billy Wright) had not been intimately associated with the club prior to his appointment. It is one of the major reasons for the club's continuity and success.

Don Howe, after 14 years as coach at the club (seven under Mee, seven under Neill) became the new manager, taking over from his close friend and room-mate from the days they played for the club together. Howe was naturally guarded at the start of his reign: 'I told the chairman I would like to have the job. He said: "We'll see." He looked as though he needed a stiff brandy.' Hill-Wood confessed to not having slept for three nights before having to make the decision to fire Neill.

Howe did not try to distance himself from Neill, though his position was a difficult one: 'There were perhaps times when I wouldn't have put out the team he put out, and there were times when he bought players I wouldn't have bought (Neill spent a total of £7.9 million on players and his sales totalled £4.6 million — arguably not an outstanding record) but I was his coach and I backed every decision he made. That's the only way a club can be run. There can only be one man making the decisions.' Neill was genuinely pleased that Howe remained: 'He had felt the draught as the axe whistled past his head,' said his old team-mate in an unusually imaginative phrase for a football autobiography, ' . . . and I was delighted that he was appointed as my successor. In my view the staff were all excellent — Don, Terry Burton, Tony Coleman and Pat Rice — I was lucky to have worked with the finest coach in the country, Don Howe, and the finest administrator, Ken Friar.'

The following season, 1984–85, saw a replay of some of the same themes heard during the last days of Neill's incumbency. After a dreadful performance at Luton, resulting in a 3–1 defeat, Howe exploded venomously. 'They should all refuse to accept their wages,' he said, 'and I'm thinking of refusing mine. Even if we beat Southampton 5–0 tomorrow, the players and I don't deserve to be paid. Sometimes I wonder what they want out of life.'

Howe's problem was the same as Neill's — he couldn't quite crack the goalscoring problem.

1980 and was sold to Crystal Palace two months later before the new season began. His cost was quoted as £1,250,000 but the sale price was confused by Paul Barron being included in the deal. Allen's only appearances for Arsenal were in a few summer tour games and practice matches. He presumably remains the only £1 million player to be sold before he ever made an appearance and Arsenal are also presumably the only club never to have played their most expensive signing.

they were, then at least, like transfer fees, it stayed within the game — they were only playing each other.) Neill continued: 'They don't seem to know what it is to hunger for goals and glory. On days like today I think they just want to pick up their money and go home.'

These were themes that were to recur only too often inside and outside Highbury in the next two years. But Neill was also impressively realistic about his team, their contemporaries and himself: 'But I'll tell you now; we'll finish in the top six again this season. Whether or not I'll be around to see it is another matter.' They did finish sixth, and Neill was not around to see it.

Neill, and everyone else for that matter, knew that his days must be numbered. The *coup de grace* came five days later, against that nightmare name from the 1930s. Walsall won 2–1, and not unluckily. Ken Friar, secretary and managing director, passed a despairing opinion that it could cost the club a quarter of a million (Arsenal ended the season losing £743,789, compared with a profit of £571,000 the year before). The chairman was magnanimous in defeat, warmly congratulating his conquerors with scotches ('. . . and bloody difficult it is too . . .'), though the fans were anything but. 'NEILL MUST GO' chants echoed into the boardroom from the street below.

Neill was philosophical, if a little bemused: 'Last night will be with me till I'm six feet under.

Though Tony Woodcock was to be a success of sorts (eventually scoring 67 goals in 169 appearances), he wasn't Ian Rush nor even Tony Cottee. Both Neill and Howe had searched far and wide for the elusive striker, their most spectacular gamble being the now legendary (some might say mythical) purchase of Clive Allen.

In August 1980 Arsenal had created a genuine sensation by paying £1¼ million for the 19-year-old QPR striker. He was only the fifth English player to cost that sum and the other four — Trevor Francis, Andy Gray, Steve Daley and Kevin Reeves — hardly represented an unbroken story of success. The noisy response to Allen's signing was, however, but a whisper compared to what happened eight weeks later.

Out of the blue, and before he had played a single game, Allen was suddenly transferred to Crystal Palace in exchange for Kenny Sansom. Paul Barron, who was tired of being back-up to Pat Jennings, went to Selhurst Park as well and served to confuse the sums involved, but the sale, like the purchase, went down in excess of one million pounds.

Everyone was baffled, particularly the fans. Allen had been the First Division's leading scorer the previous season and Sansom, despite becoming an England regular and an outstanding long-term buy, was after all, only a defender. There was a widely held belief, erroneous but persistent, that bad feelings between QPR and Palace had prevented a direct deal on Allen and Highbury was in some strange way a pre-arranged transit stop. That showed a wild misunderstanding of the nature of Arsenal's management, and the truth was far more prosaic. After pre-season training the coaching staff had decided that Allen was not the long-term answer. The club had, after all, reached two Cup finals the previous season, and Sunderland and Stapleton were then both playing well. There was no way all three could play in the same team, and Allen seemed likely to be the one left out. If the problems of 12 months later could have been foreseen, no doubt the decision would have been different. It was a view that Highbury felt to be justified right through to Allen's *anno mirabilis* of 1986–87, when he broke Jimmy Greaves Spurs' records and scored 49 first-class goals. In the classic three-legged Littlewoods Cup semi-final against Spurs that year, Arsenal conceded one goal in each game — and Allen got all three. The acid test, as everyone in the game will tell you, nonetheless, was that Arsenal won the trophy. Allen had some consolation — with both the PFA and Sportswriters' Footballer of the Year Awards.

It remains, for all that, a strange story and Arsenal are likely to remain unique in having chosen never to field a player who remains their record signing.

The search for a star continued. Yugoslavia's World Cup leader Vladimir Petrovic was eventually claimed after Neill had pursued him somewhat maniacally for a year, but he was not the answer: 'After a few weeks I knew he wasn't right, he was on the fringe of matches, not at centre-stage.' Petrovic played just 22 games before moving on to Antwerp.

By mid-1983 Neill and Howe knew a big signing was essential. The support was restive sensing, despite two semi-finals against Manchester United, that the team was going nowhere. The answer was to be Charlie Nicholas.

In a way, Arsenal made their decision to buy first and then chose Charlie Nicholas because he was the man of the moment. Manchester United and Liverpool were inevitably favourites, but Nicholas rightly felt that he would have more of a chance to shine individually at Highbury rather than at Anfield or Old Trafford.

The fact that London would probably offer more in the way of off-the-field opportunities no doubt also came into matters. Money was not a factor otherwise — all three clubs were offering roughly the same in wages and bonuses and the fee was already set at £650,000 as Nicholas was a free agent. Highbury's problem, ultimately, was that the hoopla had simply raised expectations far too high.

Nicholas' arrival certainly made a difference to attendances — they went up by nearly 4,000 a game in his first season. Despite impressions to the contrary, he also scored a fair number of goals (12, though a few were penalties). Given that he had cost only £650,000 this should have seemed a reasonable return in a first, settling-in year. But somehow the whole thing had got out of control. There were too many newspaper articles, too much of the 'booze and birds' nonsense, too many references to driving bans. Nicholas was cast in the relatively recently invented role of 'sportsman as media personality'. Steve Davis, Ian Botham and Sebastian Coe have been treated (not necessarily in accord with their wishes) similarly. Much of the hype has little to do with football. Much of it must detract from a player's performance and abilities. Much of the same emotion and a lot of the same deep-seated anxiety and dissatisfaction about the way the world seemed to be going could be detected in the long-winded, bad-tempered and often irrational debates about televised football that raged interminably through 1985.

The game seemed out of control, the issues seemed to have little to do with playing in, or watching, an enjoyable game of football. The fans were unimpressed. Everywhere they voted with their feet. At Highbury, for the first time since Herbert Chapman's early days, attendances below 20,000 became common.

The hundredth season of 1985–86 started well nonetheless (technically the centenary celebration year was not 1985–86 but 1986–87 as the hundredth birthday fell half-way through the later season) and by February Arsenal looked a good bet for both Cup finals. Then came disaster. After a convincing draw at Villa in the League Cup quarter-final, the Gunners fell incomprehensibly to the Midlanders 2–1 at home. With only Oxford and QPR otherwise left in, Arsenal seemed to have thrown away the best trophy chance they had had in years. The FA Cup was as

bad. After a 2–2 draw at Kenilworth Road, Arsenal failed to pick up their replay advantage and the second game ended 0–0. Losing the toss for a third match, the plastic of Luton proved too much and Arsenal were out of another tournament, 3–0. It was now six years since the last Cup final appearance (in Brussels) and only once since Herbert Chapman's arrival had there been a longer gap between consecutive finals or Championships (that was from 1953 to 1968, the era known as the long sleep).

The disappointment was too much. On 22 March 1986, after Arsenal had beaten Coventry 3–0 and despite it being a fourth consecutive League win, Don Howe asked to be released from his contract. He had heard, as had many others, that Terry Venables might want to come back from Barcelona. It was no secret that both Spurs and Arsenal would consider Venables a prize catch. The fact that Arsenal would only be four points behind the leaders if they won their two games in hand didn't seem to interest anyone — only 17,000 had turned out for the Coventry game. So Howe resigned with dignity and left the club their foundation for future success. It was sad, after the Double and all that had happened since, that he was unable to add his name — unlike Chapman, Whittaker, Mee and Neill — to the list of managerial winners, particularly as he had been manager in much but name in 1971.

And it was to the Double team that the club were to turn for Howe's successor. Not just to the Double team, but to the player who had even been voted Man of the Match at the moment of ultimate triumph — George Graham, 'Stroller'.

Graham's managerial experience to date had been limited. He had done a good job at troubled Millwall, not letting crowd problems deflect from a competent young team. But he was hardly a proven quantity. Nonetheless, twelve months on, the choice seemed no less than inspired. He knew Highbury, he had the confidence of the players, the board, the public (he had always had a good image as a skilful, intelligent player) and even the sponsors, JVC, who had been totally loyal to the club since the first days of real football commercialism. He was the right man at the right time.

On the pitch the season was nothing less than a revelation. Firstly Graham did not spend, saying he needed time to assess the staff and he wasn't going to buy anyone unless he was sure he was good enough. Indeed, it wasn't until season's end that he purchased Alan Smith from Leicester. So he relied on what he had — rehabilitating the impetuous Steve Williams, trusting the imperfect Niall Quinn and showing confidence in young Tony Adams at centre-back with David O'Leary. Even Charlie Nicholas was not guaranteed a place in the team, having to fight his way in from a relatively small back-up squad after a September injury.

The side settled to a steady, if unspectacular, pattern. The rock was, in Arsenal tradition, the defence. By season's end three of the back four (Anderson, Sansom and Adams) were England regulars and O'Leary, of course, had been Eire's

mainstay for years. After 27 September 1986, when they lost 1–0 at League leaders Forest, the defence locked and defeat was not to be an issue until 24 January 1987, after another 22 games, a club record for Arsenal. In that period they won 17 and drew 5, scoring 47 and conceding just 11. It was an exceptional effort, not least because little credibility was given to Arsenal's chances at the beginning of the season.

Graham was adamant from the start of the run: Arsenal were not good enough to win the Championship, he insisted, and it was definitely not said simply to generate good press copy. When the side did lose, the disappointment was, nonetheless, intense. The match was at Old Trafford, where United had been struggling all season. On this occasion Norman Whiteside seemed to have discovered a personal mission to provoke the opposition, and he succeeded so well that David Rocastle was sent off. Graham rightly blamed the referee for allowing Whiteside too much licence ('. . . I'm quite a disciplinarian and I've got to try to help the officials, but what do you do when you believe that the referee is wrong?'). Graham was more gracious to United: 'The better team won — but next time I hope we have a football match.' The truth was that the Arsenal players found it hard to accept they might lose after such a long unbroken run and the lack of old, steady heads was felt. It was to be perhaps the only negative theme in an excellent season — the players did occasionally find it hard to control their tempers when they felt that the run of the ball was against them.

By the time of the defeat by United Arsenal were well ahead of the League and going strongly in both Cups. It had been a glorious winter, capped on 27 December 1986 by a wonderful celebration of the actual centenary, which had been two days earlier, on Christmas Day itself. An enormous crowd turned out for the game against Southampton (won 1–0) and so did a great array of stars past and present. Most notable of many notables were, perhaps, Joe Mercer, Ted Drake and, above all others, George Male, the only man present to have played under Herbert Chapman (though flying wingers Bastin and Hulme were both still alive). Male played no less than 316 first-class matches for the club and never scored a goal. Though his career was sadly cut short by the war (without it he would probably have played 600 first-class matches) his very last game was in 1948 and Arsenal ended a Championship-winning season with a stunning 8–0 victory over Grimsby. A great way to go out. And 40 years on, that Boxing Day, he was there to hear the whole crowd, North Bank and all, cheering the men who had made Arsenal what it is today even more loudly than they cheered Niall Quinn's winning goal. And they had much to cheer: how appropriate that Arsenal were top of Division I that centenary day, how appropriate that Bob Wilson should be the master of ceremonies, how appropriate that the crowd was large, well behaved and appreciative; and, some might say, how appropriate that the defence did not concede a goal against Southampton. It was

Arsenal were almost out of the Littlewoods Cup in the second leg of the semi-final against Spurs at White Hart Lane when Spurs led 1-0 after having won the first leg by the same score. It seemed the centenary year, which had gone so well until after Christmas would end without a trophy. Then Viv Anderson gave Arsenal hope by squeezing in the ball by the near post past Clemence. A late second goal forced a replay.

The Littlewoods Cup semi-final replay was another home game for Spurs after David Pleat had won the toss for venue, and with eight minutes left it seemed home advantage might pay off as Spurs led 1-0. Then Allinson held off Gough and seconds after the photograph was taken scored the equalizer. When Rocastle scored the winner, Arsenal had led for only the last minute of the 300-minute marathon.

Opposite top: **Charlie Nicholas is first to the ball** in the Littlewoods Cup final and his side-footed shot beats Grobbelaar and equalizes the score after Rush had put Liverpool ahead. From then on Arsenal were always the more likely side to win.

Opposite bottom: **The winning goal** which ensured the Littlewoods Cup and a fitting centenary trophy for the Gunners. It was Charlie Nicholas again, whose future had been the question of press speculation, who scored his second goal of the match to seal victory. Nicholas (10) turns away in triumph, but it was in truth a rather scrappy goal in its final touch, but a splendid one from the point of view of Perry Groves, the 83rd-minute substitute, whose great run down the left flank set it up.

almost as if a fairy godmother had decided to shine on this great club's celebration.

And so it may have appeared three months later as the Gunners approached the series of games for which the centenary year will surely always be remembered. Having disposed of Huddersfield, Manchester City, Charlton and Forest in the League (now renamed Littlewoods) Cup, Arsenal were drawn to play a newly confident Spurs in the semi-final. Both clubs were also in the FA Cup quarter-finals. Heady days in North London.

Arsenal's League form since their defeat by Manchester United was a perfect simulation of a bursting bubble. Though they led the League at that time, they dropped 15 of the next 18 points and Liverpool, nine points behind at Christmas, were seven points ahead by the time Arsenal took the field for their memorable semi-finals against Tottenham.

The first game was at Highbury, and the home side were to be without (through injury and suspension) their critical right-sided triangle of Anderson, Rocastle and Williams. Spurs scored the only goal, inevitably through Clive Allen, and seemed to be three-quarters down Olympic Way. The cockerels no doubt thought themselves nine-tenths of the way there when, after 38 minutes of the second leg at White Hart Lane, Clive Allen scored yet again after John Lukic had flapped at a ball he should have cleared.

Spurs were well on top but Allen was uncharacteristically profligate. David Pleat, the new Spurs manager, said afterwards: 'On about four occasions I said to myself " . . . this is it" but somehow we ruined those chances. I thought Clive did well with the goal, but he missed a lot as well.' Pleat was quick enough to concede that he couldn't really complain about Allen's overall form that season.

George Graham was to be grateful for those misses when Anderson forced the ball home after a Quinn header and, towards the end, Quinn met a Rocastle cross at the left hand post quite beautifully to make the score 2–1. It was the best moment of Quinn's unexpectedly successful season.

So the tie went to a third game. The referee tossed for home advantage and the coin stuck upright in the mud. David Pleat called right the second time and had the dubious pleasure of playing the decider at home. Graham said afterwards that ' . . . I'm quite pleased with our performance. You media guys have tried to knock us down but we keep bouncing back. You did my job today; you fired my players.'

Wednesday 4 March 1987 was to be a red letter day for Arsenal. Yet again Clive Allen scored the first goal of the game (three games, three first goals and still Spurs didn't win the tie) and Spurs held that lead until the 82nd minute. Then, in quick succession, Ian Allinson squeezed the ball inside Ray Clemence's near post and David Rocastle squeezed it under the keeper's body at the last gasp and at 2–1 it was all over. As Clive White said in *The Times*: 'When the match stood at all square, there could have been no doubt,

even in the minds of Tottenham supporters, that Arsenal would eventually win. What David Pleat described as a gamble when Arsenal threw three men forward in the final minutes, to the rest of us appeared a calculated one and only accentuated the feeling that Arsenal wanted to win more badly than Tottenham.' It was the fifth time in six visits that Arsenal had won at White Hart Lane. All three of the semi-final games had been won by the away side.

Frank McLintock, captain of the Double team, watched the match with his coach that year, Don Howe: 'Like us in the 1970s, they've got players who hate to be beaten. I don't remember us losing when we were a goal up.' Spurs arguably didn't remember winning when they were a goal up against Arsenal.

McLintock went on to talk about Graham: 'He was an unusual player for Arsenal. We were a hard driving team whereas George was a bit laconic. He scored some great goals but sometimes he couldn't keep up the momentum for the whole 90 minutes. But he added that bit of class, that touch of the unexpected and we needed that at times.' McLintock also sympathised with Don Howe's position: 'I couldn't help feeling a bit sorry for him sitting there. George rightly deserves the credit, but Don encouraged a lot of this success and it's all been forgotten so quickly. He wasn't that far away. The players were all his. George hasn't bought anyone.'

Arsenal had drawn the final card no one wanted — Liverpool. After this point any pretensions in the League disappeared completely. Players who might find themselves suspended for the final were rested and, having played seven matches in 21 days, Graham's and Theo Foley's view on their League chances was clearly realistic. Liverpool came to Highbury in the League. Rush scored and that was that. Was it to be a portent? Dalglish had done a job, but Graham's young lions had contributed to the evening. At least, one no longer felt as one had in the early 1980s, that the problem was not the fact that Arsenal did not win anything, but that they did not seem likely to win anything. The game against Liverpool clearly showed that Graham, as he had said, did not have the resources in depth that he really needed to run Liverpool and Everton close over a full season. But, Highbury hoped, that would come. A quarter-final defeat (3–1) by Watford at Highbury ended the team's interest in the other Cup and all that was left to think about was Wembley and Liverpool.

No matter how good they appeared in day-to-day terms, this was not the great Liverpool side of the early 1980s. They were eventually to win nothing in 1987; shades of 1985 when they not only suffered the Heysel tragedy but (it is easily forgotten) won none of the six trophies they contested. Arsenal were not short of ability. They had their defence, which remained outstanding. Tony Adams was to become Young Player of the Year and a major asset. 'If we had that boy,' said another First Division manager, 'We'd conquer the world.' And there was always the joker, Charlie Nicholas.

Arsenal won the toss for colours and, interestingly, chose to play in their own red shirts. Twice before they had met Liverpool at Wembley. In 1950 they had played in gold shirts, in 1971 in yellow shirts and blue shorts. They had won both times but this time they reverted to the familiar. It was the first time in five finals Arsenal had worn red and only the fifth time (1951, 1968, 1970, 1972 were the others) in 12 postwar finals that they had worn their own colours.

The game was on 5 April. The press unfailingly chose Liverpool, who had already won the trophy on four consecutive occasions in the 1980s. Liverpool had, of course, won 1-0 at Highbury a month before. It was to be Ian Rush's last appearance at Wembley before his move to Juventus, perhaps his last ever. Liverpool had even set a record with a 10-0 defeat of Fulham on their way to the final. But this was, perhaps, all a little misleading. Arsenal had lacked Anderson, Rocastle and Williams when they lost 1-0 four weeks before. And while their back four was now as solid as the Bank of England, Liverpool would take the field stringing Venison, Gillespie, Hansen and Whelan across their last line of defence. These were hardly bad players, but this was surely not the cast-iron pedigree that Anfield had been putting out for the past two decades. This was surely not the Liverpool of Keegan, Smith or Souness. With Rush going, was this to be the evening of the most sustained period of success ever seen in the English game, even more successful that the Arsenal of the 1930s?

After 23 minutes Craig Johnston put Ian Rush through to open the scoring. Tediously the football world told itself, yet again, that Liverpool had never lost any of the games (almost 150) in which Ian Rush had scored. But even the oldest and most repeated records have to go eventually (he scored against Norwich in the League a week later, and Liverpool lost again) and it was to be the enigmatic Charlie Nicholas who did the damage. The Gunners seemed remarkably unaffected by Rush's goal (after all, they had never been ahead against Spurs until the 299th minute of the 300 minute semi-final marathon) and effectively took control for the remaining three-quarters of the match. Nicholas poked the ball home after a scramble on the stroke of half-time and it was Liverpool who had their backs to the wall for the second half.

Seven minutes from the end Perry Groves, nephew of Vic, and on as a substitute, roared in from the left, depositing a trail of defenders behind him and pushed the ball to Nicholas. The golden boy shot rather weakly, but the ball took a peculiarly spinning deflection and left Grobbelaar stranded as it meandered into the net. It was really Perry Groves' goal but Charlie got credit for them both and that was that.

Graham said afterwards: 'We have often played better; but the prize at the end made it one of Arsenal's most memorable performances. It makes it a dream start for me, but this is just the start.' The scorer was less subdued: 'This must have been my most memorable performance – I not only got two goals but made a real contribution to the team. It makes up for some of the bad times I've had since coming South.' In one Wembley appearance he had scored half as many goals as he scored in the League all season – but there are no prizes for which of the two statistics the world will remember.

The Times was more realistic and offered more promise: 'Arsenal had no need to win the Littlewoods Cup at Wembley. Their season has already been lined with enough golden memories. To add a touch of silver as well is not only highly lucrative but it is an unexpected bonus that no one could realistically have foreseen when their centenary season began seven months ago.'

But after that unexpected bonus to conclude their first 100 years, Arsenal and George Graham were quickly brought back to a shuddering start to the second one hundred. The very first game of Graham's second season in charge was at home to Liverpool on 15 August. A crowd of 55,000 saw the Gunners lose 2-1 and suffer a goalless draw at Old Trafford four days later. These were to be the sides which finished first and second in the League and which the Gunners only occasionally looked like emulating. A week later Arsenal were 19th in the First Division.

Although Arsenal never seemed likely to conquer Liverpool in the League in 1987-88, they did put together a run of 14 consecutive wins between 12 September and 17 November 1987. This was not only a club record, but also a record for any English club, equalling the number of games won by Bristol City in 1905, Manchester United in 1904-05 and Preston in 1951.

But, to be blunt, the season went into decline after this impressive spell. Injuries to David O'Leary and doubts about Kenny Sansom's future (Tony Adams had taken over as captain) unsettled the usually imperturbable defence, while Alan Smith's arrival did not immediately solve the basic problem – not enough goals.

There was a promising run in the FA Cup, with a good victory over Manchester United in the fifth round and a home quarter-final against Forest. But this game was a moment of truth (as a game against the same opponents was to prove a season later), with Forest playing superbly to win 2-1 and disappoint another massive crowd. Arsenal were made to appear firmly one grade below the very top in English football, although Forest themselves could finish only third behind all-conquering Liverpool.

Liverpool managed an easy double over Arsenal in January 1988, and Manchester United won at Highbury a week later. This was really the end of Highbury's pretensions for another season – although they had briefly led the League in November (they were to do the same in late autumn in all three of Graham's first seasons in charge – it was clearly a good time of year for the club.) There were relatively few consolations, despite a respectable sixth place. There was a double over Spurs to celebrate (both games ending 2-1) but these games appeared increasingly

provincial compared with the real contest – which had to be fought out and won at Anfield, Old Trafford and the City Ground. Goal-scoring remained the clear problem. Graham backed his judgement on Alan Smith, who led the scorers with a mere 11 in the League and another five in the Cup competitions. Few others contributed significantly. Michael Thomas scored nine in the League from full-back and midfield (though two were penalties), Rocastle got seven and Groves six. This was not a Championship-winning attack by anybody's standards, but Graham refused to be panicked or to buy players whom he felt did not fit.

Charlie Nicholas played just the first three games of the 1987-88 season and then disappeared into the reserves. He was eventually sold, unreplaced, to Aberdeen in January 1988 and disappeared into a rather sad, relative obscurity. Here was a classic case of unfulfilled promise.

Graham kept looking for another forward to complement Smith, but made only one serious bid – £2 million for Tony Cottee at the end of the 1987-88 season. Although Arsenal were prepared to match terms, Cottee chose to go to Everton, which was perhaps an interesting comment on the perceptions of Arsenal at that time. If Cottee had come to Highbury, his transfer would at last have superseded the nine-year-old club transfer record of $1,250,000 for the non-playing Clive Allen. Graham, perhaps more by necessity than choice, encouraged Paul Merson at the end of the 1987-88 season, partly because the previous year's leading scorer Martin Hayes had slipped into a surprising obscurity. It was very odd to find Hayes (who scored 19 goals in 35 League games and another four in the Cup competitions in 1986-87), scoring just once in 27 League appearances a season later. As it happened, Hayes also scored a sub's goal at Wembley against Luton where Arsenal reappeared in the Littlewoods Cup final.

Sunday 24 April 1988 was a delightfully bright, sunny day and an unexpectedly pleasing conclusion to a season that would probably otherwise be called disappointing. Back at Wembley for the Littlewoods Cup final, Arsenal were faced with a very different proposition from 1987, when they had defeated hot favourites Liverpool to take the trophy for the first time. In 1988 the positions were firmly reversed. Arsenal's opponents this time were Luton Town, who had never won a trophy in their 102-year history and who arrived at Wembley with morale, injury and selection problems.

Arsenal won all their seven games on the way to the final, scoring 15 goals and conceding only one. Their opponents had been Doncaster, Bournemouth, Stoke, Sheffield Wednesday and Everton and the highlight was clearly the first leg of the semi-final at Goodison Park. Perry Groves had scored the only goal to give the Gunners a comfortable lead, which was built on with a pleasing 3-1 win in the second leg at Highbury.

Luton had experienced a considerably more traumatic season. A few weeks before the final all had seemed to be going so well. Luton had reached the final of the Simod Cup (previously the Full Members Cup), the semi-final of the FA Cup and were in the Mercantile Classic Centenary celebration to be played among 16 clubs at Wembley on 17 April (Arsenal failed to qualify for this peculiar event, in the company of all major London clubs except Wimbledon). Luton were, therefore, looking to play an unprecedented four times at Wembley in the space of six weeks. It all went horribly wrong. They lost the FA Cup semi-final 2-1 to Wimbledon when they really should have done much better. Even worse, they somehow contrived to lose the Simod Cup final 4-1 to lowly Reading, who spent the rest of the season failing to avoid relegation from the Second Division. Luton were then knocked out in their first game in the 16-team Mercantile tournament and came back to Wembley for the Littlewoods Cup understandably shell-shocked.

As it happened, it was the Arsenal defence which was shell-shocked after a quarter of an hour at Wembley. After Harford had very nearly put Luton ahead with a powerful header, Foster put Brian Stein neatly through to score well and make it Luton 1 Arsenal 0. Well, Luton scored first against Reading thought the Gunners fans, and look what happened next.

The 1988 Littlewoods Cup appeared to be going Arsenal's way ten minutes from the end when Alan Smith scored this goal by squeezing the ball between the Luton keeper and the post.

Below: **With eight minutes left** in the 1988 Littlewoods Cup final, and Arsenal leading and in command, Andy Dibble made a brilliant save from Nigel Winterburn's penalty. It was a moment that turned the match.

Smith, Rocastle and Groves were conspicuous by their near absence from proceedings and, indeed, after an hour Groves was replaced by Martin Hayes. This proved an excellent substitution. Hayes gave width and pace and, with a quarter of an hour left, scored after a scramble. Five minutes later Paul Davis put the ball wide to Alan Smith, who went out to the right and then shot just between keeper Andy Dibble and the post. It was an excellent goal and, for Smith, only his second in ten games.

Only two minutes later Smith headed against the bar and Martin Hayes contrived to hit the post with the rebound from literally a yard out. Arsenal, after stuttering for an hour, were suddenly totally in charge, surging forward through a tired Luton midfield. Smith went through twice, only to see Dibble save well. Then with eight minutes left Rocastle fell in the area, the referee harshly said he was tripped and Nigel Winterburn, who had scored only once before for Arsenal, took the penalty. The shot went to Dibble's left, but the Luton reserve keeper dived beautifully and tipped it round the post. It was only the second penalty ever missed in a major Wembley final, Clive Walker's for Sunderland v Norwich in the 1985 League Cup final being the other (John Aldridge was to add a third against Wimbledon in the FA Cup final later in the season).

Winterburn and Arsenal were made to pay within seconds. Caesar stumbled and lost the ball in the penalty area. A chaos of bodies ensued, ending with Danny Wilson making it 2-2 with just five minutes left.

Arsenal's first half was no better than poor and Luton started the second half the way they did the first. After just two minutes a superb save by Lukic from a Brian Stein header saved the day and was one of the moments of the season.

That wasn't the end, for with virtually the last move of the match Ashley Grimes came round the back of Arsenal's left side, hammered the ball with the outside of his left foot to Brian Stein and into the net it went: 3-2 to Luton.

It was an astonishing finish to a peculiar game. For Arsenal the memories had to be of Smith and Hayes hitting the woodwork with successive shots, and then of Winterburn's penalty miss (or, more accurately, of Dibble's save). Arsenal were on top for just 15 minutes but in that time they scored twice and should probably have another two goals.

Although there were three League games left, this was the end of Arsenal's season. It had begun badly enough (a 2-1 home defeat by Liverpool) and ended at Wembley in a perverse defeat. Sixth place in the League was not exceptional by Highbury standards, and it was clear that the undefeated early run had flattered to deceive (10 consecutive League wins were followed by only one win in the next 11 League fixtures). But, underneath it all, the mixture was bubbling. Within 12 months events were to follow which would leave indelible memories.

After two years in charge Graham was beginning to build a pattern of his own. Unlike Liverpool, Manchester United and Spurs, he kept away from the big signings. At the same time as Liverpool were spending no less than £5.5 million to buy a forward line (Aldridge, Barnes, Beardsley and Rush, though the latter was a return ticket), Graham stuck to Alan Smith at £800,000. The only public enquiry he made was for Tony Cottee, though it was clear Highbury was not any striker's preferred destination. Apart from the Littlewoods Cup win, Arsenal had only won one trophy since the Double – the FA Cup of 1979 – and the really talented players wanted either medals (which tended to mean Liverpool) or money (which meant Italy or Spain, with Old Trafford next best).

Nonetheless, Graham was not short of talent. He had inherited Tony Adams, David Rocastle, Paul Davis and Michael Thomas. All were coming to their peak and all would attract England's attention. The full-back slots had been a problem with the decline of Kenny Sansom and the failure of Gus Caesar or Michael Thomas to replace Viv Anderson, who headed off to a final payday at Old Trafford. Graham solved the problem competently by replacing Sansom (who went, unhappily, to Newcastle for a season) with Nigel Winterburn (who cost £400,000) and buying Lee Dixon from Stoke for the same modest £400,000 ultimately to fill the right-back spot. Winterburn, still then best known for his Wembley penalty miss, had been apprehensive about replacing Sansom: 'I was worried about being compared with Kenny – after all, he's won more caps than any other England left-back. Then I realised that the comparisons would be made anyway, so I just concentrated on my own game. Highbury's a bit like Wimbledon really. When I was there we were always being criticised but we drew strength from these attacks. The mood's the same in the Arsenal dressing room. We've scored more goals than any other team in 1988-89, yet as soon as we experiment with a sweeper we're called negative.'

The shot that finally meant Arsenal's 1987-88 season would end without a trophy. In the very last minute Brian Stein scores to complete Luton's late recovery from 1-2 down and being outplayed to 3-2 winners.

Alan Smith, one of Arsenal's great successes of the Championship season, steals in to score a typical goal in a 3-2 victory at Tottenham in the season's third League game.

Graham's other signings before the Championship season of 1988-89 were equally modest – Brian Marwood from Sheffield Wednesday for £600,000, third centre-back Steve Bould from Stoke for £390,000 and Kevin Richardson for £200,000 from Watford. It was to be a particularly memorable year for Richardson, who became one of the few players to win a Champions' medal with two different clubs – he also has one from Everton in 1985.

Graham improvised well, fitting his new players to the existing structure and covering up well where he had clear deficiencies. This even led, towards the end of the season, to the three centre-back sweeper system after the ponderous offside trap had been severely battered at Highbury by both Forest and Charlton.

The team was not entirely unlike the Double side of 1971 in that it depended on perspiration rather than inspiration and, in David Lacey's words, was: '... fast, fit and pragmatic. They play the long ball towards the head of Smith and depend on the breakdown of opposition movements as a springboard for counter-attack.'

The Arsenal of 1989 were not as resilient as their predecessors of 1971. They lost and drew games the Double team would have won. Radford, Kennedy, Storey, Simpson and McLintock would force results in games where the team played badly. The 1989 team were not as dependable, particularly at Highbury where, on occasions, they looked frighteningly frail. Again, the Double team had two clear creative talents – Charlie George and George Graham – who had no real equivalents in 1989. David Rocastle came closest, winning the Barclays 'Young Eagle of the Year' Award, but there was no pretension to the pure skill of a Liam Brady or the sheer unexpected explosiveness of George at his best. To an extent, though, this was a reflection of a changing game as much as a changed Arsenal.

Middlesbrough manager Bruce Rioch said of Arsenal early in the 1988-89 season: 'They work

extremely hard to take possession. If you can't stop service into the penalty area, you're in trouble. They have massive midfield strength. Once they get the ball in your half they keep it there. They pressure you on the ball so you make mistakes. It's not easy playing them, and not very pretty either.' Arsenal were not averse to the long-ball game, and it was here that their dependence on Alan Smith became clear. As the season progressed, he played better and better, ending it as the First Division's top scorer and an international. His performance at Liverpool in the final game was quite outstanding. 'You could have fired a cannonball at him that day and he'd have controlled it and laid it off to one of the midfielders without a second thought', said one of the Liverpool defenders afterwards.

The Championship season was, in truth, a patchy one. The Gunners did not reach the top of the League until Boxing Day, and then lost the lead to Liverpool with just 13 days left. They won more games away from home than at home (12 versus 10) which was very odd indeed for a Championship side. Far more peculiar was that the sides which eventually finished second (Liverpool), third (Forest) and fourth (Norwich) effectively did the same, all having better away than home records. All the top four lost at least three home games during the season.

There were four highlights in the season – and three of these games were outstanding away wins (at Everton, Forest and Anfield) and only one at home (against Norwich).

To some extent Arsenal's League ambitions were helped by early exits in the two Cup competitions. Liverpool won a League (Littlewoods) Cup third-round tie after two replays while West Ham caused a great surprise in winning an FA Cup third-round replay 1-0 at Highbury. Arsenal had managed only to draw 2-2 at Upton Park, despite West Ham's dreadful League form which eventually led to the East Londoners' relegation. Arsenal had some minor consolation in the winning of the Mercantile Credit Trophy, another rather peculiar event which was part of the League's ill-fated centenary celebrations. The final was against Manchester United at Old Trafford and Michael Thomas and Paul Davis goals led to a 2-1 victory.

The League season had begun with one of its best displays – a 5-1 victory away at FA Cup holders Wimbledon with Alan Smith scoring a very welcome hat-trick to provide a perfect foretaste of what the season was to hold for him. It was the only hat-trick that the club recorded all season – unusual for a Championship side with a good goal-scoring record (73 in the League alone). Unfortunately this was immediately followed by a 3-2 home defeat by Villa and a 2-1 reverse at Sheffield Wednesday.

Nonetheless, other results were steady and, more as the result of a very mediocre start by the other contenders (Liverpool, Forest and Everton particularly) Arsenal found themselves in second place early in November without having had to perform particularly well to get there.

On 6 November they had an outstanding televised win at the City Ground, totally outplaying Forest in a 4-1 crushing which, for the first time, made the press take Arsenal's season seriously. The goal scorers were Bould, Adams, Smith and Marwood and, although Arsenal were now second behind a very fluent Norwich, the almost universal view was still that it was a matter of waiting for Liverpool to come good.

The situation, however, seemed to have changed completely by the second of Arsenal's memorable four performances. This was at Goodison on 14 January and, by the time that match was over, the Gunners had overtaken Norwich and were firmly placed at the top of the table five points clear. This was perhaps surprising statistically as, between Forest and Everton, Arsenal played thirteen first-class games of which they drew four, lost three and won only six. This was not exactly Championship form, but in a topsy-turvy, very open season, it was enough to put them well in front.

They were also, it must be said, playing very well when it mattered. After the 3-1 win at Goodison, Peter Ball said in *The Times*: 'In the best superstitious footballing tradition, George Graham is refusing to count the Championship until it is hatched. No one else at Goodison Park on Saturday harboured any doubts about its destination as Arsenal demolished Everton with a massively authoritative performance.' Obviously Mr Dalglish had not been at Goodison that Saturday and, indeed, Liverpool were now no fewer than 11 points behind. The gap at one time between Arsenal and Liverpool was as great as 19 points, which Liverpool clawed back between January and the ultimate dénouement on 26 May. That was an astonishing achievement by Liverpool, but not unprecedented – at Christmas time 1986 Arsenal were seven points clear at the top of the League and by the end of March 1987 Liverpool were nine points ahead – a gain of 16 points in three months. So Liverpool's ability to catch up was not in doubt – it was just that this

Another excellent goal by Alan Smith, which came in a 4-1 victory at the City Ground in November 1988. Smith and Arsenal really impressed themselves on the nation in this televised match, and Arsenal's Championship prospects were obvious as they completely outplayed Nottingham Forest.

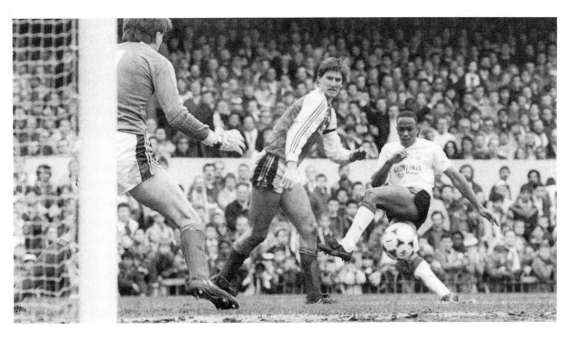

Arsenal's Championship prospects appeared to be disappearing rapidly in March 1989 when Nottingham Forest won convincingly 3-1 at Highbury. Franz Carr puts the ball past Adams and Lukic for the second Forest goal. Forest's win was almost as emphatic as Arsenal's 4-1 victory at Nottingham earlier in the season.

year it seemed so unlikely that they would, so vulnerable did they look (they had just lost 3-1 at Old Trafford).

But, above all else, it was Arsenal's performance at Goodison on 14 January which was particularly impressive. Kevin Richardson, who scored one of Arsenal's three goals for his first of the season, was exceptionally enthusiastic. 'It's like history repeating itself', he said after the game. 'The pattern, team balance and tactics are all very similar to the way Everton played in 1984-85 and that is why I find it so easy to fit in.' Richardson, who won a Championship medal with that Everton team in 1984-85, continued: 'The manager has laid down the same kind of requirements on closing down opponents, denying space and putting quality balls into the box. The Arsenal players are far more experienced now, having had two seasons when they've led the League for a while, and now we have the insurance of a five-point lead. If we don't win it now, it will be the fault of the players and nobody else.'

At Goodison Arsenal brought their impressive away record to eight wins and 29 away goals, true Championship form. This was particularly good as they were troubled by injury at the centre of defence where O'Leary and Caesar were both only second-choice options, even when available. It was David Rocastle, though, who proved Everton's downfall. The first goal was the result of a fierce cross from the right which Merson finished off with the relish of a forward enjoying his sixth goal in seven games. Just seven minutes later Rocastle went past Sheedy to the bye-line, hammered over a cross and Alan Smith flung himself at it for goal number two. Richardson scored a clever third against his old club after a neat one-two with the outstanding Smith.

One of the few advantages of Liverpool's dominance of the 1980s was that no-one else was expected to win anything, which took the pressure off them. It was only after the Everton game

that Arsenal became Championship favourites and it is an interesting comment on what happened in the next four months that the bookmakers gradually changed their quotes from odds-on at the end of January to no less than 7-1 against on 26 May.

As soon as Arsenal became favourites, the pressure was on. Instead of a steady, if not triumphal, progress towards their rightful prize, the campaign became one of slow attrition, with Liverpool gradually creeping up point by point, week by week, and most people thinking that Liverpool were bound, in the end, to win it. Between the start of the year and that dramatic dénouement on 26 May Liverpool, in fact, played 24 games undefeated. In a sense, that was irrelevant to Arsenal. All the Gunners had to do was keep winning with memorable frequency and the title would be theirs. It was not like that of course, as we all know. Of the 17 games between Goodison and Anfield, Arsenal lost three (two at home) and drew five. Those 19 points dropped could have been, and indeed seemed, crucial as Liverpool closed a gap that had been precisely that size.

A 0-1 stutter at Coventry on 21 February was perhaps excusable, but the crisis really struck when Forest destroyed the leaders at Highbury on 11 March. This was the game that everyone attended knowing Arsenal had to win, but Forest scored three times in the first half and made the defence look ponderous, unintelligent and porous. In particular, the speed of Franz Carr and the intelligence of Nigel Clough turned the supposedly well-rehearsed offside-trap into a shambles. This was the third time Forest had won at Highbury in two seasons and suddenly the Gunners, though still leading the League, looked anything but Champions. Ten days later lowly Charlton, perennial relegation candidates, drew 2-2 at Highbury and George Graham made a critical move with the change that probably secured the Championship.

Deciding his rearguard was too vulnerable, and with three experienced centre-backs now free from injury, he decided to change the pattern. Switching from the traditional four-across-the-back that Forest had so exposed, he switched to the very rare (in England) sweeper system with a third centre-back. By having David O'Leary sweep behind Bould and Adams, Graham reduced the liklihood of fast breaks cutting through a square back four. In addition, and as important, Graham perceived that, as few opponents played more than two men up front against Arsenal, the sweeper would allow the full-backs Dixon and Winterburn to push upfield to support David Rocastle and Kevin Richardson. This, in turn, released Rocastle from defensive duties and allowed him to go forward. In atack it worked perfectly – the full-backs scored three critical goals in the games that followed and midfielders Thomas and Rocastle two each. As a system it was seen at its best against Liverpool at Anfield, when the full-backs were key elements in the intense system of constant pressure that Arsenal applied to the home club and which, in the end, won them the game and the title.

It was rare for a club leading the League to change its tactics so late in the season but, as Graham said: 'I've always been a good learner and I'm prepared to apply the things I've learned. It's up to me to come up with solutions to the problems that present themselves. The players were no problem at all. I only told them about it a week before we put it into effect (against Manchester United on 2 April) but they were very willing to try it.' Tony Adams agreed: 'In my six years with the club we've always played with four across the back, but when the boss asked us to try it, we just got on with it. Good players adapt. Our usual 4-4-2 was becoming a bit stereotyped. We were all pushing up and getting caught on the break – like we did against Forest. But we've had to go for three points each time and this way we can use three attackers instead of two and the full-backs can push forward. We still have a solid base in defence.'

The Manchester United game was not the happiest for Adams, for he conceded an unlucky late own-goal when a difficult spinning ball struck him and went past Lukic. This drew peculiar response from what we must assume to be an anti-Arsenal tabloid press, the *Mirror* in particular attacking Adams in the most puerile and unimaginative way. Happily for Arsenal, the result was that it probably bonded the team closer than ever and led to Adams' most productive spell of the season. Indeed, the time between the 2-2 draw with Charlton on 21 March and the game against Derby on 13 May was really the period when Arsenal won the Championship. It was their best spell of the season, with five wins and the unlucky draw against United. Coming directly after a run of five matches in which they had picked up only four points, it restored belief and made the pulsating finish possible.

On 8 April Arsenal were finally overtaken by Liverpool and lost first place, if only for four hours. Liverpool kicked off at Anfield in the morning that day (because the Grand National was in the afternoon) and so went to the top of the table. Arsenal took the lead back again after a hard fought win over Everton (Lee Dixon scoring from 25 yards for the first goal and Niall Quinn getting the second on his first appearance of the season) but the signs were ominous. The game was hardly a classic, but chairman Peter Hill-Wood was not downhearted: 'My feeling is that whether we win the League of not, I see no reason why we shouldn't go on to have a great deal of success with this team. I've never been so hopeful about the future.'

In many respects the season had been a progressive one. The new stand, giving Highbury four-sided cover for the first time, was opened on 13 May. The 54 Clock End boxes (the famous clock was retained on top) paid for all the building work and enabled the club to add conference facilities and restaurants. Managing director Ken Friar included other developments at the same time: 'We'll be installing two electronic scoreboards – one on the East Stand and one on the West Stand – which can be seen from virtually everywhere in the ground. We're replacing every seat in the ground with upgraded seating which will take us into the 1990s and we're spending £150,000 on refurbishing all the toilet facilities and another £100,000 on new crash barriers and related works on the terraces. And there is one more important improvement we'll be carrying out during the summer – we're laying a completely new pitch.' To many, this last item was good news indeed. The poor state of the Highbury pitch – for seasons so immaculate – was thought to have contributed greatly to the team's relative failure at home. Certainly if they had played as well at home as away, the title race would not have reached anywhere near the last day. Arsenal had very carefully and cleverly avoided the considerable heat and dust generated elsewhere (and particularly at Tottenham) over the building of executive boxes. Rather than take up existing space on the side stands or completely rebuild a grandstand, they had added the boxes at the southern end and had deprived no-one of their favourite spot nor left the club open to accusations of abandoning the 'real' an in favour of corporate freeloaders. As a piece of financially astute public relations, this was of a high quality rarely associated with football clubs but in keeping with Arsenal's deserved image for competence and decency. By maintaining the classic, listed 1930s stands exactly as they are, they have also maintained a feeling of comfort *and* history which is now unmatched by any other League ground and likely to stay that way for a long time into the future. It is a remarkable credit to the club of 50 years ago that these two magnificent, matching symbols of the Chapman era should still be so suited to their purpose today.

A dull 1-0 win over Newcastle on 15 April was totally overshadowed by what happened 200 miles further north, at Hillsborough. Liverpool's sudden surge from 19 points behind, their dra-

Arsenal's 1988-89 Championship seemed to have disappeared for good when Derby County won 2-1 at Highbury in the third-last match of the League programme. Part of Arsenal's problem was the superb form of Peter Shilton, punching clear from Adams, and Rocastle.

matic unbeaten run since the New Year and the prospect of another Double had generated an astonishing amount of interest in the FA Cup semi-final against Forest, a repeat of the previous year's fixture in Sheffield. These were the two in-form clubs – having lost just two of 44 fixtures between them in 1989. The crowds at Hillsborough were massive, including thousands without tickets. The consequences are too well known to need repeating here, but the deaths of 95 fans were to cast long, long shadows over the English game for many years.

After the disaster there was considerable confusion as to what would happen next. Liverpool naturally suspended their fixtures, including the vital game against Arsenal at Anfield. Highbury refused the League's thoughtless request to continue as normal and immediately cancelled their next game. Arsenal did not take the field again for another 16 days.

When they did, on May Day, it was for a fixture which had been expected, several months before, to determine the Championship. Norwich had led the League up to Christmas and had maintained their challenge until the past few weeks. Then their collapse had been far more comprehensive than Arsenal's and this was their

last chance to struggle back into the race. The Gunners, however, chose this day for their best display of the season to date (the very best was yet to come). As Stuart Jones said in *The Times*: 'Arsenal withdrew the hand of friendship and sympathy which had been so generously extended to Liverpool. The First Division leaders, whose reaction to Hillsborough was so honourable and dignified, confirmed that now they will show no mercy to opponents or to Merseyside.'

Norwich were completely overrun. Their manager Dave Stringer said afterwards: 'We were outclassed and outplayed. It was a hammering. We finished as also-rans. On that performance, Arsenal will walk away with the title.' George Graham was more guarded: 'Even if we finish first, it will be inevitably recorded by some as meaningless and empty. But there is a time for mourning and a time when you have to go back to work.'

The display was electric, despite the fact that a key figure in winger Brian Marwood was injured and would be out for the rest of the season. Dixon and Winterburn pushed up. Smith was supported everywhere and played superbly. Norwich were as vulnerable on the wings as in the centre. Winterburn, roaring through, scored the first, Smith a spectacular volleyed second just before the interval. In the second half Thomas got the third and then Smith and Rocastle provided a gala finish. It was Arsenal's biggest win of the season and it seemed to guarantee that the League race would go all the way to the end of the season, a date at this stage still unknown because of Liverpool's fixture pile-up.

There were now just four matches left for Arsenal. The next was rather more pedestrian – away at Middlesbrough, who were fighting to stay in the First Division.

There was just one goal, the result of what appeared to be an inspired substitution by George Graham. Martin Hayes, who had not scored all season, came on in the 67th minute, was immediately fouled by Parkinson, got up and promptly scored. Lukic hammered the ball up field, Smith headed it on and Hayes just managed to squeeze it in. The rest of the game is perhaps best forgotten, though it certainly bears comparison with the hard, taut game against Stoke at the end of the Double season, when substitute Eddie Kelly scored an absolutely essential goal.

After Middlesbrough came the stumble. All Arsenal needed to do by then was keep their heads up through the next two matches – at home to Derby and Wimbledon – and then the most they would need was a draw at Anfield in the last game of the season, even assuming Liverpool won all their remaining matches. But the team seemed to crack. On Saturday 13 May Derby came to Highbury and went away with a 2-1 win. As George Graham said afterwards: 'We didn't take our chances and Peter Shilton was in superb form. If anything we were too keen. We hit too many long balls when we needed to build from the back. It's easy to demand patience from the

players but it's hard for them to keep showing it when there is so much at stake. We've got to bounce back. We've been written off so many times before that it would be silly to write us off just yet.' But in his programme notes Graham sounded a touch less confident, as if he was going through the motions, saying the right things, that not even he could really believe Liverpool would be beaten now. He declared, for instance, that he had derived great satisfaction from the developments of the past three seasons and that he wanted Arsenal to take over from Liverpool as the yardstick by which football was measured.

In the still small hours it was hard for anyone really to believe that they could now do it. It was statistically possible, but no longer very likely. Liverpool were back on top. There were two games left. The penultimate match was at home against Wimbledon on Wednesday 17 May. The Dons were never easy opponents, although Arsenal had destroyed them 5-1 at Plough Lane on the opening day of the season. That was easily Wimbledon's worst defeat of the season and they came looking for revenge. They achieved it of sorts, with a 2-2 draw that seemed to spell the end of any lingering hope for the Gunners. It descended as nothing less than a tragedy to the hordes pouring away from Highbury that night; their favourites seemed to have thrown it away by failing to win two home fixtures at the end of the season. Surely these games were the acid tests of Champions? Surely these were the games you won if you were to add your name to the panoply of greats? To take one point out of six when the Championship beckoned – it was as much as flesh and blood could bear.

Liverpool kept going. They were lucky at home to beat Forest (who were by now thoroughly sick of playing Liverpool time after time) 1-0 via a late penalty, and then ended West Ham's lingering hopes of staying in the First Division with a 5-1 win at Anfield. Two late goals in that game spelt as great a disaster for Arsenal as they did for West Ham, for they improved Liverpool's goal difference dramatically. Liverpool were now three points clear, so Arsenal had to go to Anfield and win by two clear goals. At least they had scored more than Liverpool, so two goals would do it.

Liverpool tidied up one emotional but somehow rather stunted occasion by beating Everton 3-2 in yet another Merseyside Cup final. When Liverpool won the Double in 1986 they had also beaten Everton in the FA Cup final. Here they had done it again. One game left and all Liverpool had to do was avoid defeat by two goals. A 0-1 or 1-2 defeat wouldn't be pretty, but the Double would still be theirs.

Arsenal were out of it – that was their great strength. The big bookmakers quoted them at 7-1 against, but you could have got 20-1 and better on any street corner. George Graham seemed relaxed when he was asked about the pressure a few days before: 'I hope we get this sort of pressure every year. Pressure is something the media like to talk about, but I'll tell you what

real pressure is – it's being bottom of the Third Division. This is enjoyable pressure.' When asked whether Arsenal would still win the Championship he was more guarded. 'I don't know whether we will win. I know that we can win. Any team can win one game, particularly with an away record like we've got.'

In many respects Graham was right. Arsenal's two advantages were that no-one expected them to win and, oddly, that all the top four sides had played better away than at home. This was not just a statistical freak. It was a reflection of the times and well worthy of a diversion.

Everyone now tried to build a side which could absorb pressure in defence and then score on the break. The counter-attacking game with two, or at most three, very good front players was the order of the day. Liverpool had been playing this way for some time – though with Rush, Aldridge, Barnes and Beardsley their front runners were not exactly understaffed. Forest was perhaps best at it – as Arsenal had found out to their cost – but Graham had developed along these lines with great success during the season to the point where, as a counter-attacking force, Arsenal were perhaps comparable with the James/Bastin/Hulme triangle of the early 1930s. Alan Smith was critical, his growing ability to act as a target man and control long balls forward, as well as score goals, being one of the cornerstones of the season. Brian Marwood was a key supplier, and it was fortunate that Arsenal survived his late injury so well. David Rocastle was the joker, the one man who could provide the trickery and the unexpected on the right, Michael Thomas and Kevin Richardson were the workers in midfield. Paul Merson, who filled the slot that would have been Tony Cottee's, had had a satisfactory season but ultimately did not score as many goals as he would have liked. Hence Perry Groves and Martin Hayes were always on hand as subs ready to slot into Merson's role and Graham played a 13-man team for the whole season.

To put their task in perspective, consider the following. Only twice since the 1971 Double year had Arsenal won at Anfield – the last time in November 1974. On only nine occasions since Arsenal's Double nearly 20 years before had Liverpool lost at home by two goals, the last time to Everton in 1986. The portents were not exactly encouraging.

Did it seem likely that Arsenal could perform such an unlikely feat at such an emotional moment? The game was an historian's goldmine. It was only the third time in 101 years of the Football League that the two leading clubs had met on the last day of the season with the fate of the Championship resting on the result. On one other occasion the Championsip had gone to the final match in slightly similar circumstances when the last game of the season had been the only match that day. Surprisingly, all three occasions had involved either Liverpool or Arsenal.

The first had been on 29 April 1899, when Aston Villa and Liverpool met at Villa Park, each with 43 points. Villa, with a much better goal

A 2-2 home draw with Wimbledon in the penultimate match kept Arsenal's Championship chances alive in theory, but few thought they could now win in practice. Paul Merson's goal helps Arsenal win a vital point.

average, needed only to draw, but beat Liverpool 5-0 anyway. The second occasion was a real oddity. The 1946-47 season was the most delayed ever because of an appalling winter. The final match in the First Division was not played until 14 June and it was the only game that day. It was at Bramall Lane between Sheffield United and Stoke City and Stoke needed to win to take the Championship for the only time in their history. They lost 2-1, and Liverpool became Champions.

The third occasion involved Arsenal on the last day of the 1951-52 season. They travelled to Old Trafford where Manchester United had 55 points and Arsenal 53. Arsenal's chances were only theoretical. They needed to win 7-0 (beating their best ever away win, the 7-1 Drake's game at Villa) to be Champions. Needless to say, they didn't – United won 6-1 and Arsenal came third.

In reality then, the trip to Merseyside had only one precedent in 101 years of League history – the 1899 game between Villa and Liverpool. The Stoke match was a climactic freak, the Old Trafford game a mathematical near-impossibility.

And so to Anfield. The scene was set for a tumultuous end to a deeply emotional season. There were no fences – they had been taken down after Hillsborough and the astonishing sea of scarves and flowers. There would soon be no more Kop, because Liverpool were to install seating throughout the ground. The police appealed to the crowd before the game: 'Many millions are watching. Please do not come onto the pitch at any time. If we can achieve that you will see the presentation.' The crowd obeyed. They did see the presentation, but not the one they expected.

It is impossible to recreate the atmosphere. Perhaps only United's first game after Munich or Liverpool's replayed semi-final against Forest, both played at Old Trafford, bear comparison. As David Miller said in *The Times*: 'The public came out of Merseyside's mean streets and bleak apartment blocks as the sun disappeared and poured into Anfield for the last game of the season: to share that beautiful illusion which exists inside the stadium, to enjoy the aura of reflected glory which lifts them out of the ordinariness of everyday life ... and the illusion was broken.'

The kick-off was delayed as so many Arsenal fans had been caught in traffic jams on the way to the ground. The tension was palpable, touchable. When Arsenal came out they presented a cheque for £30,000 to the Hillsborough disaster fund. All the players carried bouquets, which were taken to the supporters around the ground. It was an exceptionally thoughtful gesture, though the kindness ended here. Here was the crunch, the moment of truth, a time which these players would almost certainly never experience again in their professional lives. Liverpool had gone 24 games undefeated. It did not seem much to suppose that they would at least draw.

But Arsenal fought; fought harder than perhaps any side representing this famous club has ever fought in its history. They battled, even kicked, Liverpool out of their majestic stride. It was pressure, pressure, pressure. Dixon forced Barnes back towards his own half. Bould prevented Aldridge from controlling the ball in the way he had done all season. Richardson, Thomas and Rocastle fought and harried in midfield and gradually overwhelmed their illustrious opponents. Were Liverpool tired, or did Arsenal just make them seem tired? They were leaden, they couldn't push forward, they couldn't compete with the fury of Arsenal's fight. It seemed to be sheer willpower which kept driving Arsenal forward. Their supporters seemed to be sucking the ball towards the Liverpool goal. Yet, for all this, Liverpool only had to survive. They didn't have to score themselves, they simply had to stop Arsenal scoring twice. And at half time it was still goalless. There had only been one real chance. Thomas, outpacing the aggressive McMahon, whose spirit had personified Liverpool since Hillsborough, put over a beautiful cross from the right. Grobbelaar missed it but Bould rose beautifully. Somehow, Nicol got to the header and deflected it over the bar.

In retrospect 0-0 at half time was a good thing. If Arsenal had scored in the first half it would have given Liverpool time to regroup and to come back, to score an equaliser and make the Gunners' task impossible. The ideal scenario had always been two late goals, preferably late enough to stop Liverpool replying or allowing the Arsenal players to relax for a moment.

The second half was as frenetic as the first. Said Patrick Barclay in *The Independent*: 'The tackling was ferocious. Seldom can English football have been played with such intensity.' The first goal came after 52 minutes. Nicol was punished for a foul on the edge of the Liverpool area. Winterburn went over to take the free kick. The ball drifted across the goal to the far post, where Alan Smith suddenly appeared, unmarked, to deflect it off the side of his head into the corner of the net. The Liverpool players surrounded the referee, David Hutchinson. The linesman had briefly flagged. Why? Some Liverpool players claimed a foul, others that Smith had not touched the ball from that indirect free-kick. Hutchinson consulted the linesman. Ten million watching caught them in close up, as their conversation happened straight in front of the touchline camera. The destination of the Championship rested on that minute. The officials finally agreed: no foul, no reason to disallow the goal. Television replays showed they were absolutely right. Liverpool panicked. Rush had gone off in the first half after a distant shot (the best of the night from the home side) had caused him a leg injury. Beardsley was on in Rush's place, but Liverpool could not string their passes together. Everything foundered on the rock of the sweeper and Arsenal's determination and commitment. Never can a football team have expended so much energy in a mere 90 minutes.

But while Liverpool were panicked, Arsenal were sitting on a depreciating asset – time. The minutes ticked by and it became harder to create a clear chance anywhere. Only one good one was to appear in normal time. After 74 minutes a pass from Richardson found Thomas with an instant to spare on the penalty spot. He shot quickly, but not hard enough and too predictably and Grobbelaar saved easily going slightly to his right. Grobbelaar had not appeared on the losing side in 28 appearances so far this season. As long as it stayed 1-0, he wouldn't mind losing this one.

In the electric atmosphere of the Championship decider at Anfield, the inevitable Alan Smith helps Arsenal's cause by giving them the lead with a neat deflection from the side of his head after Adams had missed the cross. There was an extraordinary hushed delay before the goal was allowed because a nervous linesman had momentarily raised his flag.

The sands of time were running out. It was to be the nearest close-miss in history. The Kop breathed a sigh of relief as Arsenal seemed to have beaten themselves out pounding on the rock of Liverpool, a rock that seemed to be saying: 'Forget tonight, history is ours. This is the season of Hillsborough and the Double. This is what was meant to be.' With just three minutes left, a lull. Kevin Richardson was injured. Liverpool had stopped pressing completely. They had hardly had an effective attack all night. It was

easy to say afterwards that they were unlucky knowing that even a one-goal defeat was enough. If they had to win, maybe they would have played differently. Perhaps. But when the referee correctly added two minutes on for Richardson's injury, Liverpool had just five minutes left to hold out.

The game completed its allotted 90 minutes. The Kop whistled frantically for the finish, not just to the match, but to a season and to its place in the history books. The seconds ticked by as Arsenal pressed forward again. Surely one last time. A clearance from Lukic was controlled by Dixon, who pushed a long ball through to the magnificent Alan Smith, 30 yards from goal. Michael Thomas ran into the inside-right slot inside Smith. The centre-forward lobbed the ball on, straight into Thomas's path. The clock said 91 minutes and 26 seconds, 86 seconds overtime. Would there even be time for Thomas to finish the move? Steve Nicol came across to tackle. The ball bounced off the defender, onto Thomas and forward. Thomas was clear. He surged into the penalty area. Nicol and Houghton flung themselves at him in desperation. Grobbelaar, everything at stake, came out and spread himself. Thomas waited, then flicked the ball over Grobbelaar's body into the right-hand corner of the net. 2-0. There was a stunned silence and then,

Arguably the most memorable League goal ever scored. *Above:* Michael Thomas has just clipped the ball in the final minute of the final match of the season at Anfield, and the ball is on its way past Grobbelaar into the Liverpool net. It was the goal that made Arsenal, rather than Liverpool, the Champions.

Right: **A split second later** and Michael Thomas knows that he has scored the most dramatic goal in the whole history of the Football League – a climax to a season that can only happen once in 100 years.

from the Arsenal fans, euphoria. The Double was gone; the Championship surely snatched from the jaws of certain Arsenal failure. Thomas, scorer now of the most famous goal in Arsenal history, ran at the Gunners fans and took off in a flying somersault. It was a gesture of astonishment rather than excitement. For the millions watching it was beyond belief. 'Re-run the video, it can't have happened. We've strayed into a film 'script. Seasons just *don't* end like this.' It was many minutes before anyone believed it really had happened.

There were a few seconds left. Long enough for hero Thomas to intercept a Liverpool attack in his own penalty area and put the ball calmly back to Lukic. The whistle went. The most dramatic domestic season in living memory, probably ever, was at an end. Arsenal were Champions. For the first time the Championship trophy was presented as if it were the FA Cup. And how ironic that Arsenal received it at Anfield. The Kop applauded them; the dream for Liverpool was over.

The memories were inevitably of another late goal, of another Double. But that goal, from a yellow and blue shirted Charlie George against a similarly red shirted Liverpool had won a Double, whereas Michael Thomas's had prevented one. George lay down, a never to be forgotten gesture, Thomas took off in his somersault, another never to be forgotten moment.

George Graham was understandably euphoric: 'We have laid a foundation of belief at Highbury. If you lose hope, or lose belief, you may as well get out of football. Tonight was the fairytale, the unpredictable that makes us all love football. There is no doubt that we had a mountain to climb. A lot of people thought we would get carried away and try to play gung-ho football but in fact we were very controlled and content to be 0-0 at half time.' Graham gave the credit to his players, particularly Tony Adams: 'He has suffered a lot of stick which has been very undignified and done little for football. But he has proved his strength and character, and we all did that tonight. At the end of the day it is the players who go on and do it on the pitch, and we're delighted for them. It was nice to see Michael Thomas get the winner. In the first half of the season he was the most effective midfield player in the country. He has had a lapse, but exceptional players don't go bad overnight and he has soldiered on, staying in the side because of Paul Davis's injury. He's had his reward.'

Kenny Dalglish, who is now acknowledged as little short of a statesman after a desperately difficult season, retained his dignity to the end: 'We never accept second best at Liverpool, but I'm proud of the players and their achievements this season. I don't blame the end-of-season schedule pile-up for our defeat. We won the Cup final well enough. The Double just wasn't meant to be.'

The commentators found analysis almost impossible in the shadow of such unexpected and unlikely events. Rob Hughes probably got closer

Scenes that had become rather rare for the Highbury faithful. The triumphant Champions return to London, which on a sunny day seems to have turned red – even Spurs fans will not begrudge the fact that the cockerel in the foreground is on a red background.

than anyone else: 'Arsenal looked like nervous wrecks in surrendering home points to Derby and Wimbledon. They were lions at Anfield. The reason, I believe, is that they are better chasing a cause than protecting one. If the roles had been reversed, and if Arsenal had been three points ahead with the final game at Highbury, what then would have been the result?' What indeed, but it is difficult enough to explain what acutally happened without speculating on what might have been. What did happen is that Arsenal won the League Championship in circumstances which no fiction writer would have dared to create. It truly was the most remarkable end to a League season ever.

There was something unique about neutral reaction to Michael Thomas's show-stopper at Anfield. The time-honoured gripes about 'lucky Arsenal' were non-existent. And after showing such a timely sense of drama by clinching the title a minute into injury time, they could hardly

be accused of being 'boring'. Instead, the nation acclaimed George Graham. After all, he had broken the monotony of Merseyside's stranglehold on the Championship.

Liverpool and Everton had reduced the 1980s to a tug-of-war across Stanley Park and had cemented the North-West as domestic football's power base. Now, Arsenal had not only shifted the game's epicentre back to the capital; they had become the first team to seize custody of the trophy south of Birmingham since their own Double season in 1970–71.

Only Liverpool had defended the Championship successfully in that period and, in the 1989–90 season, the Gunners found themselves cast in the role of coconuts on a fairground shy.

The Charity Shield gave Dalglish's men token revenge for their last-gasp heartbreak of three months earlier, but Arsenal's opening League match — at Old Trafford — provided Graham with much more worrying evidence that his

summer transfer market inactivity would be a handicap. His policy of continuity seemed to back-fire instantly.

Manchester United, expensively refurbished by Alex Ferguson, looked irresistible candidates to succeed the Gunners as Champions in a 4–1 win that was as sobering for Graham as it was misleading for Ferguson. Arsenal repaired much of the damage by winning five of their next six games, but the United result told Graham that his team was living on borrowed time.

Brian Marwood's waning influence on the left flank, due less to declining form than deteriorating fitness, reduced to a trickle the stream of crosses on which Smith had thrived. Seven clean sheets out of nine after Old Trafford was miserly enough but Arsenal were sustained more by frugality than flair.

The run was ended, of all places, at White Hart Lane with a 2–1 defeat, although Liverpool's League Cup visit to Highbury provided

an instant tonic with Smith's goal earning the Gunners a place in the last 16. But the tone of Arsenal's season nosedived on November 23 during the home game with Norwich.

Arsenal won by the odd goal in seven, with the second of Lee Dixon's penalties converted — after a wall-pass with Canaries goalkeeper Bryan Gunn — in injury time. As Smith followed Dixon's shot into the net, he became entangled with two Norwich players, and what started as an accidental collision of limbs suddenly became an indiscriminate display of mass confrontation.

Patrick Barclay of *The Independent* observed: 'A thrilling match was spoiled by hooliganism on the pitch, which pointed to a neglected anomaly in Mrs Thatcher's Football Spectators Bill: how is it just to ban errant supporters for offences their heroes commit with impunity?'

Referee George Tyson, presumably overwhelmed by the scale of misdemeanour, took no action against those who reduced Highbury to soccer's war zone. Barclay pointed out, with some justification, the contagious qualities of feuding players: two fans felt sufficiently stirred by the prevailing pugilism to jump over the perimeter walls and join in the skirmish, which then required police intervention.

At least one Arsenal player was forcibly struck and both sides formed groups, roaming the battlefield like rival gangs. The brawl cast a long shadow over David O'Leary's club record 622nd appearance for the Gunners, a landmark he had decorated with the rare distinction of the goal which made it 3–3.

The Football Association set a new precedent within the game by levelling disciplinary charges against both clubs, the first time professional outfits had been held responsible for the conduct

David O'Leary acknowledges the crowd's tributes during his testimonial match in May 1993. He now holds Arsenal's all-time appearance record and ended his career on a remarkable high – playing in the winning team at Wembley in the FA Cup Final replay victory of 1993, as Arsenal beat Sheffield Wednesday 2-1.

of their employees. Arsenal were fined £20,000, Norwich £50,000.

At first, Graham's side showed no withdrawal symptoms from their disciplinary lapse and the following week they won 2–1 at Millwall, who had been acquitting themselves well in the top flight after gaining promotion. Not since the days when Arsenal played at Woolwich had Millwall been serious local rivals. Rocastle

An outbreak of violence at Highbury on 4 November 1989. The display of fireworks, a day early, was entirely unpredictable, particularly as Norwich are hardly renowned as a violent club. Arsenal were fined £20,000 and Norwich £50,000, but the game cast a far longer shadow. The FA deducted two points from the Gunners after a brawl at Old Trafford almost exactly a year later, and in doing so they were conscious of the earlier incident, which can have done Arsenal's cause no good at all.

survived 'the most frightening experience of my life' when he began to swallow his tongue following an off-the-ball collision with Jimmy Carter at The Den and — not for the first time — the Gunners were indebted to the swift action of physiotherapist Gary Lewin.

Arsenal were to come unstuck on Second Division Oldham's plastic pitch in the League Cup and their return to Anfield on Championship duty was less fulfilling this time, Liverpool winning 2–1. At this stage, Graham's side were showing few inhibitions in their pursuit of another title, but their season was unhinged by successive Christmas week defeats at Southampton and Aston Villa. But even worse than the 2–1 reverse at Villa Park was the spectre of ill discipline, which came back to haunt the Gunners when seven players harangued the officials after the final whistle to query the validity of the decisive goal.

All seven had to be dragged away by Lewin and assistant manager Theo Foley and, it was later revealed, they were fined £1,000 each. Significantly, Graham sacrificed the out-of-sorts Rocastle to make way for Steve Bould as the third centre-back, a throwback to the tactical triumph on which the Gunners' Championship had been founded the previous season.

For 'Rocky', it was the beginning of the end of his Highbury career. His incisive runs and

Kevin Campbell, for much of his career the foil to the more celebrated Ian Wright, volleys during the match against Chelsea on 3 October 1992. Arsenal won 2-1 with goals from Wright and Merson.

appetite for 'working the line' between both penalty boxes had been an outstanding feature of Graham's era as manager, and leaving him out of the side was condemned at the time as virtual heresy. But after Villa Park, Rocastle was never again to be an automatic choice — and Arsenal were never again allowed to forget even the slightest disciplinary indiscretion.

Adams exacted some revenge on Spurs for the setback at White Hart Lane in October by scoring the winner in the Highbury return in January 1990. It was to be the Gunners' last goal for six weeks as their season hinged on five games without a goal — three of them against Queen's Park Rangers; hardly an auspicious start to the last decade of the century.

After an FA Cup stalemate at Highbury, Arsenal were ushered from the Wembley road by two of their old employees in the Loftus Road replay: Don Howe, now in charge at Rangers, and Kenny Sansom, who scored the opening goal — his first for five years — in QPR's 2–0 win. Worse still, when the Gunners went back to Shepherds Bush on League business a fortnight later, Rangers repeated the dose and stretched Arsenal's run to just one win from 14 games. From that point, retaining the title was destined to remain no more than a pipedream and, in the end, Liverpool reclaimed their prize despite a valiant, and unexpected, challenge from Villa, which made Graham Taylor's nomination to succeed Bobby Robson as England manager a formality. Retaining the title has never been easy (in 105 years of the Championship it has happened on just 19 occasions, Arsenal succeeding in 1934 and 1935). But this was, in truth, a depressingly poor encore.

It was, all in all, a forgettable spring for Arsenal, but Graham shrewdly introduced Kevin Campbell, a raw and powerful striker who had excelled in the reserves and on loan at Leyton Orient and Leicester City, and gave him valuable experience of first-team football at Highbury. Campbell's pace was to provide a welcome injection of octane alongside Smith, who managed just three goals between New Year's Day and the end of the season, and the youngster responded to his inclusion with impressive goals against Nottingham Forest and Derby.

England's run to the World Cup semi-finals triggered the first waves of Gazzamania, but Italia 90 provided O'Leary with his own fairytale as Eire reached the last eight. 'It had been a difficult season at Arsenal,' recalls O'Leary, 'because as reigning Champions we were there to be shot at and everyone was trying to knock us off our perch. Strikers seemed to be jumping two or three inches higher for every ball and defenders appeared to be stretching an extra two or three inches for every tackle.

'Everyone wanted to beat us and we found out the hard way that the old adage is true: the only thing harder than winning titles is going out and doing it again the following year. From a personal point of view, that's what made the

World Cup finals so refreshing for me. Ireland were underdogs, nothing was expected of us and instead of everyone gnashing their teeth at us, we could relax and enjoy the competition because no-one looked on us as a credible threat.'

Ireland found themselves contesting a sudden-death penalty shoot-out with Rumania in Genoa for the right to play hosts Italy in the quarter-finals when Packie Bonner's save left you-know-who with the chance to set Ireland on the road to Rome. Arsenal fans rejoiced as much as the Gaelic hordes in Genoa when O'Leary converted his spot-kick with the aplomb of a seasoned penalty-taker.

Graham, meanwhile, had been taking a dispassionate view of his squad strength and had made up his mind that it was time for a major overhaul. The Arsenal manager, labelled a spendthrift by the media, was never converted to the school of thought which compelled some of his contemporaries to dash out and buy anyone bearing a £1 million-plus price tag. But he was not prepared to watch the likes of Villa, who had narrowly avoided relegation the previous season, leapfrog the Gunners while he merely went through the motions.

Graham broke the world record fee for a goalkeeper when he signed David Seaman from Queen's Park Rangers for £1.3 million. Most of the fee was recouped by the £1 million repatriation of John Lukic to his former club, Leeds (an unusually happy transfer for a player who was clearly the reject. Lukic had his revenge as Leeds won the League two seasons later). To be frank about it, the change of personnel between the posts was not welcomed unanimously by Arsenal supporters; Lukic had been a cornerstone of the 1989 title-winning side and few held him culpable for the 46 goals he leaked in 47 games during 1989–90 — in fact, his popularity now was greater than at any time since he left Elland Road. But Graham, always a great student of opposition strengths as well as those of his own team, had been hugely impressed by Seaman's command of his penalty box in the two FA Cup games with QPR earlier that year, and his judgement was to be thoroughly vindicated by the following May.

Also conscripted, at a total cost of £2.2 million, were Anders Limpar, an impish winger from Sweden, to fill the void left by Brian Marwood, and central defender Andy Linighan, from Norwich who was viewed by Graham as cover for Bould, Adams and O'Leary.

Were the story of 1990–91 a scriptwriter's fantasy instead of chronicled fact, publishers the length and breadth of Britain would have rejected its plot as more far-fetched than an episode of *Dynasty* and liable to capture the imagination only of those about to progress from Beatrix Potter to Hans Christian Andersen. Even by Arsenal's standards, this was a remarkable season.

Limpar's darting runs mesmerised right-backs like a bluebottle fly determined to avoid a housewife's swat. The North Bank took him instantly to their hearts. Seaman, ever-present, kept 29 clean sheets in 50 matches and commanded unqualified admiration from the terraces. And Graham's aptitude was soon to be compared with none other than Herbert Chapman.

An unbeaten run of 17 games at the start of the season was Arsenal's declaration of intent to continue the tug-of-war between Merseyside and North London for Championship supremacy. Limpar scored twice in a breathtaking display of speed and skill in the 2–2 draw at Leeds. And the Gunners avoided embarrassment in the potential banana-skin League Cup tie against Third Division Chester, who were ground-sharing with non-League Macclesfield, 20 miles away, at the time. But the two meetings with Manchester United before the end of November were firstly to remove the gloss from that flying start and then, in the League Cup, to end the Gunners' aura of invincibility.

Three seasons previously, United had been responsible for terminating the Gunners' long unbeaten run at Old Trafford; this time, they had the sheer temerity to repeat the trick at Highbury, where a Lee Sharpe hat-trick inspired them to an extraordinary 6–2 win. For Sharpe it was, despite his young age, probably to be the game of his career. Seaman had taken 17

The dependable David Seaman marshals the wall during the 1-0 defeat of Torino in the quarter-final of the European Cup Winners Cup on 15 March 1994. Arsenal won the game 1-0 with their goal coming from Tony Adams. Seaman's role in Arsenal's triumphs cannot easily be underestimated. In the four seasons from 1990 to 1994, Arsenal played 216 first class games and conceded just 165 goals. The history of the club has long been one of building on a strong defence, and it is a philosophy and a system which is unlikely to change.

Anders Limpar takes on Manchester United's Dennis Irwin in the 1993 Charity Shield at Wembley. The game was drawn 1-1, but United took the trophy home on penalties. Limpar, a crowd favourite at Highbury, was never a first team regular and, despite the lack of an inspirational alternative, George Graham sold him to Everton towards the end of the 1993-94 season.

Irwin began the furore, had their names taken by FIFA official Keith Hackett.

To their credit, both sides took instant and swingeing disciplinary measures; Alex Ferguson identified Steve Bruce, Paul Ince and Brian McClair as major perpetrators of the commotion, while Arsenal deducted a fortnight's wages from Limpar, Winterburn, Paul Davis, Michael Thomas and Rocastle. In a premeditated move to appease the FA and as a demonstration that the club was hell-bent on keeping its own house in order, Graham also forfeited a fortnight's salary after the Arsenal board sat through a video of the tempest. Chairman Peter Hill-Wood declared that the 'ultimate responsibility for conduct of the players lies with the manager' and that the Norwich and United incidents had 'sullied the name of Arsenal Football Club. Twice in one year is too often.' Graham did not volunteer to be fined by the club. It was the Arsenal board who were determined not to 'whitewash' the affair or leave the door ajar to accusations of a mere cosmetic exercise.

On November 13, a five-man FA commission deliberated for three-and-a-half hours on the Old Trafford skirmish and deducted two League points from Arsenal — precisely the punishment the directors' swift censure of their players and manager had sought to avoid. In addition, United were docked one point and both clubs were fined £50,000. To the Gunners, this amount was a drop in the ocean compared to the potential loss of revenue if they were pipped to the title by one or two points. Of the previous 30 Championships, as many as nine had been determined by such a margin. Vice-chairman David Dein estimated the commercial benefits of that glorious night at Anfield as at least £2 million to the club in sponsorship, advertising revenue and prize money.

The two-point deduction left Liverpool eight points clear at the top. The Arsenal players privately conceded that the commission's verdict was tantamount to handing the Championship to Kenny Dalglish with less than a third of the season gone. But, on the pitch, they showed no signs of a side who believed they were chasing a lost cause. Four days after the FA hearing, Southampton were trounced 4–0 at Highbury and three impressive wins over the Christmas holiday period brought the Gunners back to Liverpool's shoulder. This, in itself, was triumph over adversity after another bodyblow to Graham in the week before Christmas. Tony Adams, convicted of reckless and drunk driving at Southend Crown Court, was sentenced to four months' imprisonment.

The timing of the England defender's incarceration could scarcely have been less propitious. A first-team fixture since 1986, he had just regained his international place after losing out to Des Walker and Mark Wright in the pecking order for Italia '90. And, for Graham, who regarded Adams as the bedrock of his back line, there was no disguising the disappointment of his captain's extended leave. 'He is my eyes and

games to concede half a dozen goals — now he needed just 90 minutes for this record to be doubled. In fairness, the result — and Arsenal's collective defensive frailty on a bizarre night — turned out to be something of a freak show. Four days later, Liverpool's arrival in the capital confirmed as much when Smith, Paul Merson and a Dixon penalty sent the Champions away with their tails between their legs. Smith's strike, an exquisite half-volley with his less-favoured right foot, was the crowning moment of a personal purple patch which yielded seven goals in five games.

Six weeks earlier, however, United and Arsenal had engaged each other in an undistinguished fight for which they felt the full wrath of the FA. Richard Bott of the *Sunday Express* observed: 'Darkness closed in on English football again. The warmth and optimism generated by an Italian summer turned to the familiar chill and forboding of winter at Old Trafford.

'An astonishing free-for-all involving almost all of the game's 22 players dragged the game's reputation back into the gutter. Whether Arsenal are allowed to keep the three points they prised from the heat of battle, to prolong their unbeaten record and best start to season for four decades, becomes a relevant issue. Men of even temper and infinite wisdom will have to study the video and then act a good deal more responsibly than the participants. The powder keg always looked likely to blow. If there had not been a box of matches handy, controversy would have lit the fuse anyway when Anders Limpar scored a furiously disputed goal as the interval approached.'

As was the case in the altercation with Norwich, the referee's inertia was remarkable. Only Limpar and Nigel Winterburn, whose sandwich tackle on United full-back Dennis

Right: **The brawl at Old Trafford** on 20 October 1990 set the scene for the remarkable 1990-91 season. Even though no players were sent off, Arsenal had two points deducted and Manchester United one. This punishment was unprecedented in Football League history and, given the highly competitive nature of the First Division title race, seemed to virtually guarantee Liverpool the championship. However, things did not work out quite like that. Incidentally, Arsenal won the game at Old Trafford 1-0 with an Anders Limpar goal, one of eleven he managed in the League that season.

Below: **2 February 1991, Dennis Wise celebrates** one of the unlikeliest goals and unexpected results of the season: Chelsea's 2-1 victory over Arsenal. It was Arsenal's only League defeat of the, 38 game, season. Arsenal's was the best record of the twentieth century. The only occasions that a team had done better in Football League history were in 1888-89, when Preston did not lose any of their 22 games, and in 1893-94, when Liverpool were undefeated in 29 Second Division games (including a play-off). No other team has ever finished a League season with just one defeat.

ears in the dressing-room and my sergeant-major on the pitch,' said the manager.

Arsenal stood four-square behind their captain who, one suspects, was something of a victim of the judiciary's modern approach: making an example of a celebrity. Managing director Ken Friar pledged: 'The player has made a mistake and has been punished for it. As far as the club are concerned, he will continue to be an Arsenal player and will receive our full support.' It is to Adams' credit that he maintained a remarkable level of physical fitness; and his unequivocal refusal to sell his story of 'life on the inside' to national newspapers — who were ready to wield six-figure cheques in his direction — allowed him to resume his career with dignity.

Adams was restored to his beloved No. 6 shirt in the FA Cup fifth round at Shrewsbury

Town's Gay Meadow, where cigar-smoking John Bond's underdogs had already seen off Wimbledon in the previous round. In all, Adams missed 13 games.

Four of them comprised the fourth round FA Cup marathon with Leeds, in which Highbury witnessed two goalless draws and Elland Road most of the excitement. Limpar, with a brilliant solo goal, earned the second replay and Seaman's spectacular diversion of Gary McAllister's shot, destined for the top corner, took the sides back up the M1 for a third encore. Finally, and to the relief of both sides (who must have been sick of the sight of each other), Dixon and Paul Merson settled the issue. By this time, however, Arsenal had sacrificed the unbeaten League run of which they were justifiably proud.

The FA Cup arm-wrestle with Leeds was clearly draining the Gunners of sharpness and stamina when, on 2 February 1991, their record perished after 23 games at Stamford Bridge. Chelsea were already 2–0 up and worthy winners by the time Smith snatched a late consolation. Dixon said: 'That defeat hurt. A couple of years earlier, Liverpool had threatened to go unbeaten in the League all season until they came unstuck in the local derby with Everton. I suppose it was inevitable that we would lose our record in a local derby as well. With so many London clubs in the First Division, and all those Cup replays with Leeds, the players sometimes felt as if they were playing in a Cup Final every other week. Even so, we were disappointed with the result at Chelsea. We were beginning to believe that we really could go right through the season unbeaten in the League, even though we knew that was being unrealistic.'

It had been 103 years since a First Division team had concluded a season undefeated, Preston having not lost any of the 22 games they

played in the first ever Football League.

That setback at Stamford Bridge was to be Arsenal's last of an astonishing First Division season. They had coped so well defensively in Adams' absence that it was almost a surprise when he was recalled at Shrewsbury; less startling was the hero's reception he was afforded by the travelling fans from London, and Michael Thomas made the skipper's return a happy one with the decisive goal.

The following week, the Gunners returned to Anfield for what was becoming the annual title decider. Nothing would be cut and dried with 13 games remaining, whatever the result of this proverbial six-pointer, but Merson gave Arsenal a huge psychological advantage with the winner in a thrilling match happily spared the attrition of normal top-of-the-table dogfights. Suddenly, the talk around Highbury — though certainly not in George Graham's office — was of another Double.

The FA Cup quarter-final with Third Division Cambridge, before a season's best crowd of 42,960 at Highbury, took them a step nearer the dream. It also capped Adams' rehabilitation after his prison ordeal. Kevin Campbell put the Gunners in front with a typical opportunist effort before Cambridge, whose direct, primitive style had been described by one columnist as that of 'Wimbledon without the frills', hit back through Dion Dublin. The visitors had been galvanised into a stirring Cup run by manager John Beck's innovative methods of motivation, not least of which was pouring buckets of ice-cold water over his players before kick-off. Now, briefly, they threatened Arsenal's passage to the semi-finals before Adams, rising like a jump-jet at the far post, shattered the ambitions of Beck's would-be giant-killers.

Before the small matter of a North London semi-final with Tottenham at Wembley, the Gunners cemented their Championship challenge by taking 15 points from a possible 21, conceding just two goals in the process. Among those seven games was yet another meeting with Leeds; Campbell's double strike preserved the Gunners' unbeaten record against them and condemned Howard Wilkinson to his sixth match without a win in his exhausting personal test series with Graham.

All eyes then focused on Wembley. Twelve months previously 94 supporters had died in the disaster at Hillsborough during the Liverpool–Forest semi-final. Up to this point, the FA had never allowed a tie, other than the final, to be played at Wembley, for fear of devaluing the ultimate moment. But, apart from Wembley, no football stadium in the land, and certainly no neutral venue in the south, could have coped with the demand for tickets on a day critical to both Arsenal and Spurs.

'Common sense prevailed,' said Graham 'After Hillsborough, staging the tie at Wembley was the only acceptable solution. I don't think it devalues the glamour or pomp of the Cup final just because we're playing the semi-final there as well.' Moreover, Wembley's lush turf was a welcome change from some of the bare, heavily-sanded surfaces to which semi-finalists had been exposed in previous seasons.

For both clubs, the match was not only an historic departure from tradition but a watershed. For Arsenal, the equation was simple: lose, and another Double was gone. But for Tottenham, whose financial plight had recently come to prominence – they were reported to be

Paul Merson teases a bedraggled Standard Liege in the second leg, second round Cup Winners Cup tie in Belgium on 3 November 1993. After winning the first leg 3-0, Arsenal achieved one of their highest ever away wins with a 7-0 crushing of the Belgian side. Merson scored in both legs.

Just as Arsenal seemed set for another Double, twenty years after their first, along came Paul Gascoigne. The FA Cup semi-final of 14 April 1991 was the first to be played at Wembley. With the Hillsborough disaster fresh in the memory, it was felt that no other ground was safe enough to hold all of the Arsenal and Spurs fans who wanted to see the match. Gary Lineker is shown scoring the first of his brace of goals, this strike coming after a piece of impudent magic on the touchline from Gascoigne. But it was 'Gazza's' goal from a 30-yard free-kick which will live in the memory. Spurs went on to win 3-1 and Arsenal's Double hopes were unexpectedly dashed.

more than £10 million in the red — defeat threatened their very existence. Gascoigne's express recovery from a hernia operation gave them hope of eclipsing their rivals, installed by bookmakers as red-hot favourites . . . and although his contribution to the game lasted barely an hour, it was ultimately critical. The dramatic denouement was set to be played out with Alan Sugar and Terry Venables buying the club, it was already clear that Spurs really were in desperate straights. While we cannot play 'what might have been', it did seem that an FA Cup win and the revenue it would provide might just be the difference between survival and disappearance.

Less than five minutes of the semi-final had elapsed when Gascoigne's amazing 30-yard free-kick was too venomous for David Seaman's fingertips to alter its path towards the top left-hand corner. And when, 15 minutes later, Gary Lineker's predatory instincts finished a move inspired by Gascoigne's impudent back-heel, Arsenal's visions of another Double must have seemed like a cruel mirage to a desert explorer. Alan Smith briefly brought the dream back into view with an expertly-executed far-post header, but Lineker restored Spurs' two-goal cushion midway through the second half. Afterwards, there were tears in the Arsenal dressing-room. Graham, never arrogant in victory, managed to keep a stiff upper lip in defeat. With just five League games left, the title was still there for the taking; but the FA Cup, which had beckoned Arsenal through seven ties, was suddenly gone. It was no consolation, but Gascoigne's goal has remained one of the most startling images of a football generation. Rarely has its like been seen at such a crucial moment.

'There was nothing to choose between the sides after the first 20 minutes. That's where the match was won and lost,' reflected Graham. 'In

fact, we probably shaded it from that point onwards – but the damage had been done by then. You can't give a highly motivated team a two-goal start in Cup semi-finals because they're going to fight tooth and nail to protect it. It was a bitterly disappointing experience for my players, but the true test of their character is whether you can bounce back from these things.'

Spurs went on to win an even more remarkable final — 2–1 against Forest — during which Gascoigne committed two atrocious fouls, injuring himself so badly that he was out of the game for a season, and Gary Lineker missed a penalty. It was also the game which, in effect, spelt the end of Brian Clough's wonderful career.

Arsenal had little time to lick their wounds. Three days later, Manchester City came to Highbury and exposed the frailty of their hosts' confidence. Paul Merson and Campbell hit the target, but a 2–2 draw was by no means the tonic Graham had in mind. Liverpool, despite showing their own symptoms of fallibility, were clinging to the Gunners' shirt-tails. On the same weekend as Arsenal's Wembley heartbreak, the Mersey men — now under the management of Graeme Souness following Dalglish's shock decision to take an extended holiday on the golf course — waltzed to a 4–0 half-time lead at Leeds. That they required a fifth goal after the break to sneak home 5–4 substantiated the views of those who claimed Dalglish had baled out of a club in decline. The Liverpool of old would surely have put up the shutters and sauntered past the post instead of requiring a desperate dive at the tape.

Graham, with three of the campaign's last four games at home, knew there was no margin for error. Three points separated the sides. Arsenal had held the initiative since late February, the weekend Dalglish quit Anfield, when they thrashed Crystal Palace 4–0 at Highbury and Liverpool's internal disarray was laid bare by an unexpected 3–0 defeat at lowly Luton. Now the Gunners couldn't lose the title — they could only throw it away. Graham felt his most important task was to ensure that any tension he sensed went undetected among his squad.

Graham told startled Pressmen that his antidote to the despair which forced Dalglish into a sabbatical was gardening. 'A bunch of pansies never won the League,' said the *Today* newspaper, 'so green-fingered George grows one in his back garden to escape the managerial pressure trap. Often portrayed as a man obsessed with matching Liverpool's thirst for honours, Graham is using flower power to switch off away from the glare of publicity which claimed Dalglish.'

Nigel Winterburn, ever-present during the season and curiously overlooked by England, recalls: 'We could easily have gone unbeaten in the League all the way to February for nothing. Nobody would have remembered us for coming second in the table and going out in the FA Cup semi-finals. Or, at least, they wouldn't have remembered us for the right reasons. If we'd

blown the last few games, we'd never have lived it down. People would simply have thought we'd bottled it at Wembley and bottled it on the League run-in, and we deserved better than that for our contribution to the season.'

On April 23, with four games to go, Arsenal's lead could still have been wiped out at a stroke as Queen's Park Rangers came to Highbury. Liverpool had, on paper at least, a comfortable home game against Crystal Palace the same evening. More than 42,000 fans came armed with smelling salts and transistor radios to Highbury for 90 minutes of ritual nail-biting. This, said Graham, was the final countdown. True to Howe's word, QPR were obstinate opponents and the match was no classic. But as news filtered through of Liverpool's 3–0 canter against Palace, the Gunners dug deep. Merson scored for the second successive match and Dixon converted his fourth spot-kick of the season to keep the heat on Souness. Three games to go, no change in the cushion: three points.

It is not always easy to pinpoint the moment when Championships are won and lost, but Liverpool will always mourn the events of the May Day Bank Holiday weekend in 1991. Scotland team-mate Archie Gemmill once said of Souness: 'If he was a chocolate drop, he'd eat himself' — a reference to his self-possession — but these 48 hours must have aged the Liverpool manager more than any others. The demands of live television, becoming increasingly intrusive on the fixture calendar, twice fragmented the First Division programme, on each occasion leaving Arsenal to kick-off knowing the result of their closest rivals. On the Saturday, the Gunners were required to commence battle with Sunderland at Roker Park at the curious hour of 5.30pm — 45 minutes after the final whistle at Stamford Bridge, where Chelsea were entertaining Liverpool.

As the only team to get the better of Arsenal in 38 League games, it was perhaps appropriate that Chelsea should repay the debt by supplying their London neighbours with a giant helping hand towards the winning post. Liverpool's 4–2 demise at the Bridge left the Gunners safe in the knowledge that their leadership would be immune to any Roker revival on Wearside. As it transpired, Sunderland had neither the guile nor the firepower to breach Arsenal's dogged rearguard; Graham was far happier with a dour 0–0 draw than opposite number Denis Smith, for whom the result spelled almost certain relegation.

Monday, 6 May was, in many ways, an average Bank Holiday. Twenty-mile traffic jams along coast roads caused by day trippers who wouldn't normally venture into their back gardens in such unspecial weather; the obligatory air traffic control dispute over mainland Europe; and in the pop world, Cher was No. 1 with the Shoop Shoop Song. Arsenal's home game with Manchester United, the only team to have beaten them on home soil in 13 months, did not kick off until 8pm, yet the players congregated at the ground from lunchtime to watch Liverpool's game with Nottingham Forest.

With Arsenal now four points to the good and only 180 minutes of the season left, the algebra was elementary: if Liverpool lost, the title returned to Highbury; a draw gave them only the tiniest mathematical hope of keeping it in the Anfield boardroom. It was the ultimate irony in their season of disruption that Liverpool's flickering hopes were finally snuffed out by a 23-year-old unknown who used to cheer them on from the Kop. Ian Woan's 64th-minute winner at the City Ground made wonderful viewing for Graham's players after Nigel Clough and Jan Molby had exchanged penalties.

The result made Arsenal's fortunes against United academic. For ITV executives, who could not have foreseen Liverpool emerging pointless from their two holiday games, it was an anti-climax. But for the Highbury faithful, it turned a night of potentially unbearable nerve-jangling into a knees-up. No sooner had the Championship been clinched than the order was issued to open up the turnstiles and let 42,229 guests join the party.

Graham, returned to the boardroom from a TV interview in one of the Clock End boxes commandeered by a camera crew, found himself the recipient of a bear-hug and kiss from an East Stand season-ticket holder as he marched up the touchline, his face betraying barely a flicker of emotion. One by one the players emerged for the pre-match kick-in to thunderous acclaim. David Seaman, Lee Dixon and Michael Thomas entered the party spirit by donning a variety of headgear never previously sanctioned on match-days by Graham. North Bank fans, who filled the terrace to bursting point with more than an hour to kick-off, persuaded the players to abandon the normal practice of plying the 'keeper with shots and crosses; even Seaman happily bludgeoned 25-yarders into the arms of supporters going through their full repertoire of victorious refrains.

Dixon conducted the singing, Anders Limpar his own personal sideshow — which might have been entitled 'Twenty Things You Never Knew You Could Do With A Football'. But such was the professionalism Graham had instilled in his side that, despite all the pre-match euphoria, there was a manifest determination not to let the party fall flat. As the sun sank reluctantly behind the North Bank, Arsenal set about United as if their medals depended on it. Champions or not, they were in no mood to show their illustrious visitors — soon to defeat mighty Barcelona and lift the European Cup Winners Cup — any clemency.

Alan Smith put the Gunners in front after 19 minutes with an accomplished finish to Dixon's right-wing cross and three minutes before the break he confirmed their swaggering superiority. Kevin Campbell's pass exposed United's back line and Smith applied another uncomplicated execution to the move from 18 yards. His night was complete when referee Bob Nixon

penalised Steve Bruce for handball and regular penalty-taker Dixon stepped aside for Smith to complete his hat-trick from the spot. Perhaps the only blot on Arsenal's copybook — an eminently forgettable one — was the last-minute consolation Bruce claimed for United, which robbed Seaman of his 30th clean sheet of an outstanding term.

Graham, serenaded by the sarcastic and now ritual chants of 'Boring, Boring Arsenal' from his players in the dressing-room, modestly stayed in the tunnel while Tony Adams hoisted the trophy and led the team on a richly deserved lap of honour. 'I didn't think it was important for me to join in,' contended the manager later. 'The players are the ones who have done it. I can enjoy all the reflective glory because of their efforts, but they deserve all the credit and limelight. The fans pay their money every week to watch them play football, not to watch me sit in the dugout. I felt it was appropriate for me to stay in the background this time.' He had, after all, done it all before.

The measure of Arsenal's achievement was not lost on Graham. 'In November, we were six points behind Liverpool, we were docked another two and the majority of people wrote us off. The Championship was over, they said, and the response from my players has been absolutely first-class. Six months later, we are way ahead and we've won it with a few points to spare. I don't think anyone can begrudge us our success because we've had our fair share of knocks this season.'

The general consensus nonetheless, was that Arsenal's class of '91 were arguably less cavalier and more ruthless than Graham's earlier title-winning team. United manager Alex Ferguson acknowledged as much and was generous in his appreciation of the Gunners: 'In a league as tough as the English First Division, which I still rank as the most physically demanding in the world, it's absolutely incredible to lose only one game out of 38. And only Liverpool have found the levels of consistency and desire to rival Arsenal's achievement of winning the Championship two years out of three. They have set themselves one hell of a standard to follow. People talk about Arsenal being methodical, but there are plenty of managers up and down the country who wouldn't mind having a squad who can adapt like theirs. It's impossible to win Championships by way of a fluke — Arsenal have done it again because they are the best team in the country, no doubt about that.'

There was no shortage of 'in-house' tributes to Graham's management, one of the most glowing coming from Bertie Mee, who said: 'There is no reason why George cannot become the greatest manager in Arsenal's history. What he achieved in one season, despite the deduction of two points, equals our Double achievement of 1971. I have been very pleasantly surprised by his success. I must admit I did not envisage his managerial qualities when he was a player under me at Highbury.'

'He was known as "the Stroller" in those days because he was very, very easy-going on and off the pitch. The disciplinarian side of his nature as a manager has surprised me. He's got them playing in a similar way to when we won the Double. All round there are big similarities in talents and deficiencies between the teams. For example, both sides understood that you need discipline to achieve the result and it's not always possible to entertain and get the points. I am also impressed by the depth and quality of George's squad, which is so vital — that is illustrated by the fact that he could afford to leave out someone like David Rocastle.'

Five days after United's retreat from Highbury, Coventry City became another set of involuntary pickets at Arsenal's celebrations. The First Division's longest sitting tenants, behind the Gunners, stood between Graham and a 20th century record of just one defeat in a full League season. Leeds, in 1969, and Liverpool, in 1988, had suffered two losses each. Since the inception of the Football League there have been over 300 Divisional Championships. Of those 300 plus, just two Champions had finished undefeated (Preston in 1889 and Liverpool in the Second Division in 1894), and no club had ever finished with just one defeat.

It was always going to be the sort of occasion on which Arsenal either let their hair down or let their fans down. Happily, it turned out to be the former and Coventry's fate the latter. Limpar, shorn of defensive responsibilities was granted a licence to thrill. The maverick Swedish winger, clearly relishing his role as a free spirit up front, helped himself to a hat-trick as Arsenal's six-shooters signed off with a flourish. Smith, Perry Groves and a Trevor Peake own goal ensured that another lap of honour for Adams and company was by way of appreciation rather than apology. Domestic supremacy was highly satisfying for a squad assembled, by modern standards, for a modest premium in the transfer market. Now with English clubs granted an unqualified reprieve in European competitions, an entire continent was in theory at least, at their mercy.

Former Liverpool manager Bob Paisley once said of the European Cup: 'You could make a living out of moaning about it. You curse the hotels, raise hell about the training pitches, lug your own food about, worry about the referees, about the injuries, about the air strikes, the heating in the players' rooms, the travel weariness . . . and then the moment you are out of it, you are empty inside. The icing is off the cake. God, you don't half miss it.'

For Arsenal, the 1991–92 season promised that extra dimension of foreign adventure. In the words of John Charles, the Welsh striker who played for Juventus in the late 1950s, 'the continentals shudder when they think of the way football is played in Britain . . . what horrifies them is the British love of bodily contact.' The Gunners had every reason to believe that Europe's cream would greet their return to the

fold with some trepidation, not least because of that glorious English monopoly of the European Champions' Cup for seven years out of eight, between 1977 and 1984. In those days it wasn't just the one great club side, for when Liverpool faltered there was Forest and even Villa to claim the crown in their turn. Publicly, some commentators expressed misgivings about England's six-year exile from the European Cup since the Heysel disaster, claiming the increased skill factor among top teams on the mainland would nullify traditional British virtues of fitness and red-blooded application. Certainly there was less of the 'chip shop approach' to which former top referee Arthur Ellis once referred on the continent — but Arsenal approached the campaign with all the confidence of previous English standard-bearers.

The competition's new format, with seeded teams kept apart in the first two rounds then thrown together in two round-robin groups of four, was thought to favour Arsenal's propensity for durability and compactness. And their chances did not seem unduly diminished by an indifferent start in the League — just three wins from their opening eight games. Graham, ostensibly satisfied with his squad depth, had surprisingly declined to increase it during the close season — a repeat of his apparent inertia

after the Championship triumph of 1989.

There seemed little to concern Graham about his team's quality in a European context in the first round match with Austria Vienna, though. Drawn at home in the first leg, the Gunners secured an abyss between the sides, and 24,424 fans saluted their 6–1 rout. Liverpool trounced Finland's Kuusysi by the same score on the night and, like Arsenal, had their own hero. Colin Gibson of the *Daily Telgraph* wrote: 'Alan Smith emulated Liverpool's Dean Saunders with the four goals that must establish Arsenal as one of the most feared sides in this season's European Cup. Smith's goals, his first in Europe, but bringing his total to 20 in the last 20 games, demolished the Austrian challenge. His contribution in 14 remarkable second-half minutes was merely the cutting edge to a performance of the highest calibre by Arsenal, returning to their best form. Although Austrian football is at a low ebb, Vienna were not the worst side to have graced the competition by a long chalk. That was the frightening aspect for Arsenal's rivals.'

The Gunners could even afford the luxury of Dixon's penalty miss as Andy Linighan and Limpar completed the scoring. Vienna's 1–0 victory in the return was hollow, indeed, and by then Graham had left his domestic rivals behind with the crucial record £2.5 million outlay on Crystal Palace striker Ian Wright. Although he was ineligible for the early stages of the European Cup, Wright — capped by England seven months earlier — gave Graham an embarrassment of riches in attack.

Wright wasted little time making an impact, scoring in the 1–1 League Cup draw at Leicester and then, spectacularly, a hat-trick in his first League game for the Gunners, at Southampton. But he had to sit out the next continental expedition, which took Arsenal to Benfica's Stadium of Light, a magnificent amphitheatre in Lisbon once graced by the likes of Eusebio.

In front of 84,000 devoted Portuguese, Arsenal acquitted themselves admirably — especially Paul Davis, whose attentive marking job on Brazilian midfield player Isaias clamped the biggest single threat to the Gunners' hopes of progress. The inclusion of Isaias had raised more than a few eyebrows in the Arsenal camp in the first place, particularly when he lined up beside two Soviet internationals and two Swedish imports, an apparent contravention of UEFA's ceiling of four foreigners per team. Dissection of UEFA's smallprint revealed that Isaias qualified for Portuguese citizenship through marriage, but Arsenal had every right to express their concern: only England's cricket team offers more qualification loopholes, though playing for the Republic of Ireland can be as obscure.

In the event, the sting was in the tail. Thanks to a disciplined rearguard action and Kevin Campbell's polished equaliser, the teams came to Highbury at 1–1, with the match well-balanced. However Isaias, so well shadowed in the Stadium of Light, found a new sphere of

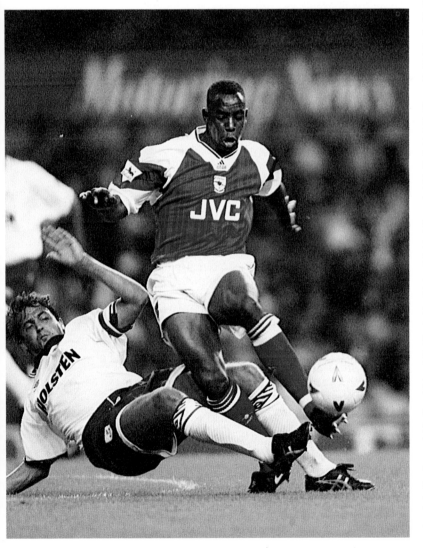

Ian Wright is robbed by Gary Mabbutt during Arsenal's 1-0 win at White Hart Lane on 16 August 1993. Wright scored the goal, which is not surprising given that he claimed 21 of the 40 goals Arsenal scored in all competitions from the start of the season to the year end. The previous season, Wright had scored no fewer than 30 of the Gunners' 73 first class goals, indicating the clubs dependence upon his mercurial talent.

influence in the second leg. Arsenal's barn-storming start yielded an early goal from Colin Pates, making only his tenth appearance in 18 months, a disallowed 'goal' from Merson and Campbell's shot against an upright. But the early optimism among expectant home supporters was to be snuffed out ruthlessly by Isaias. The Brazilian possessed that elusive ability to change the course of a match. Now, he graduated to the ability to turn the course of an entire season — Arsenal's season, that is — with one stunning swing of his boot. The 30-yard volley with which he restored parity in the tie brought all Arsenal's worst fears to the surface: they now had to chase the winner knowing that, if Benfica caught them cold at the back, the European Cup would be wrenched irrevocably from their reach. In extra time, that is exactly what happened.

The Soviet, Kulkov, and then — inevitably — Isaias left the Gunners to count the cost of failing to reach the mini-league section of the competition. Conservative estimates put the loss of revenue at £1.5 million. Worse still, another potentially lucrative avenue had been sealed off to Graham between the two games with Benfica. Following the 1–0 League Cup defeat at Coventry, he had said the result 'may yet prove a blessing in disguise' because the club's fixture commitments were already 'frightening'. But elimination from two cup competitions in the space of eight days, sandwiched by a home defeat against struggling West Ham, suddenly limited the scope of Arsenal's ambitions.

Graham effected more changes in personnel, selling Michael Thomas to the scene of his greatest triumph, Liverpool, for £1.5 million and bringing Jimmy Carter in the opposite direction for one third of that figure. Thomas, yet another product of Arsenal's fruitful youth policy, had lost his sharpness and the effervescent figure who once sparkled in the Gunners' midfield had laboured somewhat through the previous 12 months. His departure was soured by disparaging remarks he made in a Sunday newspaper about Graham's methods, and he was fined for them by the FA. It was an unnecessary post-script to a Highbury career that will always be synonymous with feats of derring-do at Anfield. Perhaps Thomas was always fated to continue his career there: certainly few players can have enjoyed such umbilical ties with Liverpool before joining them.

Wright's form continued to be irresistible — he scored all four goals in the 4–2 home win against Everton, for example — but Arsenal's, collectively, was erratic. Graham, sensing that his team was off the pace in the First Division, made the FA Cup 'a major priority'. A disastrous Christmas, in which the point gleaned from a 1–1 draw with Wimbledon was their only return from three games, increased the Gunners' sense of urgency in the Cup. The third round draw handed them a trip to fourth Division Wrexham. It was one of those heads-you-win, tails-I-lose ties that top players hate.

Deprived of the suspended Wright, Graham looked to Smith — just two goals between September 21 and the New Year — for increased productivity, and after 43 minutes of embarrassing superiority the penny finally dropped. Merson burrowed his way to the byline and presented Smith with the kind of opportunity for which all strikers in a lean spell pray. Arsenal preserved their lead without undue alarm until the 82nd minute when Mickey Thomas, a nomad with 37 years on the clock and 11 previous employers, equalised with a thunderous free-kick. Thomas had barely emerged from the scrummage of delirium when Steve Watkin hooked Gordon Davies' right-wing cross past the unsighted Seaman for a barely plausible winner. The media, predictably feasted on the biggest Cup upset since non-League Sutton's eclipse of Coventry in 1989.

Rob Hughes wrote in the *Sunday Times:* 'Oh, what lovely pandemonium, what delightful illogicality the Cup still provides! Who will believe that Arsenal, prime movers of the Premier League (and hustling) through to kill 108 years of League tradition, should fall in a theatre principally of their own making. Arsenal should have won the game by half-time . . . but this was hardly the mastery of Super Leaguers.'

Graham admitted bluntly the calamitous defeat in North Wales was 'the lowest point of my career'. Arsenal had become accustomed to adversity under his management and they were hardened against prejudice. Kicked when they were down, damned with faint praise when they won, Graham found himself almost yearning for the minor irritants of jealous epithets such as 'Boring Arsenal'. Widely regarded as one of the country's brightest and most perceptive managers, he suddenly assumed a jaundiced outlook. Out of the running for all the cups, his team were also stranded in no-man's land in the Championship they had won so vibrantly seven months earlier. It seemed a re-run of 1990.

Four days after the Wrexham debacle, Arsenal's image took another battering when Wright was fined £1,500 for spitting back at an Oldham fan as the teams left Boundary Park following the 1–1 draw in November. Merson was also docked £500 for gesticulating at fans who had barracked Wright throughout the match. Gordon Taylor, chief executive of the player's union, pointed out: 'As professionals, we are required to turn the other cheek, whatever the provocation. But being spat on is about the lowest form of degradation you can experience and, while players must expect to be punished if they retaliate in kind, I don't notice the fans responsible being hauled up before the courts to explain themselves.'

It was, nonetheless, another bodyblow for Graham the disciplinarian. His whole reputation was based on good behaviour and respecting authority. Nicknamed 'Gadaffi', he had always set great store by Bertie Mee's maxim: 'Slackness is a short cut to disaster.'

With heavy heart, Graham conceded the

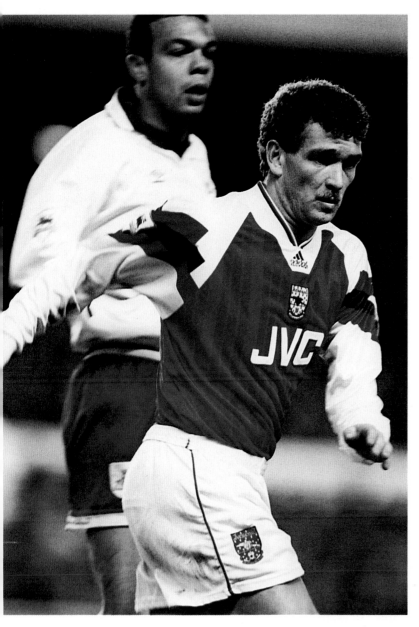

John Jensen holds off
Tottenham's Jason Dozzell during the 1-1 draw at Highbury on Monday 6 December 1993. Since the arrival of Sky Sports, North London derbies have invariably been scheduled for Sundays or Monday nights. Jensen was signed following his goalscoring performance for Denmark in the 1992 European Championship final. At the start of the 1994-95 season he was still waiting to register his first goal for Arsenal.

chairman David Dein, one of the first modern administrators to realise that aggressive marketing increased clubs' income and, in turn, provided a springboard for extra investment on facilities and players. History will judge the commercial orientation of Arsenal overseen by Dein, and the new, all-seater North Bank will perhaps come to be remembered as his personal monument to the club. A less visible driving force at the time was the Taylor Report, which obliged the top 40 clubs to incur the cost of all-seater stadia by 1994.

When the bulldozers moved in to replace the North Bank with a 12,500-seater edifice, brickbats flew over the methods chosen by Arsenal to finance the ground's biggest development in more than half a century. Bond schemes to pay for new facilities were pioneered successfully in the United States, and Glasgow Rangers' Ibrox Stadium was transformed without a murmur of dissent by way of a similar venture. In the face of a fierce recession, borrowing or flotation — the alternatives to a bond scheme — could have been monstrous burdens on Arsenal's finances. The board were very aware of two successive Spurs' boards being deposed as a result of the cost of new stands at White Hart Lane.

The reaction to the rebuilding programme at Highbury was perhaps a reflection of English football's parlous state in the summer of 1992. Graham Taylor's national side belly-flopped alarmingly in the European Championship finals in Sweden and the Premier League kicked off in funereal mood. One of the European Championship's stars, Danish midfielder John Jensen, impressed Graham so much he spent £1 million to bring him to Highbury, while Rocastle's love affair with Arsenal resulted in an amicable divorce. He joined new Champions Leeds United for £2 million, but failed to impress at Elland Road and became another of the 1989 Championship stars who seemed to have faded since the glorious night at Anfield.

Jensen, a bustling, no-nonsense player, had scored Denmark's first goal against Germany in their totally unexpected European Championship triumph after the Danes were called in as last-minute replacements for now non-existent Yugoslavia, excluded as part of a United Nations sanctions package. His arrival re-affirmed Graham's determination to atone for the previous campaign's catalogue of disappointments. In the 1992–93 Championship, however, they simply never got going. Arsenal's performances at Highbury were generally as incomplete as their North Bank. In an effort to camouflage the jungle of cranes and scaffolding, the club spent large sums of money commissioning and erecting an enormous mural, 75 yards wide and 18 yards high, to hang from corner to corner behind the North Bank goal. Thousands of painted faces peered out across Highbury in a commendable initiative to retain some of the atmosphere within the stadium (not to mention its qualities as a safety net which prevented hundreds of wayward shots sailing into the

Championship and set about building for the dawn of the Premier League. The 2–0 defeat at Liverpool, where teenager Ray Parlour made a mature debut, proved to be the Gunners' last of a forgettable season. Starting with a 1–1 draw against Manchester United in February, which featured David Rocastle's last senior goal for Arsenal, they embarked on a 17-match unbeaten run which, though ultimately unrewarded, contained several performances of distinction; England goalkeeper Chris Woods had seven put past him when Sheffield Wednesday came to Highbury, Wright's last-gasp equaliser foiled Tottenham, Anders Limpar scored a 50-yard goal of breathtaking impudence and improvisation in the 4–0 thrashing of Liverpool and Wright helped himself to his now customary hat-trick against Southampton.

The run rejuvenated Arsenal and enabled them to approach the breakaway elite division, run under the auspices of the FA rather than the Football League, with renewed confidence. The Premier League's conception owed much to a handful of visionaries including Gunners vice-

Right: **During the rebuilding of the North Bank,** Arsenal broke new ground with the, now famous, Highbury mural. It was intended to represent a crowd and ensure that balls were returned to the keeper quickly. After the new stand was completed, Arsenal offered the whole mural for sale at a knockdown five-figure sum. The game shown is against Sheffield Wednesday on 29 August 1992. Merson and Parlour scoring in a 2-1 victory.

Below: **Martin Keown clears a Newcastle attack** on 27 November 1993 during a 2-1 victory. Keown's superb defensive performances for Everton led to an England call-up, under Graham Taylor, and prompted George Graham to bring him back to Highbury for £2 million.

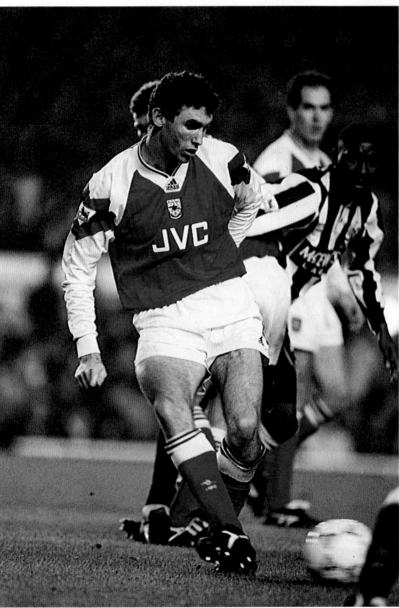

building site). It was fun and an unusually creative motif at a football ground.

The mural received more than its fair share of good-humoured criticism and even became a vehicle for political point-scoring when it came to light that none of its faces was black, an oversight quickly rectified. With ground capacity temporarily reduced to 29,000, home games were virtually sold out every week. To be frank, hardly any of them provided exceptional entertainment in the Premier League; one glowing exception was the seven-goal thriller against Southampton. But this was to be a season in which Arsenal discovered a 'home from home,' a venue at which they remained unbeaten in four games . . . Wembley.

Prospects of the Gunners winning the League Cup (now sponsored by Coca-Cola as the latest of many, the names of whom are sensibly ignored by most writers and fans) looked anything but rosy when they trailed 1–0 to Millwall at Highbury in the second round, first leg; Kevin Campbell's late introduction spared Arsenal's blushes, and he worked the oracle again at The Den a fortnight later before the Gunners scraped through on penalties with the tie deadlocked at 2–2. With Millwall moving at season's end, Arsenal were never to play again at their original 'local derby' location.

Arsenal needed two bites at the cherry to see off Derby in the next round (Campbell again scoring in both games) and two trips to the seaside before disposing of little Scarborough. The first was a wasted journey because of wintry weather, and conditions were far from ideal when Nigel Winterburn's winner earned the Gunners a quarter-final tie with Nottingham Forest. Six days and two Wright goals later, Arsenal were in the semi-finals.

By now, every other game in Arsenal's tiring schedule was a cup-tie, and Graham was almost

prepared to forgive his team for an 11-week barren spell without a League win. Wright scored from the spot against his old club and the resurgent Smith netted twice at Selhurst Park in the first leg as Crystal Palace's bid to throw the Gunners off their inexorable collision course with Wembley was sunk almost before it had begun. The return at Highbury smacked of going through the motions as Wright, inevitably, and the increasingly assured Andy Linighan cemented the first half of Arsenal's unique cup double bid and completed a 5–1 aggregate rout of Palace.

Their opponents in the League Cup final were to become frequent imposters on Graham's path to glory this season. Sheffield Wednesday, conquerors of big-spending Blackburn Rovers, arrived at Wembley with a reputation for flowing — if defensively flawed — football, and the teams treated their fans to an enthralling

afternoon. Without the injured Smith, the suspended Dixon and the cup-tied Martin Keown — repatriated from Everton for £2 million, ten times the figure Arsenal received when he was sold to Aston Villa in 1986 — the Gunners were forced to shuffle their pack. Paul Davis was recalled, to unanimous amazement, after just one comeback match in the reserves following hamstring trouble. And Northern Ireland defender Stephen Morrow, so often restricted to little more than walk-on parts in previous Arsenal productions, was pressed into service beside Davis in midfield, where he was to command centre-stage.

England manager Taylor, under fire from all quarters for his refusal to restore Wednesday's former Tottenham winger Chris Waddle to the international boards, will have drawn some minor, though valueless, comfort from Waddle's familiar retreat towards anonymity after a prom-

Right: **Steve Morrow celebrates his goal** in the Coca-Cola Cup final on 18 April 1993. He and Merson secured a 2-1 win and a psychological advantage over the team they were to meet in the FA Cup final: Sheffield Wednesday. It was the first time that the same clubs had contested the two domestic Cup finals, and the first time the same club had won both.

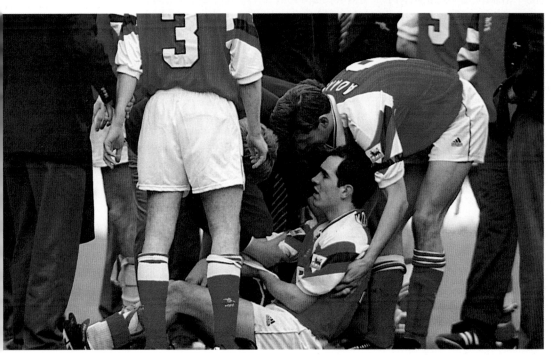

Left: **A miserable end to a joyous day** for Morrow: in the immediate post-match celebrations he climbed on Tony Adams back, fell off and broke his arm. The following day's papers were full of comments about falling off a quadruped transport of the mule family, but young Morrow had certainly made a mark on his first appearance in a major final.

ising start. He looked worthy of all Fleet Street's platitudes about his enduring skill as the Owls snatched an early lead through their excellent American import, John Harkes (the first American to score in a soccer game at Wembley). But Waddle was to be upstaged by Paul Merson, not least because of the 20th-minute equaliser which sparked an Arsenal revival.

Rob Hughes said in *The Times:* 'Like Wednesday's goal, Merson's goal came from a free-kick and finished, like Wednesday's, with a right-foot finish of class. When the ball was headed down to Merson just outside the penalty area, he hit across it to induce a kind of swerve that is sometimes mistakenly regarded in this country as the preserve of Brazilians. The ball obeyed his instruction and beat the diving Woods inside his left-hand post.'

Merson wasn't finished by any means, though. After 68 minutes, with Arsenal's vigour now firmly in the ascendency, he fashioned the winner. Thrusting deep into Wednesday territory, his low cross from the left flank caught Carlton Palmer off balance and Morrow had the simple but joyous task of thrashing it past Woods — his first senior goal for the club. For Merson, it was the perfect climax to an emotional week in which he had become a father for the second time; but for Morrow, there was to be a painful sting in the tail. On the final whistle, Tony Adams hoisted his match-winner shoulder-high by way of playful celebration . . . only for Morrow to come crashing to earth and break his arm, ruling him out of action for the last month of the season. Adams was so upset that assistant manager Stewart Houston had to persuade him to climb Wembley's famous steps to accept the trophy.

Poor Morrow required oxygen and was carted out of Wembley by ambulancemen instead of on the shoulders of adoring supporters. He was unable to collect his winner's medal, and Graham said: 'It was silly, really, a freak accident. But you can't tell players not to celebrate when they've just won a major cup competition. It did, however, remove just a little of the gloss from our victory for me — you couldn't help feeling desperately sorry for the boy.' For the press the story was obvious: 'How did you break your arm?' 'I fell off a donkey . . .', the donkey being the tabloids' less than friendly nickname for Tony Adams.

For Arsenal, the job was only half-done. They had another opportunity to test their cup-tie expertise against Wednesday in the FA Cup final, the blue riband among knockout competitions. Never has the perverse nature of cup football been so ably demonstrated as in Arsenal's fortunes in successive seasons. After Wrexham, you wouldn't have backed them to knock out a pigeon with a tranquilliser gun; now they were the name everybody wanted to avoid whenever numbered balls came out of the bag.

Not that the 1993 FA Cup started out that way. When the Gunners were required to tackle non-League Yeovil on their own patch at The

Huish, the Press descended on the West Country ready to bury Graham again. But Ian Wright's superb hat-trick, and the League Cup win at Scarborough four days later, forced them to dispense with the obituaries and instead hail Arsenal's professionalism on two thankless missions. 'Sorry you've had two wasted journeys,' Graham taunted the media corps.

Trailing 2–0 to Leeds at Highbury in the fourth round, Arsenal demonstrated their new-found belief by bouncing back to force a replay through Ray Parlour's persistence and a 25-yard Merson special. In the Elland Road encore, the Gunners again had to force the issue when they found themselves 2–1 down with eight minutes left. Smith's first goal for three months was already a symptom of Arsenal's resurgent morale before Wright, returning from suspension to spectacular effect, struck twice to sink Leeds in extra time. The significance of that comeback was not lost on Graham. Smith's previous goal, against Coventry on November 7, had helped shoot the Gunners to the Premier League's summit for the first — and last — time that season. In their next match, they surrendered pole position with a limp 3–0 capitulation at Elland Road, a performance the manager de-

Arsenal's Ray Parlour
and Spurs' Justin Edinburgh tussle for the ball during the 1993 FA Cup semi-final on 4 April 1993. Arsenal won the game with a late Adams' header from a free kick resulting from Edinburgh's foul on Parlour. Needless to say, the game was a re-run of the 1991 semi-final, right down to the Wembley setting. Unfortunately for Spurs, they no longer had Gascoigne and the result was another change of script from two years earlier.

scribed as 'wholly unacceptable'.

Arsenal's League inconsistency continued to frustrate. Points dropped at Highbury seemed largely to benefit clubs at the wrong end of the table. Of all the relegation candidates, only Crystal Palace went away empty handed. Sheffield United were among those to enjoy the Gunners' flirtation with charitable status, but their manager, Dave Bassett, was first to recognise their obsession with cup success. He said: 'Arsenal could finish in the top six, win both the major cups — and how's that for a c★★p season? If we were in Arsenal's boots and someone tried to tell me that we were having a hard time, I'd think they'd gone soft.' Bassett's prophetic analysis never looked like being far off the mark after the Blades' fortuitous 1–1 draw at Highbury in January.

Wright, whose two-goal burst accounted for Nottingham Forest in the League Cup, stamped his authority on a jittery Gunners performance with a repeat one-two in the FA Cup. For all his success, Brian Clough had never won the FA Cup as a manager in 18 attempts; Wright sent

Eddie McGoldrick, recently transferred from Crystal Palace, takes a free-kick during Arsenal's 1-0 defeat of Chelsea on 16 April 1994.

him into retirement safe in the knowledge that he never would.

Now Arsenal were through to the quarter-finals. Already in the Coca-Cola Cup final, they were 180 minutes from another medal for the mantlepiece. Ipswich, whose defensive blanket had smothered the life out of Arsenal's Boxing Day party, were more enterprising hosts at Portman Road. Much of the build-up had focused on the gash sustained by Tony Adams in a fall during a night out with friends, which forced him out of two games. More wisecracks at the captain's expense inevitably followed. Brian Woolnough sniggered in *The Sun*: 'Adams needed more stitches in his forehead than Arsenal have League points.' Typically, however, Adams had the last laugh. His return served only to inspire those around him and Ipswich were stitched up 4–2. Adams contributed to the scoring spree, which was an overdue statement of the Gunners' attacking resources . . . the previous 14 League games had yielded only four goals.

The semi-final draw was, in itself, a mandate for civil strife in Sheffield and North London: Wednesday v United and Arsenal v Tottenham. Mouth-watering prospects, but powder kegs to boot. Falling at the final hurdle before the Cup final is still the most soul-destroying experience in football. Add local pride to the equation and the stakes become even greater. Adams greeted the pairing with Spurs in a cautious, circumspect manner. 'It's one for the fans to get excited about and it obviously gives us a chance to gain revenge for our semi-final defeat in 1991,' he said. 'But semis aren't about revenge or settling old scores — they're all about getting through to the final, and we mustn't lose sight of that.'

Adams' apprehension was entirely justified. Arsenal's League match at White Hart Lane four months earlier had been pock-marked by a series of niggles and unpleasantness. Spurs' 1–0 win was a travesty and their coach, Doug Livermore, was evidently carried away by euphoria when he declared it 'a great day for football'. In truth, it was nothing of the sort. Referee Alf Buksh seemed to lose his grip as early as the second minute, when Dean Austin's palpably illegal tackle on Ray Parlour warranted a penalty.

Buksh's failure to intervene became a licence for misbehaviour. Graham complained to him in the tunnel at half-time that the game was almost out of control — which later earned him a £500 rebuke from the FA. Wright was not among the five names Buksh scribbled in his notebook, but TV cameras caught him aiming a rabbit-punch at Tottenham's David Howells and he was later suspended for three matches.

Spurs defender Justin Edinburgh admitted later that he had 'wound up' Adams by using 'the D-word' (a reference to the terrace insult aimed at Arsenal's captain by opposition fans and now so familiar that it has almost become a compliment) and warned of no truce in the Cup semi-final. For the Gunners, the ominous prom-

ise of more uncompromising attrition was compounded by tenuous portents which were deemed to favour Tottenham. According to that pillar of superstition, the Chinese calendar, 1993 was the year of the cockerel. One-nil to Spurs in the psychological war of nerves. And Paul Gascoigne, whose spell had mesmerised Arsenal at Wembley two years before, maintained his promise of a good-luck message by telephone from his new base in Italy before every round. It was an unexceptional method of motivation by a former colleague, but Spurs evidently set great store by it and believed that Arsenal would be haunted by the 'Gazza factor'.

But if Spurs were banking on historical precedent to upset the Gunners, they were mistaken. Graham, ever the shrewd tactician, gambled on a young midfield of Ian Selley, Parlour and David Hillier — combined age 58 — to cover Wembley's wide-open spaces with raw enthusiasm, and left Smith on the bench with the versatile Morrow. Selley, discarded by England's youth team after just one match of an exhausting mid-season trip to Australia for the Junior World Cup, was workmanlike and dependable; Parlour again demonstrated his phenomenal 'engine' and appetite for responsibility and Hillier, often the unsung anchorman in front of the back four, was unflappable.

Any grievance Arsenal may have felt about the penalty-that-wasn't at White Hart Lane was effectively neutralised after half-an-hour of a tense, unforgiving game. And referee Philip Don's dismissal of Tottenham's frantic appeal for a spot-kick when Andy Linighan challenged Darren Anderton uncomfortably close to his own penalty area was ultimately crucial. After conceding both the initiative and territorial advantage for 45 minutes, Arsenal gradually made their supremacy tell. Wright could and should have added to his 26 goals for the season but, even as extra-time loomed, the breakthough was looking increasingly inevitable. It duly arrived ten minutes from time.

Ironically, its origins were just inches from the spot where Linighan had felled Anderton without censure; now, Edinburgh's tackle on Parlour was penalised. After a lengthy delay for treatment to Parlour, Merson delivered the free-kick, swinging away from the goalkeeper,

towards the far post. Linighan ventured forward to contest it and his arrival caused momentary but costly confusion among Spurs' rearguard. Neil Ruddock and Gary Mabbutt both seemed to pick up Linighan and, when Merson's flighted kick cleared them both, Tony Adams was left unchallenged to head downwards and beyond Erik Thorstvedt.

Adams was merely transporting his heroics from Izmir, where England had survived a hail of missiles on World Cup duty in Turkey five days earlier, to exact revenge for the Double that got away in 1991. Spurs had no time to respond and, for the first time, the same teams had won through to contest both England's domestic cup finals. Sheffield Wednesday had beaten steel city neighbours United at Wembley 24 hours earlier after winning the right to switch their tie from Elland Road. After 70 years of banning semi-finals at Wembley, the FA had seen three there in the space of as many years.

'Adams is incredible,' enthused Graham. 'He comes back from a tiring midweek trip with England, earns nationwide respect for an outstanding performance on international duty and then produces another one for his club. It's just a pity the rest of the country took so long to recognise his quality — we've known about it at Arsenal for a long time.'

Lee Dixon's dismissal, four minutes from the end for a second bookable offence, condemned him to miss the Coca-Cola Cup final. But he was happily restored for the FA Cup reprise on May 15. Before then, however, Arsenal were ordered to undertake a preposterous pre-Wembley fixture schedule of five League games in ten days. And to add insult to injury, one of the games the Gunners were ordered to complete before the Cup final was at Hillsborough against Wednesday. Unsurprisingly, both managers fielded

unfamiliar names for a contest that served only to irritate rather than inform each other about the sides' respective strengths and weaknesses.

By the time the big day arrived, fatigue was clearly going to be a major factor. Arsenal were playing their 48th competitive match of the campaign and their 12th in six weeks. Graham preferred Jensen to Selley in midfield, while Morrow — looking perky on his return to the venue which treated him to glory and black comedy within minutes of each other — collected his League Cup winner's medal before kick-off. He was the only man to enjoy the privilege on a desperately disappointing day.

In the *Sunday Times*, Brough Scott mourned: 'Exhaustion won. Long before the end this great clawing hand had gripped the legs and minds of everyone on the pitch. Two teams had played themselves to a standstill. We went into the 15th round and beyond. The two old prizefighters had met each other so many times that they knew each other's every move. A catastrophic mistake or knockout blow was needed.'

If the rise and fall of Morrow whetted the appetite, the sequel was barely palatable viewing. Chris Waddle threatened briefly to ruffle Arsenal's feathers but, after one rasping free-kick was diverted by Seaman, he became more and more anonymous.

Wright, playing with a broken toe, struggled for 90 minutes before Graham granted him sanctuary on the bench. But he did at least make the most of his only clear-cut opportunity. After 21 minutes, Paul Davis flighted a right-wing free-kick on to Linighan's head and the big centre-half nodded it across the six-yard box. Wright, lurking with Paul Warhurst on the far post, outjumped his marker to head firmly beyond Chris Woods. Arsenal were one up, and the familiar chorus of 'Ian Wright-Wright-

Captain Tony Adams scores the only goal of the FA Cup semi-final against Spurs at Wembley on 4 April 1993, gaining revenge for the defeat at the same stage two years earlier.

May 1993 and yet another trip to Wembley, Arsenal's third of the season. This time it was the FA Cup final, in which Ian Wright played with a broken toe but maintained his remarkable goalscoring record for the season, striking with his only clear cut opportunity. After 21 minutes Wright out-jumped Paul Warhurst to give Arsenal the lead after Andy Linighan headed on a Paul Davis free-kick. The match was a repeat of the Coca-Cola Cup final, and after David Hirst equalised in the 68th minute the teams had to face each other for a third time at Wembley, in a replay.

Wright' rang round Wembley. As the lovely Emily Bell of *The Observer*, perhaps something of a fan, said: 'Wright is the yeast in the bread, the coke in the cola, the buck in the fizz, the Pardoner in Chaucer's Tales. Without him, there is a void, an impenetrable black hole of uncertain future . . .' Wednesday's renowned artistry never surfaced, but they summoned enough strength to conjure David Hirst's 68th-minute equaliser. That only hastened the onset of stalemate and neutrals agreed unanimously that parity was the only fair result.

Forty-eight hours later, Arsenal put out a full-strength side at Highbury against Manchester United in a testimonial for David O'Leary, granted a free transfer after 20 years' service. O'Leary thought the Cup final would be his last competitive appearance for the Gunners and was hoping all three major domestic trophies would be on display at his benefit game — Arsenal parading the two cups and United the Premier League trophy they had won with such panache. It turned out to be the sandwich filling between the Cup final and its replay, although 24,000 fans paid their respects to him.

O'Leary admitted: 'To be honest. I didn't want my time at Arsenal to end. But I was thrilled to be able to complete 20 full years of service with them. I would have hated to be shown the door after 19. The 20-year landmark kept me going. When I realised it was all over, that I had worn the red shirt for the last time, there was a tear or two in my eye. But I wouldn't have missed it for the world. And one day, if the club ever decide they want me back, I'd love to

return to Highbury as a coach or manager. That would be the ideal happy ending to the fairy-tale.' And if you're going to go out, an FA Cup final is the setting most players would choose.

Thursday came round and Arsenal found Wednesday waiting for them again. The FA Cup final replay attracted only 62,367 spectators, the lowest crowd ever for the fixture at Wembley and the lowest FA Cup final attendence for 71 years. But at least they saw a climax every bit as dramatic as Anfield '89. This was in direct contrast with the early portents, it must be said. With the kick-off delayed by 30 minutes and Wednesday supporters jamming the BBC switchboard with pleas for more time to reach Wembley after a motorway crash caused tail-backs on the M1, the game started in heavy rain. Maybe, as Rob Hughes put it: 'The heavens were weeping at the prospect of the renewal of Saturday's dire game.' The consensus was, sadly, that this had become the least interesting final in living memory.

But if the quality of the original tie left much to be desired, it was preferable to the brutality which scarred the opening stages of its successor. Adams (on Hirst) and Jensen (on Waddle) were given the benefit of the doubt by referee Keren Barratt for challenges which looked worse than the damage they inflicted. But Mark Bright's aerial confrontation with Linighan after 19 minutes was clearly unacceptable even to the most lenient officials. Bright appeared to use his right elbow maliciously as he jumped and the yellow card scarcely seemed sufficient punishment for an offence which left Linighan with a

broken nose, although he carried on playing.

Once football was restored to the top of the agenda, Wright deservedly put the Gunners ahead after 33 minutes. It was his 30th goal of a fragmented season, his 56th in 79 Arsenal appearances and his fourth Cup final goal in four Cup final appearances. Two of the goals came as a late substitute for Crystal Palace in 1990. It put him close to the top of the list of final scorers — only Ian Rush, with five goals, has scored more. Smith, restored to the starting line-up, provided a judicious through ball and Wright, galloping clear, belied his excitable nature to chip Woods from 12 yards. Waddle, booed for some apparent play-acting when he hit the ground as if pole-axed by Winterburn, claimed Wednesday's equaliser after 66 minutes with a deflected volley. Now, at last, tired legs were no longer able to compress space so readily and the chances came thick and fast at either end. Bright spurned the best of the lot, shaving the outside of an upright from ten yards, but perhaps his miss was divine retribution for his earlier misdemenour.

The excitement even stirred Mr Barratt, who chose to show yellow cards to Davis and — for the first time in his career — Smith for fouls innocuous compared to those which he allowed to disfigure the first half. Merson, struggling to

Andy Linighan wins the ball in a Selhurst Park tussle on 7 February 1993. This was the first leg of the Coca-Cola Cup semi-final, which Arsenal won easily 3-1. The second leg, at Highbury, was consequently a non-event, Arsenal winning 2-0. Wright scored two of the Gunner's five goals and his Cup performances that season were outstanding – claiming 15 of the 33 goals Arsenal chalked up in 17 Cup games. Notable in this picture is Arsenal's yellow second strip which, despite its garishness, became extremely popular.

live up to the high standard of his League Cup heroics, suffered from the same epidemic of profligacy which afflicted Bright, and the tie was doomed to more extra-time torture when Woods recovered a Merson shot which had squirted under his body inches from the line.

Punch-drunk and visibly dreading the prospect of a penalty shoot-out, the teams traded shots and tackles until, right on time, Arsenal won a left-wing corner. Merson dragged his weary legs across the sodden turf as Mr Barratt checked his watch. Would there be time to take it? Adams and Linighan ventured forward for one last fling. On the bench, Graham was apoplectic. What if Wednesday hoiked the ball clear and raced upfield to score? Who would take the penalties? Had they practised them enough?

O'Leary, who had again been brought on for Wright, must have let his mind wander, back to Genoa with the Republic of Ireland and to the 1980 Cup Winners Cup nightmare against Valencia, when Rix and Brady had missed. Please, God. Not penalties.

Merson's corner swung in at an inviting trajectory. Woods stayed rooted to his line and Wednesday's defence followed his lead fatally. Linighan, who had spent years as a million-pound spare part in the reserves, who had heard his name greeted with groans when it was announced on the Highbury tannoy, sensed Wednesday's collective inertia. He rose like a phoenix above Bright, whose elbows this time remained firmly by his sides, and connected with a thumping header. Its power carried it through the grasp of Woods, arching back on his line, and Nigel Worthington's attempt to hack it clear only confirmed initial impressions: it had crossed the line, Worthington's clearance hit the roof of the net and raised the roof at Arsenal's end of the stadium.

Linighan was engulfed by a tide of red-and-white delirium. Just 18 months earlier, he had asked for a transfer because he could not gain regular first-team football. Now he will be remembered as the man who scored the latest FA Cup goal of all time. The Cup has traditionally bestowed greatness on lesser lights — who, for example, remembers Roger Osborne for anything but the Ipswich goal at Wembley in 1978 or Mike Trebilcock for anything but his two goals for Everton in 1966.

The significance of Linighan's goal was not lost on Graham, the first man to win all three major domestic trophies as both a player and manager. He said: 'Andy's goal is strange because, like Stephen Morrow, he's scored the winner in a cup final and has finished with broken bones. But I'm delighted that our heroes on both occasions have been players who would not normally command such attention. They are not really the people you think of in these situations. I never thought of taking him off just because he had a broken nose. I tried to get one throughout my career because it adds some character to your face!'

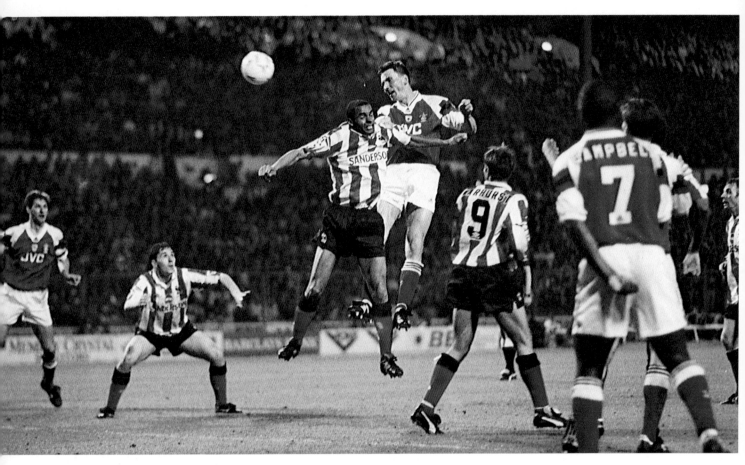

Above: **Andy Linighan scores** one of the most celebrated of all Arsenal goals – the winner in the 2-1 defeat of Sheffield Wednesday in the 1993 FA Cup final replay. The goal, from a Merson corner, came in the 120th minute and is the latest ever to have won the final. Another few seconds and Wembley would have seen the first FA Cup final to be decided by penalties. It was Arsenal's fourth trip to Wembley in 1993, and this fact was reflected by the 18,000 empty seats and the lowest ever attendance at a Wembley FA Cup final.

Linighan, his face spattered with blood when his turn came to hoist the Cup, said: 'It was a magnificent feeling to score the winner. I timed it just right, didn't I? I felt sorry for Wednesday — although no-one really wanted to settle it on penalties, they deserved to take it to a shoot-out. I'm not that bothered about the broken nose — but I know I won't be picking it for a while!'

Linighan was also the toast of his former Norwich team-mates. Arsenal's late, late winner nudged Wednesday out of Europe and put the Canaries into the UEFA Cup.

History will judge Arsenal's record-breakers. It will also be kinder to the Gunners than the Press, who curtailed the fanfares for Graham by harking back to his shortcomings in the League. There is no persecution complex at Highbury. No paranoia. But if any other club in the land had lifted two cups in one season, they would likely have been feted as heroes and celebrities.

Graham's men were, one must admit, largely ignored for their unique double. To the uncommitted, they are not cup football experts or knockout kings. Just Arsenal. Boring Arsenal. Lucky Arsenal. But two Championships and two cups in four years can't all be down to luck. Think of Arsenal and you think of greatness. The club's very strength is in its name. But it had been an odd season. The denouement had gone on too long. Arsenal and Wednesday had come to Wembley too often. To think that there were 18,000 empty seats at a Cup final with two such prominent teams playing is a remarkable comment on the season's end. Despite Manchester United finally winning the League, the new

Premier title had seemed to create uncertainty. More attention was paid to Clough and Forest's decline than to Villa's or Norwich's challenge for the title. As for Arsenal, it is hard to escape the conclusion that they owed it all to Wright. In the League the Gunners scored just 40 goals in 42 games, while in the two Cup competitions they managed 33 in 17 games. To score only 40 League goals and still end the season with two major trophies is an unlikely achievement. Of the season's 73 goals in all, no fewer than 30 were scored by Wright. No other player even reached double figures in all competitions, Campbell scoring just nine in all and Smith a depressing six, despite appearing in much of the Cup campaigning and in no fewer than 31 League matches.

So Arsenal entered the 1993–94 season as the first club to ever hold both domestic Cups. It was a significant season in many ways, not least that it was exactly 100 years since Arsenal had played their very first Football League match. That game had been against Newcastle on 2 September 1893 and the result was a 2–2 draw. At the time Arsenal were London's only professional club. The first half of the 1993–94 season, 100 years later, was to be dull but not unsuccessful. By the time Arsenal were asked to defend their FA Cup success on 10 January 1994, they were third in the Premier League and had won an astounding away leg in the UEFA cup against Standard Liege by no less than 7–0. The scorers were Adams, Selley, Smith, Merson, McGoldrick and two to Campbell. Arsenal won the tie 10–0 on aggregate. Nonetheless, that third place

in the League was not all it seemed, with Champions Manchester United no less than 14 points clear at this stage and only Blackburn showing any likelihood of catching them.

The first defence of the FA Cup was to be at the New Den, Millwall's new home. Arsenal's very first game, in 1886, had been played in the real Millwall on the other side of the Thames in the Isle of Dogs. The Arsenal side 108 years later had an apparent embarrassment of riches — starting without Linighan, Merson, Limpar, Selley, Davies, Jenson and Smith. The squad concept — also used to very good effect by Manchester United — was gradually taking hold, partially as a consequence of the Premier League's three substitute rule.

The third round game against Millwall was a poor advertisement for football. It was the 21st time in the season to date that Arsenal had kept a clean sheet, but it didn't make for the kind of spectacle that delights neutrals. In the very last minute Tony Adams came up for a corner, stubbed at a loose ball and saw it go in off Kasey Keller, Millwall's American goalkeeper.

Sadly it was to no avail. The next round saw a draw against the giant killers of the period — Bolton Wanderers. In consecutive seasons Bolton had knocked out Liverpool at Anfield and Everton at Goodison. A draw at Burnden Park seemed to give Arsenal a chance, but Bolton were totally convincing at Highbury and won 3–1 in extra time. With Villa winning 1–0 at Highbury in the League Cup (still sponsored by Coca-Cola) the Gunners had lost their grip on both the trophies they won in the previous season — and lost both at home.

With Manchester United so far ahead in the League, there was little to play for but the Cup Winners Cup. A convincing, if tight, 1–0 home win against Blackburn confirmed Arsenal's right to third place in the League, but really it was the Cup tie in Turin against Torino that mattered. Torino were not in the happiest frame of mind — facing both Italian and UEFA enquiries into allegations of bribery and the misuse of transfer fees. The first leg against Arsenal was no consolation for them. Arsenal were well on top, played a tight unadventurous formation, and went back to Highbury with a 0–0 draw. It was not a great night for the fans and it hardly set the pulse racing, but this was Arsenal's last real chance of a trophy in 1994 and caution was the only credible watchword. A 1–0 win, with another goal scored by Tony Adams, was an appropriate reward for a very tight and conservative approach.

Interestingly, George Graham chose to play Campbell rather than Wright. Campbell had been the butt of intense jeering from Arsenal fans during the debacle against Bolton. Certainly Campbell missed a number of chances, but the current Arsenal game remained directed towards Ian Wright, and Campbell has had to fill the roll of foil throughout his career. As Chris Lightbown pointed out in *The Sunday Times*, Arsenal are a team that tend to run deep from defence or knock the ball over the top for Wright to run on to. They have never been a pure, instinctive passing team in the style of Liverpool or Spurs and the Highbury crowd has had a tendency to impatience with a side which doesn't show the tenacity and grit to grind out results. The passing game was probably an essential for success in Europe — here sweepers are much more capable of plucking off the long through balls that Wright thrives on. Only Merson and Limpar of the contemporary players really exhibited the skills that can turn a game despite its tactical pattern and Limpar continued to be in and out of the team with Merson continuing to look uneasy on the left. Indeed, by the end of March, George Graham had sold Limpar to struggling Everton and, despite a good 1–0 defeat of Liverpool, it was clear that only the Cup Winners Cup counted.

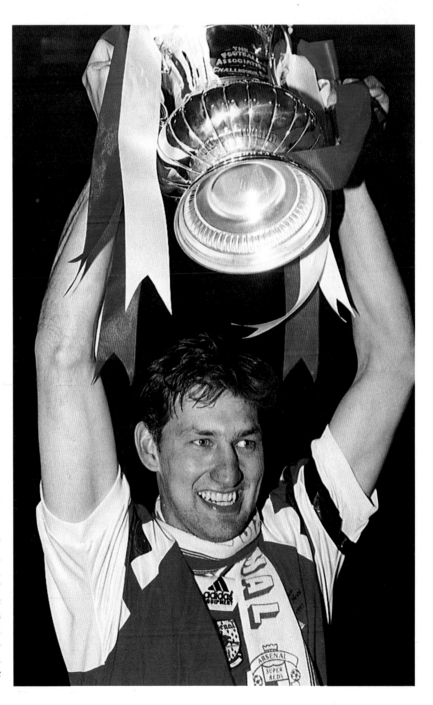

Following the previous celebratory accident with Steve Morrow after the Coca-Cola Cup final, Tony Adams keeps a tight grip on the FA Cup. He had just become the first captain to lift both major domestic Cups in the same season.

Tony Adams became an increasingly consistent and valuable goal scorer in vital matches during the 1990s. This is Arsenal's third goal in the 7-0 demolition of Standard Liege in the Cup Winners Cup, 3 November 1993.

On Thursday 29 March the team travelled to Paris for the semi-finals to play the French League leaders, Paris St Germain, who were unbeaten in 35 first-class matches. For perhaps the first time realistic memories of that shoot-out with Valencia 14 years before entered the head. Graham surprised everyone by picking Ian Wright and the striker had another outstanding game, leading the line and tirelessly running off the ball to create room for Merson and Smith. Wright had just come off an excellent away hat-trick at Ipswich and was playing as well as he ever had. In the 35th minute Graham's decision paid off, with Wright beating his marker to a Paul Davis free-kick and heading just inside the far post.

After 50 minutes St Germain equalised from a corner, but Arsenal's organisation was outstanding. At 1–1, with a precious away goal, everything was set up for the game at Highbury.

This task proved not particularly difficult by Arsenal's high standards. One goal, early on in the game from the previously abused Campbell, proved more than adequate and Arsenal held their ground in reasonable comfort. Paris St Germain were impressed. Said their manager: 'The quality of Arsenal's play surprised us. We knew they would be strong in defence but did not expect quite so much creativity upfront or in midfield.' But there were negatives, in particular a second yellow card for the irreplaceable Ian Wright. George Graham was pleased to have concluded a rather inconsistent season with another cup final, the first in Europe for so long. In an interview with Joe Lovejoy he praised

Manchester United: 'Everyone's getting out of their prams right now about United, and rightly so, but it took them 25 years to get it right. They've got more gifted individuals than us, but they've not got a Chippy Brady or Glenn Hoddle . . . The difference between them and us is that their midfield players are better than ours. I still think that Cantona will let you down at the very highest level . . . If Limpar (before he was sold) or Merson would work harder, that would improve our midfield. I'm not saying it would make it right, but it would help. What I really need is a young Peter Reid to be the boss there.'

Graham agrees that, if Manchester United wish to be personified by Cantona, then Tony Adams is the heart of Arsenal. 'We have always been strong defensively,' says Graham, 'and what's wrong with that? What I won't have is all this talk about us being a long-ball team. Sometimes we do bypass the midfield, but not all the time. Without Alan Smith (who was having an excellent end to the season) we don't hit it as long. We play better football . . . I don't know anyone who wants to be successful without playing attractive football, and I'm no different from anyone else in that respect.'

On the all too familiar subject of boring Arsenal, Graham is direct. 'We won two Championships playing super football. We played great football with a team that had great individuals. We went to Liverpool and won it in the best Championship finale there has ever been. Then we won a second title and lost one game in the whole season. That's the first time anyone's done that in a hundred years. But I

agree there was some pretty ropy stuff last season (1992–93) and in the early part of this (1993–94). We were terrible in the League last year, but we still won two cups. I know we're not right at the moment because I know what it takes to win Championships. We've got a defence as good as any in the country, but we definitely need more quality in midfield, although we've got good forwards.'

Like managers from time immemorial, Graham believes Arsenal are criticised unfairly, and he's right in seeing the prevailing attitude towards Arsenal nowadays as a cultural stereotype — almost impossible to eradicate. People who've never seen a football match in their lives seem to know that Arsenal are supposed to be boring. 'Generally, we're criticised unfairly. Who else from the south has won a Championship recently? We'll have a go. We'll go up north and take them on. Who else will?'

A fair point, and Arsenal also proved to be the only English club for three years to have progressed to the final stages of a European competition. As they flew to Copenhagen for the 1994 Cup Winners Cup final against Parma on 4 May their worries revolved around a squad hit by injury and suspension — Wright, Jensen, Hillier and Keown would all be missing. Parma were the reigning Cup Winners Cup holders, having beaten Royal Antwerp 3–1 in the final a year before. Parma were not a grand club, but they had a rich benefactor and the Swede Brolin's outstanding skills playing just behind the front two, Asprilla and Zola.

The absentees meant George Graham had to change the 4–3–3 formation he had introduced after the Cup defeat by Bolton. The traditional 4–4–2 had begun to go stale with too much being expected of Ian Wright, and the switch to Wright, Smith and Campbell upfront allowed Wright more freedom on the flanks to rove around. It was a system that depended on Alan Smith's ability to hold the ball and it was to be Alan Smith who shocked Parma in the 21st minute of the final with a stunning left foot volley from 20 yards. Dixon took a throw 40 yards out and Minotti, one of Italy's best sweepers, attempted an unnecessary overhead clearance. The ball fell to Alan Smith, who chested it down and struck it on the volley to perfection. The shot flew off the post into the net with keeper Bucci just beaten and Arsenal were 1–0 up in front of a crowded Copenhagen stadium. Just six minutes before, an excellent shot from Brolin had hit Seaman's right hand post and bounced back from the inside along the line. Parma were at this stage much the better team, with the relatively inexperienced Selley and Morrow (who seemed to save his appearance for Cup finals) holding the midfield line for Arsenal.

But that, in a sense, was that. Parma had 80 per cent of the game, Brolin was outstanding, but they could not score. Adams and, in particular, Bould were excellent and both were called up to the England squad a week later.

They defended superbly while Alan Smith held the ball up front and frustrated Parma. George Graham said later: 'Once we went a goal in front I knew we had a chance because our strength is keeping clean sheets. We had a team of heroes tonight and none more so than Alan Smith, who worked tirelessly up front.' In the end Brolin's shot against the post was the closest Parma came and Arsenal had won their first European title in 24 years. Steve Bould won the man of the match plaudits and, given their injury problems, it had been a remarkable evening for the Gunners.

Graham was rightly effusive in his praise of Parma after the match: 'They were fitter than us, they were sharper than us. Their forwards, particularly Brolin, were outstanding and it was a marvellous defensive performance by Arsenal. We're a club with marvellous team spirit and everyone — including the guys who couldn't play — was completely involved. You have to remember that around ten of the Parma squad will be in the World Cup in a month's time and, at the end of a long, hard season, they were a very tough proposition for us.'

Parma had passed the ball around well and played the game prettily. But Arsenal, as Joe

Alan Smith turns away after scoring a stunning volley against Parma in the Cup Winners Cup final on 4 May 1994 in Copenhagen. It proved to be the only goal of the game as Arsenal practised their 'we hold what we have' approach, so familiar to English fans down the years post-Herbert Chapman. It was yet another trophy, the fourth in four years, and it leaves the Gunners needing only the European Cup to complete a full set of European and domestic trophies.

Steve Bould causes problems for a clutch of Parma defenders during the 1994 Cup Winners Cup final in Copenhagen. Bould's excellent defensive performances alongside Tony Adams earnt him an England call-up under Terry Venables.

Lovejoy said, had marked and chased assiduously and kept their cleverer opponents at bay. Few teams do it better than Arsenal when it comes to defending a lead, said Lovejoy, and they slipped comfortably into the familiar 'what we have, we hold' mode. Nevio Scala, the Parma manager, also praised Arsenal: 'Tactically and technically we did not function. This was because Arsenal were the better team.'

Another final, another trophy, the fifth in six years for George Graham. It was a time to celebrate, a moment of great rejoicing for the English game. And, with a superb new all seater stadium and a solid team like this one, prospects looked good for the future.

Victory in Copenhagen came just over 107 years after that Christmas Day in 1886 when 15 men met in the Royal Oak, next to Woolwich Arsenal Station, and decided that they should take their kickabouts seriously. It was on that day that the word Arsenal was first used in a football club's title. On the Centenary Day in 1986 the Royal Oak itself was as crowded as on any Christmas Day. But there was nothing there to remind the cheerful crowd that an event of such magnitude took place exactly to the day, perhaps the very hour, a century before.

Memories that there ever was such a club south of the river have faded now. No more than a few can be left alive who remember standing on the long-gone terraces of Plumstead. In a very few years, the last remaining boys who stood on the original Spion Kop at the Manor Ground, and who witnessed the woe-begone Woolwich Arsenal of that disastrous season in 1913, will be dead. That page of history will be closed forever. No brick or pillar of the ground remains, no film exists, soon the final human memory will be consigned to oblivion. That sadness is perhaps what a history must also reflect. It is not all Wembley, champagne at the Café Royal and 'We're proud to say that name.'

Highbury, far from the Royal Oak in Woolwich, was also still on 25 December 1986. The last Christmas Day match was played there in 1954, against Champions-to-be Chelsea. The Gunners won 1–0, the great Tommy Lawton scoring the goal. Even an event as seemingly recent as football on Christmas Day is, in reality, as long ago as one-third of the club's history. 'Time driveth onwards fast,' said Tennyson. 'And in a little while our lips are dumb . . . all things are taken from us and become portions and parcels of the past.' Tennyson actually said dreadful past, a sentiment happily not applicable to Arsenal or to Highbury.

A still Christmas Day, more than a century on, would be a good time to stand and remember. The Underground station will also be closed; no mere symbol this, but probably the key to Highbury Stadium existing at all. Think of Herbert Chapman being struck by the station when he first came with long-defunct Leeds City in 1913. Think of Leslie Knighton meeting Tom Whittaker off the tube when the new signing arrived in 1919. Stand and think how many people have walked up those dank, ill-lit Edwardian tunnels in the last seven decades. Perhaps 15,000 every match Saturday for seventy years? That's around 25 million, half the population of Great Britain. And what dreams did they have, why did they come, what drew them to Gillespie Road, what did Arsenal mean to each and every one of them?

A quiet Christmas Day is a good time to think of Bastin, of James, of Drake, of Jack, of

Hapgood and Male. And, more recently, a happier, demobbed and optimistic generation of 60,000 would come every other week to see Reg Lewis and Ronnie Rooke, the immortal Joe Mercer and the golden 'Brylcreem Boy' Denis Compton, to live the two Championships and Cup finals of Tom Whittaker's brief reign.

Think of the intensity, of the hopes and fears, imagine if you can the mood on 1 May 1971, the last home game of the Double season. The tension was unbearable, nothing but a win was conceivable, and yet Arsenal's opponents, ironically, were to be Stoke City, just a month after the impossible dramas of the Hillsborough semi-final. It would be easy to go on, but each generation has its own memories. The next will hopefully have its own, just as glorious. It is the great-grandchildren of the young men who cheered Jack Lambert and Joe Hulme who are already pinning pictures of Tony Adams and Ian Wright on their bedroom walls.

In the past century Arsenal have risen to be possibly the greatest club in English history. That is inevitably a difficult argument to sustain, though the Arsenal of the 1930s must lay claim to be the greatest team in the past hundred years. Arsenal as a club probably have only two real competitors, Manchester United and Liverpool. Manchester United have the support today and the emotional backbone of Munich, but their playing record does not compare, nor did they ever dominate a generation as Liverpool and Arsenal have, nor did they ever alter the way

The players, the manager and the purpose of the whole exercise – the European Cup Winners Cup. As on so many occasions, Arsenal had dug deep into their reserves of stamina and determination, ending the season with a rather impressive piece of silverware.

the game was perceived or played. Liverpool are the other pretenders. On the field their credentials are better. They have a record in Europe second only to Real Madrid. Yet, somehow, there is an emotional element missing in Liverpool's success. Their story is not as romantic as Arsenal's or Manchester United's. We can now see that they have, despite their success in recent years, failed genuinely to occupy centre stage. Maybe their geographical position has worked against them, maybe the fact that their dominance coincided with the game's clear decline (as opposed to Arsenal's — which corresponded with its rise) somehow diminishes their achievement. Maybe the equivalent decline of their city (again, as opposed to inter-war London) took the shine away.

Arsenal are different from this Lancashire duo in more than geography. Why? Because the history of English football can be told through their story, because they did dominate a crucial generation, historically a vital decade, because they are Herbert Chapman's legacy, because they did, if unexpectedly, win the Double that established their place in the élite. All these facts suggest their claim should be stronger, though the strongest claim of all is to the emotions, for that is what football is about. Even when they are losing, Arsenal are still, somehow, the standard by which others are eventually judged.

So if you can spare the time on any Christmas Day think of Highbury, still and stolid, a repository of memories rather than cheers on the quietest day of the year. Think of 24 April 1915, of that same Nottingham Forest who donated the red shirts a century ago, coming to Highbury to lose a Second Division game 7–0, the last match fifth-placed Arsenal ever played outside top company. Think of a new, shiny Wembley, almost exactly fifteen years to the day later, on 26 April 1930, the moment when the pendulum greatly swung from north to south, the day Arsenal first won the FA Cup in a game which still defines thirty years of English football, the day the *Graf Zeppelin* sat silently above the pitch. Think of forty years further on, of 27 March 1971 at far away Hillsborough, of a clock which read 4.44pm, of the dreams of a Double which paused an instant from consignment to the dustbin of football history. That was perhaps the most unforgettable moment of all, the perfect illustration that football can be, and should be, about the emotion such set-piece dramas can evoke. Think what we would say now about the game had Frank McLintock's header hit the post rather than John Mahoney's hand, or if Gordon Banks had guessed right about Peter Storey's penalty. Think, at the end, about Michael Thomas and Bruce Grobbelaar. We will never live such a moment again.

Another hundred years will bring their own finals, their own emotions, their own dramas, their own trophies. There is not much we can say with any certainty about those hundred years, except, perhaps, that none of us will be here to help celebrate a second century in 2086.

There is so little to be sure of in a hundred years of football. In the very month that Royal Arsenal were founded in the Royal Oak in 1886, Preston North End were crushing mighty Queen's Park's pretensions north of the border with a 3–0 FA Cup win. Preston went on to the semi-final that year, the final the next and the first-ever Double the year after. A century later, at the end of the 1985–86 season, Preston sat next to bottom of the Fourth Division.

It is one of the joys of the game that we can only wait and see. Kierkegaard said that life can only be understood backwards but can only be lived forwards. He might have said the same about a football club. If the next hundred years can bring just moments like the last few seconds at Anfield in 1989, or the all-round team display at Copenhagen in 1994, then we will all have much to justify our enthusiasm and anticipation.

CHAPTER 10

The Arsenal Record Match by Match

very single first-class game that Arsenal have ever ayed in more than one hundred years is painstakingly corded in the following section. From 1919 onwards, e year they re-entered the First Division, not only each atch but also the team line-up and goalscorers are cluded. Though this information is also available for games played between 1886 and 1919, we are afraid at sheer pressure of space forced us, reluctantly, to onfine the details to the real era of modern Arsenal.

he matches covered are essentially those for which e are certain that the club played its available first am in a genuinely first-class competitive fixture. roadly this covers seven competitions – FA Cup, otball League/Premiership, Football League/Milk/ ttlewoods/Coca-Cola Cup, Charity Shield and the ree European club tournaments. Prior to the First orld War, there were also various minor tournaments hich Arsenal contested seriously – notably the ondon Cup, Kent Senior and Junior Cups and the nited League. During the two wars, Arsenal played in e senior competitions available to them, such as the ootball League South and the London League, and for e sake of completeness these games have also been cluded. Because so many players were in the forces, e club rarely turned out what might be described as s 'real' first team during the two wars, but the line- ps can usually be said to be the best available to ighbury at the time. Note also that, after the club uffered from bombing raids, home games were ayed elsewhere, usually at White Hart Lane. These ames have, however, been recorded as home atches.

etween 1886 and 1893, the only matches Royal rsenal played (except in the FA Cup) were friendlies r minor cup matches. Where we are certain (from ources such as the *Kent Messenger*) that the club as represented by the first team, then these have een included. After Arsenal joined the Football League 1893, we have generally confined the record to the even competitions mentioned above, though before e First World War other first team games have been ven for interest. Because there were fewer League ames then, some Saturdays were regularly reserved r 'important' friendlies. Where there are exceptions, eir status is made clear. Certain competitions, such s the London Cup (sometimes called, or combined ith, the London Senior Cup or London Charity Cup) ere regarded as first-class competitions for a umber of years until the club itself chose to relegate e competition to the reserve team or to a combination f first and reserve. We have tried to reflect these atterns. Modern day equivalents might be the Texaco up, Anglo-Scottish Cup or even Screen Sport Super up, which hover unhappily between the status of rst-class and supernumary. Unfortunately there are o rules and no simple answer to the status of such

matches. Obviously the club continued to play a large number of friendlies (such as testimonial games or tour matches) after the First World War, and still does so. These games can also be very hard to classify, but they are generally not competitive, nor do they necessarily involve the very best available side. We decided to err on the side of caution and, in general, exclude such matches except in very unusual cases. We have, however, included United League, Southern District Combination and London League matches in the years 1896-1904 as they were definitely contested by the first team on dates when there were no Football League fixtures.

All players are included for first-class games from 1919 onwards. We have also summarised all first-class appearances in the seven major competitions (defined above) from the time the club first entered the FA Cup. These appearance records do include the small number of games Arsenal played in the qualifying rounds of the FA Cup. Appearance records at the end of each season are for Football League matches only.

Substitutes have caused considerable statistical confusion in recent years. We have adopted the method which is becoming the norm, by awarding substitutes a full appearance when they come on the field, but only when they come on the field. A substitute who stays on the bench for the whole match is not recorded. This principle is also followed in each season's League appearance records and in the total appearance records at the end. In other words, a player with a record 38(3) might have started 34 games and come on as a substitute in 4. If he was substitute in other games but never came on the pitch, then this fact is *not* incorporated in any of these figures. The (3) refers to the number of goals scored in the relevant season/competition. Should the reader wish to check how many of the appearances were as substitute, he/she may do so by referring to the right-hand column of each season. This rule also applies in the case of Cup finals. Even if a substitute received a medal, he is not recorded as having made an appearance if he did not come onto the pitch.

Goalscorers are noted by superior numbers in each post-1919 table. We have generally taken the club's own records to be correct if there is any dispute about a goalscorer. We have also applied the accepted rule on own goals; if the ball, when struck by the last Arsenal player, was travelling in a direction which would have taken it into the goal had there been no further interference, then the goal is credited to the Arsenal player. If an opponent's interference changed the direction of a ball which would have *missed* the goal, then we have recorded it as an own-goal. Own goals are usually indicated beside the relevant

match with the word *opponents*. Goals scored in penalty shoot-outs have not been treated as first-class goals in these records.

Venues of semi-finals, finals and neutral replays of Cup matches have been given where space permits, as have the relevant round numbers. In a number of cases in the early years, no information is available on exactly where a game was played, and the venue has thus been left blank. It is quite possible that Royal Arsenal and their opponents both regularly played on Plumstead Common so both would be at home. Instances where a game was abandoned or did not run the full 90 minutes are generally indicated if the information is available, but abandoned League or Cup matches are not recorded, only the completed fixture. As this is essentially a record of matches played in chronological order, aggregate scores in two-legged matches are generally not recorded separately.

In a surprisingly large number of matches from the nineteenth century, there was either a disputed score (such as in the club's very first game), inconsistencies in recorded scores, or even the complete lack of any score at all in the newspaper information. The latter often occurred because opposing captains disagreed and the local paper preferred to offend neither club and simply did not give a result at all. Where there is no score available, we have left the space blank or introduced a question mark. There are occasions in the early years when a game was included in the official fixture list but no record of the result has ever been found. Where a score is disputed we have generally taken the report which seemed the most credible (and not necessarily the most advantageous to Arsenal). While we have tried to ensure that early friendly games were definitely played by the first team, there is often so little clarity in early reports that it is not impossible for errors to have occurred in the material. As a result, we should welcome any questions and corrections from readers.

Finally we should like to acknowledge our enormous debt to John Burt, the club statistician, who has painstakingly compiled all of this information (and very much more which space constrained us from publishing) and Daniel Feinstein who carefully put together the individual aggregate player appearances.

To conclude, between December 1886 and 4 May 1994, Arsenal played no fewer than 5968 games which we have defined as first-class. Of these they won 2779, lost 1697 and drew 1286. Based on two points for a win and one for a draw Arsenal have a percentage success rate of 57%. In their 5968 games they have scored 10,956 goals and conceded 7585.

SEASON 1886-1887
FRIENDLIES

11 Dec	Eastern W	A	W	6-0
8 Jan	Erith	H	W	6-1
15 Jan	Alexandria U	H	W	11-0
22 Jan	Eastern W	H	W	1-0
29 Jan	Erith	A	W	3-2
5 Feb	Millwall Rov	A	L	0-4
12 Feb	Alexandria U	A	W	6-0
26 Feb	2nd Rifle Brigade	H	D	0-0
12 Mar	Millwall Rov	H	W	3-0
26 Mar	2nd Rifle Brigade	A	L	0-1

	P	W	L	D	F:A
Arsenal	10	7	2	1	36:8

SEASON 1887-1888
FRIENDLIES

30 Sep	Alexandria U	H	W	5-1
15 Oct	Clapton Pilgrims		D	2-2
22 Oct	St Lukes			
5 Nov	Grange Institute		W	4-0
12 Nov	Iona Deptford		D	1-1
19 Nov	Tottenham H	A	L	1-2
26 Nov	Millwall Rov	A	L	0-3
2 Dec	Grange Park	H		
10 Dec	Brixton Rangers	H	L	1-2
16 Dec	Shrewsbury Park		W	4-0
31 Dec	Forest Gate Alliance	A	L	1-2
14 Jan	Iona Deptford	A	W	3-2
28 Jan	Champion Hill		W	6-0
3 Feb	Tottenham H	H	W	6-2
11 Feb	Millwall Rov	H	D	3-3
17 Feb	Erith		W	2-1
24 Feb	Forest Gate Alliance	H	D	1-1
2 Mar	Grange Institute		W	2-1
9 Mar	Brixton Ran		W	9-3
16 Mar	Ascham		W	5-0
30 Mar	Millwall Rov	H	W	3-0
6 Apr	Alexandria U	A	W	3-1

London Senior Cup

8 Oct	Grove House	H	W	3-1
29 Oct	Barnes		L	0-4

Junior Matches

19 Nov	Woolwich Pupils & Teachers	H	W	1-0
26 Nov	Erith	A	L	0-1
24 Feb	Thistle		L	1-2

	P	W	L	D	F:A
Arsenal	24	14	6	4	66:33

SEASON 1888-1889
FRIENDLIES

15 Sep	London Scottish		D	3-3
22 Sep	Tottenham H		L	0-1
29 Sep	Old St Pauls		W	7-3
6 Oct	Grove House		W	2-0
13 Oct	London Scottish		W	4-0
20 Oct	2nd Rifle Brigade		L	1-2
27 Oct	Brixton Ran		L	1-3
10 Nov	Millwall Rov			
17 Nov	St Lukes		D	1-1
1 Dec	Phoneix		D	0-0
22 Dec	St Brides			
5 Jan	Vulcan		D	1-1
12 Jan	Unity		D	0-0
26 Jan	St Lukes			
2 Feb	Ilford		L	1-2
16 Feb	Millwall Rov			
23 Feb	Ilford		L	0-1
2 Mar	London Caledonians		L	1-2
9 Mar	Tottenham H		W	1-0
16 Mar	South Eastern Ran		L	1-2
23 Mar	Royal Artillery		W	9-0
30 Mar	2nd Rifle Brigade		W	2-0
1 Apr	2nd Rifle Brigade		W	6-1
6 Apr	Old St Pauls		W	1-0
13 Apr	Millwall Rov		W	3-0
19 Apr	Boston T		L	1-4
20 Apr	Spartan Rov		W	6-0
23 Apr	Scots Guards		W	7-2
27 Apr	London Caledonians		L	0-1

London Association Cup

3 Nov	Phoneix		W	3-0
24 Nov	Dulwich		W	4-2
8 Dec	Old St Pauls		W	3-1
19 Jan	Clapton (Semi-Final)		L	0-2

Kent County Challenge Cup

10 Nov	Horton Kirby		W	6-2
29 Dec	Iona		W	5-1
9 Feb	Gravesend		D	3-3*

*Arsenal disqualified for refusing to play extra time.

	P	W	L	D	F:A
Arsenal	32	16	10	6	83:40

SEASON 1889-1890
FRIENDLIES

7 Sep	London Caledonians	H	D	2-2
14 Sep	Casuals	H	W	6-0
21 Sep	Tottenham H	H	W	10-1
28 Sep	Unity	H	W	8-0
19 Oct	St Old Marks College	A	W	2-1
30 Nov	Marlow	A	L	0-2
21 Dec	Ilford	A	W	2-0
25 Dec	Preston Hornets	H	W	5-0
26 Dec	Chatham	A	D	2-2
27 Dec	Reading T	H	W	5-1
4 Jan	Windsor Phoenix	H	W	3-1
18 Jan	Old Harrovians	H	W	2-1
25 Jan	Foxes	H	W	7-2
8 Feb	Chiswick Park	H	D	1-1
1 Mar	Birmingham St George	H	L	1-4
15 Mar	Ilford	A	W	4-1
28 Mar	Clapton	A	L	0-2
31 Mar	W. H. Loraine XI	H	W	3-1
7 Apr	1st Lincs. Regt.	H	W	2-1
12 Apr	Marlow	H	W	3-1
19 Apr	Chatham	H	W	1-0
26 Apr	Clapton	H	W	6-1
3 May	London Cal/Clapton Comb	H	W	3-2
10 May	Millwall Athletic	A	D	3-3

FA Cup

5 Oct	Lyndhurst (Q1)	H	W	11-0
26 Oct	Thorpe (Q2)	A	D	2-2*
16 Nov	Crusaders (Q3)	H	W	5-2
7 Dec	Swifts (Q4)	H	L	1-5

*Thorpe withdrew

London Cup

2 Nov	Unity	H	W	4-1
23 Nov	Foxes	H	W	4-1
14 Dec	St Martins Ath	H	W	6-0
11 Jan	London Caledonians	H	W	3-1
8 Mar	Old Westminster (Final)		L	0-1

London Charity Cup

1 Feb	Marlow	H	W	4-1
22 Feb	2nd Batt Scots Guards	H	W	3-0
5 Apr	Old Westminster (Final)	H	W	3-1

Kent Senior Cup

12 Oct	5th Northern Fusiliers	H	W	6-1
9 Nov	West Kent	H	W	10-1
14 Dec	Gravesend	H	W	7-2
15 Feb	Chatham	H	W	5-0
22 Mar	Thanet W (Final)		W	3-0

Six-a-Side Competition
Run by National Physical Recreation Society at Agricultural Hall

31 May	London Caledonians		W	15-7

	P	W	L	D	F:A
Arsenal	41	31	5	5	158:49

SEASON 1890-1891
FRIENDLIES

6 Sep	93rd Highlanders	H	D	1-1
13 Sep	Casuals	H	W	5-4
20 Sep	Ilford	H	W	6-0
27 Sep	London Caledonians	H	W	3-1
4 Oct	Chiswick Park	A	W	4-0
11 Oct	93rd Highlanders	H	W	4-1
18 Oct	Old St Marks	A	W	4-0
25 Oct	St Bartholomews Hospital	H	W	1-0
1 Nov	South Shore (Blackpool)	H	D	2-2
8 Nov	Ilford	A	W	3-0
15 Nov	Clapton	A	L	1-2
22 Nov	Gainsborough Trinity	H	W	2-1
1 Dec	Cambridge Univ	H	W	5-1
6 Dec	Casuals	H	D	0-0
24 Jan	Millwall Athletic	A	W	1-0
26 Jan	Everton	H	L	0-5
7 Feb	St Bartholomews Hospital	H	W	5-4
14 Mar	Old Harrovians	H	W	5-1
21 Mar	Sheffield U	H	D	1-1
27 Mar	Highland Light Infantry	H	W	3-1
28 Mar	Old Harrovians	H	W	5-0
30 Mar	Heart of Midlothians	H	L	1-5
31 Mar	Nottingham F	H	L	0-5
18 Apr	Clapton	H	W	3-1
25 Apr	Sunderland	H	L	1-3
30 Apr	London Caledonians	H	D	1-1
2 May	1st Highland Light Infantry	H	W	5-1
3 Jan	London Caledonians			(abandoned)

FA Cup

17 Jan	Derby Co (1)	H	L	1-2

London Cup

13 Dec	Old Westminster	A	W	4-1
31 Jan	Old Westminster	A	L	4-5
21 Feb	Casuals	H	W	3-2
28 Feb	Clapton	A	W	3-2
7 Mar	St Barts Hosp (Final)		W	6-0

London Charity Cup

14 Feb	Crusaders	H	W	1-0
4 Apr	Old Carthusians	A	D	1-1
8 Apr	Old Carthusians	A	D	2-2
11 Apr	Old Carthusians	A	L	1-2

	P	W	L	D	F:A
Arsenal	37	22	8	7	98:58

SEASON 1891-1892
FRIENDLIES

5 Sep	Sheffield U	H	L	0-2
12 Sep	Casuals	H	W	2-1
19 Sep	Gainsborough Trinity	H	L	1-4
26 Sep	W B A	H	D	1-1
3 Oct	St George Birmingham	H	L	1-5
8 Oct	Royal Engineers	H	W	8-0
10 Oct	Crusaders	H	W	4-1
17 Oct	Bootle	A	D	2-2
19 Oct	Sheffield Wed	H	L	1-8
24 Oct	Long Eaton Rangers	H	W	3-1
29 Oct	Royal Artillery	H	W	10-0
31 Oct	Clapton	A	W	7-0
5 Nov	Notts Co	A	L	3-4
7 Nov	London Caledonians	A	W	4-3
12 Nov	Erith	H	W	7-0
14 Nov	Cambridge University	H	W	5-1
19 Nov	Woolwich League	H	W	6-1
21 Nov	St Bartholomews Hospital	H	W	9-0
23 Nov	2nd Scots Guards	H	W	6-0
28 Nov	Canadians	H	D	1-1
30 Nov	Sheffield W	A	L	1-5
3 Dec	Canadians	H	W	4-0
5 Dec	Lincoln C	H	W	3-1
10 Dec	2nd Royal West Kent Reg	H	L	1-2
12 Dec	Chiswick Park	H	W	5-1
19 Dec	Preston N E	H	L	0-3
25 Dec	Sheffield U	A	D	3-3
26 Dec	1st Lincolnshire Reg	H	W	6-0
2 Jan	Cowlairs (Glasgow)	H	L	1-2
7 Jan	City Ramblers	H	W	3-0
9 Jan	Crusaders	H	W	4-1
21 Jan	Windsor Phoenix	H	W	3-1
23 Jan	Grimsby T	H	W	4-1
30 Jan	Burton W	H	W	3-1
4 Feb	Sheffield U	H	L	1-4
6 Feb	Cambridge University	H	W	2-1
13 Feb	Chatham	H	W	3-2
20 Feb	Burton Swifts	H	W	3-1
25 Feb	Windsor Phoenix	A	W	5-0
27 Feb	Derby Co	H	L	3-4
3 Mar	Borough Road College	H	W	5-1
5 Mar	Wolverhampton W	H	L	1-4
10 Mar	Casuals	H	W	3-1
12 Mar	Marlow	A	W	5-2
14 Mar	3rd Lanark Rovers	H	L	0-1
19 Mar	Highland Light Infantry	H	W	3-2
22 Mar	Preston N E	H	D	3-3
26 Mar	Everton	H	D	2-2
31 Mar	Notts Co	H	L	2-4
2 Apr	Chatham	H	W	5-3
9 Apr	South Shore Blackpool	H	D	1-1
15 Apr	Small Heath	H	L	1-2
16 Apr	Crewe Alexandra	H	W	2-1
18 Apr	Bootle	H	D	1-1
23 Apr	Clapton	H	W	4-1
26 Apr	Bolton W	H	W	3-2
30 Apr	Glasgow Ran	H	L	2-3

FA Cup

16 Jan	Small Heath (1)		L	1-5

	P	W	L	D	F:A
Arsenal	58	33	17	8	183:107

SEASON 1892-1893
FRIENDLIES

2 Sep	Highland Light Infantry		W	9-0
7 Sep	Gainsborough T		W	4-2
8 Sep	Scots Guards		W	5-1
10 Sep	Casuals		W	4-0
12 Sep	Sheffield U	A	L	0-1
16 Sep	Darlington		W	3-2
24 Sep	Crusaders		W	4-0
1 Oct	Marlow		W	4-0
6 Oct	3rd West Kent Rangers		W	3-0
8 Oct	Clapton		W	4-1
20 Oct	Sheffield U	H	W	1-0
22 Oct	Staffordshire Reg		W	1-0
27 Oct	Oxford University		L	0-4
5 Nov	Lincoln C	H	W	4-0
7 Nov	Fleetwood Rangers		L	1-2
12 Nov	Cambridge University		D	6-6
14 Nov	Sunderland	H	L	0-4
23 Nov	Ipswich T		W	5-0
25 Nov	Norfolk County		W	4-1
26 Nov	Clapton		W	5-0
3 Dec	W B A	H	W	3-1
12 Dec	Mr Armitage XI		W	3-1
17 Dec	Nottingham F	H	L	2-3
23 Dec	Leith Athletic	H	W	1-0
25 Dec	Burslem P V		L	1-3
26 Dec	Stockton		W	1-0
27 Dec	Blackpool	H	D	1-1
2 Jan	Glasgow Thistle	H	L	1-2
7 Jan	Middlesbrough		L	0-2
11 Jan	Sussex Martelos		W	2-0
12 Jan	Brighton		W	2-0
14 Jan	Wolverhampton W	H	L	1-3
25 Jan	Oxford University		L	0-1
28 Jan	Chatham		L	1-3
31 Jan	1st Batt Sherwood Foresters		W	3-0
3 Feb	Casuals		W	4-1
6 Feb	Royal Lancaster Regiment		W	2-0
9 Feb	Cambridge University		L	2-4
11 Feb	Small Heath	H	W	3-1
13 Feb	3rd Lanark	H	W	3-0
18 Feb	Millwall		W	5-0
25 Feb	Walsall Town Swifts	H	W	4-0
27 Feb	Notts Greenhalgh		L	1-3
3 Mar	Middlesbrough		L	0-2
11 Mar	Dumbarton	H	W	3-1
13 Mar	Aston Villa	H	L	0-1
18 Mar	Middlesbrough		W	4-2
25 Mar	Millwall		W	1-0
31 Mar	Middlesbrough		W	4-1
1 Apr	Accrington St	H	W	3-1
3 Apr	Grimsby T	H	L	3-5
8 Apr	Casuals		W	2-0
15 Apr	Crusaders		W	3-0
22 Apr	Derby Co	H	D	0-0
24 Apr	London Welsh		W	4-0
26 Apr	Sevenoaks		W	11-0
29 Apr	Stoke	H	L	0-1

FA Cup

15 Oct	Highland Light Infantry (Q1)	H	W	3-0
29 Oct	City Ramblers (Q2)	H	W	10-1
19 Nov	Millwall (Q3)	H	W	3-2
10 Dec	Clapton (Q4)	H	W	5-0
21 Jan	Sunderland (1)	A	L	0-6

	P	W	L	D	F:A
Arsenal	62	41	18	3	172:76

SEASON 1893-1894
FOOTBALL LEAGUE (DIVISION 2)

2 Sep	Newcastle U	H	D	2-2
9 Sep	Notts Co	A	L	2-3
11 Sep	Walsall	H	W	4-0
25 Sep	Grimsby T	H	W	3-1
30 Sep	Newcastle U	A	L	0-6
21 Oct	Small Heath	A	L	1-4
28 Oct	Liverpool	H	L	0-5
11 Nov	Aidwick	H	W	1-0
13 Nov	Rotherham	H	W	3-0
18 Nov	Burton Swifts	A	L	2-6
9 Dec	Northwick Victoria	A	D	2-2
25 Dec	Burslem	H	W	4-1
26 Dec	Grimsby T	A	L	1-3
30 Dec	Ardwick	A	W	1-0
1 Jan	Liverpool	A	L	0-2
6 Jan	Burslem	A	L	1-2
3 Feb	Lincoln C	A	L	0-3
6 Feb	Rotherham	A	D	1-1
10 Feb	Crewe Alexandra	H	W	3-2
12 Feb	Walsall	A	W	2-1
17 Feb	Lincoln C	H	W	4-0
24 Feb	Middlesbrough Ironopolis	A	W	6-3
3 Mar	Crewe Alexandra	A	D	0-0
10 Mar	Middlesbrough Ironopolis	H	W	1-0
23 Mar	Northwich Victoria	H	W	6-0
24 Mar	Notts Co	H	L	1-2
31 Mar	Small Heath	H	L	1-4
14 Apr	Burton Swifts	H	L	0-2

FA Cup

14 Oct	Ashford University (Q1)	H	W	12-0
4 Nov	Clapton (Q2)	H	W	6-2
25 Nov	Millwall (Q3)	H	W	2-0
16 Dec	2nd Scots Guards (Q4)	A	W	2-1
27 Jan	Sheffield W (1)	H	L	1-2

Friendlies

4 Sep	Doncaster Rov		W	4-1
16 Sep	Chatham		W	5-0
23 Sep	Middlesbrough	H	W	3-1
7 Oct	Casuals		W	5-1
9 Oct	Sunderland	H	L	1-4
12 Oct	London Caledonians		W	10-3
23 Oct	Mr Roston Bourkes XI		W	4-3
30 Oct	Wolverhampton W	H	W	1-0
30 Nov	London Caledonians		D	1-1
2 Dec	W B A	A	W	5-0
11 Dec	Preston N E		D	1-1
23 Dec	Crusaders		W	7-0
13 Jan	Accrington Stanley		W	2-0
15 Jan	Aston Villa	H	L	1-3
20 Jan	Chatham		W	4-0
29 Jan	Blackpool		W	5-2
1 Mar	London Caledonians		W	1-0
5 Mar	Luton T		W	2-0
12 Mar	Sheffield U	A	W	2-0
17 Mar	Millwall		D	2-2
26 Mar	St Mirren*		L	1-3
2 Apr	Nottingham F	H	L	1-3
7 Apr	Millwall		W	4-1
9 Apr	Sheffield U	H	L	0-1
11 Apr	New Brompton		W	4-1
12 Apr	Westerham District XI		W	6-3
16 Apr	Luton T		D	3-3
21 Apr	Burnley	H	W	2-0
25 Apr	Corinthians	A	L	3-4
28 Apr	Stoke	H	D	3-3

Position in Football League Table

	P	W	L	D	F:A	Pts	
Liverpool	28	22	0	6	77:18	50	1st
Arsenal	28	12	12	4	52:55	28	9th

SEASON 1894-1895
FOOTBALL LEAGUE (DIVISION 2)

1 Sep	Lincoln C	A	L	2-5
10 Sep	Grimsby T	H	L	1-3
15 Sep	Burton Swifts	A	L	0-3
22 Sep	Bury	H	W	4-2
29 Sep	Manchester C	H	W	4-2
6 Oct	Lincoln C	H	W	5-2
13 Oct	Newton Heath	A	D	3-3
20 Oct	Rotherham	A	W	2-1
27 Oct	Notts Co	A	D	2-2
3 Nov	Notts Co	H	W	2-1
10 Nov	Walsall	A	L	1-4
24 Nov	Newcastle U	A	W	4-2
8 Dec	Darwen	H	W	4-0
15 Dec	Manchester C	A	L	1-4
25 Dec	Burslem Port Vale	H	W	7-0
26 Dec	Grimsby T	A	L	2
1 Jan	Darwen	A	L	1
7 Jan	Leicester Fosse	A	L	1
12 Jan	Newcastle U	H	W	3
19 Jan	Burslem P V	A	W	1
26 Jan	Burton Wanderers	H	D	1
9 Feb	Rotherham	H	D	1
23 Feb	Burton Swifts	H	W	3
2 Mar	Bury	A	L	0
9 Mar	Leicester Fosse	H	D	3
23 Mar	Crewe Alexandra	A	D	0
30 Mar	Newton Heath	H	W	3
6 Apr	Crewe Alexandra	H	W	7
12 Apr	Walsall	H	W	6
20 Apr	Burton W	A	L	1

FA Cup

2 Feb	Bolton W (1)	A	L	0

Friendlies

3 Sep	Nottingham F	H	W	3
8 Sep	Fleetwood Rovers		W	4
17 Sep	W B A		L	0
24 Sep	Renton		W	6
4 Oct	Casuals		W	8
15 Oct	Sunderland	H	W	2
29 Oct	Luton T		W	5
12 Nov	R. Bourkes XI		W	6
17 Nov	Casuals		W	4
21 Nov	Marlow		W	4
1 Dec	Stoke C	H	W	3
3 Dec	St Bernards	H	L	1
24 Dec	New Brompton		L	0
29 Dec	Dresden University		W	1
5 Jan	Sheppey University		W	6
11 Feb	Luton T		W	2
16 Feb	Chatham		W	6
25 Feb	Liverpool	H	W	4
6 Mar	Eastbourne		W	5
13 Mar	Bromley & District		W	4
16 Mar	Gainsborough Trinity	H	W	2
20 Mar	Home Park Plymouth		W	2
21 Mar	Weymouth		W	5
25 Mar	Millwall	H	D	1
1 Apr	Blackburn Rov	H	D	2
8 Apr	Millwall	A	D	0
13 Apr	Dumbarton		W	5
15 Apr	Small Heath	H	L	3
25 Apr	Royal Ordnance		L	0
27 Apr	Millwall	A	W	3
30 Apr	Grimsby T		L	0

Position in Football League Table

	P	W	L	D	F:A	Pts	
Bury	30	23	5	2	78:33	48	1
Arsenal	30	14	10	6	75:58	34	8

SEASON 1895-1896
FOOTBALL LEAGUE (DIVISION 2

2 Sep	Grimsby T	H	W	3-
7 Sep	Manchester C	H	L	0-
14 Sep	Lincoln C	A	D	1-
21 Sep	Lincoln C	H	W	4-
28 Sep	Manchester C	A	L	0-
5 Oct	Rotherham	H	W	5-
12 Oct	Burton W	H	W	3-
19 Oct	Burton Swifts	H	W	5-
26 Oct	Rotherham	A	L	0-
2 Nov	Notts Co	A	W	4-
9 Nov	Newton Heath	H	W	2-
16 Nov	Liverpool	H	L	0-
30 Nov	Newton Heath	A	L	1-
7 Dec	Leicester Fosse	H	D	1-
14 Dec	Burton W	A	L	1-
21 Dec	Burton Swifts	A	L	2-
23 Dec	Crewe Alexandra	A	W	1-
25 Dec	Burslem Port Vale	H	W	2-
4 Jan	Loughborough	H	W	6-
11 Jan	Liverpool	A	L	0-
18 Jan	Newcastle U	A	L	1-
25 Jan	Leicester Fosse	A	L	0-
15 Feb	Burslem Port Vale	A	W	2-
29 Feb	Loughborough	A	L	1-
7 Mar	Notts Co	H	W	2-
14 Mar	Darwen	A	D	1-
21 Mar	Crewe Alexandra	H	W	7-
4 Apr	Grimsby T	A	D	1-
6 Apr	Newcastle U	H	W	2-
18 Apr	Darwen	H	L	1-

FA Cup

2 Feb	Burnley (1)	A	L	1-

Friendlies

9 Sep	Millwall	A	W	3-
23 Sep	Sheffield W	H	W	2-
14 Oct	Everton	H	L	0-
4 Nov	Royal Ordnance		W	3-
21 Nov	Casuals		W	3-
23 Nov	Barnsley St Peters		W	4-
9 Dec	Sunderland	H	L	1-
26 Dec	Cliftonville	H	W	10-
28 Dec	Darlington		W	6-
1 Jan	Hastings		W	12-
20 Jan	Cambridge University	H	W	7-
10 Feb	Royal Ordnance		W	6-
22 Feb	Stirlingshire		W	5-
24 Feb	Newton Heath	H	W	6-
2 Mar	Casuals		W	4-
16 Mar	Tottenham H		L	1-
23 Mar	Sheffield U	H	W	3-
26 Mar	Tottenham H		W	3-
28 Mar	Millwall	A	W	3-
2 Apr	Stockton		W	2-
3 Apr	Dundee		W	3-
7 Apr	Gravesend		W	4-
11 Apr	Millwall	H	D	2-

3 Apr	Everton	H	W	2-1
0 Apr	Whittaker XI		W	3-2
5 Apr	Luton T	H	W	5-2
7 Apr	Luton T	A	L	0-2
9 Apr	Chatham		W	1-0
0 Apr	Tottenham H		L	2-3

osition in Football League Table

	P	W	L	D	F:A	Pts	
verpool	30	22	6	2	106:32	46	1st
rsenal	30	14	12	4	59:42	32	7th

EASON 1896-1897
OOTBALL LEAGUE (DIVISION 2)

5 Sep	Manchester C	A	D	1-1
2 Sep	Walsall	H	D	1-1
4 Sep	Burton Wanderers	A	W	3-0
9 Sep	Loughborough	H	W	2-0
6 Sep	Notts Co	H	L	2-3
2 Oct	Burton Wanderers	H	W	3-0
7 Oct	Walsall	A	L	3-5
4 Oct	Gainsborough	H	W	6-1
7 Nov	Notts Co	A	L	4-7
4 Nov	Small Heath	A	L	2-5
3 Nov	Grimsby T	H	W	4-2
5 Dec	Lincoln C	A	W	3-2
2 Dec	Loughborough	A	L	0-8
9 Dec,	Blackpool	H	W	4-2
5 Dec	Lincoln C	H	W	6-2
6 Dec	Gainsborough	A	L	1-4
1 Jan	Darwen	A	L	1-4
4 Jan	Blackpool	A	D	1-1
3 Jan	Newcastle U	A	L	0-2
3 Feb	Leicester Fosse	A	L	3-6
) Feb	Burton Swifts	H	W	3-0
3 Mar	Burton Swifts	A	W	2-1
2 Mar	Newton Heath	A	D	1-1
9 Mar	Small Heath	H	L	2-3
3 Apr	Newton Heath	H	L	0-2
3 Apr	Grimsby T	A	L	1-3
5 Apr	Newcastle U	H	W	5-1
7 Apr	Leicester Fosse	H	W	2-1
9 Apr	Darwen	H	W	1-0
3 Apr	Manchester C	H	L	1-2

FA Cup

2 Dec	Leyton (Q)	H	W	5-2
2 Jan	Chatham (Q)	H	W	4-0
5 Jan	Millwall (Q)	A	L	2-4

United League

Sep	Rushden	W	3-2
3 Oct	Luton T	D	2-2
5 Oct	Rushden	L	3-5
3 Oct	Wellingborough	W	2-1
2 Nov	Kettering	D	1-1
9 Nov	Tottenham H	W	2-1
9 Nov	Kettering	W	1-0
) Nov	Wellingborough	L	1-4
9 Jan	Loughborough	W	5-3
5 Feb	Tottenham H	D	2-2
Feb	Millwall	W	3-1
Mar	Luton T	L	2-5
Apr	Loughborough	L	0-4
Apr	Millwall	L	1-3

Friendlies

Sep	Rossendale	W	4-0
) Sep	Millwall	W	2-1
) Oct	Millwall	L	1-5
Oct	Luton	L	1-3
Oct	Clyde	L	2-3
Nov	Millwall	D	2-2
Dec	Aston Villa	L	1-3
Jan	Ilkeston	W	7-0
3 Feb	Luton	W	5-1
5 Feb	Celtic	L	4-5
Mar	Reading	W	6-2
5 Mar	Casuals	L	3-5
) Mar	Reading	W	2-1
5 Mar	St Mary's, Southampton	W	2-1
Mar	Nottingham F	W	1-0
) Apr	Norfolk	L	3-4
5 Apr	Sheffield U	D	1-1

osition in Football League Table

	P	W	L	D	F:A	Pts	
otts Co	30	19	7	4	92:43	42	1st
senal	30	13	13	4	68:70	30	10th

sition in United League Table

	P	W	L	D	F:A	Pts	
illwall	14	11	2	1	43:22	23	1st
senal	14	6	5	3	28:34	15	3rd

EASON 1897-1898
OOTBALL LEAGUE (DIVISION 2)

Sep	Grimsby T	H	W	4-1
Sep	Newcastle U	A	L	1-4
Sep	Burnley	A	L	0-5
Sep	Lincoln C	H	D	2-2
Sep	Gainsborough	H	W	4-0
Sep	Manchester C	A	L	1-4
Oct	Luton T	A	W	2-0
Oct	Luton T	H	W	3-0
Oct	Newcastle U	H	D	0-0
Oct	Leicester Fosse	H	L	0-3
Nov	Walsall	A	L	2-3
Nov	Walsall	H	W	4-0
Nov	Blackpool	H	W	2-1
Dec	Leicester Fosse	A	L	1-2
Dec	Loughborough	A	W	3-1
27 Dec	Lincoln C	A	W	3-2
1 Jan	Blackpool	A	D	3-3
8 Jan	Newton Heath	H	W	5-1
15 Jan	Burton Swifts	A	W	2-1
5 Feb	Manchester C	H	D	2-2
12 Feb	Grimsby T	A	W	4-1
26 Feb	Newton Heath	A	L	1-5
5 Mar	Small Heath	H	W	4-2
12 Mar	Darwen	A	W	4-1
19 Mar	Loughborough	H	W	4-0
26 Mar	Gainsborough	A	L	0-1
2 Apr	Burnley	H	D	1-1
9 Apr	Darwen	H	W	3-1
11 Apr	Burton Swifts	H	W	3-0
23 Apr	Small Heath	A	L	1-2

FA Cup

30 Oct	St Albans (Q)	H	W	9-0
20 Nov	Sheppey United (Q)	H	W	3-0
11 Dec	New Brompton (Q)	H	W	4-2
29 Jan	Burnley (Q)	A	L	1-3

United League

22 Sep	Loughborough	A	W	3-1
4 Oct	Kettering	H	W	4-0
11 Oct	Wellingborough	A	W	3-2
13 Dec	Rushden	H	W	3-1
20 Dec	Southampton	H	D	1-1
25 Dec	Tottenham H	H	L	2-3
10 Jan	Wellingborough	H	W	3-1
22 Jan	Millwall	A	D	2-2
19 Feb	Millwall	H	D	2-2
21 Feb	Luton T	H	D	2-2
28 Mar	Rushden	A	W	3-2
1 Apr	Loughborough	H	W	4-1
4 Apr	Kettering	A	W	2-1
8 Apr	Tottenham H	A	D	0-0
13 Apr	Southampton	A	L	0-3
16 Apr	Luton T	A	L	1-2

Friendlies

15 Sep	Gravesend	A	W	3-1
1 Nov	Reading	H	W	3-1
8 Nov	Blackburn Rov	H	W	3-0
15 Nov	Bristol C	A	L	2-4
9 Feb	Maidstone	A	W	3-0
21 Mar	Bristol C	H	W	3-1
26 Apr	Thames Iron Works	A	D	2-2
28 Apr	Tottenham H	H	W	5-0
30 Apr	Millwall	A	L	0-2

Position in Football League Table

	P	W	L	D	F:A	Pts	
Burnley	30	20	2	8	80:24	48	1st
Arsenal	30	16	9	5	69:49	37	5th

Position in United League Table

	P	W	L	D	F:A	Pts	
Luton	16	13	1	2	49:11	28	1st
Arsenal	16	8	3	5	35:24	21	3rd

SEASON 1898-1899
FOOTBALL LEAGUE (DIVISION 2)

3 Sep	Luton T	A	W	1-0
5 Sep	Burslem PV	A	L	0-3
10 Sep	Leicester Fosse	H	W	4-0
17 Sep	Darwen	A	W	4-1
24 Sep	Gainsborough	H	W	5-1
1 Oct	Manchester C	A	L	1-3
15 Oct	Walsall	A	L	1-4
22 Oct	Burton Swifts	H	W	2-1
5 Nov	Small Heath	H	W	2-0
12 Nov	Loughborough	A	D	0-0
26 Nov	Grimsby T	A	L	0-1
3 Dec	Newton Heath	H	W	5-1
10 Dec	New Brighton	A	L	1-3
17 Dec	Lincoln C	H	W	4-2
24 Dec	Barnsley	A	L	1-2
31 Dec	Luton T	H	W	6-2
7 Jan	Leicester Fosse	A	L	1-2
14 Jan	Darwen	H	W	6-0
21 Jan	Gainsborough	A	W	1-0
4 Feb	Glossop	A	L	0-2
11 Feb	Walsall	H	D	0-0
13 Feb	Glossop	H	W	3-0
18 Feb	Burton Swifts	A	W	2-1
25 Feb	Burslem PV	H	W	1-0
4 Mar	Small Heath	A	L	1-4
13 Mar	Loughborough	H	W	3-1
18 Mar	Blackpool	H	W	6-0
22 Mar	Blackpool	A	D	1-1
25 Mar	Grimsby T	H	D	1-1
1 Apr	Newton Heath	A	D	2-2
3 Apr	Manchester C	A	L	0-1
8 Apr	New Brighton	H	W	4-0
15 Apr	Lincoln C	A	L	0-2
22 Apr	Barnsley	H	W	3-0

FA Cup

28 Jan	Derby Co (1)	H	L	0-6

Chatham Charity Cup

18 Jan	Chatham	A	D	1-1
20 Feb	Chatham	H	D	3-3
6 Mar	Chatham	A	L	1-2

United League

14 Sep	Reading	A	D	1-1
3 Oct	Reading	H	W	2-0
8 Oct	Millwall	A	D	1-1
10 Oct	Luton T	H	W	3-2
17 Oct	Rushden	H	W	2-0
24 Oct	Kettering	A	L	1-2
29 Oct	Southampton	A	L	1-5
31 Oct	Brighton & HA	H	W	5-2
9 Nov	Bristol C	A	W	2-1
14 Nov	Wellingborough	A	L	0-3
19 Nov	Southampton	H	W	2-1
21 Nov	Rushden	A	W	6-0
12 Dec	Bristol C	H	L	1-3
26 Dec	Millwall	H	L	0-1
27 Dec	Luton T	A	D	1-1
4 Jan	Brighton & HA	A	D	1-1
6 Feb	Kettering	H	W	4-2
11 Mar	Tottenham H	H	W	2-1
31 Mar	Wellingborough	H	W	3-0
29 Apr	Tottenham H	A	L	2-3

Friendlies

1 Sep	Gravesend	H	L	0-1
19 Sep	Thames Iron Works	H	W	4-0
25 Oct	Gravesend		W	1-0
23 Nov	Corinthians	A	L	1-4
28 Nov	Chatham	A	L	1-3
8 Dec	Thames Iron Works	A	W	2-1
25 Jan	Sevenoaks	A	W	7-1
30 Jan	Millwall	H	L	2-4
15 Feb	Gravesend	A	L	2-3
23 Feb	Clapton	A	W	3-0
9 Mar	Casuals	A	W	3-1
23 Mar	Past XI *v* Present XI	Present won		3-1
4 Apr	Millwall	A	D	0-0
24 Apr	Notts Co	H	W	2-1
26 Apr	Woolwich Locals		W	3-0

Position in Football League Table

	P	W	L	D	F:A	Pts	
Manchester C	34	23	5	6	92:35	52	1st
Arsenal	34	18	11	5	72:41	41	7th

Position in United League Table

	P	W	L	D	F:A	Pts	
Millwall	20	14	3	3	42:19	31	1st
Arsenal	20	10	6	4	40:30	24	4th

SEASON 1899-1900
FOOTBALL LEAGUE (DIVISION 2)

2 Sep	Leicester Fosse	H	L	0-2
9 Sep	Luton T	A	W	2-1
16 Sep	Burslem PV	H	W	1-0
23 Sep	Walsall	A	L	0-2
30 Sep	Middlesbrough	H	W	3-0
7 Oct	Chesterfield	A	L	1-3
14 Oct	Gainsborough	H	W	2-1
21 Oct	Bolton W	A	L	0-1
4 Nov	Newton Heath	A	L	0-2
11 Nov	Sheffield Wed	H	L	1-2
25 Nov	Small Heath	H	W	3-0
2 Dec	New Brighton	A	W	2-0
16 Dec	Burton Swifts	H	D	1-1
25 Dec	Lincoln C	A	L	0-5
30 Dec	Leicester Fosse	A	D	0-0
6 Jan	Luton T	H	W	3-1
13 Jan	Burslem PV	A	D	1-1
20 Jan	Walsall	H	W	3-1
3 Feb	Middlesbrough	A	L	0-1
10 Feb	Chesterfield	H	W	2-0
17 Feb	Gainsborough	A	D	1-1
24 Feb	Bolton W	H	L	0-1
3 Mar	Loughborough	A	W	3-2
10 Mar	Newton Heath	H	W	2-1
12 Mar	Loughborough	H	W	12-0
17 Mar	Sheffield Wed	A	L	1-3
24 Mar	Lincoln C	H	W	2-1
31 Mar	Small Heath	A	L	1-3
7 Apr	New Brighton	H	W	5-0
14 Apr	Grimsby T	A	L	0-1
16 Apr	Grimsby T	H	W	2-0
21 Apr	Burton Swifts	A	L	0-2
23 Apr	Barnsley	A	L	2-3
28 Apr	Barnsley	H	W	5-1

FA Cup

28 Oct	New Brompton (Q)	H	D	1-1
1 Nov	New Brompton (QR)	A	D	0-0
6 Nov	New Brompton (QR)	A	D	2-2
8 Nov	New Brompton (QR)	A	D	1-1
14 Nov	New Brompton (QR)	A	L	0-1

Southern District Combination

11 Sep	Millwall	L	0-1
27 Sep	Reading	W	3-0
11 Oct	Southampton	L	0-3
23 Oct	Portsmouth	L	0-2
30 Oct	Bristol C	W	3-0
10 Jan	Bristol C	W	3-1
29 Jan	Chatham	W	4-0
7 Feb	Portsmouth	L	1-3
26 Feb	Chatham	W	2-1
5 Mar	Southampton	W	1-0
19 Mar	Q P R	W	5-1
26 Mar	Reading	D	1-1
2 Apr	Millwall	L	0-1
9 Apr	Q P R	L	0-3
17 Apr	Tottenham H	L	2-4
24 Apr	Tottenham H	W	2-1*

*unfinished

Friendlies

4 Sep	Stoke	W	5-3
2 Oct	Aston Villa	W	1-0
29 Nov	Eastbourne	W	2-1
9 Dec	Southampton	D	1-1
23 Dec	Swindon T	W	2-1
27 Jan	Bedminster	W	3-0
19 Feb	Derby Co	L	0-1
13 Apr	Burnley	W	2-0

Position in Football League Table

	P	W	L	D	F:A	Pts	
Sheffield Wed	34	25	5	4	84:22	54	1st
Arsenal	34	16	14	4	61:43	36	8th

Position in Southern District Combination League

	P	W	L	D	F:A	Pts	
Millwall	16	12	2	2	30:10	26	1st
Arsenal	15	7	7	1	25:21	15	4th

(Exclusive of match unfinished 24 April, against Tottenham H, Arsenal leading 2-1)

SEASON 1900-1901
FOOTBALL LEAGUE (DIVISION 2)

1 Sep	Gainsborough	H	W	2-1
8 Sep	Walsall	H	D	1-1
15 Sep	Burton Swifts	A	L	0-1
22 Sep	Barnsley	H	L	1-2
29 Sep	Chesterfield	H	W	1-0
6 Oct	Blackpool	A	D	1-1
13 Oct	Stockport Co	H	W	2-0
20 Oct	Small Heath	A	L	1-2
27 Oct	Grimsby	H	D	1-1
3 Nov	Leicester	H	W	2-1
10 Nov	Newton Heath	H	W	2-1
17 Nov	Glossop	A	W	1-0
24 Nov	Middlesbrough	H	W	1-0
1 Dec	Burnley	A	L	0-3
8 Dec	Burslem PV	H	W	3-0
15 Dec	Leicester	A	L	0-1
22 Dec	New Brighton	H	W	2-1
24 Dec	Walsall	A	L	0-1
29 Dec	Gainsborough	A	L	0-1
12 Jan	Burton Swifts	H	W	3-1
19 Jan	Barnsley	A	L	0-3
26 Jan	Lincoln C	A	D	3-3
16 Feb	Stockport Co	A	L	1-3
19 Feb	Chesterfield	A	W	1-0
2 Mar	Grimsby T	A	L	0-1
9 Mar	Lincoln C	H	D	0-0
16 Mar	Newton Heath	A	L	0-1
23 Mar	Glossop	H	W	2-0
30 Mar	Middlesbrough	A	D	1-1
6 Apr	Burnley	H	W	3-1
8 Apr	Blackpool	H	W	3-1
13 Apr	Burslem PV	A	L	0-1
22 Apr	Small Heath	H	W	1-0
27 Apr	New Brighton	A	L	0-1

FA Cup

5 Jan	Darwen (Q)	A	W	2-0
9 Feb	Blackburn Rov (1)	H	W	2-0
23 Feb	W B A (2)	H	L	0-1

Friendlies

1 Oct	Aston Villa	H	W	3-0
21 Nov	Southampton		L	1-4
25 Dec	West Ham U		W	1-0
26 Dec	Newcastle U	H	D	1-1
1 Jan	Newcastle U		L	1-5
4 Mar	Southern League XI		W	2-1
1 Apr	Millwall		D	1-1
5 Apr	Nottingham F	H	D	1-1
20 Apr	Notts Co	H	W	3-0
25 Apr	West Ham U		D	0-0

Position in Football League Table

	P	W	L	D	F:A	Pts	
Grimsby T	34	20	5	9	60:33	49	1st
Arsenal	34	15	13	6	39:35	36	7th

SEASON 1901-1902
FOOTBALL LEAGUE (DIVISION 2)

2 Sep	Barnsley	H	W	2-1
4 Sep	Leicester	H	W	2-0
14 Sep	Preston NE	A	L	0-2
21 Sep	Burnley	H	W	4-0
28 Sep	Burslem PV	A	L	0-1
5 Oct	Chesterfield	H	W	3-2
12 Oct	Gainsborough	A	D	2-2
19 Oct	Middlesbrough	H	L	0-3
26 Oct	Bristol C	A	W	3-0
9 Nov	Stockport Co	A	D	0-0
16 Nov	Newton Heath	H	W	2-0
23 Nov	Glossop	A	W	1-0
30 Nov	Doncaster Rov	H	W	1-0
7 Dec	Lincoln C	A	D	0-0
21 Dec	Burton Un	H	L	0-1
25 Dec	Blackpool	H	D	0-0
26 Dec	Burslem PV	H	W	3-1
28 Dec	Barnsley	A	L	0-2
4 Jan	Leicester	A	L	1-2
11 Jan	Preston NE	H	D	0-0
18 Jan	Burnley	A	D	0-0
1 Feb	Chesterfield	A	W	3-1
8 Feb	Gainsborough	H	W	5-0
15 Feb	Middlesbrough	A	L	0-1
22 Feb	Bristol C	H	W	2-0
1 Mar	Blackpool	A	W	3-1
8 Mar	Stockport Co	H	W	3-0
15 Mar	Newton Heath	A	W	1-0
22 Mar	Glossop	H	W	4-0
29 Mar	Doncaster Rov	A	L	0-1
31 Mar	W B A	H	W	2-1
5 Apr	Lincoln C	H	W	2-0
12 Apr	W B A	A	L	1-2
19 Apr	Burton Un	A	L	0-2

FA Cup

14 Dec	Luton T (Q)	H	D	1-1
18 Dec	Luton T (QR)	H	W	2-0
25 Jan	Newcastle U (1)	H	L	0-2

Southern Charity Cup

7 Apr	Portsmouth	A	W	2-1
23 Apr	Tottenham H (Semi Final)	H	D	0-0
29 Apr	Tottenham H (Semi Final)	A	L	1-2

London League

16 Sep	Tottenham H	L	0-2
30 Sep	Millwall	D	1-1
21 Oct	West Ham U	L	0-1
4 Nov	Tottenham H	L	0-5
3 Feb	Q P R	D	2-2
17 Feb	Q P R	W	3-0
24 Feb	Millwall	L	1-2
28 Mar	West Ham U	W	2-0

Friendlies

2 Nov	Reading	H	W	1-0
18 Nov	Southampton	H	L	0-1
1 Apr	Blackburn Rov	H	W	2-0
25 Apr	Plymouth Arg	A	W	4-1
26 Apr	W B A	H	L	0-1

Position in Football League Table

	P	W	L	D	F:A	Pts	
W B A	34	25	4	5	82:29	55	1st
Arsenal	34	18	10	6	50:26	42	4th

Position in London League Table

	P	W	L	D	F:A	Pts	
West Ham U	8	5	2	1	19: 9	11	1st
Arsenal	8	2	4	2	9:13	6	5th

SEASON 1902-1903
FOOTBALL LEAGUE (DIVISION 2)

6 Sep	Preston NE	A	D	2-2
13 Sep	Burslem PV	H	W	3-0
20 Sep	Barnsley	A	D	1-1
27 Sep	Gainsborough	H	W	6-1
4 Oct	Bristol C	A	L	0-1
11 Oct	Bristol C	H	W	2-1
18 Oct	Glossop NE	A	W	2-1
25 Oct	Manchester U	H	L	0-1
1 Nov	Manchester C	H	W	1-0
8 Nov	Blackpool	H	W	2-1
15 Nov	Burnley	A	W	3-0
22 Nov	Doncaster Rov	A	W	1-0
29 Nov	Lincoln C	H	W	2-1
6 Dec	Small Heath	A	L	0-2
20 Dec	Manchester C	A	L	1-4
25 Dec	Burton Un	A	L	1-2
27 Dec	Burnley	H	W	5-1
1 Jan	Stockport Co	A	W	1-0
3 Jan	Preston NE	H	W	3-1
10 Jan	Burslem PV	A	D	1-1
17 Jan	Barnsley	H	W	4-0
24 Jan	Gainsborough	A	W	1-0
31 Jan	Burton Un	H	W	3-0
14 Feb	Glossop NE	H	D	0-0
28 Feb	Stockport Co	H	W	3-1
7 Mar	Blackpool	A	D	0-0
9 Mar	Manchester U	A	L	0-3
14 Mar	Chesterfield	A	D	2-2
21 Mar	Doncaster Rov	H	W	3-0
28 Mar	Lincoln C	A	D	2-2
4 Apr	Small Heath	H	W	6-1
10 Apr	Chesterfield	H	W	3-0
11 Apr	Leicester	A	W	2-0
13 Apr	Leicester	H	D	0-0

FA Cup

13 Dec	Brentford (Q)	A	D	1-1
17 Dec	Brentford (QR)	H	W	5-0
7 Feb	Sheffield U (1)	H	L	1-3

Southern Charity Cup

9 Feb	Millwall	H	L	2-3

London League

1 Sep	West Ham U	A	W	3-1
15 Sep	Q P R	H	W	3-1
27 Oct	Q P R	A	W	2-0
10 Nov	Brentford	H	W	3-0
17 Nov	Tottenham H	H	W	2-1
1 Dec	Tottenham H	A	L	0-1
26 Dec	Millwall	A	L	0-3
21 Feb	West Ham U	H	L	0-1
23 Mar	Brentford	A	W	1-0
18 Apr	Millwall	H	L	0-2

Friendlies

8 Sep	New Brompton	A	W	3-2
18 Mar	Brighton & HA	A	W	3-1
14 Apr	Northampton T	A	D	1-1
20 Apr	Bristol C	A	W	2-1
25 Apr	Chesterfield	H	W	1-0

Position in Football League Table

	P	W	L	D	F:A	Pts	
Manchester C	34	25	5	4	95:29	54	1st
Arsenal	34	20	8	6	66:30	48	3rd

Position in London League Table

	P	W	L	D	F:A	Pts	
Tottenham H	10	7	2	1	19: 4	15	1st
Arsenal	10	6	4	0	14:10	12	3rd

SEASON 1903-1904
FOOTBALL LEAGUE (DIVISION 2)

5 Sep	Blackpool	H	W	3-0
12 Sep	Gainsborough	A	W	2-0
19 Sep	Burton Un	H	W	8-0
26 Sep	Bristol C	A	W	4-0
3 Oct	Manchester U	H	W	4-0
10 Oct	Glossop	A	W	3-1
24 Oct	Burslem PV	A	W	3-2
26 Oct	Leicester	H	W	8-0
31 Oct	Barnsley	A	L	1-2
7 Nov	Lincoln C	H	W	4-0
21 Nov	Chesterfield	H	W	6-0
28 Nov	Bolton W	A	L	1-2
19 Dec	Grimsby T	H	W	5-1
25 Dec	Bradford C	H	W	4-1
26 Dec	Leicester	A	D	0-0
1 Jan	Stockport Co	A	D	0-0
2 Jan	Blackpool	A	D	2-2
9 Jan	Gainsborough	H	W	6-0
16 Jan	Burton Un	A	L	1-3
30 Jan	Manchester U	A	L	0-1
27 Feb	Barnsley	H	W	3-0
29 Feb	Burnley	H	W	4-0
5 Mar	Lincoln C	A	W	2-0
12 Mar	Stockport Co	H	W	5-2
14 Mar	Bristol C	H	W	2-0
19 Mar	Chesterfield	A	L	0-1
26 Mar	Bolton W	H	W	3-0
1 Apr	Preston NE	A	D	0-0
2 Apr	Burnley	A	L	0-1
4 Apr	Glossop	H	W	2-1
9 Apr	Preston NE	H	D	0-0
16 Apr	Grimsby T	A	D	2-2
19 Apr	Bradford C	A	W	3-0
25 Apr	Burslem PV	H	D	0-0

FA Cup

12 Dec	Bristol Rov (Q)	A	D	1-1
15 Dec	Bristol Rov (QR)	H	D	1-1
21 Dec	Bristol Rov (QR)	A*	W	1-0
6 Feb	Fulham (1)	H	W	1-0
20 Feb	Manchester C (2)	H	L	0-2

*at Tottenham

Southern Charity Cup

12 Oct	West Ham U		W	1-0
18 Jan	Reading (Semi-Final)		W	3-1
28 Apr	Millwall (Final)		L	1-2

London League

1 Sep	Tottenham H		W	1-0
7 Sep	Fulham		W	2-0
14 Sep	West Ham U		W	4-1
14 Nov	Tottenham H		D	1-1
23 Nov	Brentford		D	1-1
7 Dec	Millwall		L	1-3
11 Jan	Q P R		W	6-2
8 Feb	Brentford		W	3-2
22 Feb	West Ham U		W	4-2
7 Mar	Millwall		L	0-3
21 Mar	Q P R		L	1-3
30 Apr	Fulham		L	0-1

Friendlies

17 Oct	Luton		D	2-2
30 Nov	Army		W	4-0

Position in Football League Table

	P	W	L	D	F:A	Pts	
Preston NE	34	20	4	10	62:24	50	1st
Arsenal	34	21	6	7	91:22	49	2nd

Position in London League Table

	P	W	L	D	F:A	Pts	
Millwall	12	11	0	1	38: 8	23	1st
Arsenal	12	6	4	2	24:19	14	3rd

SEASON 1904-1905
FOOTBALL LEAGUE (DIVISION 1)

3 Sep	Newcastle U	A	L	0-3
10 Sep	Preston NE	H	D	0-0
17 Sep	Middlesbrough	A	L	0-1
24 Sep	Wolverhampton W	H	W	2-0
1 Oct	Bury	A	D	1-1
8 Oct	Aston Villa	H	W	1-0
15 Oct	Blackburn Rov	A	D	1-1
22 Oct	Nottingham F	H	L	0-3
29 Oct	Sheffield Wed	A	W	3-0
5 Nov	Sunderland	H	D	0-0
12 Nov	Stoke	H	W	2-1
19 Nov	Derby Co	A	D	0-0
3 Dec	Small Heath	A	L	1-2
10 Dec	Manchester C	H	W	1-0
17 Dec	Notts Co	A	W	5-1
24 Dec	Sheffield U	H	W	1-0
26 Dec	Aston Villa	A	L	1-3
27 Dec	Nottingham F	A	W	3-0
28 Dec	Sheffield U	A	L	0-4
31 Dec	Newcastle U	H	L	0-2
7 Jan	Preston NE	A	L	0-3
14 Jan	Middlesbrough	H	D	1-1
21 Jan	Wolverhampton W	A	L	1-4
28 Jan	Bury	H	W	2-1
11 Feb	Blackburn Rov	H	W	2-0
25 Feb	Sheffield Wed	H	W	3-0
4 Mar	Sunderland	A	D	1-1
11 Mar	Stoke	A	L	0-2
18 Mar	Derby Co	H	D	0-0
1 Apr	Small Heath	H	D	1-1
5 Apr	Everton	A	L	0-1
8 Apr	Manchester C	A	L	0-1
15 Apr	Notts Co	H	L	1-2
22 Apr	Everton	H	W	2-1

FA Cup

4 Feb	Bristol C (1)	H	D	0-0
8 Feb	Bristol C (1R)	A	L	0-1

Southern Charity Cup

10 Oct	Tottenham H	H	L	1-3

Friendlies

1 Sep	Bristol C	H	W	3-2
12 Sep	West Ham U	A	D	1-1
31 Oct	Cambridge Univ	H	W	3-0
22 Nov	Cambridge Univ	A	W	4-3
5 Dec	French International Team	H	W	26-1
18 Feb	Corinthians	A	L	1-2
27 Feb	Queens Park (Glasgow)	H	W	6-1
25 Mar	Burnley	H	W	3-0
12 Apr	Southend U	A	W	2-0
21 Apr	New Brompton	H	W	3-1
24 Apr	Dundee	H	W	3-0
26 Apr	Ipswich T	A	W	3-1
27 Apr	Norwich C	A	L	1-2
29 Apr	Sheffield U	A	L	2-3

Position in Football League Table

	P	W	L	D	F:A	Pts	
Newcastle U	34	23	9	2	72:33	48	1st
Arsenal	34	12	13	9	36:40	33	10th

SEASON 1905-1906
FOOTBALL LEAGUE (DIVISION 1)

2 Sep	Liverpool	H	W	3-1
9 Sep	Sheffield U	A	L	1-3
16 Sep	Notts Co	H	D	1-1
18 Sep	Preston NE	H	D	2-2
23 Sep	Stoke	A	L	1-2
30 Sep	Bolton W	H	D	0-0
7 Oct	Wolverhampton W	A	W	2-0
14 Oct	Blackburn Rov	A	L	0-2
21 Oct	Sunderland	H	W	2-0
28 Oct	Birmingham	A	L	1-2
4 Nov	Everton	H	L	1-2
11 Nov	Derby Co	A	L	1-5
18 Nov	Sheffield Wed	H	L	0-2
25 Nov	Nottingham F	A	L	1-3
2 Dec	Manchester C	H	W	2-0
9 Dec	Bury	A	L	0-2
16 Dec	Middlesbrough	H	D	2-2
23 Dec	Preston NE	A	D	2-2
25 Dec	Newcastle U	H	W	4-3
27 Dec	Aston Villa	A	L	1-2
30 Dec	Liverpool	A	L	0-3
1 Jan	Bolton W	A	L	1-6
6 Jan	Sheffield U	H	W	5-1
20 Jan	Notts Co	A	L	0-1
27 Jan	Stoke	H	L	1-2
10 Feb	Wolverhampton W	H	W	2-1
17 Feb	Blackburn Rov	H	W	3-2
3 Mar	Birmingham	H	W	5-0
17 Mar	Derby Co	H	W	1-0
21 Mar	Everton	A	W	1-0
24 Mar	Sheffield Wed	A	L	2-4
2 Apr	Nottingham F	H	W	3-1
7 Apr	Manchester C	A	W	2-1
13 Apr	Aston Villa	H	W	2-1
14 Apr	Bury	H	W	4-0
16 Apr	Newcastle U	A	D	1-1
21 Apr	Middlesbrough	A	L	0-2
25 Apr	Sunderland	A	D	2-2

FA Cup

13 Jan	West Ham U (1)	H	D	1-1
18 Jan	West Ham U (1R)	A	W	3-2
3 Feb	Watford (2)	H	W	3-0
24 Feb	Sunderland (3)	H	W	5-0
10 Mar	Manchester U (4)	A	W	3-2
31 Mar	Newcastle U (Semi-Final)*		L	0-2

*at Stoke

Southern Charity Cup

9 Oct	West Ham U	H	W	3-2
9 Apr	Tottenham H	A	D	0-0
28 Apr	Tottenham H	H	W	5-0
30 Apr	Reading (Final)	A	W	1-0

Friendlies

21 Sep	Faversham Rangers	A	W	9-0
18 Oct	Corinthians	A	L	1-2
30 Oct	Oxford Univ	H	W	3-1
26 Dec	Corinthians	H	D	1-1
15 Jan	Cambridge Univ	H	W	4-2
22 Jan	Oxford Univ	A	W	4-0
18 Apr	West Hartlepool	A	W	4-0

Position in Football League Table

	P	W	L	D	F:A	Pts	
Liverpool	38	23	10	5	79:46	51	1st
Arsenal	38	15	16	7	62:64	37	12th

SEASON 1906-1907
FOOTBALL LEAGUE (DIVISION 1)

1 Sep	Manchester C	A	W	4-1
3 Sep	Bury	A	L	1-4
8 Sep	Middlesbrough	H	W	2-0
15 Sep	Preston NE	H	W	3-0
22 Sep	Newcastle U	H	W	2-0
29 Sep	Aston Villa	A	D	2-2
6 Oct	Liverpool	H	W	2-1
13 Oct	Bristol C	A	W	3-1
20 Oct	Notts Co	H	W	1-0
27 Oct	Sheffield U	A	L	2-4
3 Nov	Bolton W	H	D	2-2
10 Nov	Manchester U	A	L	0-1
17 Nov	Stoke	H	W	2-1
24 Nov	Blackburn Rov	A	W	3-2
1 Dec	Sunderland	H	L	0-1
8 Dec	Birmingham	A	L	1-5
15 Dec	Everton	H	W	3-1
22 Dec	Derby Co	A	D	0-0
26 Dec	Bury	H	W	3-1
29 Dec	Manchester C	H	W	4-1
1 Jan	Sheffield Wed	A	D	1-1
5 Jan	Middlesbrough	A	L	3-5
19 Jan	Preston NE	H	W	1-0
26 Jan	Newcastle U	A	L	0-1
9 Feb	Liverpool	A	L	0-4
16 Feb	Bristol City	H	L	1-2
2 Mar	Sheffield U	H	L	0-1
16 Mar	Manchester U	H	W	4-0
27 Mar	Bolton W	A	L	0-3
28 Mar	Sheffield Wed	H	W	1-0
30 Mar	Blackburn Rov	H	W	2-0
1 Apr	Aston Villa	H	W	3-1
6 Apr	Sunderland	A	W	3-2
10 Apr	Everton	A	L	1-2
13 Apr	Birmingham	H	W	2-1
15 Apr	Stoke	A	L	0-2
17 Apr	Notts Co	A	L	1-4
27 Apr	Derby	H	W	3-2

FA Cup

12 Jan	Grimsby T (1)	A	D	1-1
16 Jan	Grimsby T (1R)	H	W	3-0
2 Feb	Bristol C (2)	H	W	2-1
23 Feb	Bristol Rov (3)	H	W	1-0
9 Mar	Barnsley (4)	A	W	2-1
23 Mar	Sheffield Wed (Semi-Final)*		L	1-3

*at Birmingham

Southern Charity Cup

10 Dec	Millwall	H	L	1-2

Friendlies

12 Sep	Reading	A	W	1-0
19 Sep	West Norwood	A	W	1-0
5 Nov	Oxford Univ	H	W	7-1
19 Nov	Clapton Orient	A	W	3-1
3 Dec	Cambridge Univ	A	W	3-1
25 Dec	Celtic	H	L	0-2
14 Jan	Cambridge Univ	H	W	6-3

On Tour

5 May	Racing Club, Brussels		W	2-1
7 May	The Hague		W	6-3
9 May	BFC Pressen, Berlin		W	9-1
12 May	SP Sportorina, Prague		W	7-5
16 May	Klub Slavia, Prague		W	4-2
18 May	Combined Vienna Team		W	4-2
19 May	Magyaren Buda Pesth		W	9-0
20 May	Buda Pesth		D	2-2

Position in Football League Table

	P	W	L	D	F:A	Pts	
Newcastle U	38	22	9	7	74:46	51	1st
Arsenal	38	20	14	4	66:59	44	7th

SEASON 1907-1908
FOOTBALL LEAGUE (DIVISION 1)

2 Sep	Notts Co	H	D	1-1
7 Sep	Bristol C	H	L	0-4
9 Sep	Bury	A	L	2-3
14 Sep	Notts Co	A	L	0-2
21 Sep	Manchester C	H	W	2-1
28 Sep	Preston NE	A	L	0-3
5 Oct	Bury	H	D	0-0
12 Oct	Aston Villa	A	W	1-0
19 Oct	Liverpool	H	W	2-1
26 Oct	Middlesbrough	A	D	0-0
2 Nov	Sheffield U	H	W	5-1
9 Nov	Chelsea	A	L	1-2
16 Nov	Nottingham F	H	W	3-1
23 Nov	Manchester U	A	L	2-4
30 Nov	Blackburn Rov	H	W	2-0
7 Dec	Bolton W	A	L	1-3
14 Dec	Birmingham	H	D	1-1
21 Dec	Everton	A	D	1-1
25 Dec	Newcastle U	H	D	2-2
28 Dec	Sunderland	H	W	4-0
31 Dec	Sheffield Wed	A	L	0-6
1 Jan	Sunderland	A	L	2-5
4 Jan	Bristol C	A	W	2-1
18 Jan	Manchester C	A	L	0-4
25 Jan	Preston NE	H	D	1-1
8 Feb	Aston Villa	H	L	0-1
15 Feb	Liverpool	A	L	1-4
22 Feb	Middlesbrough	H	W	4-1
29 Feb	Sheffield U	A	D	2-2
7 Mar	Chelsea	H	D	0-0
14 Mar	Nottingham F	A	L	0-1
21 Mar	Manchester U	H	W	1-0
28 Mar	Blackburn Rov	A	D	1-1
4 Apr	Bolton W	H	D	1-1
11 Apr	Birmingham	A	W	2-1
17 Apr	Newcastle U	A	L	1-2
18 Apr	Everton	H	W	2-1
20 Apr	Sheffield Wed	H	D	1-1

FA Cup

11 Jan	Hull C (1)	H	D	0-0
16 Jan	Hull C (1R)	A	L	1-4

Southern Charity Cup

23 Sep	Reading	H	L	0-1

Friendlies

16 Sep	Barnsley	H	W	1-0
14 Oct	Rest of Kent	A	W	3-1
26 Dec	Liverpool	H	D	2-2
1 Feb	Tottenham H	A	W	1-0

On Tour

21 Apr	Hearts		L	1-3
22 Apr	Raith Rovers		L	0-1
23 Apr	Aberdeen		L	1-4
25 Apr	Dundee		L	1-2
27 Apr	Motherwell		D	1-1
28 Apr	Glasgow Rangers		D	1-1
29 Apr	Greenock Morton		L	0-1
30 Apr	Kilmarnock		W	2-1

Position in Football League Table

	P	W	L	D	F:A	Pts	
Manchester C	38	23	9	6	81:48	52	1st
Arsenal	38	12	14	12	51:63	36	15th

SEASON 1908-1909
FOOTBALL LEAGUE (DIVISION 1)

2 Sep	Everton	H	L	0-4
5 Sep	Notts Co	A	L	1-2
7 Sep	Everton	A	W	3-0
12 Sep	Newcastle U	H	L	1-2
19 Sep	Bristol C	A	L	1-2
26 Sep	Preston NE	H	W	1-0
3 Oct	Middlesbrough	A	D	1-1
10 Oct	Manchester C	H	W	3-0
17 Oct	Liverpool	A	D	2-2
24 Oct	Bury	H	W	4-0
28 Oct	Chelsea	A	W	2-1
31 Oct	Sheffield U	A	D	1-1
7 Nov	Aston Villa	H	L	0-1
14 Nov	Nottingham F	A	W	1-0
21 Nov	Sunderland	H	L	0-4
5 Dec	Blackburn Rov	H	L	0-1
12 Dec	Bradford C	A	L	1-4
19 Dec	Manchester U	H	L	0-1
25 Dec	Leicester	A	D	1-1
26 Dec	Leicester	H	W	2-1
28 Dec	Sheffield Wed	A	L	2-6
2 Jan	Notts Co	H	W	1-0
9 Jan	Newcastle U	H	L	1-3
23 Jan	Bristol C	H	D	1-1
30 Jan	Preston NE	A	D	0-0
13 Feb	Manchester C	A	D	2-2
20 Feb	Liverpool	H	W	5-0
27 Feb	Bury	A	D	1-1
13 Mar	Aston Villa	A	L	1-2
17 Mar	Middlesbrough	H	D	1-1
20 Mar	Nottingham F	H	L	1-2
27 Mar	Sunderland	A	L	0-1
1 Apr	Sheffield U	H	W	1-0
3 Apr	Chelsea	H	D	0-0
10 Apr	Blackburn Rov	A	W	3-1
12 Apr	Sheffield Wed	H	W	2-0
17 Apr	Bradford C	H	W	1-0
27 Apr	Manchester U	A	W	4-1

FA Cup

16 Jan	Croydon Common (1)*		D	1-1
20 Jan	Croydon Common (1R)	H	W	2-0
6 Feb	Millwall (2)	H	D	1-1
10 Feb	Millwall (2R)	A	L	0-1

*at Crystal Palace

London FA Challenge Cup

28 Sep	Fulham	A	W	1-0
9 Nov	Crystal Palace	H	W	2-1
22 Feb	Clapton Orient (Semi-Final)	A	L	1-2

London Professional Charity Fund

7 Dec	Chelsea	H	W	1-0

Friendlies

7 Oct	Rest of Kent	A	W	3-0
22 Oct	Ryde	A	W	2-0
10 Mar	Hastings	A	W	3-1
9 Apr	Exeter	A	L	2-3

Position in Football League Table

	P	W	L	D	F:A	Pts	
Newcastle U	38	24	9	5	65:41	53	1st
Arsenal	38	14	14	10	52:49	38	6th

SEASON 1909-1910
FOOTBALL LEAGUE (DIVISION 1)

1 Sep	Aston Villa	A	L	1-5
4 Sep	Sheffield U	H	D	0-0
11 Sep	Middlesbrough	A	L	2-5
18 Sep	Bolton W	A	L	0-3
25 Sep	Chelsea	H	W	3-2
2 Oct	Blackburn Rov	A	L	0-7
7 Oct	Notts Co	A	L	1-5
9 Oct	Nottingham F	H	L	0-1
16 Oct	Sunderland	A	L	2-6
23 Oct	Everton	H	W	1-0
30 Oct	Manchester U	A	L	0-1
6 Nov	Bradford C	H	L	0-1
13 Nov	Sheffield Wed	A	D	1-1
20 Nov	Bristol C	H	D	2-2
27 Nov	Bury	A	W	2-1
4 Dec	Tottenham H	H	W	1-0
11 Dec	Preston NE	A	W	4-3
18 Dec	Notts Co	H	L	1-2
25 Dec	Newcastle U	H	L	0-3
27 Dec	Liverpool	H	D	1-1
1 Jan	Liverpool	A	L	1-5
8 Jan	Sheffield U	A	L	0-2
22 Jan	Middlesbrough	H	W	3-0
29 Jan	Bolton W	H	W	2-0
12 Feb	Blackburn Rov	H	L	0-1
26 Feb	Sunderland	H	L	1-2
2 Mar	Nottingham F	A	D	1-1
7 Mar	Everton	A	L	0-1
12 Mar	Manchester U	H	D	0-0
19 Mar	Bradford C	A	W	1-0
25 Mar	Newcastle U	A	D	1-1
26 Mar	Sheffield Wed	H	L	0-1
28 Mar	Chelsea	A	W	1-
2 Apr	Bristol C	A	W	1-
9 Apr	Bury	H	D	0-
11 Apr	Aston Villa	H	W	1-
16 Apr	Tottenham H	A	D	1-
23 Apr	Preston NE	H	L	1-

FA Cup

15 Jan	Watford (1)	H	W	3
5 Feb	Everton (2)	A	L	0

London FA Challenge Cup

20 Sep	Bromley	H	W	4-
11 Oct	West Ham U	H	L	0-

London Professional Charity Fun

1 Nov	Tottenham H	A	L	0-

Foord Flood Relief Fund

25 Nov	Shorncliffe Garrison and District XI (at Folkestone)		W	5-

Friendlies

22 Sep	Rest of Kent	A	W	3-
19 Feb	Fulham	H	D	2-
5 Mar	Millwall	A	D	3-
28 Apr	Colchester		W	3-
30 Apr	Ilford		L	2-

Position in Football League Table

	P	W	L	D	F:A	Pts	
Aston Villa	38	23	8	7	84:42	53	1s
Arsenal	38	11	18	9	37:67	31	18t

SEASON 1910-1911
FOOTBALL LEAGUE (DIVISION 1

1 Sep	Manchester U	H	L	1-
3 Sep	Bury	A	D	1-
10 Sep	Sheffield U	H	D	0-
17 Sep	Aston Villa	A	L	0-
24 Sep	Sunderland	H	D	0-
1 Oct	Oldham	H	D	0-
8 Oct	Bradford C	A	L	0-
15 Oct	Blackburn	H	W	4-
22 Oct	Nottingham F	A	W	3-
29 Oct	Manchester C	H	L	0-
5 Nov	Everton	A	L	0-
12 Nov	Sheffield W	H	W	1-
19 Nov	Bristol C	A	W	1-
26 Nov	Newcastle U	H	L	1-
3 Dec	Tottenham H	A	L	1-
10 Dec	Middlesbrough	H	L	0-
17 Dec	Preston NE	A	L	1-
24 Dec	Notts Co	H	W	2-
26 Dec	Manchester U	A	L	0-
31 Dec	Bury	H	W	3-
7 Jan	Sheffield U	A	L	2-
28 Jan	Sunderland	A	D	2-
11 Feb	Bradford C	H	D	0-
18 Feb	Blackburn Rov	A	L	0-
25 Feb	Nottingham F	H	W	3-
4 Mar	Manchester C	A	D	1-
6 Mar	Oldham Ath	A	L	0-
11 Mar	Everton	H	W	1-
15 Mar	Aston Villa	H	D	1-
18 Mar	Sheffield Wed	A	D	0-
25 Mar	Bristol C	H	W	3-
1 Apr	Newcastle U	A	W	1-
8 Apr	Tottenham H	H	W	2-
14 Apr	Liverpool	H	D	0-
15 Apr	Middlesbrough	A	D	1-
17 Apr	Liverpool	A	D	1-
22 Apr	Preston NE	H	W	2-
29 Apr	Notts Co	A	W	2-

FA Cup

14 Jan	Clapton Orient (1)*			
16 Jan	Clapton Orient (1)	A	W	2-
4 Feb	Swindon T (2)	A	L	0-

*match abandoned, fog

London FA Challenge Cup

19 Sep	Q P R	H	W	3-
10 Oct	Millwall	A	L	0-

London Professional Charity Fund

26 Sep	Fulham	A	W	3-

Position in Football League Table

	P	W	L	D	F:A	Pts	
Manchester U	38	22	8	8	72:40	52	1s
Arsenal	38	13	13	12	41:49	38	10t

SEASON 1911-1912
FOOTBALL LEAGUE (DIVISION 1

2 Sep	Liverpool	H	D	2-
9 Sep	Aston Villa	A	L	1-
16 Sep	Newcastle U	H	W	2-
23 Sep	Sheffield U	A	L	1-
30 Sep	Oldham Ath	H	D	1-
7 Oct	Bolton W	A	D	2-
14 Oct	Bradford C	H	W	2-
21 Oct	Preston NE	A	W	1-
28 Oct	Manchester C	A	D	3-
4 Nov	Everton	H	L	0-
11 Nov	W B A	A	D	1-
18 Nov	Sunderland	H	W	3-
25 Nov	Blackburn Rov	A	L	0-
2 Dec	Sheffield Wed	H	L	0-
9 Dec	Bury	A	L	1-
16 Dec	Middlesbrough	H	W	3-
23 Dec	Notts Co	A	L	1-
25 Dec	Tottenham H	A	L	0-

26 Dec	Tottenham H	H	W	3-1
30 Dec	Liverpool	A	L	1-4
1 Jan	Manchester U	A	L	0-2
6 Jan	Aston Villa	H	D	2-2
20 Jan	Newcastle U	A	W	2-1
27 Jan	Sheffield U	H	W	3-1
10 Feb	Bolton W	H	W	3-0
17 Feb	Bradford C	A	D	1-1
24 Feb	Middlesbrough	A	W	2-0
2 Mar	Manchester C	H	W	2-0
9 Mar	Oldham Ath	A	D	0-0
16 Mar	W B A	H	L	0-2
23 Mar	Sunderland	A	L	0-1
27 Mar	Everton	A	L	0-1
5 Apr	Manchester U	H	W	2-1
6 Apr	Sheffield Wed	A	L	0-3
8 Apr	Preston NE	H	W	4-1
13 Apr	Bury	H	W	1-0
22 Apr	Blackburn Rov	H	W	5-1
27 Apr	Notts Co	H	L	0-3

FA Cup

13 Jan	Bolton W (1)	A	L	0-1

London FA Challenge Cup

18 Sep	Q P R	A	W	2-0
16 Oct	Chelsea	H	L	2-3

London Professional Charity Fund

4 Sep	Chelsea	A	D	2-2
30 Oct	Chelsea	H	W	1-0

Charity Match Titanic Disaster

29 Apr	Tottenham H	H	W	3-0

Friendlies

25 Mar	West Ham U	H	W	3-0
20 Apr	Glasgow Rangers	A	D	0-0

On Tour

11 May	Hertha Berlin	W	5-0
12 May	Viktoria Berliner	D	2-2
16 May	Prague Deutscher	W	4-1
19 May	Furth	W	6-0
22 May	Torna Graz	W	6-0
24 May	Tottenham (Vienna)	W	4-0
26 May	Vienna Rapide	W	8-2
27 May	Wiener Athletic	W	5-0
29 May	Budapest	W	2-1

Position in Football League Table

	P	W	L	D	F:A	Pts	
Blackburn Rov	38	20	9	9	60:43	49	1st
Arsenal	38	15	15	8	55:59	38	10th

SEASON 1912-1913
FOOTBALL LEAGUE (DIVISION 1)

2 Sep	Manchester U	H	D	0-0
7 Sep	Liverpool	A	L	0-3
14 Sep	Bolton W	H	L	1-2
16 Sep	Aston Villa	H	L	0-3
21 Sep	Sheffield U	A	W	3-1
28 Sep	Newcastle U	H	D	1-1
5 Oct	Oldham Ath	A	D	0-0
12 Oct	Chelsea	H	L	0-1
19 Oct	Sunderland	H	L	1-3
26 Oct	Bradford PA	A	L	1-3
2 Nov	Manchester C	H	L	0-4
9 Nov	W B A	A	L	1-2
16 Nov	Everton	H	D	0-0
23 Nov	Sheffield Wed	A	L	0-2
30 Nov	Blackburn Rov	H	L	0-1
7 Dec	Derby Co	A	L	1-4
14 Dec	Tottenham H	H	L	0-3
21 Dec	Middlesbrough	A	L	0-2
25 Dec	Notts Co	H	D	0-0
26 Dec	Notts Co	A	L	1-2
28 Dec	Liverpool	H	D	1-1
1 Jan	Sunderland	A	L	1-4
4 Jan	Bolton W	A	L	1-5
18 Jan	Sheffield U	H	L	1-3
25 Jan	Newcastle U	A	L	1-3
8 Feb	Oldham Ath	H	D	0-0
15 Feb	Chelsea	A	D	1-1
1 Mar	Bradford PA	H	D	1-1
8 Mar	Manchester C	A	W	1-0
15 Mar	W B A	H	W	1-0
21 Mar	Manchester U	A	L	0-2
22 Mar	Everton	A	L	0-3
24 Mar	Aston Villa	A	L	1-4
29 Mar	Sheffield Wed	H	L	2-5
5 Apr	Blackburn	A	D	1-1
12 Apr	Derby Co	H	L	1-2
19 Apr	Tottenham H	A	D	1-1
26 Apr	Middlesbrough	H	D	1-1

FA Cup

11 Jan	Croydon Common (1)	A	D	0-0
15 Jan	Croydon Common (1R)	H	W	2-1
1 Feb	Liverpool (2)	H	L	1-4

London FA Challenge Cup

23 Sep	Clapton Orient	A	L	2-4

London Professional Charity Fund

30 Sep	Chelsea	A	W	3-1

Kent Senior Shield

16 Oct	Crystal Palace	A	L	0-1

Position in Football League Table

	P	W	L	D	F:A	Pts	
Sunderland	38	25	9	4	86:43	54	1st
Arsenal	38	3	23	12	26:74	18	20th

SEASON 1913-1914
FOOTBALL LEAGUE (DIVISION 2)

6 Sep	Leicester	H	W	2-1
13 Sep	Wolverhampton W	A	W	2-1
15 Sep	Notts Co	H	W	3-0
20 Sep	Hull C	H	D	0-0
27 Sep	Barnsley	A	L	0-1
4 Oct	Bury	H	L	0-1
11 Oct	Huddersfield T	A	W	2-1
18 Oct	Lincoln C	H	W	3-0
25 Oct	Blackpool	A	D	1-1
1 Nov	Nottingham F	H	W	3-2
8 Nov	Fulham	A	L	1-6
15 Nov	Grimsby T	A	D	1-1
22 Nov	Birmingham	H	W	1-0
29 Nov	Bristol C	A	D	1-1
6 Dec	Leeds C	H	W	1-0
13 Dec	Clapton Orient	A	L	0-1
20 Dec	Glossop	H	W	2-0
25 Dec	Bradford PA	A	W	3-2
26 Dec	Bradford PA	H	W	2-0
27 Dec	Leicester	A	W	2-1
1 Jan	Notts Co	A	L	0-1
3 Jan	Wolverhampton W	H	W	3-1
17 Jan	Hull C	A	W	2-1
24 Jan	Barnsley	H	W	1-0
7 Feb	Bury	A	D	1-1
14 Feb	Huddersfield T	H	L	0-1
21 Feb	Lincoln C	A	L	2-5
28 Mar	Blackpool	H	W	2-1
7 Mar	Nottingham F	A	D	0-0
14 Mar	Fulham	H	W	2-0
28 Mar	Birmingham	A	L	0-2
4 Apr	Bristol C	A	D	1-1
10 Apr	Stockport Co	A	L	0-2
11 Apr	Leeds C	A	D	0-0
13 Apr	Stockport Co	H	W	4-0
18 Apr	Clapton Orient	H	D	2-2
23 Apr	Grimsby T	H	W	2-0
25 Apr	Glossop	A	W	2-0

FA Cup

10 Jan	Bradford PA (1)	A	L	0-2

London FA Challenge Cup

22 Sep	Q P R	H	D	1-1
29 Sep	Q P R	A	W	3-2
20 Oct	Chelsea	A	W	1-0
10 Nov	Tottenham H	A	L	1-2

London Professional Charity Fund

27 Oct	West Ham U	A	L	2-3

Friendly

31 Jan	Everton	H	L	1-2

Position in Football League Table

	P	W	L	D	F:A	Pts	
Notts Co	38	23	8	7	77:36	53	1st
Arsenal	38	20	9	9	54:38	49	3rd

SEASON 1914-1915
FOOTBALL LEAGUE (DIVISION 2)

1 Sep	Glossop	H	W	3-0
5 Sep	Wolverhampton W	A	L	0-1
8 Sep	Glossop	A	W	4-0
12 Sep	Fulham	H	W	3-0
19 Sep	Stockport Co	A	D	1-1
26 Sep	Hull C	H	W	2-1
3 Oct	Leeds C	A	D	2-2
10 Oct	Clapton Orient	H	W	2-1
17 Oct	Blackpool	H	W	2-0
24 Oct	Derby Co	A	L	0-4
31 Oct	Lincoln C	H	D	1-1
7 Nov	Birmingham	A	L	0-3
14 Nov	Grimsby T	H	W	6-0
18 Nov	Nottingham F	A	D	1-1
21 Nov	Huddersfield T	A	L	0-3
28 Nov	Bristol C	H	W	3-0
5 Dec	Bury	A	L	1-3
12 Dec	Preston NE	H	L	1-2
25 Dec	Leicester	A	W	4-1
26 Dec	Leicester	H	W	6-0
1 Jan	Barnsley	A	L	0-1
2 Jan	Wolverhampton W	H	W	5-1
16 Jan	Fulham	A	W	1-0
23 Jan	Stockport Co	H	W	3-1
6 Feb	Leeds C	H	W	2-0
13 Feb	Clapton Orient	A	L	0-1
20 Feb	Blackpool	A	W	2-0
27 Feb	Derby Co	H	L	1-2
6 Mar	Lincoln C	A	L	0-1
13 Mar	Birmingham	H	W	1-0
20 Mar	Grimsby T	A	L	0-1
27 Mar	Huddersfield T	H	L	0-3
2 Apr	Hull C	A	L	0-1
3 Apr	Bristol C	A	D	1-1
5 Apr	Barnsley	H	W	1-0
1o Apr	Bury	H	W	3-1
17 Apr	Preston NE	A	L	0-3
24 Apr	Nottingham F	H	W	7-0

FA Cup

9 Jan	Merthyr T (1)	H*	W	3-0
30 Jan	Chelsea (2)	A	L	0-1

*by arrangement

London FA Challenge Cup

21 Sep	Tufnell Park	H	W	6-0
19 Oct	Q P R	H	W	2-1
9 Nov	Crystal Palace	A	W	2-0
7 Dec	Millwall (Final)	A	L	1-2

London Professional Charity Fund

2 Nov	West Ham U	H	W	1-0

Friendly

19 Dec	Swindon T	L	1-2

Position in Football League Table

	P	W	L	D	F:A	Pts	
Derby Co	38	23	8	7	71:33	53	1st
Arsenal	38	19	14	5	69:41	43	5th

SEASON 1915-1916
LONDON FOOTBALL COMBINATION

4 Sep	Tottenham H	H	W	2-0
11 Sep	Crystal Palace	A	L	1-3
18 Sep	Q P R	H	W	2-1
25 Sep	Fulham	A	L	3-4
2 Oct	Clapton Orient	H	W	2-0
9 Oct	Watford	A	L	0-1
16 Oct	Millwall	H	D	1-1
23 Oct	Croydon Common	A	W	4-1
30 Oct	Chelsea	A	L	1-3
6 Nov	Brentford	H	W	3-1
13 Nov	Tottenham H	A	D	3-3
20 Nov	Crystal Palace	H	D	2-2
27 Nov	Q P R	A	D	1-1
4 Dec	Fulham	H	W	2-1
11 Dec	Clapton Orient	A	W	2-0
18 Dec	Watford	H	W	3-1
25 Dec	West Ham U	A	L	2-8
27 Dec	West Ham U	H	W	3-2
1 Jan	Millwall	A	L	0-3
8 Jan	Croydon Common	H	W	4-2
15 Jan	Chelsea	H	L	0-6
22 Jan	Brentford	A	D	2-2

Supplementary Tournament – Section 'B'

5 Feb	Watford	H	D	1-1
12 Feb	Brentford	A	L	1-2
19 Feb	Reading	H	W	4-1
26 Feb	Clapton Orient	A	D	1-1
4 Mar	Tottenham H	H	L	0-3
11 Mar	Millwall	A	L	0-2
18 Mar	Brentford	H	W	5-2
25 Mar	Reading	A	D	1-1
1 Apr	Clapton Orient	H	W	2-1
8 Apr	Tottenham H	A	L	2-3
15 Apr	Millwall	H	D	0-0
21 Apr	Chelsea	A	L	0-9
24 Apr	Chelsea	H	L	1-3
29 Apr	Watford	A	L	1-2

Friendly

9 Jan	Fulham	H	W	2-0

Benson Fund Match

6 May	London Combination XI	H	D	2-2

Position in London Football Combination Table

	P	W	L	D	F:A	Pts	
Chelsea	22	17	2	3	71:18	37	1st
Arsenal	22	10	7	5	43:46	25	3rd

Position in Supplementary Tournament – Section 'B'

	P	W	L	D	F:A	Pts	
West Ham U	14	9	3	2	32:16	20	1st
Arsenal	14	3	7	4	19:31	10	5th

SEASON 1916-1917
LONDON FOOTBALL COMBINATION

2 Sep	West Ham U	A	L	1-2
9 Sep	Tottenham H	H	D	1-1
16 Sep	Crystal Palace	A	L	0-1
23 Sep	Brentford	H	D	0-0
30 Sep	Chelsea	A	L	0-3
7 Oct	Southampton	H	D	3-3
14 Oct	Luton	H	W	2-1
21 Oct	Portsmouth	A	L	0-1
28 Oct	Millwall	H	W	1-0
4 Nov	Watford	A	W	4-2
11 Nov	Clapton Orient	A	W	4-0
18 Nov	Fulham	A	L	0-2
25 Nov	West Ham U	H	L	0-2
2 Dec	Tottenham H	A	L	1-4
9 Dec	Crystal Palace	H	W	1-2
23 Dec	Chelsea	H	W	2-1
25 Dec	Q P R	A	W	3-2
26 Dec	Q P R	H	D	0-0
30 Dec	Southampton	A	W	1-0
6 Jan	Luton	A	W	4-1
13 Jan	Portsmouth	H	W	1-0
20 Jan	Millwall	A	L	0-1
27 Jan	Watford	H	D	1-1
3 Feb	Clapton Orient	A	D	2-2
10 Feb	Fulham	H	W	3-2
17 Feb	Chelsea	H	W	3-0
24 Feb	Southampton	A	W	2-0
3 Mar	Clapton Orient	H	W	3 1
10 Mar	West Ham U	A	W	3-2
17 Mar	Crystal Palace	A	L	0-1
24 Mar	Portsmouth	H	W	2-1
31 Mar	Chelsea	A	L	0-2
6 Apr	Tottenham H	A	D	0-0
7 Apr	Southampton	H	D	2-2
9 Apr	Tottenham H	H	W	3-2
14 Apr	Clapton Orient	A	W	3-1
21 Apr	West Ham U	H	W	2-1
26 Apr	Brentford	A	D	0-0
28 Apr	Crystal Palace	H	W	4-0
30 Apr	Portsmouth	A	D	0-0

Position in London Football Combination Table

	P	W	L	D	F:A	Pts	
West Ham U	40	30	5	5	110:45	65	1st
Arsenal	40	19	11	10	62:47	48	5th

SEASON 1917-1918
LONDON FOOTBALL COMBINATION

1 Sep	Q P R	H	W	2-0
8 Sep	Clapton Orient	A	W	5-0
15 Sep	Millwall	H	W	4-0
22 Sep	Tottenham H	A	W	2-1
29 Sep	Chelsea	H	L	0-1
6 Oct	Brentford	A	D	2-2
13 Oct	Crystal Palace	A	L	0-2
20 Oct	West Ham U	H	D	2-2
27 Oct	Q P R	A	L	0-2
3 Nov	Clapton Orient	H	W	3-1
10 Nov	Millwall	A	D	2-2
17 Nov	Tottenham H	H	L	0-1
24 Nov	Chelsea	A	L	3-4
1 Dec	Brentford	H	W	4-1
8 Dec	Crystal Palace	H	L	0-2
15 Dec	West Ham U	A	L	2-3
22 Dec	Q P R	H	W	3-0
25 Dec	Fulham	A	D	1-1
26 Dec	Fulham	H	D	1-1
29 Dec	Clapton Orient	A	W	2-1
5 Jan	Millwall	H	W	1-0
12 Jan	Tottenham H	A	L	1-4
19 Jan	Chelsea	H	W	4-1
26 Jan	Brentford	A	L	2-3
2 Feb	Crystal Palace	A	W	4-1
9 Feb	Fulham	H	L	0-3
16 Feb	Q P R	A	W	3-0
23 Feb	Clapton Orient	H	W	7-1
2 Mar	Millwall	A	W	3-0
9 Mar	Tottenham H	H	W	4-1
16 Mar	Chelsea	A	L	2-4
23 Mar	Brentford	H	L	1-3
29 Mar	West Ham U	A	L	1-4
30 Mar	Crystal Palace	H	W	3-0
1 Apr	West Ham U	H	L	1-3
6 Apr	Fulham	A	L	1-2

Supplementary Competitions

13 Apr	Millwall	H	W	4-3
20 Apr	Millwall	A	W	1-0
27 Apr	Brentford	H	W	3-1
4 May	Brentford (National War Fund)	A	D	1-1

Position in London Football Combination Table

	P	W	L	D	F:A	Pts	
Chelsea	36	21	7	8	82:39	50	1st
Arsenal	36	16	15	5	76:57	37	5th

SEASON 1918-1919
LONDON FOOTBALL COMBINATION

7 Sep	Q P R	A	W	3-2
14 Sep	Millwall	H	W	4-0
21 Sep	Fulham	A	W	2-1
28 Sep	Brentford	H	D	1-1
5 Oct	West Ham U	A	W	4-1
12 Oct	Tottenham H	H	W	3-0
19 Oct	Chelsea	A	L	1-4
26 Oct	Crystal Palace	A	L	1-2
2 Nov	Q P R	H	W	1-0
9 Nov	Millwall	A	D	3-3
16 Nov	Fulham	H	L	1-3
23 Nov	Brentford	A	L	1-4
30 Nov	West Ham U	H	L	0-2
7 Dec	Tottenham H	A	L	0-1
14 Dec	Chelsea	H	W	3-0
21 Dec	Crystal Palace	H	D	3-3
25 Dec	Clapton Orient	A	L	2-3
26 Dec	Clapton Orient	H	W	9-2
28 Dec	Q P R	A	W	2-0
4 Jan	Millwall	H	W	4-1
11 Jan	Fulham	A	L	1-3
18 Jan	Brentford	H	D	3-3
25 Jan	West Ham U	A	W	2-1
1 Feb	Tottenham H	H	L	2-3
8 Feb	Chelsea	A	W	2-1
15 Feb	Clapton Orient	H	W	4-0
22 Feb	Q P R	H	L	1-3
1 Mar	Milwall	A	W	3-0
8 Mar	Fulham	H	W	5-0
15 Mar	Brentford	A	L	0-2
22 Mar	West Ham U	H	W	3-2
29 Mar	Tottenham H	A	W	1-0
5 Apr	Chelsea	H	W	2-1
12 Apr	Clapton Orient	A	D	2-2
18 Apr	Crystal Palace	A	W	3-0
21 Apr	Crystal Palace	H	W	3-2

London Combination Victory Cup

1 Jan	Millwall	A	W	1-0
31 Mar	Fulham	H	L	1-4

Friendlies

19 Apr	Clapton Orient	W	3-1
26 Apr	Brentford	D	3-3
3 May	West Ham U	L	0-1
10 May	West Ham U	W	3-2
17 May	Chelsea	L	1-2
24 May	Tottenham H	D	0-0

Position in London Football Combination Table

	P	W	L	D	F:A	Pts	
Brentford	36	20	7	9	94:46	49	1st
Arsenal	36	20	11	5	85:56	45	2nd

The Arsenal were a Second Division club at the outbreak of the First World War, finishing fifth in the last pre-war season. After the war, the First Division was increased from 20 to 22 clubs, and The Arsenal, illogically and possibly corruptly, were elected to one of the extra places. Since then they have remained a First Division club, and from now on the records are given in more detail.

SEASON 1919-1920 FOOTBALL LEAGUE (DIVISION 1)

30 Aug	Newcastle U	H L	0-1	Williamson	Shaw	Bradshaw	Graham	Voysey	McKinnon	Rutherford	Groves	White	Blyth	Baker
1 Sep	Liverpool	A W	3-2	..	..	..	..	..	..	..	Burgess	.. [2]	.. [1]	Groves
6 Sep	Newcastle U	A L	1-3	..	..	..	..	..	..	..	..	..	..	.. [1]
8 Sep	Liverpool	H W	1-0	..	..	..	..	..	..	.. [1]	..	..	..	..
13 Sep	Sunderland	A D	1-1	..	..	Hutchins	..	..	..	..	..	.. [1]	..	..
20 Sep	Sunderland	H W	3-2	..	..	..	..	Buckley	..	..	..	.. [3]	..	..
27 Sep	Blackburn Rov	A D	2-2	..	..	Bradshaw	..	..	..	Groves	.. [1]	.. [1]	..	Baker
4 Oct	Blackburn Rov	H L	0-1	..	..	..	..	..	..	Rutherford	..	..	..	Groves
11 Oct	Everton	A W	3-2	Dunn	..	..	..	..	..	..	Groves	.. [2]	.. [1]	Toner
18 Oct	Everton	H D	1-1	Williamson	..	Hutchins	..	..	..	..	..	..	..	..
25 Oct	Bradford C	H L	1-2	..	..	..	.. [1]	..	..	..	White	Pagnam	..	..
1 Nov	Bradford C	A D	1-1	..	..	Bradshaw	Groves	Graham	..	..	.. [1]	..	Hardinge	..
8 Nov	Bolton W	H D	2-2	..	..	..	..	..	..	.. [1]	..	.. [1]	.. [1]	..
15 Nov	Bolton W	A D	2-2	..	..	..	Butler	Buckley	..	..	..	.. [2]	..	.. [1]
22 Nov	Notts Co	H W	3-1	..	..	..	..	.. [1]	..	..	..	.. [1]	..	..
29 Nov	Notts Co	A D	2-2	..	..	Hutchins	..	..	..	.. [1]	..	..	..	..
6 Dec	Chelsea	H D	1-1	..	..	Bradshaw	..	..	..	.. [1]	..	..	..	..
13 Dec	Chelsea	A L	1-3	..	..	..	.. [1]	..	..	..	..	..	..	..
20 Dec	Sheffield Wed	H W	3-1	..	..	..	..	..	..	Groves	.. [1]	.. [1]	Baker
25 Dec	Derby Co	A L	1-2	..	..	..	..	..	..	.. [1]	..	..	Lewis
26 Dec	Derby Co	H W	1-0	..	..	..	Baker	..	..	.. [1]	..	..	..
27 Dec	Sheffield Wed	A W	2-1	..	..	..	..	..	..	..	White [1]	.. [1]	.. [1]
3 Jan	Manchester C	H D	2-2	..	..	..	..	..	..	..	.. [1]	..	..
17 Jan	Manchester C	A L	1-4	Dunn	..	..	Graham[1]	Butler	..	Groves	White	Pagnam	..	..
24 Jan	Aston Villa	H L	0-1	..	..	..	..	..	Pagnam	Groves	White	Blyth	..
7 Feb	Oldham Ath	H W	3-2	..	Cownley	..	.. [1]	Buckley	..	Rutherford	White	North [1]	.. [1]	Toner
11 Feb	Aston Villa	A L	1-2	..	..	..	.. [1]	..	Baker	..	..	..	Coopland
14 Feb	Oldham Ath	A L	0-3	..	..	..	Butler	McKinnon	..	..	..	..	Toner
21 Feb	Manchester U	H L	0-3	..	..	..	Buckley	..	..	Butler	White	..	..
28 Feb	Manchester U	A W	1-0	..	Shaw	Hutchins	Butler	..	..	.. [1]	Bradshaw	Pagnam	Graham	Blyth
6 Mar	Sheffield U	A L	0-2	..	..	..	..	Butler	..	..	..	North	..
13 Mar	Sheffield U	H W	3-0	..	Peart	..	Baker	Butler	..	..	.. [2]	Graham[1]	..
20 Mar	Middlesbrough	A L	0-1	..	..	..	..	Buckley	..	Groves	..	Bradshaw	..
27 Mar	Middlesbrough	H W	2-1	..	..	..	..	..	..	.. [1]	.. [1]	Graham	..
3 Apr	Burnley	A L	1-2	..	Shaw	..	..	Butler	..	..	.. [1]	Bradshaw	..
5 Apr	W B A	H W	1-0	..	..	..	..	..	..	..	..	..	.. [1]
6 Apr	W B A	A L	0-1	..	Peart	..	Toner	Buckley	..	Greenaway	Whittaker	..	..
10 Apr	Burnley	H W	2-0	..	Shaw	..	Baker	Butler	..	Rutherford	Pagnam[1]	.. [1]	..
17 Apr	Preston NE	A D	1-1	Williamson	..	..	..	..	..	..	..	White [1]	..
24 Apr	Preston NE	H D	0-0	..	..	..	..	..	..	..	..	..	..
28 Apr	Bradford PA	A D	0-0	..	Peart	..	..	..	..	Greenaway	..	..	..
1 May	Bradford PA	H W	3-0	..	Shaw	..	..	Pattison	..	..	.. [1]	.. [1]	Bradshaw[1]	..

FA Cup

10 Jan	Rochdale (1)	H W	4-2	Williamson	Shaw	Bradshaw	Graham[1]	Butler	McKinnon	Rutherford[1]	Groves[1]	White	Pagnam[1]	Lewis
31 Jan	Bristol C (2)	A L	0-1	Dunn	..	..	..	Buckley	..	..	Pagnam	Blyth	Toner

Appearances (Goals)

Baker A 17 · Blyth W 29 (4) · Bradshaw F 33 (2) · Buckley C 23 (1) · Burgess D 7 (1) · Butler J 21 (1) · Coopland W 1 · Cownley F 4 · Dunn S 16 · Graham J 22 (5) · Greenaway D 3 · Groves F 29 (5) · Hardinge H 13 (3) · Hutchins A 18 · Lewis C 5 (1) · McKinnon A 41 · North F 4 (1) · Pagnam F 25 (13) · Pattison G 1 · Peart J 5 · Rutherford J 36 (3) · Shaw J 33 · Toner J 15 (1) · Voysey C 5 · White H 29 (15) · Whittaker T 1 · Williamson E 26 · Total: 27 players (56)

Position in League Table

	P	W	L	D	F:A	Pts	
W B A	42	28	10	4	104:47	60	1st
Arsenal	42	15	15	12	56:58	42	10th

SEASON 1920-1921 FOOTBALL LEAGUE (DIVISION 1)

28 Aug	Aston Villa	A L	0-5	Williamson	Shaw	Hutchins	Baker	Buckley	McKinnon	Smith	Groves	Pagnam	Bradshaw	Blyth
30 Aug	Manchester U	H W	2-0	..	..	..	..	..	..	.. [1]	..	.. [1]	..	..
4 Sep	Aston Villa	H L	0-1	..	..	..	..	Graham	..	..	..	..	..	..
6 Sep	Manchester U	A D	1-1	..	..	..	..	..	..	..	..	..	White[1]	..
11 Sep	Manchester C	H W	2-1	..	..	..	..	..	..	..	White	.. [1]	Groves[1]	..
18 Sep	Manchester C	A L	1-3	..	..	..	..	..	..	..	..	..	..	.. [1]
25 Sep	Middlesbrough	H D	2-2	..	..	..	..	.. [1]	..	..	..	.. [1]	..	..
2 Oct	Middlesbrough	A L	1-2	..	..	..	..	..	Rutherford	..	.. [1]	..	..	..
9 Oct	Bolton W	H D	0-0	..	..	..	..	..	..	..	.. [1]	..	Bradshaw	..
16 Oct	Bolton W	A D	1-1	..	..	..	..	..	..	..	.. [1]	..	..	..
23 Oct	Derby County	A D	1-1	..	..	..	..	..	..	..	.. [1]	..	..	..
30 Oct	Derby County	H W	2-0	..	Bradshaw	..	..	..	..	..	.. [1]	.. [1]	Blyth	Dr Paterson
6 Nov	Blackburn R	A D	2-2	..	Shaw	Bradshaw	..	Buckley[1]	.. [1]	..	..	.. [1]	Bradshaw	..
13 Nov	Blackburn R	H W	2-0	..	..	Hutchins	..	..	..	Smith	.. [1]	.. [1]	.. [1]	..
20 Nov	Huddersfield T	A W	4-0	..	..	..	..	Graham[1]	..	..	.. [1]	.. [2]	.. [1]	..
27 Nov	Huddersfield T	H W	2-0	..	..	..	..	..	Butler	..	.. [1]	.. [2]	..	..
4 Dec	Chelsea	A W	2-1	..	..	..	..	..	McKinnon	Rutherford	.. [1]	.. [2]	..	..
11 Dec	Chelsea	H D	1-1	..	..	..	..	..	..	..	..	..	.. [1]	..
18 Dec	Bradford C	A L	1-3	..	..	..	..	..	..	..	..	.. [1]	..	Toner
25 Dec	Everton	A W	4-2	..	Bradshaw	..	..	Butler	..	..	.. [1]	.. [1]	.. [1]	..
27 Dec	Everton	H D	1-1	..	Shaw	..	..	..	..	..	..	..	..	Dr Paterson
1 Jan	Bradford C	H L	1-2	..	..	..	..	Graham[1]	..	..	..	..	..	Toner
15 Jan	Tottenham	A L	1-2	..	Bradshaw	..	..	Butler	..	.. [1]	..	..	..	Dr Paterson
22 Jan	Tottenham	H W	3-2	Dunn	..	..	..	..	..	.. [2]	.. [1]	North	..	..
29 Jan	Sunderland	H L	1-2	Williamson	..	..	..	Graham	..	..	.. [1]	Pagnam[1]	..	..
5 Feb	Sunderland	A L	1-5	..	..	Cownley	..	.. [1]	..	..	Groves	..	.. [1]	..
12 Feb	Oldham Ath	A D	1-1	..	..	Hutchins	..	..	Toner	..	..	Walden	.. [1]	..
19 Feb	Oldham Ath	H D	2-2	..	..	..	..	..	McKinnon	.. [1]	..	.. [1]	..	..
26 Feb	Preston N E	A W	1-0	..	..	..	..	Butler	..	..	..	White [1]	..	..
12 Mar	Burnley	A L	0-1	..	..	..	..	Graham	..	..	Burgess	..	..	Toner
19 Mar	Burnley	H D	1-1	..	..	..	.. [1]	Pattison	..	..	..	..	..	Dr Paterson
26 Mar	Sheffield U	H L	2-6	..	..	..	.. [1]	Graham	..	..	Groves	.. [1]	..	..
28 Mar	W B A	H W	2-1	..	Shaw	..	..	.. [1]	Whittaker	..	McKenzie	North	.. [1]	..
29 Mar	W B A	A W	4-3	..	..	..	Pattison	..	..	.. [1]	.. [2]	Hopkins[1]	..
2 Apr	Sheffield U	A D	1-1	Dunn	..	..	Pattison	..	..	.. [1]	..	..	..
9 Apr	Bradford PA	H W	2-1	..	..	Bradshaw	Baker	..	McKinnon	.. [1]	..	Blyth	Toner[1]
16 Apr	Bradford PA	A W	1-0	..	..	Hutchins	..	..	..	Blyth	..	Hopkins	.. [1]
23 Apr	Newcastle U	H D	1-1	..	..	..	..	..	.. [1]	..	..	.. [1]	..
25 Apr	Preston NE	H W	2-1	..	Bradshaw	..	Pattison	..	..	..	..	.. [1]	..	..
30 Apr	Newcastle U	A L	0-1	..	Shaw	..	..	..	..	..	McKenzie	Blyth	..	..
2 May	Liverpool	H L	0-0	..	Peart	..	Whittaker	Pattison	..	..	Burgess	..	..	..
7 May	Liverpool	A L	0-3	..	Shaw	..	..	..	..	..	..	..	..	..

FA Cup

8 Jan	QPR (1)	A L	0-2	Williamson	Shaw	Hutchins	Butler	Voysey	McKinnon	Rutherford	White	Pagnam	Blyth	Toner

Appearances (Goals)

Baker A 37 (2) · Blyth W 39 (7) · Bradshaw F 21 · Buckley C 4 (1) · Burgess D 4 · Butler J 36 · Cownley F 1 · Dunn S 9 · Graham J 30 (5) · Groves G 13 (1) · Hopkins J 8 (2) · Hutchins A 39 · McKenzie A 5 (1) · McKinnon J 37 (2) · North E 8 (2) · Pagnam F 25 (14) · Paterson Dr J 20 · Pattison G 6 · Peart J 1 · Rutherford J 32 (7) · Shaw J 28 · Smith J 10 (1) · Toner J 11 (3) · Walden H 2 (1) · White H 26 (10) · Whittaker T 5 · Willamson E 33 · Total: 27 players (59)

Position in League Table

	P	W	L	D	F:A	Pts	
Burnley	42	23	6	13	79:36	59	1st
Arsenal	42	15	13	14	59:63	44	9th

SEASON 1921-1922 FOOTBALL LEAGUE (DIVISION 1)

27 Aug	Sheffield U	H L	1-2	Williamson	Shaw	Hutchins	Baker	Graham	McKinnon	Rutherford	Blyth	White[1]	North	Voysey
29 Aug	Preston NE	A L	2-3	..	..	..	Whittaker	Butler	..	..	Burgess	..[2]	..	Hopkins
3 Sep	Sheffield U	A L	1-4	..	Cownley	..	..	..	..	..	..	..[1]	..	..
5 Sep	Preston NE	H W	1-0	..	..	..	..	..	..	..	McKenzie	..	..	..
10 Sep	Manchester C	A L	0-2	..	..	..	..	..	..	..	..	..	..	..
17 Sep	Manchester C	H L	0-1	..	..	..	Baker	..	..	..	..	..	Graham	Blyth
24 Sep	Everton	A D	1-1	..	..	..	Whittaker	..	..	..	White	Baker	Bradshaw[1]	..
1 Oct	Everton	H W	1-0	..	..	..	..	..	..	..	..	..[1]	..	..
8 Oct	Sunderland	A L	0-1	..	..	..	..	..	..	..	..	..	..	..
15 Oct	Sunderland	H L	1-2	..	..	..	..	..	..	..	..	..	..[1]	Peterson
22 Oct	Huddersfield T	A L	0-2	..	Shaw	..	Baker	..	..	..	..	Henderson	..	Blyth
29 Oct	Huddersfield T	H L	1-3	..	..	..	..	..	..	..	Maxwell	North[1]	Blyth	Peterson
5 Nov	Birmingham	A W	1-0	..	Bradshaw	..	..	..	Whittaker	..	Blyth	..[1]	Hopkins	Toner
12 Nov	Birmingham	H W	5-2	..	..	..	..[1]	..	..[1]	..	..	..	..[2]	..
19 Nov	Bolton W	A L	0-1	..	..	..	..[1]	..	..	..	..	Henderson	..	..
3 Dec	Blackburn Rov	A W	1-0	..	..	..	..	..	..	..	..	..	..	..
10 Dec	Blackburn Rov	H D	1-1	..	..	..	..	..[1]	..	..	..	..	..[1]	..
12 Dec	Bolton W	H D	1-1	..	..	..	..	..	..	..	White	North	Boreham	..
17 Dec	Oldham Ath	A L	1-2	..	..	..	Whittaker	..	McKinnon	..	..	..	..	..
24 Dec	Oldham Ath	H L	0-1	..	..	..	..	..	..	..	..	..	..	..
26 Dec	Cardiff C	H D	0-0	..	..	..	..	Graham	..	..	..	Butler	Hopkins	..
27 Dec	Cardiff C	A L	3-4	..	Shaw	Turnbull	..	Pattison	Milne	..	..[1]	Henderson	Boreham[2]	Hopkins
31 Dec	Chelsea	A W	2-0	..	Bradshaw	Hutchins	Milne	Graham	Whittaker	..	Blyth	White[1]	..[1]	Toner
14 Jan	Chelsea	H W	1-0	..	..	..	Baker	..	..	Creegan	..	..	Baker	..
21 Jan	Burnley	H D	0-0	..	..	..	..	Milne	..	Rutherford	..	..	Baker	..
4 Feb	Newcastle U	H W	2-1	Dunn	..	Turnbull	Baker	..	..	..[1]	..	..	Boreham[1]	..
11 Feb	Newcastle U	A L	1-3	Williamson	..	..	..	..	..	..	..	..	..	..
20 Feb	Burnley	A L	0-1	..	..	Cownley	Milne	Pattison	..	Creegan	Butler	..	Blyth	..
25 Feb	Liverpool	A L	0-4	..	Cownley	Turnbull	Baker	Graham	..	Blyth	..	..	Boreham	..
11 Mar	Manchester U	A L	0-1	..	Hutchins	Shaw	..	Butler	..	Rutherford	Blyth	..	..	..
18 Mar	Aston Villa	A L	0-2	..	Bradshaw	Hutchins	..	Graham	..	..	Earle	..	..	..
22 Mar	Liverpool	H W	1-0	..	..	..	..[1]	..	..	Creegan	White	Young	..	..
25 Mar	Aston Villa	H W	2-0	..	..	..	..	..	..	..	..[1]	..[1]	..	..
1 Apr	Middlesbrough	H D	2-2	..	..	..	..	..	..	..	..[1]	..	..[1]	Blyth
5 Apr	Manchester U	H W	3-1	..	..	..	..	..	McKinnon	Rutherford	..[1]	Butler[1]	..[1]	Toner
8 Apr	Middlesbrough	A L	2-4	..	..	..	..[1]	..	..	..	..	..	..	..
15 Apr	Tottenham H	A L	0-2	..	..	..	..	..	Whittaker	..	..	Young	..	..
17 Apr	W B A	A W	3-0	..	..	..	..	..	..	..[1]	..	..	..	..
18 Apr	W B A	H D	2-2	..	..	..	..	..	..	..[1]	..[1]	..	..	Blyth
22 Apr	Tottenham H	H W	1-0	..	..	..	..	..	..	..[1]	..	..	..	..
29 Apr	Bradford C	A W	1-0	..·	..	..	..	..	..	..	..[1]	..[1]	..	..
6 May	Bradford C	H W	1-0	..	..	..	..	..	..	..	Young	Turnbull	..	..[1]

FA Cup

7 Jan	Q P R (1)	H D	0-0	Williamson	Turnbull	Hutchins	Milne	Pattison	Whittaker	Hopkins	Baker	White	Bradshaw	Toner
11 Jan	Q P R (1R)	A W	2-1	..	Bradshaw	..	..[1]	Graham[1]	..	Creegan	Blyth	..[2]	Baker	..
28 Jan	Bradford C (2)	A W	3-2	..	..	..	..	..	..	Rutherford	..[1]	..[2]	..	..
18 Feb	Leicester C (3)	H W	3-0	..	..	Turnbull	Baker	..	..	..[1]	Butler	..[2]	Blyth	..
4 Mar	Preston NE (4)	H D	1-1	..	..	..	..	..	..	..	..	..[1]	..	..
8 Mar	Preston NE (4R)	A L	1-2	..	..	..	..	..	..	..	..	..	..[1]	..

Appearances (Goals)

Baker A 32(4) · Blyth W 25 (1) · Boreham R 22 (10) · Bradshaw F 32 (2) · Burgess D 2 · Butler J 25 (2) · Cownley F 10 · Creegan W 5 · Dunn S 1 · Earle S 1 · Graham A 21 (3) · Henderson W 5 · Hutchins A 37 · Hopkins J 11 (3) · Maxwell T 1 · Milne W 4 · McKenzie A 3 · McKinnon A 17 · North F 11 (3) · Paterson Dr J 2 · Pattison G 2 · Rutherford J 36 (1) · Shaw J 6 · Toner J 24 (1) · Turnbull R 5 · Voysey C 1 · Whittaker T 36 (1) · White H 35 (14) · Williamson E 41 · Young A 9 (2) · Total: 30 players (47)

Position in League Table

	P	W	L	D	F:A	Pts	
Liverpool	42	22	7	13	63:36	57	1st
Arsenal	42	15	20	7	47:56	37	17th

SEASON 1922-1923 FOOTBALL LEAGUE (DIVISION 1)

26 Aug	Liverpool	A L	2-5	Williamson	Bradshaw	Hutchins	Butler	Voysey	Whittaker	Rutherford	White	Young[1]	Boreham[1]	Blyth
28 Aug	Burnley	H D	1-1	..	..	Turnbull	Baker	..	..	..	..	..[1]	..	..
2 Sep	Liverpool	H W	1-0	..	..	Hutchins[1]	..	..	..	..	..	..	..	..
4 Sep	Burnley	A L	1-4	..	..	..	..	..	..	..	..	..	Hopkins[1]	..
9 Sep	Cardiff C	A L	1-4	..	..	Turnbull	..	..[1]	..	..	..	..	Boreham	..
16 Sep	Cardiff C	H W	2-1	Dunn	..	Hutchins	..	..	..	..	..[1]	..[2]	..	Dr Paterson
23 Sep	Tottenham H	A W	2-1	..	..	..	..	..	Graham	..	..	..	..	Blyth
30 Sept	Tottenham H	H L	0-2	..	..	..	..	..	..	..	..	..	..	..
2 Oct	Sheffield U	A L	1-2	..	..	..	..	..	..	..	Townrow	..[1]	..	..
7 Oct	W B A	H W	3-1	..	Turnbull	..	..	..[1]	..	..	White[1]	..	..[1]	..
14 Oct	W B A	A L	0-7	..	Bradshaw	Turnbull	..	..	..	..	..	..	..	Dr Paterson
21 Oct	Newcastle U	A D	1-1	..	..	..	Milne	Graham	Whittaker	..	Blyth	Roe	..	Hopkins[1]
28 Oct	Newcastle U	H L	1-2	..	..	..	..	..	John	Henderson	Baker	..[1]	..	Dr Paterson
4 Nov	Everton	A L	0-1	..	..	..	..	..	Whittaker	Dr Paterson	White	..	..	Toner
11 Nov	Everton	H L	1-2	..	..	..	..	..	..	Rutherford	Blyth[1]	..	..	Dr Paterson
18 Nov	Sunderland	A D	3-3	..	..	Hutchins	..	Butler	..	..	Voysey[2]	Turnbull[1]	..	Toner
25 Nov	Sunderland	H L	2-3	..	..	..	..	..	..	..	..[1]	..[2]	..[1]	Dr Paterson
2 Dec	Birmingham	A L	2-3	..	..	Kennedy	..	Graham	John	Henderson	..[1]	..	..[1]	Toner
9 Dec	Birmingham	H W	1-0	..	Mackie	..	..	..[1]	..	Rutherford	..	..	..	Dr Paterson
16 Dec	Huddersfield T	H D	1-1	..	..	..	..	..	..	..	..	..	..	..
23 Dec	Huddersfield T	A L	0-4	..	..	..	..	..	Whittaker	..	..	..	..	Toner
25 Dec	Bolton W	A L	1-4	..	..	..	Blyth	..	Baker	..	..	..	..	..
26 Dec	Bolton W	H W	5-0	Robson	..	..	Butler	..	..	Blyth[1]	..[1]	..[4]	..[1]	Dr Paterson
30 Dec	Stoke C	H W	3-0	..	..	..	..	..	..	..[1]	..	..[1]	..	..
1 Jan	Blackburn Rov	A W	5-0	..	..	..	..	..	..	..	..[1]	..[4]	McKenzie	..
6 Jan	Stoke C	A L	0-1	..	..	..	..	Graham	..	..	..	..	Boreham	..
20 Jan	Manchester C	H W	1-0	..	..	..	..	..	..	..	..[1]	..	McKenzie	..
27 Jan	Manchester C	A D	0-0	..	..	..	..	..	..	..	..	..	..	..
3 Feb	Nottingham F	A L	1-2	..	..	..	..	..	..	..[1]	..	..	..	..
10 Feb	Nottingham F	H W	2-0	..	..	..	..	Butler	..	Rutherford	..	..	Baker[2]	..
17 Feb	Chelsea	A D	0-0	..	..	..	..	..	..	..	..[2]	..	..	..
24 Feb	Chelsea	H W	3-1	..	..	..	..	..	..	..	..	..[1]	..	..
3 Mar	Middlesbrough	A L	0-2	..	..	..	..	..	..	..	..	..	..	Toner
10 Mar	Middlesbrough	H W	3-0	..	..	..	..	..	..	..[1]	..	..[3]	..	Dr Paterson
17 Mar	Oldham Ath	H W	2-0	..	..	..	..	..	Whittaker	*opponents*	..[1]	..	..	..
24 Mar	Oldham Ath	A D	0-0	..	..	..	..	..	John	..	..	..	..	..
31 Mar	Aston Villa	H W	2-0	..	..	..	..	..	..	..	..[1]	..	..[1]	..
2 Apr	Blackburn	H D	1-1	..	..	..	..	..	..	..	..	..	McKenzie[1]	..
7 Apr	Aston Villa	A D	1-1	..	..	..	..	..	..	Clarke	..[1]	..	..	Toner
14 Apr	Preston NE	H D	1-1	..	Elvey	Baker	..	..	Young	McKenzie	..	..	Boreham[1]	Dr Paterson
21 Apr	Preston NE	A W	2-1	..	Mackie	Kennedy	..	Young	John	Baker	Earle[1]	..[1]	..	Blyth
28 Apr	Sheffield U	H W	2-0	..	..	..	..	Butler	..	Clarke	Blyth[1]	..[1]	..	Dr Paterson

FA Cup

13 Jan	Liverpool (1)	A D	0-0	Robson	Mackie	Kennedy	Milne	Butler	John	Baker	Blyth	Turnbull	Boreham	Dr Paterson
17 Jan	Liverpool (1R)	H L	1-4	..	..	..	..	Voysey	..	..	Townrow	..[1]	..	..

Appearances (Goals)

Baker A 29 (6) · Blyth W 31 (9) · Boreham R 27 (8) · Bradshaw F 17 · Butler J 18 · Clarke J 2 · Dunn S 17 · Earle S 1 (1) · Elvey J 1 · Graham A 17 (1) · Henderson W 2 · Hopkins J 2 (2) · Hutchins A 10 (1) · John R 24 · Kennedy A 24 · McKenzie A 7 (1) · Milne W 31 · Mackie J 23 · Paterson Dr J 27 · Robson J 20 · Roe A 4 (1) · Rutherford J 26 (1) · Toner J 7 · Townrow J 2 · Turnbull R 35 (20) · Voysey C 18 (4) · White H 11 (1) · Whittaker T 13 (1) · Willamson E 5 · Young A 13 (3) · Own goals 1 · Total: 30 players (61)

Position in League Table

	P	W	L	D	F:A	Pts	
Liverpool	42	26	8	8	70:31	60	1st
Arsenal	42	16	16	10	61:62	42	11th

SEASON 1923-1924   FOOTBALL LEAGUE (DIVISION 1)

25 Aug	Newcastle	H	L	1-4	Robson	Mackie	Kennedy	Milne	Butler	John	Baker	Woods	Turnbull[1]	Young	Toner
27 Aug	West Ham U	A	L	0-1	..	..	..	..	..	..	Voysey	..	..	Boreham	Haden
1 Sep	Newcastle U	A	L	0-1	..	..	..	..	..	..	Wallington	Voysey	..	Woods	..
8 Sep	W B A	A	L	0-4	..	..	..	..	..	..	Rutherford	..	..	..	..
10 Sep	West Ham U	H	W	4-1	..	..	..	..	Graham[1]	..	..	Earle[2]	..	..	..
15 Sep	W B A	H	W	1-0	..	..	..	..	..	..	..	Voysey[1]	..	Boreham	..
22 Sep	Birmingham	A	W	2-0	..	Whittaker	..	..	..	..	..	..[1]	..[1]	Blyth	..
29 Sep	Birmingham	H	D	0-0	..	Mackie	..	..	..	..	..	..	..	..	..
6 Oct	Manchester C	A	L	0-1	..	..	Whittaker	..	..	..	..	Woods	..	..	..
13 Oct	Manchester C	H	L	1-2	..	..	Kennedy	..	..	Baker	..	..	..[1]	..	Dr Paterson
20 Oct	Bolton W	A	W	2-1	..	..	..	..	Butler	Blyth	..[1]	Townrow	Young	Woods[1]	..
27 Oct	Bolton W	H	D	0-0	..	..	..	..	..	..	..[1]	..	..	..[1]	..
3 Nov	Middlesbrough	H	W	2-1	..	..	..	Graham	..	..	Dr Paterson	..[1]	..	..	Haden
10 Nov	Middlesbrough	A	D	0-0	..	..	Whittaker	..	..	..	Voysey	..	..	..	Toner
17 Nov	Tottenham H	H	D	1-1	..	..	..	..	..	..	Rutherford	..[1]	Turnbull	..	Dr Paterson
24 Nov	Tottenham H	A	L	0-3	..	..	..	..	..	..	..	..	Young	Baker	..
1 Dec	Blackburn Rov	H	D	2-2	..	..	..	Milne	Graham	..	opponents	..[1]	..	Woods	..
8 Dec	Blackburn Rov	A	L	0-2	..	..	..	..	..	..	..	Voysey	..	..	Haden
15 Dec	Huddersfield T	H	L	1-3	..	..	..	..	Graham	Butler	..	Earle	..[1]	..	Dr Paterson
22 Dec	Huddersfield T	A	L	1-6	..	..	Kennedy	..	..	..	..	Woods	..	Baker[1]	Haden
26 Dec	Notts Co	A	W	2-1	..	..	Baker	Milne	Graham	Young	..	Blyth[1]	Turnbull	Woods[1]	..
27 Dec	Notts Co	H	D	0-0	..	..	..	..	..	..	Dr Paterson	..	..	..[1]	..
29 Dec	Chelsea	H	W	1-0	..	..	..	..	..	..	..	..	..	..[1]	..
5 Jan	Chelsea	A	D	0-0	..	..	..	..	..	Voysey	..	..	..	..	..
19 Jan	Cardiff C	H	L	1-2	..	..	..	..	..	Young	..	..	..[1]	..	..
26 Dec	Cardiff C	A	L	0-4	..	..	..	..	Voysey	..	Clarke	..	..	..	..
9 Feb	Sheffield U	A	L	1-3	..	Baker	Kennedy	..	Graham	..	Rutherford	..[1]	Butler	..	Dr Paterson
16 Feb	Aston Villa	H	L	0-1	..	..	..	..	..	John	..	..	..	Haden	..
25 Feb	Sheffield U	H	L	1-3	..	Mackie	..	..[1]	Butler	..	Dr Paterson	..	Woods	Baker	Toner
1 Mar	Liverpool	H	W	3-1	..	..	..	..	Graham	..	Rutherford[1]	..[1]	..[2]	Ramsay	Haden
12 Mar	Aston Villa	A	L	1-2	..	Baker	..	..	..	..	..	..[1]	..	..[1]	..
15 Mar	Nottingham F	A	L	1-2	..	..	..	..	..	..	..	Neil	..	..[1]	..
22 Mar	Nottingham F	H	W	1-0	..	..	..	..	Butler	Young	Dr Paterson	..[1]	..	..	..
2 Apr	Liverpool	A	D	0-0	..	..	..	..	..	..	..	..[1]	..	..	..
5 Apr	Burnley	H	W	2-0	..	..	..	..	..	..	..	..	..	..[1]	..
12 Apr	Sunderland	H	W	2-0	..	..	..	..	..	..	..	..	..	..	..[1]
18 Apr	Everton	A	L	1-3	..	Mackie	..	..	..	..	Blyth	..	..	..	..[1]
19 Apr	Sunderland	A	D	1-1	..	..	..	..	..	..	..	..	..	..[1]	..
21 Apr	Everton	H	L	0-1	..	..	..	..	..	John	Rutherford	..	..	..	..
26 Apr	Preston NE	A	W	2-0	..	Baker	..	..	..	Young	Dr Paterson	..	..	..[1]	..[1]
28 Mar	Burnley	A	L	1-4	..	Mackie	..	..	Graham	..	Clarke	..	..[1]	Jones	..
3 May	Preston NE	H	L	1-2	..	Baker	..	..	Butler	..	Dr Paterson	..	Turnbull[1]	..	..

FA Cup

12 Jan	Luton (1)	H	W	4-1	Robson	Mackie	Baker	Milne[1]	Graham	Young	Dr Paterson	Blyth[1]	Turnbull[1]	Woods[1]	Haden
2 Feb	Cardiff (2)	A	L	0-1	..	..	Kennedy	..	..	..	..	..	Butler	Baker	..

Appearances (Goals)

Baker A 21(1) · Blyth W 27 (3) · Boreham R 2 · Butler J 24 · Clarke J 2 · Earle S 2 (2) · Graham A 25 (1) · Haden S 31 (3) · John R 15 · Jones F 2 · Kennedy A 29 · Mackie J 31 · Milne W 36 (1) · Neil A 11 (2) · Paterson Dr J 21 · Ramsay J 11 (4) · Robson J 42 · Rutherford J 22 (2) · Toner J 3 · Townrow F 7 (2) · Turnbull R 18 (6) · Voysey C 10 (2) · Wallington E 1 · Whittaker T 8 · Woods H 36 (8) · Young A 25 (2) · Own goals 1 · Total: 26 players (40)

Position in League Table

	P	W	L	D	F:A	Pts	
Huddersfield T	42	23	8	11	60:33	57	1st
Arsenal	42	12	21	9	40:63	33	19th

SEASON 1924-1925   FOOTBALL LEAGUE (DIVISION 1)

30 Aug	Nottingham F	A	W	2-0	Robson	Baker	Kennedy	Milne	Butler	John	Rutherford	Neil	Woods[1]	Ramsey[1]	Toner
1 Sep	Manchester C	H	W	1-0	..	..	..	..	..	..	..	..[1]	..[2]	..	..
6 Sep	Liverpool	H	W	2-0	..	..	..	..	..	..	..	..	..[2]	..	..
13 Sep	Newcastle U	A	D	2-2	..	..	..	..	..	..	..	..[1]	..	..	..
17 Sep	Manchester C	A	L	0-2	..	..	..	..	..	..	..	..	..	..	..
20 Sep	Sheffield U	H	W	2-0	..	..	..	..	..[1]	..	..[1]	..	..	..	..
27 Sep	West Ham U	A	L	0-1	..	..	..	..	..	..	Clarke	..	..	..	Blyth
4 Oct	Blackburn Rov	H	W	1-0	..	..	..	..	..	..	Rutherford	..[1]	..	..	Toner
11 Oct	Huddersfield T	A	L	0-4	..	Mackie	..	..	..	..	Blyth	..	..	..	Haden
13 Oct	Bury	H	L	0-1	..	Baker	..	..	..	..	Rutherford	..	..	..	Toner
18 Oct	Aston Villa	H	D	1-1	..	Mackie	..	..	..[1]	..	..	..	Turnbull	..	..
25 Oct	Tottenham H	H	W	1-0	..	..	..	..	..	..	..	Brain[1]	Woods	..	..
1 Nov	Bolton W	A	L	1-4	..	..	..	..	..	..	..	..[1]	..	..	..
8 Nov	Notts Co	H	L	0-1	..	Baker	..	..	..	..	..	..	..	..	..
15 Nov	Everton	A	W	3-2	Lewis	..	..	..	..	..	..	Neil	Young[1]	..[1]	..[1]
22 Nov	Sunderland	H	D	0-0	..	..	..	..	..	..	Clarke	..	..	..	..
29 Nov	Cardiff C	A	D	1-1	..	..	..	..	..	..	Hoar	Brain	..[1]	..	..
6 Dec	Preston NE	H	W	4-0	..	..	..	..	..	..	Rutherford	..	Woods[3]	..	..[1]
13 Dec	Burnley	A	L	0-1	..	..	..	..	..	..	..	..[4]	..[1]	..	..
20 Dec	Leeds U	H	W	6-1	..	..	..	..	..	..	..	..[4]	..[1]	..[1]	..
25 Dec	Birmingham	A	L	1-2	..	..	..	..	..	..	Hoar	..	..[1]	..	..
26 Dec	Birmingham	H	L	0-1	..	..	..	..	..	Young	Rutherford	..	..	..	..
27 Dec	Nottingham F	H	W	2-1	..	..	..	..	..[1]	John	Hoar	Woods	Brain	..	..
3 Jan	Liverpool	A	L	1-2	..	Mackie	..	..	..	..	..	..[1]	..	..	..
17 Jan	Newcastle U	H	L	0-2	..	Baker	..	..	..	..	..	..	Brain	..	..
24 Jan	Sheffield U	A	L	1-2	..	Mackie	..	Young	Blyth	..[1]	..	Brain	Neil	..	..
7 Feb	Blackburn Rov	A	L	0-1	..	Baker	Mackie	..	Butler	..	..	..	Woods	..	..
14 Feb	Huddersfield T	H	L	0-5	..	..	..	..	Blyth	..	..	..	..	..	..
28 Feb	Tottenham H	A	L	0-2	Robson	Mackie	Kennedy	Baker	Butler	..	..	Neil	Brain	Blyth	Haden
7 Mar	Bolton W	H	W	1-0	..	..	..	..	..	..	..	Brain	Cock	..[1]	..
14 Mar	Notts Co	A	L	1-2	..	..	..	..[1]	..	..	..	..[1]	..	..	..
21 Mar	Everton	H	W	3-1	..	..	..	..	..	..	..	..	Woods[2]	..	..
23 Mar	West Ham U	H	L	1-2	..	..	..	Whittaker	Baker[1]	..	..	..	..	..	..
28 Mar	Sunderland	A	L	0-2	..	..	..	Baker	Butler	..	..	..	..	..	..
1 Apr	Aston Villa	A	L	0-4	..	..	..	..	..	..	..	..	..	..	..
4 Apr	Cardiff C	H	D	1-1	..	Baker	..	Milne	..	..	..	..[1]	..	..	..
11 Apr	Preston NE	A	L	0-2	..	..	..	..	..	..	..	..	..	..	..
13 Apr	W B A	H	L	0-1	..	..	..	..	..	..	..	Neil	Hughes	..	..
14 Apr	W B A	H	W	2-0	..	Mackie	..	..	..	..[1]	Rutherford	Brain[1]	Young	..	..
18 Apr	Burnley	H	W	5-0	..	..	..	..	..	Ramsey	Rutherford	Woods[1]	Brain[3]	..	..[1]
25 Apr	Leeds U	A	L	0-1	Lewis	..	..	..	..	John	Hoar	..	..	Ramsey	..
2 May	Bury	A	L	0-2	..	..	..	..	..	Roe	Rutherford	..	..	Ramsey	..

FA Cup

14 Jan	West Ham U (1)	A	D	0-0	Lewis	Baker	Kennedy	Milne	Butler	John	Hoar	Woods	Brain	Ramsey	Toner
21 Jan	West Ham U (1R)	H	D	2-2	..	..	..	..	..	..	..	Brain[2]	Woods	..	..
26 Jan	West Ham U (1R)		L	0-1	..	..	..	Young	..	..		..	..	..	..
	(at Chelsea)														..

Appearances (Goals)

Baker A 32(2) · Blyth W 17 (1) · Brain J 28 (12) · Butler J 39 (3) · Clarke J 2 · Cock D 2 · Haden S 15 (1) · Hoar S 19 · Hughes J 1 · John R 39 (2) · Kennedy A 40 · Lewis D 16 · Mackie J 19 · Milne W 32 · Neil A 16 (2) · Ramsey J 30 (4) · Robson J 26 · Roe A 1 · Rutherford J 20 (2) · Toner J 26 (2) · Turnbull R 1 · Whittaker T 1 · Woods H 32 (13) · Young A 8 (2) · Total: 24 players (46)

Position in League Table

	P	W	L	D	F:A	Pts	
Huddersfield T	42	21	5	16	69:28	58	1st
Arsenal	42	14	23	5	46:58	33	20th

SEASON 1925-1926 FOOTBALL LEAGUE (DIVISION 1)

Date	Opp		Res	1	2	3	4	5	6	7	8	9	10	11
29 Aug	Tottenham H	H L	0-1	Robson	Mackie	Kennedy	Milne	Butler	John	Hoar	Buchan	Cock	Ramsey	Toner
31 Aug	Leicester	H D	2-2	..	..	..	..	..	..	..	..	Brain¹	Neil¹	..
5 Sep	Manchester U	A W	1-0	..	..	..	..	..	Blyth	..	..	..¹	..	Haden
7 Sep	Leicester C	A W	1-0	..	..	..	..	..	..	..	..	..¹	..	..
12 Sep	Liverpool	H D	1-1	..	..	..	..	..	..	..	..	..	..	..¹
19 Sep	Burnley	A D	2-2	..	..	..	Baker¹	..	..	..	..	..	..	..
21 Sep	West Ham U	H W	3-2	..	..	..	..	..	..	..	..²	..	..	..
26 Sep	Leeds U	H W	4-1	Lewis	..	..	..	..	..	..	..¹	..²	..¹	..
3 Oct	Newcastle U	A L	0-7	..	..	..	..	..	..	..	..	..	..	..
5 Oct	West Ham U	A W	4-0	..	..	..	..	..	..	opponents	..²	..¹	..	..
10 Oct	Bolton W	H L	2-3	..	..	..	..	..¹	..	..¹	..	..¹	..	..
17 Oct	Cardiff C	H W	5-0	..	..	..	..	..	..	..	..	..³	..	..
24 Oct	Sheffield U	A L	0-4	..	..	..	Blyth	..	John	..	..	..	..	..
31 Oct	Everton	H W	4-1	Robson	..	John	Baker	..	Blyth	..¹	..¹	..³	..	..¹
7 Nov	Manchester C	A W	5-2	..	..	..	..	..¹	..	..¹	..²	..³	..	..
14 Nov	Bury	H W	6-1	Harper	..	..	..¹	..	..	Rutherford JJ	..²	..³	..	..
21 Nov	Blackburn Rov	A W	3-2	..	..	..	..	..	opponents	Woods	..¹	..¹	..	..
28 Nov	Sunderland	H W	2-0	..	..	..	..	..	..	Hoar	..¹	..¹	..	..
5 Dec	Huddersfield T	A D	2-2	..	..	..	..	..	..	..	..	..	..¹	..
12 Dec	W B A	H W	1-0	..	..	..	..	..	..	..	..¹	..	..	..
19 Dec	Birmingham	A L	0-1	..	..	..	..	..	..	..	..	..	..	..
25 Dec	Notts Co	H W	3-0	..	..	..	..	..	..	..¹	..¹	..	..¹	..
26 Dec	Notts Co	A L	1-4	..	Kennedy	..	..¹	..	..	Woods	Young	..	..	..
1 Jan	Tottenham H	A D	1-1	..	Mackie	..	..¹	..	..	Hoar	Buchan	..	..	..
16 Jan	Manchester U	H W	3-2	..	..	..	..	..	..	Rutherford J	..²	..	..	..
23 Jan	Liverpool	A L	0-3	..	..	..	..	..	..	..	..	..	..	..
3 Feb	Burnley	H L	1-2	..	..	..	..	..	..	Lawson	..¹	..	..	..
6 Feb	Leeds U	A L	2-4	..	Kennedy	..	..	..	opponents	Hulme	..¹	..¹	Ramsey	Voysey
13 Feb	Newcastle U	H W	3-0	..	Mackie	..	..	Young	..¹	..	..¹	..	..	Dr Paterson¹
23 Feb	Cardiff C	A D	0-0	Lewis	..	..	..	Butler	..	Neil	..	..	..	Lawson
13 Mar	Everton	A W	3-2	Harper	..	..	..	..	..	Buchan	..³	..	..	..
17 Mar	Sheffield U	H W	4-0	..	..	..	..	..	..	..¹	..²	..	..	..
20 Mar	Manchester C	H W	1-0	..	..	..	..	..	..	..¹	..	..	..	Rutherford J
27 Mar	Bury	A D	2-2	..	..	..	..	..	..	..¹	..	..¹	..	Lawson
2 Apr	Aston Villa	A L	0-3	..	..	..	..	..	..	..	Young	..	..	..
3 Apr	Blackburn Rov	H W	4-2	Lewis	Parker	Mackie	..¹	..	..	Lawson¹	Buchan¹	..	..	Hulme
5 Apr	Aston Villa	H W	2-0	..	..	..	..	..	..	..	..	..²	..	..
10 Apr	Sunderland	A L	1-2	..	..	Kennedy	Seddon	..	..	..	..	..¹	..	..
17 Apr	Huddersfield T	H W	3-1	..¹	John	Young	..	..	..¹	..	..	..	..¹	..
24 Apr	W B A	A L	1-2	..	..	..	..	..	..¹	..	..	..	..	..
28 Apr	Bolton W	A D	1-1	..¹	..	..	..	..	..	..	..	..	..	..
1 May	Birmingham	H W	3-0	..	..¹	..	..	..	..	..	..	..²	..	..

FA Cup

Date	Opp		Res	1	2	3	4	5	6	7	8	9	10	11
9 Jan	Wolves (3)	A D	1-1	Harper	Mackie	John	Baker	Butler	Blyth	Hoar	Buchan	Brain¹	Neil	Haden
13 Jan	Wolves (3R)	H W	1-0	..	..	..	..	..	..	Woods	..¹	..	..	..
30 Jan	Blackburn R (4)	H W	3-1	..	..	..	..	..	..	Rutherford J	opponents	..¹	..	..¹
20 Feb	Aston Villa (5)	A D	1-1	..	..	..	..	..	..	Lawson	..¹	..	Ramsey	Dr Paterson
24 Feb	Aston Villa (5R)	H W	2-0	..	..	..	..	..	..	..	..	..¹	..	..¹
6 Mar	Swansea (6)	A L	1-2	..	..¹	..	..	..	..	..	..	..	..	..

Appearances (Goals)

Baker A 31 (6) · Blyth W 40 (7) · Brain J 41 (33) · Buchan C 39 (19) · Butler J 41 · Cock D 1 · Haden S 25 (2) · Harper W 19 · Hoar S 21 (3) · Hulme J 15 (2) · John R 29 · Kennedy A 16 · Lawson H 13 (2) · Lewis D 14 · Mackie J 35 · Milne W 5 · Neil A 27 (6) · Parker T 7 (3) · Paterson Dr J 1 (1) · Ramsey J 16 · Robson J 9 · Rutherford J 3 · Rutherford JJ 1 · Seddon W 1 · Toner J 2 · Voysey C 1 · Woods H 2 · Young A 7 · Own goals 3 · Total: 28 players (87)

Position in League Table

	P	W	L	D	F:A	Pts	
Huddersfield T	42	23	8	11	92:60	57	1st
Arsenal	42	22	12	8	87:63	52	2nd

SEASON 1926-1927 FOOTBALL LEAGUE (DIVISION 1)

Date	Opp		Res	1	2	3	4	5	6	7	8	9	10	11
28 Aug	Derby Co	H W	2-1	Harper	Parker¹	John	Baker	Butler	Blyth	Hulme	Buchan¹	Brain	Ramsey	Haden
1 Sep	Bolton W	H W	2-1	..	..	..	..	..	..	..²	..	..	..	..
4 Sep	Sheffield U	A L	0-4	..	..	..	..	..	..	..	..	..	..	..
6 Sep	Bolton W	A D	2-2	..	..	..	..	..	..	..¹	Lambert	..	..	Lee
11 Sep	Leicester C	H D	2-2	..	..	..	..	..	..	..¹	Buchan	..¹	Lambert	..
15 Sep	Manchester U	A D	2-2	..	..	Kennedy	..	..	John	..	Lambert	..²	Ramsey	..
18 Sep	Liverpool	H W	2-0	..	..	..	..	..	..	..	..	..	Buchan	Hoar¹
25 Sep	Leeds U	A L	1-4	..	..¹	..	..	..	..	..	..	..	..	Lee
2 Oct	Newcastle U	H D	2-2	..	..	John	..	..	Blyth	..	Buchan¹	..	Lambert	..
9 Oct	Burnley	A L	0-2	..	..	..	Young	..	..	..	..	..	..	..
16 Oct	West Ham U	H D	2-2	..	..	..	..	..	..	..	..	..¹	..	Haden
23 Oct	Sheffield Wed	H W	6-2	..	..	..	..	..	..	..	..	..⁴	..	..²
30 Oct	Everton	A L	1-3	..	..	..	..	..	..	..	Lambert	..¹	Ramsey	..
6 Nov	Blackburn Rov	H D	2-2	..	..	..	Seddon	..	..	..	Buchan¹	..¹	..	..
13 Nov	Huddersfield T	A D	3-3	..	..	..	..	..	..	..¹	Brain	Buchan	..¹	..¹
20 Nov	Sunderland	H L	2-3	..	..	..	..	..	..	..	..¹	..	..	..¹
27 Nov	W B A	A W	3-1	..	..	..	..	..	..	..¹	..¹	..	Lambert	..¹
4 Dec	Bury	H W	1-0	..	..	..	Young	..	..	..	..	..	..	..
11 Dec	Birmingham	A D	0-0	..	..	..	Butler	..	..	..	Lambert	Brain¹	Ramsey	..
18 Dec	Tottenham H	H L	2-4	..	..	..	..	..	..	..¹	Brain¹	..	..	Peel
27 Dec	Cardiff C	A L	0-2	Lewis	..	Cope	..	..	John	..	Buchan	..	..	..
28 Dec	Manchester U	H W	1-0	..	..	..	Milne	Baker	..	..	Buchan	Brain	Blyth¹	Hoar
1 Jan	Cardiff C	H W	3-2	..	..	..¹	..	Butler	..	..	..	..³	..	..
15 Jan	Derby Co	A W	2-0	..	..¹	..	..	Butler	..	..	..	..¹	..	..
22 Jan	Sheffield U	H D	1-1	..	..	..	..	..	..	..	..	..¹	..	..
5 Feb	Liverpool	A L	0-3	..	..	..	Baker	..	..	..	Lambert	..	..	..
10 Feb	Leicester C	A L	1-2	..	..	..	..	..	..	..	Buchan	..¹	Peel	..
12 Feb	Leeds	H W	1-0	Harper	..	..	Milne	Baker	Barley	..	..¹	..	Blyth	..
26 Feb	Burnley	H W	6-2	Lewis	..	..	Baker	Seddon	John	..	..¹	..⁴	..	..¹
7 Mar	West Ham U	A L	0-7	..	..	John	Seddon	Butler	Barley	Hoar	Shaw	..¹	..	Haden
12 Mar	Sheffield Wed	A L	2-4	..	..	Kennedy	Baker	..	John	Hulme	Buchan¹	..¹	..	Hoar
19 Mar	Everton	H L	1-2	Harper	..	Cope	..	Seddon	..	..	Tricker	Buchan¹	..	..
2 Apr	Huddersfield T	H L	0-2	Lewis	..	..	Milne	Butler	..	Haden	Buchan	Brain	..	..
6 Apr	Newcastle U	A L	1-6	..	..	Baker	Young	Seddon	..	Hulme	Shaw	..¹	..	..
9 Apr	Sunderland	A L	1-5	..	..	..	Butler	..	..	..	..	..¹	Peel	..
15 Apr	Aston Villa	H W	2-1	..	..	Kennedy	Baker	..	..	Hoar	..	Brain²	Blyth	Peel
16 Apr	W B A	H W	4-1	..	..¹	..	Blyth	..	..	Haden	..²	..¹	Shaw	..
18 Apr	Aston Villa	A W	3-2	..	..	..	Roberts	Butler	Barley¹	Shaw	Lambert	Tricker	Peel	John²
28 Apr	Blackburn Rov	A W	2-1	..	..	..	Baker	Seddon	John	Hulme¹	..	Brain¹	Blyth	Lee
30 Apr	Birmingham	H W	3-0	Harper	..	..	..	Butler	..	..¹	Tricker¹	Peel	..	Haden
4 May	Bury	A L	2-3	Moody	..	..	..	Seddon	..	..²	Buchan	Bowen	Brain	Peel
7 May	Tottenham H	A W	4-0	..	..	..	Roberts	Butler	..	..	Blyth	Tricker²	..²	Peel

FA Cup

Date	Opp		Res	1	2	3	4	5	6	7	8	9	10	11
8 Jan	Sheffield U (3)	A W	3-2	Lewis	Parker	Cope	Milne	Butler	John	Hulme¹	Buchan¹	Brain¹	Blyth	Hoar
29 Jan	Port Vale (4)	A D	2-2	..	..	..	Baker	..	..	..	..¹	..¹	..	..
2 Feb	Port Vale (4R)	H W	1-0	..	..	..	..	..	..	..	..¹	..	..	..
19 Feb	Liverpool (5)	H W	2-0	..	..	..	..	..	..	..	..¹	..¹	..	..
5 Mar	Wolves (6)	H W	2-1	Lewis	..	John	..	..¹	Barley	..	..	..¹	..	..
26 Mar	Southampton (SF) (at Chelsea)	W	2-1	..	..	Cope	..	..	John	..¹	..¹	..	..	
23 Apr	Cardiff (F) (at Wembley)	L	0-1	..	..	Kennedy	..	..	..	..	..	..	..	

Appearances (Goals)

Baker A 23 · Barley J 3 (1) · Blyth W 33 (3) · Bowen E 1 · Brain J 37 (31) · Buchan C 33 (14) · Butler J 31 · Cope H 11 · Haden S 17 (4) · Harper W 23 · Hoar S 16 (2) · Hulme J 37 (8) · John R 41 (3) · Kennedy A 11 · Lambert J 16 (1) · Lee J 7 · Lewis D 17 · Milne W 6 · Moody J 2 · Parker T 42 (4) · Peel H 9 · Ramsey J 12 (2) · Roberts H 2 · Seddon C 17 · Shaw J 5 (1) · Tricker R 4 (3) · Young A 6 · Total: 27 players (77)

Position in League Table

	P	W	L	D	F:A	Pts	
Newcastle U	42	25	11	6	96:58	56	1st
Arsenal	42	17	16	9	77:86	43	11th

SEASON 1927-1928 FOOTBALL LEAGUE (DIVISION 1)

27 Aug	Bury	A	L 1-5	Lewis	Parker	Kennedy	Baker	Butler	John	Hulme	Buchan	Brain[1]	Blyth	Peel
31 Aug	Burnley	H	W 4-1	..	..	Cope	..	..	..	..	..[1]	..[2]	..[1]	Hoar
3 Sep	Sheffield U	H	W 6-1	..	..[1]	..	..	..	..	..	..	..	..	..
5 Sep	Burnley	A	W 2-1	..	..	..	..	..	..	..	Blyth[1]	..[1]	Lambert	..
10 Sep	Aston Villa	A	D 2-2	..	..	..	..[1]	..	..	..	Buchan	..	Blyth[2]	..
17 Sep	Sunderland	H	W 2-1	..	..	..	..	..	..	..	..	..[1]	..	..
24 Sep	Derby Co	A	L 0-4	Moody	..	Kennedy	..	..	..	..	..	..[2]	..	..
1 Oct	West Ham U	H	D 2-2	..	..	Cope	..	..	..	..[1]	..	..[1]	..[1]	..
8 Oct	Portsmouth	A	W 3-2	Lewis	..	..	..	..	..	..	..	..[1]	..[1]	..[1]
15 Oct	Leicester C	H	D 2-2	..	..	..	..	..	..	..	..	..[1]	..	..[1]
22 Oct	Sheffield Wed	A	D 1-1	..	..	..	Seddon	..	Blyth	Hoar	..[1]	..	Lambert	Peel
29 Oct	Bolton W	H	L 1-2	..	..[1]	..	..	..	John	Hulme	..[1]	..	Blyth	Hoar
5 Nov	Blackburn Rov	A	L 1-4	..	..[1]	..	Clark	Seddon	..	..	Blyth	Buchan	Tricker	..
12 Nov	Middlesbrough	H	W 3-1	..	..	..	Roberts	Butler	..	..[1]	Tricker	..[2]	Brain	..
19 Nov	Birmingham	H	D 1-1	..	..	Hapgood	Baker	..	..	..	Brain	Blyth	..[1]
3 Dec	Huddersfield	A	L 1-2	..	..	Cope	..	..	..	..	Buchan	Brain[1]	..
10 Dec	Newcastle U	H	W 4-1	..	..[1]	..	..	..	..	..[1]	Buchan	Brain[1]	Blyth	..[1]
17 Dec	Manchester U	A	L 1-4	..	..	..	..	..	..	..[1]	Tricker	..	..[1]	..
24 Dec	Everton	H	W 3-2	..	..	..	..	..	..	..	Buchan[1]	..	..	..
27 Dec	Liverpool	A	W 2-0	..	..[1]	..	..	..	..	Hoar[1]	Lambert	..[1]	..	Peel
31 Dec	Bury	H	W 3-1	..	..	..	..	..	..	Hulme	Buchan	..	..	Hoar[1]
2 Jan	Tottenham H	H	D 1-1	Moody	..	Hapgood	..	..	..	Hulme	Buchan	..	..	Hoar[1]
7 Jan	Sheffield U	A	L 4-6	..	..	..	..	Roberts	..	..	Lambert	..[2]	Barley	..[2]
21 Jan	Aston Villa	H	L 0-3	Lewis	..	Cope	..	Butler	..	..	Blyth	..	..	..
4 Feb	Derby Co	H	L 3-4	..	Paterson	..	..	..	Seddon	..	Buchan	..[3]	Blyth	..
11 Feb	West Ham U	A	D 2e2	Lewis	..	..	Blyth	..	John	..	..[1]	..[2]	Lambert	..[1]
25 Feb	Leicester C	A	L 2-3	..	..	..	..	..	..	..	..[1]	..	..	..[1]
7 Mar	Liverpool	H	W 6-3	..	..	John	Baker	..	Blyth	..[1]	..[1]	..[3]	..[1]	Peel
10 Mar	Bolton W	A	D 1-1	Paterson	..	..	..	..	..	Hoar	..[1]	..	..	..
14 Mar	Sunderland	A	L 1-5	..	..	..	..	..	..	Hulme	..	Hoar	..[1]	..
17 Mar	Blackburn Rov	H	W 3-2	Paterson	..	..	..	..	..	..	..[2]	Brain	..	Hoar[1]
28 Mar	Portsmouth	H	L 0-2	Lewis	..	Cope	..	..	..	Hoar	Lambert	Buchan	Thompson	Peel
31 Mar	Birmingham	H	D 2-2	..	..	..	..	..	..	..	Buchan[2]	Brain	Lambert	John
6 Apr	Cardiff C	H	W 3-0	..	..	John	..	..	..	Hulme[1]	..[1]	..[1]	..	Hoar
7 Apr	Tottenham H	A	L 0-2	..	..	..	..	Roberts	..	..	Shaw	..	..	..
9 Apr	Cardiff C	A	D 2-2	Paterson	..	..	..	Butler	..	..	Buchan	..	Tricker[2]	..
14 Apr	Huddersfield	H	D 0-0	Lewis	..	..	..	..	..	..	..	..	..	..
18 Apr	Middlesbrough	A	D 2-2	..	..	..	..	..[1]	..	..[1]	Shaw	..	Peel	..
21 Apr	Newcastle U	A	D 1-1	..	..	..	..	..	..	..	..[1]	..	..	..
28 Apr	Manchester U	H	L 0-1	..	..	..	..	..	..	..	..	..	..	..
2 May	Sheffield Wed	H	D 1-1	..	..	..	..	..	..	..	..[1]	..	Lambert	Peel
5 May	Everton	A	D 3-3	Paterson	..	..	..	..	opponents	..	Buchan	Shaw[2]	Brain	..

FA Cup

14 Jan	W B A (3)	H	W 2-0	Lewis	Parker	Cope	Baker	Butler	John	Hulme[1]	Buchan	Brain[1]	Blyth	Hoar
28 Jan	Everton (4)	H	W 4-3	..	..	..	..	..	..	..[1]	..	..[2]	..	..
18 Feb	Aston Villa (5)	H	W 4-1	..	..	..	Blyth	..	..	..[1]	..	..[2]	Lambert[1]	..
3 Mar	Stoke C (6)	H	W 4-1	..	..	..	Baker	..	..	..	..[1]	..	Blyth[2]	..[1]
24 Mar	Blackburn R (SF) (at Leicester)		L 0-1	..	..	..	..	..	..	..	..	..	..	..

Appearances (Goals)

Baker A 36 (3) · Barley J 2 · Blyth W 39 (7) · Brain J 39 (25) · Buchan C 30 (16) · Butler J · Clark A 1 · Cope H 24 · Hapgood E 3 · Hoar S 38 (9) · Hulme J 36 (8) · John R 39 (1) · Kennedy A 2 · Lambert J 16 (3) · Lewis D 33 · Moody J 4 · Parker T 42 (4) · Paterson W 5 · Peel H 13 · Roberts H 3 · Seddon C 4 · Shaw J 6 (3) · Thompson L 1 · Tricker R 7 (2) · Own goals 1 · Total: 24 players (82)

Position in League Table

	P	W	L	D	F:A	Pts	
Everton	42	20	9	13	102:66	53	1st
Arsenal	42	13	14	15	82:86	41	10th

SEASON 1928-1929 FOOTBALL LEAGUE (DIVISION 1)

25 Aug	Sheffield Wed	A	L 2-3	Lewis	Parker	Cope	Baker	Butler	John	Hulme	Blyth	Brain[1]	Thompson	Jones[1]
29 Aug	Derby Co	H	L 1-3	..	..	..	..	..	..	..	..[1]	..	..	..
1 Sep	Bolton W	H	W 2-0	Paterson	..	..	..	..	..	..	Peel[1]	..[1]	Jones	Hoar
8 Sep	Portsmouth	A	L 0-2	..	..	..	..	..	..	..	Blyth	..	..	..
15 Sep	Birmingham	H	D 0-0	..	..	John	..	..	Blyth	..	Jones	..	Lambert	Peel
22 Sep	Manchester C	A	L 1-4	..	..	..	..	..	..	..	Tricker	..[1]	Thompson	Jones
26 Sep	Derby Co	A	D 0-0	Lewis	..	Cope	..	Roberts	John	..	Brain	Lambert	..	..
29 Sep	Huddersfield	H	W 2-0	..	..	..	..	..	..[1]	..	..[1]	..	..	Hoar
6 Oct	Everton	A	L 2-4	..	..	..	..	..	..	..	..[1]	..	..	Jones[1] ..[2]
13 Oct	West Ham U	H	L 2-3	..	..	..	..	..	..	..	..	..	..	..
20 Oct	Newcastle U	A	W 3-0	..	..	..	..	..	Blyth	..	Jack	Brain[1]	..[2]	..
27 Oct	Liverpool	H	D 4-4	..	..	..	..	..	opponents	..	..[1]	..[2]	..	..[1]
3 Nov	Cardiff C	A	D 1-1	..	..	..	Blyth	Butler	John	..[1]	..[1]	..	..	..
10 Nov	Sheffield U	H	W 2-0	..	..	..	..	..	Barley	..[1]	..[1]	..	..	..
17 Nov	Bury	A	L 0-1	..	..	..	..	..	Hoar	..	..	..	..	..
24 Nov	Aston Villa	H	L 2-5	..	..	..	..	John	Hulme	..[2]	Lambert	..	..	..
1 Dec	Leicester C	A	D 1-1	..	..	..	..	..	..	..	Brain[1]	Peel	..	..
8 Dec	Manchester U	H	W 3-1	..	..	..	..	..	..	..	..[2]	..[1]	..	..
15 Dec	Leeds	A	D 1-1	..	..	..	..	..	..	..	..[1]	..	..	..
22 Dec	Burnley	H	W 3-1	..	..	..	..	..	..	..[1]	..[1]	..[1]	..	..
25 Dec	Blackburn Rov	A	L 2-5	..	..	..	Baker	Roberts	..	..	..[1]	..[1]	..	..
26 Dec	Sunderland	H	D 1-1	..	..	..	..	Butler	Blyth	..	..[1]	..	..[1]	..
29 Dec	Sheffield Wed	H	D 2-2	..	..	..	..	..	..	..[1]	..	..[1]	..	..
1 Jan	Sunderland	A	L 1-5	..	..	..	..	..	John	..	Parkin[1]	..	Thompson	..
5 Jan	Bolton W	H	W 2-1	..	..	..	..	Roberts	Barley	..	Jack[2]	..	Peel	Hoar
19 Jan	Portsmouth	H	W 4-0	..	..	Hapgood	..	Butler	John	..	Jack[2]	Brain[1]	..[1]	Jones
2 Feb	Manchester C	H	D 0-0	..	..	..	..	Roberts	..	..	..	..	..	..
9 Feb	Huddersfield	A	W 1-0	..	..	..	..	..	..	Parkin	Jack[1]	..	..	..
23 Feb	West Ham U	A	W 4-3	Paterson	..	..	Blyth	..	..	..[1]	Brain[1]	..[1]	..	Hoar[1]
9 Mar	Liverpool	A	W 4-2	Lewis	..	..	Baker	..	..	..[2]	..[1]	..	..	Jones[1]
13 Mar	Birmingham	A	D 1-1	..	..	..	..	..	..	..	..[1]	..	Thompson	..
16 Mar	Cardiff C	H	W 2-1	..	..	..	..	..	..	..	..[1]	..	Peel	..
23 Mar	Sheffield U	A	D 2-2	..	..	..[1]	..	..	..	..	..[1]	..[1]	..	..
29 Mar	Blackburn Rov	H	W 1-0	..	..	..	Blyth	..	..	..	..[1]	..	..	..
30 Mar	Bury	H	W 7-1	..	..	..	Baker	..	..	..	Parkin[2]	..[4]	Thompson[1]	..
2 Apr	Newcastle U	H	L 1-2	..	..	..	..	..	..	..	..[1]	..	..	..
6 Apr	Aston Villa	A	L 2-4	..	..	..	..	Blyth	..	..	Brain[1]	..[1]	Peel	..
13 Apr	Leicester C	H	D 1-1	Paterson	..	..[1]	..	..	John	..	..[1]	..	..	..
20 Apr	Manchester U	A	L 1-4	..	..	..	..	Butler	..	..	..[1]	..	..	..
22 Apr	Everton	H	W 2-0	..	..	..[1]	..	..	..	..	..[1]	..	..	..
27 Apr	Leeds U	H	W 1-0	..	..	..	..	..	..	..	..[1]	..	..	..
4 May	Burnley	A	D 3-3	..	..	..	..	..	..	..	..[2]	..[2]	..	..

FA Cup

12 Jan	Stoke (3)	H	W 2-1	Lewis	Parker	Cope	Baker	Roberts	Barley	Hulme[1]	Jack	Brain[1]	Peel	Jones
26 Jan	Mansfield T (4)	H	W 2-0	..	..	Hapgood	..	Butler	Blyth	..[1]	..[1]	..	..	..
16 Feb	Swindon T (5)	A	D 0-0	..	..	..	..	Roberts	John	..	..	..	..	..
20 Feb	Swindon T (5R)	H	W 1-0	..	..	..	..	..	..	..	..[1]	..	..	Maycock
2 Mar	Aston Villa (6)	A	L 0-1	..	..	..	..	..	..	..	Brain	Jack	Hoar	..

Appearances (Goals)

Baker A 32 · Barley J 3 · Blyth W 20 (1) · Brain J 37 (19) · Butler J 22 · Cope H 23 · Hapgood E 17 · Hoar S 6 (1) · Hulme J 41 (6) · Jack D 31 (25) · John R 34 (1) · Jones C 39 (6) · Lambert J 6 (1) · Lewis D 32 · Parker T 42 · Parkin R 5 (3) · Paterson W 10 · Peel H 24 (5) · Roberts H 20 · Thompson L 17 (5) · Tricker R 1 · Own goals 1 · Total: 21 players (77)

Position in League Table

	P	W	L	D	F:A	Pts	
Sheffield Wed	42	21	11	10	86:62	52	1st
Arsenal	42	16	13	13	77:72	45	9th

SEASON 1929-1930   FOOTBALL LEAGUE (DIVISION 1)

Date	Opponent		Result	1	2	3	4	5	6	7	8	9	10	11
31 Aug	Leeds U	H	W 4-0	Lewis	Parker[1]	Hapgood	Baker	Roberts	John	Hulme[1]	Brain	Jack[2]	James	Jones
4 Sep	Manchester C	A	L 1-3	..	..	..	Seddon	..	..	..[1]	Jack[1]	Johnstone	Thompson	..
7 Sep	Sheffield Wed	A	W 2-0	Preedy	..	..	Seddon	..	..	..[2]				
11 Sep	Manchester C	H	W 3-2	..	..	..	..	..	..	..[1]	..[1]			..[1]
14 Sep	Burnley	H	W 6-1	..	..	..	..	..	Thompson	..[1]	Lambert[3]	James		
21 Sep	Sunderland	A	W 1-0	..	..	..	..	..	..	..		..[1]		
25 Sep	Aston Villa	A	L 2-5	..	..	..	..	..	..	..				Williams
28 Sep	Bolton W	H	L 1-2	Lewis	..	..	..	Baker	..	..	Brain			Jones[1]
5 Oct	Everton	A	D 1-1	..	..	..	..	John	..[1]	Bastin	Jack			
12 Oct	Derby Co	H	D 1-1	..	..[1]	..	..	..	..[1]	Jack	Lambert[3]			
19 Oct	Grimsby T	H	W 4-1	..	..	..	..	..	..	..				
26 Oct	Manchester U	A	L 0-1	..	..	..	..	Baker	..	..		Peel	Williams	
2 Nov	West Ham U	H	L 0-1	..	..	..	Baker	John	..[2]	Brain		James	Jones	
9 Nov	Birmingham	A	W 3-2	..	..	..	..	..	..	Jack[1]	Halliday			
23 Nov	Blackburn Rov	A	D 1-1	..	..	..	..	..	..	..[1]				
27 Nov	Middlesbrough	H	L 1-2	Preedy	..	..	..	..	..	..				
30 Nov	Newcastle U	H	L 0-1	Lewis	..	..	..	..	..[1]	..[1]				
14 Dec	Huddersfield T	H	W 2-0	..	..	..	Seddon	..	..	..[1]		Thompson		
16 Dec	Sheffield U	A	L 1-4	..	..	..	..	..	..	..		James		
21 Dec	Liverpool	A	L 0-1	..	..	..	Haynes	..	..	..		..[1]		
25 Dec	Portsmouth	A	W 1-0	..	..	..	..	Butler	..[1]	..				
26 Dec	Portsmouth	H	L 1-2	..	..	..	..	..	..	..			Bastin	
28 Dec	Leeds U	A	L 0-2	Baker	..	Jack	Haynes	..	..	Brain		Jones	..[1]	
4 Jan	Sheffield W	H	L 2-3	Parker[1]	..	Baker	Roberts	Haynes	..	James	Jack	..[1]		
18 Jan	Burnley	A	D 2-2	..	..	Haynes	..	John	..	Jack[1]	Lambert	Halliday	..[1]	
1 Feb	Bolton W	A	D 0-0	..	..	..	..	..	Williams	..		James		
8 Feb	Everton	H	W 4-0	..	..	Baker	..	..	..[1]	..[3]				
19 Feb	Derby Co	A	L 1-4	..	..	Humpish	..	..	..	Brain	Halliday[1]	Jones		
22 Feb	Grimsby T	A	D 1-1	..	..	Seddon	Jones	..	Jack	Lambert[1]	Johnstone			
8 Mar	West Ham U	A	L 2-3	..	..	Baker	Roberts	..	..[2]	..[1]	James			
12 Mar	Manchester U	H	W 4-2	..	John	..	Seddon	..	Hulme[1]	Bastin[1]	..[1]	..[1]	Williams[1]	
15 Mar	Birmingham	H	W 1-0	..	Hapgood	..	..	..	..	Jack				
29 Mar	Blackburn Rov	H	W 4-0	..	..	Haynes	..	John	..[1]	Bastin	..[2]		..[1]	
2 Apr	Liverpool	H	L 0-1	..	..	..	..	..	..	..		Jones		
5 Apr	Newcastle U	A	D 1-1	..	John	Humpish	..	Jones	..	Halliday[1]	Johnstone			
9 Apr	Middlesbrough	A	D 1-1	Preedy	..	..	Haynes	..	..[1]	Johnstone[2]	James	..[1]	Bastin	
12 Apr	Sheffield U	H	W 8-1	..	..	Hapgood	..	John	..[1]	Lambert[3]	..[1]	..[1]		
18 Apr	Leicester	H	D 1-1	..	..	..	Baker	..	..	Jack		..[1]	Jones	
19 Apr	Huddersfield	A	D 2-2	..	..	..	..	..	..[1]	Bastin[1]	Johnstone			
21 Apr	Leicester C	A	D 6-6	Lewis	..	Cope	..	Haynes	..	Jack	Halliday[4]	James	Bastin[2]	
28 Apr	Sunderland	H	L 0-1	Preedy	..	Hapgood	..	Seddon	..	..	Lambert			
3 May	Aston Villa	H	L 2-4	..	..	..	Haynes	..	..	..	..[2]			

FA Cup

11 Jan	Chelsea (3)	H	W 2-0	Lewis	Parker	Hapgood	Haynes	Roberts	John	Hulme	Jack	Lambert[1]	Thompson	Bastin[1]
25 Jan	Birmingham (4)	H	L 2-2	Preedy	..	..	Baker	..	..	..	..[1]	..	Jones	..[1]
29 Jan	Birmingham (4R)	A	W 1-0	Lewis	..	..	..[1]	..	..	Williams	..	..[1]	James	
15 Feb	Middlesbrough (5)	A	W 2-0	..	..	..	..[1]	..	..	..	..[2]	..	..	
1 Mar	West Ham U (6)	A	W 3-0	..	..	..	..	..	Jones	..	..	..	..[1]	
22 Mar	Hull C (SF) (at Leeds)		2-2	..	..	..	..	Seddon	..	Hulme	..[1]	..	..	
26 Mar	Hull C (SFR) (at Aston Villa)		1-0	..	..	..	..	..	..	Williams	..[1]	..	..	
26 Apr	Huddersfield T (F) (at Wembley)		2-0	Preedy	..	..	..	..	John	Hulme	..[1]	..[1]		

Appearances (Goals)

Baker A 19 · Bastin C 21 (7) · Brain J 6 · Butler J 2 · Cope H 1 · Halliday D 15 (9) · Hapgood E 38 · Haynes A 13 · Hulme J 37 (14) · Humpish E 3 · Jack D 33 (12) · James A 31 (5) · John R 34 · Johnstone W 7 (3) · Jones C 31 (2) · Lambert J 20 (19) · Lewis D 30 · Parker T 41 (3) · Peel H 1 · Preedy C 12 · Roberts H 26 · Seddon C 24 · Thompson L 5 (1) · Williams J 12 (3) Total: 24 Players (78)

Position in League Table

	P	W	L	D	F:A	Pts	
Sheffield Wed	42	26	8	8	105:57	60	1st
Arsenal	42	14	17	11	78:66	39	14th

SEASON 1930-1931   FOOTBALL LEAGUE (DIVISION 1)

Date	Opponent		Result	1	2	3	4	5	6	7	8	9	10	11
30 Aug	Blackpool	A	W 4-1	Keyser	Parker	Hapgood	Jones	Roberts	John	Hulme	Jack[2]	Lambert	James	Bastin[2]
1 Sep	Bolton W	A	W 4-1	..	..	..	..	..	..	..[1]	..	..[3]	..	
6 Sep	Leeds U	H	W 3-1	..	..	..	..	..	..	..	..[1]	..[2]		
10 Sep	Blackburn Rov	H	W 3-2	..	..	..	..	..	..	..	..	..[3]	Johnstone[1]	..[2]
13 Sep	Sunderland	A	W 4-1	..	..	..	Seddon	..	..	..[1]	..			
15 Sep	Blackburn Rov	A	D 2-2	..	..	..	..	..	..	..[1]	Brain	..[2]	James	
20 Sep	Leicester C	H	W 4-1	..	..	..	..	..	..	..	..	..[3]		..[1]
27 Sep	Birmingham	A	W 4-2	..	..	..	..	..	..	..	..	..[3]		..[1]
4 Oct	Sheffield U	H	D 1-1	..	..	..	..	..	..[1]	..	..			..[1]
11 Oct	Derby Co	A	L 2-4	..	..	..	..	..	..	Jack	..			..[1]
18 Oct	Manchester U	A	W 2-1	..	..	..	..	..	Williams[1]	Brain	..[1]			..[1]
25 Oct	West Ham U	H	D 1-1	..	..	..	..	..	..	..				..[1]
1 Nov	Huddersfield T	A	D 1-1	Harper	..	..	..	..	..	Jack[1]	..			
8 Nov	Aston Villa	H	W 5-2	Preedy	..	..	..	..	..	..[2]	..[1]			..[2]
15 Nov	Sheffield Wed	A	W 2-1	Harper	..	..	..	..	..	..	..[2]			
22 Nov	Middlesbrough	H	W 5-3	..	..	..	..	..	..	..[1]	..[3]	..[1]		..[2]
29 Nov	Chelsea	A	W 5-1	..	..	..	..	..	..	..	..[1]			
13 Dec	Liverpool	A	D 1-1	..	..	..	..	..	..	..[1]				
20 Dec	Newcastle U	H	L 1-2	..	..	..	..	..	..	..[1]				..[1]
25 Dec	Manchester C	A	W 4-1	..	..	..	..	..	Hulme[1]	..[1]	..[1]			..[1]
26 Dec	Manchester C	H	W 3-1	..	..	..	Jones	..	..[1]	..				..[1]
27 Dec	Blackpool	H	W 7-1	..	..	John	..	Male	Brain[3]	Jack[3]			..[1]	
17 Jan	Sunderland	H	L 1-3	..	..	Hapgood	Seddon	John	..	Jack[4]	Lambert[3]			
28 Jan	Grimsby T	H	W 9-1	Preedy	..	..	Jones	..	..[1]	Jack[4]	Lambert[3]			..[2]
31 Jan	Birmingham	H	D 1-1	..	..	..	..	..	..[1]	..[1]	..[3]			
5 Feb	Leicester	A	W 7-2	..	..	..	Seddon	..	..[1]	Brain	Jack			
7 Feb	Sheffield U	A	D 1-1	..	..	..	Jones	..	..[1]	..[1]			..[3]	
14 Feb	Derby Co	H	W 6-3	Cope	..	..	..	..	..[1]	..[1]	..[1]			..[1]
21 Feb	Manchester U	H	W 4-1	Parker	..	..	..	..	..[1]	..[1]				
28 Feb	West Ham U	A	W 4-2	..	..	..	..	..[1]	..	..[2]				
7 Mar	Huddersfield T	H	D 0-0	..	..	Baker	..	Male	..					
11 Mar	Leeds U	A	W 2-1	..	..	Male	..	Thompson	..	Lambert	..[1]			
14 Mar	Aston Villa	A	L 1-5	..	..	John	..	..	..	Jack[1]				
21 Mar	Sheffield W	H	W 2-0	Harper	..	Hapgood	..	John	Jack[1]	Lambert	..[1]			
28 Mar	Middlesbrough	A	W 5-2	..	..	..	Haynes	..	Hulme	Jack[2]	..[3]			..[1]
3 Apr	Portsmouth	A	D 1-1	..	..	..	Roberts	..	..[1]					
4 Apr	Chelsea	H	W 2-1	..	..	..	..	..	..				..[1]	
6 Apr	Portsmouth	H	D 1-1	..	..	..	..	..	..			..[1]		
11 Apr	Grimsby T	A	W 1-0	..	..	..	Haynes	..	..			..[1]		
18 Apr	Liverpool	H	W 3-1	..	..	..	Roberts	..	..			..[1]		
25 Apr	Newcastle U	A	W 3-1	..	..	..	..[1]	..	..[2]					
2 May	Bolton W	H	W 5-0	..	..	..	..	..	..[2]		..[2]			

FA Cup

10 Jan	Aston Villa (3)	H	D 2-2	Harper	Parker	Hapgood	Seddon	Roberts	John	Hulme	Jack[1]	Lambert[1]	James	Bastin
14 Jan	Aston Villa (3R)	A	W 3-1	..	..	..	..	..	..	..[2]	Brain	Jack[1]		
24 Jan	Chelsea (4)	A	L 1-2	..	..	..	..	..	..	..	Jack	Lambert		

FA Charity Shield

8 Oct	Sheffield Wed (at Chelsea)		W 2-1	Keyser	Parker	Hapgood	Seddon	Roberts	John	Hulme[1]	Brain	Lambert	Jack[1]	Bastin

Appearances (Goals)

Baker A 1 · Bastin C 42 (28) · Brain J 16 (4) · Cope H 1 · Hapgood E 38 · Harper W 19 · Haynes ? · Jack ? 35 (31) · James A 40 (5) · John R 40 (2) · Johnstone W 2 (1) · Jones C 24 (1) · Keyser G 12 · Lambert J 34 ? 41 · Preedy C 11 · Roberts H 40 (1) · Seddon C 18 · Thompson L 2 · Williams J 9 (2) Total: 22 players (127)

Position in League Table

	P	W	L	D	F:A	Pts	
Arsenal	42	28	4	10	127:59	66	1st

SEASON 1931-1932 FOOTBALL LEAGUE (DIVISION 1)

29 Aug	W B A	H L 0-1	Harper	Parker	Hapgood	Jones	Roberts	John	Hulme	Jack	Lambert	James	Bastin
31 Aug	Blackburn Rov	A D 1-1	..	..	..	..	..	..	..[1]	..	..	..	..
5 Sep	Birmingham	A D 2-2	Preedy	..	..	..	..	..	..	..[1]	..[1]	..	..
9 Sep	Portsmouth	H D 3-3	..	..	..	..	..	..	..	..	..[2]	..	..[1]
12 Sep	Sunderland	H W 2-0	..	..	..	..	..	..	..[2]	Parkin	..	..	..
16 Sep	Portsmouth	A W 3-0	..	..	..	..	..	..	..	[1]	..	..	..[2]
19 Sep	Manchester C	A W 3-1	..	..	..	..	..	..	..[1]	Jack[1]	..[1]	..	Jack[2]
26 Sep	Everton	H W 3-2	..	..	..	..	..	..	..	..	..[1]	..	Bastin
3 Oct	Grimsby T	A L 1-3	..	..	..	..	..	..	..[1]	..	..[1]	..	..
10 Oct	Blackpool	A W 5-1	..	..	..	..	..	..	..[1]	..	..	..	..[3]
17 Oct	Bolton W	H D 1-1	..	..	..	..	..	..	..	..	..	..	..
24 Oct	Leicester C	A W 2-1	..	..	..	..	..	..	opponents[2]	..	..	..	..
31 Oct	Aston Villa	H D 1-1	..	..	..	Seddon	..	..	..	..[1]	..	..	..
7 Nov	Newcastle U	A L 2-3	..	..	..	Jones	..	..	..	Parkin	..	..[1]	Jack[1]
14 Nov	West Ham W	H W 4-1	..	..	..	..	Haynes	Male	..[1]	Jack[3]	..	..	Bastin
21 Nov	Chelsea	A L 1-2	Moss	..	..	..	Seddon	John	..	..[1]	..	..	..
28 Nov	Liverpool	H W 6-0	..	..	..	..	Roberts	..	..[1]	..[2]	..[3]	..	..
5 Dec	Sheffield Wed	A W 3-1	..	..	..	..	..	..	..	..[2]	..	..	..[1]
12 Dec	Huddersfield	H D 1-1	..	..	..	..	..	..	..	..[1]	..	..	..
19 Dec	Middlesbrough	A W 5-2	..	..	..	Seddon	..	..	..	..[2]	..[1]	..	..[2]
25 Dec	Sheffield U	A L 1-4	..	..	..	..	..	..	..[1]	..	..	..	..
26 Dec	Sheffield U	H L 0-2	..	Cope	..	..	..	..	..	..	Bastin	..	Williams
2 Jan	W B A	A L 0-1	..	Hapgood	Jones	..	..	..	..	..	Lambert	..	Bastin
16 Jan	Birmingham	H W 3-0	..	..	Haynes	..	opponents	..[1]	..	..	..	..[1]	..
30 Jan	Manchester C	H W 4-0	..	..	Jones	..	..	..	..	Parkin[3]	..[1]	..	..
6 Feb	Everton	A W 3-1	..	..	..	..	..	..[1]	..[1]	..[1]	..	..	..[1]
17 Feb	Grimsby T	H W 4-0	..	..	..	..	..	..	..[1]	..[1]	..[1]	..[1]	..
20 Feb	Blackpool	H W 2-0	..	..	..	..	..	..	..[1]	..[1]	..	..	..
2 Mar	Bolton W	A L 0-1	..	..	..	..	Haynes	Male	..	..	Lambert	Thompson	..
5 Mar	Leicester C	H W 2-1	..	..	..	..	Roberts	John	..[1]	..	Coleman	James	..[1]
19 Mar	Newcastle U	H W 1-0	..	..	..	..	..	..	..[1]	Coleman	Lambert	..	..
25 Mar	Derby Co	H W 2-1	..	..	..	..	..	..	..	Jack	..[2]	..	..
26 Mar	West Ham U	A D 1-1	..	..	..	..	..	..	..	Coleman	..[1]	..	..
28 Mar	Derby C	A D 1-1	..	..	..	..	..	..	..	Lambert	Coleman	Jack[1]	..
3 Apr	Chelsea	H D 1-1	..	..	..	..	Male	..	..	Jack	Lambert[1]	John	..
6 Apr	Sunderland	A L 0-2	..	..	..	..	John	..	..	..	..	Bastin	Beasley
9 Apr	Liverpool	A L 1-2	..	..	..	..	Male	Coleman	..	..	..[1]	..	John[2]
16 Apr	Sheffield Wed	H W 3-1	..	..	..	..	..	Hulme	..	..	..	..	John[2]
25 Apr	Aston Villa	A D 1-1	Compton	..	..	Haynes	..	..	Parkin[1]	..	..	Beasley
27 Apr	Huddersfield	A W 2-1	..	..	Male	..	John	Coleman[1]	Stockill	..[1]	Jones	Bastin
30 Apr	Middlesbrough	H W 5-0	..	..	..	opponents	..	Hulme	..	..[2]	..[2]	..[2]
7 May	Blackburn Rov	H W 4-0	..	..	..	opponents	..	..	..[1]	..[2]	..	..

FA Cup

9 Jan	Darwen (3)	H W 11-1	Moss	Parker	Hapgood	Jones	Roberts	John	Hulme[2]	Jack[3]	Lambert[2]	James	Bastin[4]
23 Jan	Plymouth (4)	H W 4-2	..	..	..	..	opponents	..	..[1]	..	..	..	..[1]
13 Feb	Portsmouth (5)	A W 2-0	..	..	..	..	..	..	..	..	Parkin	..	..
27 Feb	Huddersfield (6)	A W 1-0	..	..	..	..	..[1]	..	..	..	Lambert	..	..
12 Mar	Manchester C (SF) (at Aston Villa)	W 1-0	..	..	..	..	..	..	..	..	..	..	..[1]
23 Apr	Newcastle U (F) (at Wembley)	L 1-2	..	..	..	..	Male	..	..	..	Bastin	John[1]

FA Charity Shield

7 Oct	W B A (at Aston Villa)	W 1-0	Preedy	Parker	Hapgood	Jones	Roberts	Haynes	Hulme	Jack	Lambert	James	Bastin[1]

Appearances (Goals)

Bastin C 40 (15) · Beasley A 3 · Coleman E 6 (1) · Compton L 4 · Cope H 1 · Hapgood E 41 · Harper W 2 · Haynes A 7 · Hulme J 40 (14) · Jack D 34 (20) · James J 32 (2) · John H 38 (3) · Jones C 37 · Lambert J 36 (22) · Male G 9 · Moss F 27 · Parker T 38 · Parkin R 9 (7) · Preedy C 13 · Roberts H 35 · Seddon C 5 · Stockill R 3 (1) · Thompson L 1 · Williams J 1 · Own goals 5 · Total: 24 players (90)

Position in League Table

	P	W	L	D	F:A	Pts	
Everton	42	26	12	4	116:64	56	1st
Arsenal	42	22	10	10	90:48	54	2nd

SEASON 1932-1933 FOOTBALL LEAGUE (DIVISION 1)

27 Aug	Birmingham	A W 1-0	Moss	Compton	Hapgood	Male	Roberts	John	Hulme	Jack	Stockill[1]	James	Bastin
31 Aug	W B A	H L 1-2	..	..	..	..	..	..	..	..[1]	..	..
3 Sep	Sunderland	H W 6-1	..	..	..	Jones	Haynes	..	..[3]	..[1]	Coleman[1]	..	..[1]
10 Sep	Manchester C	A W 3-2	..	..	..	..	..	..	..	..[1]	..[2]	..	..
14 Sep	W B A	A D 1-1	..	Parker	..	..	..	..	..	..[1]	..	..	..
17 Sep	Bolton W	H W 3-2	..	..	..	..	..	..	..[1]	..[1]	..	..	..[1]
24 Sep	Everton	H W 2-1	..	..	..	..	Roberts	..	..	..[1]	..[1]	..	..
1 Oct	Blackpool	A W 2-1	Preedy	..	..	..	..	..	..[1]	..	..[1]	..	..[1]
8 Oct	Derby Co	H D 3-3	Moss	..	..	..	..	..	..[1]	..	..[2]	..	..
15 Oct	Blackburn Rov	A W 3-2	..	Male	..	Hill	..	..	..	..[1]	..[1]	..	..[1]
22 Oct	Liverpool	A W 3-2	..	..	..	..	Haynes	..	..	..[1]	..[1]	..	..[2]
24 Oct	Leicester C	H W 8-2	..	..	..	..	Roberts	..	..[3]	..[1]	..[2]	..	..[2]
5 Nov	Wolverhampton W	W 7-1	..	..	..	..	..	..	..[1]	..[3]	Lambert[2]	..	..[1]
12 Nov	Newcastle U	H W 1-0	..	..	..	..	..	..	..[1]	..	Coleman	..	..
19 Nov	Aston Villa	A L 3-5	..	..	..	..	..	..	..	..[1]	Lambert[1]	..	..[1]
26 Nov	Middlesbrough	H W 4-2	..	..	..	..	..	..	..[1]	..[1]	Coleman[2]	Parkin	..[2]
3 Dec	Portsmouth	A W 3-1	..	..	..	..	..	..	..	..[1]	..	James	..[2]
10 Dec	Chelsea	H W 4-1	..	..	..	..	..	..	..	..[1]	..[1]	..	..
17 Dec	Huddersfield	A W 1-0	..	..	..	..	..	..	..	..	..	..	..[1]
24 Dec	Sheffield U	H W 9-2	..	..	..	..	..	..	..[1]	..[1]	Lambert[5]	..	..[3]
26 Dec	Leeds U	H L 1-2	..	..	..	..	..	..	..	..	..	..	..
27 Dec	Leeds U	A D 0-0	..	..	..	Sidey	Haynes	..	..	Stockill	Jack	..	..
31 Dec	Birmingham	H W 3-0	..	..	..	Hill	Roberts	..	..	Jack[1]	Coleman	..[1]	..
2 Jan	Sheffield W	A L 2-3	..	..	..	..	..	..	..	..[1]	..	..	..[1]
7 Jan	Sunderland	A L 2-3	..	..	..	..	..	..	..	..	Lambert[2]	..	..
21 Jan	Manchester C	H W 2-1	..	..	Cope	..	..	Sidey	..	..	Coleman	..	..[2]
1 Feb	Bolton W	A W 4-0	..	..	..	..	..	John	..	Parkin	..[3]	..	..[1]
4 Feb	Everton	A D 1-1	..	..	..	..	..	..	..	Jack	..[1]	..	..
11 Feb	Blackpool	H D 1-1	..	..	..	Parkin	..	..	..	..[1]	..	..	..
22 Feb	Derby Co	A D 2-2	..	..	Hapgood	..	..	..	..	..[1]	..	..	..[1]
25 Feb	Blackburn Rov	H W 8-0	..	..	..	Jones	..	..	..[2]	Stockill[1]	..[3]	..	..[2]
4 Mar	Liverpool	H L 0-1	..	..	..	..	..	..	..	Jack	..	..	..
11 Mar	Leicester C	A D 1-1	..	..	..	..	..	..	..	..	..	..[1]	..
18 Mar	Wolverhampton W	H L 1-2	..	..	..	..	..	..	..	Bowden[1]	..	..	..
25 Mar	Newcastle U	A L 1-2	..	..	..	..	..	Hill	..	Jack	..	..	..
1 Apr	Aston Villa	H W 5-0	..	..	..	Hill	..	John	Jack[1]	Bowden[1]	Lambert[2]	..[1]	..
8 Apr	Middlesbrough	A W 4-3	..	..	..	..	..	..	Hulme[3]	Parkin	..	..	..
14 Apr	Sheffield Wed	H W 4-2	..	..	..	..	..	..	..[2]	Bowden	..[1]	..	..[1]
15 Apr	Portsmouth	H W 2-0	..	..	..	..	Jones	..	..	..	..	..	..[1]
22 Apr	Chelsea	A W 3-1	..	..	..	..	..	..	Jack[1]	..	..	..	..[2]
29 Apr	Huddersfield	H D 2-2	..	..	..	..	..	..	Hulme	..	..	..	..[2]
6 May	Sheffield U	A L 1-3	..	..	..	..[1]	..	John	..	..	..	Jones	..

FA Cup

14 Jan	Walsall (3)	A L 0-2	Moss	Male	Black	Hill	Roberts	Sidey	Warnes	Jack	Walsh	James	Bastin

Appearances (Goals)

Bastin C 42 (33) · Bowden R 7 (2) · Coleman E 27 (24) · Compton L 4 · Cope H 4 · Hapgood E 38 · Haynes A 6 · Hill F 26 (1) · Hulme J 40 (20) · Jack D 34 (18) · James A 40 (3) · John H 37 · Jones C 16 · Lambert J 12 (14) · Male G 35 · Moss F 41 · Parker T 5 · Parkin R 5 · Preedy C 1 · Roberts H 36 · Sidey N 2 · Stockill R 4 (3) · Total: 22 players (118)

Position in League Table

	P	W	L	D	F:A	Pts	
Arsenal	42	25	9	8	118:61	58	1st

1933-1934

SEASON 1933-1934 FOOTBALL LEAGUE (DIVISION 1)

26 Aug	Birmingham	H	D 1-1	Moss	Male	Hapgood	Hill	Roberts	John	Hulme	Jack[1]	Coleman	James	Bastin
2 Sep	Sheffield W	A	W 2-1	..	..	..	..	..	..	Birkett	..[1]	..	Bowden	..[1]
6 Sep	W B A	H	W 3-1	..	..	..	..	..	..	Coleman	..	Lambert[1]	..	..[2]
9 Sep	Manchester C	H	D 1-1	..	..	..	..	..	..	..[1]	..	..	..	..
13 Sep	W B A	A	L 0-1	..	..	..	..	..	Jones	..	Bowden	..	James	..
16 Sep	Tottenham H	A	D 1-1	..	..	..	..	..	John	Parkin	Jack	Bowden[1]	..	..
23 Sep	Everton	A	L 1-3	..	..	..	..	..	..	..	..	..[1]	..	..
30 Sep	Middlesbrough	H	W 6-0	..	..	..	Jones	Sidey	..	Birkett[2]	Bowden[1]	Dunne	Jack[2]	..[1]
7 Oct	Blackbrn Rov	A	D 2-2	..	..	..	..	Haynes	..	..	..[1]	..	James	..[1]
14 Oct	Newcastle U	H	W 3-0	..	..	John	..	Sidey	Hill	..[1]	..[1]	*opponents*	..	Jack
21 Oct	Leicester C	H	W 2-0	..	..	Hapgood	..	..	John	..	..	..[2]	..	Bastin
28 Oct	Aston Villa	A	W 3-2	..	..	..	..	..	..	Hill	..	..[2]	..	..[1]
4 Nov	Portsmouth	H	D 1-1	..	..	..	..	..	..	..	..	..	..	..[1]
11 Nov	Wolverhampton W	A	W 1-0	..	..	..	..	..	..	..	Coleman	..	Bowden[1]	..
18 Nov	Stoke C	H	W 3-0	..	..	..	..	..	..[1]	Hulme[1]	..	..[1]	..	..
25 Nov	Huddersfield T	A	W 1-0	..	..	..	..	..	..	..	Bowden	..[1]	Coleman	..
2 Dec	Liverpool	H	W 2-1	..	..	..	..	..	..	..[1]	Coleman	..[1]	James	..
9 Dec	Sunderland	A	L 0-3	..	..	..	..	..	..	..	Bowden	Coleman	..	..
16 Dec	Chelsea	H	W 2-1	..	..	..	..	Roberts	..	Birkett	Bastin	Bowden	..	Beasley[2]
23 Dec	Sheffield U	A	W 3-1	..	..	..	..	..	..	..	Bowden[1]	Dunne	Bastin	..[2]
25 Dec	Leeds U	A	W 1-0	..	..	..	..	..	Hill	..	..	..	..[1]	..
26 Dec	Leeds U	H	W 2-0	..	..	..	..	..	John	..	..[1]	..[1]	..	..
30 Dec	Birmingham	A	D 0-0	..	..	..	..	..	Hill	..	..	..	..	..
6 Jan	Sheffield W	H	D 1-1	..	..	..	..	..	..	Coleman	..	..[1]	..	..
20 Jan	Manchester C	A	L 1-2	..	..	..	..	..	John	Birkett	..	..	..	..[1]
31 Jan	Tottenham H	H	L 1-3	..	..	..	..	..	..	..	..	..	..[1]	..
3 Feb	Everton	H	L 1-2	..	..	..	Hill	..	..	..[1]	Coleman	..	..	..
10 Feb	Middlesbrough	A	W 2-0	..	..	..	Jones	..	Sidey	..[1]	Bowden[1]	..	Dougall	..
21 Feb	Blackburn	H	W 2-1	..	..	..	Parkin	..	John	Beasley[1]	James	..	..	Bastin[1]
24 Feb	Newcastle U	A	W 1-0	..	..	..	Jones	Sidey	Hill	..[1]	Jack	..	..	..
8 Mar	Leicester C	A	L 1-4	..	..	..	..	Roberts	..	..	Bowden[1]	Cox	..	..
10 Mar	Aston Villa	H	W 3-2	Wilson	..	..	Parkin	..[1]	John	Hulme[1]	Jack[1]	..	James	Beasley
24 Mar	Wolverhampton W	H	W 3-2	Moss	..	..	Jones	..	..	..	..	Drake[1]	..[1]	Bastin[1]
30 Mar	Derby Co	H	W 1-0	Wilson	..	..	..	..	..	Beasley	Bowden	..	..[1]	..
31 Mar	Stoke C	A	D 1-1	..	..	..	..	..	Hill	..	Jack	..	Dougall	..[1]
2 Apr	Derby Co	A	W 4-2	..	..	..	Hill	..	John	..	Bowden[2]	..[2]	James	..
7 Apr	Huddersfield	H	W 3-1	Moss	..	..	..	..	..	..[1]	..[1]	..[1]	..	..
14 Apr	Liverpool	A	W 3-2	Wilson	..	John	Jones	..	Hill	Hulme[2]	..	..	..	Beasley[1]
18 Apr	Portsmouth	A	L 0-1	Moss	..	Hapgood	..	..	..	Beasley	..	..	..	Bastin
21 Apr	Sunderland	H	W 2-1	..	..	..	Parkin	..	..	Birkett	Jack	..[1]	Bastin	Beasley[1]
28 Apr	Chelsea	A	D 2-2	..	..	..	Jones	..	..	Beasley	Bowden	..	James[1]	Bastin[1]
5 May	Sheffield U	H	W 2-0	..	..	..	Hill	..	John	..	Jack	..[2]	..	..
	FA Cup													
13 Jan	Luton (3)	A	W 1-0	Moss	Male	Hapgood	Jones	Roberts	John	Coleman	Bowden	Dunne[1]	Bastin	Beasley
27 Jan	Crystal Palace (4)	H	W 7-0	Wilson	..	..	..	..	..	Birkett[1]	..	..[2]	..[2]	..[2]
17 Feb	Derby Co (5)	H	W 1-0	Moss	..	..	..	..	..	Beasley	Jack[1]	..	Dougall	Bastin
3 Mar	Aston Villa (6)	H	L 1-2	..	..	..	..	..	..	..	..	..	..[1]	..
	FA Charity Shield													
18 Oct	Everton	A	W 3-0	Moss	Male	Hapgood	Jones	Sidey	John	Birkett[2]	Colman	Bowden[1]	James	Hill

Appearances (Goals)

Bastin C 38 (13) · Beasley A 23 (10) · Birkett B 15 (5) · Bowden R 32 (13) · Coleman E 12 (1) · Cox G 2 · Dougall P 5 · Drake E 10 (7) · Dunne J 21 (9) · Hapgood E 40 · Haynes A 1 · Hill F 25 · Hulme J 8 (5) · Jack D 14 (5) · James A 22 (3) · John R 31 (1) · Jones C 29 · Lambert J 3 (1) · Male G 42 · Moss F 37 · Parkin R 5 · Roberts H 30 (1) · Sidey N 12 · Wilson A 5 · Own goals 1 · Total: 24 players (75)

Position in League Table

	P	W	L	D	F:A	Pts	
Arsenal	42	25	8	9	75:47	59	1st

1934-1935

SEASON 1934-1935 FOOTBALL LEAGUE (DIVISION 1)

25 Aug	Portsmouth	A	D 3-3	Moss	Male	John	Hill	Roberts	Copping	Hulme	Bowden[1]	Drake[1]	James	Bastin[1]
1 Sep	Liverpool	H	W 8-1	..	..	Hapgood	Crayston[1]	..	..	Beasley	..[3]	..[3]	..	..[1]
5 Sep	Blackburn Rov	H	W 4-0	..	..	..	..	..	..	..	..[1]	..[2]	..	..[1]
8 Sep	Leeds U	A	D 1-1	..	..	..	..	..	..	..	..	..[1]	..	..
15 Sep	W B A	H	W 4-3	..	..	..	..	..	..	..	..[1]	..[1]	..[1]	..[1]
17 Sep	Blackburn Rov	A	L 0-2	..	..	..	..	Sidey	John	..	..	..	Dr Marshall	..
22 Sep	Sheffield Wed	A	D 0-0	..	..	..	..	Roberts	Copping	Hulme	..	..	James	..
29 Sep	Birmingham	H	W 5-1	..	..	John	..	..	..	..	Dr Marshall	..[4]	..	..[1]
6 Oct	Stoke C	A	D 2-2	..	..	Hapgood	..	..	..	..	Bowden	..	..	..[2]
13 Oct	Manchester C	H	W 3-0	..	..	..	..	..	..	Beasley	..[2]	..	..	..[1]
20 Oct	Tottenham H	H	W 5-1	..	..	..	..	..	John	..[1]	*opponents*	..[3]	..	..
27 Oct	Sunderland	A	L 1-2	..	..	..	..	..	Copping	..	..	..[1]	..	..
3 Nov	Everton	H	W 2-0	..	..	..	..	..	..	..	..	Dunne	..	..[2]
10 Nov	Grimsby T	A	D 2-2	..	..	..	..	..	..	Hulme[1]	..	Drake[1]	..	..
17 Nov	Aston Villa	H	L 1-2	..	..	..	..	..	..	..	Dr Marshall	..	..	..[1]
24 Nov	Chelsea	A	W 5-2	..	..	..	Hill	..	..	..[1]	Bowden	..[4]	..	..
1 Dec	Wolverhampton W	H	W 7-0	..	..	..	Crayston	..	..	Birkett[2]	..[1]	..[4]	..	..
8 Dec	Huddersfield T	A	D 1-1	..	..	..	..	..	..	..	*opponents*	..	..	..
15 Dec	Leicester C	H	W 8-0	..	..	..	..	..	..	Hulme[3]	..	..[3]	..	..[2]
22 Dec	Derby Co	A	L 1-3	..	..	..	..	..	..	Birkett	..[1]	..	..	..
25 Dec	Preston NE	H	W 5-3	..	Compton	..	..	..	..	Hulme[2]	..[1]	*opponents*	..	..[1]
26 Dec	Preston NE	A	L 1-2	..	Male	..	..	Sidey	..	..	Dr Marshall	..	Bastin	Hill[1]
29 Dec	Portsmouth	H	D 1-1	..	..	..	Hill	Roberts	..	..	Bowden	..[1]	John	Bastin
5 Jan	Liverpool	A	W 2-0	..	..	..[1]	Crayston	..	..	..	..	..[1]	James	..
19 Jan	Leeds U	H	W 3-0	..	..	..	..	..	..	..	..[2]	..	Dougall	..[1]
30 Jan	W B A	A	W 3-0	..	Compton	..	Hill	Sidey	..	..[1]	Bastin[1]	..[1]	..	Beasley
2 Feb	Sheffield W	H	W 4-1	..	Male	..	Crayston	Roberts	..	..	..[1]	..	James[3]	..
9 Feb	Birmingham	A	L 0-3	..	..	..	..	..	..	..	..	..	..	..
20 Feb	Stoke C	H	W 2-0	..	..	..	..	Sidey	..	Birkett	Davidson[1]	..	Dougall	Hill[1]
23 Feb	Manchester C	A	D 1-1	..	..	John	..	Roberts	..	Bowden[1]	..	..	..	Bastin
6 Mar	Tottenham H	A	W 6-0	..	..	Compton	..	Sidey	..	Kirchen[2]	..	..[2]	..[1]	..[1]
9 Mar	Sunderland	H	D 0-0	..	..	Hapgood	..	Roberts	..	..	..	..	James	..
16 Mar	Everton	A	W 2-0	..[1]	..	..	..	..	..	..	..	..[1]	Dougall	..
23 Mar	Grimsby T	H	D 1-1	Wilson	..	..	..	..	Hill	..	..	..[1]	..	..
30 Mar	Aston Villa		W 3-1	..	..	..	..	..	..	..	..	..[1]	Bastin[1]	Beasley[1]
6 Apr	Chelsea	H	D 2-2	..	Compton[1]	John	..	..	..	..	..	..[1]	James	..
13 Apr	Wolverhampton W	A	D 1-1	..	Male	Compton	..	..	..[1]	..	Bastin	..	..	..
19 Apr	Middlesbrough	H	W 8-0	..	..	Hapgood	..	..	..	Rogers[2]	..[1]	..[4]	..	..[1]
20 Apr	Huddersfield T	H	W 1-0	..	..	..	..	..	..	..	Davidson	..	Dougall	..[1]
22 Apr	Middlesbrough	A	W 1-0	..	..	John	..	Sidey	..	..	Bowden	..[1]	James	..
27 Apr	Leicester C	A	W 5-3	..	..	Hapgood	..[2]	Roberts	..	..	Davidson[1]	..	..	..[2]
4 May	Derby Co	H	L 0-1	..	..	Trim	Hill	..	John	..	..	..	..	..
	FA Cup													
12 Jan	Brighton & HA (2)	A	W 2-0	Moss	Male	Hapgood	Crayston	Roberts	Copping	Hulme[1]	Bowden	Drake[1]	John	Bastin
26 Jan	Leicester C (3)	A	W 1-0	..	..	..	Hill	..	..	..[1]	..	..	James	..
16 Feb	Reading (4)	A	W 1-0	..	..	..	Crayston	..	..	Birkett	Bastin[1]	..	..	Beasley
2 Mar	Sheffield W (5)	A	L 1-2	..	..	John	..	..	*opponents*	Beasley	Davidson	..	..	Bastin
	FA Charity Shield													
28 Nov	Man City	H	W 4-0	Moss	Male	Hapgood	Hill	Sidey	Copping	Birkett[1]	Dr Marshall[1]	Drake[1]	John	Bastin[1]

Appearances (Goals)

Bastin C 36 (20) · Beasley A 20 (6) · Birkett R 4 (2) · Bowden E 24 (14) · Compton L 5 (1) · Copping W 31 · Crayston J 37 (3) · Davidson R 11 (2) · Dougall P 8 (1) · Drake E 41 (42) · Dunne J 1 · Hapgood E 34 (1) · Hill F 15 (3) · Hulme J 16 (8) · James A 30 (4) · John R 9 · Kirchen A 7 (2) · Male C 39 · Marshall Drj 4 · Moss F 33 (1) · Roberts L 36 · Rogers L 5 (2) · Sidey N 6 · Trim R 1 · Wilson A 9 · Own Goals 3 · Total: 25 players (115)

Position in League Table

	P	W	L	D	F:A	Pts	
Arsenal	42	23	7	12	115:46	58	1st

SEASON 1935-1936 FOOTBALL LEAGUE (DIVISION 1)

1935-1936

31 Aug	Sunderland	H	W	3-1	Wilson	Male	Hapgood	Crayston	Roberts	Copping	Milne	Davidson	Drake[2]	James	Bastin[1]
3 Sep	Grimsby T	A	L	0-1	..	..	Compton	..	..	..	..	..	..	..	..
7 Sep	Birmingham	A	D	1-1	..	..	..	..	..	..	..	..	.. [1]	Bastin	Beasley
11 Sep	Grimsby T	H	W	6-0	..	..	..	..	..	..	Beasley[1]	Bowden[1]	.. [1]	Davidson	Milne[3]
14 Sep	Sheffield Wed	H	D	2-2	..	..	Hapgood	..	..	..	..	..	.. [1]	..	.. [1]
18 Sep	Leeds U	A	D	1-1	..	..	..	..	..	..	..	Bastin	.. [1]	..	..
21 Sep	Manchester C	H	L	2-3	..	..	..	..	..	Hill	Milne	Davidson	..	James[1]	Bastin[1]
28 Sep	Stoke C	A	W	3-0	..	..	..	.. [1]	..	..	..	Bowden	Dunne	..	.. [2]
5 Oct	Blackburn Rov	H	W	5-1	..	..	..	..	..	..	.. [1]	.. [3]	Drake	..	.. [1]
12 Oct	Chelsea	A	D	1-1	..	..	..	.. [1]	..	..	..	..	..	..	..
19 Oct	Portsmouth	A	L	1-2	..	Compton	John	..	..	Copping	.. [1]	Davidson	..	..	..
26 Oct	Preston NE	H	W	2-1	..	Male	Hapgood	..	..	..	Hulme	Bowden	.. [1]	..	.. [1]
2 Nov	Brentford	A	L	1-2	..	..	..	..	..	..	..	Parkin[1]	..	..	..
9 Nov	Derby Co	H	D	1-1	..	..	..	..	..	..	..	Bowden	.. [1]	Bastin	Milne
16 Nov	Everton	A	W	2-0	..	..	..	..	..	..	..	..	.. [1]	.. [1]	Rogers
23 Nov	Wolverhampton W	H	W	4-0	..	..	..	..	..	..	.. [1]	..	.. [2]	..	.. [1]
30 Nov	Huddersfield T	A	D	0-0	..	..	..	..	..	..	Rogers	..	..	..	Beasley
9 Dec	Middlesbrough	H	W	2-0	..	..	..	..	..	..	.. [2]	..	..	..	..
14 Dec	Aston Villa	A	W	7-1	..	..	..	..	..	..	..	..	.. [7]	..	..
25 Dec	Liverpool	A	W	1-0	..	..	..	..	Sidey	..	Hulme[1]	..	..	..	..
26 Dec	Liverpool	H	L	1-2	..	..	..	..	..	..	.. [1]	Bastin	..	James	..
28 Dec	Sunderland	A	L	4-5	Moss	..	..	..	Roberts	*opponents*	Rogers	Bowden[1]	.. [1]	Bastin[1]	..
4 Jan	Birmingham	H	D	1-1	..	..	..	..	..	..	Hulme	..	.. [1]	..	..
18 Jan	Sheffield Wed	A	L	2-3	..	..	..	..	.. [1]	..	..	Bastin	.. [1]	James	..
1 Feb	Stoke C	H	W	1-0	..	..	..	..	Sidey	..	..	Bowden	.. [1]	..	Bastin
8 Feb	Blackburn Rov	A	W	1-0	..	..	Compton	.. [1]	..	..	..	Davidson	Hill	Dougall	Beasley
22 Feb	Portsmouth	H	L	2-3	Wilson	Compton[1]	Hapgood	Cartwright	..	..	..	..	Dunne	.. [1]	..
4 Mar	Derby Co	A	W	4-0	..	Male	..	Crayston[1]	..	Cartwright	Kirchen[1]	Bastin	Cox[1]	.. [1]	..
7 Mar	Huddersfield T	H	D	1-1	..	..	..	Cartwright	Roberts	Copping	Hulme	.. [1]	..	..	..
11 Mar	Manchester City	A	L	0-1	..	Compton	..	..	Sidey	..	Kirchen	Bowden	..	..	..
14 Mar	Preston NE	A	L	0-1	..	Male	..	..	Roberts	John	Hulme	Rogers	Dunne	Davidson	Milne
25 Mar	Everton	H	D	1-1	..	..	Compton	Hill	Crayston	Copping	.. [1]	Bastin	Cox	Dougall	Rogers
28 Mar	Wolverhampton W	A	D	2-2	..	Compton	Hapgood	Crayston	Tuckett	Hill	Kirchen[1]	Bowden	Westcott	..	Beasley[1]
1 Apr	Bolton W	H	D	1-1	..	..	John	Hill	Joy	Copping	Hulme	Rogers	.. [1]	James	..
4 Apr	Brentford	H	D	1-1	..	..	..	..	..	..	..	..	Dunne	Dougall[1]	..
10 Apr	W B A	H	W	4-0	..	Male	Hapgood	Crayston[1]	Roberts	..	.. [1]	Bastin	.. [1]	James[1]	..
11 Apr	Middlesbrough	A	D	2-2	..	..	..	..	Sidey	Hill	..	Bowden[1]	..	Bastin[1]	..
13 Apr	W B A	A	L	0-1	..	Compton	John	..	Roberts	Copping	Kirchen	Rogers	Bowden	Davidson	..
18 Apr	Aston Villa	H	W	1-0	..	Male	Hapgood	..	Sidey	..	..	Bastin	Drake[1]	James	..
27 Apr	Chelsea	H	D	1-1	..	..	..	..	..	..	Hulme	Bowden	.. [1]	Bastin	..
29 Apr	Bolton W	A	L	1-2	..	..	..	..	..	..	.. [1]	Davidson	Cox	James	Milne
2 May	Leeds U	H	D	2-2	..	..	..	..	Tuckett	John	Kirchen[1]	Bastin[1]	Bowden	..	Beasley

FA Cup

11 Jan	Bristol Rov (3)	A	W	5-1	Moss	Male	Hapgood	Crayston	Roberts	Copping	Hulme	Bowden[1]	Drake[2]	Davidson	Bastin[2]
25 Jan	Liverpool (4)	A	W	2-0	..	..	..	..	Sidey	..	.. [1]	.. [1]	..	James	..
15 Feb	Newcastle (5)	A	D	3-3	Wilson	..	..	..	..	..	.. [1]	Bastin	Bowden[2]	..	Beasley
19 Feb	Newcastle (5R)	H	W	3-0	..	..	..	..	Roberts	..	..	.. [2]	..	..	.. [1]
29 Feb	Barnsley (6)	H	W	4-1	..	..	..	..	..	..	..	.. [1]	.. [1]	..	.. [2]
21 Mar	Grimsby T (SF) (at Huddersfield)		W	1-0	..	..	..	..	..	..	..	.. [1]	..	..	..
25 Apr	Sheffield U (F) (at Wembley)		W	1-0	..	..	..	..	..	..	..	Bowden	Drake[1]	..	Bastin

FA Charity Shield

23 Oct	Sheffield Wed	H	L	0-1	Wilson	Male	Hapgood	Hill	Joy	Copping	Milne	Crayston	Dunne	Davidson	Bastin

Appearances (Goals)

Bastin C 31 (11) · Beasley A 26 (2) · Bowden R 22 (6) · Cartwright S 5 · Compton L 12 (1) · Copping W 33 · Cox G 5 (1) · Crayston J 36 (5) · Davidson R 13 · Dougall R 8 (3) · Drake E 26 (24) · Dunne J 6 (1) · Hapgood E 33 · Hill F 10 · Hulme J 21 (6) · James A 17 (2) · John R 6 · Joy B 2 · Kirchen A 6 (3) · Male G 35 · Milne J 14 (6) · Moss F 5 · Parkin R 1 (1) · Roberts H 26 (1) · Rogers E 11 (3) · Sidey N 11 · Tuckett E 2 · Westcott R 2 (1) · Wilson A 37 · Own goals 1 · Total: 29 players (78)

Position in League Table

	P	W	L	D	F:A	Pts	
Sunderland	42	25	11	6	109:74	56	1st
Arsenal	42	15	12	15	78:48	45	6th

SEASON 1936-1937 FOOTBALL LEAGUE (DIVISION 1)

1936-1937

29 Aug	Everton	H	W	3-2	Wilson	Male	Hapgood[1]	Crayston	Roberts	Copping	Hulme	Bowden[1]	Drake	James[1]	Bastin
3 Sep	Brentford	A	L	0-2	Swindin	..	..	..	..	..	..	Bastin	..	Davidson	Beasley
5 Sep	Huddersfield T	A	D	0-0	..	..	..	Cartwright	..	John	..	..	Kirchen	James	..
9 Sep	Brentford	H	D	1-1	..	..	..	Crayston	Sidey	Copping	Milne	..	Drake[1]	..	..
12 Sep	Sunderland	H	W	4-1	..	..	..	.. [1]	Roberts[1]	..	Beasley[1]	Bowden	..	..	Bastin[1]
19 Sep	Wolverhampton W	A	L	0-2	..	..	..	..	Sidey	..	..	..	..	..	..
26 Sep	Derby Co	H	D	2-2	..	..	..	..	Roberts	..	..	..	.. [1]	Bastin	Compton D[1]
3 Oct	Manchester U	A	L	0-2	..	..	..	..	..	..	..	..	..	..	..
10 Oct	Sheffield Wed	H	D	1-1	..	..	..	..	..	..	Kirchen	..	.. [1]	..	..
17 Oct	Charlton Ath	A	W	2-0	..	..	..	..	..	..	..	Davidson[1]	Bowden	James	.. [1]
24 Oct	Grimsby T	H	D	0-0	..	..	..	..	..	..	..	..	..	..	Bastin
31 Oct	Liverpool	A	L	1-2	..	..	..	Cartwright	..	..	.. [1]	Bastin	..	Davidson	Compton D
7 Nov	Leeds U	H	W	4-1	..	..	..	Bastin	..	..	.. [1]	Bowden	Drake[1]	.. [1]	Milne[1]
14 Nov	Birmingham	A	W	3-1	..	..	..	..	..	Crayston	.. [1]	..	.. [2]	..	..
21 Nov	Middlesbrough	H	W	5-3	..	..	..	.. [1]	..	Copping	..	.. [1]	.. [1]	..	.. [2]
28 Nov	W B A	A	W	4-2	..	..	..	Crayston	..	..	..	..	.. [2]	..	.. [2]
5 Dec	Manchester City	H	L	1-3	Wilson	Compton L	..	..	..	..	..	..	.. [1]	..	..
12 Dec	Portsmouth	A	W	5-1	Swindin	Male	Compton L	Bastin	..	..	..	James	.. [1]	.. [4]	..
19 Dec	Chelsea	H	W	4-1	..	..	..	Crayston	..	..	.. [2]	..	.. [1]	.. [1]	..
25 Dec	Preston NE	H	W	4-1	..	..	..	..	..	..	.. [1]	..	.. [2]	..	.. [1]
26 Dec	Everton	A	D	1-1	..	..	..	..	..	..	.. [1]	..	..	..	..
28 Dec	Preston NE	A	W	3-1	Boulton	Compton L	Hapgood	..	Joy	..	Nelson[1]	Bastin	Kirchen[1]	Bowden	.. [1]
1 Jan	Bolton W	A	W	5-0	..	Male	Compton L	..	Sidey	..	Kirchen	..	Drake[4]	James	.. [1]
2 Jan	Huddersfield T	H	D	1-1	..	..	..	..	..	..	.. [1]	..	..	..	..
9 Jan	Sunderland	A	D	1-1	..	..	..	Bastin	Roberts	..	..	James	..	Nelson	.. [1]
23 Jan	Wolverhampton W	H	W	3-0	..	..	..	.. [1]	..	..	..	Bowden[1]	.. [1]	Davidson	..
3 Feb	Derby Co	A	L	4-5	..	..	..	.. [1]	*opponents*	..	.. [1]	..	.. [1]	..	..
6 Feb	Manchester U	H	D	1-1	..	..	..	..	..	..	..	James	..	.. [1]	..
13 Feb	Sheffield Wed	A	D	0-0	..	Compton L	Hapgood	Crayston	Joy	..	..	Bastin	Bowden	..	..
24 Feb	Charlton Ath	H	D	1-1	..	Male	..	..	Roberts	..	.. [1]	Bowden	Drake	..	Bastin
27 Feb	Grimsby T	A	W	3-1	..	..	..	..	Joy	..	Milne	..	Kirchen[3]	John	Compton D
10 Mar	Liverpool	H	W	1-0	..	..	..	Copping	Roberts	John	Kirchen[1]	Davidson	Bowden	Bastin	..
13 Mar	Leeds U	A	W	4-3	..	..	..	Bastin[1]	..	..	.. [2]	Bowden[1]	Drake	Davidson	..
20 Mar	Birmingham	H	D	1-1	..	..	..	Crayston	..	..	..	Bastin	Bowden[1]	..	..
26 Mar	Stoke C	H	D	0-0	..	..	..	..	..	Copping	..	Bowden	Drake	James	..
27 Mar	Middlesbrough	A	D	1-1	..	..	..	..	Joy	..	..	Bastin	Bowden[1]	Davidson	..
29 Mar	Stoke C	A	D	0-0	..	Compton L	..	Bastin	Roberts	..	Nelson	James	Biggs	..	..
3 Apr	W B A	H	W	2-0	..	Male	..	Crayston	..	..	Kirchen	Bastin	Bowden	.. [1]	Nelson[1]
10 Apr	Manchester City	A	L	0-2	..	..	..	..	Joy	..	..	..	..	..	..
17 Apr	Portsmouth	H	W	4-0	..	Compton L	..	..	..	..	Nelson[1]	James	Kirchen[1]	..	Compton D[2]
24 Apr	Chelsea	A	L	0-2	..	Male	..	..	Sidey	..	..	Bastin	Bowden	..	..
1 May	Bolton W	H	D	0-0	..	..	..	..	..	..	..	James	Kirchen	..	Bastin

FA Cup

16 Jan	Chesterfield (3)	A	W	5-1	Boulton	Male	Compton L	Bastin	Roberts	Copping	Kirchen[2]	James	Drake[2]	Davidson[1]	Milne
30 Jan	Manchester U (4)	H	W	5-0	..	..	..	.. [1]	..	*opponents*	.. [1]	..	.. [1]	.. [1]	..
20 Feb	Burnley (5)	A	W	7-1	..	..	Hapgood	Crayston[1]	..	..	.. [1]	Bowden	.. [4]	James	Bastin[1]
6 Mar	W B A (6)	A	L	1-3	..	..	..	..	..	..	Milne	..	Kirchen	..	.. [1]

FA Charity Shield

28 Oct	Sunderland	A	L	1-2	Swindin	Compton L	Hapgood	Crayston	Joy	Copping	Milne	Bowden	Kirchen[1]	Davidson	Compton D

Appearances (Goals)

Bastin C 33 (5) · Beasley A 7 (1) · Biggs A 1 · Boulton F 21 · Bowden R 28 (6) · Cartwright S 2 · Compton D 14 (4) · Compton L 15 · Copping W 38 · Crayston J 30 (1) · Davidson R 28 (9) · Drake E 26 (20) · Hapgood E 32 (1) · Hulme J 3 · James A 19 (1) · John R 5 · Joy B 6 · Kirchen A 33 (18) · Male G 37 · Milne J 19 (9) · Nelson D 8 (3) · Roberts H 30 (1) · Sidey N 6 · Swindin G 19 · Wilson A 2 · Own goals 1 · Total 25 players (80)

Position in League Table

	P	W	L	D	F:A	Pts	
Manchester C	42	22	7	13	107:61	57	1st
Arsenal	42	18	8	16	80:49	52	3rd

SEASON 1937-1938 FOOTBALL LEAGUE (DIVISION 1)

28 Aug	Everton	A W 4-1	Wilson	Male	Hapgood	Crayston	Roberts	Copping	Kirchen	Bowden	Drake³	Bastin¹	Milne
1 Sep	Huddersfield T	H W 3-1	..	..	..	..¹	..	..	Hulme	..	..²	..¹	..
4 Sep	Wolverhampton W	H W 5-0	..	..	..	..¹	..	..	..¹	..¹		..¹	..
8 Sep	Huddersfield T	A L 1-2	..	..	..	..	..	..	Milne	..	..¹	..	Compton D
11 Sep	Leicester C	A D 1-1	Boulton	..	..	..	..	..	..	..			Biggs
15 Sep	Bolton W	A L 0-1	..	Compton L	..	..	..	..	Hulme¹	Bastin	..	Davidson¹	Milne¹
18 Sep	Sunderland	H W 4-1	..	Male	..	..	..	..			..		..¹
25 Sep	Derby Co	A L 0-2	Wilson	..	..	..	..	..	Kirchen¹	..	Hunt	..	..
2 Oct	Manchester C	H W 2-1	..	Compton L	..	..	..	..	..²	Bowden	..	Bastin	..
9 Oct	Chelsea	A D 2-2	Boulton	..	..	..	..	..	..	..	..¹	Davidson¹	..
16 Oct	Portsmouth	H D 1-1	..	..	..	Bastin	..	Collett	..	..			..¹
23 Oct	Stoke C	A D 1-1	Wilson	..	..	Crayston	..	Copping	Hulme	Bastin	Bowden		
30 Oct	Middlesbrough	H L 1-2	..	..	..		Joy	Copping	Milne	Jones L¹	Hunt	Bastin	Compton D
6 Nov	Grimsby T	A L 1-2	..	..	..¹	..			Biggs	Kirchen	Jones L		
13 Nov	W B A	H D 1-1	..	..		..	opponents	..	Kirchen	Hunt	Drake¹		Bastin¹
20 Nov	Charlton Ath	A W 3-0	Boulton	Male	..	..		..	..¹		..²		..¹
27 Nov	Leeds U	H W 4-1	..	..	..	Cartwright¹	..	Collett					..¹
4 Dec	Birmingham	A W 2-1	..	..	..	..	..	Copping	Milne¹	..	..		..¹
11 Dec	Preston NE	H W 2-0	..	..	..		..	..	Hulme	..	..		
18 Dec	Liverpool	A L 0-2	..	..	..	Crayston	..	..	Kirchen	..	..		..¹
25 Dec	Blackpool	A L 1-2	..	..	..	Cartwright¹	..	..		..	..		..¹
27 Dec	Blackpool	H W 2-1	..	..	..		Sidey	..	..	..¹	Lewis¹		
1 Jan	Everton	H W 2-1	..	..	..	Crayston	Joy	..	..	..¹	Drake¹		Compton D
15 Jan	Wolverhampton W	A L 1-3	..	..	..	..	..	..	..		Lewis		Bastin
29 Jan	Sunderland	A D 1-1	..	..	..	..²	..	..	Griffiths		Drake¹	..¹	..¹
2 Feb	Leicester C	H W 3-1	Swindin	..	..		..	..			Lewis¹		
5 Feb	Derby Co	H W 3-0	..	..	..	..	..	..	Kirchen	Jones L	Drake¹	Carr	Compton D¹
16 Feb	Manchester C	A W 2-1	..	..	..	..	..	..	Griffiths¹	..	..¹		Bastin
19 Feb	Chelsea	H W 2-0	..	..	..	..	..	..	..²	..		Hunt	
26 Feb	Portsmouth	A D 0-0	..	..	..	..	..	Collett		..	..¹	Carr¹	
5 Mar	Stoke C	H W 4-0	..	..	..	..	..		..²	..		Drury	..¹
12 Mar	Middlesbrough	A L 1-2	..	..	..	..	Sidey	Copping		..¹	Carr		..²
19 Mar	Grimsby	H W 5-1	..	..	..	..	Joy	..	..²	Carr	Drake		
26 Mar	W B A	A D 0-0	..	..	..	Collett		..	Drury	Jones L	..¹	Carr¹	
2 Apr	Charlton Ath	H D 2-2	..	..		Crayston	..	Collett	Bremner¹	..	Carr	Drury	Compton D
9 Apr	Leeds U	A W 1-0	..	..	Compton L	Cartwright	..	Copping	Griffiths	..	Drake		Bastin
15 Apr	Brentford	H L 0-2	..	..	Hapgood	Jones L	..		Kirchen	Carr	Lewis		
16 Apr	Birmingham	H D 0-0	..	..	..		..	..		Drury	Drake	Bastin	Compton D
18 Apr	Brentford	A L 0-3	..	..	..	Crayston	..	..		Jones L	Carr²	Drury	Bastin¹
23 Apr	Preston NE	A W 3-1	..	..	..		..	..	Drake	..	..¹		
30 Apr	Liverpool	H W 1-0	..	..	..	Jones L	..	..	Kirchen¹	Bremner	..²		..²
7 May	Bolton W	H W 5-0	..	..	..								

FA Cup

Date	Opponent												
8 Jan	Bolton W (3)	H W 3-1	Boulton	Male	Hapgood	Crayston	Joy	Copping	Kirchen¹	Hunt	Drake	Jones L	Bastin²
22 Jan	Wolves (4)	A W 2-1	..	..	..	..	..	..	..¹	..	..¹	..	..
12 Feb	Preston NE (5)	H L 0-1	Swindin	..	..	..	..	..	..	..	..	..	..

Appearances (Goals)

Bastin C 38 (15) · Biggs A 2 · Boulton F 15 · Bowden R 10 (1) · Bremner G 2 (1) · Carr E 11 (7) · Cartwright S 6 (2) · Collett E 5 · Compton D 7 (1) · Compton L 9 (1) · Copping W 38 · Crayston J 31 (4) · Davidson R 5 (2) · Drake E 27 (17) · Drury J 11 · Griffiths W 9 (5) · Hapgood E 41 · Hulme J 7 (2) · Hunt G 18 (3) · Jones L 28 (3) · Joy B 26 · Kirchen A 19 (6) · Lewis R 4 (2) · Male G 34 · Milne J 16 (4) · Roberts H 13 · Sidey N 3 · Swindin G 17 · Wilson A 10 · Own goals 1 · Total 29 players (77)

Position in League Table

	P	W	L	D	F:A	Pts	
Arsenal	42	21	11	10	77:44	52	1st

SEASON 1938-1939 FOOTBALL LEAGUE (DIVISION 1)

Date	Opponent												
27 Aug	Portsmouth	H W 2-0	Swindin	Male	Hapgood	Crayston	Joy	Copping	Kirchen	Jones L o.g.	Drake	Jones B¹	Bastin
3 Sep	Huddersfield T	A D 1-1	..	..	..	..	..	..	..	..	..¹	..	..
8 Sep	Brentford	A L 0-1	..	..	..	..	..	..	Nelson	..	Carr	..	..
10 Sep	Everton	H L 1-2	..	..	..	..	..	..	..	Bremner	Drake¹	..¹	Cumner¹
14 Sep	Derby Co	H L 1-2	..	..	..	Jones L	..	..	..	..	..	..	..
17 Sep	Wolverhampton W	A W 1-0	..	..	..	Crayston	..	..	Kirchen	..	..	..	..
24 Sep	Aston Villa	H D 0-0	..	..	..	..	..	..	Nelson	Jones L	..	..	..
1 Oct	Sunderland	A D 0-0	..	..	..	..	..	..	Kirchen¹	Bremner¹	..	..	..
8 Oct	Grimsby T	H W 2-0	..	..	..	Jones L	..	..	..¹	Bastin	..	..	..¹
15 Oct	Chelsea	A L 2-4	..	..	..	Crayston	..	..	..	Bremner	..	Drury	Bastin
22 Oct	Preston NE	H W 1-0	..	..	Compton L	opponents	..	Collett	Walsh	Jones B¹	..¹	..	..
29 Oct	Bolton W	A D 1-1	..	..	Hapgood	Jones L	..	Copping		Jones B¹	..	..	..¹
5 Nov	Leeds U	H L 2-3	..	..	Compton L	..	..	..	Kirchen¹	..¹	..	Bastin	Cumner
12 Nov	Liverpool	A D 2-2	..	..	Hapgood	Crayston	..	..			..¹	..	..
19 Nov	Leicester C	H D 0-0	..	..	..	..	..	..		Jones L		Drury¹	..
26 Nov	Middlesbrough	A D 1-1	..	Compton L	..	..	..¹	..	Nelson¹	..¹			Bastin
3 Dec	Birmingham	H W 3-1	..	..	..	..	..	..	..	Jones B	..¹	Cumner	
10 Dec	Manchester U	A L 0-1	..	..	..	..	..	..	..	Jones L	Lewis²	..¹	Bastin¹
17 Dec	Stoke C	H W 4-1	Wilson	..	..	..	..	..	Drake	..		Jones B	..
24 Dec	Portsmouth	A D 0-0	..	..	..	..	..	..	..¹	Bremner	..	Drury	..
27 Dec	Charlton Ath	A L 0-1	..	..	..	..	..	..	..	Drury	..	Jones B	..
31 Dec	Huddersfield T	H W 1-0	..	Male	..	..	..¹	..	..	..	..²	..	Kirchen
14 Jan	Everton	A L 0-2	..	..	..	..	..	..	Collett	..			..¹
21 Jan	Charlton Ath	H W 2-0	..	..	..	Pryde	..	Kirchen	Bremner	..¹	..	Drury	Bastin¹
28 Jan	Aston Villa	A W 3-1	..	..	..	..	..	Copping	Drake	..	..	..	Kirchen
1 Feb	Wolverhampton W	H D 0-0	..	..	..	..	..	..	Bastin	..	..¹	Jones B	Bastin¹
4 Feb	Sunderland	H W 2-0	..	Compton L	..	Crayston	opponents	Collett	Kirchen	Drury	Drake²	..	Cumner
18 Feb	Chelsea	H W 1-0	..	..	..	..	..	Collett	..	..¹	..	..	Bastin
21 Feb	Grimsby T	A L 1-2	..	..	..	..	..	..	..	..	..¹	..	
25 Feb	Preston NE	A L 1-2	..	..	..	..	Fields	Cartwright	Jones B	Jones L	..	Drury¹	Kirchen¹
4 Mar	Bolton W	H W 3-1	..	..	..	..	Joy	Pugh	Cartwright	Jones B	Drake¹	Curtis	..
11 Mar	Leeds U	A L 2-4	Swindin	..	Compton L¹	..	..	Cartwright	Drake¹	Jones B	Lewis	..	Cumner
18 Mar	Liverpool	H W 2-0	..	..	..	..		Jones L	Bremner	..¹	..	Bastin	
25 Mar	Leicester C	A W 2-0	..	..	..	..	..	Kirchen	Farr¹	Drake¹	..	Compton D	Cumner
1 Apr	Middlesbrough	H L 1-2	..	..	..	..	..	..	..¹	..¹	..	..	Nelson
7 Apr	Blackpool	A L 0-1	Marks	Compton L	..	..	..	..					
8 Apr	Birmingham	A W 2-1	..	Male	..								
10 Apr	Blackpool	H W 2-1	Swindin	..	Compton L¹	..¹							
15 Apr	Manchester U	H W 2-1	..	..	..	Hapgood							
22 Apr	Stoke C	A L 0-1	..	..	..								
29 Apr	Derby Co	A W 2-1	Marks	Compton L	..								
6 May	Brentford	H W 2-0	..	..	..								

FA Cup

Date	Opponent												
7 Jan	Chelsea (3)	A L 1-2	Wilson	Male	Hapgood	Crayston	Joy	Copping	Drake	Jones B	Lewis	Drury	Bastin¹

FA Charity Shield

Date	Opponent												
26 Sep	Preston	H W 2-1	Swindin	Male	Compton L	Crayston	Joy	Copping	Kirchen	Jones L	Drake²	Jones B	Cumner

Appearances (Goals)

Bastin C 23 (3) · Bremner G 13 (3) · Carr E 1 · Cartwright S 3 · Collett G 9 · Compton D 1 · Compton L 18 (2) · Copping W 26 · Crayston J 34 (3) · Cumner R 12 (2) · Curtis G 2 · Drake E 38 (14) · Drury G 23 (2) · Farr A 2 (1) · Fields A 3 · Hapgood E 38 · Jones B 30 (4) · Jones L 18 · Joy B 39 · Kirchen A 27 (9) · Lewis R 15 (7) · Male G 28 · Marks G 2 · Nelson D 9 (1) · Pryde D 4 · Pugh S 1 · Swindin G 21 · Walsh W 3 · Wilson A 19 · Own Goals 3 · Total: 29 players (55)

Position in League Table

	P	W	L	D	F:A	Pts	
Everton	42	27	10	5	88:52	59	1st
Arsenal	42	19	14	9	55:41	47	5th

SEASON 1939-1940
FOOTBALL LEAGUE (DIVISION 1)
(Prior to outbreak of War)

26 Aug Wolverhampton W 2 Arsenal 2 (Kirchen, Lewis)
Arsenal Team: Marks, Male, Hapgood, Crayston, Joy B, Jones L, Kirchen, Drury, Lewis, Jones B, Bastin

30 Aug Arsenal 1 Blackburn Rov 0 (Bastin)
Arsenal Team: Marks, Male, Hapgood, Crayston, Joy B, Jones L, Kirchen, Bremner, Lewis, Jones B, Bastin.

2 Sep Arsenal 5 Sunderland 2 (Drake 4, Drury 1)
Arsenal Team: Marks, Male, Hapgood, Crayston, Joy B, Jones L, Kirchen, Drury, Drake, Jones B, Bastin

21 Aug Jubilee Match
Arsenal 1 Tottenham H 1 (Drury)
Arsenal Team: Marks, Male, Hapgood, Crayston, Joy, Jones L, Kirchen, Drury, Lewis, Jones B, Nelson

Goal Scorers (Football League)

Drake 4 · Bastin 1 · Drury 1 · Lewis 1 · Kirchen 1

SEASON 1939/40 ALL MATCHES

	Opponents (Comp)		
21 Oct	Charlton Ath (Lge)	H	8-4
28 Oct	Clapton Orient (Lge)	A	6-1
4 Nov	Crystal Palace (Lge)	H	5-0
11 Nov	Norwich C (Lge)	A	1-1
18 Nov	Tottenham H (Lge)	H	2-1
25 Nov	Millwall (Lge)	A	3-3
2 Dec	West Ham U (Lge)	H	3-0
9 Dec	Watford (Lge)	A	3-1
16 Dec	Southend U (Lge)	H	5-1
25 Dec	Clapton Orient (Lge)	H	3-0
26 Dec	Crystal Palace (Lge)	A	3-0
30 Dec	Norwich C (Lge)	H	2-2
1 Jan	Charlton Ath (Lge)	A	6-2
13 Jan	Millwall (Lge)	H	4-1
20 Jan	West Ham U (Lge)	A	0-3
25 Jan	Tottenham H (Lge)	A	1-0
8 Feb	Watford (Lge)	H	2-2
10 Feb	Brentford (Lge)	H	3-1
24 Feb	Millwall (Lge)	H	4-1
2 Mar	Fulham (Lge)	A	1-1
9 Mar	Southampton (Lge)	A	2-3
16 Mar	West Ham U (Lge)	H	2-3
22 Mar	Charlton (Lge)	A	2-1
23 Mar	Chelsea (Lge)	H	3-0
25 Mar	Charlton (Lge)	H	1-1
30 Mar	Tottenham H (Lge)	A	1-1
3 Apr	Southend (Lge)	A	5-0
6 Apr	Brentford (Lge)	A	4-2
8 Apr	West Ham U (Lge)	A	1-2
13 Apr	Portsmouth (Lge)	H	3-2
17 Apr	Chelsea (Lge)	A	2-2
20 Apr	Notts Co (Cup R1)	H	4-0
24 Apr	Tottenham H (Lge)	H	2-4
27 Apr	Notts Co (Cup R1)	A	5-1
4 May	Crystal Palace (Cup R2)	H	3-1
11 May	Crystal Palace (Cup R2)	A	2-0
13 May	Millwall (Lge)	A	2-0
18 May	Birmingham C (Cup R3)	H	1-2
22 May	Fulham (Lge)	H	2-1
25 May	Portsmouth (Lge)	A	1-1
1 Jun	Southampton (Lge)	H	5-0

Position in Regional League South (A Division)

	P	W	L	D	F	A	Pts
Arsenal	18	13	1	4	62	22	30 1st

Position in Regional League South (C Division)

	P	W	L	D	F	A	Pts
Tottenham	18	11	3	4	43	30	26 1st
Arsenal	18	9	4	5	41	26	23 3rd

SEASON 1940/41 ALL MATCHES

	Opponents (Comp)		
31 Aug	Southend U (Lge)	A	7-1
7 Sep	Fulham (Lge)	H	5-0
14 Sep	Fulham (Lge)	A	1-0
21 Sep	Brentford (Lge)	H	3-1
28 Sep	Q P R (Lge)	A	2-3
5 Oct	Southend U (Lge)	H	7-0
12 Oct	Tottenham H (Lge)	A	3-2
19 Oct	Northampton T (Lge)	H	5-4
26 Oct	Brentford (Lge)	A	3-3
2 Nov	Charlton Ath (Lge)	H	2-2
16 Nov	Tottenham H (Lge)	H	1-1
23 Nov	Northampton T (Lge)	A	8-1
30 Nov	Crystal Palace (Lge)	H	2-2
7 Dec	Charlton Ath (Lge)	A	0-5
14 Dec	Q P R (Lge)	H	3-2
21 Dec	Crystal Palace (Lge)	A	3-3
25 Dec	West Ham U (Lge)	H	2-4
28 Dec	Luton T (Lge)	A	8-1
4 Jan	Reading (Cup Q)	A	0-2
11 Jan	Reading (Cup Q)	H	0-1
25 Jan	West Ham U (Cup Q)	A	3-1
1 Feb	Clapton Orient (Cup Q)	A	3-3
8 Feb	Clapton Orient (Cup Q)	H	15-2
15 Feb	Brighton & HA (Cup R1)	A	4-1
22 Feb	Brighton & HA (Cup R1)	H	3-1
1 Mar	Watford (Cup R2)	A	4-0
8 Mar	Watford (Cup R2)	H	5-0
15 Mar	West Ham U (Cup R3)	A	1-0
22 Mar	Millwall (Cup Q)	A	6-1
29 Mar	West Ham U (Cup R3)	H	2-1
5 Apr	Tottenham H (Cup R4)	H	2-1
12 Apr	Tottenham H (Cup R4)	A	1-1
14 Apr	Chelsea (Lge)	A	1-3
19 Apr	Leicester C (Cup SF)	H	1-0
26 Apr	Leicester C (Cup SF)	A	2-1
3 May	Tottenham H (Cup Q)	H	3-3
6 May	Tottenham H (Cup Q)	A	0-3
10 May	Preston NE (Cup F)	Wembley	1-1
17 May	West Ham U (Cup Q)	H	3-0
24 May	Millwall (Cup Q)	A	5-2
31 May	Preston NE (Cup F)	Blackburn	1-2

Position in Regional League South

	P	W	L	D	F	A	Pts
Crystal Palace	27	16	4	7	86	44	39 1st
Arsenal	19	10	5	4	66	38	24 4th

London War Cup
(Qualifying Competition, marked Q)

	P	W	L	D	F	A	Pts
Reading	10	6	0	4	29	8	16 1st
Arsenal	10	5	3	2	38	18	12 4th

SEASON 1941/42 ALL MATCHES

	Opponents (Comp)		
30 Aug	Brentford (Lge)	A	1-4
6 Sep	Crystal Palace (Lge)	H	7-2
13 Sep	Fulham (Lge)	A	5-2
20 Sep	Tottenham H (Lge)	H	4-0
27 Sep	Portsmouth (Lge)	A	5-1
4 Oct	Chelsea (Lge)	H	3-0
11 Oct	Charlton Ath (Lge)	A	3-1
18 Oct	West Ham U (Lge)	H	4-1
25 Oct	Watford (Lge)	A	1-3
1 Nov	Aldershot (Lge)	H	3-2
8 Nov	Millwall (Lge)	A	2-2
15 Nov	Clapton Orient (Lge)	H	5-2
22 Nov	Q P R (Lge)	H	4-1
29 Nov	Reading (Lge)	H	3-1
6 Dec	Brighton (Lge)	A	3-2
13 Dec	Brentford (Lge)	H	1-3
25 Dec	Fulham (Lge)	H	2-0
27 Dec	Tottenham H (Lge)	A	2-1
3 Jan	Portsmouth (Lge)	H	6-1
10 Jan	Chelsea (Lge)	A	5-1
17 Jan	Charlton Ath (Lge)	H	3-2
24 Jan	West Ham U (Lge)	A	0-3
31 Jan	Watford (Lge)	H	11-0
7 Jan	Aldershot (Lge)	A	0-1
14 Feb	Millwall (Lge)	H	10-0
21 Feb	Clapton Orient (Lge)	A	3-1
28 Feb	Q P R (Lge)	A	1-0
7 Mar	Reading (Lge)	A	4-1
14 Mar	Brighton & HA (Lge)	H	4-2
21 Mar	Clapton Orient (Cup Q)	H	4-1
28 Mar	West Ham U (Cup Q)	A	4-0
4 Apr	Clapton Orient (Cup Q)	A	2-1
6 Apr	West Ham U (Cup Q)	H	1-4
11 Apr	Brighton & HA (Cup Q)	A	3-0
18 Apr	Brighton & HA (Cup Q)	H	5-1
2 May	Brentford (Cup SF)	Chelsea	0-0
9 May	Crystal Palace (Lge)	A	3-3
16 May	Brentford (Cup SF)	Tottenham	1-2

Position in London League

	P	W	L	D	F	A	Pts
Arsenal	30	23	5	2	108	43	48 1st

London War Cup
(Qualifying Competition, marked Q)

	P	W	L	D	F	A	Pts
Arsenal	6	5	1	0	19	7	10 1st

SEASON 1942/43 ALL MATCHES

	Opponents (Comp)		
29 Aug	Charlton Ath (Lge)	A	6-2
5 Sep	Southampton (Lge)	H	6-1
12 Sep	Millwall (Lge)	A	2-1
19 Sep	Luton T (Lge)	H	2-0
26 Sep	Portsmouth (Lge)	A	2-2
3 Oct	Fulham (Lge)	A	4-3
10 Oct	Clapton Orient (Lge)	A	4-1
17 Oct	Brentford (Lge)	H	0-2
24 Oct	Reading (Lge)	H	4-1
31 Oct	Crystal Palace (Lge)	A	7-1
7 Nov	Tottenham H (Lge)	A	0-1
14 Nov	Q P R (Lge)	H	3-0
21 Nov	Aldershot (Lge)	A	7-4
28 Nov	Charlton Ath (Lge)	H	3-0
5 Dec	Southampton (Lge)	A	3-1
12 Dec	Millwall (Lge)	H	6-0
19 Dec	Luton T (Lge)	A	4-0
25 Dec	Chelsea (Lge)	A	2-5
26 Dec	Chelsea (Lge)	H	1-5
2 Jan	Portsmouth (Lge)	H	5-0
9 Jan	Fulham (Lge)	H	7-2
16 Jan	Clapton Orient (Lge)	H	6-0
23 Jan	Brentford (Lge)	A	1-0
30 Jan	Reading (Lge)	A	5-4
6 Feb	Crystal Palace (Lge)	H	9-0
13 Feb	Tottenham H (Lge)	H	1-0
20 Feb	Q P R (Lge)	A	2-3
27 Feb	Aldershot (Lge)	H	0-1
6 Mar	Brighton (Cup Q)	A	5-1
13 Mar	Watford (Cup Q)	H	4-1
20 Mar	West Ham U (Cup Q)	A	3-1
27 Mar	Brighton & HA (Cup Q)	H	5-0
3 Apr	Watford (Cup Q)	A	1-1
10 Apr	West Ham U (Cup Q)	H	3-1
24 Apr	Q P R (Cup SF)	Chelsea	4-1
1 May	Charlton Ath (Cup F)	Wembley	7-1
15 May	Blackpool (Cup play-off)	Chelsea	2-4

Position in Football League (South)

	P	W	L	D	F	A	Pts
Arsenal	28	21	6	1	102	40	43 1st

League Cup (South)
(Qualification Competition, marked Q)

	P	W	L	D	F	A	Pts
Arsenal	6	5	0	1	21	5	11 1st

SEASON 1943/44 ALL MATCHES

	Opponents (Comp)		
28 Aug	Charlton Ath (Lge)	A	0-1
4 Sep	Southampton (Lge)	H	4-1
11 Sep	West Ham U (Lge)	A	2-2
18 Sep	Portsmouth (Lge)	H	1-2
25 Sep	Brighton & HA (Lge)	A	1-1
2 Oct	Fulham (Lge)	A	4-3
9 Oct	Clapton Orient (Lge)	A	1-1
16 Oct	Brentford (Lge)	H	3-3
23 Oct	Watford (Lge)	H	4-2
30 Oct	Crystal Palace (Lge)	A	1-1
6 Nov	Chelsea (Lge)	H	6-0
13 Nov	Q P R (Lge)	H	5-0
27 Nov	Charlton Ath (Lge)	H	6-2
4 Dec	Southampton (Lge)	A	2-1
11 Dec	West Ham U (Lge)	H	1-1
18 Dec	Tottenham H (Lge)	A	1-2
25 Dec	Millwall (Lge)	A	5-1
26 Dec	Millwall (Lge)	H	1-1
1 Jan	Portsmouth (Lge)	A	1-2
8 Jan	Chelsea (Lge)	A	0-2
22 Jan	Fulham (Lge)	H	1-1
29 Jan	Clapton Orient (Lge)	H	1-0
5 Feb	Brentford (Lge)	A	1-4
12 Feb	Watford (Lge)	A	2-0
19 Feb	Luton T (Cup Q)	H	7-1
26 Feb	Q P R (Cup Q)	A	1-1
4 Mar	Reading (Cup Q)	H	2-3
11 Mar	Luton T (Cup Q)	A	1-1
18 Mar	Q P R (Cup Q)	H	1-4
25 Mar	Reading (Cup Q)	A	1-5
1 Apr	Aldershot (Lge)	A	3-0
8 Apr	Crystal Palace (Lge)	H	5-2
10 Apr	Brighton & HA (Lge)	H	3-1
22 Apr	Tottenham H (Lge)	H	3-3
29 Apr	Q P R (Lge)	A	1-1
6 May	Aldershot (Lge)	H	3-1

Position in Football League (South)

	P	W	L	D	F	A	Pts
Tottenham H	30	19	3	8	71	36	46 1st
Arsenal	30	14	6	10	72	42	38 4th

League Cup (South)
(Qualifying Competition, marked Q)

	P	W	L	D	F	A	Pts
Reading	6	6	–	–	23	6	12 1st
Arsenal	6	1	3	2	13	15	4 4th

SEASON 1944/45 ALL MATCHE

	Opponents (Comp)	
26 Aug	Luton T (Lge)	A
2 Sep	Tottenham H (Lge)	A
9 Sep	Aldershot (Lge)	H
16 Sep	Southampton (Lge)	A
23 Sep	Q P R (Lge)	H
30 Sep	Millwall (Lge)	A
7 Oct	Brighton & HA (Lge)	H
14 Oct	Fulham (Lge)	A
21 Oct	West Ham U (Lge)	H
28 Oct	Crystal Palace (Lge)	A
4 Nov	Reading (Lge)	A
11 Nov	Charlton Ath (Lge)	H
18 Nov	Watford (Lge)	H
25 Nov	Chelsea (Lge)	A
2 Dec	Luton T (Lge)	H
9 Dec	Tottenham H (Lge)	H
16 Dec	Aldershot (Lge)	A
23 Dec	Brentford (Lge)	H
30 Dec	Southampton (Lge)	H
6 Jan	Q P R (Lge)	A
13 Jan	Millwall (Lge)	H
20 Jan	Brighton & HA (Lge)	A
27 Jan	Fulham (Lge)	H
3 Feb	Reading (Cup Q)	A
10 Feb	Clapton Orient (Cup Q)	H
17 Feb	Portsmouth (Cup Q)	A
24 Feb	Reading (Cup Q)	H
3 Mar	Clapton Orient (Cup Q)	A
10 Mar	Portsmouth (Cup Q)	H
17 Mar	Millwall (Cup SF)	N
24 Mar	Crystal Palace (Lge)	H
31 Mar	Reading (Lge)	H
2 Apr	Brentford (Lge)	A
14 Apr	Charlton Ath (Lge)	A
21 Apr	Watford (Lge)	A
28 Apr	Chelsea (Lge)	H
5 May	West Ham U (Lge)	A

Football League (South)

	P	W	L	D	F	A
Tottenham H	30	23	1	6	81	3
Arsenal	30	14	13	3	77	6

League Cup (South)
(Qualifying Competition, marked Q)

	P	W	L	D	F	A
Arsenal	6	5	1	0	20	8

SEASON 1945/46 ALL MATCHES

	Opponents (Comp)	
25 Aug	Coventry C (Lge)	A
27 Aug	West Ham U (Lge)	A
1 Sep	Coventry C (Lge)	H
3 Sep	Wolverhampton W (Lge)	A
8 Sep	Luton T (Lge)	H
15 Sep	Luton T (Lge)	A
22 Sep	Aston Villa (Lge)	H
29 Sep	Aston Villa (Lge)	A
6 Oct	Swansea T (Lge)	H
13 Oct	Swansea T (Lge)	A
20 Oct	Charlton Ath (Lge)	H
27 Oct	Charlton Ath (Lge)	A
3 Nov	Fulham (Lge)	A
10 Nov	Fulham (Lge)	H
17 Nov	Plymouth Arg (Lge)	H
24 Nov	Plymouth Arg (Lge)	A
1 Dec	Portsmouth (Lge)	A
8 Dec	Portsmouth (Lge)	H
15 Dec	Nottingham F (Lge)	H
22 Dec	Nottingham F (Lge)	A
25 Dec	Newport Co (Lge)	A
26 Dec	Newport Co (Lge)	H
29 Dec	Wolverhampton W (Lge)	H
5 Jan	West Ham U (Cup R3)	A
9 Jan	West Ham U (Cup R3)	H
12 Jan	W B A (Lge)	H
19 Jan	W B A (Lge)	A
26 Jan	Leicester C (Lge)	A
2 Feb	Birmingham (Lge)	H
9 Feb	Tottenham H (Lge)	H
16 Feb	Tottenham H (Lge)	A
23 Feb	Brentford (Lge)	A
9 Mar	Chelsea (Lge)	H
13 Mar	Birmingham (Lge)	A
16 Mar	Chelsea (Lge)	A
23 Mar	Millwall (Lge)	A
30 Mar	Millwall (Lge)	H
6 Apr	Southampton (Lge)	H
13 Apr	Southampton (Lge)	A
19 Apr	Derby Co (Lge)	A
20 Apr	Leicester C	H
22 Apr	Derby Co (Lge)	H
29 Apr	Brentford (Lge)	H
4 May	West Ham U (Lge)	H

Position in League Table (South)

	P	W	L	D	F	A
Birmingham	42	28	9	5	96	45
Arsenal	42	16	15	11	76	73

SEASON 1946-1947 FOOTBALL LEAGUE (DIVISION 1)

Date	Opponent				1	2	3	4	5	6	7	8	9	10	11
31 Aug	Wolverhampton W	A	L	1-6	Swindin	Scott	Male	Nelson	Joy	Curtis	McPherson	Sloan	Lewis[1]	Logie	Bastin
4 Sep	Blackburn Rov	H	L	1-3	..	..	Joy	..	Compton L	Waller	Dr O'Flanagan	McPherson	..[1]	Drury	Hodges
7 Sep	Sunderland	H	D	2-2	..	..	..	..	..	..	..	..	..[2]	Logie	Smith A
11 Sep	Everton	A	L	2-3	..	..	..	Bastin	..	..	Nelson	..	..[2]	..	..
14 Sep	Aston Villa	A	W	2-0	..	..	..	..	..	Logie	McPherson	Drury	..[1]	Curtis	Dr O'Flanagan[1]
17 Sep	Blackburn Rov	A	W	2-1	..	..	..	..	..	..	..	..	..[2]	Jones B	Nelson
21 Sep	Derby Co	H	L	0-1	..	..	..	..	..	..	..	..	Dr O'Flanagan	..	..
28 Sep	Manchester U	A	L	2-5	..	Male	..	..	..	..	..	Sloan	Lewis[1]	..	..
5 Oct	Blackpool	A	L	1-2	..	Scott	..	Male	..	Jones B	Nelson	Logie[1]	Sloan	Curtis	Hodges
12 Oct	Brentford	H	D	2-2	..	Joy	Collett	Waller	..	..	McPherson	..	Lewis[1]	..	Dr O'Flanagan
19 Oct	Stoke C	H	W	1-0	..	Scott	Joy	Male	..	Waller	..	Gudmundsson	..[1]	..	..
26 Oct	Chelsea	A	L	1-2	..	..	..	Waller	..	Jones B	Nelson	..	..[1]	..	..
2 Nov	Sheffield U	H	L	2-3	..	..	..	Male	..	Waller	McPherson	Logie[1]	..	Jones B	Smith A
9 Nov	Preston NE	A	L	0-2	..	..	Barnes	..	..	Collett	..	Lewis	Grant	Curtis	Nelson
16 Nov	Leeds U	H	W	4-2	Platt	..	Wade	Sloan	..	..	..[1]	Logie[1]	Lewis[2]	..	Dr O'Flanagan
23 Nov	Liverpool	A	L	2-4	..	..	..	..	..	..	..	..	..	..	..[1]
30 Nov	Bolton W	H	D	2-2	..	..	Barnes	..	..	Mercer	..	..	..	Jones B	..
7 Dec	Middlesbrough	A	L	0-2	..	Male	..	Mercer	..	Collett	..	..	Grant	..	..
14 Dec	Charlton Ath	H	W	1-0	Swindin	..	..	Sloan	..	Mercer	..	..	Rooke[1]	..	..
21 Dec	Grimsby T	A	D	0-0	..	..	..	..	..	..	..	..[1]	..[1]	..	Morgan
25 Dec	Portsmouth	H	W	2-1	..	..	..	..	..	..	..	..	..	..	Dr O'Flanagan
26 Dec	Portsmouth	A	W	2-0	..	Compton	..	..	Fields	..	Jones B	..	..[2]	Curtis	Morgan
28 Dec	Wolverhampton W	H	D	1-1	..	Scott	..	..	Compton L	..	McPherson	..	..[1]	Jones B	Dr O'Flanagan
4 Jan	Sunderland	A	W	4-1	..	Compton	..	..	Fields	..	..	Lewis[2]	..[2]	..	Logie
18 Jan	Aston Villa	H	L	0-2	..	..	Collett	..	..	Waller	..	..	..	Logie	Rudkin
1 Feb	Manchester U	H	W	6-2	..	Male	Barnes	..	Compton L	Mercer	..[1]	Logie[1]	..[3]	Jones B	..
8 Feb	Blackpool	H	D	1-1	..	..	..	..	..	..	..	..	..[1]	Curtis	..
22 Feb	Stoke C	A	L	1-3	..	Scott	..	..	..	..	..	..	..[1]	Jones B	..[1]
1 Mar	Chelsea	H	L	1-2	..	..	..	..	..	..	..	..	..	..	..[1]
15 Mar	Preston NE	H	W	4-1	..	..	..	..	..	..	..	Rooke[1]	Lewis[3]	..	Calverley
22 Mar	Leeds U	A	D	1-1	..	..	..	..	..	..	..	..	..	..[1]	..
4 Apr	Huddersfield T	H	L	1-2	..	..	..	..	..	..	..	..	..	..	..
5 Apr	Bolton W	A	W	3-1	..	..	..	..	..	..	..	Logie	..[1]	Rooke[2]	..
7 Apr	Huddersfield T	A	D	0-0	..	..	..	..	..	..	Jones B	..	..	..[4]	..
12 Apr	Middlesbrough	H	W	4-0	..	Male	..	..	..	..	McPherson[1]	..[1]	Rooke	Jones B	..
19 Apr	Charlton Ath	A	D	2-2	..	Scott	..	..	..	..	..	..	Lewis[4]	Rooke	Compton D[1]
26 Apr	Grimsby T	H	W	5-3	..	..	..	..	..	..	..	..	..	..[1]	Calverley
10 May	Derby Co	A	W	1-0	..	..	..	..	Fields	..	..	..[1]	..	..	..
24 May	Liverpool	H	L	1-2	..	Male	..	..[1]	..	..	..	..	Rooke	Jones B	..
26 May	Brentford	A	W	1-0	..	..	..	..[1]	..	..	..	..	Lewis[1]	Rooke[1]	..
31 May	Everton	H	W	2-1	..	Scott	..	..	..	..	..[1]	..	..	..	..
7 June	Sheffield U	A	L	1-2	..	..	..	..	..	..	..	..	..	..	Jones B

FA Cup

Date	Opponent				1	2	3	4	5	6	7	8	9	10	11
11 Jan	Chelsea (3)	A	D	1-1	Swindin	Scott	Barnes	Sloan	Compton L	Mercer	McPherson[1]	Lewis	Rooke	Jones B	Logie
15 Jan	Chelsea (3R)	H	D	1-1	..	Male	..	..	..	..	..[1]	..	..	Logie	Curtis
20 Jan	Chelsea (3R) (at Tottenham)		L	0-2	..	..	..	..	..	..	..	..	..	Jones B	Logie

Appearances (Goals)

Barnes W 26 · Bastin C 6 · Calverley A 11 · Collett E 6 · Compton D 1 (1) · Compton L 36 · Curtis G 11 · Drury G 4 · Fields A 8 · Grant C 2 · Gudmundsson A 2 · Hodges C 2 · Jones B 26 (1) · Joy B 13 · Lewis R 28 (29) · Logie J 35 (8) · Male G 15 · McPherson I 37 (6) · Mercer J 25 · Morgan S 2 · Nelson D 10 · Dr O'Flanagan K 14 (3) · Platt T 4 · Rooke R 24 (21) · Rudkin T 5 (2) · Scott L 28 · Sloan P 30 (1) · Smith A 3 · Swindin 38 · Wade J 2 · Waller H 8 · Total: 31 players (72)

Position in League Table

	P	W	L	D	F:A	Pts
Liverpool	42	25	10	7	84:52	57 1st
Arsenal	42	16	17	9	72:70	41 13th

SEASON 1947-1948 FOOTBALL LEAGUE (DIVISION 1)

Date	Opponent				1	2	3	4	5	6	7	8	9	10	11
23 Aug	Sunderland	H	W	3-1	Swindin	Scott	Barnes	Macaulay	Fields	Mercer	Roper	Logie[1]	Lewis	Rooke[1]	McPherson[1]
27 Aug	Charlton Ath	A	W	4-2	..	..	..	..	..	..	..[1]	..	..[1]	..	..
30 Aug	Sheffield U	A	W	2-1	..	..	..	..	..	..	..	..[1]	..	..	..
3 Sep	Charlton Ath	H	W	6-0	..	..	..	..	..	..	..	..[4]	..[2]	..	..
6 Sep	Manchester U	H	W	2-1	..	..	..	..	..	..	..	..	..[1]	..	..
10 Sep	Bolton W	H	W	2-0	..	..	..	..	..	..	..	..	..[1]	..	..[1]
13 Sep	Preston NE	A	D	0-0	..	..	..	..	Compton L	..	..	Sloan	..	..	..
20 Sep	Stoke C	H	W	3-0	..	Male	..	..	..	..	..[1]	Rooke	Jones B	..	..[2]
27 Sep	Burnley	A	W	1-0	..	Scott	..	..	..	Sloan	..	Lewis[1]	Rooke	..	..
4 Oct	Portsmouth	H	D	0-0	..	..	..	Male	..	..	..	..	..	..	..
11 Oct	Aston Villa	H	W	1-0	..	..	Wade	Macaulay	..	Mercer	..	Rooke[1]	Jones B	..	..
18 Oct	Wolverhampton W	A	D	1-1	..	Male	Wade	..	..	..	..	Lewis	Rooke[1]	..	..
25 Oct	Everton	H	D	1-1	..	Scott	Barnes	..	..	..	..	..[1]	..	..	..
1 Nov	Chelsea	A	D	0-0	..	..	..	..	..	..	..	..	..	..	..
8 Nov	Blackpool	H	W	2-1	..	..	..	..	..	..	..[1]	Lewis	Rooke[1]	Logie	..
15 Nov	Blackburn Rov	A	W	1-0	..	..	..	..	..	..	..	..[1]	..	..	..
22 Nov	Huddersfield T	H	W	2-0	..	..	..	..	..	..	..	..[1]	..	..	..
29 Nov	Derby Co	A	L	0-1	..	..	..	..	..	..	..	..	..	..	..
6 Dec	Manchester C	H	D	1-1	..	..	..	..	..	..	..[1]	Logie[1]	..	..	..
13 Dec	Grimsby T	A	W	4-0	..	..	..	..	..	..	..	Logie[1]	..[2]	Jones B	..
20 Dec	Sunderland	A	D	1-1	..	..	Wade	..	..	..	..[1]	..	..	..	..
25 Dec	Liverpool	A	W	3-1	..	..	Wade	..	..	..	..	..	Lewis	Rooke[2]	..
27 Dec	Liverpool	H	L	1-2	..	..	..	..	..	..	..[1]	..	..	..	..
1 Jan	Bolton W	A	W	1-0	..	Male	Scott	..	..	..	..	..	..	..[1]	..
3 Jan	Sheffield U	H	W	3-2	..	..	..	..	..	..	..	..	..	..[2]	..
17 Jan	Manchester U	A	D	1-1	..	Scott	Barnes	..	..	..	..	Lewis[1]	Rooke	Logie	..
31 Jan	Preston NE	H	W	3-0	..	..	..	..	..	..	..	Logie	Lewis[2]	..	..
7 Feb	Stoke C	A	D	0-0	..	..	..	..	..	..	..	..	..[2]	..	..
14 Feb	Burnley	H	W	3-0	..	..	..	..	..	..	..	..	Jones B	..	Compton D
28 Feb	Aston Villa	A	L	2-4	..	..	..	..	opponents	..	..	Lewis	..[1]	..	..
6 Mar	Wolverhampton W	H	W	5-2	..	..	..	..	..	..	..	Logie[1]	..[2]	Forbes[1]	..
13 Mar	Everton	A	W	2-0	..	..	..	..	..	..	Lewis	..	..	..	..[2]
20 Mar	Chelsea	H	L	0-2	..	..	..	..	..	..	Roper	..	..	..	..
26 Mar	Middlesbrough	H	W	7-0	..	..	..	..	opponents	..	..	..[3]	Lewis	..[2]	..
27 Mar	Blackpool	A	L	0-3	..	..	..	..	..	..	McPherson	..	Lewis	..	..
29 Mar	Middlesbrough	A	D	1-1	..	..	..	..	..	..	Roper	..[1]	Forbes	..	..
3 Apr	Blackburn Rov	H	W	2-0	..	..	..	..	..	..	..[1]	..	..	..	..
10 Apr	Huddersfield T	A	D	1-1	..	Male	..	Forbes	..	..	..[1]	..	Lewis	..	..
17 Apr	Derby Co	H	L	1-2	..	Scott	..	Macaulay	..	..	..[1]	..	Forbes	..	..
21 Apr	Portsmouth	A	D	0-0	..	..	..	..	..	..	..	Jones B	..	..	..
24 Apr	Manchester C	A	D	0-0	..	Male	Scott	..	..	..	..	Lewis	..[4]	..[1]	..
1 May	Grimsby T	H	W	8-0	..	..	..	Smith L	..	..	Logie[1]	..[4]	..[1]	..[2]	..

FA Cup

Date	Opponent				1	2	3	4	5	6	7	8	9	10	11
10 Jan	Bradford C (3)	H	L	0-1	Swindin	Male	Scott	Macaulay	Compton L	Mercer	Roper	Logie	Lewis	Rooke	McPherson

Appearances (Goals)

Barnes W 35 · Compton D 14 (6) · Compton L 35 · Fields A 6 · Forbes A 11 (2) · Jones B 7 (1) · Lewis R 28 (14) · Logie J 39 (8) · Macaulay A 40 · Male G 8 · McPherson I 29 (5) · Mercer J 40 · Rooke R 42 (33) · Roper D 40 (10) · Scott L 39 · Sloan W 3 · Smith L 1 · Swindin G 42 · Wade J 3 · Own goals 2 · Total: 19 players (81)

Position in League Table

	P	W	L	D	F:A	Pts
Arsenal	42	23	6	13	81:32	59 1st

SEASON 1948-1949 FOOTBALL LEAGUE (DIVISION 1)

1948-1949

21 Aug	Huddersfield T	A D 1-1	Swindin	Barnes	Smith	Macaulay	Fields	Mercer	Roper	Logie	Rooke[1]	Forbes	McPherson
25 Aug	Stoke C	H W 3-0	..	..	..	..	Compton L	..	..[1]	..[1]	..	..[1]	..
28 Aug	Manchester U	H L 0-1	..	..	..	..	..	..	..	..	..	..	..
30 Aug	Stoke C	A L 0-1	..	..	..	..	..	..	..	..	..	..	..
4 Sep	Sheffield U	A D 1-1	..	..	..	..	..	*opponents*	..	..	..	Lishman	Vallance
8 Sep	Liverpool	H D 1-1	..	..	..	..	..	..	..	..	..[1]	..	..
11 Sep	Aston Villa	H W 3-1	..	Scott	Barnes	..	..	..	..[1]	Jones B	..[2]	..	Compton D
15 Sep	Liverpool	A W 1-0	..	..	..	..	..	Jones B	..	Lewis[1]	..	..	..
18 Sep	Sunderland	A D 1-1	..	..	..	..	..	Mercer	..	Jones B[1]	Lewis	..	..
25 Sep	Wolverhampton W	H W 3-1	..	Barnes	Smith	Forbes	..	..	..	Macaulay	..[2]	Jones B	..[1]
2 Oct	Bolton W	A L 0-1	..	Scott	Barnes	..	..	..	McPherson	..	..	..	Roper
9 Oct	Burnley	H W 3-1	..	Barnes	Smith	Macaulay	..	..	Roper	Logie[1]	..[2]	Rooke	Jones B
16 Oct	Preston NE	A D 1-1	..	Scott	Barnes	..	..	..	..	..	Rooke[1]	Forbes	..
23 Oct	Everton	H W 5-0	..	..	Smith	..	..	..	..	..[2]	..[2]	..[1]	McPherson
30 Oct	Chelsea	A W 1-0	..	..	Barnes	..	..	..	..	..	..[1]	..	..
6 Nov	Birmingham C	H W 2-0	..	..	..	..	..	..	..	..	Lewis[1]	..[1]	..
13 Nov	Middlesbrough	A W 1-0	..	Barnes	Smith	..	..	..	..	..	..[1]	..	..
20 Nov	Newcastle U	H L 0-1	..	..	..	..	..	..	..	..	..	..	Rooke
27 Nov	Portsmouth	A L 1-4	..	..	..	..	..	..	..	..	..[1]	..	McPherson
4 Dec	Manchester C	H D 1-1	..	..	..	..	..	..	..	..	Rooke[1]	..	..
11 Dec	Charlton Ath	A L 3-4	Platt	..	..	..	..	..	..[1]	..	..	Lewis[1]	..[1]
18 Dec	Huddersfield T	H W 3-0	Swindin	..	..	..	..	..	..	..	..[3]	..	..
25 Dec	Derby Co	H D 3-3	..	..	..	..	..	..	..	..[1]	..[1]	..	..[1]
27 Dec	Derby Co	A L 1-2	..	..	..	..	..	..	..	..	..	..[1]	..
1 Jan	Manchester U	A L 0-2	..	..	..	..	..	..	..	Lewis	..	Lishman	..
15 Jan	Sheffield U	H W 5-3	..	..	..	..	..	..	..	Logie[2]	..[1]	..[1]	..[1]
22 Jan	Aston Villa	A L 0-1	..	..	..	..	..	..	..	..	..	..	..
5 Feb	Sunderland	H W 5-0	Platt	..	..	..[1]	..	..	McPherson[1]	..	Lewis[1]	..[1]	Vallance[1]
19 Feb	Wolverhampton W	A W 3-1	..	..	..	..	..	..	..	..[1]	..[2]	..	..
26 Feb	Bolton W	H W 5-0	..	..	..	..	..	Forbes	..[1]	..[2]	..[1]	..	..[1]
5 Mar	Burnley	A D 1-1	..	..	..	..	..	..	..	..	..	..[1]	..
12 Mar	Preston NE	H D 0-0	..	Scott	..	..	..	Mercer	..	..	..	..	..
19 Mar	Newcastle U	A L 2-3	..	..	Barnes	..	..	Forbes[1]	..	..	..[1]	..	..
2 Apr	Birmingham C	A D 1-1	..	..	..	..	..	..	..	..	..	..[1]	..
9 Apr	Middlesbrough	H D 1-1	..	..	..	..	..	..	..	..	..	..[1]	..
15 Apr	Blackpool	A D 1-1	..	Barnes	Smith	..	..	..	..	..	..[1]	..	..
16 Apr	Everton	A D 0-0	Swindin	..	..	Mercer	..	..	..	Jones B	Rooke	..	Roper
18 Apr	Blackpool	H W 2-0	..	..	..	..	..	..	..	Logie	Lewis	..[2]	Compton D
23 Apr	Chelsea	H L 1-2	..	..	..	Macaulay	..	..	..	..	..	..	..[1]
27 Apr	Manchester C	A W 3-0	..	..	..	..	..	Mercer	..	..	Roper[1]	..[2]	Vallance
4 May	Portsmouth	H W 3-2	..	..	..	..	..	Forbes	..	..[1]	..	..[2]	..
7 May	Charlton Ath	H W 2-0	..	..	..	Mercer	Daniel	..	..	..	..[1]	..[1]	..
	FA Cup												
8 Jan	Tottenham H (3)	H W 3-0	Swindin	Barnes	Smith	Macaulay	Compton L	Mercer	Roper[1]	Logie	Rooke	Lishman[1]	McPherson[1]
29 Jan	Derby Co (4)	A L 0-1	..	..	..	..	Mercer	Forbes	..	..	Lewis	..	..
	FA Charity Shield												
6 Oct	Manchester U	H W 4-3	Swindin	Barnes	Smith	Macaulay	Compton L	Mercer	Roper	Logie	Lewis[2]	Rooke[1]	Jones B[1]

Appearances (Goals)

Barnes W 40 · Compton D 6 (2) · Compton L 40 · Daniel R 1 · Fields A 1 · Forbes A 25 (4) · Jones B 8 (1) · Lewis R 25 (16) · Lishman D 23 (12) · Logie J 35 (11) · Macaulay A 39 (1) · McPherson I 33 (5) · Mercer J 33 · Platt E 10 · Rooke R 22 (14) · Roper D 31 (5) · Scott L 12 · Smith L 32 · Swindin G 32 · Vallance T 14 (2) · Own goals 1 · Total: players 20 (74)

Position in League Table

	P	W	L	D	F:A	Pts	
Portsmouth	42	25	9	8	84:42	58	1st
Arsenal	42	18	11	13	74:44	49	5th

SEASON 1949-1950 FOOTBALL LEAGUE (DIVISION 1)

1949-1950

20 Aug	Burnley	H L 0-1	Swindin	Barnes	Smith	Mercer	Daniel	Forbes	McPherson	Macaulay	Roper	Lishman	Vallance
24 Aug	Chelsea	A W 2-1	..	..	..	Macaulay	..	..	..	Logie	Goring[1]	..[1]	Roper
27 Aug	Sunderland	A L 2-4	..	..	..	..	..	..	*opponents*	..[1]	..	..	..
31 Aug	Chelsea	H L 2-3	..	Scott	Barnes	Mercer	Compton L	Shaw	..	..	..[2]	..	..
3 Sep	Liverpool	H L 1-2	..	..	..	..	..	Forbes	..	..	..	..[1]	..
7 Sep	W B A	A W 2-1	..	Barnes[1]	Smith	Logie	..	Mercer	..	Lewis[1]	..	Shaw	..
10 Sep	Huddersfield T	A D 2-2	..	..	..	..	..	..	..	..[1]	..[1]	..	..
14 Sep	W B A	H W 4-1	Platt	..[1]	..	Macaulay	..	..	Cox	..[1]	..[1]	Logie	..[1]
17 Sep	Bolton W	A D 2-2	..	..[1]	..	..	..	..	..	..[1]	..	Roper	McPherson
24 Sep	Birmingham C	H W 4-2	..	..	..	..	..	..	..	..[1]	..[2]	Logie[1]	Roper
1 Oct	Derby Co	A W 2-1	..	..	..	..	..	..	..	Logie	..	Lewis[2]	..
8 Oct	Everton	H W 5-2	..	..	..	..	..	..	..	..	..[2]	..[2]	..[1]
15 Oct	Middlesbrough	A D 1-1	..	Wade	..	..	..	..	..	..	Roper[1]	..	McPherson
22 Oct	Blackpool	H W 1-0	..	Barnes	..	..	..	..	..	..	..	..[1]	..
29 Oct	Newcastle U	A W 3-0	..	..	..	..	Daniel	..	..	..	..[3]	..	..
5 Nov	Fulham	H W 2-1	..	..[1]	..	..	Compton L	..	..	..	..	..	..[1]
12 Nov	Manchester C	A W 2-0	..	..	..	..	..	..	..[1]	..[1]	..	..	..
19 Nov	Charlton Ath	H L 2-3	..	..	..	..	..	..	..	..[1]	..	..[1]	..
26 Nov	Aston Villa	A D 1-1	..	..	..	Forbes	..	..	..	..	..	..[1]	..
3 Dec	Wolverhampton W	H D 1-1	..	..	..	..	..	..	..	..	..[1]	..	..
10 Dec	Portsmouth	A L 1-2	..	..	..	..	..	..	..	..	Goring[1]	..	Roper
17 Dec	Burnley	A D 0-0	..	..	..	..	..	..	..	..	..	..	..
24 Dec	Sunderland	H W 5-0	..	..	..	..[1]	..	..	..	..[1]	..[1]	..[1]	McPherson[1]
26 Dec	Manchester U	A L 0-2	..	..	..	..	..	..	..	Macaulay	..	..	..
27 Dec	Manchester U	H D 0-0	Swindin	Scott	Barnes	Macaulay	..	Forbes	..	Logie	..	..	..
31 Dec	Liverpool	A L 0-2	..	..	..	Forbes	..	Mercer	..	..	..	Macaulay	..
14 Jan	Huddersfield T	H W 1-0	..	..	..	..	..	..	..	..	..	Lewis[1]	..
21 Jan	Bolton W	H D 1-1	..	..	..	Macaulay	..	Forbes	..	..	..	..[1]	Compton D
4 Feb	Birmingham C	A L 1-2	..	..	..	Forbes	Smith	Mercer	..	..	..[1]	..	McPherson
18 Feb	Derby Co	H W 1-0	..	..	..	..	Compton L	..	Roper	..[1]	..	..	Compton D
25 Feb	Everton	A W 1-0	..	..	..	..	..	..	Cox[1]	Kelly	Roper	Lishman	..
8 Mar	Middlesbrough	H D 1-1	..	..	Smith	Macaulay	..	Forbes[1]	McPherson	Logie	..	..	..
11 Mar	Charlton Ath	A D 1-1	..	..	..	..	Daniel	Mercer	Cox	Lewis	Goring	..	..[1]
25 Mar	Fulham	A D 2-2	..	..	..	..	Compton L	..	..[1]	Logie[1]	Roper	..	McPherson
29 Mar	Aston Villa	H L 1-3	Platt	Barnes	..	..	..	..	McPherson	..	Cox	..[1]	Compton D
1 Apr	Manchester C	H W 4-1	Swindin	..	..	Forbes	..	Shaw	Cox	Lewis[2]	Goring[1]	..[1]	..
8 Apr	Blackpool	A L 1-2	..	..	..	..	..	Mercer	..	..	..[1]	..	..
10 Apr	Stoke C	H W 6-0	Platt	..[1]	..	Macaulay	*opponents*	Shaw	McPherson	Logie	..[2]	..[2]	Roper
15 Apr	Newcastle U	H W 4-2	Swindin	..	..	..	..	Mercer	Cox	..	..[3]	Lewis[1]	Compton D
22 Apr	Wolverhampton W	A L 0-3	..	Scott	Barnes	Forbes	..	..	..	..	..	..	..
3 May	Portsmouth	H W 2-0	..	..	..	..	..	..	..	..	..[2]	..	..
6 May	Stoke C	A W 5-2	..	..	..	..	Daniel	..	..	Lewis[1]	..	Lishman[3]	McPherson[1]
	FA Cup												
7 Jan	Sheffield W (3)	H W 1-0	Swindin	Scott	Barnes	Forbes	Compton L	Mercer	Cox	Logie	Goring	Lewis[1]	McPherson
28 Jan	Swansea T (4)	H W 2-1	..	..	..[1]	..	..	..	..	..[1]	..	..	..
11 Feb	Burnley (5)	H W 2-0	..	..	..	..	..	..	..	..	..	..[1]	Compton D[1]
4 Mar	Leeds U (6)	H W 1-0	..	..	..	..	..	..	..	..	Roper	..[1]	..
18 Mar	Chelsea (SF) (at White Hart Lane)	D 2-2	..	..	..	..	..[1]	..	..[1]	..	Goring	..	..
22 Mar	Chelsea (SFR) (at White Hart Lane)	W 1-0	..	..	..	Macaulay	..	..	..[1]	..	..	..	..
29 Apr	Liverpool (F) (at Wembley)	W 2-0d	..	..	..	Forbes	..	..	..	..	..	..[2]	..

Appearances (Goals)

Barnes W 38 (5) · Compton D 11 (1) · Compton L 35 · Cox F 32 (3) · Daniel R 6 · Forbes A 23 (2) · Goring P 29 (21) · Kelly N 1 · Lewis R 31 (19) · Lishman D 14 (9) · Logie J 34 (7) · Macaulay A 24 · McPherson I 27 (3) · Mercer J 35 · Platt E 19 · Roper D 27 (7) · Scott L 15 · Shaw A 5 · Smith L 31 · Swindin G 23 · Vallance T 1 · Wade J 1 · Own goals 2 – Total: 22 players (79)

Position in League Table

	P	W	L	D	F:A	Pts	
Portsmouth	42	22	11	9	74:38	53	1st
Arsenal	42	19	12	11	79:55	49	6th

SEASON 1950-1951 FOOTBALL LEAGUE (DIVISION 1)

19 Aug	Burnley	A	W 1-0	Swindin	Barnes	Smith	Forbes	Fields	Mercer	Cox	Logie	Goring	Lishman	Roper[1]
23 Aug	Chelsea	H	D 0-0	..	..	..	..	Compton	..	..	..	..	..	..
26 Aug	Tottenham H	H	D 2-2	..	..[1]	..	Shaw	..	..	..[1]	..	..	..	..[1]
30 Aug	Chelsea	A	W 1-0	..	..	..	..	..	..	..[1]	..[2]	..	..	McPherson
2 Sep	Sheffield W	H	W 3-0	Platt	Scott	Barnes	..	..	..	..[1]	..	..	..[1]	..
6 Sep	Everton	H	W 2-1	..	..	..[1]	Forbes	..	..	..[1]	..	..	..	..
9 Sep	Middlesbrough	A	L 1-2	..	..	..	..	..	..	..	..	..	..	Roper
13 Sep	Everton	A	D 1-1	Swindin	Barnes	Smith	..	..	McPherson	..	..[2]	..[1]	..	..
16 Sep	Huddersfield T	H	W 6-2	..	..	..	Shaw	..	Forbes	..	..[2]	..[3]	..[1]	..
23 Sep	Newcastle U	A	L 1-2	..	..	..	..	..	Mercer	..	..[1]	..	..	..
30 Sep	W B A	H	W 3-0	..	..	..	Forbes	..	..	..	..[1]	..	..[2]	..
7 Oct	Charlton Ath	A	W 3-1	..	..	..	..[1]	..	..	..	..	..[1]	..[1]	..[1]
14 Oct	Manchester U	H	W 3-0	..	..	..	..	..	..	..	opponents	..[1]	..[1]	..
21 Oct	Aston Villa	A	D 1-1	..	Scott	..	Shaw	..	..	..	..[1]	..	..	..
28 Oct	Derby Co	H	W 3-1	Platt	Barnes	..	Forbes[1]	..	..	..	..	..[1]	..[1]	..
4 Nov	Wolverhampton W	A	W 1-0	..	..	..	..	..	..	..	..	..	..[4]	..[1]
11 Nov	Sunderland	H	W 5-1	..	..	..	..	..	..	..	..[1]	..	..[1]	..[1]
18 Nov	Liverpool	A	W 3-1	..	..	..	..[1]	..	..	..	..	..[1]	..[1]	..
25 Nov	Fulham	H	W 5-1	..	..	..	..[1]	..	..	..	..[1]	..	..[3]	..
2 Dec	Bolton W	A	L 0-3	..	..	..	..[1]	..	..	..	..	..	..	..
9 Dec	Blackpool	H	D 4-4	Swindin	..[1]	..	..	..	..	..	..	..[1]	..[1]	..
16 Dec	Burnley	H	L 0-1	..	Scott	Barnes	..	..	..	..	..	..	..	Cox
23 Dec	Tottenham H	A	L 0-1	..	..	..	..	..	..	..	..	..	..	..
25 Dec	Stoke C	H	L 0-3	..	..	..	Shaw	..	Forbes	..	..	..	..	..
26 Dec	Stoke C	A	L 0-1	Platt	Barnes	Smith	..	..	Mercer	Cox	Goring	Holton	Lewis	Roper
30 Dec	Sheffield W	A	W 2-0	..	Scott	..	Forbes	Daniel	..	..	Logie	Goring[2]	..[2]	..
13 Jan	Middlesbrough	H	W 3-1	..	Barnes	..	Shaw	Compton	Forbes	McPherson	..	..[1]	..[2]	..
20 Jan	Huddersfield T	A	D 2-2	..	..	..	..	..	..	..	..	..	..	..
3 Feb	Newcastle U	H	D 0-0	..	..	..	Forbes	..	Mercer	..	..	..	..	..
17 Feb	W B A	A	L 0-2	..	..	..	Shaw	..	Forbes	Cox	..	..	..	..
24 Feb	Charlton Ath	H	L 2-5	Kelsey	..	..	..	..	..	McPherson	..[2]	..	..	..
3 Mar	Manchester U	A	L 1-3	..	Scott	Barnes	Mercer	..	..	..	..	Holton[1]	Goring	Marden
10 Mar	Aston Villa	H	W 2-1	Platt	Barnes	Smith	Shaw	Daniel	..	Milton	..	..	Lewis[2]	..
17 Mar	Derby Co	A	L 2-4	..	..	..	..	..	..	Cox	..	Goring[1]	..[1]	..
23 Mar	Portsmouth	H	L 0-1	Kelsey	Scott	..	Mercer	Compton	Shaw	Roper	..	..	..	..
24 Mar	Wolverhampton W	H	W 2-1	..	..	..	..	..	Bowen	..	..	Holton[2]	Forbes	..
26 Mar	Portsmouth	A	D 1-1	Swindin	..	..	Shaw	Daniel	..	..	..[1]	..	..	..[1]
31 Mar	Sunderland	A	W 2-0	..	..	..	Mercer	Compton	..	..	..	..[1]	Lewis	..[1]
7 Apr	Liverpool	H	L 1-2	..	..	..	..	..	..	..	..	..[1]	..	..
14 Apr	Fulham	A	L 2-3	..	..	Barnes	Forbes	..	..	..	..	..[1]	..[1]	..
21 Apr	Bolton W	H	D 1-1	..	..	..	Mercer	..	..	McPherson	Roper	..	Lishman[1]	..
2 May	Blackpool	A	W 1-0	..	..	..	Forbes	Daniel	..	Roper[1]	Lewis	..	..	..

FA Cup

6 Jan	Carlisle U (3)	H	D 0-0	Platt	Barnes	Smith	Forbes	Daniel	Mercer	Cox	Logie	Goring	Lewis	Roper
11 Jan	Carlisle U (3R)	A	W 4-1	..	..	..	Shaw	Compton	Forbes	McPherson	..[1]	..[1]	..[2]	..[1]
27 Jan	Northampton (4)	H	W 3-2	..	..	..	Forbes	..	Mercer	..	..	..[1]	..[2]	..[1]
10 Feb	Manchester U (5)	A	L 0-1	..	..	..	..	..	..	..	..	..	..	..

Appearances (Goals)

Barnes W 35 (3) · Bowen D 7 · Compton L 36 · Cox F 13 (2) · Daniel R 5 · Fields A 1 · Forbes A 32 (4) · Goring P 34 (15) · Holton C 10 (5) · Kelsey J 4 · Lewis R 14 (8) · Lishman B 26 (17) · Logie J 39 (9) · McPherson 26 · Marden B 11 (2) · Mercer J 31 · Milton A 1 · Platt E 17 · Roper D 34 (7) · Scott L 17 · Shaw A 16 · Smith L 32 · Swindin G 21 · Own goals 1 · Total: 23 players (73)

Position in League Table

	P	W	L	D	F:A	Pts	
Tottenham H	42	25	7	10	82:44	60	1st
Arsenal	42	19	14	9	73:56	47	5th

SEASON 1951-1952 FOOTBALL LEAGUE (DIVISION 1)

18 Aug	Huddersfield T	H	D 2-2	Swindin	Scott	Barnes	Forbes	Daniel	Bowen	Roper	Logie	Holton[1]	Lishman	Marden[1]
22 Aug	Chelsea	A	W 3-1	..	..	..	..	..	Mercer	..[1]	..	..[1]	..	..[1]
25 Aug	Wolverhampton W	A	L 1-2	..	..	..	..	..	..	..	..	..[1]	..	..
29 Aug	Chelsea	H	W 2-1	..	..	..	..	..	..	..	..	..[1]	..[1]	..
1 Sep	Sunderland	H	W 3-0	..	Barnes	Smith	..	..	..	..	..	..	..[3]	Cox
5 Sep	Liverpool	H	D 0-0	..	..	..	..	..	..	..	..	..	..	..
8 Sep	Aston Villa	A	L 0-1	..	..	..	..	..	Bowen	..	..	..	..	..
12 Sep	Liverpool	A	D 0-0	..	..	..	..	..	Mercer	Milton	..	..	..	..
15 Sep	Derby Co	H	W 3-1	..	..	..	..	..	..	..	..[2]	..	..[1]	..
22 Sep	Manchester C	A	W 2-0	..	..	..	..	..	..	..	..[1]	..	..[1]	..
29 Sep	Tottenham H	H	D 1-1	..	..	..	..	..	..	..	..[1]	..	..	..
6 Oct	Preston NE	A	L 0-2	..	..	..	..	..	..	..	..	..	..	..
13 Oct	Burnley	H	W 1-0	..	..	..	..	..	..	Logie	Lewis[1]	..	..	Roper
20 Oct	Charlton Ath	A	W 3-1	..	Chenhall	Wade	..	Compton	..	Milton[1]	Logie	..[2]	..	..
27 Oct	Fulham	H	W 4-3	..	Barnes	Smith	..	Daniel	..	..[1]	..	..[1]	..[1]	..
3 Nov	Middlesbrough	A	W 3-0	..	..	..	..	..	..	..	..	..[1]	..	..
10 Nov	W B A	H	W 6-3	..	..	Wade	..	..	..	..	..	..	..[1]	..
17 Nov	Newcastle U	A	L 0-2	..	..	..	..	..	..	..	..	..	..[3]	..
24 Nov	Bolton W	H	W 4-2	..	Chenhall	Barnes	..	..	..	..	..	..	..	..[1]
1 Dec	Stoke C	A	L 1-2	..	..	..	..	..	..	..	..	..	Lewis[1]	..
8 Dec	Manchester U	H	L 1-3	..	Barnes	Smith	..	..	..	..	..[1]	..	Lishman	..
15 Dec	Huddersfield T	A	W 3-2	..	..	..	..	..	Bowen	..	Lewis[1]	Goring	..	..[2]
22 Dec	Wolverhampton W	H	D 2-2	..	..	..	..	..	..	..	..[2]	..	..	..
25 Dec	Portsmouth	H	W 4-1	..	..	..	..	..	Mercer	Cox[1]	Logie[1]	Lewis[1]	Goring[1]	Marden
26 Dec	Portsmouth	A	D 1-1	..	..	Wade	Shaw	..	Bowen	..[1]	Lewis	Goring	Lishman	..
29 Dec	Sunderland	A	L 1-4	..	..	Smith	Forbes	Compton	Mercer	..	Logie	..[1]	..	..
5 Jan	Aston Villa	H	W 2-1	..	..	..	..	Daniel	..	..	..[1]	..	..	Roper[2]
19 Jan	Derby Co	A	W 2-1	..	..	..	..	..	..	..	..	..	..	..[1]
26 Jan	Manchester C	H	D 2-2	..	..	..	..[1]	..	..	..	..	..	..[2]	..[1]
9 Feb	Tottenham H	A	W 2-1	..	..	..	..	..	..	..	Lewis	..	..	..[1]
16 Feb	Preston NE	H	D 3-3	..	..	..	..	..	..	..	..[2]	..	..	..[1]
1 Mar	Burnley	A	W 1-0	..	..	..	Shaw	..	..	Milton[1]	..	Goring	..	Cox
13 Mar	Charlton	H	W 2-1	..	..	..	..	..	..	Cox	Goring[2]	Holton	..	Roper
15 Mar	Fulham	A	D 0-0	..	..	..	..	..	..	Milton	..	..[1]	..	Cox
22 Mar	Middlesbrough	H	W 3-1	..	..	..	Forbes	..	..	..[1]	Logie	..[1]	..[1]	Roper
11 Apr	Blackpool	A	D 0-0	..	..	..	..[1]	..	..	Cox	..	Goring	..	Roper
12 Apr	Bolton	A	L 1-2	..	..	..	..[1]	Compton	..	..	..	..	Shaw	..
14 Apr	Blackpool	H	W 4-1	..	..[1]	Wade	..	Shaw	opponents	..	..	Holton	Lishman[2]	..
16 Apr	Newcastle U	H	D 1-1	..	..	..	..	Mercer	Bowen	Milton[1]	..	Goring	..	..
19 Apr	Stoke C	H	W 4-1	..	..[1]	..	Mercer	Compton	Cox	Forbes	..	Holton[2]	..[1]	..
21 Apr	W B A	A	L 1-3	..	..	..	Forbes	..	Shaw	..	Milton	Goring	..[1]	Robertson
26 Apr	Manchester U	A	L 1-6	..	..	Smith	..	..	Mercer	Cox[1]	..	..	Lewis	Roper

FA Cup

12 Jan	Norwich C (3)	A	W 5-0	Swindin	Barnes	Smith	Forbes	Daniel	Mercer	Cox	Logie[1]	Goring[1]	Lishman[2]	Roper[1]
2 Feb	Barnsley (4)	H	W 4-0	..	..	..	..	..	..	..	..	Lewis[3]	..[2]	..
23 Feb	Leyton Orient (5)	A	W 3-0	..	..	..	Shaw	..	..	..	..	..[1]	..[2]	..
8 Mar	Luton T (6)	A	W 3-2	..	..	..	..	..	..	..[2]	Milton[1]	Goring	..	..
5 Apr	Chelsea (SF) (at Tottenham)		D 1-1	..	..	..	Forbes	..	..	..[1]	Logie	Lewis	..	..
7 Apr	Chelsea (SFR) (at Tottenham)		W 3-0	..	..	..	..	..	..	..[2]	..	Goring	..[1]	..
3 May	Newcastle (F) (at We...)		L 0-1	..	..	..	..	..	..	..	..	Holton	..	..

Appearances (Goals)

Barnes W 41 (2) · Bowen D 8 · Chenhall J 3 · Compton L 4 · Cox F 25 (3) · Daniel R 34 · Forbes A 38 (3) · Goring P 16 (4) · Holton C 28 (17) · Lewis R 9 (8) · Lishman D 38 (23) · Logie J 34 (4) · Marden R 7 (2) · Mercer J 36 · Milton A 20 (5) · Robertson J 1 · Roper D 30 (9) · Scott L 4 · Shaw A 8 · Smith L 28 · Swindin G 42 · Wade J 8 · Own goals 1 · Total: 22 players (80)

Position in League Table

	P	W	L	D	F:A	Pts	
Manchester U	42	23	8	11	95:52	57	1st
Arsenal	42	21	10	11	80:61	53	3rd

SEASON 1952-1953 FOOTBALL LEAGUE (DIVISION 1)

23 Aug	Aston Villa	A W 2-1	Swindin	Wade	Smith	Shaw	Daniel	Mercer	Forbes	Oakes[1]	Goring	Lishman[1]	Roper
27 Aug	Manchester U	H W 2-1	..						Cox[1]		[1]		' [1]
30 Aug	Sunderland	H L 1-2		Chenhall	Wade					Goring	Holton	[1]
3 Sep	Manchester U	A D 0-0						Bowen				
6 Sep	Wolverhampton W	A D 1-1		Wade	Smith			Mercer					[1]
10 Sep	Portsmouth	H W 3-1				Forbes			Milton[1]	Logie	Goring[1]	Shaw	[1]
13 Sep	Charlton Ath	H L 3-4					[1]					
17 Sep	Portsmouth	A D 2-2	Platt	Chenhall		Shaw		Bowen	Forbes	Holton[2]	Goring
20 Sep	Tottenham H	A W 3-1						Forbes	Logie[1]	Goring[1]	Lishman
27 Sep	Derby Co	A L 0-2			Wade						
4 Oct	Blackpool	H W 3-1	Kelsey						[1]		[2]
11 Oct	Sheffield W	H D 2-2							[1]		[1]
25 Oct	Newcastle U	H W 3-0		Wade	Smith	Forbes		Mercer			[1]	[2]
1 Nov	W B A	A L 0-2							[1]	
8 Nov	Middlesbrough	H W 2-1				Shaw		Forbes		Holton[1]
15 Nov	Liverpool	A W 5-1		Chenhall	Wade	Forbes		Mercer		[3]		Marden[2]
22 Nov	Manchester C	H W 3-1		Wade	Smith				[2]		[1]	Roper
29 Nov	Stoke C	A D 1-1		Chenhall	Wade				[1]
13 Dec	Burnley	A D 1-1		Wade	Smith				[1]
20 Dec	Aston Villa	H W 3-1				Shaw			[1]		[1]	[1]
25 Dec	Bolton W	A W 6-4					[1]		[1]		[2]		[1]
3 Jan	Sunderland	A L 1-3				Forbes			[1]
17 Jan	Wolverhampton W	H W 5-3					[1]	Shaw	[1]		[2]
24 Jan	Charlton Ath	A D 2-2						Mercer			[1]	[1]
7 Feb	Tottenham H	H W 4-0					[2]	Shaw		[1]	[1]
18 Feb	Derby Co	H W 6-2						Shaw	Goring	[2]	[2]
21 Feb	Blackpool	A L 2-3			Chenhall			Mercer[1]		[1]
2 Mar	Sheffield W	A W 4-1				Shaw			Cox		[4]
7 Mar	Cardiff	H L 0-1			Smith					Logie
14 Mar	Newcastle U	A D 2-2							Milton		Goring	[2]
19 Mar	Preston NE	H D 1-1				Forbes		[1]
21 Mar	W B A	H D 2-2				Shaw		Forbes	Cox		Holton[1]		[1]
28 Mar	Middlesbrough	A L 0-2				Forbes		Mercer		Goring
3 Apr	Chelsea	A D 1-1				Shaw		Forbes		Logie	Goring[1]		[2]
4 Apr	Liverpool	H W 5-3					opponents		Milton		[1]	[2]
6 Apr	Chelsea	H W 2-0	Swindin			Forbes		Mercer	Roper		[1]	Marden[1]
11 Apr	Manchester C	A W 4-2								[2]
15 Apr	Bolton W	H W 4-1			Chenhall		Dodgin			[1]	[2]	[1]
18 Apr	Stoke C	H W 3-1					Daniel				[3]	'
22 Apr	Cardiff	A D 0-0			Smith			Shaw		
25 Apr	Preston NE	A L 0-2							
1 May	Burnley	H W 3-2				[1]		Mercer		[1]		[1]

FA Cup

10 Jan	Doncaster Rov (3)	H W 4-0	Kelsey	Wade	Smith	Shaw	Daniel	Forbes	Milton	Logie[1]	Holton[1]	Lishman[1]	Roper[1]
31 Jan	Bury (4)	H W 6-2				Forbes	opponents	Mercer	[1]		[1]	[1]	[1]
14 Feb	Burnley (5)	A W 2-0							[1]		[1]	[1]
28 Feb	Blackpool (6)	H L 1-2							[1]			

Appearances (Goals)

Bowen D 2 · Chenhall J 13 · Cox F 9 (1) · Daniel R 41 (5) · Dodgin W 1 · Forbes A 33 (1) · Goring P 29 (10) · Holton C 21 (19) · Kelsey J 25 · Lishman D 39 (22) · Logie J 32 (10) · Marden R 8 (4) · Mercer J 28 (2) · Milton A 25 (7) · Oakes D 2 (1) · Platt E 3 · Roper D 41 (14) · Shaw A 25 · Smith L 31 · Swindin G 14 · Wade J 40 · Own goals 1 · Total: 21 players (97)

Position in League Table

	P	W	L	D	F:A	Pts
Arsenal	42	21	9	12	97:64	54 1st

SEASON 1953-1954 FOOTBALL LEAGUE (DIVISION 1)

19 Aug	W B A	A L 0-2	Kelsey	Wade	Smith	Forbes	Dodgin	Mercer	Roper	Logie	Holton	Lishman	Marden
22 Aug	Huddersfield T	H D 0-0			Evans								Ward
24 Aug	Sheffield U	A L 0-1						Bowen			Goring
29 Aug	Aston Villa	A L 1-2						Mercer					Marden
1 Sep	Sheffield U	H D 1-1				Bowen		Forbes	opponents		Holton
5 Sep	Wolverhampton W	H L 2-3				Forbes		Bowen		[1]		[1]
8 Sep	Chelsea	H L 1-2	Swindin	Barnes	Smith			Milton		[1]	Tilley	Roper
12 Sep	Sunderland	A L 1-7			Evans			Mercer			Lishman[1]
15 Sep	Chelsea	A W 2-0	Kelsey	Wade	Barnes	Shaw		Bowen	Forbes		[2]
19 Sep	Manchester C	H D 2-2								Lawton	[2]
26 Sep	Cardiff	A W 3-0				Forbes	opponents	Mercer	Walsh	Holton	[2]
3 Oct	Preston NE	H W 3-2			[1]				Milton	[1]		[2]
10 Oct	Tottenham H	A W 4-1		Wills	Evans	[1]			[1]	[2]	Lawton	[1]
17 Oct	Burnley	H L 2-5			Barnes	[1]						[1]
24 Oct	Charlton Ath	A W 5-1				Dickson			Roper[1]		Holton[1]	Marden[3]
31 Oct	Sheffield W	H W 4-1								[2]	[2]
7 Nov	Manchester U	A D 2-2						Forbes	[1]	[3]
14 Nov	Bolton W	H W 4-3							[1]		[1]
21 Nov	Liverpool	A W 2-1							Milton	[1]		[1]	Roper
28 Nov	Newcastle U	H W 2-1							[1]	[1]
5 Dec	Middlesbrough	A L 0-2			Smith					
12 Dec	W B A	H D 2-2						Mercer	Roper		[2]	Marden
19 Dec	Huddersfield T	A D 2-2							Milton[1]	[1]	Roper
26 Dec	Blackpool	A D 2-2									[1]
28 Dec	Blackpool	H D 1-1			Barnes				[1]
16 Jan	Wolverhampton W	A W 2-0			Wade			Forbes	[1]
23 Jan	Sunderland	H L 1-4							Lawton	[1]
6 Feb	Manchester C	A D 0-0			Barnes	Forbes		Mercer	Walsh	Logie	Lawton
13 Feb	Cardiff	H D 1-1							[1]
24 Feb	Preston NE	A W 1-0						Dickson		Goring	Holton	[1]
27 Feb	Tottenham H	H L 0-3						Mercer		Logie
6 Mar	Burnley	A L 1-2			Evans			Bowen		[1]		Marden
13 Mar	Charlton Ath	H D 3-3						Dickson[1]		[1]		Milton
20 Mar	Sheffield W	A L 1-2							[1]
27 Mar	Manchester U	H W 3-1			Smith	Dickson		Forbes	[2]	Goring	Roper
3 Apr	Bolton W	A L 1-3			Barnes						Lishman
6 Apr	Aston Villa	H D 1-1			Wade			Mercer	Milton	Lawton[1]	[1]
10 Apr	Liverpool	H W 3-0				Bowen	Dickson			Tapscott[2]	Lawton	[1]
16 Apr	Portsmouth	H W 3-0				Goring		Bowen	[2]	[1]
17 Apr	Newcastle U	A L 2-5	Sullivan						[1]	Holton[1]
19 Apr	Portsmouth	A D 1-1	Kelsey				Dodgin	Dickson			[1]
24 Apr	Middlesbrough	H W 3-1								Logie	Tapscott[1]	[1]	[1]

FA Cup

9 Jan	Aston Villa (3)	H W 5-1	Kelsey	Wills	Wade	Dickson	Dodgin	Forbes	Milton[1]	Logie[1]	Holton[1]	Lishman	Roper[2]
30 Jan	Norwich (4)	H L 1-2			Smith					[1]		

FA Charity Shield

12 Oct	Blackpool	H W 3-1	Kelsey	Wills	Barnes	Forbes	Dodgin	Mercer	Holton	Logie	Lawton[1]	Lishman[2]	Roper

Appearances (Goals)

Barnes W 19 (1) · Bowen D 10 · Dickson W 24 (1) · Dodgin W 39 · Evans D 10 · Forbes A 30 (4) · Goring P 9 · Holton C 32 (17) · Kelsey J 39 · Lawton T 9 (1) · Lishman D 39 (18) · Logie J 35 (8) · Marden R 9 (3) · Mercer J 19 · Milton A 21 (3) · Roper D 39 (12) · Shaw A 2 · Smith L 7 · Sullivan C 1 · Swindin G 2 · Tapscott D 5 (5) · Tilley P 1 · Wade J 18 · Walsh B 10 · Ward G 3 · Wills L 30 · Own goals 2 · Total: 26 players (75)

Position in League Table

	P	W	L	D	F:A	Pts
Wolverhampton W	42	25	10	7	96:56	57 1st
Arsenal	42	15	14	13	75:73	43 12th

SEASON 1954-1955   FOOTBALL LEAGUE (DIVISION 1)

Date	Opponent		Result	1	2	3	4	5	6	7	8	9	10	11
21 Aug	Newcastle U	H	L 1-3	Kelsey	Wills	Wade	Forbes	Dickson	Shaw	Walsh	Logie	Holton	Lishman[1]	Roper
25 Aug	Everton	A	L 0-1	..	..	Evans	..	..	Goring	Bloomfield	..	..	Tapscott	Haverty
28 Aug	W B A	A	L 1-3	..	..	Barnes	Goring	Forbes	Bowen	Walsh	Tapscott	Lawton	Lishman[1]	..
31 Aug	Everton	H	W 2-0	..	..	..	..	..	..	Tapscott	Logie	..	..[1]	Roper[1]
4 Sep	Tottenham H	H	W 2-0	..	..	..	..	..	..	..	..	..	..[1]	..[1]
8 Sep	Manchester C	A	L 1-2	Guthrie	..	..	..	..	..	..	..	..	..[1]	..
11 Sep	Sheffield U	H	W 4-0	Kelsey	..	..	..	..[1]	..	..[1]	..	..	..[1]	..[1]
14 Sep	Manchester C	H	L 2-3	..	..	..	..	..	..	..[1]	..	Holton	..[1]	..
18 Sep	Preston NE	A	L 1-3	..	..	..	..	..	..	..	..[1]	Lawton	..	..
25 Sep	Burnley	H	W 4-0	..	Barnes	Wade	Forbes	Dickson	Goring	..	..[2]	..[2]	..[1]	..[1]
2 Oct	Leicester C	A	D 3-3	..	..	..	Goring	Forbes	Bowen	..	..[2]	..[2]	..	..
9 Oct	Sheffield W	A	W 2-1	..	..	..	..	Dickson	Forbes	Walsh	Tapscott	..	Bloomfield[1]	..[1]
16 Oct	Portsmouth	H	L 0-1	Guthrie	Wills	..	..	Dodgin	..	..	Logie	Holton	..	..[1]
23 Oct	Aston Villa	A	L 1-2	Kelsey	Barnes	..	..	..	..	..	..	Lawton	..	..[1]
30 Oct	Sunderland	H	L 1-3	..	..	..	..	..	..	Milton	Tapscott	Holton	..	..[1]
6 Nov	Bolton W	A	D 2-2	..	..	..	..	..[1]	Fotheringham	..	..[2]	Bloomfield	Lawton	Lishman[1]
13 Nov	Huddersfield T	H	L 3-5	..	..	..	..	..	..	..	Tapscott	Roper	..[1]	Marden
20 Nov	Manchester U	A	L 1-2	..	Wills	..	..	..	Bowen	..	Logie	Tapscott[1]	..	Roper
27 Nov	Wolverhampton W	H	D 1-1	..	..	..	..	..	Forbes	..	Tapscott	Roper[1]	..[1]	Marden
4 Dec	Blackpool	A	D 2-2	..	..	..	..	..	Bowen	..	..[1]	..[1]	..	..
11 Dec	Charlton Ath	H	W 3-1	..	..	..	..	..	..	..	..[2]	..	..	..
18 Dec	Newcastle U	A	L 1-5	..	..[1]	..	..	..	..	Walsh	..	..	..	..
25 Dec	Chelsea	H	W 1-0	..	Barnes	Evans	..	..	..	Clapton	..	Lawton[1]	..	Haverty
27 Dec	Chelsea	A	D 1-1	..	..	..	..	..	..	..	..[1]	..	..	..
1 Jan	W B A	H	D 2-2	..	..	..	..	..	..	..	..	..[1]	..[1]	..
15 Jan	Tottenham H	A	W 1-0	..	..	..	..	..	..	Milton	..	..[1]	..	Holton
5 Feb	Preston NE	H	W 2-0	..	..	..	..	..	..	Roper[1]	..[1]	..	..	..
12 Feb	Burnley	A	L 0-3	..	..	..	..	..	..	..	..	..	..	..
19 Feb	Leicester C	H	D 1-1	..	..	..	..	..	..	Tapscott	Herd	Wilkinson	..	Roper[1]
26 Feb	Sheffield W	H	W 3-2	..	..	..	..	..	..	Clapton	Tapscott[3]	Roper	Bloomfield	Haverty
5 Mar	Charlton Ath	A	D 1-1	..	..	..	..	..	Forbes	..	..	..[1]	..	Marden
12 Mar	Aston Villa	H	W 2-0	..	..	..	..	..	Bowen	..	..	..[1]	..	..[1]
19 Mar	Sunderland	A	W 1-0	..	..	..	..	..	Forbes	..	..	Lawton	Lishman	Bloomfield[1]
26 Mar	Bolton W	H	W 3-0	Sullivan	Wills	..	..	..	Oakes	..	..	Roper[1]	..[2]	..
2 Apr	Huddersfield T	A	W 1-0	Kelsey	..	..	..	..	..	..	..	..[1]	..	..
8 Apr	Cardiff	H	W 2-0	..	..	..	..	..	..	..	..[2]	..	Bloomfield	Swallow
9 Apr	Blackpool	H	W 3-0	..	..	..	..	..	..	..	..	..[1]	Lishman[2]	Bloomfield
11 Apr	Cardiff	A	W 2-1	..	..	..	..	..	..	..	..	..	..[1]	..[1]
16 Apr	Wolverhampton W	A	L 1-3	..	..	..	..	..	..	..	..	..	..[1]	..
18 Apr	Sheffield U	A	D 1-1	Sullivan	..	..	..	..	..	..	Herd	..[1]	..	..
23 Apr	Manchester U	H	L 2-3	Kelsey	..	..	..	..	..	..	Tapscott	..	..[2]	..
30 Apr	Portsmouth	A	L 1-2	..	..	..	..	..	..	..	Herd[1]	..	Tapscott	..

FA Cup

Date	Opponent		Result	1	2	3	4	5	6	7	8	9	10	11
8 Jan	Cardiff (3)	H	W 1-0	Kelsey	Barnes	Evans	Goring	Fotheringham	Bowen	Milton	Tapscott	Lawton[1]	Lishman	Haverty
29 Jan	Wolves (4)	A	L 0-1	..	..	..	..	..	..	..	..	..	..	Holton

Appearances (Goals)

Barnes W 25 · Bloomfield J 19 (4) · Bowen D 21 · Clapton Danny 16 · Dickson W 4 · Dodgin W 3 · Evans D 21 · Forbes A 20 (1) · Fotheringham J 27 · Goring P 41 (1) · Guthrie R 2 · Haverty J 6 · Herd D 3 (1) · Holton C 8 · Kelsey J 38 · Lawton T 18 (6) · Lishman D 32 (19) · Logie J 13 (3) · Marden R 7 · Milton A 8 (3) · Oakes D 9 · Roper D 35 (17) · Shaw A 1 · Sullivan C 2 · Swallow R 1 · Tapscott D 37 (13) · Wade J 14 · Walsh J 6 · Wilkinson J 1 · Wills L 24 (1) · Total: players 30 (69)

Position in League Table

	P	W	L	D	F:A	Pts	
Chelsea	42	20	10	12	81:57	52	1st
Arsenal	42	17	16	9	69:63	43	9th

SEASON 1955-1956   FOOTBALL LEAGUE (DIVISION 1)

Date	Opponent		Result	1	2	3	4	5	6	7	8	9	10	11
20 Aug	Blackpool	A	L 1-3	Kelsey	Barnes	Evans	Goring	Dickson	Bowen	Clapton	Tapscott[1]	Holton	Lishman	Bloomfield
23 Aug	Cardiff C	H	W 3-1	..	..	..	..	Fotheringham	..	..	..	Lawton[3]	..	..
27 Aug	Chelsea	H	D 1-1	..	..	..	..	..	..	..	..[1]	..	..	Roper
31 Aug	Manchester C	A	D 2-2	..	..	..	..	..	..	..	..	..	..	..[1]
3 Sep	Bolton W	A	L 1-4	..	..	..	..	..	..	..	Herd	..[1]	..	Tapscott
6 Sep	Manchester C	H	D 0-0	..	..	..	..	..	..	..	Tapscott	..	Roper	Bloomfield
10 Sep	Tottenham H	A	L 1-3	..	..	..	..	..	..	..	..	..	..	Walsh
17 Sep	Portsmouth	H	L 1-3	..	..	..	..	..	..	..	..	..	Lishman[1]	Roper
24 Sep	Sunderland	A	L 1-3	..	Wills	..	..	..	..	Tiddy	Roper	..	..	Nutt
1 Oct	Aston Villa	H	W 1-0	..	..	..	..	Holton	..	..	Bloomfield	Roper	..	..[1]
8 Oct	Everton	A	D 1-1	..	..	..	..	Fotheringham	Holton	..	..	..	..[1]	..
15 Oct	Newcastle U	H	W 1-0	..	..	..	..	..	..	..	..	..[1]	..	Clapton
22 Oct	Luton T	A	D 0-0	Sullivan	..	..	..	..	..	Clapton	..	..	..	Tiddy
29 Oct	Charlton Ath	H	L 2-4	Kelsey	..	..	..	..	..	..[1]	..	..	..[1]	..
5 Nov	Manchester U	A	D 1-1	..	..	..	..	..	..	..	Tapscott	..	..[1]	..
12 Nov	Sheffield U	H	W 2-1	..	..	..	..	..	..	..[1]	Roper[1]	Groves[1]	..	..
19 Nov	Preston NE	A	W 1-0	..	..	..	..	..	..	..	Tapscott	..	Roper	..
26 Nov	Burnley	H	L 0-1	..	..	..	..	..	..	..	..	Roper	Lishman	..
3 Dec	Birmingham C	A	L 0-4	..	..	..	..	..	..	..	..	..	Bloomfield	..
10 Dec	W B A	H	W 2-0	Sullivan	..	..	..	..	..	opponents	..[1]	Groves	..	..
17 Dec	Blackpool	H	W 4-1	..	Charlton	..	..	..	..	..[1]	..	..	..[1]	..[1]
24 Dec	Chelsea	A	L 0-2	..	Charlton	..	..	..	..	..	..	..	..	..
26 Dec	Wolverhampton W	A	D 3-3	..	..	..	..	..	..	..	..[2]	..	..	..
27 Dec	Wolverhampton W	H	D 2-2	..	..	..	..	..	..	..	..[2]	..	..	..
31 Dec	Bolton W	H	W 3-1	..	..	..	..	..	..	..	..[2]	..[1]	..	..
14 Jan	Tottenham H	H	L 0-1	Kelsey	Wills	..	Forbes	..	..	..	..	..	..	Nutt
21 Jan	Portsmouth	A	L 2-5	Sullivan	..	..	..	..	..	..	..[2]	..	..	Tiddy
4 Feb	Sunderland	H	W 3-1	Kelsey	Charlton	..	Goring	Dodgin	Bowen	..	Herd[2]	..[1]	..	..
11 Feb	Aston Villa	A	D 1-1	..	..	..	..	..	..	..	Tapscott[2]	..[1]	..	..
21 Feb	Everton	H	W 3-2	Sullivan	..	..	..	..	..	..	Tapscott[2]	..[1]	..	..
25 Feb	Newcastle U	A	L 0-2	..	..	..	..	Holton	..	..	Herd	..	..	Nutt
6 Mar	Preston NE	H	W 3-2	Kelsey	..	..	..	..	..	..	Tapscott[2]	..	..	..
10 Mar	Charlton Ath	A	L 0-2	..	..	..	..	..	..	..	Herd	Tapscott	..	..
17 Mar	Manchester U	H	D 1-1	..	..	..	..	Goring	..	..	Tapscott	Holton[1]	..	Haverty
24 Mar	Sheffield U	A	W 2-0	..	..	..	..	..	..	..	..[1]	..[2]	..	..[1]
31 Mar	Luton T	H	W 3-0	..	..	..	..	..	..	..	..[2]	..[1]	..	..[1]
2 Apr	Huddersfield T	H	W 2-0	..	..	..	..	..	..	..[1]	..	..	..	..
3 Apr	Huddersfield T	A	W 1-0	..	..	..	..	..	..	..	..	..	..	..
7 Apr	Burnley	A	W 1-0	..	..	..	..	..	..	..	Bloomfield	..	Swallow[1]	..
14 Apr	Birmingham C	H	W 1-0	..	..	..	..	..	Forbes	..	Tapscott[1]	..	Bloomfield	..
21 Apr	W B A	A	L 1-2	..	..	..	..	..	..	..	..[1]	..	..	..
28 Apr	Cardiff C	A	W 2-1	..	..	..	..	..	..	..	..[1]	..[1]	..	Nutt

FA Cup

Date	Opponent		Result	1	2	3	4	5	6	7	8	9	10	11
7 Jan	Bedford Town (3)	H	D 2-2	Sullivan	Charlton	Evans	Goring	Fotheringham	Holton	Clapton	Tapscott[1]	Groves[1]	Bloomfield	Tiddy
12 Jan	Bedford Town (3R)	A	W 2-1	Kelsey	..	..[1]	..	..	..	Groves[1]	..[1]	Roper	..	..
28 Jan	Aston Villa (4)	H	W 4-1	..	..	..	..	Dodgin	..	Clapton	..[2]	Groves[1]	..	..
18 Feb	Charlton Ath (5)	A	W 2-0	..	..	..	..	..	Bowen	..	..	..[1]	..	..
3 Mar	Birmingham C (6)	H	L 1-3	..	..	..[1]	..	..	..	..	..	..	..	Nutt

Appearances (Goals)

Barnes W 8 · Bloomfield J 32 (3) · Bowen D 22 · Charlton S 19 · Clapton Danny 39 (2) · Dickson W 1 · Dodgin W 15 · Evans D 42 · Forbes A 5 · Fotheringham J 25 · Goring P 37 · Groves V 15 (8) · Haverty J 8 (2) · Herd D 5 (1) · Holton C 31 (8) · Kelsey J 32 · Lawton T 8 (6) · Lishman D 15 (5) · Nutt G 8 (1) · Roper D 16 (4) · Sullivan C 10 · Swallow R 1 (1) · Tapscott D 31 (17) · Tiddy M 21 · Walsh B 1 · Wills L 15 · Own goals 1 · Total: 26 players (60)

Position in League Table

	P	W	L	D	F:A	Pts	
Manchester U	42	25	7	10	83:51	60	1st
Arsenal	42	18	14	10	60:61	46	5th

SEASON 1956-1957 FOOTBALL LEAGUE (DIVISION 1)

Date	Opponent	Ven	Res	Kelsey	Charlton	Evans	Goring	Dodgin	Bowen	Clapton	Tapscott	Holton	Bloomfield	Tiddy
18 Aug	Cardiff C	H	D 0-0	Kelsey	Charlton	Evans	Goring	Dodgin	Bowen	Clapton	Tapscott	Holton	Bloomfield	Tiddy
21 Aug	Burnley	H	W 2-0	..	..	..	Wills	..	Goring	..	..	..	..[1]	..[1]
25 Aug	Birmingham C	A	L 2-4	..	..	..	..	..	Holton[1]	..	..	Roper[1]	..	..[1]
28 Aug	Burnley	A	L 1-3	..	..	..	..	..	..	..	..	..	..	..[1]
1 Sep	W B A	H	W 4-1	..	..	..	..	..	..	..	..[1]	..[2]	..[1]	..[1]
4 Sep	Preston NE	H	L 1-2	..	..	..	..	..	..	..	..	..	..	..[1]
8 Sep	Portsmouth	A	W 3-2	..	..	..	..	..	Goring	..	Bloomfield[1]	Holton[1]	Swallow	..[1]
10 Sep	Preston NE	A	L 0-3	..	..	..	..	..	..	..	..	Tapscott	..	..
15 Sep	Newcastle U	H	L 0-1	..	..	..	..	..	..	..	..	Tapscott	..	..
22 Sep	Sheffield W	A	W 4-2	..	..	..	..	Holton	..	..	Tapscott[1]	Groves	Bloomfield[2]	..[1]
29 Sep	Manchester U	H	L 1-2	..	..	..[1]	Goring	Dodgin	Bowen	..	..	..	..	..
6 Oct	Manchester C	H	W 7-3	..	..	..[1]	..	..	..	..[1]	..[2]	Holton[4]	..[1]	Haverty[1]
13 Oct	Charlton Ath	A	W 3-1	..	..	..	..	..	..	..	..	..	..	..[1]
20 Oct	Tottenham H	H	W 3-1	Sullivan	..	..	Wills	..	Holton	..	..	Herd[2]	..	..
27 Oct	Everton	A	L 0-4	Kelsey	..	..	..	..	..	..	..	..	..	..
3 Nov	Aston Villa	H	W 2-1	..	..	..	..	..	Bowen	Groves[2]	..	Holton	..	..
10 Nov	Wolverhampton W	A	L 2-5	..	..	..	..	..	..	Clapton	..[1]	..[2]	..	..[1]
17 Nov	Bolton W	H	W 3-0	Sullivan	..	..	..	..	..	..	..[2]	..[1]	..	..
24 Nov	Leeds U	A	D 3-3	..	..	..	Goring	..	..	..	..[1]	..	..[1]	Tiddy
1 Dec	Sunderland	H	D 1-1	..	..	..	..	..	..	..	..[1]	..	..	Haverty
8 Dec	Luton T	A	W 2-1	..	..	..	..	..	..	..	..	Herd	..	..[1]
15 Dec	Cardiff C	A	W 3-2	..	..	..[1]	Holton	..	..	..	..	..[2]	..	..[1]
22 Dec	Birmingham C	H	W 4-0	..	..	..	..[1]	..	..	opponents	..	..	..[1]	..
25 Dec	Chelsea	A	D 1-1	..	..	..	..	..	..	..	..[1]	..	..[1]	..
26 Dec	Chelsea	H	W 2-0	Kelsey	..	..	..	..	..	..	..[1]	..[1]	..	..
29 Dec	W B A	A	W 2-0	..	..	..	..	..	..	..	..[1]	..[1]	..	..[1]
12 Jan	Portsmouth	H	D 1-1	Sullivan	..	..[1]	..	..	..	..	..	..	..	..
19 Jan	Newcastle U	A	L 1-3	..	..	..	..	..	..	..	..[2]	..[3]	..[1]	..
2 Feb	Sheffield W	H	W 6-3	..	..	..	..	..	..	..	..	..[2]	..	..
9 Feb	Manchester U	A	L 2-6	..	..	..	..	..	..	..	Swallow	..	..	..
23 Feb	Everton	H	W 2-0	Kelsey	..	Wills	..[1]	..	..	..	Tapscott[1]	Groves	..	..
9 Mar	Luton T	H	L 1-3	..	..	Evans	..	..	..	..	..[1]	Herd	..	..
13 Mar	Tottenham H	A	W 3-1	..	Wills	..	..	..	..[2]	..	..	..	..	..
16 Mar	Aston Villa	A	D 0-0	..	..	..	..	..	..	..	..	..	..	Nutt
20 Mar	Manchester C	A	W 3-2	..	Charlton	..	..	..	Goring	..	..[1]	..	..[1]	Tiddy[1]
23 Mar	Wolverhampton W	H	D 0-0	..	..	..	..	..	Bowen	..	..	..	..	Haverty
30 Mar	Bolton W	A	L 1-2	..	..	..	..	..	..	..	..[1]	..	..	..
6 Apr	Leeds U	H	W 1-0	..	..	..	..	..	..	..	..[1]	..	..	..
13 Apr	Sunderland	A	L 0-1	..	..	..	..	..	..	..	Barnwell	..	..	..
19 Apr	Blackpool	H	D 1-1	..	..	..	..[1]	..	..	..	Tapscott[1]	..	..	..
20 Apr	Charlton Ath	H	W 3-1	..	..	Wills	..	..	..	Tiddy	..[2]	Groves	..	..[1]
22 Apr	Blackpool	A	W 4-2	..	..	Wills	..	..	..	..	..[2]	Herd[1]	..	..

FA Cup

Date	Opponent	Ven	Res	Kelsey	Charlton	Evans	Holton	Dodgin	Bowen	Clapton	Tapscott	Herd	Bloomfield	Haverty
5 Jan	Stoke C (3)	H	W 4-2	Sullivan	Charlton	Evans	Holton	Dodgin	Bowen	Clapton	Tapscott[1]	Herd[2]	Bloomfield	Haverty[1]
26 Jan	Newport Co (4)	A	W 2-0	..	..	..	..	..	..	..	..[1]	..[1]	..	..
16 Feb	Preston NE (5)	A	D 3-3	..	..	..	..	..	opponents	..	..[1]	..[1]	..	..
19 Feb	Preston NE (5R)	H	W 2-1	Kelsey	..	..	..	..[1]	..	..	..	..[1]	..	..
2 Mar	W B A (6)	A	D 2-2	..	..[1]	Wills	..	..	..	..	..	..[1]	..	Groves
5 Mar	W B A (6R)	H	L 1-2	..	..	..	..	..	..	..	..	..[1]	..	..

Appearances (Goals)

Barnwell J 1 · Bloomfield J 42 (10) · Bowen D 30 (2) · Charlton S 40 · Clapton Danny 39 (2) · Dodgin W 41 · Evans D 40 (4) · Goring P 13 · Groves V 5 (2) · Haverty J 28 (8) · Herd D 22 (12) · Holton C 39 (10) · Kelsey J 30 · Nutt G 1 · Roper D 4 (3) · Sullivan C 12 · Swallow R 4 · Tapscott D 38 (25) · Tiddy M 15 (6) · Wills L 18 · Own goals 1 · Total: 20 players (85)

Position in League Table

	P	W	L	D	F:A	Pts	
Manchester U	42	28	6	8	103:54	64	1st
Arsenal	42	21	13	8	85:69	50	5th

SEASON 1957-1958 FOOTBALL LEAGUE (DIVISION 1)

Date	Opponent	Ven	Res	Kelsey	Charlton	Evans	Holton	Fotheringham	Bowen	Clapton	Herd	Groves	Bloomfield	Haverty
24 Aug	Sunderland	A	W 1-0	Kelsey	Charlton	Evans	Holton	Fotheringham	Bowen	Clapton	Herd	Groves[1]	Bloomfield	Haverty
27 Aug	W B A	H	D 2-2	..	..	..	..	..	..	..	..[2]	..[1]	..	..
31 Aug	Luton T	H	W 2-0	..	..	Wills	..[1]	..	..	..	..	..	..	..
4 Sep	W B A	A	W 2-1	..	..	Evans	..	Dodgin	..	..	Bloomfield[1]	Herd	Swallow[1]	..
7 Sep	Blackpool	A	L 0-1	..	..	..	..	..	..	..	Herd	Groves	Bloomfield	..
10 Sep	Everton	H	L 2-3	..	..	..	..	..	..	..	..[1]	..[2]	..	..
14 Sep	Leicester C	H	W 3-1	..	..	..	..	..	..	..	..[1]	..[2]	..	..
21 Sep	Manchester U	A	L 2-4	Sullivan	..	..	..	..	..	..	..	..	..	Tiddy[1]
28 Sep	Leeds U	H	W 2-1	Kelsey	Wills	..	..	..	..	..	Swallow	Herd[2]	..	..
2 Oct	Aston Villa	H	W 4-0	Kelsey	..	..	..	..	..	..	..[1]	..[1]	..[1]	..[1]
5 Oct	Bolton W	A	W 1-0	..	..	..	..	..	..	..	..	..[1]	..	..
12 Oct	Tottenham H	A	L 1-3	..	Charlton	..	..[1]	..	..	Tapscott	Groves	..	..	..
16 Oct	Everton	A	D 2-2	..	..	..	..	..	..	Nutt	Swallow	..[1]	..	..
19 Oct	Birmingham C	H	L 1-3	Sullivan	..	..	..	..	Goring	..	..	..	..	..
26 Oct	Chelsea	A	D 0-0	Kelsey	..	..	Goring	..	Wills	Clapton	Tapscott	Holton	..	Haverty
2 Nov	Manchester C	H	W 2-1	..	..	..	Holton	..	Bowen	..	Herd	..	..	..
9 Nov	Nottingham F	A	L 0-4	..	..	..	..	..	Goring	..	..	..	..	..
16 Nov	Portsmouth	H	W 3-2	..	..	..	..	..	Bowen	..[1]	Groves[2]	..	..	..
23 Nov	Sheffield W	A	L 0-2	..	..	..	..	..	..	..	Swallow	..	..	..
30 Nov	Newcastle U	H	L 2-3	..	..	..	Wills	..	..	..	Herd	Holton[1]	..	Tiddy
7 Dec	Burnley	A	L 1-2	Standen	..	..	Goring	..	..	Le Roux	..[1]	..	..	Nutt
14 Dec	Preston NE	H	W 4-2	Kelsey	..	..	Holton	..	opponents	..	..[2]	Groves[1]	..[1]	..[1]
21 Dec	Sunderland	H	W 3-0	..	..	..	..	..	..	..	..[2]	..[1]	..	..
26 Dec	Aston Villa	A	L 0-3	..	..	..	..	..	..	..	..	..	..	..
28 Dec	Luton T	A	L 0-1	..	..	..	..	..	Goring	..	..	..	..	..
11 Jan	Blackpool	H	L 2-3	..	Wills	..	Goring	..	Bowen	Clapton	Tapscott	Herd[2]	Groves	..
18 Jan	Leicester C	A	W 1-0	..	Charlton	..	..	Fotheringham	..	..	Groves	..	..[1]	..
1 Feb	Manchester U	H	L 4-5	..	..	..	Ward	..	..	..	Groves	..	Bloomfield[2]	..
8 Feb	Bolton W	H	L 1-2	..	..	..	..	..	Petts	..	..	..	..[1]	..
22 Feb	Tottenham H	H	D 4-4	..	..	..	..	opponents	..	Clapton[1]	Groves	..	..[1]	..
1 Mar	Birmingham C	A	L 1-4	..	..	..	..	..	..	..	..[1]	..[3]	..[1]	..
8 Mar	Chelsea	H	W 5-4	..	..	Wills	..	..	..	..	..[1]	..[3]	..	..
15 Mar	Manchester C	A	W 4-2	..	..	..	..	..	..	..	..	..	..	..
19 Mar	Leeds U	A	L 0-2	..	..	..	..	..	Holton	..	..	..	..	..
22 Mar	Sheffield W	H	W 1-0	..	..	..	..	..	Petts	..	..	..	..	..
29 Mar	Portsmouth	A	L 4-5	..	..	..	Bowen	..	..	..[1]	opponents	..	..[1]	..[1]
7 Apr	Wolverhampton W	H	L 0-2	..	..	..[1]	..	..	Bowen	..	Biggs	..	..	Haverty
8 Apr	Wolverhampton W	A	W 2-1	..	..	..	Goring	..	Bowen	Tiddy	Herd[1]	..	..[1]	Nutt
12 Apr	Newcastle U	A	D 3-3	..	Wills	Evans	..	..	..	..	Biggs	..	..	Haverty
19 Apr	Burnley	H	D 0-0	..	Wills	Evans	..	..	..	..	Herd	..	..	..
21 Apr	Nottingham F	H	D 1-1	..	Charlton	Wills	Ward	..	Petts	..	Biggs	..	..[1]	Haverty
26 Apr	Preston NE	A	L 0-3	..	Wills	Evans	..	..	Bowen	..	Herd	..	..	..

FA Cup

Date	Opponent	Ven	Res	Kelsey	Charlton	Evans	Holton	Dodgin	Bowen	Clapton	Herd	Groves	Bloomfield	Nutt
4 Jan	Northampton (3)	A	L 1-3	Kelsey	Wills	Evans	Holton	Dodgin	Bowen	Clapton[1]	Herd	Groves	Bloomfield	Nutt

Appearances (Goals)

Biggs A 2 · Bloomfield J 40 (16) · Bowen D 30 · Charlton S 36 · Clapton Danny 28 (5) · Dodgin W 23 · Evans D 32 · Fotheringham J 19 · Goring P 10 · Groves V 30 (10) · Haverty J 15 · Herd D 39 (24) · Holton C 26 (4) · Kelsey J 38 · Le Roux D 5 · Nutt G 21 (3) · Petts J 9 · Standen J 1 · Sullivan C 3 · Swallow R 7 (3) · Tapscott D 8 (2) · Tiddy M 12 (2) · Ward G 10 · Wills L 18 (1) · Own goals 3 · Total: 24 players (73)

Position in League Table

	P	W	L	D	F:A	Pts	
Wolverhampton W	42	28	6	8	103:47	64	1st
Arsenal	42	16	19	7	73:85	39	12th

1958-1959

SEASON 1958-1959 FOOTBALL LEAGUE (DIVISION 1)

23 Aug	Preston NE	A	L 1-2	Kelsey	Charlton	Evans	Ward	Dodgin	Bowen	Clapton	Groves	Herd	Bloomfield[1]	Haverty
26 Aug	Burnley	H	W 3-0	..	..	..	..	..	Docherty[1]	..	..	Holton[1]	..[1]	Nutt
30 Aug	Leicester C	H	W 5-1	..	..	..[1]	..	..	..	..[1]	..	..[2]	..	..[1]
2 Sep	Burnley	A	L 1-3	..	..	..	..	..	..	..	..[1]	..	..	..
6 Sep	Everton	A	W 6-1	..	Wills	..	..	..	..	..	..[1]	Herd[4]	..[1]	..
9 Sep	Bolton W	H	W 6-1	..	..	..[1]	..	..	..	..[1]	..	..[1]	..[1]	..[2]
13 Sep	Tottenham H	H	W 3-1	..	..	..	..	..	..	..	..	..[2]	..	..[1]
17 Sep	Bolton W	A	L 1-2	..	..	..	..	..	..	..	..	..	..[1]	..
20 Sep	Manchester C	H	W 4-1	..	..	..[1]	..	..	..	..	..	..[2]	..[1]	..
27 Sep	Leeds U	A	L 1-2	..	..	..	..	..	..	..	..	..[1]	..	..
4 Oct	W B A	H	W 4-3	..	..	..	..	..	*opponents*	..	..	..[1]	..	Henderson[2]
11 Oct	Manchester U	A	D 1-1	..	..	..	..[1]	..	..	..	..	..	..	..
18 Oct	Wolverhampton W	H	D 1-1	Standen	..	..	..	..	Petts	..	..	Biggs[1]	..	Nutt
22 Oct	Aston Villa	A	W 2-1	Kelsey	..	..	..[1]	..	Docherty	..	..	Herd	..	..[1]
25 Oct	Blackburn Rov	A	L 2-4	..	..	..[1]	..[1]	..	..	..	..	..	..	..
1 Nov	Newcastle U	H	W 3-2	..	..	..	..	..	..	..	..[1]	..	..	Henderson[2]
8 Nov	West Ham U	A	D 0-0	..	..	..	..	..	..	..	..	..	..	..
15 Nov	Nottingham F	H	W 3-1	..	..	..	..	..	..	*opponents*	..	..[1]	..	..[1]
22 Nov	Chelsea	A	W 3-0	..	..	..	Docherty	..	Bowen	..[1]	Barnwell[1]	Henderson[1]	..	Haverty
29 Nov	Blackpool	H	L 1-4	..	..	..	..	..	Petts	..[1]	..	Biggs	..	..
6 Dec	Portsmouth	A	W 1-0	..	..	..	Ward	..	Docherty	..	..	Henderson	..	Nutt[1]
13 Dec	Aston Villa	H	L 1-2	..	..	..	Goring	..	..	..	Ward	..[1]	..	..
20 Dec	Preston NE	H	L 1-2	..	..	..	Ward	..	..	..	Groves	Barnwell	..	Henderson[1]
26 Dec	Luton T	A	L 3-6	..	..	..[1]	..	Fotheringham	..	..	..	Julians[1]	..[1]	..
27 Dec	Luton T	H	W 1-0	..	..	McCullough	Docherty	Dodgin	Petts	..	..	..	..[1]	..
3 Jan	Leicester C	A	W 3-2	..	..	..	..	..	Bowen	..	Julians[2]	Herd	..[1]	..
17 Jan	Everton	H	W 3-1	Standen	..	Evans	Ward	Docherty	..	..	Groves[2]	..	..[1]	..
31 Jan	Tottenham	A	W 4-1	Kelsey	..	..	Docherty	Dodgin	..	..	..[1]	..[1]	Julians	..[2]
7 Feb	Manchester C	A	D 0-0	..	..	..	Ward	..	..	..	..	..	Barnwell	..
21 Feb	W B A	A	D 1-1	Standen	..	..	Docherty	..	..	Groves	Julians[1]	..	..	..
24 Feb	Leeds U	H	W 1-0	Goy	..	..	..	..	..	Herd[1]	Goulden	Goring	..	Haverty
28 Feb	Manchester U	H	W 3-2	Standen	..	..	..	..	..	Clapton	Ward	Herd[1]	..[2]	..
7 Mar	Wolverhampton W	A	L 1-6	..	..	..	..	..	..	..	..	..	..	..[1]
14 Mar	Blackburn Rov	H	D 1-1	..	..[1]	McCullough	..	..	..	..	Barnwell	..	Julians	..
21 Mar	Newcastle U	A	L 0-1	..	..	..	..	..	..	..	Groves	..	Barnwell	Nutt
28 Mar	West Ham U	H	L 1-2	..	Evans	..	Ward	..	Docherty	..	..	Henderson[1]	Julians	..
4 Apr	Nottingham F	A	D 1-1	..	..	..	Docherty	..	Bowen	..	..	Herd	Barnwell	Haverty[1]
11 Apr	Chelsea	H	D 1-1	..	..	..	Ward[1]	..	..	Henderson	..	Julians	..	..
14 Apr	Birmingham C	A	L 1-4	..	..	..	..	..	Docherty	Clapton[1]	..	Herd	..	Henderson
18 Apr	Blackpool	A	W 2-1	..	..	..	..	..	..	..	..	Julians[1]	..	Haverty[1]
25 Apr	Portsmouth	H	W 5-2	..	Wills	..	Docherty	..	Bowen	*opponents*	..[3]	..	Bloomfield	Henderson[1]
4 May	Birmingham C	H	W 2-1	Goy	..	Evans	Ward	Docherty	..	..[1]	Barnwell	Groves[1]	..	..
	FA Cup													
10 Jan	Bury (3)	A	W 1-0	Kelsey	Wills	McCullough	Docherty	Dodgin	Bowen	Clapton	Julians	Herd[1]	Bloomfield	Henderson
24 Jan	Colchester U (4)	A	D 2-2	..	..	Evans	Ward	Docherty	..	..	Groves[2]	..	..	..
28 Jan	Colchester U (4R)	H	W 4-0	..	..	..[1]	..	..	..	..	..	..[2]	Julians[1]	..
14 Feb	Sheffield U (5)	H	D 2-2	..	..	..[1]	..	Dodgin	..	..	..	..	..[1]	Haverty
18 Feb	Sheffield U (5R)	A	L 0-3	..	..	..	Docherty	..	..	..	..	..	..	Henderson

Appearances (Goals)

Barnwell J 16 (3) · Biggs A 2 (1) · Bloomfield J 29 (10) · Bowen D 16 · Charlton S 4 · Clapton Danny 39 (6) · Docherty T 38 (1) · Dodgin W 39 · Evans D 37 (5) · Fotheringham J 1 · Goring P 2 · Goulden R 1 · Goy P 2 · Groves V 33 (10) · Haverty J 10 (3) · Henderson J 21 (12) · Herd D 26 (15) · Holton C 3 (3) · Julians L 10 (5) · Kelsey J 27 · McCullough W 10 · Nutt G 16 (6) · Petts J 3 · Standen J 13 · Ward G 31 (4) · Wills L 33 (1) · Own goals 3 · Total: 26 players (88)

Position in League Table

	P	W	L	D	F:A	Pts	
Wolverhampton W	42	28	9	5	110:49	61	1st
Arsenal	42	21	13	8	88:68	50	3rd

1959-1960

SEASON 1959-1960 FOOTBALL LEAGUE (DIVISION 1)

22 Aug	Sheffield W	H	L 0-1	Standen	Wills	Evans	Docherty	Charles	Ward	Clapton D R	Groves	Herd	Bloomfield	Henderson
26 Aug	Nottingham F	A	W 3-0	..	..	..	Charles ..	Dodgin	Groves	..[3]	Barnwell	..	..	Haverty
29 Aug	Wolverhampton W	A	D 3-3	..	..	..	..	..	..	..[1]	..	..[2]	Henderson	..
1 Sep	Nottingham F	H	D 1-1	..	..	McCullough	..	..	..	..	..	..[1]	Bloomfield	..
5 Sep	Tottenham H	H	D 1-1	..	..	..	..	..	Docherty	..	..[1]	..	..	..
9 Sep	Bolton W	A	W 1-0	..	..	..	..	..	..	..	..	..[1]	Henderson	..
12 Sep	Manchester C	H	W 3-1	..	..	..	..	..	..	..[1]	..[1]	..	Bloomfield	..[1]
15 Sep	Bolton W	H	W 2-1	..	..	..	Ward	..	..	..[1]	..	..[1]	..	Henderson
19 Sep	Blackburn Rov	A	D 1-1	..	..	..	Groves	..	..	..	..	..[1]	..	..
26 Sep	Blackpool	H	W 2-1	..	..	..	..	..	..	..	..[1]	..[1]	..	Haverty
3 Oct	Everton	A	L 1-3	..	..	..	..	..	..	..	..[1]	..	..	..
10 Oct	Manchester U	A	L 2-4	..	..	..	Docherty	..	Groves	..	Bloomfield	..[1]	Henderson[1]	..
17 Oct	Preston NE	H	L 0-3	..	..	..	..	..	..	Henderson	..	Julians	Herd	..
24 Oct	Leicester C	A	D 2-2	Kelsey	..	..	Groves	..	Ward	Herd	..[1]	..	Barnwell[1]	Henderson
31 Oct	Birmingham C	H	W 3-0	..	..	..	..	..	Petts	Henderson[1]	Barnwell[1]	Herd[1]	Bloomfield	Haverty
7 Nov	Leeds U	A	L 2-3	Standen	..	..	..	..	..	..[1]	..	..[1]	..	..
14 Nov	West Ham U	H	L 1-3	Kelsey	..	..	Charles	..	..	Clapton D R	Herd	Groves	..[1]	..
21 Nov	Chelsea	A	W 3-1	..	..	..	Groves	..	..	..	Barnwell	Henderson	..[1]	..[2]
28 Nov	W B A	H	L 2-4	..	..	..	Barnwell	..	..	..	Henderson	Groves[1]	..[1]	..
5 Dec	Newcastle U	A	L 1-4	..	..	..	..	Charles	..	..	..	..	..	..[1]
12 Dec	Burnley	H	L 2-4	..	..	..	Groves	Dodgin	Ward	..	Barnwell	Henderson	..[1]	..[1]
19 Dec	Sheffield W	A	L 1-5	Standen	Magill	Wills	..	..	Barnwell	..	Henderson	Julians[1]	..	..
26 Dec	Luton T	H	L 0-3	..	..	Evans	Ward	..	Petts	Herd	Barnwell	..	..	Clapton D R
28 Dec	Luton T	A	W 1-0	..	..	..	Wills	..	Barnwell	Nutt	Herd	..[1]	..	Haverty
2 Jan	Wolverhampton W	H	D 4-4	..	..	..[1]	Barnwell	..	Wills[1]	Henderson	..	Charles[1]	..	..[1]
16 Jan	Tottenham H	A	L 0-3	..	..	..	Wills	Snedden	Barnwell	Clapton D R	..	Julians	..	..
23 Jan	Manchester C	A	W 2-1	Kelsey	..	McCullough	Ward	Docherty	Wills	..	*opponents*	Charles[1]	..	..
6 Feb	Blackburn Rov	H	W 5-2	..	..	..	..	..	..	Henderson	..[1]	..[3]	..	..[1]
13 Feb	Blackpool	A	L 1-2	..	..	..	Barnwell	..	..	..	..	..[1]	..	..
20 Feb	Everton	H	W 2-1	..	..	..	Ward	Dodgin	Docherty	..	Barnwell	..[2]	Groves	..
27 Feb	Newcastle U	H	W 1-0	..	..	..	..	..	..	..	..[1]	..	..	..
5 Mar	Preston NE	A	W 3-0	..	..	..	..	..	..	..[1]	Groves	..	Bloomfield[1]	..[1]
15 Mar	Leicester C	H	D 1-1	Standen	..	..	..	..	..	..	Herd[1]	..	Groves	..
19 Mar	Burnley	A	L 2-3	Kelsey	..	..	..	..	Groves	..[2]	..	Clapton D P	Barnwell	..
26 Mar	Leeds U	H	D 1-1	..	..	..	Charles	..	..	..	Barnwell	Herd[1]	Bloomfield	..
2 Apr	West Ham U	A	D 0-0	..	..	..	..	Docherty	..	..	Herd	Julians	..	..
9 Apr	Chelsea	H	L 1-4	..	..	..	Docherty	Dodgin	..	..	Barnwell	Herd	..[1]	..
15 Apr	Fulham	H	W 2-0	..	Wills	..	Groves	Docherty	Everitt	..[1]	Herd[1]	Clapton D P	..	..
16 Apr	Birmingham C	A	L 0-3	..	Magill	Wills	Everitt	..	Groves	..	..	..	..	Nutt
18 Apr	Fulham	A	L 0-3	..	Wills	McCullough	..	..	Ward	..	Julians	Charles	..	..
23 Apr	Manchester U	H	W 5-2	..	..	..	Ward[1]	..	Everitt	Clapton D R[1]	Henderson	Groves	..[3]	Haverty
30 Apr	W B A	A	L 0-1	..	..	..	..	..	..	..	..	..	..	..
	FA Cup													
9 Jan	Rotherham U (3)	A	D 2-2	Standen	Magill	Evans	Docherty	Dodgin	Wills	Henderson	Barnwell	Julians[1] o.g.	Bloomfield	Haverty
13 Jan	Rotherham U (3R)	H	D 1-1	..	..	..	Wills	Docherty	Barnwell	Clapton D R	Henderson	Herd	..[1]	..
18 Jan	Rotherham U (3R) (at Sheffield Wed)		L 0-2	..	..	..	Docherty	Snedden	..	..	Julians	Charles	..	Henderson

Appearances (Goals)

Barnwell J 28 (7) · Bloomfield J 36 (10) · Charles M 20 (8) · Clapton D P (Denis) 3 · Clapton D R (Danny) 23 (7) · Docherty T 24 · Dodgin W 30 · Evans D 7 (1) · Everitt M 5 · Groves V 30 (1) · Haverty J 35 (8) · Henderson J 31 (7) · Herd D 31 (14) · Julians L 8 (2) · Kelsey J 22 · Magill E 17 · McCullough W 33 · Nutt G 3 · Petts J 7 · Snedden J 1 · Standen J 20 · Ward G 15 (1) · Wills L 33 (1) · Own goals 1 · Total: 23 players (68)

Position in League Table

	P	W	L	D	F:A	Pts	
Burnley	42	24	11	7	85:61	55	1st
Arsenal	42	15	18	9	68:80	39	13th

SEASON 1960-1961 FOOTBALL LEAGUE (DIVISION 1)

Date	Opponent				GK	2	3	4	5	6	7	8	9	10	11
20 Aug	Burnley	A	L	2-3	Kelsey	Wills	McCullough	Everitt	Snedden	Docherty	Skirton	Barnwell	Herd[1]	Bloomfield[1]	Henderson
23 Aug	Preston NE	H	W	1-0	..	..	..	Ward	Docherty	Everitt[1]	..	..	..	..	..
27 Aug	Nottingham F	H	W	3-0	..	..	..	Everitt	Snedden	Docherty	..[2]	..	..	..	..[1]
30 Aug	Preston NE	A	L	0-2	..	..	..	..	..	..	..	..	..	..	..
3 Sep	Manchester C	A	D	0-0	..	..	..	Ward	..	..	..	Bloomfield	..	Kane	..
6 Sep	Birmingham C	H	W	2-0	..	..	..	..	..	..	Clapton D R	..	..[1]	..[1]	..
10 Sep	Tottenham H	H	L	2-3	..	..	..	..[1]	..	..	..	..	..[1]	..	..
14 Sep	Birmingham C	A	L	0-2	..	..	..	..	..	..	Skirton	..	..	..	..
17 Sep	Newcastle U	H	W	5-0	..	..	..	..	..	Groves	Clapton D R[1]	Herd[3]	Strong[1]	Bloomfield	..
24 Sep	Cardiff C	A	L	0-1	..	..	..	..	..	..	..	..[1]	..	..	..
1 Oct	W B A	H	W	1-0	..	..	..	Docherty	..	..	..	..	..[1]	..	..
8 Oct	Leicester C	A	L	1-2	..	..	..	..	..	..	..	..	..	..	..[1]
15 Oct	Aston Villa	H	W	2-1	..	Standen	..	..	..	..	..	Barnwell	..[1]	Herd[1]	..
22 Oct	Blackburn Rov	A	W	4-2	Standen	..	..	..	..	..	Strong[2]	..	Charles[1]	..[1]	..
29 Oct	Manchester U	H	W	2-1	Kelsey	..	..	..	..	..	..	..[1]	..	..[1]	..
5 Nov	West Ham U	A	L	0-6	..	..	..	..	..	..	..	..	..[1]	..	Haverty
12 Nov	Chelsea	H	L	1-4	..	..	..	..	..	..	..	..	..	..	Henderson
19 Nov	Blackpool	A	D	1-1	..	..	..	Clapton D P	..	..	Clapton D R	..	Strong	..[1]	..
26 Nov	Everton	H	W	3-2	..	..	..	Docherty	..	..	..	..	..	..[3]	..
3 Dec	Wolverhampton W	A	L	3-5	..	..	..	..	..	..	..	..[1]	..	..[2]	..
10 Dec	Bolton W	H	W	5-1	..	..	..	..	..	..	..	..[1]	..[2]	Eastham[2]	..
17 Dec	Burnley	H	L	2-5	..	..	..	..	..	..	..	Eastham	..[1]	Herd[1]	..
23 Dec	Sheffield W	A	D	1-1	..	Magill	..	Neill[1]	..	..	..	..	Herd	Henderson	Skirton
26 Dec	Sheffield W	H	D	1-1	..	..	..	..	Young	..	Skirton	Barnwell	..	Eastham[1]	Henderson
31 Dec	Nottingham F	A	W	5-3	..	..	..	..	Charles	..	O'Neill	..	..[3]	..	..[1]
14 Jan	Manchester C	H	W	5-4	..	..	..	..	..	..	Clapton D R[1]	Eastham	..[3]	Henderson[1]	Haverty
21 Jan	Tottenham H	A	L	2-4	McClelland	..	..	..	Young	Docherty	Skirton	..	..[1]	Strong[2]	..
4 Feb	Newcastle U	A	D	3-3	..	Wills	..	Docherty	..	Groves	Skirton	..	Strong[1]	Strong[2]	..
11 Feb	Cardiff C	H	L	2-3	..	..	..	Charles	..	..	..	Strong	Herd[2]	Eastham	..
18 Feb	W B A	A	W	3-2	..	Bacuzzi	..	Neill	Charles	..	..[1]	Barnwell	..	..	..[2]
25 Feb	Leicester C	H	L	1-3	Kelsey	..	..	..	..	..	..	Eastham	..	Henderson[1]	..
4 Mar	Aston Villa	A	D	2-2	..	..	..	Ward	..	..	Henderson	Barnwell[1]	..	Eastham	..[1]
11 Mar	Blackburn Rov	H	D	0-0	..	..	..	..	..	..	..	..	..	..	..
18 Mar	Manchester U	A	D	1-1	..	..	..	Charles[1]	Snedden	..	..	Eastham	..	Barnwell	..
25 Mar	West Ham U	H	D	0-0	..	..	..	..	Neill	..	..	..	..	..	..
31 Mar	Fulham	A	D	2-2	..	..	..	..	..	..	Clapton D R	..	..[2]	Henderson	..
1 Apr	Bolton W	A	D	1-1	..	..	Magill	..	..	..	..	Barnwell	..	..[1]	Skirton
3 Apr	Fulham	H	W	4-2	..	..	McCullough	Petts	..	..	..	..[2]	..	..[2]	..
8 Apr	Blackpool	H	W	1-0	..	..	..	Charles	..	..	O'Neill	..[1]	..	..	..
15 Apr	Chelsea	A	L	1-3	..	..	..	..	..	..	Strong[1]	..	..	Eastham	Henderson
22 Apr	Wolverhampton W	H	L	1-5	..	..	..	..	..	Barnwell	..	Griffiths	..	..	..[1]
29 Apr	Everton	A	L	1-4	..	..	..	Barnwell	Charles	Groves	Skirton	Eastham	Strong	Herd[1]	..

FA Cup

Date	Opponent				GK	2	3	4	5	6	7	8	9	10	11
7 Jan	Sunderland (3)	A	L	1-2	Kelsey	Magill	McCullough	Neill	Charles	Groves	Barnwell	Herd[1]	Strong	Eastham	Henderson

Appearances (Goals)

Bacuzzi D 13 · Barnwell J 26 (6) · Bloomfield J 12 (1) · Charles M 19 (3) · Clapton D R (Danny) 18 (2) · Clapton D P (Denis) 1 · Docherty T 21 · Eastham G 19 (5) · Everitt M 4 (1) · Griffiths A 1 · Groves J 32 · Haverty J 12 (4) · Henderson J 39 (10) · Herd D 40 (29) · Kane P 4 (1) · Kelsey J 37 · Magill E 6 · McClelland J 4 · McCullough W 41 · Neill T 14 (1) · O'Neill F 2 · Petts J 1 · Skirton A 16 (3) · Snedden J 23 · Standen J 1 · Strong G 19 (10) · Ward G 9 (1) · Wills L 24 · Young D 4 · Total: 29 players (77)

Position in League Table

	P	W	L	D	F:A	Pts	
Tottenham H	42	31	7	4	115:55	66	1st
Arsenal	42	15	16	11	77:85	41	11th

SEASON 1961-1962 FOOTBALL LEAGUE (DIVISION 1)

Date	Opponent				GK	2	3	4	5	6	7	8	9	10	11
19 Aug	Burnley	H	D	2-2	Kelsey	Magill	McCullough	Brown	Snedden	Neill	McLeod	Eastham	Charles[2]	Henderson	Skirton
23 Aug	Leicester C	A	W	1-0	McClelland	..	..	..	..	..	..	..	..[1]	..	..
26 Aug	Tottenham H	A	L	3-4	..	..	..	..	..	..	..	..	..[2]	..	..[1]
29 Aug	Leicester C	H	D	4-4	..	..	..	..	..	..	..[1]	..[1]	..[1]	..	..[1]
2 Sep	Bolton W	A	L	1-2	..	..	..	Neill	Petts	..	..	..	..[1]	..	..
9 Sep	Manchester C	H	W	3-0	Kelsey	..	..	Snedden	Neill	opponents	Griffiths[1]	Henderson	Eastham	..	..[1]
16 Sep	W B A	A	L	0-4	..	..	..	..	..	..	..	Charles	..	..	..
20 Sep	Sheffield W	A	D	1-1	..	..	..	..	..	..	..	Eastham	..	Henderson	..
23 Sep	Birmingham C	H	D	1-1	..	..	..	..	..	..	..	..	..[1]	..	..
30 Sep	Everton	A	L	1-4	..	..	..	..	..	..	..	..	Groves	..	..[1]
7 Oct	Blackpool	H	W	3-0	..	Bacuzzi	..	Ward[1]	Brown	Groves	Skirton	..	..[2]	Henderson	McLeod
14 Oct	Blackburn Rov	A	D	0-0	McKechnie	..	..	..	..	..	McLeod	..	Strong	Barnwell	Skirton
21 Oct	Manchester U	H	W	5-1	Kelsey	..	..	..[1]	..	..	..	Barnwell[1]	Charles	Eastham[1]	..[2]
28 Oct	Cardiff C	A	D	1-1	..	..	..	..	..	..	..	..	..	..[1]	..
4 Nov	Chelsea	H	L	0-3	..	Magill	..	..	..	..	..	..	..	..	..
11 Nov	Aston Villa	A	L	1-3	..	Bacuzzi	..	..	..	..	..	Eastham	..	Henderson	..[1]
14 Nov	Sheffield W	H	W	1-0	McKechnie	..	..	..	..	..	..	..	Strong[1]	..	..
18 Nov	Nottingham F	H	W	2-1	Kelsey	..	..	Clamp	..	..	..[1]	..	..	..	..
25 Nov	Wolverhampton W	A	W	3-2	..	..	..	..	..	..	..	Ward[2]	..	Eastham	..[1]
2 Dec	West Ham U	H	D	2-2	..	..	..	..	..	..	..	..	..[1]	..	..[1]
9 Dec	Sheffield U	A	L	1-2	..	..	..	..	Snedden	..	..	..	..[1]	..	..
16 Dec	Burnley	A	W	2-0	..	..	..	..	..	..	..	Barnwell	Charles[1]	..	..[1]
23 Dec	Tottenham H	H	W	2-1	..	..	..	..	..	..	..	..	..[1]	..	..[1]
26 Dec	Fulham	H	W	1-0	..	..	..	..	..	..	..	Griffiths	..[1]	..	..
13 Jan	Bolton W	H	L	1-2	..	..	Magill	..	..	..	Skirton[2]	Barnwell	..	..	McLeod
20 Jan	Manchester C	A	L	2-3	..	..	McCullough	..	..	Petts	Ward	Barnwell	..	Griffiths	McLeod
3 Feb	W B A	H	L	0-1	..	..	..	..	..	Petts	Ward	Charles	..	Griffiths	..
10 Feb	Birmingham C	A	L	0-1	..	..	..	Neill	..	..	Charles	Strong	Barnwell	..	..
24 Feb	Blackpool	A	W	1-0	..	..	..	..	..	Armstrong	Strong[1]	Groves	Eastham	Skirton	..
3 Mar	Blackburn	H	D	0-0	..	..	..	Clamp	..	Groves	Skirton	..	..	..	Armstrong
17 Mar	Cardiff C	H	D	1-1	..	..	..	Clamp	..	Groves	Clapton	Barnwell	Strong[1]	..	Skirton
24 Mar	Chelsea	A	W	3-2	..	Clarke	..	..	..	..	McLeod[1]	..	..[2]	Barnwell	..[2]
31 Mar	Aston Villa	H	L	4-5	..	Magill	McCullough	Brown	Neill	Clamp	..	Griffiths	..[1]	Barnwell	..[2]
7 Apr	Nottingham F	A	W	1-0	McKechnie	Magill	McCullough	Brown	Neill	Clamp	..[1]	..	..	Eastham	..[1]
11 Apr	Fulham	A	L	2-5	McKechnie	..	..	Clamp	Brown	Petts	..	..[1]	..	..	..[1]
14 Apr	Wolverhampton W	H	W	3-1	Kelsey	..	..	Brown	Neill	Clamp	..	..[2]	Barnwell	..	..[1]
16 Apr	Manchester U	A	W	3-2	..	..	..	..	..	Petts	opponents	..	Eastham[1]	..	..[1]
20 Apr	Ipswich T	A	D	2-2	..	..	..	Clamp	..	..	Clapton[1]	..	..	..	McLeod[1]
21 Apr	West Ham U	A	D	3-3	..	..	..	..	..	..	Clapton[1]	..	..	..[1]	McLeod[1]
23 Apr	Ipswich T	H	L	0-3	..	..	..	Clamp	..	..	..	..	..	..	..
28 Apr	Sheffield U	H	W	2-0	..	..	..	Brown	..	..	..	..[1]	Barnwell[1]	..[1]	Armstrong
1 May	Everton	H	L	2-3	..	..	..	..	..	..	..	Strong	..	..	..

FA Cup

Date	Opponent				GK	2	3	4	5	6	7	8	9	10	11
6 Jan	Bradford C (3)	H	W	3-0	Kelsey	Bacuzzi	McCullough	Clamp	Brown	Snedden	McLeod	Barnwell o.g.	Charles[2]	Eastham	Skirton
31 Jan	Manchester U (4)	A	L	0-1	..	..	..	Snedden	..	Clamp	Skirton	..	..	..	McLeod

Appearances (Goals)

Armstrong G 4 (1) · Bacuzzi D 22 · Barnwell J 14 (3) · Brown L 41 · Charles M 21 (15) · Clamp L 18 · Clapton Danny 5 (1) · Clarke F 1 · Eastham G 38 (6) · Griffiths A 14 (2) · Groves V 16 · Henderson J 12 · Kelsey J 35 · McLeod J 37 (6) · Magill E 21 · McClelland J 4 · McCullough J 40 · McKechnie I 3 · Neill T 20 · Petts J 12 · Skirton A 38 (19) · Snedden J 15 · Strong G 20 (12) · Ward J 11 · Own goals 2 · Total: 24 players (71)

Position in League Table

	P	W	L	D	F:A	Pts	
Ipswich	42	24	10	8	93:67	56	1st
Arsenal	42	16	15	11	71:72	43	10th

SEASON 1962-1963 FOOTBALL LEAGUE (DIVISION 1)

18 Aug	Leyton Orient	A W 2-1	McKechnie	Magill	McCullough	Brown	Neill	Snedden	Armstrong	Strong[1]	Baker[1]	Barnwell	Skirton
21 Aug	Birmingham C	H W 2-0	..	..	..[1]	..	..	..	..	..	..[1]	..	..
25 Aug	Manchester U	H L 1-3	..	..	..	Clamp[1]	Brown	..	..	Eastham	Strong	..	..
29 Aug	Birmingham C	A D 2-2	..	..	..	..	..	..	..	Strong[2]	Baker	..	..
1 Sep	Burnley	A L 1-2	..	Bacuzzi	..	..	..	..	..	..	..	..	..[1]
4 Sep	Aston Villa	H L 1-2	McClelland	..	..	..	..	..	..	Barnwell	..	Eastham	..[1]
8 Sep	Sheffield W	H L 1-2	..	Magill	..	Brown	Neill	..	..	Eastham	..[1]	Barnwell	..
10 Sep	Aston Villa	A L 1-3	McKechnie	..	..	..	..	..	..	Court	..[1]	..	..
15 Sep	Fulham	A W 3-1	..	..	..	Smithson	Brown	..	MacLeod[1]	..	..[1]	Ward	..[1]
22 Sep	Leicester C	H D 1-1	..	..	..	Brown	Neill	..	..	Barnwell	..[1]	Strong	..
29 Sep	Bolton W	A L 0-3	..	..	..	Smithson	Brown	Ward	..	Strong	..	Barnwell	..
6 Oct	Tottenham H	A D 4-4	McClelland	..	..	Snedden	..	Groves	..[1]	..[1]	Court[2]	Eastham	..
13 Oct	West Ham U	H D 1-1	..	..	..	Neill	..	Snedden	..	..	Baker[1]	..	..
27 Oct	Wolverhampton W	H W 5-4	..	..	..	..	..	..	..	..	..[3]	..[2]	..
3 Nov	Blackburn Rov	A D 5-5	..	..	..	Snedden	..	Groves	..	..	..[2]	..[1]	..[2]
10 Nov	Sheffield U	H W 1-0	..	..	..	..	..	..	..	..[1]	..	..	..
14 Nov	Liverpool	A L 1-2	..	..	..	..	..	..	..	..[1]	..	..	..
17 Nov	Nottingham F	A L 0-3	..	..	..	..	..	..	..	..	..	..	..
24 Nov	Ipswich T	H W 3-1	..	..	..	Barnwell[1]	Neill	Snedden	..	Court	..[1]	..	Armstrong[1]
1 Dec	Manchester C	A W 4-2	..	..	..	..	..	..	..[2]	Strong[1]	..[1]	..	..
8 Dec	Blackpool	H W 2-0	..	..	..	..	..	*opponents*	..	..[1]	..	..	..
15 Dec	Leyton Orient	H W 2-0	..	..	..	..	..	..	..	..	..[2]	..	..
9 Feb	Leicester C	A L 0-2	..	..	..	..	Brown	Neill	Court	..	..	..	MacLeod
16 Feb	Bolton W	H W 3-2	..	..	..	..	..[1]	Snedden	MacLeod[1]	..	..	..	Armstrong[1]
23 Feb	Tottenham H	H L 2-3	..	..	..	..	..	..	..	..[1]	..[1]	..	..
2 Mar	West Ham U	A W 4-0	..	..	..[1]	..	..	..	..	..[1]	..[2]	..	..
9 Mar	Liverpool	H D 2-2	..	..	..[1]	..	..	..	..[1]	..	..	..	Anderson
23 Mar	Blackburn Rov	H W 3-1	..	..	..	..	..	..	..[1]	..[2]	..	..	..
26 Mar	Everton	H W 4-3	..	..	..	..	..	..	..[1]	..[1]	..[1]	..	Skirton[1]
30 Mar	Ipswich T	A D 1-1	..	..	..	..	..	Neill	*opponents*	..	..	..	..
6 Apr	Nottingham F	H D 0-0	..	Bacuzzi	..	..	..	..	..	..	..	..	..
8 Apr	Wolverhampton W	A L 0-1	..	..	..	..	..	..	..	..	..	..	..
12 Apr	W B A	H W 3-2	..	..	..	..	..	..	..	..[2]	..	..	..[1]
13 Apr	Sheffield U	A D 3-3	..	Magill	Bacuzzi	..[1]	..	..	Anderson[1]	..	..[1]	..	McCullough
15 Apr	W B A	A W 2-1	..	Clarke	McCullough	..	..	Groves	MacLeod	..	..[2]	..	Anderson
20 Apr	Manchester C	H L 2-3	..	Magill	..	..	..	..	..[1]	..[1]	..	..	..
24 Apr	Everton	A D 1-1	..	..	Clarke	..	..	McCullough	..	..[1]	..	..	Skirton
27 Apr	Blackpool	A L 2-3	..	..	..	..	..	..	..	Sammels[1]	Strong	..	..[1]
6 May	Manchester U	A W 3-2	..	..	..	..	..	..	..	Strong[1]	Baker[1]	Sammels	..[1]
11 May	Burnley	H L 2-3	..	..	..	..	..	..	..	..	..[1]	Eastham	..[1]
14 May	Fulham	H W 3-0	..	..	McCullough	..	..	Groves	..	..	..[3]	..	Armstrong
18 May	Sheffield W	A W 3-2	..	..	..	..	..	..	..	Court[1]	..[1]	..[1]	Skirton
	FA Cup												
30 Jan	Oxford U (3)	H W 5-1	McClelland	Magill	McCullough	Barnwell	Brown	Snedden	Court	Strong[2]	Baker[2]	Eastham	MacLeod[1]
12 Mar	Sheffield W (4)	H W 2-0	..	..	..	..	..	..	MacLeod[1]	..[1]	..	..	Skirton
19 Mar	Liverpool (5)	H L 1-2	..	..	..	..	..	..	..[1]	..	..	..	..

Appearances (Goals)

Anderson T 5 (1) · Armstrong G 16 (2) · Bacuzzi D 6 · Baker J 39 (29) · Barnwell J 34 (2) · Brown L 38 (1) · Clamp E 4 (1) · Clarke F 5 · Court D 6 (3) · Eastham G 33 (4) · Groves V 9 · MacLeod J 33 (9) · Magill E 36 · McClelland J 33 · McCullough W 42 (3) · McKechnie I 9 · Neill T 17 · Sammels J 2 (1) · Skirton A 28 (10) · Smithson R 2 · Snedden J 27 · Strong G 36 (18) · Ward G 2 · Own goals 2 · Total: 23 players (86)

Position in League Table

	P	W	L	D	F:A	Pts	
Everton	42	25	6	11	84:42	61	1st
Arsenal	42	18	14	10	86:77	46	7th

SEASON 1963-1964 FOOTBALL LEAGUE (DIVISION 1)

24 Aug	Wolverhampton W	H L 1-3	McClelland	Magill	McCullough	Barnwell	Ure	Brown	Skirton	Strong[1]	Baker	Eastham	Armstrong
27 Aug	W B A	H W 3-2	..	..	..	..	..	..	MacLeod	..[1]	..[2]	..	Skirton
31 Aug	Leicester C	A L 2-7	..	..	..	..[1]	..	..	..[1]	..	..	..	..
4 Sep	W B A	A L 0-4	McKechnie	..	..	Neil	..	Barnwell	..	..	..	..	..
7 Sep	Bolton W	H W 4-3	..	Bacuzzi	..	..	Brown	Ure[1]	..	..	..[1]	..	..[2]
10 Sep	Aston Villa	H W 3-0	..	Magill	..	Brown	Ure	Groves	..	..	..[3]	..	..
14 Sep	Fulham	A W 4-1	..	..	..	..	..	..	..[1]	..[2]	..[1]	..	..
21 Sep	Manchester U	H W 2-1	..	..	..	..	..	..	..	..	..[1]	..[1]	..
28 Sep	Burnley	A W 3-0	..	..	..	..	..	..	..	..[2]	..	..[1]	Armstrong
2 Oct	Everton	A L 1-2	..	..	..	..	..	..	..	..[1]	..	..	..
5 Oct	Ipswich	H W 6-0	..	..	..	..	..	..	..[1]	..[3]	..[2]	..	..
9 Oct	Stoke C	A W 2-1	..	..	..	..	..	..	..	Court	..[2]	Barnwell	..
15 Oct	Tottenham H	H D 4-4	..	..	..	..	..	..	..	Strong[1]	..[1]	Eastham[2]	..
19 Oct	Aston Villa	A L 1-2	..	..	..	..	..	..	..[1]	..	..	Barnwell	..
26 Oct	Nottingham F	H W 4-2	Wilson	..	..	..	..	Barnwell	*opponents*	..[2]	..	Eastham	Anderson[1]
2 Nov	Sheffield U	A D 2-2	..	..	..	..	..	..	..	..[1]	..[1]	..	..
5 Nov	Birmingham C	H W 4-1	..	..	Clarke F	..	Neill	..	..	..[1]	..[3]	..	..
9 Nov	West Ham U	H D 3-3	..	..	McCullough	..	Ure	..	..[1]	..	..	..[1]	..[1]
16 Nov	Chelsea	A L 1-3	..	..	..	..	..	..	..	..	..	..[1]	..
23 Nov	Blackpool	H W 5-3	Furnell	Clarke F	..	..[1]	..	..[1]	..	..[2]	..	..[1]	..
30 Nov	Blackburn Rov	A L 1-4	..	Magill	..	..	..	..	Court	..	..[1]	..	Skirton
7 Dec	Liverpool	H D 1-1	..	..	..	Barnwell	..	Snedden	MacLeod	..	..[1]	..	Armstrong
10 Dec	Everton	H W 6-0	..	..	..	..	..	..	..	..[1]	..[2]	..[2]	..[1]
14 Dec	Wolverhampton W	A D 2-2	..	..	..	..	..	..	..	..[2]	..	..	..
21 Dec	Leicester C	H L 0-1	..	..	..	Brown	..	..	..	..	..	..	..
28 Dec	Birmingham C	A W 4-1	..	..	..	..	..	..	..[2]	..	..[1]	Barnwell	..[1]
11 Jan	Bolton W	A D 1-1	..	..	..	Barnwell	..	..	..	..	..[1]	Eastham	..
18 Jan	Fulham	H D 2-2	..	Bacuzzi	..	..	..	..	..	..[1]	..[1]	..	..
1 Feb	Manchester U	A L 1-3	..	Magill	..[1]	Groves	..	..	Skirton	..	..	..	..
8 Feb	Burnley	H W 3-2	..	..	..	..	..	..	Armstrong[1]	..[1]	..	..	Anderson[1]
18 Feb	Ipswich	A W 2-1	..	..	Clarke F	..	..	..	Skirton	..[1]	..	..[1]	Armstrong
22 Feb	Tottenham H	A L 1-3	McClelland	Clarke F	McCullough	..	..	..	MacLeod	..[1]	..	..	..
29 Feb	Stoke C	H D 1-1	..	Bacuzzi	..	..	..	..	..	..	..[1]	..	..
7 Mar	Nottingham F	A L 0-2	Furnell	..	..	..	..	..	..	..	..	..	..
14 Mar	Chelsea	H L 2-4	..	..	..	Neill[1]	..	Simpson	..	..	..[1]	..	..
21 Mar	West Ham U	A D 1-1	..	Magill	..	..	..	..	Skirton[1]	Court	Radford	..	Anderson
24 Mar	Sheffield W	H D 1-1	..	..	..	..	..	..	Armstrong	Strong[1]	Court	..	..
28 Mar	Sheffield U	H L 1-3	..	..	..	..	..	..	..	..[1]	..	..	..
30 Mar	Sheffield W	A W 4-0	..	..	..	..	..	..	Skirton[3]	Court[1]	Baker	..	Armstrong
4 Apr	Blackpool	A W 1-0	..	..	..	..	..	..	..[1]	..	..	..	..
11 Apr	Blackburn Rov	H D 0-0	..	..	Clarke F	..	..	McCullough	..	Strong	..	Court	..
18 Apr	Liverpool	A L 0-5	..	..	McCullough	..	..	Snedden	..	..	..	Eastham	..
	FA Cup												
4 Jan	Wolves (3)	H W 2-1	Furnell	Magill	McCullough	Barnwell	Ure	Snedden	MacLeod	Strong[1]	Baker[1]	Eastham	Armstrong
25 Jan	W B A (4)	A D 3-3	..	..	..	Groves	..	..	..[1]	..	..[1]	..	..[1]
29 Jan	W B A (4R)	H W 2-0	..	..	..	..	..	..	Skirton	..[1]	..	..	..[1]
15 Feb	Liverpool (5)	H L 0-1	..	..	..	..	..	..	MacLeod	..	..	..	..
	Inter-Cities Fairs Cup												
25 Sep	Staevnet (1)	A W 7-1	McKechnie	Magill	McCullough	Brown	Ure	Groves	MacLeod[1]	Strong[3]	Baker[3]	Eastham	Armstrong
22 Oct	Staevnet (1)	H L 2-3	..	..	..	..	..	..	Skirton[1]	..	Court	Barnwell[1]	..
13 Nov	FC Liege (2)	H D 1-1	Wilson	..	..	..	..	Barnwell	MacLeod	..	Baker	Eastham	Anderson[1]
18 Dec	FC Liege (2)	A L 1-3	Furnell	..	..[1]	Barnwell	..	Snedden	..	..	Court	..	Armstrong

Appearances (Goals)

Anderson T 10 (3) · Armstrong G 28 (3) · Bacuzzi D 5 · Baker J 39 (26) · Barnwell J 19 (2) · Brown L 22 (1) · Clarke F 5 · Court D 8 (1) · Eastham G 38 (10) · Furnell J 21 · Groves V 15 · MacLeod J 30 (7) · Magill E 35 · McClelland J 5 · McCullough W 40 (1) · McKechnie 1 11 · Neill T 11 (1) · Radford J 1 · Simpson P 6 · Skirton A 15 (7) · Snedden J 14 · Strong G 38 (26) · Ure I 41 (1) · Wilson R 5 · Own goals 1 · Total: 24 players (90)

Position in League Table

	P	W	L	D	F:A	Pts	
Liverpool	42	26	11	5	92:45	57	1st
Arsenal	42	17	14	11	90:82	45	8th

SEASON 1964-1965 FOOTBALL LEAGUE (DIVISION 1)

22 Aug	Liverpool	A L 2-3	Furnell	Howe	McCullough	Snedden	Ure	Simpson	Armstrong	Strong[1]		Baker[1]		Eastham	Anderson
25 Aug	Sheffield W	H D 1-1	..	..					McCullough	MacLeod[1]	.. [1]		..		..	Armstrong[1]
29 Aug	Aston Villa	H W 3-1	..	..	Clarke F	Simpson	..	McCullough	MacLeod[1]	.. [1]		..		..	Armstrong[1]
2 Sep	Sheffield W	A L 1-2	..	..		Strong	Ferry	..	Skirton	Court		.. [1]		..	
5 Sep	Wolverhampton W	A W 1-0	..	..	McCullough	..	..	Neill	..	.. [1]		.. [1]		..	
8 Sep	Blackburn Rov	H D 1-1	..	..		.. [1]		..	..	..		.. [1]	.. 2	..	
12 Sep	Sunderland	H W 3-1	..	..	Clarke F			..	..	..		.. [1]		..	.. 1
16 Sep	Blackburn Rov	A W 2-1	..	..				..	..	.. [1]		.. [1]	.. 1	..	
19 Sep	Leicester C	A W 3-2	..	..				..	..	.. [1]		.. [1]		..	
26 Sep	Chelsea	H L 1-3	↙	..				..	..	..		..		..	
6 Oct	Nottingham F	H L 0-3	..	Clarke	McCullough	McLintock		..	Simpson	Strong		..		..	
10 Oct	Tottenham H	A L 1-3	..	Howe	Clarke F	..		..	Simpson	Anderson		.. [1]		..	
17 Oct	Burnley	H W 3-2	Burns	..		..		..	.. [1]	Sammels[1]		.. [1]		..	
24 Oct	Sheffield U	A L 0-4	..	..	McCullough	..		Neill	Court	.. [1]		.. 2		..	
31 Oct	Everton	H W 3-1	..	..		..		Neill	Court	.. [1]		.. [1]		.. 1	
7 Nov	Birmingham C	A W 3-2	..	..				..	..	.. [1]		..		..	
11 Nov	Leeds U	A L 1-3	..	..				..	Skirton	Radford		..		..	
14 Nov	West Ham U	H L 0-3	..	..				..	Skirton	Radford		..		..	
21 Nov	W B A	A D 0-0	..	..				..	Tawse			..		.. 1	
28 Nov	Manchester U	H L 2-3	..	..		Sneddon		..	Anderson[1]	McLintock		..		..	
5 Dec	Fulham	A W 4-3	..	..		McLintock	..	..	Skirton[1]	Sammels	.. 2			..	.. 1
12 Dec	Liverpool	H D 0-0	..	..				..	..	..		.. [1]		..	
19 Dec	Aston Villa	A L 1-3	..	..		..	Ure	..	..	..		.. [1]		..	
26 Dec	Stoke C	H W 3-2	..	..		.. 1		..	..	..		.. [1]		..	
28 Dec	Stoke C	A L 1-4	..	..			Neill	..	..	.. [1]		..		..	
2 Jan	Wolverhampton W	H W 4-1	..	..	Clarke F	..	Ure	..	..	Radford[3]		.. [1]		..	
16 Jan	Sunderland	A W 2-0	..	..				..	..	..		.. [1]		..	
23 Jan	Leicester C	H W 4-3	..	..				..	..	..	.. 2			.. 1	.. 1
6 Feb	Chelsea	A L 1-2	..	..		Neill		..	..	..		.. [1]		..	
13 Feb	Leeds U	H L 1-2	..	..		..		..	Anderson	..		..		..	
20 Feb	Fulham	H W 2-0	..	..	McCullough	..		..	Tawse	.. [1]		.. [1]		..	
23 Feb	Tottenham H	H W 3-1	..	..				..	..	.. [1]	.. 2			..	
27 Feb	Burnley	A L 1-2	..	..				.. [1]	Skirton	..		..		..	
6 Mar	Sheffield U	H D 1-1	..	..				.. 1	Armstrong	..		..		Sammels	Eastham
13 Mar	Nottingham F	A L 0-3	..	Magill				..	Skirton	Eastham		..		Radford	Tawse
27 Mar	West Ham U	A L 1-2	..	Howe		McLintock		Neill	Tawse	Radford		.. [1]		Eastham	Armstrong
3 Apr	W B A	H D 1-1	Furnell	..		Neill		McLintock	Skirton	Sammels		.. [1]		.. 1	
6 Apr	Birmingham C	H W 3-0	..	..		McLintock[1]		Court	Sammels	Baldwin		.. [1]		..	Skirton[1]
16 Apr	Blackpool	A D 1-1	..	..		Neill		McLintock	..	Court		.. [1]		.. 1	Armstrong
19 Apr	Blackpool	H W 3-1	..	..		.. 1		..	..	..	.. 2			..	
24 Apr	Everton	A L 0-1	..	..		..		..	..	..		.. 1		..	
26 Apr	Manchester U	A L 1-3	..	..		..		..	..	..		..		..	

FA Cup

9 Jan	Darlington (3)	A W 2-0	Burns	Howe	Clarke F	McLintock	Ure	Court	Skirton	Radford[1]	Baker	Eastham	Armstrong[1]
30 Jan	Peterborough (4)	A L 1-2	..	..	..	..	..	..	..	.. [1]	..	..	..

Appearances (Goals)

Anderson T 10 (2) · Armstrong G 40 (4) · Baker J 42 (25) · Baldwin T 1 · Burns A 24 · Clarke F 15 · Court D 33 (3) · Eastham G 42 (10) · Ferry G 11 · Furnell J 18 · Howe D 40 · MacLeod J 1 · Magill E 1 · McCullough W 30 · McLintock F 25 (2) · Neill T 29 (1) · Radford J 13 (7) · Sammels J 17 (5) · Simpson P 6 (2) · Skirton A 22 (3) · Snedden J 3 · Strong G 12 (3) · Tawse B 5 · Ure I 22 (1) · Total: 24 players (69)

Position in League Table

	P	W	L	D	F:A	Pts
Manchester U	42	26	7	9	89:39	61 1st
Arsenal	42	17	18	7	69:75	41 13th

SEASON 1965-1966 FOOTBALL LEAGUE (DIVISION 1)

21 Aug	Stoke C	H W 2-1	Furnell	Howe	McCullough	McLintock	Ure	Neil	Baldwin	Eastham	Baker[2]	Court	Armstrong
25 Aug	Northampton T	A D 1-1	Wilson	..	..	Neill	..	McLintock	.. [1]	.. [1]	.. [1]	..	..
28 Aug	Burnley	A D 2-2	..	..	..	..	..		Sammels	.. [1]	.. [1]	..	..
4 Sep	Chelsea	H L 1-3	Furnell	..	..				..	.. [1]	.. [1]		
7 Sep	Nottingham F	A W 1-0	..	..	..	Court	Neill	..	Armstrong	Radford	.. [1]	Sammels[1]	Eastham
11 Sep	Tottenham H	A D 2-2	..	..	..	McLintock	..	Court	opponents	..	.. [1]	..	..
14 Sep	Nottingham F	H W 1-0	..	..	..	..	..	..	..	..	.. [1]	..	.. 1
18 Sep	Everton	A L 1-3	..	..	..	..	..	Simpson	..	..	.. [1]	..	..
25 Sep	Manchester U	H W 4-2	..	..	..	..	..	Court	.. 1	.. [1]	.. [1]	..	.. 1
28 Sep	Northampton T	H D 1-1	..	..	..	..	..	..	..	.. [1]	..	..	Skirton for Sammels Simpson for Baker
2 Oct	Newcastle U	A W 1-0	..	..	..	..	.. 1	Ure	..	..	..	..	
9 Oct	Fulham	H W 2-1	..	..	..	..	..	Neill	..	.. [1]	.. 1	..	
16 Oct	Blackpool	A L 3-5	..	..	..	..	..	opponents	.. 1	.. [1]	.. [1]	..	
23 Oct	Blackburn Rov	H D 2-2	Burns	..	..	..	..	.. 1	..	.. [1]	.. [1]	..	
30 Oct	Leicester C	A L 1-3	Furnell	..	Storey	..	..	..	.. 1	..	..	..	
6 Nov	Sheffield U	H W 6-2	Burns	..	..	..	..	..	Skirton[2]	Sammels	.. 2	Eastham	Armstrong[2]
13 Nov	Leeds U	A L 0-2	..	..	..	..	..	..	.. [2]	..	.. [1]	..	..
20 Nov	West Ham U	H W 3-2	..	..	..	..	..	..	.. [2]	..	.. 1	..	
4 Dec	Aston Villa	H D 3-3	..	..	..	..	..	..	.. [2]	Radford	.. 1	..	
11 Dec	Liverpool	A L 2-4	..	..	..	..	..	..	..	.. [1]	Baldwin[1]	..	
27 Dec	Sheffield W	A L 0-4	..	..	..	..	..	Simpson	..	Sammels	Baker	..	Walley for Armstrong
28 Dec	Sheffield W	H W 5-2	Wilson	..	..	Neill	Ure	Walley	.. 1	Radford	.. [1]	Sammels[1]	Eastham[2]
1 Jan	Fulham	A L 0-1	..	..	..	..	..	McLintock	..	Sammels	..	Eastham	Armstrong
8 Jan	Liverpool	H L 0-1	Furnell	..	..	McLintock	Neill	Court	..	..	Radford	Eastham	
15 Jan	Blackburn Rov	A L 1-2	..	..	..	..	..	..	..	Eastham	.. [1]	Armstrong	
29 Jan	Stoke C	A W 3-1	..	..	.. 1	..	..	Ure	..	Sammels	Radford[2]	Court	
5 Feb	Burnley	H D 1-1	..	..	..	..	..	Court	..	Baldwin	.. [1]	Sammels[1]	..	Walley for Sammels
19 Feb	Chelsea	A D 0-0	..	..	..	..	..	Ure	..	Sammels	..	Court	
5 Mar	Blackpool	H D 0-0	..	..	..	..	..	..	..	..	..	..	Simpson for Howe
8 Mar	Tottenham H	H D 1-1	..	Storey	McCullough	Neill	Ure	Court[1]	..	Eastham	..	Eastham	..
12 Mar	Everton	H L 0-1	..	..	..	McLintock	..	Neill	Neilson	Eastham	Court	..	
19 Mar	Manchester U	A L 1-2	..	..	..	..	Neill	Ure	Armstrong	Sammels	..	Walley[1]	Simpson for McCullough
26 Mar	Newcastle U	H L 1-3	..	..	Simpson	Court	Ure	Neill	Skirton	opponents	..	Eastham	Armstrong
5 Apr	W B A	H D 1-1	..	Court	Storey	McLintock	..	.. [1]	..	Radford	Baldwin	..	..
11 Apr	W B A	A D 4-4	..	..	..	..	Neill	Ure	..	.. [1]	Baldwin[2]	..	.. 1
16 Apr	West Ham U	A L 1-2	..	..	..	..	Ure	Neill	..	..	..	..	
20 Apr	Sunderland	A W 2-0	..	..	..	..	..	..	.. [1]	Sammels[1]	Radford	..	Walley
23 Apr	Sunderland	H D 1-1	..	..	..	..	..	Walley	..	..	..	..	Armstrong
25 Apr	Sheffield U	A L 0-3	..	..	..	Neill	..	..	..	..	..	..	
30 Apr	Aston Villa	A L 0-3	..	..	..	Simpson	..	..	..	..	..	..	
5 May	Leeds U	H L 0-3	..	Pack	..	McGill	..	Court	Armstrong	Baldwin	Ure	Sammels	Eastham
7 May	Leicester C	H W 1-0	..	Court	opponents	..	Ure	Walley	Neilson	Simpson	Radford	Eastham	Armstrong

FA Cup

22 Jan	Blackburn (3)	A L 0-3	Furnell	Howe	Storey	McLintock	Neill	Walley	Skirton	Sammels	Baker	Eastham	Armstrong

Appearances (Goals)

Armstrong G 39 (6) · Baker J 24 (13) · Baldwin T 8 (5) · Burns A 7 · Court D 38 (1) · Eastham G 37 (6) · Furnell J 31 · Howe D 29 (1) · McCullough W 17 · McGill A 2 · McLintock F 36 (2) · Neill T 39 · Neilson G 2 · Pack R 1 · Radford J 32 (8) · Sammels J 32 (6) · Simpson P 8 · Skirton A 24 (9) · Storey P 28 · Ure I 21 · Walley J 9 (1) · Wilson R 4 · Own goals 4 · Total: 22 players (62)

Position in League Table

	P	W	L	D	F:A	Pts
Liverpool	42	26	7	9	79:34	61 1st
Arsenal	42	12	17	13	62:75	37 14th

SEASON 1966-1967 FOOTBALL LEAGUE (DIVISION 1)

20 Aug	Sunderland	A W 3-1	Furnell	Court	Storey	McLintock	Ure	Neill	Skirton[2]	Baldwin	Radford	Sammels	Armstrong[1]	McGill for Court
23 Aug	West Ham U	H W 2-1	..	..	..	..	..	..	..	..	..	..	..	Simpson for Skirton
27 Aug	Aston Villa	H W 1-0	..	..	..	..	..	..	Coakley	.. [1]	..	..	..	
29 Aug	West Ham U	A D 2-2	..	Simpson	..	..	.. 1	..	..	McGill	Baldwin	.. [1]	..	
3 Sep	Tottenham H	A L 1-3	..	Court	Simpson	..	..	..	..	Baldwin	Radford	.. [1]	..	
6 Sep	Sheffield W	H D 1-1	..	..	..	..	..	..	..	..	..	.. [1]	..	McGill for Simpson
10 Sep	Manchester C	A D 1-1	..	Howe	McGill	..	..	..	..	..	..	..	..	

1966-1967 *continued*

17 Sep	Blackpool	H	D	1-1	Furnell	Simpson	Storey	McLintock	Ure	Neill	Coakley[1]	Addison	Radford	Sammels	Armstrong	McGill for Radford
24 Sep	Chelsea	A	L	1-3	..	..	..	..	..	McGill	..	..[1]	Baldwin	..	Walley	
1 Oct	Leicester C	H	L	2-4	..	..	..	..	..	Neill	..	..[1]	Graham[1]	..	Armstrong	McGill for Neill
8 Oct	Newcastle U	H	W	2-0	..	..	..	Boot[1]	..	Woodward	*opponents*	McLintock	..	..	..	
15 Oct	Leeds U	A	L	1-3	..	McNab	..	..[1]	..	Simpson	Walley	..	..	..	..	
22 Oct	W B A	H	L	2-3	..	..	..	McLintock	..	..	Boot	Graham	Radford	..	..[2]	
29 Oct	Manchester U	A	L	0-1	..	..	..	..	Neill	..	Sammels	Addison	Graham	Radford	..	
5 Nov	Leeds U	H	L	0-1	..	Storey	Walley	..	..	..	..	Radford	..	Addison	..	Boot for Sammels
12 Nov	Everton	A	D	0-0	..	McNab	Storey	..	Ure	Neill	Radford	Sammels	..	Simpson	Addison	
19 Nov	Fulham	H	W	1-0	..	..	..	..[1]	..	..	Neilson	Addison	..	Sammels	Armstrong	
26 Nov	Nottingham F	A	L	1-2	..	..	..	..	..	..	..[1]	..	..	..	..	
3 Dec	Burnley	H	D	0-0	..	..	..	..	..	..	..	Radford	..	..	..	Simpson for McNab
10 Dec	Sheffield U	A	D	1-1	..	Simpson	..	..	..	..	..	..	..[1]	..	..	Woodward for Sammels
17 Dec	Sunderland	H	W	2-0	..	McNab	..	..[1]	..	..	Addison	..	..	..[1]	..	
26 Dec	Southampton	H	W	4-1	..	..	..	..	..	Simpson	Neilson	..[2]	..	..	..[2]	
27 Dec	Southampton	A	L	1-2	..	..	..	McGill	..	..	Addison[1]	..	..	..	..	
31 Dec	Aston Villa	A	W	1-0	..	..	..	McLintock[1]	..	..	Neilson	Addison	..	..	..	
7 Jan	Tottenham	H	L	0-2	..	..	..	..	..	..	..	Radford	..	..	..	
14 Jan	Manchester C	H	W	1-0	..	Simpson	..	..[1]	..	Neill	..	..	..	..	..	
21 Jan	Blackpool	A	W	3-0	..	..	..	..	..	..	..[1]	..	..	..[2]	..	Walley for Radford
4 Feb	Chelsea	H	W	2-1	..	..	..	..	..	..	..	Addison	..[1]	..	..[1]	McNab for Addison
11 Feb	Leicester C	A	L	1-2	..	..	..	..	..	..	..	..	..[1]	..	..	
25 Feb	Newcastle U	A	L	1-2	..	McNab	..	..	Neill	Simpson	..	Radford	..[1]	..	..	Court for Sammels
3 Mar	Manchester U	H	D	1-1	..	..	..	..	..	..	Addison	..	..	..[1]	..	Court for McLintock
18 Mar	W B A	A	W	1-0	..	..	..	..[1]	..	..	Court	..	..	..	..	
25 Mar	Sheffield U	H	W	2-0	..	..	Simpson	..[1]	Ure	Neill	..	..	..	..[1]	..	
27 Mar	Liverpool	A	D	0-0	..	..	..	..	..	..	..	..	..	..	..	
28 Mar	Liverpool	H	D	1-1	..	..	..	..	..	..	..	..	..[1]	..	..	
1 Apr	Stoke C	A	D	2-2	..	..	..	..	..	..	..	..	..[2]	..	..	
19 Apr	Fulham	A	D	0-0	..	..	Storey	..	Neill	Ure	Simpson	..	..	..	..	
22 Apr	Nottingham F	H	D	1-1	..	..	..[1]	..	..	..	..	..	..	..	..	
25 Apr	Everton	H	W	3-1	..	..	..	..[1]	..	..	..	Addison	..[1]	..[1]	..	
29 Apr	Burnley	A	W	4-1	..	..	..	..	..	..	..[1]	..[1]	..[1]	..	..[1]	Court for Addison
6 May	Stoke C	H	W	3-1	..	..	..	..[1]	..	..	*opponents*	Radford[1]	..	..	..	
13 May	Sheffield W	A	D	1-1	..	..	Woodward	Radford	..	..	..	Addison	..[1]	..	..	
	FA Cup															
28 Jan	Bristol Rov (3)	A	W	3-0	Furnell	Simpson	Storey	McLintock	Neill	Ure	Neilson[1]	Addison	Graham[1]	Sammels	Armstrong[1]	
18 Feb	Bolton W (4)	A	D	0-0	..	..	..	..	..	..	..	Radford	..	..	..	
22 Feb	Bolton W (4R)	H	W	3-0	..	..	..	..	..	..	..	..[3]	..	..	..	
11 Mar	Birmingham C (5)	A	L	0-1	..	McNab	..	Court	..	Simpson	Addison	..	..	..	..	
	Football League Cup															
13 Sep	Gillingham (2)	H	D	1-1	Furnell	Howe	Walley	McLintock	Ure	Neill	Coakley	Tyrer	Baldwin[1]	Sammels	Armstrong	
21 Sep	Gillingham (2R)	A	D	1-1	..	McGill	Storey	Ure	Neill	Walley	..	Radford	..[1]	..	Jenkins	Tyrer for Jenkins
28 Sep	Gillingham (2R)	H	W	5-0	..	..	..	McLintock[2]	Ure	Neill	..[1]	Baldwin[2]	Simpson	..	Armstrong	
5 Oct	West Ham U (3)	H	L	1-3	..	Simpson	..	Boot	..	Woodward	..	Jenkins[1]	Walley	..	..	

Appearances (Goals)

Armstrong G 40 (7) · Addison C 17 (4) · Baldwin T 8 (2) · Boot M 4 (2) · Coakley T 9 (1) · Court D 13 · Furnell J 42 · Graham G 33 (11) · Howe D 1 · McNab R 26 · McGill J 8 · McLintock F 40 (9) · Neill T 34 · Neilson G 12 (2) · Radford J 30 (4) · Sammels J 42 (10) · Simpson P 36 (1) · Skirton A 2 (2) · Storey P 34 (1) · Ure I 37 · Walley J 4 · Woodward J 3 · Own Goals 2 · Total: 22 players (58)

Position in League Table

	P	W	L	D	F:A	Pts	
Manchester U	42	24	6	12	84:45	60	1st
Arsenal	42	16	12	14	58:47	46	7th

1967-1968

SEASON 1967-1968 FOOTBALL LEAGUE (DIVISION 1)

19 Aug	Stoke C	H	W	2-0	Furnell	Court	Storey	McLintock	Neill	Simpson	Johnston	Radford	Graham[1]	Sammels[1]	Armstrong	
22 Aug	Liverpool	A	L	0-2	..	McNab	..	..	..	..	..	..	Court	..	..	
26 Aug	Nottingham F	A	L	0-2	..	Court	..	..	..	..	..	..	Graham	..	..	
28 Aug	Liverpool	H	W	2-0	..	Simpson	..	..	..	Ure	Addison	*opponents*	..	..[1]	..	Johnston for Radford
2 Sep	Coventry C	H	D	1-1	..	Storey	McNab	..	..	Simpson	Johnston	Addison	..[1]	..	..	Court for McNab
6 Sep	W B A	A	W	3-1	..	..	Simpson	..	..	Ure	..	..[1]	..	..[1]	..[1]	
9 Sep	Sheffield U	A	W	4-2	..	..	..	..[1]	..	..	Radford	..[1]	..[2]	..	..	
16 Sep	Tottenham H	H	W	4-0	..	..	..	..	..[1]	..	..[1]	..[1]	..[1]	..	..	
23 Sep	Manchester C	H	W	1-0	..	..	..	..	..	..	..[1]	..	..	..	..	
30 Sep	Newcastle U	A	L	1-2	..	..	..	..	..	..	..	..	..[1]	..	..	
7 Oct	Manchester U	A	L	0-1	..	..	McNab	..	..	..	..	Simpson	..	..	..	
14 Oct	Sunderland	H	W	2-1	..	..	..	..	..	..	..[1]	..	..[1]	..	..	Addison for Simpson
23 Oct	Wolverhampton W	A	L	2-3	..	..	..	..	..	..	..	Addison	..[1]	..	..[1]	
28 Oct	Fulham	H	W	5-3	..	..	..	..	..	..	..[3]	..[2]	..	..	..	
4 Nov	Leeds U	A	L	1-3	..	..	..	..[1]	..	Simpson	..	..	..	..	..	
11 Nov	Everton	H	D	2-2	..	..	..	..	..	..	..	Johnston[1]	..	..[1]	..	
18 Nov	Leicester C	A	D	2-2	..	..	..	..	..	..	..[1]	..[1]	..	..	..	
25 Nov	West Ham U	H	D	0-0	..	..	..	..	..	..	..	..	..	..	..	Jenkins for Graham
2 Dec	Burnley	A	L	0-1	..	..	..	..	..	..	..	..	..	..	..	Rice for Graham
16 Dec	Stoke C	A	W	1-0	..	..	..	..	Ure	..	..	..	..[1]	..	..	Rice for McLintock
23 Dec	Nottingham F	H	W	3-0	..	..	..	..	Neill	Ure	..	..	..[2]	Simpson	..[1]	
26 Dec	Chelsea	A	L	1-2	..	..	..	..	..[1]	..	..	..	..	..	..	
30 Dec	Chelsea	H	D	1-1	..	..	..	..	..	..	..[1]	Sammels	..	..	..	
6 Jan	Coventry C	A	D	1-1	..	..	..	Simpson	..	..	..	Johnston	..[1]	Sammels	..	
13 Jan	Sheffield U	H	D	1-1	..	Rice	..	..	..	..	..	..	..[1]	..	..	
20 Jan	Tottenham H	A	L	0-1	..	Simpson	..	McLintock	..	..	..	Jenkins	..	..	..	Rice for Jenkins
3 Feb	Manchester C	A	D	1-1	..	..	Storey	..	..	..	..	Gould	..[1]	..	..	
10 Feb	Newcastle U	H	D	0-0	..	..	..	..	..	..	..	..	..	..	..	
24 Feb	Manchester U	H	L	0-2	..	McNab	..	..	..	Simpson	Jenkins	..	..	..	..	
16 Mar	Wolverhampton W	H	L	0-2	Wilson	..	..	..	Simpson	Neill	Radford	..	..	..	..	Davidson for Simpson
23 Mar	Fulham	A	W	3-1	..	Rice	..	..	Neill	Simpson	..	..[1]	..[1]	Court[1]	..	
29 Mar	West Ham U	A	D	1-1	..	Storey	McNab	..	..	..	..	Court	..	Gould	..[1]	
6 Apr	Everton	A	L	0-2	..	..	..	..	Ure	..	..	..	..	..	..	
10 Apr	Southampton	A	L	0-2	..	McNab	Storey	..	..	..	..	..	..	..	..	
13 Apr	Leicester C	H	W	2-1	..	Storey	McNab	..	Neill	..	..	..	..[1]	..[1]	..	
15 Apr	Southampton	H	L	0-3	..	..	..	..	..	..	..	..	..	..	..	Sammels for McLintock
20 Apr	Sunderland	A	L	0-2	..	..	..	..	..	..	..	..	..	Sammels	..	Gould for Court
27 Apr	Burnley	H	W	2-0	..	McNab	Storey	Court[1]	..	..	..	Sammels	..	Gould	..[1]	
30 Apr	Sheffield W	H	W	3-2	..	..	..	..[1]	..	..	..[1]	..	..	..[1]	..	Rice for Graham
4 May	Sheffield W	A	W	2-1	..	Storey	McNab	McLintock	Simpson	Court	..[1]	Johnston	Gould[1]	Sammels	..	
7 May	Leeds U	H	W	4-3	..	McLintock[1]	Storey	Court	Neill	Simpson	*opponents*	..[1]	Sammels	Gould[1]	..	
11 May	W B A	H	W	2-1	..	McNab	McLintock[1]	..	..	..	..	..	..	..[1]	..	
	FA Cup															
27 Jan	Shrewsbury T (3)	A	D	1-1	Furnell	Storey	McNab	McLintock	Simpson	Ure	Radford[1]	Jenkins	Graham	Sammels	Armstrong	Neill for Radford
30 Jan	Shrewsbury T (3R)	H	W	2-0	..	Simpson	Storey	..	Neill	..	..	..[1]	..	..[1]	..	Court for Jenkins
17 Feb	Swansea T (4)	A	W	1-0	..	Storey	Simpson	..	..	..	..	Gould[1]	..	..	..	
9 Mar	Birmingham C (5)	H	D	1-1	..	..	McNab	..	Simpson	Neill	..[1]	..	..	..	..	
12 Mar	Birmingham C (5R)	A	L	1-2	Wilson	..	..	..	..	..	..	..[1]	..	..	..	
	Football League Cup															
12 Sep	Coventry C (2)	A	W	2-1	Furnell	Storey	Simpson	McLintock	Neill	Ure	Radford	Addison	Graham[1]	Sammels[1]	Armstrong	
11 Oct	Reading T (3)	H	W	1-0	..	..	McNab	..	..	..	..	Simpson[1]	..	..	..	
1 Nov	Blackburn Rov (4)	H	W	2-1	..	..	..	..	..	Simpson	..	Addison[1]	..[1]	..	..	Johnston for Radford
29 Nov	Burnley (5)	A	D	3-3	..	..	..	..[1]	..	..	..	Johnston	..[2]	..	..	
5 Dec	Burnley (5R)	H	W	2-1	..	..	Rice	..	..[1]	..	..[1]	..	..	..	..	
17 Jan	Huddersfield (SF)	H	W	3-2	..	Simpson	McNab[1]	..	..	Ure	..[1]	..	..[1]	..	..	
6 Feb	Huddersfield (SF)	A	W	3-1	..	..	Storey	..[1]	..	..	..	Jenkins[1]	..	..[1]	..	
2 Mar	Leeds (F) (at Wembley)		L	0-1	..	Storey	McNab	..	Simpson	..	..	..	..	..	..	Neill for Jenkins

Appearances (Goals)

Addison C 11 (5) · Armstrong G 42 (5) · Court D 16 (3) · Davidson R 1 · Furnell J 29 · Gould R 16 (6) · Graham G 38 (16) · Jenkins D 3 · Johnston G 18 (3) · McLintock F 38 (4) · McNab R 30 · Neill T 38 (2) · Radford J 39 (10) · Rice P 6 · Sammels J 35 (4) · Simpson P 40 · Storey P 39 · Ure I 21 · Wilson R 13 · Own goals 2 · Total: 19 players (60)

Position in League Table

	P	W	L	D	F:A	Pts	
Manchester C	42	26	10	6	86:43	58	1st
Arsenal	42	17	15	10	60:56	44	9th

SEASON 1968-1969 FOOTBALL LEAGUE (DIVISION 1)

10 Aug	Tottenham H	A	W 2-1	Wilson	Storey	McNab	McLintock *og*	Neill	Simpson	Radford[1]	Sammels	Graham	Jenkins	Court	
13 Aug	Leicester C	H	W 3-0	..	..	..	..	..	..	..	..	..	Court[1]	Jenkins	Gould[2] for Graham
17 Aug	Liverpool	H	D 1-1	..	..	..	..	..	..	..[1]	..	Gould	..	..	
21 Aug	Wolverhampton W	A	D 0-0	..	..	..	..	..	..	..	..	..	..	..	
24 Aug	Ipswich T	A	W 2-1	..	..	..	..	..	..	..[1]	..	..	..	..[1]	
27 Aug	Manchester C	H	W 4-1	..	..	..	..	..	..	..[1]	..[1]	..	..	..[2]	
31 Aug	Q P R	H	W 2-1	..	..	..	..[1]	..[1]	..	..	..	..	..	..	
7 Sep	Southampton	A	W 2-1	..	..	..	..	..	..	..[2]	..	..	..	..	Johnston for Jenkins
14 Sep	Stoke C	H	W 1-0	..	..	..	..	..[1]	..	..	..	..	..	..	Armstrong for Radford
21 Sep	Leeds U	A	L 0-2	..	..	..	..	..	..	Armstrong	..	..	..	..	Johnston for Jenkins
28 Sep	Sunderland	H	D 0-0	..	..	..	..	..	..	Radford	..	..	..	..	
5 Oct	Manchester U	A	D 0-0	..	..	..	..	..	..	..	..	..	..	..	
9 Oct	Manchester C	A	D 1-1	..	..	..	..	..	..	..[1]	..	..	..	..	Armstrong for Sammels
12 Oct	Coventry C	H	W 2-1	..	..	..	Ure	..	..	..[1]	Armstrong	..	..[1]	..	Graham for Jenkins
19 Oct	W B A	A	L 0-1	..	..	..	McLintock	..	Ure	..	Simpson	Graham	..	Armstrong	Gould for Graham
26 Oct	West Ham U	H	D 0-0	..	..	..	..	..	..	Robertson	Radford	..	Simpson	..	
9 Nov	Newcastle U	H	D 0-0	..	..	..	Court	..	..	..	..	..	Sammels	..	Gould for Robertson
16 Nov	Nottingham F	A	W 2-0	..	..	..	..	..	Simpson	Radford[1]	McLintock	Sammels	Graham	..[1]	
23 Nov	Chelsea	H	L 0-1	..	..	..	McLintock	Ure	..	..	Court	..	..	..	Gould for Graham
30 Nov	Burnley	A	W 1-0	..	..	..	..	..	..	Robertson[1]	..	..	Gould	..	
7 Dec	Everton	H	W 3-1	..	..	..	..	..	..	Radford[1]	..[1]	..	..	Robertson	Graham[1] for Sammels
14 Dec	Coventry	A	W 1-0	..	..	..	..	..	..	..	Robertson	Court	..[1]	Graham	
21 Dec	W B A	H	W 2-0	..	..	..	..	*opponents*	..	..	..	..	..[1]	..	
26 Dec	Manchester U	H	W 3-0	..	..	..	..	..	..	..[1]	Graham	..[1]	..	Armstrong[1]	
11 Jan	Sheffield W	H	W 2-0	..	..	..	..	Neill	..	..[1]	Sammels	..	..[1]	..	
18 Jan	Newcastle U	A	L 1-2	..	..	..	..	Ure	..	..	..	Graham	..[1]	..	Robertson for Graham
1 Feb	Nottingham F	H	D 1-1	..	..	..	..	..	..	..	..	Court	..[1]	Robertson	Armstrong for Court
15 Feb	Burnley	H	W 2-0	..	..	..	Graham	..	..	Robertson	..	..	..[2]	Armstrong	
18 Feb	Ipswich	H	L 0-2	..	..	..	..	..	..	..	..	..	..	..	Johnston for Robertson
1 Mar	Sheffield W	A	W 5-0	..	..	..	..	..	..	Radford[3]	..[1]	..	..[1]	..	
22 Mar	Q P R	A	W 1-0	..	..	..	McLintock	..	..	..	..	..	..	..[1]	
24 Mar	Tottenham H	H	W 1-0	..	..	..	..	..	..	..	..[1]	..	..	..	
29 Mar	Southampton	H	D 0-0	..	..	..	..	..	..	..	..	..	..	..	
31 Mar	Liverpool	A	D 1-1	..	..	..	..	..	Graham	Robertson[1]	..	..	..	..	
5 Apr	Sunderland	A	D 0-0	..	..	..	..	..	..	..	..	..	..	..	Radford for Gould
7 Apr	Wolverhampton W	H	W 3-1	..	..	..	..	..	..[1]	..[1]	..	..	..	..[1]	
8 Apr	Leicester C	A	D 0-0	..	..	..	..	..	..	..	..	..	..	..	
12 Apr	Leeds U	H	L 1-2	..	..	..	..	..	..[1]	..	..	..	..	..	Radford for Gould
14 Apr	Chelsea	A	L 1-2	..	..	..	..	Simpson	..	..	..	..[1]	Radford	..	Neill for Graham
19 Apr	Stoke C	A	W 3-1	..	..	..	..	Neill	*opponents*	..	..	..[1]	Gould	..[1]	
21 Apr	West Ham U	A	W 2-1	..	..	..	..	Simpson	..[1]	..	..[1]	..	Radford	..	Gould for Simpson
29 Apr	Everton	A	L 0-1	..	..	..	..	Neill	..	..	..	..	Gould	..	Radford for Sammels
	FA Cup														
4 Jan	Cardiff (3)	A	D 0-0	Wilson	Storey	McNab	McLintock	Ure	Simpson	Radford	Armstrong	Court	Gould	Graham	
7 Jan	Cardiff (3R)	H	W 2-0	..	..	..	..	..	..	..	Sammels	..	..[1]	Armstrong[1]	
25 Jan	Charlton Ath (4)	H	W 2-0	..	..	..	..	..	..	..	..[1]	..	..	Robertson[1]	
12 Feb	W B A (5)	A	D 0-1	..	..	..	..	..	..	..	..	..	..	..	Armstrong for Sammels
	Football League Cup														
4 Sep	Sunderland (2)	H	W 1-0	Wilson	Storey	McNab	McLintock	Neill[1]	Simpson	Radford	Sammels	Gould	Court	Jenkins	
25 Sep	Scunthorpe U (3)	A	W 6-1	..	..	..	..	..	..	Armstrong	..[1]	..[1]	..[1]	..[3]	
15 Oct	Liverpool (4)	H	W 2-1	..	..	..	..	..	Ure	Radford[1]	Simpson[1]	Graham	..	Armstrong	Gould for Simpson
29 Oct	Blackpool (5)	H	W 5-1	..	..	..	..	..	..	..[1]	Gould[1]	..	Simpson[1]	..[2]	Court for McLintock
20 Nov	Tottenham H (SF)	H	W 1-0	..	..	..	..	Ure	Simpson	..[1]	Court	Sammels	Graham	..	Gould for Graham
4 Dec	Tottenham H (SF)	A	D 1-1	..	..	..	..	..	..	..[1]	..	..	Gould	..	Graham for McNab
15 Mar	Swindon T (F) (at Wembley)		L 1-3*	..	..	..	..	..	..	..	Sammels	Court	..[1]	..	Graham for Simpson

*aet, 1-1 at 90 mins

Appearances (Goals)

Armstrong G 29 (5) · Court D 40 (6) · Gould R 38 (10) · Graham G 25 (4) · Jenkins D 14 (3) · Johnston G 3 · McLintock F 37 (1) · McNab R 42 · Neill T 22 (2) · Radford J 34 (15) · Robertson J 19 (3) · Sammels J 36 (4) · Simpson P 34 · Storey P 42 · Ure I 23 · Wilson R 42 · Own goals 3 · Total: 16 players (56)

Position in League Table

	P	W	L	D	F:A	Pts	
Leeds	42	27	2	13	66:26	67	1st
Arsenal	42	22	8	12	56:27	56	4th

SEASON 1969-1970 FOOTBALL LEAGUE (DIVISION 1)

9 Aug	Everton	H	L 0-1	Wilson	Rice	McNab	McLintock	Neill	Simpson	Robertson	George	Gould	Graham	Radford	
13 Aug	Leeds U	A	D 0-0	..	..	..	..	Ure	..	..	Storey	..	..	..	Court for Rice
16 Aug	W B A	A	W 1-0	..	..	..	Court	..	..	..	George[1]	Storey	..	..	
19 Aug	Leeds U	H	D 1-1	..	..[1]	..	..	..	..	..	..	..	..	..	
23 Aug	Nottingham F	H	W 2-1	..	..	..[1]	McLintock	Neill	..	..	..	Sammels	..[1]	..	Gould for George
25 Aug	West Ham U	A	D 1-1	..	Storey	..	..	..	..	*opponents*	..	Court	..	..	
30 Aug	Newcastle U	A	L 1-3	..	..	..	..	..	..	..[1]	..	..	..	..	
6 Sep	Sheffield W	H	D 0-0	..	Rice	..	Sammels	..	..	..	Gould	..	..	Armstrong	Kelly for Court
13 Sep	Burnley	A	W 1-0	..	Storey	..	McLintock	..	..	..	Sammels	Gould	..[1]	..	Court for Gould
16 Sep	Tottenham H	H	L 2-3	Webster	..	..	..	..	..	..[1]	George	Radford[1]	..	Sammels	
20 Sep	Manchester U	H	D 2-2	..	..	Rice	..	Court	..	..	Armstrong	..	..[1]	..[1]	
27 Sep	Chelsea	A	L 0-3	..	..	McNab	Court	McLintock	..	..	Sammels	..	..	George	
4 Oct	Coventry C	H	L 0-1	Barnett	..	..	McLintock	Roberts	..	..	..	Court	..	Gould	George for Court
7 Oct	W B A	H	D 1-1	..	..	..	..	..	..	..	..	Graham	Gould	Radford[1]	
11 Oct	Stoke C	A	D 0-0	..	..	..	..	..	..	..	..	Gould	Graham	..	
18 Oct	Sunderland	A	D 1-1	..	..	..	..	Neill	..	..	..[1]	Graham	Gould	..	Kennedy for McNab
25 Oct	Ipswich T	H	D 0-0	..	..	Nelson	..	..	..	..	..	Gould	Graham	..	George for Gould
1 Nov	Crystal Palace	A	W 5-1	..	..	McNab	Court	..	..	..	..	Radford[3]	..[1]	Armstrong[1]	
8 Nov	Derby Co	H	W 4-0	..	..	..	..	..	..	..	..[2]	..	..	..[1]	George[1] for Neill
15 Nov	Wolverhampton W	A	L 0-2	..	..	..	..	..	..	..	..	..	..	..	George for Graham
22 Nov	Manchester C	H	D 1-1	..	..	..	..	..[1]	..	..	..	..	..	..	George for Armstrong
29 Nov	Liverpool	A	W 1-0	..	..	..	..	McLintock	..	..[1]	..	..	..	..	
6 Dec	Southampton	H	D 2-2	..	..	Nelson	..	..	..	..	..[1]	..[1]	..	..	
13 Dec	Burnley	H	W 3-2	Wilson	..	McNab	..	..	..	..[1]	..	..[1]	..	..[1]	Kelly for McLintock
20 Dec	Sheffield W	A	D 1-1	..	..	..	..	Neill	..	..	..[1]	..	Kelly	..	George for McNab
26 Dec	Nottingham F	A	D 1-1	..	..	..[1]	..	..	..	..	..	..	..	..	
27 Dec	Newcastle U	H	D 0-0	..	..	..	George	..	..	..	..	..	..	..	
10 Jan	Manchester U	A	L 1-2	..	..	Nelson	Court	..	..	Marinello[1]	..	..	George	..	
17 Jan	Chelsea	H	L 0-3	..	..	McNab	McLintock	Roberts	..	..	..	..	Kelly	Kennedy	George for Kelly
31 Jan	Coventry C	A	L 0-2	..	..	..	..	..	..	..	..	..	Graham	Armstrong	
7 Feb	Stoke C	H	D 0-0	..	..	..	..	..	..	..	..	..	George	..	
14 Feb	Everton	A	D 2-2	..	..	..	..	..	..	..	..	..[1]	Graham	George[1]	Gould for Simpson
18 Feb	Manchester C	A	D 1-1	..	..	..	..	..	Kelly	..	George	..	Sammels	Graham[1]	
21 Feb	Derby Co	A	L 2-3	..	..	..	..	..[1]	..	..	..	..[1]	..	..	
28 Feb	Sunderland	H	W 3-1	..	..[1]	..	..	..	..[1]	..	Sammels	..	Kennedy[1]	..	Court for Sammels
14 Mar	Liverpool	H	W 2-1	..	..	..	Kelly	McLintock	Simpson	..	..[1]	..[1]	George	..	
21 Mar	Southampton	A	W 2-0	..	..	..	..	..	..	..	..[1]	..	..[1]	..	
28 Mar	Wolverhampton W	H	D 2-2	..	..	..	..	..	..	..	..	..	..	..[2]	
30 Mar	Crystal Palace	H	W 2-0	..	..	Nelson	..	..	..	..	..	..[1]	..[1]	..	
31 Mar	Ipswich T	A	L 1-2	..	..	McNab	..	..	..	..	..	..	..[1]	..	
4 Apr	West Ham U	H	W 2-1	..	..	..	..[1]	..	..	..	..	..[1]	..	..	
2 May	Tottenham H	A	L 0-1	..	..	..	..	Roberts	..	Armstrong	..	..	..	..	Kennedy for Kelly
	FA Cup														
3 Jan	Blackpool (3)	H	D 1-1	Wilson	Storey	Nelson	Court	Neill	Simpson	Robertson	Sammels	Radford[1]	Graham	Armstrong	
15 Jan	Blackpool (3R)	A	L 2-3	..	..	McNab	George	..	..	..	..[1]	..[1]	..	..	

Football League Cup

2 Sep	Southampton (2)	A D	1-1	Wilson	Storey	McNab[1]	McLintock	Roberts	Simpson	Robertson	George	Court	Graham[2]	Radford	Gould for Roberts
4 Sep	Southampton (2R)	H W	2-0	..	..	..	..	..	..	..	Sammels	Radford	..	Armstrong	
24 Sep	Everton (3)	H D	0-0	Webster	..	..	Court	McLintock	..	..	Sammels	Radford	..	Armstrong	
1 Oct	Everton (3R)	A L	0-1	..	Rice	..	McLintock	Neill	..	..	..	Gould	..	Storey	Court for McLintock

European Fairs Cup

9 Sep	Glentoran (1)	H W	3-0	Wilson	Storey	McNab	McLintock	Simpson	Graham[2]	Robertson	Court	Gould[1]	Sammels	Armstrong	Nelson for McNab, Kelly for Court
29 Sep	Glentoran (1)	A L	0-1	Webster	Rice	..	Court	Neill	Simpson	..	Sammels	Radford	Gould	George	Kennedy for Radford
20 Oct	Sp Cb de Port (2)	A D	0-0	Barnett	Storey	..	..	..	..	..	..	..	Graham[1]	Armstrong	
26 Nov	Sp Cb de Port (2)	H W	3-0	..	..	..	..	..	..	..	..	..	Graham[2]	Armstrong	
17 Dec	Rouen (3)	A D	0-0	Wilson	..	..	..	..	..	..	..	..	..	..	Kelly for Graham
13 Jan	Rouen (3)	H W	1-0	..	..	Nelson	..	..	..	Marinello	..[1]	..[1]	George	..	Graham for Court
11 Mar	Dinamo Bacau (4)	A W	2-0	..	..	McNab	Kelly	McLintock	..	..[1]	..[1]	..	..	George	
18 Mar	Dinamo Bacau (4)	H W	7-1	..	..	..	..	..	..	..[2]	..[2]	..[2]	..	Graham	Armstrong for Graham
8 Apr	Ajax (SF)	H W	3-0	..	..	..	..	..	..	..[1]	..[1]	..	..	..	Armstrong for Marinello
15 Apr	Ajax (SF)	A L	0-1	..	..	..	..	..	Armstrong	..	..	..	..	..	
22 Apr	Anderlecht (F)	A L	1-3	..	..	..	..	..	..	..[1]	..[1]	..	..	..	Kennedy[1] for George
28 Apr	Anderlecht (F)	H W	3-0	..	..	..	..[1]	..	..	..	..	..	..	..	

Appearances (Goals)

Armstrong G 17 (3) · Barnett G 11 · Court D 21 · George C 28 (6) · Gould R 11 · Graham G 36 (7) · Kelly E 16 (2) · Kennedy R 4 (1) · Marinello P 14 (1) · McLintock F 30 · McNab R 37 (2) · Neill T 17 (1) · Nelson S 4 · Radford J 39 (12) · Rice P 7 (1) · Roberts J 11 (1) · Roberston J 27 (4) · Sammels J 36 (8) · Simpson P 39 · Storey P 39 (1) · Ure I 3 · Webster M 3 · Wilson R 28 · Own goals 1 · Total: 23 players (51)

Position in League Table

	P	W	L	D	F:A	Pts	
Everton	42	29	5	8	72:34	66	1st
Arsenal	42	12	12	18	51:49	42	12th

SEASON 1970-1971 FOOTBALL LEAGUE (DIVISION 1)

Starting line-up (15 Aug): Wilson · Rice · McNab · Kelly · Roberts · McLintock · Armstrong · Storey · Radford · George · Graham

15 Aug	Everton	A D	2-2	Marinello for George
17 Aug	West Ham U	A D	0-0	Marinello for Radford
22 Aug	Manchester U	H W	4-0	Nelson for Radford
25 Aug	Huddersfield T	H W	1-0	
29 Aug	Chelsea	A L	1-2	
1 Sep	Leeds U	H D	0-0	
5 Sep	Tottenham	H W	2-0	Nelson for McLintock
12 Sep	Burnley	A W	2-1	
19 Sep	W B A	H W	6-2	opponents
26 Sep	Stoke C	A L	0-5	
3 Oct	Nottingham F	H W	4-0	
10 Oct	Newcastle U	A D	1-1	
17 Oct	Everton	H W	4-0	
24 Oct	Coventry C	A W	3-1	
31 Oct	Derby Co	H W	2-0	
7 Nov	Blackpool	A W	1-0	
14 Nov	Crystal Palace	H D	1-1	
21 Nov	Ipswich T	A W	1-0	
28 Nov	Liverpool	H W	2-0	Graham[1] for Kelly
5 Dec	Manchester C	A W	2-0	
12 Dec	Wolverhampton W	H W	2-1	
19 Dec	Manchester U	A W	3-1	
26 Dec	Southampton	H D	0-0	
9 Jan	West Ham U	H W	2-0	
16 Jan	Huddersfield T	A L	1-2	
30 Jan	Liverpool	A L	0-2	
6 Feb	Manchester C	H W	1-0	
20 Feb	Ipswich	H W	3-2	
27 Feb	Derby Co	A L	0-2	Graham for Rice
2 Mar	Wolverhampton W	A W	3-0	
13 Mar	Crystal Palace	A W	2-0	Sammels[1] for George
20 Mar	Blackpool	H W	1-0	
3 Apr	Chelsea	H W	2-0	Kelly for Armstrong
6 Apr	Coventry C	H W	1-0	
10 Apr	Southampton	A W	2-1	
13 Apr	Nottingham F	A W	3-0	
17 Apr	Newcastle U	H W	1-0	
20 Apr	Burnley	H W	1-0	
24 Apr	W B A	A D	2-2	opponents
26 Apr	Leeds U	A L	0-1	Sammels for Rice
1 May	Stoke C	H W	1-0	Kelly[1] for Storey
3 May	Tottenham H	A W	1-0	

FA Cup

Starting line-up (6 Jan): Wilson · Rice · McNab · Storey · McLintock · Simpson · Armstrong · Sammels · Radford · Kennedy · Graham

6 Jan	Yeovil T (3)	A W	3-0	Kelly for McNab
23 Jan	Portsmouth (4)	A D	1-1	George for Rice
1 Feb	Portsmouth (4R)	H W	3-2	
17 Feb	Manchester C (5)	A W	2-1	
6 Mar	Leicester C (6)	A D	0-0	
15 Mar	Leicester C (6R)	H W	1-0	
27 Mar	Stoke C (SF) (at Sheffield W)	D	2-2	Sammels for George
31 Mar	Stoke C (SFR) (at Birmingham)	W	2-0	
8 May	Liverpool (F) (at Wembley) *aet, 0-0 at 90 mins	W	2-1*	Kelly[1] for Storey

Football League Cup

Starting line-up (8 Sep): Wilson · Rice · McNab · Kelly · McLintock · Roberts · Armstrong · Storey · Nelson · Kennedy · Graham

8 Sep	Ipswich T (2)	A D	0-0	
28 Sep	Ipswich T (2R)	H W	4-0	
6 Oct	Luton T (3)	A W	1-0	
28 Oct	Crystal Palace (4)	A D	0-0	
9 Nov	Crystal Palace (4R)	H L	0-2	

European Fairs Cup

Starting line-up (16 Sep): Wilson · Rice · McNab · Kelly · McLintock · Roberts · Armstrong · Storey · Radford · Kennedy · Graham

16 Sep	Lazio Roma (1)	A D	2-2	Nelson for Graham
23 Sep	Lazio Roma (1)	H W	2-0	
21 Oct	Sturm Graz (2)	A L	0-1	
4 Nov	Sturm Graz (2)	H W	2-0	
2 Dec	Beveren Waas (3)	H W	4-0	
16 Dec	Beveren Waas (3)	A D	0-0	Marinello for Armstrong, George for Radford
9 Mar	FC Koln (4)	H W	2-1	
23 Mar	FC Koln (4)	A L	0-1	

Appearances (Goals)

Armstrong G 42 (7) · George C 17 (5) · Graham G 38 (11) · Kelly E 23 (4) · Kennedy R 41 (19) · Marinello P 3 · McLintock F 42 (5) · McNab R 40 · Nelson S 4 · Radford J 41 (15) · Rice P 41 · Roberts J 18 · Sammels J 15 (1) · Simpson P 25 · Storey P 40 (2) · Wilson R 42 · Own Goals 2 · Total: 16 Players (71)

Position in League Table

	P	W	L	D	F:A	Pts	
Arsenal	42	29	6	7	71:29	65	1st

SEASON 1971-1972 FOOTBALL LEAGUE (DIVISION 1)

14 Aug	Chelsea	H	W 3-0	Wilson	Rice	McNab	Storey	McLintock[1]	Simpson	Armstrong	Kelly	Radford[1]	Kennedy[1]	Graham	
17 Aug	Huddersfield T	A	W 1-0	..	..	..	..	..	..	..	..	..	..[1]	..	
20 Aug	Manchester U (Liverpool)	A	L 1-3	..	..	..	..	..[1]	..	..	..	..	..	..	
24 Aug	Sheffield U	H	L 0-1	..	..	..	..	..	..	..	..	..	..	..	
28 Aug	Stoke C	H	L 0-1	..	..	..	..	..	..	..	..	..	..	..	Roberts for Rice
4 Sep	W B A	A	W 1-0	..	..	..	..	..	Roberts[1]	..	..	..	..	..	
11 Sep	Leeds U	H	W 2-0	..	..	..	..[1]	..	..	..	Simpson	..	..	..[1]	
18 Sep	Everton	A	L 1-2	..	..	..	..	..	..	..	..	..	..[1]	..	Kelly for McLintock
25 Sep	Leicester C	H	W 3-0	..	..[1]	Nelson	..	Simpson	..	..	Kelly	..[2]	..	..	George for Storey
2 Oct	Southampton	A	W 1-0	..	..	..	McLintock	..[1]	..	..	..	..	..	..	
9 Oct	Newcastle U	H	W 4-2	..	..	..	..	..	George	..[1]	..[1]	..	..[1]	..[1]	Davies for Radford
16 Oct	Chelsea	A	W 2-1	..	..	..	..	Roberts	..	..	..	..	..[2]	..	Simpson for Kelly
23 Oct	Derby Co	A	L 1-2	..	..	..	..	..	..	..	..	..	..	..[1]	Simpson for Kelly
30 Oct	Ipswich T	H	W 2-1	..	..	..	Storey	..	McLintock	*opponents*	George[1]	..	..	..	
6 Nov	Liverpool	A	L 2-3	..	..	..	..	..	..	*opponents*	..	..	..[1]	..	
13 Nov	Manchester C	H	L 1-2	..	..	..[1]	..	..	..	..	..	..	..	..	
20 Nov	Wolverhampton W	A	L 1-5	..	..	..	..	..	..	..	..	..	..[1]	..	
24 Nov	Tottenham H	A	D 1-1	..	..	McNab	..	..	..	..	Kelly	..	..[1]	..	
27 Nov	Crystal Palace	H	W 2-1	..	..	..	..	..	..	..	..[1]	..[1]	..	..	
4 Dec	West Ham U	A	D 0-0	..	..	..	..	McLintock	Simpson	..	..	..	..	..	
11 Dec	Coventry C	H	W 2-0	..	..	..	..	..	..	..	..	..[2]	..	..	Marinello for Simpson
18 Dec	W B A	H	W 2-0	..	..	..	..	..	Roberts[2]	..	..	..	..	..	
27 Dec	Nottingham F	A	D 1-1	..	..	..	Kelly	..	Simpson	..	Ball	..	..	..[1]	
1 Jan	Everton	H	D 1-1	..	..	..	..	Roberts	..[1]	..	..	..	..	..	George for Armstrong
8 Jan	Stoke C	A	D 0-0	..	..	..	..	McLintock	..	..	..	..	..	..	
22 Jan	Huddersfield T	H	W 1-0	..	..	Nelson	..	..	..	..[1]	..	..	..	..	George for Ball
29 Jan	Sheffield U	A	W 5-0	..	..	..	Roberts	..	..[1]	..	..	George[2]	..[1]	..[1]	
12 Feb	Derby Co	H	W 2-0	..	..	..	Kelly	..	..	..	..	..[2]	..	..	
19 Feb	Ipswich T	A	W 1-0	..	..	..	..	..	..	..	..	..[1]	..	..	
4 Mar	Manchester C	A	L 0-2	..	..	..	Storey	..	..	..	..	..	Radford	..	
11 Mar	Newcastle U	A	L 0-2	..	..	..	..	Simpson	Graham	..	..	..	Kennedy	Radford	Batson for George
25 Mar	Leeds U	A	L 0-3	..	..	..	..	McLintock	Simpson	..	..	..	..	Roberts	Marinello for Roberts
28 Mar	Southampton	H	W 1-0	..	..	..	..	..	..	..	..	..	..	Marinello[1]	
1 Apr	Nottingham F	H	W 3-0	..	..	..	..	Roberts	..	..	..	..[1]	..[1]	..	Graham[1] for Kennedy
4 Apr	Leicester C	A	D 0-0	..	..	..	..	McLintock	..	..	..	..	Graham	..	
8 Apr	Wolverhampton W	H	W 2-1	..	..	..	..	..	..	Marinello	..	..	Kennedy	Graham[2]	Armstrong for Marinello
11 Apr	Crystal Palace	A	D 2-2	..	..	..	..	Roberts	..	Armstrong	..[1]	Radford[1]	George	..	
22 Apr	West Ham U	H	W 2-1	Barnett	..	McNab	..	McLintock	..	..	..[2]	..	..	..	Batson for McLintock
25 Apr	Manchester U	H	W 3-0	..	..	..	Roberts	..	..[1]	..	Nelson	..[1]	Kennedy[1]	..	Marinello for Graham
1 May	Coventry C	A	W 1-0	..	..	..	Storey	..[1]	..	..	Ball	..	George	..	
8 May	Liverpool	H	D 0-0	..	..	Nelson	..	..	..	..	..	..	Kennedy	..	Roberts for Rice
11 May	Tottenham H	H	L 0-2	..	..	McNab	Nelson	..	Roberts	..	Simpson	..	..	..	Marinello for Simpson

FA Cup

15 Jan	Swindon T (3)	A	W 2-0	Wilson	Rice	Nelson	Kelly	McLintock	Simpson	Armstrong[1]	Ball[1]	Radford	Kennedy	Graham	
5 Feb	Reading (4)	A	W 2-1	..	..[1]	..	..	..	*opponents*	..	..	George	..	..	
26 Feb	Derby Co (5)	A	D 2-2	..	..	..	..	..	..	..	..	..[2]	..	..	Storey for Kelly
29 Feb	Derby Co (5R)	H	D 0-0	..	..	..	Storey	..	..	..	..	..	..	..	Radford for Kennedy
13 Mar	Derby Co (5R) (at Leicester)		W 1-0	..	..	..	..	..	..	..	..	..	..[1]	..	
18 Mar	Orient (6)	A	W 1-0	..	..	..	..	..	..	..	..[1]	..	..	..	
15 Apr	Stoke C (SF) (at Villa Park)		D 1-1	Wilson injured Radford in goal	..	McNab	..	..	..	..[1]	..	Radford	George	..	Kennedy for Wilson
19 Apr	Stoke C (SFR) (at Everton)		W 2-1	Barnett	..	..	..	..	..	..	..	..[1]	..[1]	..	
6 May	Leeds (F) (at Wembley)		L 0-1	..	..	..	..	..	..	..	..	..	..	..	Kennedy for Radford

Football League Cup

8 Sep	Barnsley (2)	H	W 1-0	Wilson	Rice	McNab	Storey	McLintock	Roberts	Marinello	Kelly	Radford	Kennedy[1]	Graham	
6 Oct	Newcastle U (3)	H	W 4-0	..	..	Nelson	McLintock	Simpson	..	Armstrong	..	..[2]	..[1]	..[1]	
26 Oct	Sheffield U (4)	H	D 0-0	Barnett	..	..	Storey	Roberts	McLintock	..	George	..	..	..	
8 Nov	Sheffield U (4R)	A	L 0-2	Wilson	..	..	Kelly	..	..	..	..	..	..	..	McNab for McLintock

European Cup

15 Sep	St't Drammen (1)	A	W 3-1	Wilson	Rice	Simpson[1]	McLintock	McNab	Roberts	Kelly[1]	Marinello[1]	Graham	Radford	Kennedy	Davies for Marinello
29 Sep	St't Drammen (1)	H	W 4-0	..	..	Nelson	Kelly	Simpson	..	Armstrong[1]	George	Radford[2]	Kennedy[1]	Graham	
20 Oct	Gr'pers Zurich (2)	A	W 2-0	..	..	..	McLintock	Roberts	George	..	Kelly	..	..[1]	..[1]	
3 Nov	Gr'pers Zurich (2)	H	W 3-0	..	..	..	Storey	..	McLintock	..	George[1]	..[1]	..[1]	..	Simpson for Roberts, McNab for McLintock
8 Mar	Ajax Ams'dam (3)	A	L 1-2	..	..	..	..	McLintock	Simpson	..	..	..	..[1]	..	
22 Mar	Ajax Ams'dam (3)	H	L 0-1	..	..	..	..	..	..	..	..	Marinello	..	..	Roberts for Nelson

Appearances (Goals)

Armstrong G 42 (2) · Ball A 18 (3) · Batson B 2 · Barnett G 5 · Davies P 1 · George C 23 (7) · Graham G 40 (8) · Kelly E 23 (2) · Kennedy R 37 (12) · McNab R 20 · McLintock F 37 (3) · Marinello P 8 (1) · Nelson S 24 (1) · Radford J 34 (8) · Rice P 42 (1) · Roberts J 23 (3) · Simpson P 34 (4) · Storey P 29 (1) · Wilson R 37 · Own goals 2 · Total: 19 players (58)

Position in League Table

	P	W	L	D	F:A	Pts	
Derby Co	42	24	8	10	69:33	58	1st
Arsenal	42	22	12	8	58:40	52	5th

SEASON 1972-1973 FOOTBALL LEAGUE (DIVISION 1)

12 Aug	Leicester C	A	W 1-0	Barnett	Rice	McNab	Storey	McLintock	Simpson	Armstrong	Ball[1]	Radford	Kennedy	Graham	
15 Aug	Wolverhampton W	H	W 5-2	..	..	..[1]	..	..	..[1]	..	..	..[2]	..[1]	..	Roberts for Simpson
19 Aug	Stoke C	H	W 2-0	..	..	..	..	..	Roberts	..	..	..	..[2]	..	
22 Aug	Coventry C	A	D 1-1	..	..[1]	..	..	..	Simpson	..	..	..	..	..	
26 Aug	Manchester U	A	D 0-0	..	..	..	..	..	..	..	..	George	..	..	
29 Aug	West Ham U	H	W 1-0	..	..	..	..	..	..	..	..[1]	Radford	..	..	George for Armstrong
2 Sep	Chelsea	H	D 1-1	..	..	..	..	..	*opponents*	..	..	..	..	..	George for Armstrong
9 Sep	Newcastle U	A	L 1-2	..	..	..	..	..	Roberts	Marinello	..	..	..[1]	..	
16 Sep	Liverpool	H	D 0-0	..	..	..	..	..	..	..	..	..	..	..	
23 Sep	Norwich C	A	L 2-3	..	..	..	..[1]	..	..	..	..	..[1]	..	..	
26 Sep	Birmingham C	H	W 2-0	..	..	..	..[1]	..	..	..	..	..	..	George[1]	
30 Sep	Southampton	H	W 1-0	..	..	..	..	..	..	..	..	..	..	..	Graham[1] for Kennedy
7 Oct	Sheffield U	A	L 0-1	..	..	..	..	..	Blockley	..	..	..	Graham	..	
14 Oct	Ipswich T	H	W 1-0	..	..	..	..	..	..	..	..	..	..[1]	..	
21 Oct	Crystal Palace	A	W 3-2	..	..[1]	..	..	..	..	..	Kelly	..[1]	..	..[1]	Nelson for Kelly
28 Oct	Manchester C	H	D 0-0	..	..	..	..	..	..	..	..	..	George	Graham	
4 Nov	Coventry C	H	L 0-2	..	..	..	..	..	..	..	Ball	..	..	Kelly	Graham for Kelly
11 Nov	Wolverhampton W	A	W 3-1	..	..	..	..	..	..	..[1]	..	..[2]	..	..	
18 Nov	Everton	H	W 1-0	..	..	..	..	Simpson	..	..	..	..[1]	..	..	
25 Nov	Derby Co	A	L 0-5	Wilson	..	..	..	McLintock	Simpson	..	..	..	..	..	Armstrong for Marinello
2 Dec	Leeds U	H	W 2-1	..	..	..	..	Blockley	..	Armstrong	..[1]	..[1]	Kennedy	..	
9 Dec	Tottenham H	A	W 2-1	..	..	..	..[1]	..	..	..	..	..[1]	..	..	McLintock for Simpson
16 Dec	W B A	H	W 2-1	Barnett	..	..	..	McLintock	*opponents*	..	..	..[1]	..	..	George for Rice
23 Dec	Birmingham C	A	D 1-1	Wilson	Nelson	..	..	Blockley	..	..	..	..	..	..[1]	
26 Dec	Norwich C	H	W 2-0	..	..	..	..	..	..	..	..[1]	..[1]	..	..	George for Nelson
30 Dec	Stoke C	A	D 0-0	..	Rice	..	..	..	..	..	..	..	..	..	
6 Jan	Manchester U	H	W 3-1	..	..	..	..	..	..	..[1]	..[1]	..	..[1]	..	
20 Jan	Chelsea	A	W 1-0	..	..	..	..	..	..	..	..	..	..[1]	..	McLintock for Kelly
27 Jan	Newcastle U	H	D 2-2	..	..	..	..	..	..	..	..[1]	..	..[1]	..	George for Armstrong
10 Feb	Liverpool	A	W 2-0	..	..	..	..	..	..	..	..[1]	..[1]	..	..	George for Radford
17 Feb	Leicester C	H	W 1-0	..	..	..	..	..	McLintock	*opponents*	..	..	..	..	George for Blockley
28 Feb	W B A	A	L 0-1	..	..	..	Batson	McLintock	George	..	..	..	..	..	
3 Mar	Sheffield U	H	W 3-2	..	..	..	George[2]	..	Batson	..	..[1]	..	..	..	Nelson for Batson
10 Mar	Ipswich T	A	W 2-1	..	..	..	Storey	..	Simpson	..	..[1]	..[1]	..	..	
24 Mar	Manchester C	A	W 2-1	..	..	..	..	..	..	..	..	George[1]	..[1]	..	Nelson for Kelly
26 Mar	Crystal Palace	H	W 1-0	..	..	..	..	..	..	..	..[1]	..	..	..	
31 Mar	Derby Co	H	L 0-1	..	..	..	..	..	..	..	..	..	..	..	Nelson for McLintock

Date	Opponent	V	Result												Notes
14 Apr	Tottenham H	H D	1-1	Wilson	Rice	McNab	Storey[1]	Blockley	Simpson	Armstrong	Ball	Radford	Kennedy	Kelly	George for Kelly
21 Apr	Everton	A D	0-0	..	..	..	..	..	..	..	..	..	..	..	George for Blockley
23 Apr	Southampton	A D	2-2	..	..	..	..	Kelly	..	..	..	..[1]	George[1]	Kennedy	
28 Apr	West Ham U	A W	2-1	..	..	..	..	..	..	..	..	..[1]	Kennedy[1]	George	
9 May	Leeds U	A L	1-6	..	Batson	..	..	Blockley	..	..[1]	..	..	..	Hornsby	Price for Hornsby

FA Cup

Date	Opponent	V	Result												Notes
13 Jan	Leicester C (3)	H D	2-2	Wilson	Rice	McNab	Storey	Blockley	Simpson	Armstrong[1]	Ball	Radford	Kennedy[1]	Kelly	
17 Jan	Leicester C (3R)	A W	2-1	..	..	..	..	..	..	..	..[1]	..	..	..[1]	
3 Feb	Bradford C (4)	H W	2-0	..	..	..	..	..	..	..	..[1]	George[1]	..	..	Marinello for George
24 Feb	Carlisle U (5)	A W	2-1	Barnett	..	..	..	McLintock[1]	..	..	..[1]	Radford	..	..	Nelson for Storey
17 Mar	Chelsea (6)	A D	2-2	Wilson	..	..	..	..	..	..	..[1]	George[1]	..	..	
20 Mar	Chelsea (6R)	H W	2-1	..	..	..	..	..	..	..	..[1]	..[1]	..[1]	..	
7 Apr	Sunderland (SF) (at Sheffield W)	A L	1-2	..	..	..	..	Blockley	..	..	..	..[1]	..	..	Radford for Blockley

Football League Cup

Date	Opponent	V	Result												Notes
5 Sep	Everton (2)	H W	1-0	Barnett	Rice	McNab	Storey[1]	McLintock	Simpson	Marinello	Ball	Radford	Kennedy	Graham	
3 Oct	Rotherham U (3)	H W	5-0	..	..	Nelson	..[1]	..	Roberts	..[1]	Ball	..[2]	Graham	George[1]	
31 Oct	Sheffield U (4)	A W	2-1	..	..	McNab	..	..	Simpson	..	Kelly	..[1]	..	..[1]	
21 Nov	Norwich C (5)	H L	0-3	..	..	..	..	..	..	..	Ball	..	George	Kelly	

Appearances (Goals)

Armstrong G 30 (2) · Ball A 40 (10) · Barnett G 20 · Batson B 3 · Blockley J 20 · George C 27 (6) · Graham G 16 (2) · Hornsby B 1 · Kelly E 27 (1) · Kennedy R 34 (9) · McLintock F 29 · McNab R 42 (1) · Marinello P 13 (1) · Nelson S 6 · Price D 1 · Radford J 38 (15) · Rice P 39 (2) · Roberts J 7 · Simpson P 27 (1) · Storey P 40 (4) · Wilson R 22 · Own goals 3 · Total: 21 players (57)

Position in League Table

	P	W	L	D	F:A	Pts	
Liverpool	42	25	7	10	72:42	60	1st
Arsenal	42	23	8	11	57:43	57	2nd

SEASON 1973-1974   FOOTBALL LEAGUE (DIVISION 1)

Date	Opponent	V	Result												Notes
25 Aug	Manchester U	H W	3-0	Wilson	Rice	McNab	Price	Blockley	Simpson	Armstrong	Ball[1]	Radford[1]	Kennedy[1]	George	Hornsby for Radford
28 Aug	Leeds U	H L	1-2	..	..	..	Storey	..[1]	..	..	..	Kelly	..	..	Price for Simpson
1 Sep	Newcastle U	A D	1-1	..	..	..	Price	..	Storey	..	..	Kelly	..	..[1]	
4 Sep	Sheffield U	A L	0-5	..	..	..	Batson	..	..	..	..	..	..	..	
8 Sep	Leicester C	H L	0-2	..	..	..	Storey	..	Simpson	Kelly	..	Radford	..	..	Armstrong for Kelly
11 Sep	Sheffield U	H W	1-0	..	..	..	..[1]	..	..	Armstrong	..	..	..[1]	Kelly	
15 Sep	Norwich C	A W	4-0	..	..	..[1]	..	..	George[1]	..[1]	..	..[1]	..		
22 Sep	Stoke C	H W	2-1	..	..	..	..	..	Simpson	..[1]	..	..	George	Kelly for George
29 Sep	Everton	A L	0-1	..	..	..	..	..	..	..	..	..	..	Kelly for George
6 Oct	Birmingham C	H W	1-0	..	..	..	..	..	..	..	Chambers	..[1]	Kelly	Brady for Blockley
13 Oct	Tottenham H	A L	0-2	..	..	..	..	Simpson	Kelly	..	George	..	Brady	Batson for Radford
20 Oct	Ipswich T	H D	1-1	..	..	..	..	..[1]	..	..	..	Batson	..	Price
27 Oct	Q P R	A L	0-2	..	..	..	..	..	..	..	..	..	Powling	
3 Nov	Liverpool	H L	0-2	..	..	..	..	Powling	..	..	Radford	..	Kelly	Batson for Kelly
10 Nov	Manchester C	A W	2-1	..	..	..	..	Kelly[1]	Ball	..	Hornsby[1]	Armstrong		
17 Nov	Chelsea	H D	0-0	..	..	..	..	..	..[2]	..[1]	..	..		
24 Nov	West Ham U	A W	3-1	..	..	..	..	..	..	..[1]	..	..		
1 Dec	Coventry C	H D	2-2	..	..	..	..	..	..	..	..	Nelson[1] for Kelly
4 Dec	Wolverhampton W	H D	2-2	..	..	..	..	..	..	..[1]	Radford	..	Hornsby[1] for George
8 Dec	Derby Co	A D	1-1	..	..	..	..	opponents	..	Blockley	..	..	
15 Dec	Burnley	A L	1-2	..	..	Nelson	..	..	..	..	..[1]	..	
22 Dec	Everton	H W	1-0	..	..	McNab	..	Blockley	Simpson	Armstrong	Ball[1]	Hornsby	..	Kelly
26 Dec	Southampton	A D	1-1	..	..	Nelson	..	..	..	..[1]	Radford	..	..	Hornsby for Kelly
29 Dec	Leicester C	A L	0-2	..	..	..	..	..	..	..	..	..	Hornsby
1 Jan	Newcastle U	H L	0-1	..	..	..	..	..	..	..	..	..	Kelly
12 Jan	Norwich C	H W	2-0	..	..	Storey	Kelly	..	..	..[2]	..	Brady
19 Jan	Manchester U	A D	1-1	..	..	McNab	Storey	..	..	..	..[1]	Kelly
2 Feb	Burnley	H D	1-1	..	..	Storey	Kelly	..	..	..[1]	Brady
5 Feb	Leeds U	A L	1-3	..	..	Nelson	Storey	..	..	..[1]
16 Feb	Tottenham H	H L	0-1	..	..	..	..	Simpson	Kelly	..	..	..
23 Feb	Birmingham C	A L	1-3	..	..	..	..	George	..[1]	Armstrong
2 Mar	Southampton	H W	1-0	..	..	..	..	..[1]	..
16 Mar	Ipswich T	A D	2-2	McNab	..	..	..[1]	Brady	..	..[1]
23 Mar	Manchester C	H W	2-0	Rice	..	..	..	Ball	..[2]	George
30 Mar	Stoke C	A D	0-0	..	..	Blockley	..	Armstrong	..	George	Simpson for Kelly
6 Apr	West Ham U	H D	0-0	..	..	..	..	..	..	..[2]	Simpson for Kelly
13 Apr	Chelsea	A W	3-1	..	..	..	..	..	..[1]	..[1]	Brady for Radford
15 Apr	Wolverhampton W	A L	1-3	..	..	..	Simpson	..	..	..	Simpson for George
20 Apr	Derby Co	H W	2-0	..	..	..	Kelly	..	George[1]	..	Brady	Simpson for Blockley
24 Apr	Liverpool	A W	1-0	Rimmer	..	..	..	..	Radford	..[1]
27 Apr	Coventry	A D	3-3	Wilson	..[1]	..	Simpson	..	..[1]	..[1]	George
30 Apr	Q P R	H D	1-1	..	..	..	..	..	..	Brady[1] for Ball

FA Cup

Date	Opponent	V	Result												Notes
5 Jan	Norwich (3)	A W	1-0	Wilson	Rice	McNab	Storey	Blockley	Simpson	Kelly[1]	Ball	Radford	Kennedy	Armstrong	
26 Jan	Aston Villa (4)	H D	1-1	..	..	..	..	..	..	Armstrong	..	..	..[1]	Kelly	
30 Jan	Aston Villa (4R)	A L	0-2	..	..	..	..	..	..	..	..	..	..	Brady for McNab

Football League Cup

Date	Opponent	V	Result												Notes
2 Oct	Tranmere Rov (2)	H L	0-1	Wilson	Rice	McNab	Storey	Blockley	Simpson	Armstrong	Ball	Radford	Kennedy	Kelly	Chambers for Ball

FA Cup (1972-73)
Third Place Play-off

Date	Opponent	V	Result												
18 Aug	Wolverhampton	H L	1-3	Wilson	Batson	McNab	Price	Blockley	Simpson	Chambers	Ball	Radford	Kennedy	Hornsby[1]	

Appearances (Goals)

Armstrong G 41 · Ball A 36 (13) · Batson B 5 · Blockley J 26 (1) · Brady L 13 (1) · Chambers B 1 · George C 28 (5) · Hornsby B 9 (3) · Kelly E 37 (1) · Kennedy R 42 (12) · McNab R 23 (1) · Nelson S 19 (1) · Powling R 2 · Price D 4 · Radford J 32 (7) · Rice P 41 (1) · Rimmer J 1 · Simpson P 38 (2) · Storey P 41 · Wilson R 41 · Own goals 1 · Total 20 players (49)

Position in League Table

	P	W	L	D	F:A	Pts	
Leeds U	42	24	4	14	66:31	62	1st
Arsenal	42	14	14	14	49:51	42	10th

17 Aug	Leicester C	A W 1-0	Rimmer	Matthews	Nelson	Storey	Simpson	Kelly	Armstrong	Brady	Radford	George	Kidd[1]	Price for Kelly
20 Aug	Ipswich T	H L 0-1	..	Storey	..	Kelly	..	Matthews	..	Hornsby	Kidd	Brady	
24 Aug	Manchester C	H W 4-0	..	Rice	..	..	..	Storey	Matthews	George	..²	²	Armstrong for Simpson
27 Aug	Ipswich T	A L 0-3	..	..	..	..	..	Matthews	Brady	..	..	..	Storey	
31 Aug	Everton	A L 1-2	..	..	..	Storey	..	Kelly	Blockley	Brady	..	George	Kidd[1]	Powling for Kelly
7 Sep	Burnley	H L 0-1	..	..	..	..	Blockley	Matthews	Armstrong	..	..	..	..	Simpson for Rice
14 Sep	Chelsea	A D 0-0	..	Kelly	Simpson	..	..	..	..	George	..	Kidd	Brady	
21 Sep	Luton T	H D 2-2	..	Simpson	Nelson	..	..	..	..	Kelly	..	..²	..	
28 Sep	Birmingham C	A L 1-3	..	Storey	Simpson	Kelly	..	..	George[1]	Ball	..	..	..	
5 Oct	Leeds U	A L 0-2	..	..	..	..	..	..	Armstrong	..	..	..[1]	..[1]	Powling for Blockley
12 Oct	Q P R	H D 2-2	..	..	..	..	Powling	..	..	..	..	..	Armstrong	
16 Oct	Manchester C	A L 1-2	..	..	..	Nelson	..	Kelly	Ball	Brady	..[1]	..		
19 Oct	Tottenham H	A L 0-2	..	..	Nelson	Kelly	..	Simpson	Armstrong	Ball	..	Brady	Kidd	
26 Oct	West Ham U	H W 3-0	..	..	McNab	..	Mancini	..	Rice	..	..[1]	..[1]	..[1]	Armstrong for Rice
2 Nov	Wolverhampton W	H D 0-0	..	..	..	..	..	..	..	..	..	..	..	
9 Nov	Liverpool	A W 3-1	..	Rice	..	..	..	..	Storey	..²	..	Kidd	Brady[1]	
16 Nov	Derby Co	H W 3-1	..	..	..	..	..	..	..	..²	..	..[1]		
23 Nov	Coventry C	A L 0-3	..	..	..	..	Simpson	Powling	Armstrong	..	..	..	..[1]	George for Brady
30 Nov	Middlesbrough	H W 2-0	..	..	..	..	..	..	George	..[1]	..	..	..	
7 Dec	Carlisle U	A L 1-2	..	..	..	..	Mancini	..	Storey	..	..	..[1]	Cropley	
14 Dec	Leicester C	H D 0-0	..	..	..	..	Mancini	Simpson	..	..	..	..	..	
21 Dec	Stoke C	A W 2-0	..	..	..	..	..	..	..	..	..	..²	..	
26 Dec	Chelsea	H L 1-2	..	..	..	..	..	..	..	..[1]	..	..	..	
28 Dec	Sheffield U	A D 1-1	..	..	..	..	..	..	..	..	George[1]	..	..	Armstrong for Kelly
11 Jan	Carlisle U	H W 2-1	..	..	..	..	..	..	Armstrong	..	Radford[1]	..	..[1]	
18 Jan	Middlesbrough	A D 0-0	..	..	..	..	..	..	..	..	Storey	..	..	
1 Feb	Liverpool	H W 2-0	..	..	..	Matthews	..	..	..	..²	Brady	..	Storey	Ross for Ball
8 Feb	Wolverhampton W	A L 0-1	..	..	..	Ross	..	..	..	Brady	Radford	..	..	
22 Feb	Derby Co	A L 1-2	..	..	..	Storey	..	..	..	Ball	..[1]	..	Brady	
1 Mar	Everton	H L 0-2	..	..	..	..	..	..	..	..	..	..	..	
15 Mar	Birmingham C	H D 1-1	..	..	Nelson	..	..	..	Matthews	..	..	..[1]	..	
18 Mar	Newcastle U	H W 3-0	..	..	..	Rostron[1]	..	..	..	..[1]	Hornsby	..[1]	..	
22 Mar	Burnley	A D 3-3	..	..	..	Matthews	..	..	Rostron[1]	..	..²	..	..	Powling for Matthews
25 Mar	Luton T	A L 0-2	..	..	..	Storey	..	..	..	Radford	Hornsby	..	..	
29 Mar	Stoke C	H D 1-1	..	..	McNab	..	Kelly[1]	..	Matthews	..	Stapleton	Rostron	Hornsby	Brady for Stapleton
31 Mar	Sheffield U	H W 1-0	..	..	Nelson	..	Mancini	..	..	Kelly	Hornsby	Kidd[1]	Armstrong	
8 Apr	Coventry C	H W 2-0	..	..	..	..	..	..	..	..	..	..²	..	
12 Apr	Leeds U	H L 1-2	..	..	..	..	..	..	..	..	..	..[1]	..	Brady for Nelson
19 Apr	Q P R	A D 0-0	..	..	..	..	..	Ball	..	..	..	..	..	
23 Apr	Newcastle U	A L 1-3	Barnett	..	Matthews	..	..	Brady	..	..	..[1]	..	Rostron	Nelson for Kelly
26 Apr	Tottenham H	H W 1-0	Barnett	..	Nelson	..	..	Simpson	..	Brady	..	..[1]	Armstrong	
28 Apr	West Ham U	A L 0-1	..	Storey	..	Kelly	..	Matthews	..	..	..	..	Rostron	

FA Cup

4 Jan	York C (3)	H D 1-1	Rimmer	Rice	McNab	Kelly[1]	Mancini	Powling	Storey	Ball	Armstrong	Kidd	Cropley	
7 Jan	York C (3R)	A W 3-1	..	..	..	..	Simpson	Mancini	Armstrong	..[1]	Radford	..³	..	
25 Jan	Coventry (4)	A D 1-1	..	..	..	Storey	Mancini	Simpson	..	..[1]	..	..	George	Matthews for George
29 Jan	Coventry (4R)	H W 3-0	..	..	..	Matthews[1]	..	..	..	..²	..	..	Storey	Brady for Radford
15 Feb	Leicester C (5)	H D 0-0	..	..	..	Storey	..	..	..	..	..	..	Brady	
19 Feb	Leicester C (5R)	A D 1-1	..	..	..	..	..	..	..	..	..[1]	..	Matthews	Brady for Matthews
24 Feb	Leicester C (5R)	A W 1-0	..	..	..	..	..	..	..	..	..[1]	..	..	Brady for Matthews
8 Mar	West Ham (6)	H L 0-2	..	..	..	..	..	..	Matthews	..	..	..	Brady	Armstrong for Radford

Football League Cup

10 Sep	Leicester C (2)	H D 1-1	Rimmer	Kelly	Simpson	Storey	Blockley	Mathews	Armstrong	George	Radford	Kidd[1]	Brady	
18 Sep	Leicester C (2R)	A L 1-2	..	Simpson	Nelson	..	..	..	..	Kelly	..	..	..[1]	

Appearances (Goals)

Armstrong G 24 · Ball A 30 (9) · Barnett G 2 · Blockley J 6 · Brady L 32 (3) · Cropley A 7 (1) · George C 10 (2) · Hornsby B 12 (3) · Kelly E 32 (1) · Kidd B 40 (19) · Mancini T 26 · McNab N 18 · Matthews J 20 · Nelson S 20 · Powling R 8 · Price D 1 · Radford J 29 (7) · Rice P 32 · Rimmer J 40 · Ross T 2 · Rostron W 6 (2) · Simpson P 40 · Stapleton F 1 · Storey P 37 · Total: 24 players (47)

Position in League Table

	P	W	L	D	F:A	Pts	
Derby	42	21	10	11	67:49	53	1st
Arsenal	42	13	18	11	47:49	37	16th

16 Aug	Burnley	A D 0-0	Rimmer	Rice	Nelson	Kelly	Mancini	O'Leary	Armstrong	Cropley	Hornsby	Kidd	Brady	
19 Aug	Sheffield U	A W 3-1	..	..[1]	..	..	..	..	..	..	..	..[1]	..[1]	
23 Aug	Stoke C	H L 0-1	..	..	..	..	..	..	..	..	..	..	..	
26 Aug	Norwich C	H W 2-1	..	..	Storey	..[1]	..	..	..	..	Ball[1]	..	..	
30 Aug	Wolverhampton W	A D 0-0	..	..	Nelson	..	..	..	Ball	..	Radford	..	..	
6 Sep	Leicester C	H D 1-1	..	..	..	..	..	..	..	..	Stapleton[1]	..	..	
13 Sep	Aston Villa	A L 0-2	..	..	..	..	..	..	..	..	..	..	..	
20 Sep	Everton	H D 2-2	..	..	..	..	..	..	..	..	..	..[1]	..[1]	
27 Sep	Tottenham H	A D 0-0	..	..	..	..	..	..	..	..	..	..	Rostron	Brady for Rostron
4 Oct	Manchester C	H L 2-3	..	..	..	..	Simpson	..	..[1]	..[1]	..	..	Brady	Rostron for Kelly
11 Oct	Coventry C	H W 5-0	..	..	..	Powling	..	..	..[1]	..²	..	..²	..	Rostron for Cropley
18 Oct	Manchester U	A L 1-3	..	..	..	Kelly[1]	O'Leary	Simpson	..	..	..	..	..	
25 Oct	Middlesbrough	H W 2-1	..	..	..	..	..	..	..	..[1]	..	..	..	Powling for Kelly
1 Nov	Newcastle U	A L 0-2	..	..	..	..	..	..	Powling	..	..	..	..	
8 Nov	Derby Co	H L 0-1	..	..	Storey	..	..	Powling	Cropley	..	Hornsby	..	..	
15 Nov	Birmingham C	A L 1-3	..	..	..	..	..	..	..[1]	..	Kidd	..	Matthews for Cropley
22 Nov	Manchester U	H W 3-1	..	..	..	Nelson	..	opponents	..[1]	Armstrong[1]	..	..	..	
29 Nov	West Ham U	A L 0-1	..	..	Nelson	Storey	..	..	..	..	..[1]	..	..	
2 Dec	Liverpool	A D 2-2	..	..	Storey	Nelson	..	..	..[1]	..	..	..[1]	..	
6 Dec	Leeds U	H L 1-2	..	..	Nelson	Storey	..	..	Armstrong	Ball	..	..	..[1]	
13 Dec	Stoke C	A L 1-2	Barnett	..	..	..	..	..	..[1]	..	..	..	..	Simpson for Nelson
20 Dec	Burnley	H W 1-0	Rimmer	..	Simpson	Kelly	Mancini	..	..	..	Radford[1]	..	..	Stapleton for Brady
26 Dec	Ipswich	A L 0-2	..	..	Kelly	Storey	O'Leary	..	..	..	..	..	..	
27 Dec	Q P R	H W 2-0	..	..	Nelson	..	..	..	..	..[1]	Stapleton	..[1]	..	
10 Jan	Aston Villa	H D 0-0	..	..	..	Powling	..	Mancini	..	..	..	..	..	
17 Jan	Leicester C	A L 1-2	..	..	..	Ross[1]	..	..	..	..	..	..	..	
31 Jan	Sheffield U	H W 1-0	..	..	..	..	Mancini	Powling	..	..	..	..	..[1]	Rostron for Nelson
7 Feb	Norwich C	A L 1-3	..	..	Storey	..	..	Simpson	..	..	..	..[1]	..	
18 Feb	Derby Co	A L 0-2	..	..	Nelson	..	..	Powling	..	..	Radford	..	..	
21 Feb	Birmingham C	H W 1-0	..	..	..	..	..	..	..	..	..	..	..[1]	Simpson for Brady
24 Feb	Liverpool	H W 1-0	..	..	..	..	..	..	..	..	..	..[1]	..	
28 Feb	Middlesbrough	A W 1-0	..	..	..	..	..	..	..	..	..	..[1]	..	
13 Mar	Coventry C	A D 1-1	..	..	..	..	..	..	..	..[1]	..	..	..	
16 Mar	Newcastle U	H D 0-0	..	..	..	..	..	..	..	..	..	..	..	
20 Mar	West Ham U	H W 6-1	..	..	..	..	..	..	..[1]	..²	..	..³	..	Stapleton for Rice
27 Mar	Leeds U	A L 0-3	..	..	..	..	..	..	..	..	..	..	..	
3 Apr	Tottenham H	H L 0-2	..	..	..	..	..	..	..	..	..	..	..	
10 Apr	Everton	A D 0-0	..	..	..	..	..	..	..	..	..	Cropley	..	
13 Apr	Wolverhampton W	H W 2-1	..	..	..	..	..	..[1]	..	..	..	..[1]	..	
17 Apr	Ipswich T	H L 1-2	..	..	..	..	O'Leary	..	Rostron	..	Stapleton[1]	..	..	
19 Apr	Q P R	A L 1-2	..	..	..	..	..	..	Kidd[1]	..	Radford	..	..	Armstrong for Radford
24 Apr	Manchester C	A L 1-3	..	..	..	..	Mancini	..	Armstrong[1]	..	Stapleton	..	..	

FA Cup

3 Jan	Wolves (3)	A L 0-3	Rimmer	Rice	Nelson	Storey	O'Leary	Powling	Armstrong	Ball		Stapleton	Kidd	Brady

Football League Cup

9 Sep	Everton (2)	A D 2-2	Rimmer	Rice	Nelson	Kelly	Mancini	O'Leary	Ball	Cropley[1]	Radford	Kidd	Brady	Stapleton[1] for Mancini
23 Sep	Everton (2R)	H L 0-1	..	..	..	..	..	..	..	..	Stapleton	..	Rostron	

Appearances (Goals)

Armstrong G 29 (4) · Ball A 39 (9) · Barnett J 1 · Brady L 42 (5) · Cropley A 20 (4) · Hornsby B 4 · Kelly E 17 (2) · Kidd B 37 (11) · Mancini T 26 (1) · Matthews J 1 · Nelson S 36 · O'Leary D 27 · Powling R 29 (4) · Radford J 15 (3) · Rice P 42 (1) · Rimmer J 41 · Ross T 17 (1) · Rostron W 5 · Simpson P 9 · Stapleton F 25 (4) · Storey P 11 · Own goals 1 · Total 21 players (47)

Position in League Table

	P	W	L	D	F:A	Pts
Liverpool	42	23	5	14	66:31	60 1st
Arsenal	42	13	19	10	47:53	36 17th

SEASON 1976-1977 FOOTBALL LEAGUE (DIVISION 1)

21 Aug	Bristol C	H L 0-1	Rimmer	Rice	Nelson	Ross	O'Leary	Simpson	Ball	Armstrong	Macdonald	Radford	Cropley	Storey for Cropley
25 Aug	Norwich C	A W 3-1	..	..	..¹	..¹	..	..	..	..	..¹	Stapleton¹	Brady	
28 Aug	Sunderland	A D 2-2	..	..	..	..¹	..	..	..	..	..¹			
4 Sep	Manchester C	H D 0-0	..	..	..	..	..	Howard	..	Brady	..	..	Armstrong	Cropley for Stapleton
11 Sep	West Ham U	A W 2-0	..	..	..	..¹	..	Howard	..	..¹	Cropley	..	..	Storey for O'Leary
18 Sep	Everton	H W 3-1	..	..	..	..	Howard	Powling	..	..	Macdonald¹	..¹	..	
25 Sep	Ipswich T	A L 1-3	..	..	..	..	O'Leary	Howard	*opponents*	..	..¹	..	..	
2 Oct	Q P R	H W 3-2	..¹	..	..	..	..	..	..	..	..¹	..	..¹	
16 Oct	Stoke C	H W 2-0	..¹	Storey	..	..	..	..	..¹	..	..¹	..	..	Storey for Nelson
20 Oct	Aston Villa	A L 1-5	..	..	..	..	..	..	..¹	..	..	..	..	Radford for Stapleton
23 Oct	Leicester C	A L 1-4	..	..	..	..	Matthews	..	..	..	..	..¹	..	
30 Oct	Leeds U	A L 1-2	..	Nelson	..	..	Simpson	..	Matthews¹	..	..	..	..	
6 Nov	Birmingham C	H W 4-0	..	..¹	..	..¹	O'Leary	Simpson	..	..	..¹	..¹	..¹	Storey for O'Leary
20 Nov	Liverpool	H D 1-1	..	..	..	..	..	..	Ball	..	..	..	..	
27 Nov	Coventry C	A W 2-1	..	..	..	..¹	..	..	..	..	..¹	..¹	..	
4 Dec	Newcastle U	H W 5-3	..	..	..	..	..	Howard	..	..	..³	..¹	..	Matthews for Rice
15 Dec	Derby Co	A D 0-0	..	..	..	..	..	Simpson	Storey	..	..	..	..	
18 Dec	Manchester U	H W 3-1	..	Powling	..	..	..	..	..	..¹	..²	..	..	Rostron for Stapleton
27 Dec	Tottenham H	A D 2-2	..	..	..	..	..	..	Hudson	..	..²	Rostron		
3 Jan	Leeds U	H D 1-1	..	..	..	..	..	..	Hudson	..	..¹	Armstrong		
15 Jan	Norwich C	H W 1-0	..¹	Nelson	..	..	..	..	..	..	..	..	..	
18 Jan	Birmingham C	A D 3-3	..	..	..	..	..	..	..	..	..³	Rostron		
22 Jan	Bristol C	A L 0-2	..	..	..	Storey	..	..	..	..	..	Rostron		
5 Feb	Sunderland	H D 0-0	..	..	..	Ross	..	..	..	..	..	..		
12 Feb	Manchester C	A L 0-1	..	..	..	..	..	..	..	..	..	Howard	Matthews for O'Leary	
15 Feb	Middlesbrough	A L 0-3	..	..	..	..	Howard	..	Matthews	Hudson	..	Rostron	Powling for Howard	
19 Feb	West Ham U	H L 2-3	..	..	..	..	Powling	..	Hudson	Brady¹	..	..¹	Armstrong	
1 Mar	Everton	A L 1-2	..	..	..	..	Howard	Powling	Brady	Hudson	..¹	..	..	
5 Mar	Ipswich	H L 1-4	..	..	Young	..	..	..	..	Matthews	..¹	..	..	Nelson for Matthews
8 Mar	W B A	H L 1-2	..	..	Nelson	Price	Young	Howard	..	Powling	..¹	..	..	Price for Hudson
12 Mar	Q P R	A L 1-2	..	..	..	Powling	..¹	..	..	Hudson	..	..	..	
23 Mar	Stoke C	A D 1-1	..	..	..	..	O'Leary²	Young	..	..	Price¹	..	..	Matthews for Powling
2 Apr	Leicester C	H W 3-0	..	..	..	..	O'Leary²	Young	Rix¹	Price	Stapleton	..	..	
9 Apr	W B A	A W 2-0	..	..	Matthews	Price	..	..	..	Hudson	..¹	..¹	..	Brady for Rix
11 Apr	Tottenham H	H W 1-0	..	..	..	..	..	..	..	..	..¹	..	..	
16 Apr	Liverpool	A L 0-2	..	..	..	..	..	..	Brady	..	..	..	..	Rix for Ross
23 Apr	Coventry C	H W 2-0	..	..	..	Ross	..	..	..	..	..¹	..¹	..	Rix for Young
25 Apr	Aston Villa	H W 3-0	..	..	Nelson¹	Matthews	..	..	..	..	..¹	..	..¹	Howard for O'Leary
30 Apr	Newcastle U	A W 2-0	..	..	..	..¹	..	..	..	..	..¹	..	..	Rix for Young
3 May	Derby Co	H D 0-0	..	..	..	..	..	..	..	..	..	..	..	Price for Matthews
7 May	Middlesbrough	H D 1-1	..	..	..	..	..	..	..	Rix	..	..¹	..	Rix for Young
14 May	Manchester U	A L 2-3	..	..	..	..	..	..	..¹	Hudson	..	..¹	..	

FA Cup

8 Jan	Notts Co (3)	A W 1-0	Rimmer	Rice	Nelson	Ross¹	O'Leary	Simpson	Hudson	Brady	Macdonald	Stapleton	Armstrong	
29 Jan	Coventry C (4)	H W 3-1	..	..	..	..	..	..	..	..	..²	..¹	..	Storey for Macdonald
26 Feb	Middlesbrough (5)	A L 1-4	..	..	..	..	..	..	Brady	Hudson	..¹	..	..	Matthews for O'Leary

Football League Cup

31 Aug	Carlisle U (2)	H W 3-2	Rimmer	Rice	Nelson	Ross²	O'Leary	Simpson	Ball	Brady	Macdonald¹	Stapleton	Armstrong	
21 Sep	Blackpool (3)	A D 1-1	..	..	..	..	Powling	Howard	..	..	..	..	..	
28 Sep	Blackpool (3R)	H D 0-0	..	..	..	..	O'Leary	..	..	..	..	..	..	Storey for Nelson
5 Oct	Blackpool (3R)	H W 2-0	..	..	Storey	Matthews	..¹	..	..	..	..	..¹	..	
26 Oct	Chelsea (4)	H W 2-1	..	..	Nelson	Ross¹	Simpson	..	..	..	..	..¹	..	
1 Dec	Q P R (5)	A L 1-2	..	..	..	..	O'Leary	Simpson	..	..	..	..¹	..	

Appearances (Goals)

Armstrong G 37 (2) · Ball A 14 (1) · Brady L 38 (5) · Cropley A 3 · Howard P 16 · Hudson A 19 · Macdonald M 41 (25) · Matthews J 17 (2) · Nelson S 32 (3) · O'Leary A 33 (2) · Powling R 12 · Price D 8 (1) · Radford J 2 · Rice P 42 (3) · Rimmer J 42 · Rix G 7 (1) · Ross T 29 (4) · Rostron W 5 · Simpson P 19 · Stapleton F 40 (13) · Storey P 11 · Young W 14 (1) · Own goals 1 · Total: 22 players (64)

Position in League Table

	P	W	L	D	F:A	Pts
Liverpool	42	23	8	11	62:33	57 1st
Arsenal	42	16	15	11	64:59	43 8th

SEASON 1977-1978 FOOTBALL LEAGUE (DIVISION 1)

20 Aug	Ipswich T	A L 0-1	Jennings	Rice	Nelson	Ross	Young	O'Leary	Powling	Brady	Macdonald	Stapleton	Rix	Price for Brady
23 Aug	Everton	H W 1-0	..	..	..	Powling[1]	O'Leary	Young	Brady	Ross	..	..	..	
27 Aug	Wolverhampton W	A D 1-1	..	..	..	..[1]	Young	O'Leary	Ross	Brady	..	Price	..	
3 Sep	Nottingham F	H W 3-0	..	..	..	..	O'Leary	Young	Brady[1]	Ross	..	Stapleton[2]	..	
10 Sep	Aston Villa	A L 0-1	..	..	..	Hudson	..	..	..	..	..	..	..	
17 Sep	Leicester C	H W 2-1	..	..	..	Price ..	..	..	..	..	..[1]	..[1]	..	
24 Sep	Norwich C	A L 0-1	..	..	..	..	..	Simpson	Matthew	..	..	..	..	Walford for Matthews
1 Oct	West Ham U	H W 3-0	..	..[1]	..	..	..	..	Brady[1]	..	..	..[1]	..	
4 Oct	Liverpool	H D 0-0	..	..	..	..	..	..	..	..	..	..	..	Matthews for Ross
8 Oct	Manchester C	A L 1-2	..	..	..	..	..	..	..	Matthews	..[1]	..	..	
15 Oct	Q P R	H W 1-0	..	..	..	..	..	Young	..	Hudson	..[1]	..	..	
22 Oct	Bristol C	A W 2-0	..	..	..	..	Young	Simpson	..	..	..[1]	..	..[1]	
29 Oct	Birmingham C	H D 1-1	..	..[1]	..	..	O'Leary	..	..	Ross	..	..	..	Heeley for Price
5 Nov	Manchester U	A W 2-1	..	..	..	..	..	Young	..	Sunderland	..[1]	..[1]	..	
12 Nov	Coventry C	H D 1-1	..	..	..	..	..	..	*opponents*	..	..	..	..	
19 Nov	Newcastle U	A W 2-1	..	..	..	..	..	..	..	..[1]	Hudson	..[1]	..	
26 Nov	Derby Co	H L 1-3	..	..	..[1]	..	..	..	..	..	Macdonald	..	..	
3 Dec	Middlesbrough	A W 1-0	..	..	..	..	..	..	*opponents*	..	..	..	..	
10 Dec	Leeds U	H D 1-1	..	..	..	..	..	..[1]	..	..	..	..	..	
17 Dec	Coventry C	A W 2-1	..	..	..	..	..	..	..	..	..	..[2]	..	
26 Dec	Chelsea	H W 3-0	..	..	..	..[1]	..[1]	..	..	..	..	..	..[1]	Simpson for Stapleton
27 Dec	W B A	A W 3-1	..	..	..	..	..	..	..[1]	..[1]	..[1]	..	..	
31 Dec	Everton	A L 0-2	..	..	..	..	..	..	..	..	..	..	..	Simpson for Macdonald
2 Jan	Ipswich T	H W 1-0	..	..	..	..[1]	..	..	..	..	..	Heeley	..	Simpson for Heeley
14 Jan	Wolverhampton W	H W 3-1	..	..	..	..	..	..	..[1]	..	..[1]	Stapleton[1]	..	
21 Jan	Nottingham F	A L 0-2	..	..	..	..	..	..	..	..	..	..	..	
4 Feb	Aston Villa	H L 0-1	..	..	..	..	..	..	..	..	..	Hudson	..	
11 Feb	Leicester C	A D 1-1	..	..	..	..	..	..	..[1]	..	..	Stapleton	..	
25 Feb	West Ham U	A D 2-2	..	..	..	..	..	..	..	..	..[2]	..	..	Walford for Rix
28 Feb	Norwich C	H D 0-0	..	..	..	..	..	..	..	..	..	..	Hudson	Heeley for Macdonald
4 Mar	Manchester C	H W 3-0	..	..	..	..[1]	..	..[1]	..	..[1]	Hudson	..	Heeley	Walford for Price
18 Mar	Bristol C	H W 4-1	..	..	..	..[1]	..	..	..	..[1]	Macdonald	..[2]	Hudson	Rix for Sunderland
21 Mar	Birmingham C	A D 1-1	..	..	..	..	..	..	..[1]	..	..	..	..	
25 Mar	W B A	H W 4-0	..	..	..	..	..	..[1]	..	..	..[3]	..	..	Rix for Sunderland
27 Mar	Chelsea	A D 0-0	..	..	..	..	..	..	..	Rix	..	..	..	
1 Apr	Manchester U	H W 3-1	..	..	..	..	..	..	..[1]	..	..[2]	..	..	
11 Apr	Q P R	A L 1-2	..	..	..	..	..	..	..[1]	Hudson	..	..	Rix	Matthews for Young
15 Apr	Newcastle U	H W 2-1	..	..	..	..[1]	..	Walford	..[1]	Rix	..	..	Hudson	
22 Apr	Leeds U	A W 3-1	..	Devine	..	..	..	Young	*opponents*	..	..[1]	..[1]	Matthews	
25 Apr	Liverpool	A L 0-1	..	..	..	..	..	..	..	..	..	..	Hudson	Matthews for Brady
29 Apr	Middlesbrough	H W 1-0	..	..	..	..	..	..	Sunderland	..	..	..[1]	..	
9 May	Derby Co	A L 0-3	..	Price	Matthews	Harvey	..	Walford	Heeley	..	Sunderland	..	..	
	FA Cup													
7 Jan	Sheffield U (3)	A W 5-0	Jennings	Rice	Nelson	Price	O'Leary[1]	Young	Brady	Sunderland	Macdonald[2]	Stapleton[2]	Rix	
28 Jan	Wolves (4)	H W 2-1	..	..	..	..	..	..	..	..[1]	..[1]	Hudson	..	
18 Feb	Walsall (5)	H W 4-1	..	..	..	..	..	..	..	..[1]	..[1]	Stapleton[2]	..	
11 Mar	Wrexham (6)	A W 3-2	..	..	..	..	..	..[1]	..	..[1]	..[1]	..	Hudson	
8 Apr	Orient (SF) (at Chelsea)	A W 3-0	..	..	..	..	..	..	..	Rix[1]	..[2]	..	..	
6 May	Ipswich (F) (at Wembley)	A L 0-1	..	..	..	..	..	..	..	Sunderland	..	..	..	Rix for Brady
	Football League Cup													
30 Aug	Manchester U (2)	H W 3-2	Jennings	Rice	Nelson	Powling	O'Leary	Young	Brady[1]	Ross	Macdonald[2]	Stapleton	Rix	
25 Oct	Southampton (3)	H W 2-0	..	..	..	Price	Young	Simpson	..[1]	Hudson	..	..[1]	..	
29 Nov	Hull C (4)	H W 5-1	..	..	..	..	O'Leary	Young	..[1]	Matthews[2]	..[1]	..[1]	..	Simpson for O'Leary
18 Jan	Manchester C (5)	A D 0-0	..	..	..	..	..	..	..	..	..	..	..	
24 Jan	Manchester C (5R)	H W 1-0	..	..	..	..	..	..	..[1]	..	..	..	..	Hudson for Matthews
7 Feb	Liverpool (SF)	A L 1-2	..	..	..	..	..	..	..	Hudson	..[1]	..	..	
14 Feb	Liverpool (SF)	H D 0-0	..	..	..	..	..	..	..	..	..	..	..	

Appearances (Goals)

Brady L 39 (9) · Devine J 3 · Harvey J 1 · Heeley M 4 · Hudson A 17 · Jennings P 42 · Macdonald M 39 (15) · Matthews J 5 · Nelson S 41 (1) · O'Leary D 41 (1) · Powling R 4 (2) · Price D 39 (5) · Rice P 38 (2) · Rix G 39 (2) · Ross T 10 · Simpson P 9 · Stapleton F 39 (13) · Sunderland A 23 (4) · Walford S 5 · Young W 35 (3) · Own goals 3 · Total 20 players (60)

Position in League Table

	P	W	L	D	F:A	Pts	
Nottingham F	42	25	3	14	69:24	64	1st
Arsenal	42	21	11	10	60:37	52	5th

SEASON 1978-1979 FOOTBALL LEAGUE (DIVISION 1)

19 Aug	Leeds U	H D 2-2	Jennings	Devine	Nelson	Price	O'Leary	Young	Brady[2]	Sunderland	Macdonald	Stapleton	Harvey	Kosmina for Price
22 Aug	Manchester C	A D 1-1	Barron	Rice	..	..	..	..	Devine	..	..[1]	..	Walford	
26 Aug	Everton	A L 0-1	..	..	..	..	..	..	Brady	..	..	..	Devine	Walford for Devine
2 Sep	Q P R	H W 5-1	Jennings	..	..	..	..	..	..[1]	..	Walford	..[2]	Rix[2]	
9 Sep	Nottingham F	A L 1-2	..	..	..	..	..	..	..[1]	..	..	..	..	Harvey for O'Leary
16 Sep	Bolton W	H W 1-0	..	..	..	..	Walford	..	..	..	Stapleton[1]	Heeley	..	
23 Sep	Manchester U	H D 1-1	..	..	..	..[1]	O'Leary	..	..	..	..	Walford	..	Heeley for Walford
30 Sep	Middlesbrough	A W 3-2	..	..	..	..[1]	..[1]	..	..	..	..	Devine	..	Walford[1] for Devine
7 Oct	Aston Villa	H D 1-1	..	..	..	..	..	..	..	..[1]	..	Walford	..	
14 Oct	Wolverhampton W	A L 0-1	..	..	..	..	..	..	..	..	..	..	..	Stead for Sunderland
21 Oct	Southampton	H W 1-0	..	..	..	Stead	Gatting	..	..[1]	Heeley	..	..	..	
28 Oct	Bristol C	A W 3-1	..	..	..	Price	O'Leary	..	..[2]	Gatting	..[1]	Heeley	..	Walford for O'Leary
4 Nov	Ipswich T	H W 4-1	..	..	..[1]	..	..	..	..	Sunderland	..[3]	Gatting	..	
11 Nov	Leeds U	A W 1-0	..	..	..	..	..	..	..	..	..	..[1]	..	
18 Nov	Everton	H D 2-2	..	..	..	..	..	..	..[2]	..	..	..	..	
25 Nov	Coventry C	A D 1-1	..	..	..	..	..	..	..	..	..[1]	Walford	..	Heeley for Price
2 Dec	Liverpool	H W 1-0	..	..	..	..[1]	..	..	..	..	..	Gatting	..	
9 Dec	Norwich C	A D 0-0	..	..	..	..	..	..	..	..	..	..	..	Walford for Nelson
16 Dec	Derby Co	H W 2-0	..	..	Walford	..[1]	..	..	..	..	..[1]	..	..	
23 Dec	Tottenham H	A W 5-0	..	..	..	..	..	..	..[1]	..[3]	..[1]	..	..	
26 Dec	W B A	H L 1-2	..	..	..	..	..	..	..[1]	..	..	..	..	
30 Dec	Birmingham C	H W 3-1	..	..[1]	..	..	..	..	..	..[1]	..[1]	..	..	
13 Jan	Nottingham F	H W 2-1	..	Walford	Nelson	Talbot	..	..	..	..	..[1]	Price[1]	..	
3 Feb	Manchester U	A W 2-0	..	Rice	..	..	..	..	..	..[2]	..	..	..	
10 Feb	Middlesbrough	H D 0-0	..	..	..	..	..	..	..	..	..	..	..	
13 Feb	Q P R	A W 2-1	..	..	..	..	..	..	..[1]	..	..	..[1]	..	Walford for Young
24 Feb	Wolverhampton W	H L 0-1	..	..	Gatting	..	..	Walford	..	..	..	..	..	
3 Mar	Southampton	A L 0-2	..	..	Nelson	..	..	..	..	Gatting	..	..	..	Heeley for Gatting
10 Mar	Bristol C	H W 2-0	..	..	..	..	..	..	..	Heeley	..[1]	..	..[1]	McDermott for Heeley
17 Mar	Ipswich T	A L 0-2	..	..	..	..	..	..	..	Sunderland	..	..	..	Gatting for Price
24 Mar	Manchester C	H D 1-1	..	..	..	..	..	Young	Heeley	..[1]	..	..	..	McDermot for Young
26 Mar	Bolton W	A L 2-4	..	..	..	..	..	Walford	Gatting	..	..	..[1]	..	Heeley[1] for Talbot
3 Apr	Coventry C	H D 1-1	..	..	..[1]	..	..	Young	..	..	..	Heeley	..	Walford for Heeley
7 Apr	Liverpool	A L 0-3	..	..	Walford	..	..	..	..	..	..	Price	..	Brignall for Stapleton
10 Apr	Tottenham H	H W 1-0	..	..	..	..	..	..	Brady	..	..[1]	..	..	
14 Apr	W B A	A D 1-1	..	..	Nelson	..	..	Walford	..[1]	..	..	..	..	Gatting for Rix
16 Apr	Chelsea	H W 5-2	..	..	..	..	..[1]	..	..	..[1]	..[2]	..[1]	..	
21 Apr	Derby Co	A L 0-2	..	..	Walford	..	Gatting	Young	..	..	..	..	..	
25 Apr	Aston Villa	A L 1-5	..	..	..	..	..	Devine	..	..	..[1]	..	..	
28 Apr	Norwich C	H D 1-1	..	Devine	Nelson	..	..	Walford[1]	..	..	..	..	..	
5 May	Birmingham C	A D 0-0	Barron	Rice	..	..	O'Leary	Young	..	..	..	..	..	Walford for Barron – Price in goal
14 May	Chelsea	A D 1-1	Jennings	..	..	..	..	..	..	Vaessen	Macdonald[1]	Devine	..	
	FA Cup													
6 Jan	Sheffield W (3)	A D 1-1	Jennings	Rice	Walford	Price	O'Leary	Young	Brady	Sunderland[1]	Stapleton	Gatting	Rix	
9 Jan	Sheffield W (3R)	H D 1-1	..	..	Nelson	..	..	..	..[1]	..	..	..	..	
15 Jan	Sheffield W (3R) (at Leicester)	D 2-2	..	..	..	..	..	..	..[1]	..[1]	..	..	..	

1978-1979 *continued*

17 Jan	Sheffield W (3R) (at Leicester)		D 3-3	Jennings	Rice	Nelson	Price	O'Leary	Young[1]	Brady	Sunderland	Stapleton[2]	Gatting	Rix	
22 Jan	Sheffield W (3R) (at Leicester)		W 2-0	..	..	..	..	..	..	..	..	..[1]	..[1]	..	Walford for Nelson
27 Jan	Notts County (4)	H	W 2-0	..	..	..	Talbot[1]	..	..[1]	..	..	..	Price	..	
26 Feb	Nottingham F (5)	A	W 1-0	..	..	..	..	..	Walford	..	..	..[1]	..	..	
19 Mar	Southampton (6)	A	D 1-1	..	..	..	..	..	Young	..	..	..	..[1]	..	Walford for Price
21 Mar	Southampton (6R)	H	W 2-0	..	..	..	..	..	..	..	..[2]	..	..	..	Walford for Brady
31 Mar	Wolves (SF) (at Aston Villa)		W 2-0	..	..	..	..	..	..	Gatting	..[1]	..[1]	..	..	
12 May	Manchester U (F) (at Wembley)		W 3-2	..	..	..	..[1]	..	..	Brady	..[1]	..[1]	..	..	Walford for Price

Football League Cup

29 Aug	Rotherham U (2)	A	L 1-3	Jennings	Rice	Nelson	Price	O'Leary	Young	Brady	Sunderland	Macdonald	Stapleton[1]	Rix	

UEFA Cup

13 Sep	L'motive Leipzig (1)	H	W 3-0	Jennings	Rice	Nelson	Price	Walford	Young	Brady	Sunderland[1]	Stapleton[2]	Harvey	Rix	Gatting for Brady, Heeley for Harvey
27 Sep	L'motive Leipzig (1)	A	W 4-1	..	..	..	..	O'Leary	..	..[1]	..[1]	..[2]	Devine	..	Vaessen for Price, Walford for Young
18 Oct	Hajduk Split (2)	A	L 1-2	..	..	..	..	..	..	..[1]	Heeley	..	Kosmina	..	
1 Nov	Hajduk Split (2)	H	W 1-0	..	..	..	..	..	..[1]	..	Gatting	..	Heeley	..	Kosmina for Heeley, Vaessen for Kosmina
22 Nov	Red Star Belgrade (3)	A	L 0-1	..	..	..	..	..	..	Heeley	Sunderland	..	Walford	..	
6 Dec	Red Star Belgrade (3)	H	D 1-1	..	..	..	..	..	..	..	..[1]	..	Gatting	..	Kosmina for Heeley, Macdonald for Rix

Appearances (Goals)

Barron P 3 · Brady L 37 (13) · Brignall S 1 · Devine J 7 · Gatting S 21 (1) · Harvey J 1 · Heeley M 10 (1) · Jennings P 39 · Kosmina A 1 · McDermott B 2 · Macdonald M 4 (2) · Nelson S 33 (2) · O'Leary D 37 (2) · Price D 39 (8) · Rice P 39 (1) · Rix G 39 (3) · Stapleton F 41 (17) · Stead K 2 · Sunderland A 37 (9) · Talbot B 20 · Vaessen P 1 · Walford S 33 (2) · Young W 33 · Total: 23 players (61)

Position in League Table

	P	W	L	D	F:A	Pts	
Liverpool	42	30	4	8	85:16	68	1st
Arsenal	42	17	11	14	61:48	48	7th

1979-1980

SEASON 1979-1980 FOOTBALL LEAGUE (DIVISION 1)

18 Aug	Brighton & HA	A	W 4-0	Jennings	Rice	Nelson	Talbot	O'Leary	Young	Brady[1]	Sunderland[2]	Stapleton[1]	Price	Rix	Hollins for Brady
21 Aug	Ipswich T	H	L 0-2	..	..	..	..	..	..	..	..	..	..	..	Hollins for Price
25 Aug	Manchester U	H	D 0-0	..	..	..	..	..	..	Gatting	..	..	Hollins	..	Walford for Gatting
1 Sep	Leeds U	A	D 1-1	..	..	..[1]	..	..	..	..	..	..	..	..	
8 Sep	Derby Co	A	L 2-3	..	..	..	..	..	..	Brady	..[1]	..[1]	..	..	
15 Sep	Middlesbrough	H	W 2-0	..	..	..	..	..	..	..	..[1]	..[1]	..	..	
22 Sep	Aston Villa	A	D 0-0	Barron	..	..	..	..	..	..	..	..	..	..	
29 Sep	Wolverhampton W	H	L 2-3	Jennings	..	..	..	Walford	..	..	..	..[1]	..[1]	..	Price for Talbot
6 Oct	Manchester C	H	D 0-0	..	..	..	..	O'Leary	..	..	..	..	..	..	
9 Oct	Ipswich T	A	W 2-1	..	Walford	..	..	..	..	..	..[1]	..	..	..[1]	
13 Oct	Bolton W	A	D 0-0	..	Rice	..	..	..	..	..	..	..	..	..	
20 Oct	Stoke C	H	D 0-0	..	..	..	..	..	..	..	..	..	..	..	
27 Oct	Bristol C	A	W 1-0	..	..	..	..	..	..	..	..[1]	..	..	..	
3 Nov	Brighton & HA	H	W 3-0	..	Devine	..	..	..	..	..[1]	..[1]	..	..	..[1]	Gatting for Sunderland
10 Nov	Crystal Palace	A	L 0-1	..	..	..	..	..	..	..	Gatting	..	Price	..	Walford for Devine
17 Nov	Everton	H	W 2-0	..	..	..	..	..	..	..	Vaessen	..[2]	..	..	Gatting for Brady
24 Nov	Liverpool	H	D 0-0	..	..	..	..	..	..	Gatting	Sunderland	..	..	..	
1 Dec	Nottingham F	A	D 1-1	..	..	..	..	..	Walford	..	..	..[1]	..	..	
8 Dec	Coventry C	H	W 3-1	..	..	..	..	..[1]	..	Brady	..[1]	..[1]	Hollins	..	Gatting for Nelson
15 Dec	W B A	A	D 2-2	..	..	..[1]	..	..	..	..	..	..[1]	..	..	
21 Dec	Norwich C	H	D 1-1	..	..	..	..	..	..	..	..	..[1]	..	..	McDermott for Nelson
26 Dec	Tottenham H	H	W 1-0	..	..	Rice	..	..	Young	..	..[1]	..	..	..	
29 Dec	Manchester U	A	L 0-3	..	..	..	..	..	..	..	..	..	..	..	Walford for O'Leary
1 Jan	Southampton	A	W 1-0	..	..	..	..	Walford	..[1]	Gatting	..	..	..	..	
12 Jan	Leeds U	H	L 0-1	..	Rice	Nelson	..	..	..	Brady	..	..	..	..	
19 Jan	Derby Co	H	W 2-0	..	..	..	..	..	..[1]	..[1]	..	..	Price	..	
9 Feb	Aston Villa	H	W 3-1	..	..	..	..	O'Leary	..	..	..[2]	..	..	..[1]	
23 Feb	Bolton W	H	W 2-0	..	..	..	..	..	..[1]	..	..	..[1]	..	..	Vaessen for Rice
1 Mar	Stoke C	A	W 3-2	..	Devine	..	..	..	..	..[1]	..[1]	..	..[1]	..	
11 Mar	Bristol C	H	D 0-0	..	..	..	..	..	..	..	Vaessen	..	..	..	
15 Mar	Manchester C	A	W 3-0	..	..	..	..	..	..	..[2]	..	..[1]	..	..	Gatting for Stapleton
22 Mar	Crystal Palace	H	L 1-1	..	..	..	..	..	..	..[1]	Sunderland	..	..	..	
28 Mar	Everton	A	W 1-0	Barron	Rice	..	..	..	..	Gatting[1]	..	Vaessen	..	..	
2 Apr	Norwich C	A	D 1-2	Jennings	Devine	..	..	..	..	Brady	..	Stapleton	..	..[1]	Vaessen for Nelson
5 Apr	Southampton	H	D 1-1	..	..	Walford	..	..	..	..	..[1]	..	..	..	Vaessen for Price
7 Apr	Tottenham H	A	W 2-1	Barron	Rice	..	..	..	..	..	Devine	Vaessen[1]	Hollins	Davis	Sunderland[1] for Brady
19 Apr	Liverpool	A	D 1-1	Jennings	..	..	..[1]	..	..	Gatting	Sunderland	Stapleton	Price	Hollins	Vaessen for Stapleton
26 Apr	W B A	H	D 1-1	Barron	..	Devine	..	Walford	..	Brady	..	[1]	Hollins	Vaessen	Gatting for Young
3 May	Coventry C	A	W 1-0	..	..	Nelson	..	..	..	Gatting	..	Vaessen[1]	Price	Hollins	Davis for Price
5 May	Nottingham F	H	D 0-0	Jennings	Devine	..	..	O'Leary	..	Brady	Vaessen	Stapleton	..	Rix	Hollins for Stapleton
16 May	Wolverhampton W	A	W 2-1	..	Rice	..	..	Walford[1]	..	..	Sunderland	..[1]	..	..	Vaessen for Price
19 May	Middlesbrough	A	L 0-5	..	..	..	..	..	..	..	..	..	..	..	Vaessen for Walford

FA Cup

5 Jan	Cardiff C (3)	A	D 0-0	Jennings	Rice	Devine	Talbot	Walford	Young	Gatting	Sunderland	Stapleton	Hollins	Rix	
8 Jan	Cardiff C (3R)	H	W 2-1	..	..	Nelson	..	..	..	..	..[2]	..	..	..	
26 Jan	Brighton & HA (4)	H	W 2-0	..	..	..[1]	..[1]	O'Leary	..	Brady	..	..	Price	..	
5 Feb	Bolton W (5)	A	D 1-1	..	..	..	..	..	..	..	..	..[1]	..	..	
19 Feb	Bolton W (5R)	H	W 3-0	..	..	..	..	..	..	..	..[2]	..[1]	..	..	
8 Mar	Watford (6)	A	W 2-1	..	Devine	..	..	..	..	..	..	..[2]	..	..	Gatting for Sunderland
12 Apr	Liverpool (SF) (at Sheffield W)		D 0-0	..	Rice	..	..	..	..	..	..	..	..	..	Walford for Nelson
16 Apr	Liverpool (SFR) (at Aston Villa)		D 1-1	..	..	Walford	..	..	..	..	..[1]	..	..	..	
28 Apr	Liverpool (SFR) (at Aston Villa)		D 1-1	..	..	Devine	..	..	..	..	..[1]	..	..	..	
1 May	Liverpool (SFR) (at Coventry)		W 1-0	..	..	..	..[1]	..	..	..	..	..	..	..	
10 May	West Ham U (F) (at Wembley)		L 0-1	..	..	..	..	..	..	..	..	..	..	..	Nelson for Devine

Football League Cup

29 Aug	Leeds (2)	A	D 1-1	Jennings	Rice	Nelson	Talbot	O'Leary	Young	Brady	Sunderland	Stapleton[1]	Hollins	Rix	
4 Sep	Leeds (2R)	H	W 7-0	..	..	..[1]	..	..	..	..[2]	..[3]	..[1]	..	..	
25 Sep	Southampton (3)	H	W 2-1	..	..	..	..	Walford	..	..[1]	..	..[1]	..	..	
30 Oct	Brighton & HA (4)	A	D 0-0	..	..	..	..	O'Leary	..	..	..	..	..	..	Gatting for Rice
13 Nov	Brighton & HA (4R)	H	W 4-0	..	Devine	..	..	..	..	..	Vaessen[2]	..[2]	Price	..	
4 Dec	Swindon T (5)	H	D 1-1	..	..	..	..	..	Walford	Gatting	Sunderland[1]	..	..	..	Hollins for Price
11 Dec	Swindon T (5R)	A	L 3-4	..	..	Walford	..[1]	..	Young	Brady[2]	..	..	Hollins	..	

FA Charity Shield

11 Aug	Liverpool (at Wembley)		L 1-3	Jennings	Rice	Nelson	Talbot	O'Leary	Walford	Brady	Sunderland[1]	Stapleton	Price	Rix	Young for Nelson, Hollins for Price

European Cup-Winners Cup

19 Sep	Fenerbahce (1)	H	W 2-0	Jennings	Rice	Nelson	Talbot	O'Leary	Young[1]	Brady	Sunderland[1]	Stapleton	Hollins	Rix	
3 Oct	Fenerbahce (1)	A	D 0-0	..	..	..	..	..	..	..	..	..	..	..	
24 Oct	Magdeburg (2)	H	W 2-1	..	..	..	..	..	..[1]	..	..[1]	..	..	..	
7 Nov	Magdeburg (2)	A	D 2-2	..	Devine	..	..	..	..	..[1]	Gatting	..	..	..	Price[1] for Hollins, Walford for Nelson
5 Mar	IFK Gothenburg (3)	H	W 5-1	..	..	..	..	..	..[1]	..[1]	Sunderland[2]	..	Price[1]	..	Hollins for Brady, McDermott for Sunderland
19 Mar	IFK Gothenburg (3)	A	D 0-0	..	..	..	..	..	..	..	Vaessen	..	..	..	
9 Apr	Juventus (SF)	H	D 1-1	..	..	Walford	..	*opponents*	..	..	Sunderland	..	..	..	Vaessen for Devine, Rice for O'Leary
23 Apr	Juventus (SF)	A	W 1-0	..	Rice	Devine	..	..	..	..	..	..	..	..	Vaessen[1] for Price, Hollins for Talbot
14 May	Valencia (F) (at Brussels)		D 0-0*	..	..	Nelson	..	..	..	..	..	..	..	..	Hollins for Price

*lost 4-5 on penalties

Appearances (Goals)

Barron P 5 · Brady L 34 (7) · Davis P 2 · Devine J 20 · Gatting S 14 (1) · Hollins J 26 (1) · Jennings P 37 · McDermott B 1 · Nelson S 35 (2) · O'Leary D 34 (1) · Price D 22 (1) · Rice P 26 · Rix G 38 (4) · Stapleton F 39 (14) · Sunderland A 37 (14) · Talbot B 42 (1) · Vaessen P 14 (2) · Walford S 19 (1) · Young W 38 (3) · Total: 19 players (52)

Position in League Table

	P	W	L	D	F:A	Pts	
Liverpool	42	25	7	10	81:30	60	1st
Arsenal	42	18	8	16	52:36	52	4th

SEASON 1980-1981 FOOTBALL LEAGUE (DIVISION 1)

1980-1981

16 Aug	W B A	A W 1-0	Jennings	Devine	Sansom	Talbot	O'Leary	Young	Vaessen	Price	Stapleton[1]	Hollins	Rix	
19 Aug	Southampton	H D 1-1	..	..	..	..	..	..	Hollins	Vaessen	Price	Stapleton[1]	..	McDermott for Talbot
23 Aug	Coventry C	A L 1-3	..	..	..	..	..	..	..	Sunderland	Stapleton[1]	Price	..	Rice for Price
30 Aug	Tottenham H	H W 2-0	..	..	..	..	..	..	..	..	..[1]	..[1]	..	
6 Sep	Manchester C	A D 1-1	..	..	..	..	..	..[1]	..	..	..	..	..	
13 Sep	Stoke C	H W 2-0	..	..	..[1]	..	..	..	..[1]	..	..	..	..	
20 Sep	Middlesbrough	A L 1-2	Wood	..	..	..	..	..	..	..	..	..	..[1]	
27 Sep	Nottingham F	H W 1-0	..	..	..	..	..	..	..	..	..	Gatting	..[1]	
4 Oct	Leicester C	H W 1-0	..	..	..	..	Walford	..	..	..	..[1]	..	..	
7 Oct	Birmingham C	A L 1-3	..	..	..	..	..	..	..	..[1]	..	..	..	
11 Oct	Manchester U	A D 0-0	..	..	..	..	..	..	..	..	..	..	..	
18 Oct	Sunderland	H D 2-2	..	..	..	..	..	..[1]	..	..	..	..[1]	..	McDermott for Talbot
21 Oct	Norwich C	H W 3-1	..	..	..[1]	..[1]	..	..	..	..	..	..	..	McDermott[1] for Hollins
25 Oct	Liverpool	A D 1-1	..	..	..	..	..	..	..	..[1]	..	Price	..	Rice for Price
1 Nov	Brighton & HA	H W 2-0	..	..	..	..	..	..	..	..	..	McDermott[1]	..[1]	
8 Nov	Leeds U	A W 5-0	..	..	..	..[1]	..	..	..[2]	..[1]	Gatting[1]	..	..	
11 Nov	Southampton	A L 1-3	..	..	..	..	..	..	..	..	McDermott	Gatting	..[1]	Price for Gatting
15 Nov	W B A	H D 2-2	Jennings	..	..	..	O'Leary	..	*opponents*	..[1]	Stapleton	..	..	
22 Nov	Everton	H W 2-1	..	..	..	..	..	Walford	..	..	..[1]	McDermott[1]	..	Gatting for Sanson
29 Nov	Aston Villa	A D 1-1	..	..	..	..[1]	Walford	Young	..	..	..	Gatting	..	
6 Dec	Wolverhampton W	H D 1-1	..	..	..	..	..	..	..	McDermott	..[1]	..	..	Vaessen for Hollins
13 Dec	Sunderland	A L 0-2	..	..	..	..	..	..	Price	..	..	..	Davis	Vaessen for Gatting
20 Dec	Manchester U	H W 2-1	..	..	..	..	..	..	Vaessen[1]	..	..	..	Rix[1]	
26 Dec	Crystal Palace	A D 2-2	..	..	..	..	..	..	Hollins	Vaessen	..[1]	McDermott[1]	..	
27 Dec	Ipswich T	H D 1-1	..	..	..	..	..	..	..	Sunderland[1]	..	Gatting	..	
10 Jan	Everton	A W 2-1	..	..	..	Davis	..	..	..	Vaessen[1]	..	..[1]	McDermott	Price for Hollins
17 Jan	Tottenham H	A L 0-2	..	..	..	McDermott	..	..	..	Sunderland	..	..	Rix	
31 Jan	Coventry C	H D 2-2	..	Hollins	..	Talbot[1]	..	..	McDermott	..	..[1]	..	..	
7 Feb	Stoke C	A D 1-1	..	..	..	..	O'Leary	..	..	..	..[1]	..	..	
21 Feb	Nottingham F	A L 1-3	..	..	..	..	..	..	..	..	..[1]	..	..	Devine for Gatting
24 Feb	Manchester C	H W 2-0	..	Devine	..	..[1]	..	..	Hollins	..[1]	..	..	..	
28 Feb	Middlesbrough	H D 2-2	..	..	..	..	..	Walford	..[1]	..	..[1]	..	..	McDermott for Sunderland
7 Mar	Leicester C	A L 0-1	..	..	..	..	..	Young	..	..	..	..	..	Price for Hollins
21 Mar	Norwich C	A D 1-1	..	..	..	..[1]	..	..	Nicholas	..	..	McDermott	..	
28 Mar	Liverpool	H W 1-0	..	..	..	..	..	..	Hollins	..[1]	..	Nicholas	..	Davis for Hollins
31 Mar	Birmingham C	H W 2-1	..	..	..	..	..[1]	..	Davis	..	..[1]	..	..	McDermott for Devine
4 Apr	Brighton & HA	A W 1-0	..	..	..	..	..	..	..	..	..	Hollins[1]	..	
11 Apr	Leeds U	H D 0-0	..	..	..	..	..	..	Hollins	..	..	Nicholas	Davis	McDermott for Hollins
18 Apr	Ipswich T	A W 2-0	..	..	..[1]	..	..	..	..	..	..	..[1]	..	
20 Apr	Crystal Palace	H W 3-2	..	..	..	..[1]	..	..[1]	..	..	..	..	..[1]	McDermott for Sunderland
25 Apr	Wolverhampton W	A W 2-1	..	..	..	..	..	..	*opponents*	McDermott	..[1]	..	..	
2 May	Aston Villa	H W 2-0	..	Hollins	..	..	..	..[1]	McDermott[1]	Sunderland	..	..	..	Nelson for Talbot
	FA Cup													
3 Jan	Everton (3)	A L 0-2	Jennings	Devine	Sansom	Talbot	O'Leary	Young	Hollins	Sunderland	Stapleton	Gatting	Rix	McDermott for Talbot
	Football League Cup													
26 Aug	Swansea (2)	A D 1-1	Jennings	Devine	Sansom	Talbot	O'Leary	Young	Hollins	Sunderland	Stapleton[1]	Price	Rix	
2 Sep	Swansea (2R)	H W 3-1	..	..	..	..	Walford[1]	..	..[1]	..[1]	..	..	..	
22 Sep	Stockport Co (3)	A W 3-1	Wood	..	..	..	O'Leary	..	..[1]	..[1]	..[1]	Gatting	..	
4 Nov	Tottenham (4)	A L 0-1	..	..	..	..	Walford	..	..	..	..	..	..	McDermott for Hollins

Appearances (Goals)

Davis P 10 (1) · Devine J 39 · Gatting S 23 (3) · Hollins J 38 (5) · Jennings P 31 · McDermott B 23 (5) · Nelson S 1 · Nicholas P 8 (1) · O'Leary D 24 (1) · Price D 12 (1) · Rice P 2 · Rix G 35 (5) · Sansom K 42 (3) · Stapleton F 40 (14) · Sunderland A 34 (7) · Talbot B 40 (7) · Vaessen P 7 (2) · Walford S 20 · Wood G 11 · Young W 40 (4) · Own goals 2 · Total: 20 players (61)

Position in League Table

	P	W	L	D	F:A	Pts	
Aston Villa	42	26	8	8	72:40	60	1st
Arsenal	42	19	8	15	61:45	53	3rd

SEASON 1981-1982 FOOTBALL LEAGUE (DIVISION 1)

1981-1982

29 Aug	Stoke C	H L 0-1	Jennings	Devine	Sansom	Talbot	O'Leary	Young	Davis	Sunderland	McDermott	Nicholas	Rix	Vaessen for Devine
2 Sep	W B A	A W 2-0	..	..	..	..[1]	..	..	..	..[1]	..	..	..	
5 Sep	Liverpool	A L 0-2	..	..	..	..	..	..	Hollins	..	..	..	..	Davis for Nicholas
12 Sep	Sunderland	H D 1-1	..	Hollins	..	..	..	..	Davis	..[1]	..	..	..	
19 Sep	Leeds U	A D 0-0	..	..	..	..	..	..	..	..	..	..	..	Devine for Nicholas
22 Sep	Birmingham C	H W 1-0	..	Devine	..	..[1]	..	..	..	..	..	Hollins	..	
26 Sep	Manchester U	H D 0-0	..	..	..	..	..	..	Hollins	..	Hawley	Nicholas	Davis	
3 Oct	Notts Co	A L 1-2	..	Hollins	..	..	..	..	Davis	..	..[1]	..	Rix	McDermott for Hawley
10 Oct	Swansea C	A L 0-2	..	Devine	..	..	..	..	..	..	..	..	Hollins	
17 Oct	Manchester C	H W 1-0	..	Hollins	..	..	..	Whyte	McDermott	..	Meade[1]	..	Rix	
24 Oct	Ipswich T	A L 1-2	..	..	..	..	..	Young	Davis	..[1]	..	..	..	
31 Oct	Coventry C	H W 1-0	..	..	..	..	*opponents*	Whyte	McDermott	Vaessen	Hawley	..	..	
7 Nov	Aston Villa	A W 2-0	..	Devine	..	..[1]	..	..	Hollins	..	Davis	..	..[1]	
21 Nov	Nottingham F	A W 2-1	..	..	..	..[1]	..	..	..	Sunderland[1]	..	..	..	
28 Nov	Everton	H W 1-0	..	..	..	..	..	..	..	..	..	..	..	McDermott[1] for Devine
5 Dec	West Ham U	A W 2-1	..	Robson	..	..	..	..[1]	..[1]	..	..	..	..	
20 Jan	Stoke C	A W 1-0	Wood	..	..	..	..	..	..	..[1]	..	..	..	
23 Jan	Southampton	A L 1-3	..	..	..	..	..[1]	..	..	..	..	..	..	McDermott for O'Leary
26 Jan	Brighton & HA	H D 0-0	..	..	..	..	Hollins	..	McDermott	..	..	..	..	Meade for Davis
30 Jan	Leeds U	H W 1-0	..	Hollins	..	..	O'Leary	..	Vaessen[1]	..	..	..	..	
2 Feb	Wolverhampton W	H W 2-1	..	..	..	..	..	..	..[1]	..	..	..	..[1]	Hawley for Sunderland
6 Feb	Sunderland	A D 0-0	..	..	..	..	..	..	..	..	..	..	..	
13 Feb	Notts Co	H W 1-0	..	..	..	..	..	..	..	..	..	..	..	Meade[1] for Nicholas
16 Feb	Middlesbrough	H W 1-0	..	..	..	..	..	..	..	..	..	..	..[1]	Meade for Nicholas
20 Feb	Manchester U	A D 0-0	..	..	..	..	..	..	..	..	..	..	..	Meade for Vaessen
27 Feb	Swansea C	H L 0-2	..	..	..	..	..	..	..	..	..	..	..	Meade for Vaessen
6 Mar	Manchester C	A D 0-0	..	..	..	..	..	..	Gorman	..	..	Robson	..	
13 Mar	Ipswich T	H W 1-0	..	..	..	..	..	..	..	..	..	..[1]	..	
16 Mar	W B A	H D 2-2	..	..	..	..	..	..	..	..[1]	..	..	..	Meade[1] for Gorman
20 Mar	Coventry C	A L 0-1	..	..	..	..	Devine	..	..	..	..	..	..	Meade for Gorman
27 Mar	Aston Villa	H W 4-3	..	..	..	..	O'Leary	..	Meade[1]	..[1]	..	..	..[2]	
29 Mar	Tottenham H	A D 2-2	..	..	..	..	..	..	..	..[2]	..	..	..	Nicholas for Davis
3 Apr	Wolverhampton W	A D 1-1	..	..	..	..	..	..	..	..	..[1]	..	..	Hawley for Meade
10 Apr	Brighton & HA	A L 1-2	..	..	..	..[1]	..	..	..	..	..	..	Nicholas	
12 Apr	Tottenham H	H L 1-3	..	..	..	..	..	..	..	Hawley[1]	Nicholas	..	Rix	McDermott for Robson
17 Apr	Nottingham F	H W 2-0	..	..	..	..[1]	..	..	..	..	Davis	..	..[1]	
24 Apr	Everton	A L 1-2	..	..	..	..	..	..	Hawley	Sunderland	..	..	..[1]	Nicholas for Hollins
1 May	West Ham U	H W 2-0	..	..	..	..	..	..	..	..[1]	..	..	..[1]	
4 May	Birmingham C	A W 1-0	..	..	..	..	..	..[1]	..	..	..	..	..	
8 May	Middlesbrough	A W 3-1	..	..	..	..[1]	..	..	..	..	..[1]	..	..[1]	Nicholas for Davis
11 May	Liverpool	H D 1-1	..	..	..	..	..	..	Nicholas	..[1]	Hawley	..	..	Meade for Hawley
15 May	Southampton	H W 4-1	..	..	..	..	..	..	Davis[2]	..	..[1]	..[1]	..	
	FA Cup													
2 Jan	Tottenham H (3)	A L 0-1	Jennings	Robson	Sansom	Talbot	O'Leary	Whyte	Hollins	Sunderland	Rix	Nicholas	Davis	Meade for Jennings
	Milk Cup													
6 Oct	Sheffield U (2)	A L 0-1	Jennings	Devine	Sansom	Talbot	O'Leary	Young	Hollins	Sunderland	Hawley	Nicholas	Davis	
27 Oct	Sheffield U (2R)	H W 2-0	..	Hollins	..	..	..	..[1]	McDermott	..[1]	Meade	..	Rix	Vaessen for Meade
10 Nov	Norwich C (3)	H W 1-0	..	..	..	..	..	Whyte	..	..	Davis	..[1]	..	Meade for Sunderland
1 Dec	Liverpool (4)	H D 0-0	..	..	..	..	..	..	..	..	..	..	..	Hankin for McDermott
8 Dec	Liverpool (4R)	A L 0-3	Wood	Robson	..	..	..	..	Hollins	..	..	..	..	Hankin for Nicholas

1981-1982 *continued*

UEFA Cup

16 Sep	Panathinaikos (1)	A	W	2-0	Jennings	Hollins	Sansom	Talbot	O'Leary	Young	Davis	Vaessen	McDermott[1]	Nicholas	Rix	Meade[1] for Vaessen
30 Sep	Panathinaikos (1)	H	W	1-0	..	Devine	..	..[1]	..	..	Hollins	Sunderland	..	..	..	Whyte for O'Leary
20 Oct	Winterslag (2)	A	L	0-1	..	..	..	..	..	..	..	..	Meade	..	..	McDermott for Meade
3 Nov	Winterslag (2)	H	W	2-1	..	Hollins[1]	..	..	..	Whyte	McDermott	Vaessen	..	..	..[1]	Davis for Vaessen

Appearances (Goals)

Davis P 38 (4) · Devine J 11 · Gorman P 4 · Hawley J 14 (3) · Hollins J 40 (1) · Jennings P 16 · McDermott B 13 (1) · Meade R 16 (4) · Nicholas P 31 · O'Leary D 40 (1) · Rix G 39 (9) · Robson S 20 (2) · Sansom K 42 · Sunderland A 38 (11) · Talbot B 42 (7) · Vaessen P 10 (2) · Whyte C 32 (2) · Wood G 26 · Young W 10 · Own goals 1 · Total 19 players (48)

Position in League Table

	P	W	L	D	F:A	Pts	
Liverpool	42	26	7	9	80:32	87	1st
Arsenal	42	20	11	11	48:37	71	5th

1982-1983

SEASON 1982-1983 FOOTBALL LEAGUE (DIVISION 1)

28 Aug	Stoke C	A	L	1-2	Wood	Hollins	Sansom	Talbot	O'Leary	Whyte	Robson	Sunderland[1]	Chapman	Woodcock	Rix	Davis for Sunderland
31 Aug	Norwich C	H	D	1-1	..	..	..	..	Davis	..	..	..	..	..[1]	..	Devine for Sansom
4 Sep	Liverpool	H	L	0-2	..	..	Devine	..	O'Leary	..	..	Davis	..	..	..	
7 Sep	Brighton & HA	A	L	0-1	..	..	..	..	..	..	..	..	..	..	..	Hawley for Talbot
11 Sep	Coventry C	A	W	2-0	..	..	Sansom	..	..	..	Davis	Robson	..[1]	..[1]	..	
18 Sep	Notts Co	H	W	2-0	..	..[1]	..	..	..	..	..	..	..	..	..[1]	
25 Sep	Manchester U	A	D	0-0	..	..	..	..	..	..	..	..	..	..	..	
2 Oct	West Ham U	H	L	2-3	..	..	..	..[1]	..	..	..[1]	Sunderland	..	..	..	
9 Oct	Ipswich T	A	W	1-0	..	..	..	..	..	..	..	..	Robson	..[1]	..	Hawley for Hollins
16 Oct	W B A	H	W	2-0	..	Devine	..	..	..	..	..	..[1]	..	..[1]	..	
23 Oct	Nottingham F	A	L	0-3	..	Hollins	..	..	..	..	..	..	..	..	..	Chapman for Robson
30 Oct	Birmingham C	H	D	0-0	..	O'Shea	..	..	..	..	..	..	..	..	..	Chapman for Woodcock
6 Nov	Luton T	A	D	2-2	..	..	..	..[1]	..	..	..	..	..	..	..[1]	
13 Nov	Everton	H	D	1-1	Jennings	..	..	..	..	..	..	Chapman	..	..	..	McDermott[1] for O'Leary
20 Nov	Swansea C	A	W	2-1	Wood	..	..	..	..	..	..	Sunderland	..	..[1]	..	Chapman[1] for Woodcock
27 Nov	Watford	H	L	2-4	..	..	..	..[1]	..	..	..	..	..[1]	..	..	
4 Dec	Manchester C	A	L	1-2	..	..	..	..	..	..	..	..	Chapman	Robson	..	McDermott[1] for O'Shea
7 Dec	Aston Villa	H	W	2-1	..	Hollins	..	..	..	..[1]	..	..	Robson	Woodcock[1]	..	
18 Dec	Sunderland	A	L	0-3	Jennings	..	..	..	..	..	..	..	..	..	..	Chapman for Davis
27 Dec	Tottenham H	H	W	2-0	..	..	..	..	..	Robson	..	..[1]	Nicholas	..[1]	..	
28 Dec	Southampton	A	D	2-2	..	..	..	..	..	..	..	..	..	..[1]	..	Chapman[1] for Woodcock
1 Jan	Swansea C	H	W	2-1	..	..	..	..	..	..	..	..[1]	Petrovic	..[1]	..	Chapman for Sunderland
3 Jan	Liverpool	A	L	1-3	..	..	..	..[1]	..	..	Nicholas	Chapman	..	..	..	
15 Jan	Stoke C	H	W	3-0	..	..[1]	..	Whyte	..	Nicholas	Davis	Sunderland	..[1]	..	..[1]	Talbot for O'Leary
22 Jan	Notts Co	A	L	0-1	..	..	..	Robson	..	..	..	..	..	..	..	Talbot for Davis
5 Feb	Brighton & HA	H	W	3-1	..	..	..	..	..	..	Talbot	Meade[2]	..	Davis	..[1]	
26 Feb	W B A	A	D	0-0	..	Kay	..	..	Whyte	..	Devine	Davis	Meade	Woodcock	..	Talbot for Rix
5 Mar	Nottingham F	H	D	0-0	..	Hollins	..	..	..	..	Talbot	..	Sunderland	..	..	Meade for Sunderland
15 Mar	Birmingham C	A	L	1-2	..	..	..	..	..	..	Petrovic	..	..[1]	..	..	Talbot for Petrovic
19 Mar	Luton T	H	W	4-1	..	O'Leary	..	..	..	..	Talbot	..[1]	..	..[3]	..	Meade for O'Leary
22 Mar	Ipswich T	H	D	2-2	Wood	Hollins	..	Devine	..[1]	..	..	..	..	..	..[1]	
26 Mar	Everton	A	W	3-2	..	Robson[1]	..	Whyte	O'Leary	..	..	..	..[1]	..[1]	..	
2 Apr	Southampton	H	D	0-0	..	Kay	..	..	..	..	..	..	..	..	..	
4 Apr	Tottenham H	A	L	0-5	..	Robson	..	..	..	..	..	..	..	..	..	Petrovic for Whyte
9 Apr	Coventry C	H	W	2-1	..	..	..	..	Kay	..	..	..	Petrovic	..[1]	..[1]	Chapman for Nicholas
20 Apr	Norwich C	A	L	1-3	..	Kay	..	Talbot	O'Leary	Whyte	McDermott	Hill	Davis[1]	Chapman	..	Hollins for Rix
23 Apr	Manchester C	H	W	3-0	Jennings	..	..	Whyte	..	Nicholas	Talbot[3]	Davis	McDermott	Woodcock	Hill	Hawley for Woodcock
30 Apr	Watford	A	L	1-2	..	..	..	..	..	..	..	..	..[1]	Hawley	..	Petrovic for Hawley
2 May	Manchester U	H	W	3-0	..	Devine	..	..	..[1]	..	..[2]	..	..	..	..	Petrovic for Hawley
7 May	Sunderland	H	L	0-1	..	..	..	..	..	..	..	..	Petrovic	McDermott	..	Hawley for Devine
10 May	West Ham U	A	W	3-1	..	Kay	..	..[1]	..	..	..	..	..[1]	..[1]	..	
14 May	Aston Villa	A	L	1-2	..	Devine	..	..	..	..	..	..[1]	McDermott	Petrovic	..	

FA Cup

8 Jan	Bolton W (3)	H	W	2-1	Jennings	Hollins	Sansom	Talbot	O'Leary	Robson	Davis[1]	Sunderland	Nicholas	Woodcock	Rix[1]	
29 Jan	Leeds U (4)	H	D	1-1	..	..	..	Robson	..	Nicholas	Talbot	..[1]	Petrovic	..	..	
2 Feb	Leeds U (4R)	A	D	1-1	..	..	..	..	..	..	..	..	..	..	..[1]	Davis for Sunderland
9 Feb	Leeds U (4R)	H	W	2-1	..	..	..	..	..	..	..	Meade	..	..[1]	..[1]	
19 Feb	Middlesbrough (5)	A	D	1-1	..	..	..	..	Whyte	..	..	Davis	..	..	..[1]	
28 Feb	Middlesbrough (5R)	H	W	3-2	..	..	..	..	..	..	..[1]	..[1]	Sunderland	..[1]	..	
12 Mar	Aston Villa (6)	H	W	2-0	..	..	..	..	..	..	Petrovic[1]	..	..	..[1]	..	
16 Apr	Manchester U (SF) (at Aston Villa)		L	1-2	Wood	Robson	..	Whyte	O'Leary	Hollins	Talbot	..	Petrovic	..[1]	..	Chapman for Robson

Milk Cup

5 Oct	Cardiff C (2)	H	W	2-1	Wood	Hollins[1]	Sansom	Talbot	O'Leary	Whyte	Davis[1]	Sunderland	Robson	Woodcock	Rix	
26 Oct	Cardiff C (2)	A	W	3-1	..	..	..	..	..	..	..[1]	..[1]	..	..[1]	..	
9 Nov	Everton (3)	A	D	1-1	Jennings	O'Shea	..	..	..	..	..	..	..[1]	..	..	Chapman for Sunderland
23 Nov	Everton (3R)	H	W	3-0	Wood	..	..	..	..	..	..	..[3]	..	..	..	Chapman for Sunderland
30 Nov	Huddersfield T (4)	H	W	1-0	..	..	..	..	..	..	..	..[1]	..	..	..	
18 Jan	Sheffield W (5)	H	W	1-0	Jennings	Hollins	..	Nicholas	..	Robson	..	..	Petrovic	..[1]	..	
15 Feb	Manchester U (SF)	H	L	2-4	..	..	..	Robson	..	Nicholas[1]	Talbot	Meade	..	..[1]	..	Davis for O'Leary
23 Feb	Manchester U (SF)	A	L	1-2	..	..	..	..	Whyte	..	..	..[1]	..	..	..	Davis for Hollins

UEFA Cup

14 Sep	Spartak Moscow (1)	A	L	2-3	Wood	Hollins	Sansom	Talbot	O'Leary	Whyte	Davis	Robson[1]	Chapman[1]	Woodcock	Rix	
29 Sep	Spartak Moscow (1)	H	L	2-5	..	..	..	..	..	*opponents*	..	..	..[1]	..	..	Sunderland for Hollins, McDermott for Davis

Appearances (Goals)

Chapman L 19 (3) · Davis P 41 (4) · Devine J 9 · Hawley J 6 · Hill C 7 · Hollins J 23 (2) · Jennings P 19 · Kay J 7 · McDermott B 9 (4) · Meade R 4 (2) · Nicholas P 21 · O'Leary D 36 (1) · O'Shea D 6 · Petrovic V 13 (2) · Rix G 36 (6) · Robson S 31 (2) · Sansom K 40 · Sunderland A 25 (6) · Talbot B 42 (9) · Whyte C 36 (3) · Wood G 23 · Woodcock A 34 (14) · Total: 22 players (58)

Position in League Table

	P	W	L	D	F:A	Pts	
Liverpool	42	24	8	10	87:37	82	1st
Arsenal	42	16	16	10	58:56	58	10th

1983-1984

SEASON 1983-1984 FOOTBALL LEAGUE (DIVISION 1)

27 Aug	Luton T	H	W	2-1	Jennings	Robson	Sansom	Talbot	O'Leary	Hill	McDermott[1]	Davis	Woodcock[1]	Nicholas	Rix	
29 Aug	Wolverhampton W	A	W	2-1	..	..	..	..	..	..	..	..	..	..[2]	..	
3 Sep	Southampton	A	L	0-1	..	..	..	..	..	..	..	..	..	..	..	Whyte for McDermott
6 Sep	Manchester U	H	L	2-3	..	..	..	..[1]	..	..	..	..	..[1]	..	..	Sunderland for McDermott
10 Sep	Liverpool	H	L	0-2	..	..	..	..	..	..	Sunderland	..	..	..	..	
17 Sep	Notts Co	A	W	4-0	..	..	..	Whyte	..	*opponents*	..	..	..[1]	..	..[1]	Talbot[1] for Nicholas
24 Sep	Norwich C	H	W	3-0	..	..	..	..	..	..	..[2]	..	Chapman[1]	..	..	McDermott for Nicholas
1 Oct	Q P R	A	L	0-2	..	..	..	..	..	..	..	..	..	..	..	
15 Oct	Coventry C	H	L	0-1	..	..	..	..	..	..	..	..	..	..	..	McDermott for Whyte
22 Oct	Nottingham F	H	W	4-1	..	..	..	..	..	..[1]	..[1]	..	Woodcock[2]	..	..	McDermott for Nicholas
29 Oct	Aston Villa	A	W	6-2	..	..	..	..	..	..	..	..	..[5]	..	..	McDermott for Robson
5 Nov	Sunderland	H	L	1-2	..	..	..	..	Adams	..	..	Talbot	..[1]	..	..	McDermott for Sunderland
12 Nov	Ipswich T	A	L	0-1	..	..	..	..	O'Leary	..	..	Davis	..	..	..	Gorman for Sunderland
19 Nov	Everton	H	W	2-1	..	..[1]	..	..	..	..	..[1]	Gorman	McDermott	..	..	Meade for Sunderland
26 Nov	Leicester C	A	L	0-3	..	..	..	..	..	Kay	..	Davis	Woodcock	..	..	Chapman for Rix
3 Dec	W B A	H	L	0-1	..	..	..	Caton	Adams	Hill	Madden	..	..	..	Allinson	Meade for Robson
10 Dec	West Ham U	A	L	1-3	..	Hill	..	Kay	Whyte[1]	Caton	..	..	..	..	..	Meade for Hill
17 Dec	Watford	H	W	3-1	..	..	..	Cork	..	..	Meade[3]	..	..	..	..	
26 Dec	Tottenham H	A	W	4-2	..	..	..	Robson	O'Leary	..	..[2]	..	..	..[2]	..	Cork for Robson
27 Dec	Birmingham C	H	D	1-1	..	..	..	Cork	Whyte	..	..	..	..	..[1]	..	McDermott for Caton
31 Dec	Southampton	H	D	2-2	..	..	..	..[1]	O'Leary	..	..	..	..	..[1]	..	
2 Jan	Norwich C	A	D	1-1	..	..	..	..	..	..	..	..	..[1]	..	..	
14 Jan	Luton T	A	W	2-1	..	Kay	..[1]	Talbot	..	..	..	..	..[1]	..	Rix	
21 Jan	Notts Co	H	D	1-1	..	..	..	..	Adams	..	..	..	..	..[1]	..	McDermott for Adams
28 Jan	Stoke C	A	L	0-1	..	..	..	..	O'Leary	..	McDermott	..	..	..	..	
4 Feb	Q P R	H	L	0-2	..	..	..	..	..	..	Meade	..	..	..	..	Cork for Meade

1983-84 *continued*

11 Feb	Liverpool	A	L	1-2	Jennings	Hill	Sansom	Talbot	O'Leary	Caton	Cork	Davis	Woodcock	Nicolas	Rix[1]	Allinson for Cork
18 Feb	Aston Villa	H	D	1-1	..	..	..	..	..	..	Davis	Nicholas	Mariner	Woodcock	..[1]	
25 Feb	Nottingham F	A	W	1-0	..	..	..	..	..	..	..	..	..[1]	..	..	
3 Mar	Sunderland	A	D	2-2	..	..	..	..	..	..	..	..[1]	..	..[1]	..	
10 Mar	Ipswich T	H	W	4-1	..	..	..	..[1]	..	..	..	..	..[2]	..[1]	..	Allinson for Rix
17 Mar	Manchester U	A	L	0-4	..	..	..	..	..	..	Robson	..	..	..	..	
24 Mar	Wolverhampton W	H	W	4-1	..	..	..	..	..	..	..[1]	..[1]	..	..[1]	..[1]	
31 Mar	Coventry C	A	W	4-1	..	..	Sparrow	..[1]	..	Whyte[1]	..[1]	..	..[1]	..	..	Kay for Jennings (Robson in goal)
7 Apr	Stoke C	H	W	3-1	Lukic	..	..	..	..	Caton	..	..[1]	..[1]	..[1]	..	Meade for Nicholas
9 Apr	Everton	A	D	0-0	..	..	Sansom	..	..	..	..	..	..	..	..	
21 Apr	Tottenham H	H	W	3-2	..	..	..	..	..	..	..[1]	..[1]	..	..[1]	..	Davis for Rix
23 Apr	Birmingham C	A	D	1-1	..	..	..	..	..	..	..	..	..	..[1]	Davis	
28 Apr	Leicester C	H	W	2-1	Jennings	..	..	..	..	..	..	..	..	..[1]	Rix	Davis[1] for Talbot
5 May	W B A	A	W	3-1	..	..	..	..[1]	..	..	..[1]	..	..[1]	..	..	Davis for Robson
7 May	West Ham U	H	D	3-3	..	..	..	..[1]	..	..	..	..	..[1]	..[1]	..	Davis for Rix
12 May	Watford	A	L	1-2	..	..	..	..	..	..	..[1]	Davis	..	Meade	..	
	FA Cup															
7 Jan	Middlesbrough (3)	A	L	2-3	Jennings	Hill	Sansom	Cork	O'Leary	Caton	Meade	Davis	Woodcock[1]	Nicholas[1]	Rix	Talbot for Cork
	Milk Cup															
4 Oct	Plymouth Arg (2)	A	D	1-1	Jennings	Robson	Sansom	Whyte	O'Leary	Hill	Sunderland	Davis	Woodcock	Nicholas	Rix[1]	Talbot for Woodcock
25 Oct	Plymouth Arg (2)	H	W	1-0	..	..	..	..	..	..	..[1]	..	..	..	..	
9 Nov	Tottenham H (3)	A	W	2-1	..	..	..	..	..	..	..	..	..[1]	..[1]	..	
29 Nov	Walsall (4)	H	L	1-2	..	..[1]	..	..	..	..	..	..	..	..	Allinson	

Appearances (Goals)

Adams T 3 · Allinson I 9 · Caton T 26 · Chapman L 4 (1) · Cork D 7 (1) · Davis P 35 (1) · Gorman P 2 · Hill C 37 (1) · Jennings P 38 · Kay J 7 · Lukic J 4 · Madden D 2 · Mariner P 15 (7) · Meade R 13 (5) · McDermott B 13 (2) · Nicholas C 41 (11) · O'Leary D 36 · Rix G 34 (4) · Robson S 28 (6) · Sansom K 40 (1) · Sparrow B 2 · Sunderland A 12 (4) · Talbot B 27 (6) · Whyte C 15 (2) · Woodcock A 37 (21) · Own goals 1 · Total: 25 players (74)

Position in League Table

	P	W	L	D	F:A	Pts	
Liverpool	42	22	6	14	73:32	80	1st
Arsenal	42	18	15	9	74:60	63	6th

SEASON 1984-1985 FOOTBALL LEAGUE (DIVISION 1)

1984-1985

25 Aug	Chelsea	H	D	1-1	Jennings	Anderson	Sansom	Talbot	O'Leary	Caton	Robson	Davis	Mariner[1]	Woodcock	Allinson	
29 Aug	Nottingham F	A	L	0-2	..	..	..	..	..	..	..	Nicholas	..	..	Davis	Allinson for Talbot
1 Sep	Watford	A	W	4-3	..	..	..	..[1]	..	..	..	Davis	..	..[1]	Nicholas[2]	
4 Sep	Newcastle U	H	W	2-0	..	..[1]	..	..[1]	..	..	..	..	..	..	..	
8 Sep	Liverpool	H	W	3-1	..	..	..	..[2]	..	..	..	..	..	..[1]	..	
15 Sep	Ipswich T	A	L	1-2	..	..	..	..	..	..	..	Rix	..	..	..[1]	
22 Sep	Stoke C	H	W	4-0	..	..	..[1]	..	..	..	..	..	..[1]	..[2]	..	
29 Sep	Coventry C	A	W	2-1	..	..	..	..	..	..	..	..	..[1]	..[1]	..	Davis for Talbot
6 Oct	Everton	H	W	1-0	..	..	..	..	..	..	..	..	..	..	..[1]	
13 Oct	Leicester C	A	W	4-1	..	..[1]	..	..[2]	..	..	..	..[1]	Allinson	..	..	
20 Oct	Sunderland	H	W	3-2	..	..	..	..[1]	..	..[1]	..	..	..[1]	..	..	Davis for Woodcock
27 Oct	West Ham U	A	L	1-3	..	..	..	..	..	Hill	..	..	..[1]	Davis	..	
2 Nov	Manchester U	A	L	2-4	Lukic	..	..	..	..	Caton	Davis	..	..[1]	Woodcock[1]	..	Adams for Rix
10 Nov	Aston Villa	H	D	1-1	Jennings	..	..	..	..	..	Robson	Davis	Mariner[1]	..	..	Allinson for Caton
17 Nov	QPR	H	W	1-0	..	..	..	..	..	Adams	..	..	Allinson	..[1]	..	
25 Nov	Sheffield W	A	L	1-2	..	..	..	..	..	..	..	..	Mariner	..[1]	..	Allinson for O'Leary
1 Dec	Luton T	H	W	3-1	Lukic	..[1]	..	..	Adams	Caton	..	..	..	..[1]	Allinson[1]	
8 Dec	Southampton	A	L	0-1	..	..	..	..	O'Leary	Adams	..	..	..	..	..	Meade for Allinson
15 Dec	WBA	H	W	4-0	..	..	..	..[1]	Adams	Caton	..	..[1]	..	..	..[2]	
22 Dec	Watford	H	D	1-1	..	O'Leary	Hill	..	..	..	..	Nicholas	..	..	..[1]	
26 Dec	Norwich C	A	L	0-1	..	Anderson	Sansom	..	O'Leary	Adams	..	Caton	..	..	..	Nicholas for Allinson
29 Dec	Newcastle U	A	W	3-1	..	..	Caton	..[1]	..	..	..	Nicholas[2]	..	..	..	
1 Jan	Tottenham H	H	L	1-2	..	..	..	..	..	..	..	Allinson	..	..[1]	Nicholas	Williams for Nicholas
19 Jan	Chelsea	A	D	1-1	..	..	Sansom	..	..	Caton	..	Williams	..[1]	..	..	
2 Feb	Coventry C	H	W	2-1	..	..	..	..	..	..	..	..	..	Meade[1]	Allinson[1]	Nicholas for Caton
12 Feb	Liverpool	A	L	0-3	..	..	..	..	..	Adams	..	..	..	..	..	Nicholas for Allinson
23 Feb	Manchester U	H	L	0-1	..	..	..	Williams	..	Caton	..	Davis	..	Woodcock	Nicholas	Talbot for Davis
2 Mar	West Ham U	H	W	2-1	..	..	..	..	..	..	..[1]	..	..[1]	..	..	
9 Mar	Sunderland	A	D	0-0	..	..	..	Talbot	..	..	..	..	..	..	..	
13 Mar	Aston Villa	A	D	0-0	..	..	..	..	..	..	..	..	..	..	..	Meade for Woodcock
16 Mar	Leicester C	H	W	2-0	..	..	..	Williams[1]	Adams	..	..	..	..	Meade[1]	..	Talbot for Nicholas
19 Mar	Ipswich T	H	D	1-1	..	..	..	..	..	..	..	..	..	..[1]	..	Talbot for Davis
23 Mar	Everton	A	L	0-2	..	..	..	..	O'Leary	..	..	Rix	..	..	..	Talbot for Robson
30 Mar	Stoke C	A	L	0-2	..	..	..	..	..	..	Talbot	..	..	..	..	Allinson for Meade
6 Apr	Norwich C	H	W	2-0	..	..	..	..	..	..	Robson[1]	..	..	Talbot	..[1]	Allinson for Mariner
13 Apr	Nottingham F	H	D	1-1	..	..	..	..	..	..	..	..	Allinson[1]	..	..	
17 Apr	Tottenham H	A	W	2-0	..	..	..	..	..	..	..	..	..	..[1]	..[1]	Mariner for O'Leary
20 Apr	QPR	A	L	0-1	..	..	..	..	Adams	..	..	..	..	..	..	Mariner for Adams
27 Apr	Sheffield W	H	W	1-0	..	..	..	..	O'Leary	..	..	..	Mariner[1]	..	..	Allinson for Robson
4 May	Luton T	A	L	1-3	..	..	..	Talbot	..	..	..	..	..	Allinson	..[1]	Davis for Caton
6 May	Southampton	H	W	1-0	..	..	..	..	Adams	Davis	..	..[1]	..	..	..	
11 May	WBA	A	D	2-2	..	..	*opponents*	..	O'Leary	Adams	..	..	..	Davis	..	Allinson[1] for Nicholas
	FA Cup															
5 Jan	Hereford (3)	A	D	1-1	Lukic	Anderson	Caton	Talbot	O'Leary	Adams	Robson	Williams	Mariner	Woodcock[1]	Nicholas	Allinson for Nicholas
22 Jan	Hereford (3R)	H	W	7-2	..	..[1]	Sansom	..[2]	..	Caton	..	..	..[2]	..[1]	..[1]	
26 Jan	York C (4)	A	L	0-1	..	..	..	..	..	..	..	..	..	..	..	Allinson for Nicholas
	Milk Cup															
25 Sep	Bristol R (2)	H	W	4-0	Jennings	Anderson[1]	Sansom	Talbot	O'Leary	Caton	Robson	Rix	Mariner	Woodcock[1]	Nicholas[2]	
9 Oct	Bristol R (2)	A	D	1-1	..	..	..	..	..	..[1]	..	..	..	..	..	
31 Oct	Oxford U (3)	A	L	2-3	..	..	..	..	..	..	..	..[1]	Allinson[1]	..	..	Adams for Robson

Appearances (Goals)

Adams T 16 · Allinson I 27 (10) · Anderson V 41 (3) · Caton T 35 (1) · Davis P 24 (1) · Hill C 2 · Jennings P 15 · Lukic J 27 · Mariner P 36 (7) · Meade R 8 (3) · Nicholas C 38 (9) · O'Leary D 36 · Rix G 18 (2) · Robson S 40 (2) · Sansom K 39 (1) · Talbot B 41 (10) · Williams S 15 (1) · Woodcock T 27 (10) · Own goals (1) · Total: 18 players (61)

Position in League Table

	P	W	L	D	F:A	Pts	
Everton	42	28	8	6	88:43	90	1st
Arsenal	42	19	14	9	61:49	66	7th

SEASON 1985-1986 FOOTBALL LEAGUE (DIVISION 1)

1985-1986

17 Aug	Liverpool	A	L	0-2	Lukic	Anderson	Sansom	Williams	O'Leary	Caton	Robson	Allinson	Nicholas	Woodcock	Rix	
20 Aug	Southampton	H	W	3-2	..	..	..	..	..	..[1]	..[1]	..	..	..[1]	..	
24 Aug	Manchester U	H	L	1-2	..	..	..	..	..	..	..	..[1]	..	..	..	Davis for Williams
27 Aug	Luton T	A	D	2-2	..	..	..	Davis	..	..	..	*opponent*	..	..[1]	..	Mariner for O'Leary
31 Aug	Leicester C	H	W	1-0	..	..	..	..	Mariner	..	..	..	..	..[1]	..	
3 Sep	QPR	A	W	1-0	..	..	..	..	O'Leary	..	..	..[1]	..	..	..	
7 Sep	Coventry C	A	W	2-0	..	..	..	..	..	..	..	..	..[1]	..[1]	..	
14 Sep	Sheffield W	H	W	1-0	..	..	..	..	..	..	..	..[1]	..	..	..	
21 Sep	Chelsea	A	L	1-2	..	..	..	..	..	..	..	..	..[1]	..	..	
28 Sep	Newcastle U	H	D	0-0	..	..	..	..	..	..	Rocastle	..		..	..	Whyte for Allinson
5 Oct	Aston Villa	H	W	3-2	..	..[1]	..	..	..	..	Whyte[1]	..	..	..[1]	..	
12 Oct	West Ham U	A	D	0-0	..	..	..	..	..	..	..	..	..	..	..	Rocastle for O'Leary
19 Oct	Ipswich T	H	W	1-0	..	..	..	..[1]	..	..	..	..	..	..	..	Rocastle for Nicholas
26 Oct	Nottingham F	A	L	2-3	..	..	..	..[1]	..	..	..	..	..	..	..[1]	Rocastle for Allinson
2 Nov	Manchester C	H	W	1-0	..	..	..	..[1]	..	..	Williams	..	..	..	..	Whyte for Allinson
9 Nov	Everton	A	L	1-6	..	..	..	..	..	..	..	..	..[1]	..	..	
16 Nov	Oxford U	H	W	2-1	..	..	..	..[1]	..	..	..	Robson	..	..[1]	Hayes	Allinson for Woodcock
23 Nov	WBA	A	D	0-0	..	..	..	..	Keown	..	..	..	..	..	..	Whyte for Hayes
30 Nov	Birmingham C	H	D	0-0	..	..	..	..	O'Leary	..	..	..	..	..	..	Allinson for Williams
7 Dec	Southampton	A	L	0-3	..	..	..	..	..	..	..	..	..	..	..	Allinson for Hayes
14 Dec	Liverpool	H	W	2-0	..	..	..	..	..	Keown	Allinson	..	..[1]	Quinn[1]	Rix	
21 Dec	Manchester U	A	W	1-0	..	Caesar	..	..	..	..	..	..	..[1]	..	..	
28 Dec	QPR	H	W	3-1	..	..	..	..	..	..	..	..	..[1]	..	..[1]	Woodcock[1] for Robson
1 Jan	Tottenham H	H	D	0-0	..	Anderson	..	..	..	..	..	Rocastle	..	..	..	Woodcock for Quinn
18 Jan	Leicester C	A	D	2-2	..	..	..	..	..	..	..	Robson[1]	..[1]	..	..	
1 Feb	Luton T	H	W	2-1	..	..	..	Rocastle	..	..	..[1]	Mariner	..	..	..[1]	

1985-86 *continued*

SEASON 1985-1986 FOOTBALL LEAGUE (DIVISION 1)

1 Mar	Newcastle U	A	L 0-1	Lukic	Anderson	Sansom	Williams	O'Leary	Keown	Allinson	Rocastle	Nicholas	Woodcock	Rix	Mariner for Woodcock
8 Mar	Aston Villa	A	W 4-1	Wilmot	..	..	..	*opponents*	..	Hayes[1]	..[1]	..[1]	..	..	
11 Mar	Ipswich T	A	W 2-1	..	..	..	..	..	..	..	..	..[1]	..[1]	..	Mariner for O'Leary
15 Mar	West Ham U	H	W 1-0	Lukic	..	..	..	..	..	..	..	..	..[1]	..	
22 Mar	Coventry C	H	W 3-0	..	Adams	..	..	*opponents*	..	..[1]	..	..	..[1]	..	
29 Mar	Tottenham H	A	L 0-1	..	Anderson	..	..	..	..	..	..	..	Quinn	..	Mariner for Quinn
31 Mar	Watford	H	L 0-2	..	..	..	..	..	..	..	..	..	Mariner	..	Robson for Hayes
1 Apr	Watford	A	L 0-3	..	..	..	..	Adams	..	Robson	..	..	Woodcock	..	Allinson for Williams
5 Apr	Manchester C	A	W 1-0	..	..	..	Allinson	..	..	..[1]	..	..	Quinn	..	Mariner for Quinn
8 Apr	Nottingham F	H	D 1-1	..	..	..	..[1]	..	..	..	..	..	..	..	Mariner for Rocastle
12 Apr	Everton	H	L 0-1	..	..	..	..	..	..	..	Davis	..	..	..	
16 Apr	Sheffield W	A	L 0-2	..	..	..	..	..	..	..	..	..	Woodcock	..	
26 Apr	WBA	H	D 2-2	..	..	..	..[1]	O'Leary	Adams	..[1]	..	Hayes	..	..	Quinn for Woodcock
29 Apr	Chelsea	H	W 2-0	..	..[1]	..	Keown	..	..	..	..	Nicholas[1]	..	..	Quinn for Rix
3 May	Birmingham C	A	W 1-0	..	..	..	..	..	..	..	..	..	..[1]	..	
5 May	Oxford U	A	L 0-3	..	..	..	..	..	..	..	..	..	..	..	Allinson for O'Leary

FA Cup

4 Jan	Grimsby T (3)	A	W 4-3	Lukic	Anderson	Sansom	Davis	O'Leary	Keown	Allinson	Rocastle	Nicholas[3]	Quinn	Rix[1]	
25 Jan	Rotherham U (4)	H	W 5-1	..	..	..	Rocastle	..	..	..[2]	Robson[1]	..[1]	..	..[1]	Woodcock for Robson
15 Feb	Luton T (5)	A	D 2-2	..	..	..	Williams	..	..	..[1]	Rocastle[1]	..	Woodcock	..	Mariner for Nicholas
3 Mar	Luton T Extra Time (5R)	H	D 0-0	..	..	..	..	..	..	..	..	..	Mariner	..	
5 Mar	Luton T (5 2nd Rep)	A	L 0-3	..	..	..	..	..	..	..	..	..	..	Hayes	Quinn for Hayes

Milk Cup

25 Sep	Hereford U (2)	A	D 0-0	Lukic	Anderson	Sansom	Davis	O'Leary	Caton	Robson	Allinson	Nicholas	Woodcock	Rix	Mariner for Robson
8 Oct	Hereford U (2 extra time)	H	W 2-1	..	..[1]	..	..	..	..	Whyte	..	..[1]	..	..	Rocastle for Davis
30 Oct	Manchester C (3)	A	W 2-1	..	..	..	..	..	..	Williams	..[1]	..[1]	..	..	
19 Nov	Southampton (4)	H	D 0-0	..	..	..	..	..	..	..	Robson	..	..	Hayes	Allinson for Hayes
26 Nov	Southampton (4R)	A	W 3-1	..	..	..	..	..	..	..	..[1]	..[1]	..	..[1]	
22 Jan	Aston Villa (5)	A	D 1-1	Wilmot	..	..	Rocastle	..	..	Allinson	..	..[1]	Quinn	Rix	Woodcock for Robson
4 Feb	Aston Villa (5R)	H	L 1-2	Lukic	..	..	..	..	..	..	Mariner[1]	..	..	..	Woodcock for Allinson

Appearances (Goals)

Adams T 10 · Allinson I 33 (6) · Anderson V 39 (2) · Ceasar G 2 · Caton T 20 (1) · Davis P 29 (4) · Hayes M 11 (2) · Keown M 22 · Lukic J 40 · Mariner P 9 · Nicholas C 41 (10) · O'Leary D 35 · Quinn N 12 (1) · Rix G 38 (3) · Robson S 27 (4) · Rocastle D 16 (1) · Sansom K 42 · Whyte C 7 (1) · Williams S 17 · Wilmot R 2 · Woodcock T 33 (11) · Own Goals (3) · Total: 21 players (49)

Position in League Table

	P	W	L	D	F:A	Pts
Liverpool	42	26	6	10	89:37	88 1st
Arsenal	42	20	13	9	49:47	69 7th

1986-1987

SEASON 1986-1987 FOOTBALL LEAGUE (DIVISION 1)

23 Aug	Manchester U	H	W 1-0	Lukic	Anderson	Sansom	Robson	O'Leary	Adams	Rocastle	Davis	Quinn	Nicholas[1]	Rix	Hayes for Rocastle
26 Aug	Coventry C	A	L 1-2	..	..[1]	..	..	..	..	..	..	..	..	..	Hayes for Rix
30 Aug	Liverpool	A	L 1-2	..	..	..	..	..	..[1]	..	..	..	..	..	Williams for Robson
2 Sep	Sheffield W	H	W 2-0	..	..	..	..	..	..[1]	..	..	..[1]	..	..	Hayes for Rocastle
6 Sep	Tottenham H	H	D 0-0	..	..	..	..	..	..	..	..	..	..	..	Hayes for Rocastle
13 Sep	Luton T	A	D 0-0	..	..	..	Williams	..	..	..	..	..	..	..	Groves for Rix
20 Sep	Oxford U	H	D 0-0	..	..	..	..	..	..	..	..	..	..	..	Groves for Rix
27 Sep	Nottingham F	A	L 0-1	..	..	..	..	..	..	..	..	..	..	Groves	Allinson for Nicholas
4 Oct	Everton	A	W 1-0	..	..	..	..[1]	..	..	..	..	..	Allinson	..	Caesar for Groves
11 Oct	Watford	H	W 3-1	..	..	..	..	..	..	..	..	..[1]	Groves[1]	Hayes[1]	Allinson for O'Leary
18 Oct	Newcastle U	A	W 2-1	..	..[1]	..	..[1]	..	..	..	..		..	..	Caesar for Quinn
25 Oct	Chelsea	H	W 3-1	..	..	..	..	..	..	..[1]	..		..	..[2]	Allinson for Quinn
1 Nov	Charlton A	A	W 2-0	..	..	..	..	..	..[1]	..	..		..	..[1]	Caesar for Groves
8 Nov	West Ham U	H	D 0-0	..	..	..	..	..	..	..	..	..	..	..	
15 Nov	Southampton	A	W 4-0	..	..[1]	..	..	..	..	..	..	..[1]	..[1]	..[1]	Caesar for Rocastle
22 Nov	Manchester C	H	W 3-0	..	..[1]	..	..	..	..[1]	..	..	..[1]	Allinson	..	Merson for Hayes
29 Nov	Aston Villa	A	W 4-0	..	..	*opponents*	..	..	..	..[1]	..	..	Groves[1]	..[1]	
6 Dec	QPR	H	W 3-1	..	..	..	..	..	..	..	..	..[1]	..	..[2]	Nicholas for Groves
13 Dec	Norwich C	A	D 1-1	..	..	..	..	..	..	..	..	..	..	..[1]	Caesar for Groves
20 Dec	Luton T	H	W 3-0	..	..	..	..	..	..[1]	..	..	..[1]	..	..[1]	Nicholas for Groves
26 Dec	Leicester C	A	D 1-1	..	..	..	..	..	..	..	..	..	..	..[1]	Caesar for Groves
27 Dec	Southampton	H	W 1-0	..	..	..	..	..	..	..	..	..[1]	Nicholas	..	Allinson for Hayes
1 Jan	Wimbledon	H	W 3-1	..	..	..	..	..	..	..	..	..	..[2]	..[1]	Allinson for Rocastle
4 Jan	Tottenham H	A	W 2-1	..	..	..	..	..	..[1]	..	..[1]	..	..	..	Rix for Quinn
18 Jan	Coventry C	H	D 0-0	..	..	..	..	..	..	..	..	..	..	..	Rix for Hayes
24 Jan	Manchester U	A	L 0-2	..	..	..	..	..	..	..	..	..	..	..	Caesar for Nicholas
14 Feb	Sheffield W	A	D 1-1	..	Thomas	..	..	..	..	Groves	..	..[1]	Rix	..	Allinson for Williams
25 Feb	Oxford U	A	D 0-0	..	Anderson	..	Thomas	..	..	Rocastle	..	..	Groves	..	Nicholas for Groves
7 Mar	Chelsea	A	L 0-1	..	..	..	..	..	..	..	Caesar	..	Allinson	..	Merson for Hayes
10 Mar	Liverpool	H	L 0-1	..	..	..	..	..	..	..	Groves	..	..	..	Caesar for Hayes
17 Mar	Nottingham F	H	D 0-0	..	..	..	Williams	Caesar	..	..	..	..	Nicholas	Thomas	Allinson for Groves
21 Mar	Watford	A	L 0-2	..	Caesar	..	Thomas	O'Leary	..	Allinson	Davis	..	..	Hayes	Rix for Quinn
28 Mar	Everton	H	L 0-1	..	Anderson	..	Williams	..	..	Rocastle	..	..	..	..	Groves for Hayes
8 Apr	West Ham U	A	L 1-3	Wilmot	..	Thomas	..	..	..	..	..	Groves	..	..[1]	Rix for Hayes
11 Apr	Charlton A	H	W 2-1	Lukic	..	Sansom	..	..	..	..	..[1]	Quinn	..	..[1]	Groves for Quinn
14 Apr	Newcastle U	H	L 0-1	..	..	Thomas	..	..	..	..	..	Groves	..	..	Rix for Rocastle
18 Apr	Wimbledon	A	W 2-1	..	..	Caesar	..	..	..	..	..[1]	Merson[1]	..	Rix	Allinson for Rocastle
20 Apr	Leicester C	H	W 4-1	Wilmot	..	Sansom	..	..	..	Hayes[2]	..[1]	..	..[1]	..	Caesar for O'Leary
25 Apr	Manchester C	A	L 0-3	..	..	Thomas	..	Caesar	..	..	..	..	..	..	Allinson for Merson
2 May	Aston Villa	H	W 2-1	..	..	..	..	O'Leary	..	Rocastle	..	Quinn	..	Hayes[2]	Groves for Quinn
4 May	QPR	A	W 4-1	..	..	..	..	Caesar	..	Rix[2]	..	Merson[1]	..	..[1]	
9 May	Norwich C	H	L 1-2	..	..	..	..	O'Leary	..	..	..	..[1]	..	..	Groves for Anderson

FA Cup

10 Jan	Reading (3)	A	W 3-1	Lukic	Anderson	Sansom	Williams	O'Leary	Adams	Rocastle	Davis	Quinn	Nicholas[2]	Hayes[1]	
31 Jan	Plymouth A (4)	H	W 6-1	..	..[2]	..	..	..	..	..[1]	..[1]	..[1]	..[1]	..	Groves for Hayes/Caesar for Groves
21 Feb	Barnsley (5)	H	W 2-0	..	..	..	Allinson	..	..	..	..	..	Groves	..[1]	Nicholas[1] for Quinn/Thomas for Hayes
14 Mar	Watford (QF)	H	L 1-3	..	..	..	Williams	..	..	..	Groves	..	Allinson[1]	..	Nicholas for Allinson/Thomas for Hayes

Football League (Littlewoods) Cup

23 Sep	Huddersfield T (2)	H	W 2-0	Lukic	Anderson	Sansom	Williams	O'Leary	Adams	Rocastle	Davis[1]	Quinn[1]	Nicholas	Rix	Groves for Quinn
7 Oct	Huddersfield T (2)	A	D 1-1	..	..	..	..	..	..	..	..	..	Allinson	Groves	Hayes[1] for Allinson
28 Oct	Manchester C (3)	H	W 3-1	..	..	..	..	..	..	..[1]	..[1]	..	Groves	Hayes[1]	Allinson for Quinn
18 Nov	Charlton A (4)	H	W 2-0	..	..	..	*opponents*	..	..	..	..	..[1]	..	..	Allinson for Groves
21 Jan	Nottingham F (QF)	H	W 2-0	..	..	..	..	..	..	..	..	..	Nicholas[1]	..[1]	Rix for Quinn
8 Feb	Tottenham H (SF1)	H	L 0-1	..	Caesar	..	..	..	..	Groves	..	..	..	..	Thomas for Caesar/Rix for Nicholas
1 Mar	Tottenham H (SF2)	A	W 2-1	..	Anderson[1]	..	Thomas	..	..	Rocastle	..	..[1]	..	..	Allinson for Nicholas
4 Mar	Tottenham H (SFR)	A	W 2-1	..	..	..	..	..	..	..[1]	..	..	..	..	Allinson[1] for Thomas
5 Apr	Liverpool (F) (at Wembley)		W 2-1	..	..	..	Williams	..	..	..	..	..	..[2]	..	Groves for Quinn/Thomas for Hayes

Appearances (Goals)

Adams T 42 (6) · Allinson I 14 · Anderson V 40 (4) · Caesar G 15 · Davis P 39 (4) · Groves P 25 (3) · Hayes M 35 (19) · Lukic J 36 · Merson P 7 (3) · Nicholas C 28 (4) · O'Leary D 39 · Quinn N 35 (8) · Rix G 18 (2) · Robson S 5 · Rocastle D 36 (2) · Sansom K 35 · Thomas M 11 · Williams S 34 (2) · Wilmot R 6 · Own Goals 1 · Total: 19 players (58 goals)

Position in League Table

	P	W	L	D	F:A	Pts
Everton	42	26	8	8	76:31	86 1st
Arsenal	42	20	12	10	58:35	70 4th

NOTE Tables for Seasons 1987-88 and 1988-89 will be found on pages 269 and 270

SEASON 1987-88 FOOTBALL LEAGUE (DIVISION 1)

Date	Opp	Vn	Res	Score	Lukic	Thomas	Sansom	Williams	O'Leary	Adams	Rocastle	Davis[1]	Smith	Nicholas	Hayes	Substitutes
15 Aug	Liverpool	H	L	1-2	Lukic	Thomas	Sansom	Williams	O'Leary	Adams	Rocastle	Davis[1]	Smith	Nicholas	Hayes	Groves for Rocastle
19 Aug	Manchester U	A	D	0-0	..	..	..	..	..	..	..	..	..	..	..	Groves for Nicholas
22 Aug	QPR	A	L	0-2	..	..	..	..	..	..	..	..	..	..	..	Rix for Rocastle
29 Aug	Portsmouth	H	W	6-0	..	..	..	..	..	..[1]	..[1]	..[1]	..[3]	Groves	Rix	Merson for Groves/ Richardson for Rix
31 Aug	Luton	A	D	1-1	..	..	..	..	..	..	..	..[1]	..	..	..	—
12 Sep	Nottingham F	A	W	1-0	..	..	..	..	..	..	..	..	..[1]	..	..	
19 Sep	Wimbledon	H	W	3-0	..	..[1]	..	..	..	..	..[1]	..	..[1]	..	..	Hayes for Rocastle / Merson and Richardson for Groves and Williams
26 Sep	West Ham	H	W	1-0	..	..	..	..[1]	..	..	..	..	..	..	..	Hayes for Rocastle
3 Oct	Charlton	A	W	3-0	..	..[1]	..	..	..	..[1]	..	..	..	..[1]	..	Hayes for Rocastle
10 Oct	Oxford	H	W	2-0	..	..	..	..[1]	..	..	..	..[1]	..	..	Richardson	Hayes and Caesar for Rocastle and Smith
18 Oct	Tottenham	A	W	2-1	..	..[1]	..	..	..	..	..	..	..[1]	..	..	Hayes for Groves
24 Oct	Derby C	H	W	2-1	..	..[1]	..	..	..	..	..	..	..[1]	..	..[1]	Merson for Groves
31 Oct	Newcastle	A	W	1-0	..	..	..	..	..	..	..	..	..[1]	..	..	Caesar and Hayes for Williams and Adams
3 Nov	Chelsea	H	W	3-1	..	..[1]	..	.. o.g.	..	..	..	..	..	..	..[2]	—
14 Nov	Norwich	A	W	4-2	..	..[1]	..	..	..	..[2]	..	..	..	..[1]	..	Caesar for Adams
21 Nov	Southampton	H	L	0-1	..	..	..	..	..	..	..	..	..	..	..	Quinn for Groves, Winterburn for Quinn
28 Nov	Watford	A	L	0-2	..	..	..	..	..	..	..	..	..	..	..	Hayes for Richardson
5 Dec	Sheffield W	H	W	3-1	..	..	..	..	..	..	..	..	..	..[1]	..[1]	Merson[1] for Davis
13 Dec	Coventry	A	D	0-0	..	..	..	..	..	..	..	Hayes	..	..	..	Merson for Hayes
19 Dec	Everton	H	D	1-1	..	..	..	..	..	..	..[1]	Davis	..	..	..	Merson for Richardson
26 Dec	Nottingham F	H	L	0-2	..	..	..	..	..	..	..	Merson	Quinn	..	..	Smith and Caesar for Merson and O'Leary
28 Dec	Wimbledon	A	L	1-3	..	..	..	..	Caesar	..	..	Hayes	..[1]	..	..	Smith for Hayes
1 Jan	Portsmouth	A	D	1-1	..	..	Winterburn	..	..	..	..	..	..	..	..	Smith[1] and Merson for Quinn and Groves
2 Jan	QPR	H	D	0-0	..	Winterburn	Sansom	..	..	..	..	..	Smith	Merson	..	Groves for Merson
16 Jan	Liverpool	A	L	0-2	..	..	..	..	..	..	..	..	..	Quinn	..	Thomas and Groves for Caesar and Rocastle
24 Jan	Manchester U	H	L	1-2	..	Thomas	Winterburn	..	O'Leary	..	..	Rix	..	..[1]	..	Groves for Rix
13 Feb	Luton	H	W	2-1	..	Dixon	..	Thomas[1]	..	..	..[1]	Hayes	..	..	..	Caesar for Adams
27 Feb	Charlton	H	W	4-0	..	Winterburn	Sansom	..[1]	Caesar	..	..	..	..[1]	Merson[2]	..	Davis and Quinn for Merson and Richardson
6 Mar	Tottenham	H	W	2-1	..	..	..	..	..	..	..	..	..[1]	Groves[1]	..	—
19 Mar	Newcastle	H	D	1-1	..	Dixon	Winterburn	..	..	..	..	Davies	..	..[1]	Hayes	Quinn for Smith
26 Mar	Derby	A	D	0-0	..	..	..	..	..	..	..	..	..	..	..	Richards and Quinn for Rocastle and Smith
30 Mar	Oxford	A	D	0-0	..	Winterburn	Sansom	..	..	..	..	..	..	..	Marwood	Merson and Quinn for Rocastle and Marwood
2 Apr	Chelsea	A	D	1-1	..	Dixon	Winterburn	Williams	..	..	.. o.g.	..	Quinn	..[1]	Hayes	—
4 Apr	Norwich	H	W	2-0	..	Winterburn	Sansom	..	..	..	..	Smith[1]	..[1]	..	..	—
9 Apr	Southampton	A	L	2-4	..	..	..	..	Thomas	..	..	..[1]	..	.. o.g.	..	Merson for Groves
12 Apr	West Ham	A	W	1-0	..	..	..	Thomas[1]	..	Adams	..	..	..	Merson	Richardson	Rix for Richardson
15 Apr	Watford	H	L	0-1	..	..	..	..	..	..	..	..	..	..	..	Hayes for Richardson
30 Apr	Sheffield W	A	D	3-3	..	..	..	..	..	..	..	..[1]	..	..[2]	Marwood	Richardson and Hayes for Davis and Winterburn
2 May	Coventry	H	D	1-1	..	Dixon	..	..	..	..	..	..	..	..	..[1]	Hayes and Groves for Merson and Richardson
7 May	Everton	A	W	2-1	..	..	..	..[1]	..	..	..	..	..	Hayes[1]	..	Rix and Campbell for Caesar and Hayes

FA Cup

Date	Opp	Vn	Res	Score	Lukic	Winterburn	Sansom	Williams	O'Leary	Adams	Rocastle[1]	Hayes[1]	Smith	Merson	Richardson	Substitutes
9 Jan	Millwall (3)	H	W	2-0	Lukic	Winterburn	Sansom	Williams	O'Leary	Adams	Rocastle[1]	Hayes[1]	Smith	Merson	Richardson	Groves for Merson
30 Jan	Brighton (4)	A	W	2-1	..	..	..	..	..	..	Rix	Groves[1]	Quinn	..[1]		Hayes for Rix
20 Feb	Manchester U (5)	H	W	2-1	..	..	..	Thomas	..	.. o.g.	Hayes	Smith[1]	Groves			Rix for O'Leary
12 Mar	Nottingham F (6)	H	L	1-2	..	..	..	..	..	..[1]	..	..	..			Davis and Quinn for O'Leary and Hayes

Football League (Littlewoods) Cup

Date	Opp	Vn	Res	Score	Lukic	Thomas	Sansom	Williams[1]	O'Leary	Adams	Rocastle	Davis	Smith[1]	Groves[1]	Rix	Substitutes
23 Sep	Doncaster (2)	A	W	3-0	Lukic	Thomas	Sansom	Williams[1]	O'Leary	Adams	Rocastle	Davis	Smith[1]	Groves[1]	Rix	Richardson and Quinn for Groves and Rix
6 Oct	Doncaster (2)	H	W	1-0	..	..[1]	..	..	Caesar	..	..	..	..	..	Hayes	—
27 Oct	Bournemouth (3)	H	W	3-0	..	..[1]	..	..	O'Leary	..	..	..	..[1]	..	Richardson[1]	Merson for Groves
17 Nov	Stoke C (4)	H	W	3-0	..	..	..	..[1]	..	..	..[1]	..	..	..	..[1]	Hayes for Groves
20 Jan	Sheffield W (5)	A	W	1-0	..	Winterburn[1]	..	..	..	..	..	Rix	..	Quinn	..	Groves for Quinn
7 Feb	Everton (SF)	A	W	1-0	..	..	..	Thomas	..	..	..	Hayes	..	Groves[1]	..	Caesar and Quinn for Rocastle and Smith
24 Feb	Everton (SF)	H	W	3-1	..	..	..	..[1]	..	..	..[1]	..	..[1]	..	..	Davis for O'Leary
24 Apr	Luton (F) (at Wembley)		L	2-3	..	..	..	..	Caesar	..	..	Davis	..[1]	..	..	Hayes[1] for Groves

---

Appearances League only (Goals)

Lukic 40 · Rocastle 40 (7) · Adams 39 (2) · Smith 39 (11) · Thomas 37 (9) · Groves 34 (6) · Sansom 34 (1) · Richardson 29 (4) · Williams 29 (1) · Davis 29 (5) · Hayes 27 (1) · O'Leary 23 · Caesar 22 · Winterburn 17 · Merson 15 (5) · Quinn 11 (2) · Rix 10 · Dixon 6 · Marwood 4 (1) · Nicholas 3 · Campbell 1 · Own goals 3 · Total: 21 players (58)

Position in League Table

	P	W	L	D	F:A	Pts	
Liverpool	40	26	2	12	87:24	90	1st
Arsenal	40	18	10	12	58:39	66	6th

The Arsenal Record for 1988-89

Date	Opponent		Result	Lukic	Dixon	Winterburn	Thomas	Bould	Adams	Rocastle	Davis	Smith[3]	Merson[1]	Marwood[1]	Substitutes
27 Aug	Wimbledon	A	W 5-1	Lukic	Dixon	Winterburn	Thomas	Bould	Adams	Rocastle	Davis	Smith[3]	Merson[1]	Marwood[1]	–
3 Sep	Aston Villa	H	L 2-3	..	..	..	..	O'Leary	..	..	..	..[1]	..	..[1]	Groves for Rocastle
10 Sep	Tottenham H	A	W 3-2	..	..	..[1]	..	..	..	..	..	..[1]	..	..[1]	Groves/Richardson for Rocastle/Marwood
17 Sep	Southampton	H	D 2-2	..	..	..	..	..	..	..	..	..[1]	..	..[1]	Hayes/Richardson for Davis/Merson
24 Sep	Sheffield W	A	L 1-2	..	..	..	..	..	..	..	..	..[1]	..	..	Groves for Merson
1 Oct	West Ham U	A	W 4-1	..	..	..	..[1]	Bould	..	..[1]	..	..[2]	Groves	..	Hayes for Groves
22 Oct	QPR	H	W 2-1	..	..	..	..	..	..[1]	..	Richardson	..[1]	Merson	..	Groves for Merson
25 Oct	Luton T	A	D 1-1	..	..	..	..[1]	..	..[1]	..	..	..[1]	..	..	–
29 Oct	Coventry C	H	W 2-0	..	..	..	..[1]	..	..[1]	..	..	..	..	..	Groves/Hayes for Rocastle/Merson
6 Nov	Nottingham F	A	W 4-1	..	..	..	..	..[1]	..[1]	..	..	..[1]	..	..[1]	Hayes for Merson
12 Nov	Newcastle U	A	W 1-0	..	..	..	..	..[1]	..	..	..	..	Hayes	.	Merson for Rocastle
19 Nov	Middlesbrough	H	W 3-0	..	..	..	..	..	..	..[1]	..	..	Merson[2]	..	Hayes for Marwood
26 Nov	Derby Co	A	L 1-2	..	..	..	..[1]	..	..	..	..	..	..	Hayes	Groves for Richardson
4 Dec	Liverpool	H	D 1-1	..	..	..	..	..	..	..	..	..[1]	..	Marwood	Hayes for Marwood
10 Dec	Norwich C	A	D 0-0	..	..	..	..[1]	..	..	..	..	..	..	..	Hayes for Marwood
17 Dec	Manchester U	H	W 2-1	..	..	..	..[1]	..	..	..	..	..	..[1]	..[2]	–
26 Dec	Charlton A	A	W 3-2	O'Leary	..	..	..	..	..	..	..	..[1]	..[1]	..	–
31 Dec	Aston Villa	A	W 3-0	..	..	..	..[1]	..	..	..[1]	..	..[1]	..[1]	..	Groves[1] for Merson
2 Jan	Tottenham H	H	W 2-0	..	..	..	..[1]	..	..	..	..	..[1]	..[1]	..	Davis/Groves for Richardson/Marwood
14 Jan	Everton	A	W 3-1	..	Dixon	..	Davis	O'Leary	Caesar	..	..[1]	..[1]	..[1]	..	Groves/Thomas for Merson/Marwood
21 Jan	Sheffield W	H	D 1-1	..	..	..	..	..	..	..	..	..	..[1]	..	Groves/Thomas for Caesar/Rocastle
4 Feb	West Ham U	H	W 2-1	..	..	..	Thomas	..	Adams	..	..	..[1]	..	Groves[1]	Bould/Hayes for O'Leary/Merson
11 Feb	Millwall	A	W 2-1	..	..	..	..	..	..	..	..	..[1]	..	Marwood[1]	Bould for O'Leary
18 Feb	QPR	A	D 0-0	..	..	..	..	..	..	..	..	..	..	..	Bould/Hayes for Dixon/Merson
21 Feb	Coventry C	A	L 0-1	..	Bould	..	..	..	..	..	..	..	..	..	Hayes for Marwood
25 Feb	Luton T	H	W 2-0	..	..	..	..	..	..	..	..	..[1]	Groves[1]	..	Merson for Rocastle
28 Feb	Millwall	H	D 0-0	..	..	..	..	..	..	..	..	..	..	..	Merson/Dixon for Rocastle/Richardson
11 Mar	Nottingham F	H	L 1-3	..	..	..	..	..	..	..	..	..[1]	..	..	Merson/Dixon for Bould/Groves
21 Mar	Charlton A	H	D 2-2	..	Dixon	..	Davis[1]	..	..	..[1]	..	..	Merson	..	Groves/Thomas for Richardson/Merson
25 Mar	Southampton	A	W 3-1	..	..	..	..	..	..	..[1]	..	..	Groves[1]	..	Merson[1] for Groves
2 Apr	Manchester U	A	D 1-1	..	..	..	..	..	..[1]	..	..	..	Bould	..	Thomas/Merson for Davis/Marwood
8 Apr	Everton	H	W 2-0	..	..[1]	..	Thomas	..	..	..	..	Quinn[1]	..	..	Merson for Marwood
15 Apr	Newcastle U	H	W 1-0	..	..	..	..	..	..	..	..	..	..	..[1]	Merson/Groves for O'Leary/Rocastle
1 May	Norwich C	H	W 5-0	..	..	..[1]	..[1]	..	..	..[1]	..	Smith[2]	..	Merson	Quinn/Hayes for Bould/Merson
6 May	Middlesbrough	A	W 1-0	..	..	..	..	..	..	..	..	..[1]	..	..	Hayes[1] for Merson
13 May	Derby Co	A	L 1-2	..	..	..	..	..	..	..	..	..[1]	..	..	Hayes/Groves for Bould/Merson
17 May	Wimbledon	H	D 2-2	..	..	..[1]	..	..	..	..	..	..	..[1]	..	Groves/Hayes for Bould/Merson
26 May	Liverpool	A	W 2-0	..	..	..	..[1]	..	..	..	..	..[1]	..	..	Groves/Hayes for Bould/Merson

FA Cup

Date	Opponent		Result	Lukic	Dixon	Winterburn	Thomas	Bould	Adams	Rocastle	Richardson	Smith	Merson[2]	Marwood	Substitutes
8 Jan	West Ham U (3)	A	D 2-2	Lukic	O'Leary	Winterburn	Thomas	Bould	Adams	Rocastle	Richardson	Smith	Merson[2]	Marwood	Davis and Groves for Bould and Marwood
11 Jan	West Ham U (3R)	H	L 0-1	..	Dixon	..	..	O'Leary	..	..	..	..	..	..	Davis and Groves for Rocastle and Marwood

Football League (Littlewoods) Cup

Date	Opponent		Result	Lukic	Dixon	Winterburn	Thomas	Bould	Adams	Rocastle	Davis	Smith	Groves	Marwood[1]	Substitutes
28 Sep	Hull C (2)	A	W 2-1	Lukic	Dixon	Winterburn[1]	Thomas	Bould	Adams	Rocastle	Davis	Smith	Groves	Marwood[1]	Hayes and Richardson for Groves and Rocastle
12 Oct	Hull C (2)	H	W 3-0	..	..	..	..	..	..	..	..	..[2]	Merson[1]	..	Hayes and Richardson for Davis and Marwood
2 Nov	Liverpool (3)	A	D 1-1	..	..	..	..	..	..	..[1]	Richardson	..	..	..	Groves for Merson
9 Nov	Liverpool (3R)	H	D 0-0	..	..	..	..	..	..	..	..	..	..	..	Hayes for Merson
23 Nov	Liverpool (3R2)	A	L 1-2	..	..	..	..	..	..	..	..	..	..[1]	..	Hayes for Marwood

---

Appearances League Only (Goals)

Lukic 38 · Rocastle 38 (6) · Winterburn 38 (3) · Thomas 37 (7) · Merson 37 (9) · Adams 36 (4) · Smith 36 (24) · Richardson 34 (1) · Dixon 33 (1) · Marwood 31 (9) · Bould 30 (2) · O'Leary 26 · Groves 21 (4) · Hayes 17 (1) · Davis 12 (1) · Quinn 3 (1) · Caesar 2 · Total 17 players (73)

Position in League Table

	P	W	L	D	F:A	Pts	
Arsenal	38	22	6	10	73:36	76	1st

SEASON 1989–90 FOOTBALL LEAGUE (DIVISION 1)

Date	Opponent			Score	Lukic	Dixon	Winterburn	Thomas	O'Leary	Adams	Rocastle	Richardson	Smith	Merson	Marwood	Substitutions
19 Aug	Manchester U	A	L	1–4	Lukic	Dixon	Winterburn	Thomas	O'Leary	Adams	Rocastle[1]	Richardson	Smith	Merson	Marwood	Caesar/Groves for Adams/Merson
22 Aug	Coventry C	H	W	2–0	..	..	..	..[1]	..	..	..	..	..	..	..[1]	Groves for Rocastle
26 Aug	Wimbledon	H	D	0–0	..	..	..	..	..	..	..	..	..	..	..	Groves for Merson
09 Sep	Sheffield W	H	W	5–0	..	..	..	..[1]	..	..[1]	..	..	..[1]	..[1]	..[1]	
16 Sep	Nottingham F	A	W	2–1	..	..	..	..	..	..	..	..	..[1]	..[1]	..	Groves for Merson
23 Sep	Charlton A	H	W	1–0	..	..	..	..	..	..	..	..	..	..	..[1p]	Groves for Rocastle
30 Sep	Chelsea	A	D	0–0	..	..	..	..	..	..	..	..	..	Groves	Hayes	Merson for Rocastle
14 Oct	Manchester C	H	W	4–0	..	..	..	..[1]	..	..	..	..	..[2]	..	Marwood	Jonsson/Merson[1] for Richardson/Marwood
18 Oct	Tottenham H	A	L	1–2	..	..	..	..[1]	..	..	..	..	..	..	Hayes	Jonsson/Merson for Richardson/Smith
21 Oct	Everton	A	L	0–3	..	..	..	..	..	..	..	Quinn	Merson	..	..	Smith for Hayes
28 Oct	Derby Co	H	D	1–1	..	..	..	..	..	..	..	Smith[1]	Quinn	Merson	..	Jonsson/Campbell for Winterburn/Quinn
4 Nov	Norwich C	H	W	4–3	..	..[2,1p]	..	..[1]	..	..	..	..	..	..[1]	..	Groves for Merson
11 Nov	Millwall	A	W	2–1	..	..	..	..[1]	..	..	..	..	..[1]	..	Marwood	Groves for Quinn
18 Nov	QPR	H	W	3–0	..	..[1p]	..	..	..	..	..	..[1]	..	..	..	Groves/Jonsson[1] for Rocastle/Marwood
26 Nov	Liverpool	A	L	1–2	..	..	..	..	..	..	..	..[1]	..	..	Groves	Hayes/Jonsson for Quinn/O'Leary
3 Dec	Manchester U	H	W	1–0	..	..	..	..	..	..	..	..	..	Groves[1]	Marwood	Merson for Marwood
9 Dec	Coventry C	A	W	1–0	..	..	..	..	..	..	..	..	..	..	..	Merson[1] for Marwood
16 Dec	Luton T	H	W	3–2	..	..	..	..	..	..	..	..[1]	..	Groves	..[1]	Merson[1]/Jonsson for Smith/Groves
26 Dec	Southampton	A	L	0–1	..	..	..	..	..	..	..	..	..	Merson	..	Davis/Groves for Marwood/Merson
30 Dec	Aston Villa	A	L	1–2	..	..	..	..	..	..[1]	Groves	..	..	Bould	Merson	Rocastle for Bould
1 Jan	Crystal Palace	H	W	4–1	..	..[1]	..	..	..	..[1]	..	..[2]	..	..	..	Rocastle/Davis for Smith/Winterburn
13 Jan	Wimbledon	A	L	0–1	..	..	Davis	..	..	..	..	..	..	..	..	Caesar/Rocastle for O'Leary/Smith
20 Jan	Tottenham H	H	W	1–0	..	Davis	Thomas	..	..[1]	..	Rocastle	..	..	..	Groves	
17 Feb	Sheffield W	A	L	0–1	..	Pates	Davis	..	..	..	..	..	..	..	Merson	Caesar/Campbell for Pates/Richardson
27 Feb	Charlton A	A	D	0–0	..	..	Winterburn	Thomas	Bould	..	..	..	..	Merson	Marwood	Campbell for Marwood
3 Mar	QPR	A	L	0–2	..	..	..	..	..	..	..	..	..	..	Groves	O'Leary/Campbell for Thomas/Smith
7 Mar	Nottingham F	H	W	3–0	..	..	..	..	..	..[1]	..	..	..	..	..[1]	Campbell[1]/O'Leary for Merson/Groves
10 Mar	Manchester C	A	D	1–1	..	..	..	..	..	..	..	..	..	Campbell	Marwood[1]	Hayes for Rocastle
17 Mar	Chelsea	H	L	0–1	..	..	..	..	..	..	..	..	..	..	Groves	Hayes/O'Leary for Rocastle/Campbell
24 Mar	Derby Co	A	W	3–1	..	..	..	..	..	..	Hayes[2]	..	..[1]	..	..	O'Leary/Ampadu for Bould/Campbell
31 Mar	Everton	H	W	1–0	..	..	..	..	..	..	..	..[1]	..	..	..	O'Leary/Ampadu for Richardson/Campbell
11 Apr	Aston Villa	H	L	0–1	..	..	..	..	..	..	..	O'Leary	..	..	..	Merson for Hayes
14 Apr	Crystal Palace	A	D	1–1	..	..	..	..	..	..	..[1]	..	..	..	..	Davis/Merson for Bould/Campbell
18 Apr	Liverpool	H	D	1–1	..	..	..	..	..	..	Davis	..	..	Merson[1]	..	Campbell/Pates for Groves/Bould
21 Apr	Luton T	A	L	0–2	..	..	..	..	..	..	..	..	..	..	Campbell	Hayes/Rocastle for O'Leary/Merson
28 Apr	Millwall	H	W	2–0	..	..	..	..	..	..	Rocastle	Davis[1]	..	..[1]	Marwood	Campbell/Richardson for Marwood/Thomas
2 May	Southampton	H	W	2–1	..	..[1p]	..	..	..	..	Richardson	..	..	..	..	Rocastle[1]/Groves for Richardson/Marwood
5 May	Norwich C	A	D	2–2	..	..	Hayes	..	..	..	Rocastle	..[2]	..	Campbell	Groves	O'Leary/Thomas for Bould/Davis

FA Cup

Date	Opponent			Score	Lukic	Dixon	Winterburn	Thomas	O'Leary	Adams	Rocastle	Richardson	Smith	Merson	Marwood	Substitutions
6 Jan	Stoke C (3)	A	W	1–0	Lukic	Dixon	Davis	Thomas	O'Leary	Adams	Quinn[1]	Richardson	Groves	Bould	Merson	Jonsson/Rocastle for Thomas/Merson
27 Jan	QPR (4)	H	D	0–0	..	..	Winterburn	Davis	..	Rocastle	..	Smith	..	..	Groves	Thomas/Merson for Davis/Bould
31 Jan	QPR (4R)	A	L	0–2	..	..	..	Thomas	..	..	..	..	..	..	..	Merson for Groves

Football League (Littlewoods) Cup

Date	Opponent			Score	Lukic	Dixon	Winterburn	Thomas	O'Leary	Adams	Rocastle	Richardson	Smith	Merson	Marwood	Substitutions
19 Sep	Plymouth (2)	H	W	2–0	Lukic	Dixon	Winterburn	Thomas	O'Leary	Adams	Rocastle	Richardson	Smith[1]	Bould	Groves	Merson for Groves
3 Oct	Plymouth (2)	A	W	6–1	..	Dixon *og opponents*	..	..[3]	..	..	..	..[1]	Groves[1]	Hayes	..	Caesar/Merson for Dixon/Groves
25 Oct	Liverpool (3)	H	W	1–0	..	..	..	..	..	..	..	Quinn	Merson	..	..	Smith[1] for Hayes
22 Nov	Oldham A (4)	A	L	1–3	..	..	..	..	..	..	..	Smith	Quinn[1]	Jonsson	..	Groves for Jonsson

FA Charity Shield

Date	Opponent			Score	Lukic	Dixon	Winterburn	Thomas	O'Leary	Adams	Rocastle	Richardson	Smith	Merson	Marwood	Substitutions
12 Aug	Liverpool (at Wembley)		L	0–1	Lukic	Dixon	Winterburn	Thomas	O'Leary	Adams	Rocastle	Richardson	Smith	Caesar	Merson	Marwood/Quinn for Caesar/Smith

Appearances (Goals)

Lukic 38 · Dixon 38(5) · Adams 38(5) · Smith 38(10) · Winterburn 36 · Thomas 36(5) · O'Leary 34(1) · Richardson 33 · Rocastle 33(2) · Groves 30(4) · Merson 29(7) · Bould 19 · Marwood 17(6) · Campbell 15(2) · Hayes 12(3) · Davis 11(1) · Quinn 6(2) · Jonsson 6(1) · Caesar 3 · Pates 2 · Ampadu 2

Position in League Table

	P	W	D	L	F:A	Pts	
Liverpool	38	23	10	5	78:37	79	1st
Arsenal	38	18	8	12	54:38	62	4th

SEASON 1990-91 FOOTBALL LEAGUE (DIVISION 1)

Date	Opponent			Score		Dixon	Winterburn	Thomas	Bould	Adams	Rocastle	Davis	Smith[1]	Merson[1]	Limpar	Substitutes
25 Aug	Wimbledon	A	W	3–0	Seaman	Dixon	Winterburn	Thomas	Bould	Adams	Rocastle	Davis	Smith[1]	Merson[1]	Limpar	Groves[1] for Limpar
29 Aug	Luton T	H	W	2–1	..	..	..	..[1]	..	..	..	..	..	..[1]	..	Groves for Limpar
1 Sep	Tottenham H	H	D	0–0	..	..	..	..	..	..	..	..	..	..	..	Groves for Merson
8 Sep	Everton	A	D	1–1	..	..[1p]	..	..	..	..	..[1]	..	..	..[1]	..[1]	Groves[1] for Smith
15 Sep	Chelsea	H	W	4–1	..	..[1p]	..	..	..	..	..	..	Groves	..[1]	..[1]	Campbell/Linighan for Groves/Bould
22 Sep	Nottingham F	A	W	2–0	..	..	..	..	..	..	..[1]	..	..	..	..[1]	Smith for Rocastle
29 Sep	Leeds U	A	D	2–2	..	..	..	Jonsson	..	..	..	..	Smith	..	..[2]	Hillier/Groves for Winterburn/Merson
6 Oct	Norwich C	H	W	2–0	..	..	..	..	..	..	..	..[2]	..	..	..	Hillier/Groves for Limpar/Merson
20 Oct	Manchester U	A	W	1–0	..	..	..	Thomas	..	..	..	..	..	..	..[1]	Groves for Rocastle
27 Oct	Sunderland	H	W	1–0	..	..[1p]	..	..	..	..	..	..	..	..	..[2]	Groves for Rocastle
3 Nov	Coventry C	A	W	2–0	..	..	..	..	..	..	Groves	..	..	..	..	Campbell/O'Leary for Smith/Groves
10 Nov	Crystal Palace	A	D	0–0	..	..	..	..	..	..	O'Leary	..	Campbell	..	..	Groves/Smith for Merson/Limpar
17 Nov	Southampton	H	W	4–0	..	..	..	..	..	..	Groves	..	Smith[2]	..[1]	..[1]	O'Leary/Campbell for Dixon/Groves
24 Nov	QPR	A	W	3–1	..	..	..	..	..	..	..	..	..[1]	..[1]	..	Campbell[1]/O'Leary for Groves/Adams
2 Dec	Liverpool	H	W	3–0	..	..[1p]	..	..	..	..	O'Leary	..	..[1]	..[1]	..	
8 Dec	Luton T	A	D	1–1	..	..	..	..	..	..	..	..	..[1]	..[1]	..	Groves for Limpar
15 Dec	Wimbledon	H	D	2–2	..	..	..	..	..	..[1]	Groves	..	..	..[1]	..	O'Leary for Winterburn
23 Dec	Aston Villa	A	D	0–0	..	..	..	..	..	Linighan	..	..	..	..	..	Rocastle for Limpar
26 Dec	Derby Co	H	W	3–0	..	..	..	..	..	..	Rocastle	..	..[2]	..[1]	..	Campbell/O'Leary for Rocastle/Limpar
29 Dec	Sheffield U	H	W	4–1	..	..[1p]	..	..[1]	..	..	Groves	..	..[2]	..	..	Cole/O'Leary for Groves/Winterburn
1 Jan	Manchester C	A	W	1–0	..	..	..	..	..	..	O'Leary	..	..[1]	..	..	Hillier/Groves for O'Leary/Limpar
12 Jan	Tottenham H	A	D	0–0	..	..	..	..	..	..	..	..	..	..	..	Hillier/Groves for Davis/Merson
19 Jan	Everton	H	W	1–0	..	..	..	..	..	Groves	..	..	..	..[1]	..	Campbell/Hillier for Limpar/Bould
2 Feb	Chelsea	A	L	1–2	..	..	..	..	..	Linighan	Groves	..	..[1]	..	..	Hillier/Campbell for Bould/Limpar
23 Feb	Crystal Palace	H	W	4–0	..	..	..	..	..	..	O'Leary[1]	..	..[1]	..[1]	Campbell[1]	Pates/Rocastle for Linighan/Merson
3 Mar	Liverpool	A	W	1–0	..	..	..	..	..	Adams	..	Hillier	..	..[1]	..	Rocastle/Davis for Campbell/Adams
17 Mar	Leeds U	H	W	2–0	..	..	..	..	..	..	..	..	..	..	..[2]	
20 Mar	Nottingham F	H	D	1–1	..	..	..	..	..	..	..	Davis	..	..	..[1]	Groves/Limpar for Davis/Merson
23 Mar	Norwich C	A	D	0–0	..	..	..	Rocastle	..	..	..	..	..	Campbell	Limpar	Groves/Linighan for Limpar/Rocastle
30 Mar	Derby Co	A	W	2–0	..	..	..	Campbell	..	..	Rocastle	..	..[2]	Merson	..	Groves/Hillier for Limpar/Rocastle
3 Apr	Aston Villa	H	W	5–0	..	..	..	Hillier	..	..	Campbell[2]	..[1]	..[2]	..	..	Thomas/Groves for Hillier/Merson
6 Apr	Sheffield U	A	W	2–0	..	..	..	..	..	..	..[1]	..	..[1]	..	..	Groves/Thomas for Merson/Limpar
9 Apr	Southampton	A	D	1–1	..	opponents	..	..	..	..	..	..	..	Groves	..	Thomas/Merson for Hillier/Limpar
17 Apr	Manchester C	H	D	2–2	..	..	..	Thomas	..	..	..[1]	..	..	Merson[1]	Groves	Limpar/O'Leary for Merson/Dixon
23 Apr	QPR	H	W	2–0	..	..[1p]	..	Hillier	..	..	..	..	..	..[1]	Limpar	O'Leary/Groves for Merson/Limpar
4 May	Sunderland	A	D	0–0	..	..	..	..	..	..	..	..	..	..	Groves	O'Leary for Groves
6 May	Manchester U	H	W	3–1	..	..	..	..	..	..	..	..	..3.1p	..	Limpar	Thomas/O'Leary for Hillier/Limpar
11 May	Coventry C	H	W	6–1	..	opponents	..	..	..	..	..	..	..[1]	..	..[3]	Linighan/Groves[1] for Merson/Campbell

FA Cup

Date	Opponent			Score		Dixon	Winterburn	Thomas	Bould	Linighan	Groves	Davis	Smith[1]	Merson	Limpar[1]	Substitutes
5 Jan	Sunderland (3)	H	W	2–1	Seaman	Dixon	Winterburn	Thomas	Bould	Linighan	Groves	Davis	Smith[1]	Merson	Limpar[1]	O'Leary for Limpar
27 Jan	Leeds U (4)	H	D	0–0	..	..	..	..	..	Groves	O'Leary	..	..	..	..	Hillier/Campbell for O'Leary/Limpar
30 Jan	Leeds U (4R)	A	D	1–1*	..	..	..	..	..	Linighan	Hillier	..	..	..	..[1]	
13 Feb	Leeds U (4R/2)	H	D	0–0*	..	..	..	..	..	Groves	O'Leary	..	..	..	..	Campbell/Linighan for Groves/Limpar
16 Feb	Leeds U (4R/3)	A	W	2–1	..	..[1]	..	..	..	Linighan	..	..	..	..[1]	Campbell	Rocastle for Merson
27 Feb	Shrewsbury T (5)	A	W	1–0	..	..	..	..[1]	..	Adams	..	Hillier	..	..	..	Davis for Hillier
9 Mar	Cambridge U (6)	H	W	2–1	..	..	..	..	..	..[1]	..	..	..	..	..	Groves for Limpar
14 Apr	Tottenham H (S/F) (at Wembley)	L	1–3		..	..	..	..	..	..	Campbell	Davis	..[1]	..	Limpar	

*after extra time

Football League (Rumbelows) Cup

Date	Opponent			Score		Dixon	Winterburn	Hillier	Bould	Adams	Rocastle	Davis	Smith	Merson[1]	Groves	Substitutes
25 Sep	Chester (2)	A	W	1–0	Seaman	Dixon	Winterburn	Hillier	Bould	Adams	Rocastle	Davis	Smith	Merson[1]	Groves	Cambell for Rocastle
9 Oct	Chester (2)	H	W	5–0	..	..	..	..	..	..[1]	..	..	..[1]	..[1]	..[2]	Campbell/O'Leary for Rocastle/Bould
30 Oct	Manchester C (3)	A	W	2–1	..	..	..	Thomas	..	..[1]	Groves[1]	..	..	..	Limpar	Campbell for Limpar
28 Nov	Manchester U (4)	H	L	2–6	..	..	..	..	..	..	..	..	..[2]	..	..	Campbell for Limpar

Appearances (Goals)

Bould 38(5) · Dixon 38(5) · Seaman 38 · Winterburn 38 · Davis 37(3) · Merson 37(13) · Smith 37(22) · Limpar 34(11) · Groves 32(3) · Thomas 31(2) · Adams 30(1) · Campbell 22 (9) · O'Leary 21(1) · Rocastle 16(2) · Hillier 16 · Linighan 10 · Jonsson 2 · Cole 1 · Pates 1 · own goals (2)

Position in League Table

	P	W	D	L	F:A	Pts	
Arsenal	38	24	13	1	74:18	83**	1st

**two points deducted

SEASON 1991–92 FOOTBALL LEAGUE (DIVISION 1)

Date	Opponent			Score												Substitutions
17 Aug	QPR	H	D	1–1	Seaman	Dixon	Winterburn	Hillier	O'Leary	Adams	Campbell	Davis	Smith	Merson[1]	Limpar	Rocastle/Groves for O'Leary/Campbell
20 Aug	Everton	A	L	1–3	..	..	..[1]	..	..	..	Rocastle	..	..	..	..	Groves/Linighan for Limpar/Hillier
24 Aug	Aston Villa	A	L	1–3	..	..	..	Linighan	..	..	..	..	..[1]	..	..	Groves/Thomas for O'Leary/Rocastle
27 Aug	Luton T	H	W	2–0	..	..	..	Thomas	Linighan	..	..	..	..[1]	..[1]	..	
31 Aug	Manchester C	H	W	2–1	..	..	..	..	..	..	..	..	..[1]	..	..[1]	Campbell/Pates for Rocastle/Limpar
3 Sep	Leeds U	A	D	2–2	..	..	..	..	..	..	O'Leary	..	..[2]	..	Campbell	Rocastle for Thomas
7 Sep	Coventry C	H	L	1–2	..	..	..	Campbell	..	..[1]	Rocastle	..	..	..	Limpar	O'Leary/Thomas for Limpar/Davis
14 Sep	Crystal Palace	A	W	4–1	..	..	..	Hillier	..	..	..	Groves	..[1]	..	Campbell[2]	Thomas[1]/O'Leary for Groves/Hillier
21 Sep	Sheffield U	H	W	5–2	..	..[1]	..	Campbell[1]	..	..	..[1]	Davis	..[1]	..	Groves[1]	O'Leary/Thomas for Winterburn/Groves
28 Sep	Southampton	A	W	4–0	..	..	..	Thomas	..	..	..[1]	Wright[3]	..	..	Limpar	Campbell for Merson
5 Oct	Chelsea	H	W	3–2	..	..[1]p	..	..	..	Pates	..	..[1]	..	Campbell[1]	..	Merson/O'Leary for Limpar/Wright
19 Oct	Manchester U	A	D	1–1	..	..	..	Davis	Pates	Adams	..[1]	..[1]	..[1]	Merson	Campbell	
26 Oct	Notts Co	H	W	2–0	..	..	..	..	..	..	..	..[1]	..	..	..	Limpar for Campbell
2 Nov	West Ham	H	L	0–1	..	..	..	Thomas	..	Linighan	..	..	..	..	Limpar	Groves for Thomas
16 Nov	Oldham A	A	D	1–1	..	..	..	Hillier	Bould	..	..	..[1]	..	..	Pates	O'Leary/Groves for Bould/Pates
23 Nov	Sheffield W	A	D	1–1	..	..	..	..	..[1]	..	..	..	..	..	..	O'Leary for Hillier
1 Dec	Tottenham H	H	W	2–0	..	..	..	..	..	..	..	..[1]	..	..	Campbell[1]	Limpar/O'Leary for Wright/Rocastle
8 Dec	Nottingham F	A	L	2–3	..	..	..	..	..	..	Campbell	..[1]	..[1]	..	Limpar	Carter/O'Leary for Limpar/Bould
21 Dec	Everton	H	W	4–2	..	..	..	..	..	Adams	..	Wright[4]	..	..	..	O'Leary/Campbell for Rocastle/Merson
26 Dec	Luton T	A	L	0–1	..	..	..	O'Leary	..	..	..	..	..	..	..	Campbell for Limpar
28 Dec	Manchester C	A	L	0–1	..	..	..	..	..	..	..	..	..	..	Davis	Linighan/Groves for Bould/O'Leary
1 Jan	Wimbledon	H	D	1–1	..	..	..	Hillier	Linighan	..	..	..	..	..[1]	Carter	Campbell for Wright
11 Jan	Aston Villa	H	D	0–0	..	..	..	..	O'Leary	..	..	Campbell	..	..	..	Groves for Merson
18 Jan	QPR	A	D	0–0	..	..	..	Davis	..	..	..	Wright	..	..	..	
29 Jan	Liverpool	A	L	0–2	..	..	..	Parlour	..	..	..	..	..	..	..	Bould/Groves for O'Leary/Parlour
1 Feb	Manchester U	H	D	1–1	..	..	..	Hillier	Bould	..	..[1]	..	..	..	..	Pates/Limpar for Rocastle/Carter
8 Feb	Notts Co	A	W	1–0	..	..	..	..	..	..	Pates	..	..[1]	..	Groves	Parlour/Campbell for Winterburn/Groves
11 Feb	Norwich C	H	D	1–1	..	..	..	..	..	..	..	..	..	..[1]	Limpar	Campbell/Parlour for Limpar/Winterburn
15 Feb	Sheffield W	H	W	7–1	..	..	..	..	..	..	Rocastle	..[1]	..[1]	..[1]	..[2]	Campbell[2] for Smith
22 Feb	Tottenham H	A	D	1–1	..	..	..	..	..	Pates	..	..[1]	..	..	Campbell	O'Leary/Limpar for Hillier/Rocastle
10 Mar	Oldham A	H	W	2–1	..	..	..	..	..	Adams	..	..[1]	..	..[1]	Limpar	O'Leary for Limpar
14 Mar	West Ham U	A	W	2–0	..	..	..	..	..	..	..	..[2]	..	..	Groves	Campbell/O'Leary for Smith/Groves
22 Mar	Leeds U	H	D	1–1	..	..	..	..	..	..	..	..	O'Leary	..[1]	Campbell	Parlour/Limpar for Hillier/Rocastle
28 Mar	Wimbledon	A	W	3–1	..	..	..	..	..	..	Parlour[1]	..[1]	Campbell[1]	..	Groves	Limpar/Lydersen for Groves/Merson
31 Mar	Nottingham F	H	D	3–3	..	..[1]p	..	..	..	..[1]	Rocastle	..	..	..[1]	Limpar	Lydersen/Smith for Rocastle/Wright
4 Apr	Coventry C	A	W	1–0	..	..	..	..	..	..	Lydersen	..	..[1]	..	..	Rocastle/Smith for Winterburn/Limpar
8 Apr	Norwich C	A	W	3–1	..	O'Leary	Lydersen	..	..	..	Rocastle	..[2,1p]	..[1]	..	..	Morrow/Smith for O'Leary/Limpar
11 Apr	Crystal Palace	H	W	4–1	..	Lydersen	Winterburn	..	..	..	..	..[1]	..[3]	..	..	Smith/Morrow for Limpar/Winterburn
18 Apr	Sheffield U	A	D	1–1	..	..	..	..[1]	..	..	..	Campbell[1]	Smith	..	..	Heaney for Limpar
20 Apr	Liverpool	H	W	4–0	..	..	..	..	..	..	..	Wright[2]	Campbell	..	..[1]	O'Leary for Lydersen
25 Apr	Chelsea	A	D	1–1	..	Dixon[1]	..	..	..	..	..	..	..	..	..	Smith/Merson for Limpar/O'Leary
2 May	Southampton	H	W	5–1	..	..	..	..	..	..	..	..[3,1p]	..[1]	..	..	Smith[1]/Parlour for Limpar/Merson

FA Cup

4 Jan	Wrexham (3)	A	L	1–2	Seaman	Dixon	Winterburn	Hillier	O'Leary	Adams	Rocastle	Campbell	Smith[1]	Merson	Carter	Groves for Campbell

Football League (Rumbelows) Cup

25 Sep	Leicester C (2)	A	D	1–1	Seaman	Dixon	Thomas	Campbell	Linighan	Adams	Rocastle	Davis	Wright[1]	Merson	Groves	O'Leary for Linighan
8 Oct	Leicester C (2)	H	W	2–0	..	..	Winterburn	Thomas	Pates	..	..	Wright[1]	Smith	..[1]	Campbell	Groves for Writht
30 Oct	Coventry C (3)	A	L	0–1	..	..	..	Davis	..	..	..	..	..	..	Limpar	Groves/Linighan for Limpar/Pates

FA Charity Shield

18 Aug	Tottenham H (at Wembley)		D	0–0	Seaman	Dixon	Winterburn	Hillier	O'Leary	Adams	Rocastle	Davis	Smith	Merson	Campbell	Thomas/Cole for Rocastle/Campbell

European Cup

18 Sept	FK Austria (1)	H	W	6–1	Seaman	Dixon	Winterburn	Campbell	Linighan[1]	Adams	Rocastle	Davis	Smith[4]	Merson	Limpar[1]	Groves for Limpar
2 Oct	FK Austria (1)	A	L	0–1	..	..	..	Thomas	..	..	..	Campbell	..	..	O'Leary	Groves for Merson
23 Oct	Benfica (2)	A	D	1–1	..	..	..	Davis	Pates	..	..	..[1]	..	..	Limpar	Groves/Thomas for Campbell/Limpar
6 Nov	Benfica (2)	H	L	1–3*	..	..	..	..	..[1]	..	..	..	..	..	..	

*after extra time

Appearances (Goals)

Seaman 42 · Merson 42(12) · Winterburn 41(1) · Rocastle 39(4) · Smith 39(12) · Dixon 38(4) · Adams 35(2) · Campbell 31(13) · Wright 30(24) · Limpar 29(4) · Hillier 27(1) · Bould 25(1) · O'Leary 25 · Linighan 17 · Groves 13(1) · Davis 12 · Pates 11 · Thomas 10(1) · Lydersen 7 · Carter 6 · Parlour 6(1) · Morrow 2 · Heaney 1

Position in League Table

	P	W	D	L	F:A	Pts	
Leeds U	42	22	16	4	74:37	82	1st
Arsenal	42	19	15	8	81:46	72	4th

SEASON 1992–93 FOOTBALL LEAGUE (DIVISION 1)

Date	Opponents	V	R	Score	1	2	3	4	5	6	7	8	9	10	11	Substitutes
15 Aug	Norwich C	H	L	2–4	Seaman	Dixon	Winterburn	Hillier	Bould[1]	Adams	Jensen	Smith	Campbell[1]	Merson	Limpar	Wright for Merson
18 Aug	Blackburn Rov	A	L	0–1	..	..	..	..	..	..	..	..	..	Carter	..	Pates/Groves for Jensen/Limpar
23 Aug	Liverpool	A	W	2–0	..	..	..	..	Pates	..	..	Wright[1]	..	Parlour	..[1]	Merson for Limpar
26 Aug	Oldham	A	W	2–0	..	..	..[1]	..	Bould	..	Parlour	..[1]	..	Merson	Morrow	Pates/Smith for Merson/Wright
29 Aug	Sheffield W	H	W	2–1	..	..	..	..	..	..	Jensen	..	..	..[1]	Parlour[1]	Smith for Merson
2 Sep	QPR	A	D	0–0	..	..	..	..	..	..	..	..	..	..	..	Pates/Smith for Hillier/Merson
5 Sep	Wimbledon	A	L	2–3	..	..	..	Pates	..	..	..	..[2]	..	..	..	O'Leary/Smith for Jensen/Adams
12 Sep	Blackburn Rov	H	L	0–1	..	..	..	Selley	..	..	..	..	Smith	..	..	Campbell/Morrow for Parlour/Jensen
19 Sep	Sheffield U	A	D	1–1	..	..	..	Parlour	..	..	..	..[1]	..	..	Limpar	Linighan/Flatts for Merson/Limpar
28 Sep	Manchester C	H	W	1–0	..	..	..	Hillier	..	..	..	..[1]	..	..	Campbell	Limpar for Smith
3 Oct	Chelsea	H	W	2–1	..	..	..	..	..	..	..	..[1]	..[1]	..	..	Limpar for Merson
17 Oct	Nottingham F	A	W	1–0	..	..	..	..	..	..	..	..[1]	..	..	..	Limpar/Pates for Wright/Jensen
24 Oct	Everton	H	W	2–0	..	..	..	..	..	..	..	..[1]	..	..	..	Pates/Limpar[1] for Dixon/Wright
2 Nov	Crystal P	A	W	2–1	..	..	Morrow	..	..	..	..	..[1]	..[1]	..[1]	..	Limpar for Wright
7 Nov	Coventry C	H	W	3–0	..	..	..	..	..	..	..	..[1]	..[1]	..	..[1]	Limpar for Campbell
21 Nov	Leeds U	A	L	0–3	..	..	..	..	..	..	..	..	Campbell	..	Limpar	Parlour/Miller for Hillier/Seaman
28 Nov	Manchester U	H	L	0–1	..	..	..	..	..	..	..	..	..	..	..	Parlour/Flatts for Jensen/Limpar
5 Dec	Southampton	A	L	0–2	..	..	..	..	..	..	Parlour	..	..	..	Flatts	Jensen/Limpar for Dixon/Flatts
12 Dec	Tottenham H	A	L	0–1	..	Lydersen	Winterburn	..	..	..	Jensen	..	..	..	Parlour	Limpar for Jensen
19 Dec	Middlesbrough	H	D	1–1	..	..	..	..	Linighan	..	Flatts	..[1]	Smith	..	..	Jensen/Campbell for Merson/Parlour
26 Dec	Ipswich T	H	D	0–0	..	..	..	..	Bould	Linighan	Jensen	..	..	Campbell	Flatts	O'Leary/Limpar for Jensen/Campbell
28 Dec	Aston Villa	A	L	0–1	..	..	..	..	..	..	O'Leary	..	..	..	Parlour	Flatts/Limpar for Parlour/Hillier
9 Jan	Sheffield U	H	D	1–1	..	Dixon	..	..[1]	Linighan	Adams	Jensen	..	..	Merson	Limpar	O'Leary for Merson
16 Jan	Manchester C	A	W	1–0	..	..	..	..	Bould	..	..	Campbell	..	..[1]	Flatts	Campbell for Limpar
31 Jan	Liverpool	H	L	0–1	..	..	..	..	Linighan	..	Carter	..	..	..	Parlour	O'Leary/Heaney for Hillier/O'Leary
10 Feb	Wimbledon	H	L	0–1	..	Keown	..	..	..	..	Selley	Wright	..	..	Campbell	Carter/Morrow for Merson/Smith
20 Feb	Oldham A	A	W	1–0	..	..	Morrow	..	..[1]	..	Jensen	Selley	Campbell	..	Limpar	Carter for Limpar
24 Feb	Leeds U	H	D	0–0	..	..	Winterburn	..	..	..	Selley	Wright	Smith	..	..	Campbell for Limpar
1 Mar	Chelsea	A	L	0–1	..	Dixon	Morrow	..	..	Keown	Jensen	Campbell	..	..	Flatts	Lydersen/Carter for Hillier/Campbell
3 Mar	Norwich C	A	D	1–1	..	..	Winterburn	Davis	..	..	..	Wright[1]	Parlour	Carter	Limpar	Campbell for Limpar
13 Mar	Coventry C	A	W	2–0	..	..	Keown	..	..	Adams	Parlour	..[1]	Campbell[1]	Merson	Morrow	Limpar/Hillier for Wright/Merson
20 Mar	Southampton	H	W	4–3	..	Keown	Winterburn	..	..[1]	..	Carter[2]	Morrow	..	..[1]	Limpar	Hillier/Dickov for Davis/Limpar
24 Mar	Manchester U	A	D	0–0	..	Dixon	Keown	Morrow	..	..	Jensen	Wright	..	..	Carter	Parlour/Hillier for Carter/Adams
6 Apr	Middlesbrough	A	L	0–1	..	O'Leary	Winterburn	Hillier	..	..	..	..	Smith	Carter	Limpar	Morrow/Keown for Hillier/O'Leary
10 Apr	Ipswich T	A	W	2–1	..	..	..	Morrow	..	Keown	..	Campbell	..[1]	Merson[1]	Carter	Adams/Parlour for O'Leary/Jensen
12 Apr	Aston Villa	H	L	0–1	..	Dixon	..	Selley	Keown	Adams	Morrow	Wright	..	..	Campbell	Parlour/Linighan for Wright/Campbell
21 Apr	Nottingham F	H	D	1–1	..	..	..	..	Linighan	Keown	Jensen	..[1]	..	Parlour	Carter	Adams/Campbell for Winterburn/Parlour
1 May	Everton	A	D	0–0	..	O'Leary	Lydersen	Davis	..	Bould	Keown	Selley	..	Campbell	..	Jensen/Heaney for Lydersen/Carter
4 May	QPR	H	D	0–0	Miller	Dixon	Keown	..	..	Adams	Jensen	Campbell	..	Merson	Heaney	Carter for Merson
6 May	Sheffield W	A	L	0–1	..	Lydersen	..	Marshall	O'Leary	Bould	..	Selley	..	Heaney	Carter	McGowan/Flatts for Jensen/Lydersen
8 May	Crystal P	H	W	3–0	Seaman	Dixon	Winterburn	Davis	Linighan	Adams	Carter	Wright[1]	Campbell[1]	Merson	Parlour	Dickov[1]/O'Leary for Carter/Wright
11 May	Tottenham H	H	L	1–3	Miller	Lydersen	Keown	Marshall	O'Leary	Bould	Flatts	Selley	Smith	Dickov[1]	Heaney	McGowan/Carter for Lydersen/Flatts

FA Cup

Date	Opponents	V	R	Score	1	2	3	4	5	6	7	8	9	10	11	Substitutes
2 Jan	Yeovil T (3)	A	W	3–1	Seaman	Dixon	Winterburn	Hillier	Bould	Adams	O'Leary	Wright[3]	Smith	Merson	Limpar	
25 Jan	Leeds U (4)	H	D	2–2	..	..	..	..	Linighan	..	Jensen	Campbell	..	..[1]	Parlour[1]	Carter for Jensen
3 Feb	Leeds U (4R)	A	W	3–2*	..	..	..	Selley	..	..	Morrow	Wright[2]	..[1]	..	..	Campbell/O'Leary for Parlour/Winterburn
13 Feb	Nottingham F (5)	H	W	2–0	..	..	..	Hillier	..	..	Jensen	..[2]	Selley	..	Limpar	Campbell/Morrow for Wright/Limpar
6 Mar	Ipswich T (6)	A	W	4–2	..	opponents	..	Davis	..	..[1]	Carter	..[1p]	Smith	..	Morrow	Hillier/Campbell[1] for Carter/Smith
4 Apr	Tottenham H (SF) (at Wembley)		W	1–0	..	..	..	Hillier	..	..[1]	Parlour	..	Campbell	..	Selley	Smith/Morrow for Wright/Campbell
15 May	Sheffield W (F) (at Wembley)		D	1–1*	..	..	..	Davis	..	..	Jensen	..[1]	..	..	Parlour	Smith/O'Leary for Parlour/Wright
20 May	Sheffield W (FR) (at Wembley)		W	2–1*	..	..	..	..	..[1]	..	..	..[1]	..	Smith	Campbell	O'Leary for Wright

*after extra time

Football League (Coca-Cola) Cup

Date	Opponents	V	R	Score	1	2	3	4	5	6	7	8	9	10	11	Substitutes
22 Sep	Millwall (2)	H	D	1–1	Seaman	Dixon	Winterburn	Hillier	Bould	Adams	Parlour	Wright	Smith	Merson	Limpar	Campbell[1] for Limpar
7 Oct	Millwall (2)	A	D	1–1*	..	..	..	..	..	..	Jensen	..	..	..	Campbell[1]	Parlour for Merson
28 Oct	Derby Co (3)	A	D	1–1	..	Lydersen	Morrow	..	..	..	..	Campbell[1]	..	..	Limpar	
1 Dec	Derby Co (3R)	H	W	2–1	..	Dixon	..	..	..	..	Parlour	Wright[1]	Campbell[1]	..	Flatts	
6 Jan	Scarborough (4)	A	W	1–0	..	..	Winterburn[1]	..	..	..	O'Leary	Smith	..	..	Limpar	Campbell for Merson
12 Jan	Nottingham F (5)	H	W	2–0	..	..	..	..	Linighan	..	Jensen	..[2]	..	Campbell	..	Morrow for Wright
7 Feb	Crystal P (SF)	A	W	3–1	..	..	..	..	..	..	Selley	..[1p]	..[2]	..	Campbell	Morrow for Wright
10 Mar	Crystal P (SF)	H	W	2–0	..	..	..	Davis	..[1]	..	Carter	..[1]	..	..	Morrow	Hillier/Campbell for Winterburn/Smith
18 Apr	Sheffield W (F) (at Wembley)		W	2–1	..	O'Leary	Morrow[1]	..	..	..	..	Campbell	Davis	..[1]	Parlour	

*(won 3–1 on penalties)

Appearances (Goals)

Seaman 39 · Campbell 37(4) · Adams 35 · Merson 33(6) · Jensen 32 · Wright 31(15) · Smith 31(3) · Hillier 30(1) · Dixon 29 · Winterburn 29(1) · Bould 24(1) · Limpar 23(2) · Linighan 21(2) · Parlour 21(1) · Morrow 16 · Carter 16(2) · Keown 16 · O'Leary 11 · Flatts 10 · Selley 9 · Lydersen 8 · Pates 7 · Davis 6 · Heaney 5 · Miller 4 · Dickov 3(2) · Marshall 2 · McGowan 2 · Groves 1

Position in League Table

	P	W	D	L	F:A	Pts	
Manchester U	42	24	12	6	67:31	84	1st
Arsenal	42	15	11	16	40:38	56	10th

SEASON 1993–94 FA CARLING PREMIERSHIP

Date	Opponent			Score	Seaman	Dixon	Winterburn	Davis	Linighan	Adams	Jensen	Wright	Campbell	Merson	Limpar	Substitutes
14 Aug	Coventry C	H	L	0–3	Seaman	Dixon	Winterburn	Davis	Linighan	Adams	Jensen	Wright	Campbell	Merson	Limpar	McGoldrick/Keown for Jensen/Dixon
16 Aug	Tottenham H	A	W	1–0	..	Keown	..	..	..	..	..	..[1]	..	McGoldrick	Parlour	
21 Aug	Sheffield W	A	W	1–0	..	..	..	..	..	..	..	..[1]	..	..	..	Merson for Parlour
24 Aug	Leeds U	H	W	2–1	..	opponents	..	..	..	Selley	Merson[1]	..	..	McGoldrick	Parlour	Hillier for Davis
28 Aug	Everton	H	W	2–0	..	..	..	Hillier	..	Adams	Jensen	..[2]	..	..	..	Merson for Hillier
1 Sep	Blackburn Rov	A	D	1–1	..	..	..	Merson	..	..	..	..	..[1]	..	..	Selley for Merson
11 Sep	Ipswich T	H	W	4–0	..	..	..	Davis	..	..	..	..[1]	..[3]	Merson	McGoldrick	Hillier/Limpar for Jensen/Merson
19 Sep	Manchester U	A	L	0–1	..	..	..	Hillier	..	..	..	..	..	..	..	Davis/Smith for Hillier/Merson
25 Sep	Southampton	H	W	1–0	..	..	..	Davis	..	..	..	..	..	..[1]	..	Hillier for Davis
2 Oct	Liverpool	A	D	0–0	..	Dixon	..	..	..	..	..	..	..	..	..	
16 Oct	Manchester C	H	D	0–0	..	..	..	..	..	..	Heaney	..	Smith	Parlour	..	Campbell for Heaney
23 Oct	Oldham A	A	D	0–0	..	..	..	..	..	..	Hillier	..	..	Merson	..	Campbell for Hillier
30 Oct	Norwich C	H	D	0–0	..	..	..	..	Bould	..	Jensen	..	..	..	Limpar	Keown/Campbell for Winterburn/Smith
6 Nov	Aston Villa	H	L	1–2	..	..	..	Selley	Keown	..	..	..[1]	Campbell	Merson	Limpar	
20 Nov	Chelsea	A	W	2–0	..	..	..	Davis	Linighan	Bould	Keown	..[1]p	Smith[1]	..	Selley	Morrow for Winterburn
24 Nov	West Ham U	A	D	0–0	..	..	..	Keown	..	..	Morrow	..	..	..	Limpar	Campbell/Miller for Limpar/Wright
27 Nov	Newcastle	H	W	2–1	..	..	..	Morrow	Keown	..	Jensen	..[1]	..[1]	..	McGoldrick	
4 Dec	Coventry C	A	L	0–1	..	..	..	Davis	..	Adams	Selley	..	..	..	..	Bould/Campbell for Adams/McGoldrick
6 Dec	Tottenham H	H	D	1–1	..	..	Keown	Selley	Bould	..	Jensen	..[1]	..	..	Limpar	Campbell for Smith
12 Dec	Sheffield W	H	W	1–0	Miller	..	Morrow	..	Keown	..	..	..[1]	..	..	..	Bould/Campbell for Keown/Merson
18 Dec	Leeds U	A	L	1–2	Seaman	..	Winterburn	..	Bould	..	..	..	..	Campbell[1]	..	Parlour/Morrow for Smith/Dixon
27 Dec	Swindon T	A	W	4–0	..	..	..	Parlour	..	..	..	..[1]	Campbell[3]	Hillier	McGoldrick	Merson/Keown for Parlour/Adams
29 Dec	Sheffield U	H	W	3–0	..	..	..	..	..	..	..	..[1]	..[2]	..	..	Merson/Keown for Wright/Parlour
1 Jan	Wimbledon	A	W	3–0	..	..	..	..[1]	..	..	..	..[1]	..[1]	..	•	Keown/Merson for Dixon/Jensen
3 Jan	QPR	H	D	0–0	..	..	..	..	..	..	..	..	..	..	..	Keown for Jensen
15 Jan	Manchester C	A	D	0–0	..	..	..	..	..	..	..	..	..	..	..	Merson/Keown for McGoldrick/Jensen
22 Jan	Oldham A	H	D	1–1	..	..	..	..	..	..	..	..[1]p	..	..	..	Merson/Keown for McGoldrick/Jensen
13 Feb	Norwich C	A	D	1–1	..	..	..	Davis	..	..	..	Campbell[1]	Smith	Merson	Parlour	
19 Feb	Everton	A	D	1–1	..	..	..	..	..	..	..	..	..	..[1]	..	Keown/Hillier for Adams/Jensen
26 Feb	Blackburn Rov	H	W	1–0	..	..	..	..	..	..	..	..	..	..[1]	..	
5 Mar	Ipswich T	A	W	5–1	..	opponents	..	Selley	..	..	Parlour[1]	Wright[3]1p	..	Hillier	Limpar	Merson/Keown for Limpar/Hillier
19 Mar	Southampton	A	W	4–0	..	..	..	Keown	Linighan	..	..	..[3]1p	Campbell[1]	Selley	..	Smith for Limpar
22 Mar	Manchester U	H	D	2–2	..	opponents	..	Davis	Bould	..	Jensen	..	Smith	Merson[1]	Selley	Campbell for Davis
26 Mar	Liverpool	H	W	1–0	..	..	Keown	Parlour	..	Linighan	..	..	Campbell	..[1]	..	Morrow/Smith for Jensen/Wright
2 Apr	Swindon T	H	D	1–1	..	..	..	Davis	Linighan	Adams	..	..	Smith[1]	..	Parlour	Campbell/McGoldrick for Merson/Jensen
4 Apr	Sheffield U	A	D	1–1	..	Keown	Winterburn	Parlour	Bould	..	..	Campbell[1]	..	Selley	McGoldrick	Dixon/Merson for Keown/McGoldrick
16 Apr	Chelsea	H	W	1–0	..	Dixon	Morrow	Hillier	Keown	..	Selley	..[1]	Campbell	Parlour	..	Smith for Hillier
19 Apr	Wimbledon	H	D	1–1	..	..	Keown	Davis	Bould[1]	..	Campbell	..	Smith	..	Selley	Flatts for Davis
23 Apr	Aston Villa	A	W	2–1	..	..	..	..	..	Linighan	..	..[2]1p	..	Morrow	Flatts	Parlour for Davis
27 Apr	QPR	A	D	1–1	..	..	..	Morrow	Linighan	Adams	Flatts	..	..	Merson[1]	Parlour	Selley/McGoldrick for Flatts/Keown
30 Apr	West Ham U	H	L	0–2	..	McGoldrick	Winterburn	Davis	Bould	Linighan	Parlour	..	Campbell	..	Selley	Morrow/Dickov for McGoldrick/Merson
7 May	Newcastle	A	L	0–2	..	Dixon	..	..	..	Adams	McGoldrick	..	Smith	Morrow	Selley	Parlour/Linighan for Davis/Dixon

FA Cup

Date	Opponent			Score												Substitutes
10 Jan	Millwall (3)	A	W	1–0	Seaman	Dixon	Winterburn	Parlour	Bould	Adams[1]	Keown	Wright	Campbell	Hillier	McGoldrick	Merson/Jensen for Wright/Hillier
31 Jan	Bolton W (4)	A	D	2–2	..	..	..	..	..	..[1]	..	..[1]	..	..	Merson	Smith for Parlour
9 Feb	Bolton W (4R)	H	L	1–3*	..	..	..	Hillier	..	..	..	Campbell	..	Smith[1]	Merson	Parlour	Keown/McGoldrick for Hillier/Wright

* aet

Football League (Coca-Cola) Cup

Date	Opponent			Score												Substitutes
21 Sep	Huddersfield T (2)	A	W	5–0	Seaman	Keown	Winterburn	Davis	Linighan	Adams	Jensen	Wright[3]	Campbell[1]	Merson[1]	McGoldrick	Hillier/Smith for Jensen/Merson
5 Oct	Huddersfield (2)	H	D	1–1	..	Dixon	..	Parlour	..	Bould	..	Smith[1]	..	Limpar	..	Selley/Heaney for Jensen/McGoldrick
26 Oct	Norwich C (3)	H	D	1–1	..	..	..	..	..	Adams	..	Wright[1]	Smith	Merson	..	Campbell/Davis for Merson/McGoldrick
10 Nov	Norwich C (3R)	A	W	3–0	..	Keown	Selley	..	Bould	..	..[2]	..	..[1]	Limpar	Campbell/Davis for Jensen/Dixon
30 Nov	Aston Villa (4)	H	L	0–1	..	Winterburn	Morrow	Keown	..	..	..	..	..	McGoldrick	Campbell/Davis for Jensen/Dixon

FA Charity Shield

Date	Opponent			Score												Substitutes
7 Aug	Manchester U (at Wembley)		D	1–1	Seaman	Dixon	Winterburn	Davis	Linighan	Adams	Jensen	Wright[1]	Campbell	Merson	Limpar	Keown/McGoldrick for Dixon/Limpar

European Cup Winners' Cup

Date	Opponent			Score												Substitutes
15 Sep	Odense (1)	A	W	2–1	Seaman	Selley	Winterburn	Davis	Linighan	Keown	Jensen	Wright[1]	Campbell	Merson[1]	McGoldrick	Smith for Wright
29 Sep	Odense (1)	H	D	1–1	..	Dixon	..	..	Keown	Adams	..	..	..[1]	..	..	Smith for Wright
20 Oct	Standard Liege (2)	H	W	3–0	..	..	..	..	..	..	..	..[2]	Smith	..[1]	..	Campbell/Linighan for Wright/Keown
3 Nov	Standard Liege (2)	A	W	7–0	..	..	..	..	..	..[1]	..	Selley[1]	..[1]	..[1]	Campbell[2]	McGoldrick[1]/Bould for Smith/Keown
2 Mar	Torino (3)	A	D	0–0	..	..	..	..	Bould	..	..	Campbell	..	Hillier	Selley for Davis
15 Mar	Torino (3)	H	W	1–0	..	..	..	..	..	..[1]	..	Wright	..	..	Selley/Keown for Hillier/Jensen
29 Mar	Paris St-Germain (SF)	A	D	1–1	..	..	..	..	..	..	..	..[1]	..	..	Selley	Keown/Campbell for Davis/Smith
12 Apr	Paris St-Germain (SF)	H	W	1–0	..	..	..	..	..	..	..	..	..	Campbell[1]	Selley	Hillier/Keown for Davis/Winterburn
4 May	Parma (F) (at Copenhagen)		W	1–0	..	..	..	..	..	..	Campbell	Morrow	..[1]	Merson	..	McGoldrick for Merson

Appearances (Goals)

Seaman 39 · Wright 39(23.5p) · Campbell 37(14) · Adams 35 · Winterburn 34 · Dixon 33 · Keown 33 · Merson 33(7) · Jensen 27 · Parlour 27(2) · McGoldrick 26 · Bould 25(1) · Smith 25(3) · Davis 22 · Linighan 21 · Selley 18 · Hillier 15 · Morrow 11 · Limpar 10 · Miller 4 · Flatts 3 · Dickov 1 · Heaney 1 · own goals (3)

Position in League Table

	P	W	D	L	F-A	Pts	
Manchester U	42	27	11	4	80:38	92	1st
Arsenal	42	18	17	7	53:28	71	4th

Complete First Class Appearances 1886-1994

The list below includes all players who have made appearances in recognised first-class competitions since the club was founded in 1886 until 1 August 1994. We have defined seven qualifying first-class competitions, viz: Football League, FA Cup, League/Milk/Littlewoods/Coca-Cola Cup, the three major European Cups and the Charity Shield. All other leagues in which Arsenal appeared (such as the United League) or extra cups (such as the Coronation Cup) or wartime competitions are excluded.

Arsenal regularly appeared in the qualifying rounds of the FA Cup in the last decade of the nineteenth century. So that the record may be complete, we have regarded these matches as first-class although some were against poor opposition (this fact is reflected in the appearance records – for instance A. Elliott scored 11 goals in 10 FA Cup qualifying matches between 1892 and 1894).

The appearance record is the first figure in each section, goals scored in that competition are in brackets. To avoid an overwhelming volume of numbers it has now become the statistical convention to record any occasion when a substitute comes onto the pitch (even for 60 seconds) as a full appearance, but not to record an occasion when the sub stays on the bench throughout. We have followed that convention here and all appearances *on the field* as substitute are included in the record. The years indicated generally refer to seasons with the first-team appearances, and the year given is the year the season ended. Hence 1921-24 refers to seasons 1920-21 to 1923-24. We are indebted to Daniel Feinstein for preparing the original material.

Name	Career	League	FA Cup	Lg/Milk Cup	Euro Comp	CS
Adams, Tony	1984-	319(20)	29(5)	45(2)	2	3
Addison, Colin	1966-67	28(9)	2	2(1)		
Allinson, Ian	1983-87	83 (16)	9(4)	13(3)		
Ambler, C J	1893-95	1	1			
Anderson, J W	1897-1903	145(10)	9			
Anderson, Terry	1961-65	25(6)		1(1)	1(1)	
Anderson, Viv	1984-87	120(9)	12(3)	18(3)		
Anderson, W	1902-04	27(10)	2(1)			
Armstrong, George	1961-77	500(53)	60(10)	35(3)	26(2)	
Arnold, T	1906	2				
Ashcroft, Jimmy	1900-08	273	30			
Aston, J	1900	11(3)	4(2)			
Bacuzzi, Dave	1959-64	46	2			
Baker, Alf	1920-31	310(23)	41(3)			
Baker, Joe	1962-66	144(93)	10(4)		2(3)	
Baldwin, Tommy	1962-66	17(7)		3(4)		
Ball, Alan	1971-76	177(45)	28(7)	12		
Bannister, W	1903-04	18	4			
Barbour, H	1889-93		5(4)			
Barley, B C	1927-29	8(1)	2			
Barnes, Walley	1943-55	267(11)	25(1)			2
Barnett, Geoff	1969-76	39	3	5	2	
Barnwell, John	1956-64	138(23)	10		3(1)	
Barron, Paul	1978-80	8				
Bassett, S J	1909	1				
Bastin, Cliff	1930-46	350(150)	42(26)			4(2)
Bates, Maurice	1886-92		3			
Bateup, E	1906-11	34	2			
Batson, Brendan	1971-74	10				
Beardsley, Fred	1886-93		2			
Beasley, Pat	1931-36	79(19)	10(5)			
Bee, E	1890-93		4			
Bell, C	1914	1(2)				
Bellamy, Jimmy	1905-07	29(4)				
Beney, W	1909-10	16(6)	1			
Benson, Bob	1914-15	52(7)	2			
Bigden, J H	1905-08	75(1)	12			
Biggs, Anthony	1956-58	4(1)				
Biggs, Arthur	1936	3				
Birkett, Ralph	1934-35	19(7)	2(1)		2(3)	
Black, Tommy	1933		1			
Blackwood, J	1901	17(6)	1(1)			
Blair, J	1906-07	13(3)				
Blockley, Jeff	1972-75	52(1)	7	3		
Bloomfield, Jimmy	1954-60	210(54)	17(2)			
Blyth, Billy	1915-29	314(45)	29(6)			
Boot, Micky	1964-66	4(2)	4(2)	1		
Booth, C	1894-96	16(2)	10(10)			
Boreham, Reg	1922-24	51(18)	2			
Bould, S	1988-	161(5)	16	17	7	
Boulton, Frank	1936-38	36	6			
Bowden, Ray	1933-37	123(42)	13(5)			2(1)
Bowden, Dave	1950-59	146(2)	16			
Bowen, E	1927	1				
Boyd, H	1895-97	40(31)	1			

Name	Career	League	FA Cup	Lg/Milk Cup	Euro Comp	CS
Boylan, P A	1897		11			
Boyle, J	1894-97	61(7)	5(2)			
Bradshaw, Frank	1915-23	132(14)	10			
Bradshaw, W	1903-04	4(1)				
Brady, Liam	1973-80	235(43)	35(2)	23(10)	13(4)	1
Brian, Jimmy	1924-31	204(125)	27(14)			1
Bremner, Gordon	1938-39	15(4)				
Briercliffe, Tommy	1902-05	122(33)	11(1)			
Briggs, S	1894	2				
Brignall, Steve	1979	1				
Brock, J S	1897-99	57(19)	1(1)			
Brown, Laurie	1961-63	101(2)	5		3	
Bryan, T	1894	9(1)				
Buchan, Charles	1925-28	102(49)	18(7)			
Buchan, James	1905	8				
Buchanan, R	1895-96	42(16)	2			
Buckenham, W E	1910	21(5)				
Buckley, Chris	1915-27	56(3)	3			
Buist, Bobby	1891-97	17	10			
Burdett, G	1911-13	28				
Burgess, D	1920-22	13(1)				
Burns, Tony	1963-66	31	2			
Burrell, G	1913-14	23(3)	1			
Burrows, L	1894-96	10				
Busby, W	1904	5(2)	1			
Butler, Jack	1920-30	266(7)	29(1)			
Caesar, Gus	1985-90	44	1	5		
Cale, A	1897	8(4)				
Calder, L A	1911	1				
Caldwell, J	1895-98	93(2)	2			
Caldwell, J H	1913	3				
Calverley, Alf	1947	11				
Calvert, F	1911-12	2(1)				
Campbell, K	1988-	143(42)	17(2)	19(5)	12(5)	2
Carr, Eddie	1938-39	12(7)				
Carter, Jimmy	1991-	22(2)	3	1		
Cartright, S	1936-39	16(2)				
Carver, G	1897	1				
Cassidy, H	1897	1				
Caton, Tommy	1983-86	81(2)	4	10		
Chalmers, Jackie	1911-12	48(21)	3(1)			
Chambers, Brian	1973-74	1		1		
Chapman, Lee	1982-83	23(4)	1	2	2(2)	
Charles, Mel	1959-62	60(26)	4(2)			
Charlton, Stan	1955-58	99	11(3)			
Charteris, W	1889		1			
Chenhall, John	1944-53	16				
Chisholm, N W	1909	3				
Christmas, A	1889		1			
Clamp, Eddie	1961- 62	22(1)	2			
Clapton, Danny	1953-62	207(26)	17(2)			
Clapton, Dennis	1958-61	4				
Clark, J	1924-25	4				
Clark, J M	1898-99	4				
Clark, W	1928	1				
Clarke, Fred	1960-64	26	2			
Clarke, G B	1923	2				
Coakley, Tom	1966	9(1)		4(1)		
Cock, D J	1925-26	3				
Cole, Andy	1990-1992	1				1
Coleman, Ernie	1932-34	45(26)	1			1
Coleman, Tim	1903-08	172(81)	18(4)			
Coles, F G	1901-04	78(2)	3			
Collett, Ernie	1938-47	20				
Common, Alf	1911-13	77(23)	3			
Compton, Denis	1935-50	54(15)	5(1)			1
Compton, Leslie	1932-51	253(5)	17(1)			3
Connolly, Peter	1889-93		6(2)			
Connor, M, J	1903	14(2)				
Cooper, L	1892-94	7	3(2)			
Cope, Horace	1926-33	65	11			
Copping, Wilf	1935-39	166	19			4
Cork, David	1980-85	7(1)	1			
Cottrell, E H	1899-1901	24(12)				
Counley, F F	1920-22	15				
Coupland, Ernest	1920	1				
Court, David	1959-70	174(17)	5	11(1)	8	
Cox, Freddie	1949-53	79(8)	15(7)			
Cox, George	1934-36	7(1)				
Crawford, Gavin	1890-98	125(17)	9(1)			
Crawford, H S	1911-13	26	1			
Crayson, Jack	1934-39	168(16)	16(1)			
Creegan, W W	1922	5	1			
Cropley, Alex	1974-76	30(5)	2	2(1)		
Cross, Archie	1900-10	133	13			

Name	Career	League	FA Cup	Lg/Milk Cup	Euro Comp	CS
Crowe, A	1905-07	7(4)				
Crozier, J	1895	1				
Cumner, Horace	1939	12(2)				
Curie, W	1909	3				
Curtis, George	1939-47	13	1			
Dailly, H	1899	8(4)				
Daniel, Ray	1946-53	87	12			
Davidson, A	1904	1				
Davidson, Bobby	1935-38	57(13)	4(2)			1
Davidson, Roger	1965-69	1				
Davie, D	1892-93		2(1)			
Davies, Paul	1969-72	1		1		
Davis, F W	1893-99	134(8)	5			
Davis, Paul	1979-	347(29)	27(3)	49(4)	16	2
Devine, Andy	1913-14	24(5)				
Devine, D	1894	2				
Devine, John	1976-83	89	6	8	8	
Devlin, J	1898	1				
Dick, John	1899-1910	263(13)	9			
Dickov, Paul	1993-	4(2)				
Dickson, Bill	1953-56	29(1)	2			
Dixon, Lee	1988-	215(5)	24(1)	27	12	3
Docherty, Tommy	1958-61	83(1)	7			
Dodgin, Bill	1952-61	191	16(1)			1
Dougall, Peter	1934-36	21(4)	2(1)			
Drain, T	1910	2				
Drake, Ted	1934-39	168(124)	14(12)			2(3)
Drury, George	1938-46	38(3)	1			
Ducat, Andy	1904-12	175(19)	13(2)			
Duff, H	1898	1(1)				
Duncan, D	1913	3(1)	2(1)			
Dunn, S	1919-22	42	1			
Dunne, Jimmy	1934-36	28(10)	4(3)			1
Dunsbie, R C	1900	7				
Dyer, G	1892-93		5			
Earle, S J C	1922-24	4(3)				
Eastham, George	1960-66	207(41)	13			
Edgar, J	1902	10(1)	1			
Elliott, A	1892-94	24(11)	10(11)			
Elvey, J R	1922	1				
Evans, Dennis	1951-61	189(10)	18(2)			
Evans, R	1913	1	1			
Everitt, Mike	1958-61	9(1)				
Fairclough, W	1896	26				
Farmer, G A	1897	1				
Farr, Andy	1939	2(1)				
Farrell, P	1898	19(3)				
Ferguson, J	1907	1				
Ferry, Gordon	1961-65	11				
Fidler, Joe	1913-14	24				
Fields, Alf	1939-50	19				
Firth, F	1898	1				
Fisher, G	1910	2				
Fitchie, Tommy	1902-09	56(27)	9(2)			
Flannigan, J	1911-15	114(28)	6(1)			
Flatts, Mark	1992-	13		1		
Fletcher, A	1915	3				
Forbes, Alex	1948-56	217(21)	22			1
Ford, G E	1913-14	9	1			
Foster, W	1889-90		2			
Fotheringham, Jim	1951-59	72	4			
Foxall, A	1902	31(3)				
Freeman, Bert	1905-07	44(20)	5(3)			
Furnell, Jim	1963-68	141	13	12	1	
Fyfe, J	1899	7				
Garbutt, Bill	1906-08	51(8)	13(6)			
Garton, J	1899	5				
Gatting, Steve	1977-81	58(5)	10(1)	4	4	
Gaudie, R	1900-01	48(21)	2			
Gemmell, D	1894	5				
George, Charlie	1968-75	123(31)	22(11)	8(2)	16(5)	
Gilmer, H P	1896	3				
Gloak, D	1889-92		2			
Gooing, Bill	1902-05	94(44)	6(2)			
Gordon, R	1896	20(6)				
Goring, Peter (H)	1948-60	220(51)	20(2)			
Gorman, Paul	1980-84	6				
Gould, Bobby	1968-70	65(16)	7(3)	9(3)	2(1)	
Goulden, Roy	1954-61	1				
Goy, Peter	1955-60	2				
Graham, Alec	1913-24	166(16)	13(3)			
Graham, George	1966-72	227(60)	27(2)	27(9)	25(7)	
Graham, H	1892		1			
Graham, J	1900	1				
Grant, Cyril	1946	2				
Grant, G M	1912-15	54(5)	3			
Grant, J W	1912	4(3)				
Gray, Archie	1905-12	183	16			
Gray, W	1899	1				
Greenaway, D	1909-21	162(1)	9			
Grice, N C	1906	1				
Grieve, T	1901	6				
Griffiths, Arfon	1961-62	15(2)	9(1)			
Griffiths, Mal	1937-39	9(5)				
Groves, Freddie	1913-21	50(5)	3(1)			
Groves, Perry	1986-92	156(21)	17(1)	26(6)	4	
Groves, Vic	1955-63	185(31)	16(6)		2	
Gudmundsson, Albert	1946	2				
Guthrie, Ralph	1953-56	2				
Haden, Sammy	1924-27	88(10)	5(1)			
Halliday, David	1930	15(9)				
Hamilton, T S	1898-1900	7				
Hankin, Ray	1981-82			2		
Hanks, E	1913	4(2)				
Hannah, D	1898-99	47(13)	2			
Hannigan, R	1900	1				
Hapgood, Eddie	1928-39	393(2)	41			
Hardinge, Wally	1914-20	54(14)	1			
Hare, C B	1895-96	19(7)	1			
Harper, Bill	1925-31	63	10			
Hartley, A	1900	5(1)				
Harvey, Jimmy	1977-80	3			1	
Hatfield, T	1895-96	2				
Haverty, Joe	1954-61	114(25)	8(1)			
Hawley, John	1981-83	20(3)		1		
Hayes, Martin	1985-90	102(26)	9(3)	21(5)		
Haynes, A E	1930-34	29	1			1
Haywood, A	1896-99	71(32)	2			
Heaney, Neil	1992-94	7		1		
Heath, J	1894-95	10(5)	2(2)			
Heeley, Mark	1977-80	15(1)			5	
Henderson, J	1894-95	37(17)	6(8)			
Henderson, Jackie	1958-62	103(29)	8			
Henderson, W	1922-23	7				
Heppinstall, F	1910-11	23				
Herd, David	1954-61	166(97)	14(10)			
Hill, Colin	1981-85	46(1)	1	4		
Hill, Frank	1933-35	76(4)	2			3
Hillier, David	1990-	88(2)	13	11	3	1
Hoar, Sid	1925-29	99(18)	17(1)			
Hoare, G R	1908-12	30(12)	4(1)			
Hodges, Cyril	1946-47	2				
Hollins, John	1979-83	127(9)	12	20(3)	13(1)	1
Holton, Cliff	1947-58	198(83)	18(5)			1
Hopkins, Jimmy	1921-23	21(7)	1			
Hornsby, Brian	1972-76	26(6)				
Housington, D	1890		2(1)			
Howard, Pat	1976-77	16		4(1)		
Howat, Davie	1894-96	55(3)	13(1)			
Howe, Don	1964-66	70(1)	3	1		
Hudson, Alan	1976-78	36	7	4		
Hughes, J	1925	1				
Hulme, Joe	1926-38	333(108)	39(17)			2
Humpish, E	1930	3				
Hunt, F	1898-1903	73(30)	2			
Hunt, George	1938	18(3)	3			
Hunter, J	1905	22(4)				
Hutchins, Arthur	1920-23	104(1)	4			
Hynds, Tommy	1907	13	4			
Jack, David	1929-34	181(110)	25(10)			2(1)
Jackson, Jimmy	1900-05	181	8			
Jacques, G H	1894	2(2)				
James, Alex	1929-37	231(26)	28(1)			2
Jeffreys, W W	1894	22	9			
Jenkins, David	1963-68	17(3)	2(1)	6(5)		
Jenkyns, Caesar	1896	27(6)				
Jennings, Pat	1977-85	237	38	32		1
Jensen, John	1992-	59	5	8	8	1
Jobey, George	1914	28(3)				
John, Bob	1922-37	421(12)	46(1)			3
Johnston, George	1967-69	21(3)		4		
Johnstone, W	1930-31	9(4)				
Jones, Bryn	1938-49	71(7)	3			2(1)
Jones, Charlie	1929-34	176(8)	17			2
Jones, F J	1921-24	3				

Complete First Class Appearances 1886-1994

Name	Career	League	FA Cup	Lg/Milk Cup	Euro Comp	CS
Jones, Leslie	1937-39	46(3)	3			1
Jonsson, Siggi	1989-91	8(1)	1	1		
Joy, Bernard	1936-46	86	4			3
Julian, J W	1889-93		4			
Julians, Len	1958-60	19(7)	6(3)			
Kaine, E T	1900-01	1				
Kane, Peter	1960-63	4(1)				
Kay, John	1981-84	14				
Kelly, Eddie	1968-76	175(13)	17(4)	15	15(2)	
Kelly, Noel	1947-50					
Kesley, Jack	1949-62	327	24		1	
Kemp, F	1906	2				
Kempton, A	1915		1			
Kennedy, Andy	1923-28	122	7			
Kennedy, Ray	1968-74	158(53)	27(6)	11(4)	16(8)	
Keown, Martin	1985-86	22	5			
	1993-	49	3	3	7	1
Keyser, Gerrie	1931	12				1
Kidd, Brian	1974-76	77(30)	9(3)	4(1)		
King, E	1913	11	2			
King, H E	1915	37(26)	2(2)			
Kirchen, Alf	1935-39	92(38)	7(6)			2(1)
Kirk, F W	1894	1				
Kosima, John	1978-79	1			3	
Kyle, Peter	1907-08	52(21)	8(1)			
Laidlaw, J A	1902	3(2)				
Lambert, Jack	1926-34	143(98)	16(11)			2
Lawrence, E T	1903	21(4)	1			
Lawrence, W H	1910	25(5)	1			
Lawson, Herbert	1926	13(2)	3			
Lawton, Tommy	1953-55	35(13)	2(1)			1(1)
Leather, J	1896	8				
Lee, H J	1908-10	41(15)				
Lee, J H	1927	7				
Leroux, Daniel	1957-58	5				
Lewis, C H	1908-20	206(30)	14(4)			
Lewis, Danny	1924-30	142	25			
Lewis, Reg	1937-52	154(103)	20(13)			1(2)
Liddell, Neil	1915	2				
Lievesley, Joe	1913-15	73	2			
Limpar, Anders	1990-94	96(17)	7(2)	9	3(1)	1
Linighan, Andy	1990-	69(2)	11(1)	10(1)	4(1)	1
Linward, Bill	1903-05	46(9)	2			
Lishman, Doug	1948-56	225(125)	17(10)			1(2)
Lloyd, F	1900	16(3)				
Logan, A	1900	20(4)				
Logan, H M	1911	11				
Logan, P	1900-02	8(1)				
Logie, Jimmy	1939-55	296(68)	29(8)			2
Low, A B	1907	2				
Low, T P	1901	24(1)	2(1)			
Lukic, John	1983-90	233	21	32		1
Lydersen, Pal	1992-	15	1			
Macanlis, D	1892		1			
Macaulay, Archie	1947-50	103(1)	4			1
Macdonald, Malcolm	1976-80	84(42)	9(10)	14(5)	1	
Mackie, Alex	1923-26	108	10			
MacLeod, John	1961-64	101(23)	8(4)		3(1)	
Madden, David	1983-84	2				
Magill, Eddie	1959-65	116	11		4	
Main, A	1900-03	64(14)	3			
Male, George	1930-48	285	27			4
Mancini, Terry	1974-76	52(1)	8	2		
Marden, Ben	1950-55	42(11)				
Marinello, Peter	1970-73	35(3)	5(1)	7(1)		
Mariner, Paul	1984-86	60(14)	6(2)	4(1)		
Marks, George	1939	2				
Marshall, Jimmy	1935	4			1(1)	
Marshall, Scott	1993-	2				
Marwood, Brian	1988-90	52(16)	2	6(1)		
Matthews, John	1973-78	45(2)	6(1)	6(2)		
Maxwell, J M	1909	1				
Maxwell, T	1922	1				
Maycock, W	1929	1				
McAuley, J	1898	24	1			
McAvoy, John	1896-1899	60(8)	2			
McBean, James	1889-92		6			
McClelland, John	1960-64	46	3			
McConnell, A	1898-99	36(1)	1			
McCowie, A	1900-01	29(10)				
McCullough, Billy	1958-66	253(4)	11		4(1)	
McDermott, Brian	1979-84	61(12)	1	4	6(1)	

Name	Career	League	FA Cup	Lg/Milk Cup	Euro Comp	CS
McDonald, D	1910-11	26	2			
McDonald, H	1906-13	94	9			
McEachrane, Roddie	1902-14	313	30			
McFarlane, A	1897	5				
McGeoch, A	1898-99	36(14)	1			
McGibbon, C E	1910	4(3)				
McGill, Jimmy	1965-67	10		2		
McGoldrick, Eddie	1993-	26	2	4	5(1)	1
McGowan, Gavin	1993-	2				
McKechnie, Ian	1954-64	23		2		
McKellar, M T	1910	3(1)	2(1)			
McKenzie, A	1921-23	15(2)		2		
McKinnon, Angus	1909-22	211(4)	6			
McLaughlin, J	1912-13	16(3)				
McLintock, Frank	1964-73	315(26)	36(1)	35(4)	19(1)	
McNab, Bob	1966-75	278(4)	39	26(2)	21	
McNab, W	1894	2(1)				
McNichol, David	1900-03	101	3			
McPhee, J	1899	7	1			
McPherson, Ian	1946-51	152(19)	11(2)			
McQuilkie, A	1892		1			
Mead, Tommy	1895-97	11(5)				
Meade, Raphael	1980-85	41(14)	3	4(1)	3(1)	
Meggs, J	1889-92		5(4)			
Mercer, Joe	1946-54	249(2)	25			2
Merson, Paul	1986-	233(63)	26(4)	28(8)	12(3)	3
Miller, Alan	1992-	8				
Mills, S	1896	23(4)	1			
Milne, Billy	1920-27	114(1)	10(2)			
Milne, Jackie	1935-38	49(19)	3			2
Milton, Arthur	1946-55	75(18)	4(3)			
Mitchell, A	1899	10(2)				
Moir, J G	1899-1900	41(1)	1			
Monteith, J	1898	6(1)				
Moody, J	1927-28	6				
Mordue, Jackie	1907-08	26(1)	2			
Morgan, Stan	1938-48	2				
Morrow, Stephen	1992-	29	4	6(1)	1	
Mortimer, P	1895-96	50(20)				
Moss, Frank	1931-36	143(1)	16			2
Murphy, J	1900	27				
Murrell, E H	1900	6				
Neave, David	1904-12	154(29)	14(2)			
Neil, Andy	1924-26	54(9)	3			
Neill, Terry	1959-70	241(8)	13	16(2)	5	
Neilson, Gordon	1964-68	14(2)	3(1)			
Nelson, Dave	1936-46	27(4)				
Nelson, Sammy	1966-81	345(1)	35(1)	27(1)	21	1
Nicholas, Charlie	1983-88	149(34)	13(10)	20(10)		
Nicholas, Peter	1981-83	60(1)	8(1)	8(2)	4	
Norman, J	1915	4				
North, E J	1920-22	23(6)				
Nutt, Gordon	1955-60	49(10)	2			
Oakes, Donald	1946-54	11(1)				
O'Brien, P	1895-97	64(27)	2(1)			
Offer, H	1889-92		4(1)			
O'Flanagan, Kevin	1947	14(3)				
O'Leary, David	1975-1993	558(11)	70(1)	70(2)	21	3
Oliver, H	1910	1				
O'Neill, Frank	1959-61	2				
Ord, Roger	1897-1900	88	2			
O'Shea, Danny	1980-84	6		3		
Owens, I	1902	9(2)	2			
Pack, Roy	1963-66	1				
Pagnam, Tom	1920-21	50(26)	3(1)			
Parker, Tom	1926-33	258(17)	34(1)			2
Parkin, R	1929-36	25(11)	1			
Parlour, Ray	1992-	54(4)	7(1)	6		
Paterson, Jimmy	1921-26	71(2)	7(1)			
Paterson, W	1928-29	15				
Pates, Colin	1990-1993	21		2	2(1)	
Pattison, G C	1920-22	9	1			
Payne, G C	1913	3				
Peachey, J	1891		1			
Peart, J C	1911-21	64	3			
Peel, H	1927-30	47(5)	5(1)			
Petrovic, Vladimir	1982-83	13(2)	6(1)	3		
Petts, John	1956-62	32				
Place, W	1901-02	41(6)	1			
Platt, Ted	1939-53	53	4			
Powell, Joe	1894-97	86(1)	3			
Powling, Ritchie	1974-81	55(3)	2	2		

Name	Career	League	FA Cup	Lg/Milk Cup	Euro Comp	CS
Pratt, T	1904	8(3)				
Preedy, Charlie	1930-33	37	2			
Price, David	1972-81	126(16)	26(1)	11	12(2)	1
Pryde, Dave	1939	4				
Quayle, J	1911	1				
Quinn, N	1985-90	67(14)	10(2)	16(4)		
Radford, John	1962-76	379(111)	44(15)	34(12)	24(11)	
Ramsey, J H	1924-27	69(11)	6			
Randall, C E	1912-14	43(12)	1			
Rankin, J	1892-93		3			
Rawson, F	1904	1				
Raybould, S	1909	26(6)	4(1)			
Reece, G	1895	1				
Rice, Pat	1966-80	397(11)	67(11)	36	27	1
Richardson, Kevin	1987-90	96(5)	9(1)	16(2)		
Rimmer, Jimmy	1974-77	124	12	10		
Rippon, W	1911	9(2)				
Rix, Graham	1975-89	351(41)	44(7)	47(2)	21(1)	1
Roberts, Herbie	1926-38	297(4)	36(1)			
Roberts, John	1969-72	59(4)		12(1)	10	
Robertson, B	1889		3(4)			
Robertson, James	1948-53	1				
Robertson, Jimmy	1968-70	46(7)	4(1)	4	5	
Robson, Jock	1923-26	97	4			
Robson, Stewart	1981-87	151(16)	13(1)	20(3)	2(1)	
Rocastle, David	1985-92	218(23)	19(4)	33(6)	4	2
Rodger, J	1908	1				
Roe, A	1923-25	5(1)				
Rodgers, E	1935-36	16(5)				
Rooke, Ronnie	1946-49	88(68)	5(1)			1(1)
Roose, Leigh	1912	13				
Roper, Don	1948-57	297(88)	22(7)			2
Ross, Trevor	1974-77	58(5)	3(1)	6(3)		
Rostron, Wilf	1973-77	17(2)		1		
Rudkin, Tom	1947	5(2)				
Russell, J	1896-97	23(4)	1			
Rutherford, J J	1926	3				
Rutherford, Jock	1914-26	223(25)	10(2)			
Sammels, Jon	1961-71	215(39)	21(3)	19(3)	15(7)	
Sanders, M	1900	4				
Sands, Percy	1904-15	327(9)	23(2)			
Sansom, Kenny	1980-88	314(6)	26	48	6	
Satterthwaite, Charlie	1905-08	109(42)	12			
Satterthwaite, J N	1908-10	25(5)	2			
Scott, A	1889		3(5)			
Scott, Laurie	1937-51	115	9			
Seddon, W C	1926-32	69	6			1
Selley, Ian	1992-	27	3	3	7(1)	
Shanks, Tommy	1903-04	44(29)	2(1)			
Sharp, Jimmy	1906-08	102(4)	14(1)			
Sharpe, W H	1895	11(4)	1			
Shaw, Arthur	1948-55	57	4			
Shaw, H	1899-1900	26(9)	1			
Shaw, J	1927-28	11(4)				
Shaw, Joe	1908-22	308(4)	16			
Shaw, W	1894-95	19(11)	3			
Shortt, M	1911	4				
Shrewsbury, T P	1897-98	3				
Sidey, Norman	1933-38	40	3			2
Simpson, Peter	1960-78	359(10)	53	33(3)	21(1)	
Sinclair, F	1897	26				
Skirton, Alan	1959-67	144(53)	8		1(1)	
Slade, D	1914	12(4)				
Sloan, Paddy	1947-48	33(1)	3			
Smith, Alan	1947	3				
Smith, Alan	1987-	245(84)	25(6)	35(15)	13(6)	2
Smith, J	1921	10(1)				
Smith, Lionel	1939-54	162	18			1
Smithson, Rod	1959-64	2				
Sneddon, John	1959-65	83	10		1	
Sparrow, Brian	1980-84	2				
Spicer, T A	1900-01	4				
Spittle, W A	1913-14	7				
Standen, Jim	1953-61	35	3			
Stapleton, Frank	1973-80	225(75)	32(15)	27(14)	15(4)	1
Stead, Kevin	1977-78	2				
Stevens, A	1898	5(1)				
Stevens, R C	1910	7(1)				
Stevenson, R	1895	8				
Stewart, W S	1891-92		2			
Stockhill, R	1932-33	7(4)				
Stonley, S	1913-14	38(14)	1			

Name	Career	League	FA Cup	Lg/Milk Cup	Euro Comp	CS
Storer, Harry	1895-96	40	1			
Storey, Peter	1961-77	39(9)	51(4)	37(2)	22(2)	
Storrs, J A	1893-94	13	4			
Strong, Geoff	1958-64	125(69)	8(5)		4(3)	
Stuart, J	1898	2(1)				
Sullivan, Con	1954-58	28	4			
Sunderland, Alan	1977-84	206(55)	34(16)	26(13)	14(7)	1(1)
Swallow, Ray	1953-58	13(4)				
Swann, A	1902	7(3)				
Swindin, George	1937-54	271	23		3	
Talbot, A	1897	5				
Talbot, Brian	1979-85	254(40)	30(7)	27(1)	15(1)	1
Tapscott, Derek	1953-58	119(62)	13(6)			
Tawse, Brian	1963-65	5				
Templeton, Bobby	1905-06	33(1)	6(1)			
Tennant, J	1900-01	51(7)	2(1)			
Theobald, S W	1903-09	24				
Thomas, M	1986-91	163(24)	19(1)	24(5)	2	2
Thompson, Len	1928-32	26(6)	1			
Thompson, M	1909-14	60(1)	5			
Thorpe, H	1904	10				
Tiddy, Mike	1955-58	48(8)	4			
Tilley, Peter	1952-53	1				
Toner, Joe	1920-26	87(6)	11			
Townrow, F A	1923-24	8(2)	1			
Tricker, R W	1927-29	12(5)				
Trim, R	1935	1				
Tuckett, E W	1936	2				
Turnbull, Bobby	1922-25	59(26)	7(2)			
Turner, P	1901	32(5)	2			
Tyrer, Alan	1966-67			2		
Ure, Ian	1963-69	168(2)	16	14	4	
Vaessen, Paul	1979-82	32(6)		2(2)	5(1)	
Vallance, Tom	1947-50	15(2)				
Vaughan, W	1902		1			
Voysey, C R	1920-26	35(6)	2			
Wade, Joe	1944-56	86	5			
Walden, H A	1921	2				
Walford, Steve	1977-81	77(3)	10	7	5	1
Waller, Henry	1947	8				
Walley, Tom	1964-67	14(1)	1	3		
Wallington, E E	1924	1				
Walsh, Brian	1949-55	17				
Walsh, Charlie	1933		1			
Walsh, W	1939	3				
Ward, A	1896	7				
Ward, Gerry	1953-63	95(10)	3			
Warnes, Billy	1933		1			
Watson, R	1904-05	9	1			
Webster, Malcolm	1968-69	3		2	1	
Westcott, Ronnie	1936	2(1)				
White, H A	1920-23	102(40)	8(5)			
White, W	1898-99	40(17)	1			
Whitfield, J	1897	2				
Whittaker, Tom	1920-25	64(2)	6			
Whyte, Chris	1978-85	89(8)	5	16	4	
Wilkinson, John	1954-56	1				
Williams, Charlie	1894-95	18	4			
Williams, Edward	1889		1			
Williams, J J	1930-32	22(5)	4			
Williams, Steve	1984-	95(4)	11	16(1)		
Williams, W	1894	1(1)				
Williamson, Ernie	1920-23	105	8			
Wilmot, Rhys	1986-	8		1		
Wills, Len	1949-62	195(4)	13			1
Wilson, Alex	1934-39	82	7			1
Wilson, Bob	1963-74	234	32	18	24	
Wilson, O	1913	1				
Winship, I	1911-15	55(7)	1			
Winterburn, N	1987-	55(3)	6	9(2)		
Wolfe, G	1901-03	6				
Wood, George	1980-83	60	1	7	2	2
Woodcock, Tony	1982-86	131(56)	14(6)	22(5)	2	
Woods, H	1924-26	70(21)	5(1)			
Woodward, John	1967	3		1		
Worrall, A	1894	4				
Wright, D	1905	1				
Wright, Ian	1991-	100(62)	10(11)	15(13)	6(4)	1(1)
Young, A	1922-27	68(9)	3			
Young, Alan	1959-61	4				
Young, Willie	1977-81	170(11)	28(3)	20(1)	18(4)	1

Index

Note: The statistical section on pages 253–302, which includes all Arsenal teams and scorers season-by-season, also includes an alphabetical list of all Arsenal players. These pages are not indexed below.

Page numbers in *italic* refer to captions.

303